A More Perfect Union

A More Perfect Union

Federal Union in Political Theory and Practice, 1500-1951

Joshua Livestro

Amsterdam University Press

For Sarah, Daniel, Hannah, and Ruben

Cover illustration: The 1777 flag of the United States and the flag of the European Union
Cover design: Coördesign, Leiden
Lay-out: Crius Group, Hulshout

ISBN	978 90 4856 377 7
e-ISBN	978 90 4856 378 4 (pdf)
DOI	10.5117/9789048563777
NUR	697

"There is (...) an association between sovereignty and historiography; a community writes its own history when it has the autonomous political structure needed if it is to command its own present, and typically the history it writes will be the history of that structure."

J. G. A. Pocock, "Deconstructing Europe," *London Review of Books*, vol. 13, no. 24, 19 December 1991.

Table of Contents

Introduction

In his *Alarums and Excursions*, the Dutch political philosopher Luuk van Middelaar described the Brexit vote of June 2016 as a moment of existential crisis for the European Union: "The divorce disturbed its long-cherished self-image and for a moment it feared for its survival" (Van Middelaar 488). In the end, the EU's will to survive helped it to steer a course out of the crisis, towards a renewed sense of purpose.

Van Middelaar proceeded to give metaphysical meaning to this crisis by calling it a "Machiavellian moment," a reference to arguably one of the finest works of intellectual history from the past half-century, written by the New Zealand historian J. G. A. Pocock. Pocock's study reconstructed the rise of an Atlantic tradition of republican political thought that linked the Renaissance Florence of Niccolo Machiavelli to the England of the Civil War period and the America of the Revolutionary era.

As Van Middelaar read it, the Machiavellian moment was an episode in which, "[o]ut of the experience of a democratic republic's own transience and mortality there may arise a political will to manifest itself as a sovereign player in historical time" (Van Middelaar 486). This European Machiavellian moment, which according to him effectively started with the international banking crisis of 2008, would see the Union gradually become an independent actor on the world stage. Like the original early-sixteenth-century Machiavellian moment, Van Middelaar claimed, this European moment also had an aspect of "theological liberation" (487), the theology in this case being the European belief in the idea of the Union's perpetuity, and in the universality of the ideals on which it was founded. Freed from these eschatological shackles, Europe could now, finally, as the former German Chancellor Angela Merkel put it, "take its destiny into its own hands" (512). Using Machiavelli's image of fortune as a stream, Van Middelaar placed the EU squarely in the middle of this stream, ready to respond to the changing tides – "an existential experience" (487).

Livestro, Joshua: *A More Perfect Union. Federal Union in Political Theory and Practice, 1500-1951.*
Amsterdam: Amsterdam University Press, 2024.
DOI: 10.5117/9789048563777_INTRO

It is difficult to disagree with Van Middelaar's assertion that the EU needs to fully grasp its "Machiavellian moment" and develop the capacity to become a credible actor on the world stage.[1] And his point is well made that the EU has only been able to survive by periodically ignoring its own ground rules, through acts of pure political creativity. But it would be dangerous to rely exclusively on the EU's powers of improvisation as a means of maintaining itself in the stream of events. To put it in Machiavellian terms: to do so would require an extraordinary amount of *virtù*, more than any organisation or individual is likely to possess. Sooner or later an event would take the Union by surprise, and *fortuna*'s stream would wash over it.

If the Union is to survive in the long term, it needs to take measures not just to withstand the stream of fickle fortune but to protect itself against it structurally, as far as possible. As Machiavelli himself put it:

> I am disposed to hold it that Fortune is the arbiter of one-half of our actions, but that it lets us control roughly the other half. I compare fortune to one of those dangerous rivers that, when they become enraged, flood the plains, destroy trees and buildings, move earth from one place and deposit it in another. Everyone flees before it, everyone gives way to its thrust, without being able to halt it in any way. But this does not mean that, when the river is not in flood, men are unable to take precautions, by means of dykes and dams, so that when it rises next time, it will either not overflow its banks or, if it does, its force will not be so uncontrolled or damaging.
> (*The Prince* 85)

In political terms, "take precautions" and creating "dykes and dams" principally means *constitution building*.

Machiavelli is known to us today mainly for his advice on how to respond with *virtú* to the caprices of fortune, but he was no less productive as a philosopher of constitutional theory. He devoted part of his main reflection on the troubles of republics, the famous *Discourses on the First Ten Books of Titus Livy*, to precisely this issue. The same subject also cropped up in his most notorious work, *The Prince*, specifically in chapter VI. Here he observed

---

1   For an interesting elaboration of this point, see Hans Kribbe's *The Strongmen: European Encounters With Sovereign Power*. It is noteworthy that Kribbe also talks about the EU experiencing a Machiavellian moment: "Bereft of the help of the United States and without safety lines, the continent is forced to confront the maelstrom of events on its own. It forms a test of strength, a 'Machiavellian moment'" (Kribbe 121–122).

that the greatest *virtù* belonged to the founders of new principalities: "I consider that the most outstanding were Moses, Cyrus, Romulus, Theseus and others of that stamp" (20). These framers didn't just found cities, empires, and religions: they also defined them constitutionally, as authors of their founding legal and moral codes. As Machiavelli explained in a seminal essay published in 1520 as the *Discursus about the Reforming of Florence*, there was no better way of preventing internal chaos than to create a solid constitution. In fact, it may well be the *only* way: "There is no other way for escaping [arms, violence and plunder] than to give the city institutions that can by themselves stand firm" (*Collected Works* 1: 115).

It is this other kind of *virtù*, the constitution-making kind, that is the focus of this book. In terms of the Machiavellian moment, that means we must begin by reassessing Machiavelli's own reflections on the theory of the cycle of political regimes: more specifically on the idea of the mixed regime as the optimal regime form, and on the practical translation of that idea into concrete constitutional arrangements, both their founding and their maintenance. We will look at the development of these ideas in confrontation with their most important historical counter-concepts – universal monarchy and sovereignty – tracing the gradual transformation of the ideal of the mixed regime from a division based on estates or social classes to a division by constitutional functions or powers. And we will trace how this new conception of the mixed regime was eventually integrated into federal theory in the form of the separation of powers and checks and balances – the latter idea developed most fully as an organisational principle for the American federal constitution of 1787.

In the spirit of Machiavelli, we will also consider the options for the republic to maintain itself in the world – or, indeed, to impose itself upon it through expansion. Because one important lesson we can draw from studying the theorists who lived and worked within this tradition of constitution-making Machiavellian moments is the stress they placed on the link between a republic's constitution and its place in the world. In their view, the choice for a certain type of political regime was as much about its external dimension as about its internal order. This quest to secure the republic's place in the world was what gave shape to the kind of political entity discussed in Machiavelli's *Discourses* (bk 2, ch. 4). The federation, or "league," as he called it, featured as one of three possible models of territorial expansion, the other two being violent expansion and what he called "the method of Rome," where a great power placed itself at the head of an expansionist alliance, eventually bringing the other members under its rule. After some deliberation Machiavelli concluded that for the Florence of his day the most practical option was "the method of the Etruscans"; that is, "forming a league consisting of several republics in which no one of them had preference, authority or rank above the others" (*Discourses on the First Ten Books of Titus Livy* 283; bk 2, ch. 4).

In his study of practical examples of leagues, Machiavelli not only praised the useful qualities of leagues like those of the Etruscans or the Swiss, he also identified several problematic aspects that characterised their functioning. The first was one of *organisation*: the weakness of the league's political centre, and the inefficiency of its decision-making process. The second was one of *extent:* there seemed to be a limit to how far a federation could expand, at least if it wanted to maintain some form of cohesion. The third was one of *duration.* This was a challenge the league had in common with other regime forms, such as empires and city states: the challenge of sustaining itself over time.

Machiavelli's writings furnished political thought on international affairs with two important conceptual tools for analysing international affairs. One was the key distinction of three different modes of expansion. Over the next four and a half centuries, between 1500 and 1950, politicians and political thinkers would come back to these three modes time and again to analyse their contemporary geostrategic predicaments. Over the course of the seventeenth century the league option would also come to serve as the foundation for the development of a new concept that was eventually called "federal union." In the early modern period, the Machiavellian taxonomy of modes of expansion would give birth to a second taxonomy for different types of multi-state regimes. During the period of European state formation, the new concept of "federal union" would take the place of Machiavelli's league. Federal union served as a counter-concept to the dominant concepts of the age: first, the idea of universal monarchy; and later, as Europe experienced a series of devastating wars, the martial idea of the balance of power.

—

In his book *The Machiavellian Moment*, Pocock defined his central concept in two different ways. He saw it first of all as an individual event, "the moment in time when a republic was seen as confronting its own temporal finitude, as attempting to remain morally and politically stable in a stream of irrational events conceived as essentially destructive of all systems of secular stability" (viii). In essence, this is the Machiavellian image Van Middelaar was working with, that is, communities as historical actors standing in the river of events, being tested by the tide.

A More Perfect Union contains many descriptions of that type of moment
– both European and American moments, even transatlantic moments.
Ultimately, however, it is focused as much, if not more, on the second meaning of the concept. Here, Pocock stressed not uniqueness but continuity:
"'[T]he Machiavellian moment' had a continuing history, in the sense that
secular political self-consciousness continued to pose problems in historical
self-awareness, which form part of the journey of Western thought from the
mediaeval Christian to the modern historical period" (viii). This certainly
applies to the history of the "federal union." Though there are obvious
differences between the way Machiavelli, writing in the 1510s, used the
word *league* and the way Monnet used the term *federation* in the 1950s, the
key argument of this book is that the two were part of the same tradition
of federal political thought and action.

Reconstructing this other, continuous constitutional tradition of Machiavellian moments is part of an effort to map the development of the concept
of federal union over time. Here, this book owes an intellectual debt to the
German historian Reinhart Koselleck (1923–2006). Koselleck was a historian
who played an important role in the development of what has been termed
the "linguistic turn" in the study of history. His name is associated with the
German school of *Begriffsgeschichte*, the study of conceptual history. By a
concept he meant any term that "bundles together the richness of historical
experience and the sum of theoretical and practical lessons drawn from it"
(Koselleck and Richter 20). This meant there was an essential difference
between mere words and concepts: "[T]he meaning of words can be defined
exactly, but concepts can only be interpreted" (20). According to Koselleck,
the meaning of political concepts is always contested. The focus of his
research was on lines of conceptual contestation, and the changes that
resulted from these contests. Koselleck's original insight was that, in order
to understand concepts more fully, we have to study their development over
time, in the contexts in which they were used, while also paying attention
to the evolving relationship with their counter-concepts: "In and of itself,
words' persistence over time is an insufficient index of their unchanging
content. Only through a diachronic investigation of the layers of meaning
contained in a concept can we uncover long-term structural transformations"
(Koselleck and Richter 18).

In doing the research for this book, it has been my contention that, when
the post–Second World War European Founders reached for the concept
of federal union in constructing a new order for (the Western part of) their
continent, they inevitably loaded it with all the historical content and problematics contained within it. I therefore set out to apply Koselleck's insight

in an attempt to uncover the concept's many layers of meaning. In doing so, my ultimate aim is to open the past as a source of self-understanding for today's European Union.

This effort will take us on a long journey lasting the better part of five centuries, following the concept from its early-sixteenth-century Florentine source all the way to the extraordinary period just after the Second World War, which saw the creation of a number of different organisations based on competing interpretations of the concept of federal union. The chapters are broadly structured chronologically, tracing the prehistory, birth, and development of the concept of federal union through the centuries. However, this is not just, or even primarily, a linguistic study. It is also a study of the contexts in which the concept was debated, the lived political experiences of the past five centuries on both sides of the Atlantic. The concept was developed in concrete political situations, in answer to problems the historical actors in these situations were struggling with: problems involving the establishment or maintenance of internal order, or external security, or indeed, expansion. It is therefore a study of constitutional and geopolitical history as much as a study of conceptual history.

The first chapter focuses on Machiavelli's discussion of the modes of expansion that are available to a republic facing a "Machiavellian moment" – an existential crisis that brings the risk of decline and fall. The next chapter then surveys the rich variety of regional leagues that already existed in Machiavelli's time, or which were formed in the early modern period: the Swiss Republic, the Polish-Lithuanian Commonwealth, the Dutch United Provinces, and the Holy Roman Empire (the post-1648 form that is). The chapter ends at the turn of the eighteenth century with the English and Scottish debate on the Union of the Crowns. It is in this debate that Machiavelli's analysis of the modes of expansion was used to create a taxonomy of different types of union, one of which was called *federal union*.

It is important to emphasise here that the reader must let go of any present-day conceptions attached to this term (or to its counterpart, *confederation*). Much of the historical debate covered by this book focused on the development of an interpretation of *league, confederation,* or *federal union,* that was not just plausible in political theory but also workable in the practice of political life. That debate had still not been fully settled by the time the European Founders sat down to negotiate the European Coal and Steel Community in the early 1950s. In this book, *federal union* is generally used in the sense that the people in question used it in their own respective languages, times, and places.

In Chapter Three, we track how the model of federal union was introduced into the debate about European order. The collapse of the old dual order of empire and papacy, commonly referred to as the *Respublica Christiana*, triggered the search for a new conceptual framework for the maintenance of political order on the continent. During the process of state formation in Europe, federal union became one of the options for the organisation of relationships between states, and between the collective of states and the outside world.

The ideas of the seventeenth century and early-eighteenth-century authors who looked for a quasi-constitutional settlement of relationships between states on the European continent were eventually picked up by later generations of politicians. This happened first on the other side of the Atlantic Ocean. Chapter Four presents an analysis of the proceedings at the Philadelphia Convention of 1787, whose delegates drafted the Constitution of the United States. Recent American scholarship has interpreted the Convention as an attempt to negotiate the kind of peace plan that had been the subject of political and philosophical speculation in Europe in the two centuries prior to the American Revolution. The constitution that finally emerged from these negotiations was based on a number of compromises, predominantly on representation and on one of federal union's main counter-concepts, namely sovereignty. Yet, though the new constitution was in itself a remarkable achievement, it did not settle the debate about the relationship between the new political centre and the states. Chapter Five tracks the often fractious and unstable relationship between the two layers of the American government in the first seventy years after its founding. At critical moments, the Union was held together only by a Great Compromise that reaffirmed the commitment of all sides to the original Philadelphia compromise. When that compromise became impossible to sustain, a large group of Southern states seceded from the Union, with the American Civil War of the 1860s as the inevitable result.

Chapter Six discusses how the same ideas that, at least in part, inspired the American constitution also influenced proceedings at the great European peace conferences of 1815, after the hardship of the Napoleonic wars. The Congress System was in effect an attempt to implement the peace plan idea in an entirely different setting from the American one – not a collection of smaller and medium-sized newly established republics, but a small number of large, long-established monarchies, as well as a large number of medium-sized and smaller monarchies and republics.

Though the Congress method was a breakthrough in practical terms, it would only survive for a decade, and was eventually replaced by the much less formal Concert system. At the theoretical level, the Congress System would leave its mark chiefly in the form of the Holy Alliance, which was

treated by later generations of students of the concept of federal union as both
a model worth studying and a practical example of the kind of union to avoid
(owing mainly to its antidemocratic and generally repressive character).

The greater impact would be that of the American example. At the
theoretical level, its influence would be greatest in the debate that would
eventually lead to the formation of the German Reich. This German
debate, which is covered in Chapter Seven, covers both the theoretical
breakthrough – which owed a lot to the works of the French philosopher
Alexis de Tocqueville – and the practical shortcomings of the kind of federal
union that was eventually created: a monarchical union dominated by a
single state, Prussia. In its practical workings it was closer to Machiavelli's
theoretically preferred option, that of the expansionist Roman empire, than
to his pragmatically chosen one, the Etruscan league.

Chapter Eight discusses the other track along which the American
example influenced the European debate about federal union: that of the
peace movement. Participants in this debate would embrace the idea of
the formation of a United States on the continent of Europe as a kind of
"sister federation" to its American counterpart. By tying these two unions
together through a transatlantic bond, they also introduced a wholly new
idea: something in between continental and global federation. As far as the
European federal union was concerned, less intellectual energy was spent
on its constitutional features than on the means for its establishment. Over
the course of the nineteenth century, the peace movement also succeeded
in defining its own version of federal union as the alternative to two types
of monarchical regime: the Holy Alliance of monarchs, and the Caesarean
empires of Napoleon III and Bismarck.

Chapter Nine looks at the practical successes of the peace movement:
the Peace Conferences at The Hague of 1899 and 1907, and the Versailles
Treaty of 1919, which led to the creation of the League of Nations. Through
the latter, the peace movement's ideal of a transatlantic league was implemented on a global scale – though subsequent events in Washington, D.C.
would effectively reduce it to a European rump-league (albeit with some
South American and Asian involvement). In the second half of the 1920s,
it looked for a while as though the League of Nations could provide a legal
framework for the maintenance of political order on the continent, when the
three main powers – France, England, and Germany – used it to structure
their relations as part of the Locarno process. The legal-philosophical
debate about the nature of the League, meanwhile, showed the extent of
the conceptual confusion surrounding the idea of federal union even as
late as the mid-1920s.

In Chapter Ten, the focus shifts to the geopolitical causes and consequences of the First World War. In the political debate about these issues,
Machiavelli's other modes of expansion came to dominate. In the eyes of
anti-federalists during this post-war period, violent conquest and the use
of alliances to extend control over neighbouring territories were seen as
superior to the federal union option.

In this Interbellum debate, supporters of the federal idea fought back on
two different fronts. On the one front, they worked to outlaw the method of
violent conquest. On the other, they strove to present the option of federal
union in the form of "Pan-Europe" or "The United States of Europe" as a
practical alternative to empire-building by the great powers, highlighting
both its economic benefits and its ability to maintain peace and security
on a continental scale.

The last part of the Interbellum formed the nadir in the story of federal
union on the European side of the Atlantic. On the level of practical politics,
federalism seemed to have been crushed by its old systemic rival, which
now took on the guise of fascist or communist totalitarianism. The defeat
seemed to have been extended to the theoretical level, with the "great dictators" Stalin and Hitler dismissing federalism as an outdated concept, made
superfluous by technological developments. The sense of federalist defeatism
was deepened by the miserable failure of the League of Nations to prevent
the return of balance of power politics and the continent's subsequent slide
into war. Defeat would not lead to resignation, however. The war years,
between 1939 and 1945, were a period of incredible creativity among political
thinkers engaging with the topic of federal union. The Allies, also referred
to as the "United Nations," would come out of the war with a renewed sense
of federal purpose, and a large number of blueprints for implementation.

Chapter Eleven discusses the post-war debate about the practical value
of federal union. This debate would lead to a number of international,
transatlantic, and European experiments. The book closes with a chapter
on the founding moment of the European Union: the 1951 creation of the
European Coal and Steel Community.

—

Students of this second European Machiavellian moment generally claimed
it to be "without precedent,"[2] and have consequently treated the period prior

2   See, for example, Haas (526) and Milward (494). The most notable exception here is Andrew
Moravcsik, whose aim it was to subsume "European integration wherever possible under general

to the founding of the ECSC as largely irrelevant to any attempt at understanding of its nature. As this book will demonstrate, that is a fundamental
mistake. The union that was created, represented the culmination of the
rich variety of schemes developed in previous centuries for the construction
of a European federal union. Its core elements – the idea of incremental
progress towards full federation, the use of a small vanguard of suitable
member states to kickstart the process, and the use of an economic project
as a first step towards a more complete federal union – had by then been
around for nearly 150 years. The other supposedly unique element of Europe's
new federal union, shared sovereignty, had been present in European debate
since it was discussed by Tocqueville in the 1830s, after its establishment
in the United States in 1787.

This lack of historical awareness concerning the importance of previous
Machiavellian moments in Europe's long struggle with the theory and
practice of federal union wasn't just down to an error of interpretation
on the part of these scholars. It was also, or perhaps mainly, the result of
a parallel development in the field of historical studies. Just as Europe's
federal union was taking shape constitutionally, the historical profession
took a collective turn away from long-term studies, instead focusing on
ever-shorter timescales. The idea of comparing a political event from 1951
with one in 1919 became anathema, let alone with one from 1787 or 1500. This
shift in focus to the so-called "Short Past" led to the virtual disappearance
of narrative history (Guldi and Armitage 53).

To the extent that historians did produce a longer-term view of the past,
they offered an interpretation of it that made meaningful comparison
with the present almost impossible, at least for students of European
integration. After all, why study the past when no less an authority than
the (co-)founder of the modern discipline of the history of political thought,
Quentin Skinner, had concluded that the history of European political
thought since 1600 was essentially the history of thinking about *the state*

theories rather than treating it as *sui generis*" (500). His interpretation has recently been followed
by Kiran Klaus Patel, who claimed that "it is easy to overemphasise the legal and administrative
differences between the EC and other efforts of regional cooperation and integration, such
as the UNECE, the Brussels Pact, the OECD or the Council of Europe, at least for the first and
formative years in their existence. The characterisation of the EC as *sui generis* (of its own kind;
exceptional) which already existed in the 1950s and was pushed for by its own supporters is
quite misleading" (204). This book argues that, though some form of comparison with other
organisations founded in this period is justified, Patel misses the point that, in some fundamental
aspects, the ECSC *was* different from the other organisations established in this period. This did
not, however, make it *sui generis*. It was part of a long tradition (on both sides of the Atlantic)
of thinking about, and experimenting with, federal unions.

– the one thing the European Coal and Steel Community clearly wasn't, and didn't aspire to become (*Foundations of Modern Political Thought* 2: 349–351)?

The turn of the millennium saw two parallel developments that together have helped to unlock the pre-ECSC past as an object of study for EU purposes. One was the increased awareness among historians of political thought that "the state" was in fact only one among a number of competing terms and concepts used in early modern political discourse to describe the basic units of study, and that it remained so until well into the twentieth century. This insight was a product of the development of the history of international political thought as a separate field of study. The other development was the renewed interest in the *longue durée* approach in the wider field of historical studies.

Encouraged by these developments, this book sets out to do what the diplomats who negotiated the founding treaty of the ECSC did not have the time or inclination to do: to embed the union created in 1951 in the European and transatlantic federal tradition. By studying the European Union's prehistory, we will gain a clearer grasp of exactly what was negotiated in the early 1950s – and, by extension, of what the Union is today, and what it may well become tomorrow.

Bibliography

Guldi, Jo, and David Armitage. *The History Manifesto*. 2014. Cambridge University Press, 2019.

Haas, Ernst B. *The Uniting of Europe: Political, Social, and Economic Forces, 1950–1957*. 1958. University of Notre Dame Press, 2004.

Koselleck, Reinhart, and Michaela Richter. "Introduction and Prefaces to the Geschichtliche Grundbegriffe." *Contributions to the History of Concepts*, vol. 6, no. 1, 2011, pp. 1–37.

Kribbe, Hans. *The Strongmen: European Encounters with Sovereign Power*, Agenda Publishing, 2020.

Machiavelli, Niccolo. *The Discourses*. 1517. Edited with an introduction by Bernard Crick, using the translation of Leslie J. Walker, S. J., with revisions by Brian Richardson. Penguin Books, 1998.

Machiavelli, Niccolo. *Discursus about the Reforming of Florence*. 1520. *Collected Works of Niccoló Machiavelli*, Delphi Classics, 2017.

Machiavelli, Niccolo. *The Prince*, edited by Quentin Skinner and Russell Price. 1520. Cambridge University Press, 2000.

Middelaar, Luuk van. *Alarums and Excursions: Improvising Politics on the European Stage*. 2017. Agenda Publishing, 2019.

Milward, Alan S. *The Reconstruction of Western Europe 1945–1951*. 1984. Routledge, 2006.

Moravcsik, Andrew. *The Choice for Europe: Social Purpose and State Power from Messina to Maastricht*. Cornell University Press, 1998

Patel, Kiran Klaus. "Why the EU Became 'Europe': Towards a New History of European Union." *Annals of the Fondazione Luigi Einaudi*, vol. 54, 2020, pp. 199–216.

Pocock, J. G. A. *The Machiavellian Moment: Florentine Political Thought in the Atlantic Republican Tradition*. Princeton University Press, 1975.

Skinner, Quentin. *Foundations of Modern Political Thought*. Cambridge University Press, 1978. 2 vols.

1 The Machiavellian Moment: On Modes of Expansion

Abstract

In his Discourses, Machiavelli presented a taxonomy of the means of territorial expansion. Among them was a concept that would take on a life of its own in the centuries that followed – a league of states in which none had authority over others.

Keywords: Machiavelli, league, federal union, expansion, sovereignty, universal monarchy

The original Machiavellian Moment

For the Florentine republic, the original Machiavellian moment was a moment of rupture, a tear in the historical fabric. Through it would pour the forces of disruption – literally, in the form of invading armies. The rise of the newly united Spanish kingdom had made conflict with France over the Italian peninsula all but inevitable. After all, the power that controlled Italy would control the major trade routes in the Mediterranean. Florence would experience the full disruptive force of this conflict in the 1490s and 1500s, when the Italian peninsula was repeatedly invaded by French, Spanish, and (German) Imperial armies. The first invasion, by the French king Charles VIII, had led to the collapse of the Medici regime. Subsequent offensives would bring the Medici back to power, see the French take control of the duchy of Milan, and the Spanish seize the kingdom of Naples; meanwhile, Venice would lose all its territory outside the Veneto. Pope Julius II, with his anti-French Holy League, was briefly successful in his effort to "free Italy from the barbarians," but his successes would be overturned immediately after his death in 1513. This left the Florentines with an urgent question: how could a city state like theirs avoid getting swept away by the rising tide of monarchies striving for universal rule?

Livestro, Joshua: *A More Perfect Union. Federal Union in Political Theory and Practice, 1500-1951.*
Amsterdam: Amsterdam University Press, 2024.
DOI: 10.5117/9789048563777_CH01

The republic's demise in 1512, and the Medici family's return to power, constituted a moment of maximum danger for the city. Not because the Medici might succeed in their aim of subjugating the city's population, but because they might *not*. While the republican experiment of 1494 to 1512 had clearly ended in failure, its mere existence had inculcated in the people of Florence a love of liberty that might have left the city unsuited to any other form of government. It made the task of forming a stable rule by one family much more difficult.

The additional problem the Medici faced when they took back control of the city was that for them, the connection between past and present had been severed, and with it the connection between tradition and legitimacy (Pocock, *The Machiavellian Moment* 158). They couldn't simply justify their claim to power by pointing to the rule of their ancestors. After all, that rule had ended with Piero and the rest of the Medici family being forced to flee the city in disgrace twenty years earlier, in 1494. The family would therefore face an immediate challenge to its authority from those who lost out because of the transition away from republicanism: the *popolo*, chiefly the city's middle class. With nobody able to present a credible alternative, it threatened to leave Florence divided and rudderless.

The situation the city found itself in was, essentially, a *new* situation requiring a *new* solution. This only aggravated the problem. After all, as Machiavelli observed, innovation was the most difficult challenge of all: "[T]here is nothing more difficult to take in hand, more perilous to conduct, or more uncertain in its success, than to take the lead in the introducing of a new order of things" (*The Prince*, ch. 6). Still, this was the challenge the Florentines were facing: to create a new regime that had a chance of *maintaining its state*, in Italy and in Europe, remaining stable in time and able to withstand fortune's caprices.

—

Machiavelli's *The Prince* was primarily an attempt to explain to the "new prince" Lorenzo de' Medici that because he had obtained control of the city through *fortuna* rather than his own merit or inheritance, his situation was precarious. Only by showing extreme *virtù*, like the book's *exemplum virtutis* Cesare Borgia, could he hope to maintain his state, and perhaps even expand his dominion. The kind of *virtù* that Machiavelli described, however, could only help the prince establish his claim to power in the short term. The fact that the Medici owed their position to fortune in the form of outside intervention, and therefore lacked legitimacy, made it likely that they would not be able to maintain their state in the longer term. The latter would have required a degree of good fortune that was usually beyond mere mortals (as it was for Cesare, whose fate was sealed when his father was succeeded by his arch enemy Giuliano della Rovere as Pope Julius II). Long-term stability required something more than the *virtù* of an exceptional prince. That something more was the right kind of constitution.

Regarding constitutions, Machiavelli and his contemporaries drew inspiration from two different, though related, classical sources. The first was Greek and Roman medical writing. The term constitution (*constituzione*) had clear medical overtones: its roots were in the "body politic" analogy used in Roman times, where the various parts of the commonwealth were associated with different body parts, each with its own social function. From this tradition the Florentine writers copied the use of medical terms to describe the flourishing or decay of the republic, frequently invoking the example of doctors in their analyses and prescriptions. Hence Machiavelli, in the context of discussing the preservation of the freedom of a republic, observed that "in every large city there inevitably occur unfortunate incidents which call for the physician, and the more important the incidents the wiser should be the physician one looks for" (Machiavelli, *Discourses*, 3: 49, 526). If untreated, these incidents could cause the body politic to suffer from *corruption* – a problem that would feature prominently in the writing of Renaissance political philosophers.

The medical analogy was extended by use of the theory of the humours (bodily fluids) developed in the second century CE by the Greek medical writer Galen. Just as Galen associated different humours with different character traits, classical philosophers (and their Florentine students) associated these humours with different social classes and their different ambitions. The main objective of a constitution was to do justice to the distribution of humours within its territory. The founder's task was to identify the mix of humours within the city, and then to design a constitution based on this mix. This way the city would be given a stable and potentially lasting framework. A healthy constitution was one in which the humours were in balance, each in its appropriate place.[1]

The other source was classical regime theory. This tradition of constitutional reflection started with Plato. In book VIII of his *Republic* he had Socrates describe five regime types: aristocracy (rule of the most talented and virtuous), timocracy (referring mainly to Sparta, which he defined as rule of land-owners), oligarchy (rule of the rich), democracy (rule of the

---

1   On the importance of the humours to Machiavellian constitutional thinking, see Fabio Raimondi, *Constituting Freedom: Machiavelli and Florence*, especially 42–48, "The Virtue of the Florentines and the Humours."

people), and tyranny (rule of one). Each regime type was based on a type of ruler and represented a stage in the development of the constitution, from best to worst.

The next phase in the development of classical regime theory came when Aristotle reorganised and systematised the categories introduced by Plato. He discussed the various regime types in his *Politics*, distinguishing a proper and a corrupt form of each regime type. By proper forms he meant "governments which have a regard towards the common interest [and] are constituted in accordance with strict principles of justice." The corrupt forms were those that "regard only the interest of the rulers" (Aristotle, *The Politics* 61).

The rule of one created the pairing of monarchy and tyranny; the rule of the few, that of aristocracy and oligarchy. Similarly, Aristotle considered democracy to be a corrupt form of what he called *politeia* – a kind of re-publican regime based on a selective but egalitarian concept of citizenship. All who met the requirements for full citizenship would devote their lives to the giving of laws, the keeping of order, the settling of legal disputes, the defence of the city and the maintenance of relations with other cities. What made it a "good" regime form was its focus on *eudaimonia*, or good living – that of these citizen-politicians themselves and of the *polis* as a whole – through the pursuit of justice.

Corruption was inevitable, though. Sooner or later the selfish pursuit of personal or factional interests would lead to the rise of either a rule of one or the rule of a few. To counter the corrosive effects of these selfish and emotional tendencies in the people, Aristotle suggested combining *politeia* with an aristocratic and a monarchical element. The result of this was a *mixed regime*: a system that took the best qualities of the pure regime forms and blended them into a constitution that successfully combined dynamism with stability.

Aristotle would use the later chapters of the *Politics* to nuance this rather schematic version of his regime theory, effectively excluding monarchy as irrelevant in a Greek setting and listing various different forms of the two other main regimes (aristocracy and *politeia*) while also allowing for combinations. It was the schematic rather than the nuanced version of his theory, however, to which the Greek historian Polybius (born around 200 BCE) would add the idea of the regime cycle, through which one type of regime evolved into the next. Together, the ideas of the three main regime forms, the regime cycle, and the mixed regime as the optimal constitution came to dominate political theory from the classical era to the early modern period.

—

Machiavelli's *Discourses on the First Ten Books of Titus Livy* contained an extensive reflection on classical regime theory. In book 1, chapter 2, he first introduced the six Aristotelian regime types, before explaining why each of the three good forms would inevitably be reduced to its corrupt counterpart: "[I]f anyone who is organizing a commonwealth sets up one of the first three forms of government, he sets up what will last but for a while, since there are no means whereby to prevent it passing into its contrary, on account of the likeness which in such a case virtue has to vice." Using Polybian imagery, he called this a "cycle through which all commonwealths must pass" (106). Observing that "all the forms of government mentioned above are far from satisfactory, the three good ones because their life is so short, the three bad ones because of their inherent malignity," he then presented the standard classical solution in the form of the mixed regime: "[P]rudent legislators, aware of their defects, refrained from adopting as such any one of these forms, and chose instead one that shared in them all, since they thought such a government would be stronger and more stable" (109).

According to Machiavelli, Roman history had seen two periods where such mixed regimes were established. One was after the end of the monarchy, when the last king, Tarquinius Superbus, was chased out of the city and the kings were replaced by consuls (110). At this stage, the republic represented two of the three regime forms, namely monarchy and aristocracy. The Roman republic became a properly mixed regime when democracy was added several decades later in the form of the tribunes, "when the Roman nobility became so overbearing (...) that the populace rose against them, and they were constrained by the fear that they might lose all, to grant the populace a share in the government" (111). According to Machiavelli, this first "perfect commonwealth" – which was established through "the blending of these estates" (111) – would last until the end of the second century BCE, when first Marius and then Sulla would exploit the inevitable corruption of the old republic, accelerated by the Agrarian Laws, to seize power for their respective factions.[2]

The other example of a Roman mixed regime mentioned by Machiavelli was presented in *Discourses* I, chapter 10, where he talked about the era when the emperors obtained their position through adoption rather than inheritance, "the period which extends from Nerva to Marcus [96–180 CE]." In this period "good men governed (...), the senate maintaining its authority, the magistrates enjoying their honours (...) rank and merit held in respect."

---

2   Most fully described in *Discourses*, I, ch. 37.

However, this period lasted an even time: "[As] soon as the empire fell once more to the heirs by birth, its ruin recommenced" (137).

Machiavelli's description of the "golden age" of the adopted emperors contained a reference to the importance of freedom of speech to the maintenance of a free republic. What made the age of elected emperors golden was in part the fact that "everyone is free to hold and to defend his own opinion" (*Discourses* 137). This kind of freedom of speech was not just an indication of the health of the republic: it also served an important constitutional function through the ability of all to formulate accusations against any citizen who had "committed any offence prejudicial to the freedom of the state" (124). This "legal outlet for [popular] anger" served as a kind of constitutional check in the form of an impeachment process against those in power. The freedom to formulate a well-founded accusation against a fellow citizen should be distinguished, however, from unfounded attacks on the character of another. Such libellous speech should be in contempt in any free city, and "with a view to checking them no institution which serves this end should be neglected" (129).

The *Discourses* mentioned three essential functions of government whose shape was to be determined through a constitution: the administration of justice (both criminal and civil), the distribution of public offices through appointment or election, and the conduct of foreign policy through diplomacy and warfare. To these powers were added the powers required to execute them, such as the levying of taxes. Machiavelli did recognise the importance of legislation to the health of a commonwealth: "The main foundations of all states (whether they are new, old or mixed) are good laws and good armies" (*The Prince* 42). But the making of laws as such was not included in his overview of the core powers of government.[3]

—

So far there was nothing unorthodox about Machiavelli's analysis. His assertion in *Discourses* book I, chapter 2 that a mixed regime would guarantee stability because "if in one and the same state there was principality, aristocracy and democracy each would keep watch over the other" (109) seemed an echo of Cicero's claim in *The Republic,* book I, chapter 69 ("A mixed

---

3   A reflection perhaps of the fact that, to Machiavelli, politics was prior to legislation. See Geuna, who observes that it was "[s]ocial and political conflict [that] produced good orders and good laws," and that therefore "[f]rom a genetic perspective, politics is a *primum* and law is a *posterum* or a *derivatum*" (17).

constitution is the best") that "although those simple forms often change into others, such things rarely happen in a political structure which represents a combination and a judicious mixture" (32). Hence Quentin Skinner's contention when underlining Machiavelli's observation that "no free city can ever uphold a free way of life unless it maintains a republican constitution," that he "not only presents a wholehearted defence of traditional republican values; he also presents that defence in a wholeheartedly traditional way" ("Pre-Humanist Origins of Republican Ideas" 141).

But though Machiavelli's presentation and source material may have been wholeheartedly traditional, his conclusions on constitutional issues were in fact quite innovative. In the course of discussing the Roman republic, he would introduce one such innovation: the functions of a regime could be separated from their traditional personal representation. In this way, he claimed in *Discourses* book I, chapter 2, at the end of the period of the monarchy the Romans had been able to "[expel] the title of king, not the royal power."[4] (Discourses, 110) This idea was further developed in his *History of Florence and of the Affairs of Italy* (published posthumously in 1532). In book II, chapter 9, Machiavelli described how, around 1350, the people of Florence, after chasing the nobility's leadership out of the city and reducing the remaining noblemen to the rank of ordinary citizens, designed a kind of mixed regime founded entirely upon itself: "The nobility being thus overcome, the people reformed the government; and as they were of three kinds, the higher, the middle, and the lower class, it was ordered that the first should appoint two signors; the two latter three each, and that the Gonfaloniere should be chosen alternately from either party" (Machiavelli, *Collected Works* 6610).

In two short treatises devoted to the designing of new institutions for Florence, written in the early 1520s, he would elaborate on this idea by sketching a system of institutions that reflected the powers of the original mixed regime but were effectively based entirely on the people.[5] Here the

---

4   There is a suggestion that Machiavelli took his material for this chapter from book 6 of Polybius' *Histories* (Hexter 75). If this is correct, chapter 11 of that same book (which deals with the Roman Constitution) would be a plausible source of inspiration for Machiavelli's conception of the consular royal power existing separate from its monarchical source ("for if we confine our observation to the power of the Consuls we should be inclined to regard it as despotic"; Polybius, *Histories* 380).

5   *Discursus on Remodelling the Government of Florence* (1520) and the *Minuta di provvisione per la riforma dello stato di Firenze* (1522). They were written in response to the invitation by Cardinal Giulio de' Medici's announcement in 1519 that he wanted to consult the citizens of Florence on their ideas about the right constitution of the city. The *Discursus* was dedicated

Galenic theory of the bodily humours helped to revolutionise the mixed regime theory: in the course of its functioning, the new constitution would lead to the gradual mixing of the two dominant humours (of the *grandi* and the *popolo*) until there was no longer a meaningful difference between them.[6]

Another innovative aspect of Machiavelli's constitutional theory was his claim that the founding of a republic didn't necessarily have to be the most important moment in its constitutional history, or at least not the decisive one. A constitution, in other words, was a *living* entity, capable of development. This development in turn was linked to another innovative idea, namely that of discord as the driving force of constitutional development.

Conventional Renaissance humanist constitutional theory had claimed with Cicero that the ultimate aim of the mixed regime was stability through unity (*concordia*). It could achieve that because "there is no reason for change in a country where everyone is firmly established in his own place" (Cicero, *The Republic* 32). The ideal example here as discussed by Machiavelli's contemporaries was that of Venice, the *Serenissima* – a republic whose constitution had seemingly guaranteed permanent stability by freezing relations between one, few, and many. It was the Venetian model that had inspired the reform of the Florentine republican constitution after 1502, especially the introduction of a lifetime position for the Gonfaloniere as highest-ranked official in government – similar to the position of the Doge in the Venetian constitution. Even after the fall of the republic, the Venetian model would retain a prominent position in Florentine political thought.

In book I, chapter 2 of his *Discourses*, Machiavelli argued for the exact opposite approach: the mixed regime would work best when it *didn't* guarantee stability, when all estates continually pursued their own ambitions, and when conflicts between the estates ("tumults") were frequent. It wasn't peace and quiet but "friction between the plebs and the senate that brought this perfection about" (111). Against Venice's stability, he put Rome's restless ambition. Dynamism and internal friction together helped to form the ideal constitution as described by Machiavelli: the Rome of the early Republic. It was its initial ability to adapt that allowed the Roman republican constitution gradually to take on the aspects of an optimal mixed regime: "In spite of the fact that Rome had no Lycurgus to give it at the outset such a constitution as would ensure to it a long life of freedom, yet, owing to

to the Medici Pope Leo X and was written with him in mind; the *Minuta* was a revised version written after Leo X's death in 1521.

6   Here I am following the interpretation of the two treatises by Raimondi.

friction between the plebs and the senate, so many things happened that chance effected what had not been provided by a lawgiver" (110).

This adaptability was itself also something that could be lost, if not valued properly by those in charge of the constitution's maintenance. It was the Roman republic's lack of ability to keep on adapting its constitution that would eventually lead to its downfall. A longer life for the republic might have been possible, he observed in book I, chapter 18, "had the introduction of new laws [to tackle various forms of corruption] been accompanied by a modification of the institutions" (161). It led Machiavelli to formulate his famous maxim of *riddure ai principii*, set out in *Discourses* III, chapter 1: that in order that "a state should long survive, it should frequently be restored to its original principles" (385). There were two ways this could happen: either by "its own intrinsic good sense" or, more likely, "by some external event" or "some internal occurrence" (386). His contemporaries treated these kinds of shocks to the system as problems because they threatened to disturb the republic's constitutional balance and internal peace. But to Machiavelli, they were useful because it was "essential that men who live under any constitution should frequently have their attention called to themselves" (387).

The purpose served by such internal or external challenges was so important to him that he even suggested planning for the occasions when *fortuna* was too kind to the republic: "[B]etween one case of action of this type and the next there ought to elapse at most ten years, because by this time men begin to change their habits and to break the laws" (*Discourses* 388). It was in fact for this reason that in the pre-republican period (1434–1494) the governing class of Florence "used to say that it was necessary to reconstitute the government every five years; otherwise, it was difficult to maintain it" (388). Should a republic ignore to update its constitutional arrangements, Machiavelli further observed in *Discourses* III, chapter 9, this would almost inevitably lead to its demise: "It thus comes about that a man's fortune changes, for she changes his circumstances, but he doesn't change his way. The downfall of cities also comes about because institutions in republics do not change with the times" (432).

Empire and Liberty

To maintain itself in time, the republic would also have to find a way of maintaining itself in space. This wasn't just a matter of holding one's own. Strengthening a territory by expanding it was, to Machiavelli, a perfectly acceptable strategy: "Wanting to annex territory is indeed very natural and normal, and when capable men undertake it, they are always praised or, at least, not criticised" (*The Prince* 13). Rome was the most obvious example here. After all, the city had shown the world how to combine republican liberty with the expansionist ambitions of empire. Machiavelli explicitly stated that the purpose of the *Discourses* was to instruct "those who plan to convert a city into a great empire" (281; II: ch. 3).

In embracing expansion as a constitutional objective, Machiavelli firmly placed himself in the Florentine republican humanist tradition. Based on a foundation myth about the city in which it was presented as an offshoot of the Roman republic, authors like Leonardo Bruni (1370–1444) had argued that as "true Roman race, heirs of Romulus" (Bruni 86) it was Florence's "destiny" (94) to "gain power and mastery over the whole earth" (...) "by right of succession" (112).

It is important to understand that to these authors, the Roman empire as we know it – that of the Caesars, born after the demise of the republic in the first century BCE – was a corruption of the original *republican* empire. In post-republican Roman political theory, the republic had come to be interpreted as categorically different from the empire. Where the empire represented order, the republic represented liberty. But to the early Renaissance Florentine thinkers, this was a misinterpretation of Roman history. The republic was itself an empire: an empire of liberty.[7]

This embrace of republican expansionism pitted Machiavelli against his contemporaries, most of whom looked to Venice as the prime example of a successful republic. The secret of Venice's success, according to them, was its ability to control its impulses. By ignoring the natural urge to conquer and dominate, the Venetian republic had been able to keep itself aloof from world affairs for nearly eight hundred years. It achieved this in part by keeping arms, and the martial instincts that came with using them, out of Venetian politics. Its fighting was done by mercenary armies, allowing the citizenry of Venice to devote itself exclusively to politics, commerce, and the arts. To make sure the city stayed free of internal troubles, it had also fixed citizenship rules so that only those whose families participated in the founding of the city could participate in running its affairs. Families who arrived afterwards were excluded from active citizenship – in perpetuity. This made Venetian politics extremely stable and predictable. It may have seemed lacking in dynamism compared to other more ambitious

---

7   On Machiavelli's relationship with the Florentine republican tradition, specifically on the issue of territorial expansion, see Mikael Hörnqvist, *Machiavelli and Empire*.

Italian states, but according to its admirers, this was exactly what made it successful.

Machiavelli would discuss the choice between Venice and Rome in some depth in book I, chapter 6 of his *Discourses*. He was willing to accept in principle that, "to set up a republic which is to last a long time, the way to set about it is to constitute it like (…) Venice; to place it in a strong position, and so to fortify it that no one will dream of taking it by a sudden assault" (122; I: ch. 6. Subsequent quotations in this section are drawn from the same chapter).

If life was predictable and stable, this might have been an ideal solution. But since, Machiavelli observed, "human affairs are ever in a state of flux and cannot stand still, either there will be improvement or decline" (123). Planning for every eventuality meant anyone seeking to construct a new constitution would also have to consider the question of expansion as a way of protecting its liberty: "Should, then, anyone be about to set up a republic, he should first inquire whether it is to expand as Rome, both in dominion and in power, or is to be confined to narrow limits" (122). Here, he argued, history clearly favoured Rome over Venice. Whereas the Romans managed to conquer and control all of Italy and then large parts of Europe, North Africa, and the Middle East, Venice was incapable of defending her dominions: "[W]hen its strength was put to the test, [she] lost everything in a single battle" (122).[8]

According to Machiavelli, this defeat was an accident waiting to happen. Having always prioritised stability over everything else, Venice was simply not equipped for the kind of exposure to fortune that expansion of its territory would bring. Thus, "if a commonwealth be constituted with a view to its maintaining the *status quo*, but not with a view to expansion, and by necessity it be led to expand, its basic principles will be subverted and it will soon be faced with ruin" (123).

Even if a long peace was virtually guaranteed, the Venetian option was the less desirable of the two since it would lead to the kind of vices that would leave the republic weakened. In his characteristically misogynistic prose, Machiavelli concluded that, "should heaven (…) be so kind to [a commonwealth] that it has no need to go to war, it will then come about that idleness will either render it effeminate or give rise to factions; and these two things, either in conjunction or separately, will bring about its downfall" (123). Instead of planning for stability, the more prudent option was therefore to

---

8   The battle of Agniadello of 1509, in which a French army routed part of the Venetian army. In *The Prince*, Machiavelli would write about this battle that in a single day, the Venetians had "lost what they gained with so much effort over eight hundred years" (46).

follow the method of the Romans and put up with "[s]quabbles between the populace and the senate" as the best way of "arriving at the greatness of Rome" (123–124). His preference for Rome over Venice made sense given the changed circumstances of the early sixteenth century. But choosing the method of the Romans inevitably meant that the republic would also have to decide whether it wanted to pursue a strategy of territorial expansion – and if so, how.

—

In Book II, chapter 4 of the *Discourses*, Machiavelli reflected on what he described as the three main methods of expansion for republics. One was that of conquest followed by subjection – making new states subjects instead of allies: "[T]o undertake the responsibility of governing cities by force, especially such as have been accustomed to self-government, is a difficult and tiresome business. And unless you have armed forces, and they are strong forces, you can neither impose obedience on, nor rule, them" (284–285; II: ch. 4. Subsequent quotes are also from this chapter). This method was therefore "quite useless" (284), as the examples of Sparta and Athens had shown.

The second method, the one used by republican Rome, was the one that Machiavelli thought worked best under ideal circumstances. It was "forming alliances in which you reserve to yourself the headship, the seat in which the central authority resides, and the right of initiative" (284.) A republic bent on expansion would be wise to use this method, "for experience has shown that there is no other that is so certain or so sure." However, to imitate Rome was probably too great a challenge for Florence: "[A] great many institutions observed in Rome, pertaining to both internal and to foreign affairs, are not only not imitated at the present time, but are deemed to be of no account" (287). As a result, the Florentines had "become the prey of anybody who wanted to overrun this land" (288). With the barbarians almost constantly at the city gates, there was no time to design and implement an ideal strategy. The search was for a solution that worked in the here and now.

That left the third method which, though not ideal, was "next best to that of the Romans" (286) – that of "forming a league consisting of several republics in which no one of them had preference, authority or rank above the others" (283). Expansion here could happen by conquest but was usually a consensus process, based on equal treatment. In several places in the *Discourses* Machiavelli discussed the Amphictyonic and Achaean Leagues in ancient Greece, and the Swiss Confederacy and Holy Roman Empire in contemporary Europe, as examples of confederate leagues consisting of free republics. His preferred historical example, however, was that of the

Etruscans, whose success in maintaining their state for hundreds of years was based on a league for mutual defence and governance: "[W]hen other cities were acquired, they made them constituent members in the same way as the Swiss act in our time and as in Greece the Achaeans and the Aetolians acted in olden times" (283).

Though he saw some advantages – not being drawn into wars unnecessarily and being able to hold onto new territory without any effort – there was a problem which set it behind the Roman method. It involved its mode of decision-making: "[I]ts members are distinct and each has its own capital; which makes it difficult for them to consult and to make decisions" (286). "A league is governed by a council," he observed, and this meant it "must needs be slower in arriving at any decision than those who dwell within one and the same circle" (286).

An additional problem was that leagues seemed to have a natural limit beyond which expansion invariably tended to lead to problems:

> Experience shows (...) that such a method of forming a confederation has a fixed limit, and that there is no case which indicates that this limit can be transcended. For, having attained the stage at which it seems to them they can defend themselves against all comers, they do not try to extend their dominion. (...) Those who went beyond the appropriate limit were speedily ruined.
> (287)

This was chiefly a matter of organisational capacity, but it also had an internal political aspect. Expanding the league would mean decreasing the power of the existing member states. That, Machiavelli thought, would make it less likely that they would support continued expansion: "[T]hey do not appreciate further acquisitions as does a single republic which hopes to enjoy the whole" (286).

Despite these problematic aspects, Machiavelli ended up recommending this option as the more practical one for Florence: "[I]f to imitate the Roman way seems to be difficult, that of the Tuscans of old should not appear so difficult, especially to the Tuscans of today [i.e., the Florentines]. For, though they were unable, for the reasons assigned, to form an empire like that of Rome, they did succeed in acquiring in Italy such power as this method of proceeding allowed" (288).[9] The league option left the Tuscans "for a long time secure, resulting in the greatest glories of empire" (288).

---

9   Though he doesn't mention it in this passage, it's entirely possible that Machiavelli had in mind the Italic League of 1454, established through the Treaty of Lodi, which for forty years

Empire in the form of a league of city states might be the most secure way in which a republic like Florence could maintain its state and its liberty over time. In the end, though, Machiavelli observed that empires were as vulnerable to the laws of corruption as republics. In fact, expansion might even hasten its disintegration: "Had the Romans not prolonged offices and military commands, they would not have attained such great power in so short a time, and, had they been slower in making conquests, they would also have been slower to arrive at servitude" (*Discourses* 474; III: ch. 24). Even for empires there was no escaping the iron law of corruption as formulated by Machiavelli: decline and fall was inevitable whatever path was chosen. The problem of time would remain, even for the most successful republics. This being the case, he argued, a republic might as well get there by going down the empire route. At least that way it could achieve *grandezza*, greatness, before it faded into nothingness.

Intermezzo: Leagues in Ancient Greece

Although the dominant regime form during the brief golden age of classical democracy in the fifth century BCE was the city-state (*polis*), Greek antiquity also produced numerous examples of leagues (*koinè*).

The one that would be most often mentioned in the period covered in this book (1500–1951), the *Amphictyonic League*, actually predated the Athenian golden age. Though at times it took political positions, it was not strictly speaking a political league but a religious one, centred on the Mysteries at Delphi. What made it remarkable was that it was based on the tribes that had first settled Greece rather than the normal carriers of political authority in the classical period: the city-states and regional communities.

The first federal moment in Greek history came after the decline of Athens, Sparta, and Thebes, in the early part of the fourth century BCE. The lack of a major power that maintained a sense of order in the Greek civilisational area likely forced the many smaller cities to form defensive confederations (Freeman 185).

The most remarkable of the many leagues formed in this period was that of Lykia. What little is known of its constitution is derived from the work of the Greek philosopher Strabo, who lived in the first century BCE. He described it as having a "general congress" of "23 cities that share in the vote." For voting, they used a form of proportional representation, giving

kept the peace between the five main powers of Italy (Florence, the Papal States, Venice, Milan, and Naples) and united them in a league for defensive purposes.

the larger cities three votes, the middle-sized two, and the smaller ones a single vote each. The congress had the power of appointment, electing a president called Lykiarch as well as a number of other executive officials. It also elected judges and magistrates to keep the peace and help settle legal disputes, which suggests the existence of a common legal code. The congress further had the power to decide on matters of war and peace, and to send and receive diplomatic missions (Behrwald 408).

In the period of federal revival, from 280 BCE onwards, two leagues competed for dominance: the Achaean league, on the Peloponnesos, and the Aetolian league in central Greece. We know most about the Achaean League, thanks to an extensive discussion of its history and features by Polybius, who was a native of the region. In his *Histories*, he described it as having "adopted the same laws, weights and measures, and coinage," and sharing "statesmen, council, and law courts" (bk II, ch. 37). Foreign policy and matters of war and peace were considered the exclusive preserve of the league. In all other matters the member cities governed themselves. And though the League did fight wars of conquest, the conquered territories would as a rule be offered membership on equal terms with the existing member cities. The Achaean League came to an end through a Roman victory in the final battle of the Achaean war, at Corinth (146 BCE).

The end of the *Respublica Christiana*

The Europe in which Machiavelli lived and worked was based on a geopolitical framework that had been around for hundreds of years. The many powers and principalities of Europe were bound together in what would eventually be termed the *Respublica Christiana* (Tuck 27–29). It was a political fiction through which European countries and territories maintained the suggestion of political unity in the absence of actual unity. If it ever had existed, it was only temporary, in the face of a common threat, and would dissolve as soon as the danger had abated.

The medieval use of the imperial title was not without its theoretical challenges. After all, strictly speaking, it belonged to the Roman era. To a neutral observer it would seem that this period had clearly come to an end but accepting that conclusion would have caused a significant religious problem. The Book of Daniel had presented the prophecy of the Four Empires. History would see a sequence of four realms that would have to appear and decline before the coming of "one like a son of man," who would be given "everlasting dominion that will not pass away" (Daniel 7:13–14). Given that in Christian eschatology, the four empires had come to be interpreted as referring to the Babylonian, the Persian, the Greek, and the Roman empires, it was therefore essential that any new European empire could find a way of presenting itself as a continuation of the Roman one.

The process that was eventually developed under the Carolingians, the *translatio imperii* (translation of empire), helped to solve this problem. In doing so, however, it created another. At the theoretical level, the empire was considered to be singular, universal, and therefore indivisible (Wilson 38–40). If this was the case, how then to explain the presence of a second empire in the form of Byzantium? For centuries, the two empires would basically solve this dilemma by denying the other's existence, though they did at times flirt with the idea of unification through marriage. It may not have been a convincing strategy, but it was more attractive than the alternative, which was a fight for supremacy (140–141). In the end, the fall of Constantinople would solve the Two emperors problem for the Holy Roman Empire – until, that is, Napoleon reintroduced it with a vengeance by crowning himself emperor in 1804. After that, the nineteenth century would see a proliferation of empires – at the peak, Europe counted no fewer than four of them.[10] A hundred years later, they had all disappeared.

—

The second of the "Two Swords" that supposedly ruled Europe was the spiritual power – the papacy. This would come under increased pressure from two directions. One source of pressure came from rulers who treated the Vatican as a rival political power in their own lands. In the eleventh and twelfth centuries, this struggle focused on the power of both sides to fill clerical posts with their own candidates (the Investiture Controversy). In the fourteenth century the papal election itself, and the seat of its authority, became the focus. During the Western Schism in the late fourteenth century, the College of Cardinals had elected two different popes, each with a separate seat of authority – the official pope had been forcibly returned to Rome, while a politically backed antipope continued to rule from Avignon, where the papacy had settled in the early part of that century.

10　The second half of the nineteenth century would see five different heads of state claim the title: the Austrian emperor, the Russian Tsar, the French emperor, the German emperor, and Victoria as empress of India. But the five would not rule simultaneously. The French Empire ended with the abdication of Napoleon III in 1871, mere months before the coronation of the first German emperor, Wilhelm I. And Victoria would not assume the title of empress until 1877.

With its political authority under threat, the papacy also saw its spiritual authority undermined through early Reformation movements in Central and Eastern Europe. One of the earliest European federal schemes, proposed by King George of Bohemia in 1463, would see the two issues unite in a single, direct challenge to the Pope's authority. The crisis had been provoked by the Papal Curia's decision to revoke the Compacts of Basle of 1433. This agreement, which settled the Bohemian civil war, had given moderate Hussite priests the right to share both bread and wine with the laity during the Eucharist. Pope Pius II's decision to annul this meant that once again, only priests would be allowed to drink the wine – a seemingly small issue but politically highly significant because it reinstated a hierarchy that the Hussite revolt had sought to abolish.

Scrapping the Compacts also posed a political problem of the first order for King George. The peace on which his realm was based was suddenly under threat. Even worse, when he refused to accept the Pope's demand, the latter declared him a heretic – a status that would have undermined his ability to represent his kingdom on the international stage (Kavka et al. 42). He had to come up with a plan to outflank the Pope, by placing himself at the heart of European affairs (53).

The initial idea was to propose that Bohemia would lead a crusade by an anti-Turkish defence league as a European response to the fall of Constantinople ten years earlier, in 1453. But when the Pope beat him to it by proposing his own crusader coalition, George proposed something entirely different: a union (*unio*) of the rulers of Europe to establish peace and justice in internal European relations. Through an act of creative legal interpretation, he was able to propose the formation of a new kind of body: international, with all the characteristics of an artificial person as established in Roman private law clauses about the corporation (Kavka et al. 23). Following the principle of regional representation established in the Church Councils of the fifteenth century, groups of monarchs of selected regions called *nationes* – France, Spain, Germany, and Italy – were each to nominate one ruler to represent them in an assembly, where matters would be decided by majority decisions on a one member, one vote basis (*Treaty on the Establishment of Peace throughout Christendom*, Article 19; cited in Kavka et al. 90). Article 9 provided for the creation of a Court, "which will sit in the name of all of us" would help to "settle individual matters in proper order" so that "rivulets of justice will flow to all sides" (87).

Though George had managed to secure backing for the proposal from the kings of the Polish-Lithuanian Commonwealth and the Kingdom of Hungary, the plan died a quiet death when its proposed leader, the French king Louis

XI, refused to support it. His courtiers told the Bohemian delegation that "it would appertain best to the Holy Father to negotiate this with the Emperor; and that the King of Bohemia ought not to interfere in the matter" (Kavka et al. 56). As compensation, Louis granted their other request by signing a friendship treaty between the two crowns.

There are two ways to interpret this episode. The French reply suggests that even in the second half of the fifteenth century the papacy was still one of the two pillars of the European order. And the fact that Louis felt compelled to placate the papal faction at his court showed how powerful the Pope still was in European politics. But George's proposal, and the support it received from his neighbours, also showed that the Pope's position was, even then, far from undisputed.

—

In the temporal realm, during the later Middle Ages the dominant power was the Holy Roman Empire. Its history has usually been read as one of continued decline since its founding in the tenth century. Voltaire's famous quip – "Neither Holy nor Roman nor an Empire" – is typical of this interpretation. In Machiavelli's time however, the Empire was very much in the ascendancy. It would reach its zenith in 1519, when it merged with the rising power of the newly created Spanish kingdom. The two crowns were united in the person of the young Spanish king Charles V, who through inheritance and marriage would also add the Portuguese kingdom and the duchy of Burgundy to his realm.

Charles's election as Holy Roman Emperor in 1519 would expand his empire still further. It stretched from the Strait of Gibraltar all the way to the Baltic Sea, incorporating the European commercial and cultural centres of Italy and the Low Countries. Even if it didn't span the entire continent, it was still as powerful an empire as Europe had seen since the time of Charlemagne. Significantly, his vast empire also included a number of territories on the other side of the Atlantic Ocean, in both North and South America. Charles's realm therefore combined the old *territorial* idea of empire, which had been around since Roman times, with the new *colonial* one that would come to dominate the next five hundred years.

In 1513, when Machiavelli published *The Prince*, it was still possible to imagine that this system under the dual supervision of empire and papacy would continue indefinitely. In reality, it was already in its death throes. Luther's Ninety-Five Theses, published four years later, reflected broadly shared critical positions on issues of Catholic dogma developed by Christian humanist authors and early Reformation theologians.[11] In capturing the essence of this religious-intellectual movement, Luther managed to put his own stamp on it, making it an almost unstoppable force.

Charles V would spend most of his life trying to stop the Reformation's momentum and establish himself as the uncontested monarch of Europe. The closest he came to achieving the latter objective was arguably in 1525, when his army defeated a French force at the siege of Pavia in Northern Italy. The battle ended with Spanish troops taking the French king Francis I captive and sending him to Spain as Charles's prisoner. One year later, the emperor would force him to sign the humiliating Treaty of Madrid, which not only forced Francis to cede vast tracts of land to the Spanish crown, but also confirmed Charles's status as the political head of Christianity, referring to the French king as his junior partner (Lessafer 31).

Predictably, Francis I would resume hostilities immediately after being set free. He joined the English king, the Pope, the Italian republics of Florence and Venice, and the Duchy of Milan in the League of Cognac (1526). However, the end result was the same: a convincing victory for the imperial troops. After the Sack of Rome (1527), and a series of French defeats, Charles V was able to persuade the individual members of the coalition to abandon their hostilities and sign peace treaties with him. The only coalition member to hold out until the end of the war was the Florentine republic. Its fall, after an extended siege in the summer of 1530, also meant the end of the republican experiment in the city. It gave Charles a *de facto* claim to the overlordship of Italy, and therewith to the whole of Western and Central Europe.

In the end, it wasn't an external enemy but a Protestant revolt within his own Holy Roman Empire that would end Charles's domination. A decisive defeat during the Second Schmalkaldic War in 1552 against the army of a German league of Protestant principalities forced him to accept his own humiliating peace in the form of the Treaty of Augsburg (1555). This treaty established for the first time at the legal and political level the split within Europe's Christian community.[12] It was on the basis of the compromise enshrined within this treaty that legal scholars would eventually develop the doctrine of *cuius regio, eius religio* – giving local rulers the freedom to determine the religious denomination for their territory.

---

11   See Skinner, *The Foundations of Modern Political Thought* 2: 20–64.

12   There had, of course, been an earlier split in the wider Christian community in the form of the Great Schism of 1054, which separated the Eastern (Greek) Orthodox community from the Western (Latin) one.

The Peace of Augsburg was not in itself a turning point – that had come earlier. By 1540, references to papal authority had already disappeared from new international treaties, even treaties signed between Catholic parties (Lessafer 27). What Augsburg did do was confirm that Europe no longer possessed the fiction of a moral-political framework for controlling the tensions between its constituent parts. Neither the papacy nor the empire could be invoked as absolute authority in the settlement of conflicts. There was no way back to the old order.

An attempt at re-unification: universal monarchy

The decline of the *Respublica Christiana* created room for a new unifying idea. One school would seek to adapt Machiavelli's method of Rome to a modern setting. It would go by the name of *universal monarchy*. The concept was described most fully by the early Renaissance Florentine poet and sometime politician Dante Alighieri (1265–1321). In his *De Monarchia*, while making the case for "the unity of universal monarchy," Dante provided a clear sketch of its essential qualities (Dante 397). It was to be "a single sovereign authority set over all others in time, that is to say over all authorities which operate in those things and over those things which are measured by time" (143). Though placed in time, the empire was itself a manifestation of man's striving to escape from time into a realm where history was at an end – a realm of universal peace, "the goal to which all our human actions are directed as to their final end" (154–155). It was also a post-political space. Its essential quality was harmony or concord – harmony of society as a whole with God's intentions (165) and of individuals within society with each other. The required "unity of wills" (197) left no room for fundamental disagreements, least of all about the authority of the universal monarch.

———

The idea of universal monarchy seemed to have lost its significance with the relative decline of the Holy Roman Empire in the later Middle Ages. It was reintroduced in Machiavelli's own time by the chancellor of the new emperor Charles V, Mercurino di Gattinara (1465–1530). Gattinara was an Italian lawyer of relatively modest descent – though his father and grandfather had served on the local town council, his family had opposed his wish to study the law because of the costs involved. The decision to ignore his family's opinion on the matter would prove to be a fortuitous one. He quickly made a name for himself as a creative and tenacious advocate, and came to serve first the Holy Roman Emperor's sister, Margaret of Austria, who had married the local ruler in Gattinara's home region of Savoy, and then her nephew, the young monarch Charles V.

It was in the service of the king, and ultimately the emperor, that Gattinara would revive the concept of universal monarchy, to legitimate his master's ambitious expansionist agenda.[13] Like most political concepts, it was first and foremost a rhetorical tool. By appealing to Christian eschatological expectations – the promise of a post-historical realm of eternal peace – it helped to mobilise Charles's faithful subjects for his expansionist agenda. During the campaign to establish a global empire the theory could also be used as a weapon against local resistance movements, who would place themselves on the wrong side of God and history by opposing expansion. If possible, Gattinara preferred expansion by peaceful means to military conquest. The latter invariably had to be financed through new taxes at home, risking rebellion at the very moment when military forces were already stretched.[14] It made him one of the first modern proponents of the use of soft power as a diplomatic strategy (Boone 17).

"Universal" monarchy may sound ambitious to a modern audience, but with extensive Spanish possessions in both Asia and the Americas, it certainly seemed a plausible objective to Gattinara's contemporaries. In European debate, universal was also interpreted not so much as "covering the whole world" as "covering all of Europe." As such, it was very much considered a realistic aspiration, by supporters and detractors alike.

While Charles would never fulfil his – or Gattinara's – ambition of uniting all of Europe under his rule, the *idea* of universal monarchy would remain a powerful force in European politics and political thought for centuries to come. One of its most eloquent, and certainly one of its most interesting defenders was the Italian monk Tommaso Campanella (1561–1639). Campanella would spend most of his adult life in prison on charges of heresy

---

13   Gattinara would try to bring back not just the *idea* of universal monarchy but even its most eloquent spokesman, Dante. He approached the humanist scholar Erasmus to produce a critical edition of the text – something Erasmus ultimately refused. See Boone 127. On the reasons for Erasmus' refusal, see also Van Gelderen, "Universal Monarchy, the Rights of War and Peace and the Balance of Power" 51–54.

14   Gattinara's wisdom would be ignored by subsequent Spanish monarchs, to their cost. In the late 1560s, a ten per cent levy ("Tiende Penning," basically a value added tax) imposed by Philip II's governor of the Low Countries on the sale of food and drink provoked the ire of the Dutch provinces, and became one of the reasons for the escalation of the Dutch Revolt. And in 1640, Catalonia would rise up in revolt over Philip IV's government's violation of its long-established right to be excluded from both taxation and troop levies by the Spanish crown.

and involvement in a plot against Spanish rule. While in prison he wrote a number of books, including a tract titled *On the Spanish Monarchy* (1600), advising the Spanish emperor on how to achieve universal rule.

The book gained notoriety for a number of reasons. One was the instrumental way in which he wrote about organised religion, especially about the use of the clergy to the emperor. In chapter 6, "How the Clergy Are to Be Dealt Withal," he suggested that "it is not sufficient we have the clergy on our side." To make sure the church really worked for the empire, "we are further to labour that at length we get a Spaniard to be elected Pope, or rather, one of the House of Austria" (Campanella 25). Whereas in the old order of the *Respublica Christiana* emperor and pope were rivals, as well as the dual pillars on which the order rested, Campanella suggested that in the new order the Pope was a political pawn, there to serve the emperor's purpose (though the emperor's purpose in turn was to serve the Catholic faith, of which the Pope was the living embodiment).

The book also contained several chapters advising the Spanish monarch on how to divide and conquer the other parts of Europe. All strategic suggestions were connected with the overarching goal of establishing a universal monarchy. Bringing the rebelling Dutch provinces onside helped to control the German hinterland. Infiltrating the Polish court by getting a Habsburg prince elected as Polish-Lithuanian monarch could, in turn, help to keep the Baltic fleet free for campaigns against England. Campanella also gave advice on how to divide and destabilise English society: apart from setting the Scots and Irish against the English, and hiring all the fleets of Western Europe to harass and incapacitate the English fleet, he suggested fostering divisions within England by sponsoring Protestant religious sects. This advice caused such a scandal among the English elite that they gave him the moniker "the second Machiavel."

The Spanish monarchy would eventually not prove equal to the task of establishing a universal monarchy. It had probably already passed its zenith by the time Campanella wrote his book (the death of Philip II in 1598 is generally seen as a turning point). By the time he was finally released from prison, Campanella therefore set himself the task of addressing the same challenge to the state that was, in his view, the most likely successor to the candidacy: the French monarchy.[15] In *On the French Monarchy*, he would

---

15   This is not as inconsistent as it seems. In *On the Spanish Monarchy*, he had already written that "there is no Christian Kingdome, that is more able to oppose, and put a stop to the growing of the *Spanish Monarchy,* than *France*" (144). With Spain's relative decline, France became the natural successor.

repeat the same exercise he had completed in 1600, this time offering his advice to the French court on how to infiltrate the higher ranks of the clergy and divide and conquer the other territories of Europe.

The counter-concept: sovereignty

Universal monarchy would provoke a number of competing counter-ideas. One of these was a concept that would take the same idea of an omnipotent monarch but impose a geographical and logical limit on it.

—

The period 1550–1650 would be dominated by some of the bloodiest wars in European history. These conflicts, though not without territorial and dynastic motives, were mostly a product of the growing Catholic–Protestant divide. The schism, which had already shown glimpses of its violent potential during the Second Schmalkaldic War (1551–1555), would fully erupt during the French Wars of Religion (1562–1598), pitting Catholics against Huguenot Protestants.

France in 1560 was a country on the brink. Royal grip on power was far from secure, with the fifteen-year-old King Francis II unable to impose order on rival noble factions at the court. His untimely death that same year only increased uncertainty. Meanwhile, religious fanaticism was reaching fever pitch, with Protestant iconoclastic furies in several cities putting Catholics on high alert. The queen regent Catherine de' Medici pursued a policy of practical toleration – issuing a series of edicts emphasising the status of Catholicism as the official religion but calling for all violence against Protestant worshippers to cease. This approach ended in catastrophe when the leader of one of the main factions at the court, the Duc de Guise, led a band of his soldiers in a massacre of Protestant worshippers in Wassy in early 1562.

It was the opening salvo of three decades of civil war. Among its most notorious episodes was the St Bartholomew's Day Massacre (1572), a week of anti-Protestant pogroms that saw the slaughter of thousands of Huguenots in Paris and cities up and down the land. The conflict would finally end in 1598 when the new king Henry IV passed the Edict of Nantes, which made religious toleration the official policy of the French state.

—

It is in this context of bloody, religiously inspired civil war that we must read the work of the French legal scholar Jean Bodin (1530–1596). His *Six Livres de la Republique* (1576) formed a conscious attempt to provide a theoretical solution to the conflict – not on religious grounds, but on constitutional ones. He did it by taking a well-established concept and giving an entirely new meaning to it.

In the writings of Machiavelli, the word *imperium* was used in two different ways. One was what we would call "empire," which in Machiavelli's work referred to both the reality of the republic, with its current conquests, as well as the ambition of further expansion. The other meaning was the "rule" or "power" of the persons administering a territory, also translated as "sovereignty." He talked about princes "holding the sovereignty" over dominions (Machiavelli, *Collected Works* 326), of persons "rising to sovereignty" (398), of Caesar being "one of those who sought the sovereignty of Rome" (1065). Sovereignty seemed to be everywhere: a prince could possess it and so could a local ruler. The fact that the latter's sovereignty was limited was of no consequence: they were still a sovereign in their own right. An important aspect of this second use of the concept of *imperium* was its divisibility. It followed almost naturally out of Machiavelli's embrace of the concept of the mixed regime. If the king, the nobles, and the people all had a share in the government of the *res publica*, all were to a certain extent holders of sovereignty.

These were the ideas that Bodin set out to challenge. He started by arguing that sovereignty, by definition, had to be the *highest* power, "the absolute and perpetual power of a commonwealth" (Bodin 1). Since it had to be the ultimate power, it therefore made no sense to speak of the sovereignty of lower ranked local rulers or noblemen at the court. From claiming there were no other forms of sovereignty apart from the highest (*summum imperium*), it was a small step to conclude that sovereignty could not in fact have any kind of limits imposed on it – not even from other constitutional actors. Sovereignty as defined by Bodin was "not limited in power, or in function, or in length of time" (3).

This conclusion led Bodin to reject categorically the idea, embraced by Machiavelli, that the ideal regime was a mix of monarchy, aristocracy, and democracy. Against the classical and Renaissance tradition he argued that "no such state has ever existed, and none can be made or even imagined, because the prerogatives of sovereignty are indivisible" (104). Since the sovereign's power to legislate could never be limited by "any greater, equal or below him" (56), Bodin could only accept three possible regime forms, all based on complete and undivided sovereignty: either the sovereignty of one (monarchy), the sovereignty of the few (aristocracy), or the sovereignty of the many (democracy).[16]

Having thus eliminated the option of a mixed regime by showing that within any constitution the sovereign power could never accept any limits on itself, the final step in his argument was to show that there was also no regime cycle that could transform a monarchy into something else. The sovereign's actions and decisions could not be subject to a right of revolt, as claimed by radical Protestant theologians. "To induce the subjects to rebel against their natural princes," Bodin warned, would mean "opening the door to a licentious anarchy, which is worse than the harshest tyranny in the world" (quoted in Skinner, *Foundations* 2: 285).

To Bodin, this vision of "licentious anarchy" was more than a theoretical observation: he had witnessed firsthand the bloodshed during the St Bartholomew's Day massacres. The shock of this personal experience of political violence must have been great, because he went on to argue that no action of the sovereign could ever justify attempting to remove him from power, "even if he has committed all the wickedness, impiety and cruelty that one could mention" (Bodin 115). Contrary to the argument in the most famous of the Huguenot tracts, *Vindiciae Contra Tyrannos*, published anonymously a few years later (1579), Bodin claimed that even in such circumstances regime change was not only not called for but actually illegitimate. A sovereign never stopped being sovereign, no matter how bad his rule. He acknowledged that subjects did have the right to ignore manifestly unjust edicts, but it was not for them to remove from power the king that issued them.

The fact that Bodin thought of the sovereign's power as unimpeachable did not mean he thought that it should also be unlimited. He accepted certain limits on sovereign power in the form of custom and natural law: "[T]here is no prince in all the world who has the power to levy taxes on the people at his pleasure any more than he has the power to take another's goods" (Bodin 21). In Bodin's scheme, the core of a sovereign's power lay in their monopoly on the power of legislation, which was elevated above all other powers of government: "We thus see that the main point of sovereign majesty and absolute power consists of giving law to the subjects in general

---

16   In book 2, chapter 1, Bodin did admit that there are practical examples of mixed regimes, for example in Denmark: "[W]e might say that the king of Denmark and his nobility each have a share of sovereignty." But, he concluded, "one can also say that this commonwealth has no assured repose." His fundamental objection to mixed regimes was therefore not that they couldn't exist but that they couldn't *persist* (105).

without their consent" (23), or more pithily: "Law is the command of the sovereign" (51). But this power, which he called "the one prerogative of sovereignty, inasmuch as all the other rights are comprehended in it," could only be used in a limited number of areas.[17] These enumerated powers he called "the marks of sovereignty":

> [D]eclaring war or making peace, hearing appeals in last instance from the judgments of any magistrate; instituting and removing the highest officers; imposing taxes and aids on subjects or exempting them; granting pardons and dispensations against the rigour of the law; determining the name, value, and measure of the coinage; requiring subjects and liege vassals to swear that they will be loyal without exception.
> (58–59)

Bodin's book was a spectacular success, going through no fewer than twenty-four editions by the end of the sixteenth century. Translated versions would appear in Latin (edited by Bodin himself), English, German, Italian, and Spanish.[18] The text would play a crucial role in shaping the debate about the emerging concept of the state. The traditional view of society as based on a hierarchy of ever-expanding social circles was confronted with the possibility of an upper limit in the form of the sovereign's realm. Over land beyond their borders, monarchs could not claim sovereignty. Conversely, no foreign monarch could make a claim to match the sovereignty of a realm's own sovereign. In redefining the concept of *imperium* as sovereignty, Bodin had thus both increased its scope nationally and limited it internationally (Onuf 48–49).

—

The latter argument would be developed more fully by the English philosopher Thomas Hobbes (1588–1679). Like Bodin, Hobbes was confronted with a bloody civil war, the result of a conflict between King Charles I and Parliament in the 1640s. His first priority was therefore to find a way to safeguard internal stability. He sought it by providing a theoretical justification for absolute kingship; and,

17   Even Bodin's sovereign, it seems, couldn't fully escape the paradoxical nature of sovereignty: the more absolute the position of the sovereign was, the more limited their power tended to be. This paradox is described at some length by David Graeber and David Wengrow in chapter 10 of their study *The Dawn of Everything* ("Why The State Has No Origin: The Humble Beginnings of Sovereignty, Bureaucracy and Politics").

18   See Bodin's Biography, part 2, Harvard Bodin Project, https://projects.iq.harvard.edu/bodinproject/biography-bodin-page-2

like Bodin, he found his solution in a definition of sovereignty as the indivisible superior power in a commonwealth and in the rejection of the regime cycle, which in classical regime theory was linked to the idea that each legitimate regime type had its corrupt form. He would specifically reject the latter idea, in his *De Cive* (*On the Citizen*, 1642), in a chapter titled "On the Three Kinds of Commonwealth": "[T]hese are not three further kinds of commonwealth, but three alternative names, which have been bestowed by people who were annoyed with a government or its members" (Hobbes, *On the Citizen* 418).

In his magnum opus *Leviathan*, published at the very end of the Civil War (1651), he further defined the solution as the creation of a "Power (...) great enough for our security." The idea of a covenant (*foedus*) was not in itself enough to establish a commonwealth. After all, "Covenants, without the Sword, are but Words, and of no strength to secure a man at all" (494). Safety was to be found in strength. And in numbers: what was required was the consent not of a few but of a multitude, "not determined by any certain number, but by comparison with the Enemy we feare" (497). This multitude in turn would have to be directed by a single power, continuously. It was upon this common power, whose aim was to "defend them from the invasion of Forraigners, and the injuries of one another," that "all power and strength" was conferred, thereby "[reducing] all their Wills, by plurality of voices, unto one Will" (507). And though he admitted that in theory this Leviathan or state could take the form of either the rule of one or the rule of many, Hobbes was clear that, ultimately, it was only the rule of one that could secure the long term stability of the commonwealth: "[A] Monarch cannot disagree with himself, out of envy, or interest; but an Assembly may, and that to such a height, as may produce a Civill Warre" (569).

Having established the solution, Hobbes then set out the factors that could undermine the health of the commonwealth. The most important factor here was "imperfect institutions." He rejected the idea of division of powers. Where Machiavelli saw the potential for creative friction between these powers, Hobbes feared their destructive potential. Such a scenario was "plainly and directly against the essence of a Common-wealth. (...) For what is it to divide the Power of a Common-wealth but to Dissolve it; for Powers divided mutually destroy each other" (Hobbes, *Leviathan* 997). For that same reason he rejected the idea of a mixed regime: "This endangereth the Common-wealth. (...) For although few perceive, that such government, is not government, but division of the Common-wealth into three Factions, and call it mixt Monarchy; yet the truth is, that it is not one independent Common-wealth, but three independent factions; not one Representative Person, but three" (1009).

Health for a commonwealth was about more than just good institutions though. It was also a matter of the right attitude. Hobbes warned against the effect on the spirit, of both the citizen and the Commonwealth as a whole, of imitation of models alien to the commonwealth, both those of neighbouring nations and, especially, of the Greeks and Romans: "[A]s to Rebellion in particular against Monarchy; one of the most frequent causes of it, is the Reading of the books of Policy, and Histories of the ancient Greeks, and Romans" (Hobbes, *Leviathan* 1000). Young men, easily impressed by "the great exploits of warre," would rush headlong to imitate these examples, failing to consider "the frequent Seditions, and Civill Warres, produced by the imperfection of their Policy" (1001).

The ultimate objective of the Hobbesian commonwealth was the opposite of the kind of violent ambition praised by Machiavelli as the driving force of human development. He valued above all the virtue of *contentment*, which he made the central objective of all human striving: "[T]he voluntary actions, and inclinations of all men, tend not only to the procuring, but also to the assuring of a contented life" (Hobbes, *Leviathan*, 260). It was intimately tied up with the covenant through which a multitude could create its own Leviathan or commonwealth: "The finall Cause, End, or Designe of men (who naturally love Liberty, and Dominion over others), in the introduction of that restraint upon themselves, (in which wee see them live in Common-wealths) is the foresight of their own preservation, and of a more contented life thereby" (492).

Hobbes used the word contentment both in the material sense of "every man (...) contented with his share" (Hobbes, *Leviathan* 341) and in the sense of accepting their station, "a more contented life" (492). Contentment wasn't just a required quality in the citizen; it was also a core virtue of the sovereign. The alternative was a restlessness which expressed itself in "insatiable appetite, or Bulimia, of enlarging Dominion" (1018). The problem here wasn't just the potential cost of war, "the incurable Wounds thereby many times received from the enemy" (1018). There was also the potential cost of victory, "of ununited conquests, which are many times a burden, and with lesse danger lost, than kept" (1019). Expansion, a natural ambition for a commonwealth in Machiavelli's work, was transformed by Hobbes into one of the main destabilising forces of the commonwealth.

—

By limiting its reach geographically, and by making it antithetical to the idea of expansion as propagated by Machiavelli, Bodin, and Hobbes had introduced a concept that would pose a significant challenge to aspiring universal monarchs. By stressing its indivisibility, they also created a significant challenge for another answer to the collapse of the old *Respublica Christiana*: a number of territories uniting under a common governing structure, for the purpose of guaranteeing their joint security.

Bibliography

Aristotle. *The Politics*, edited by Stephen Everson, Cambridge University Press, 1988.

Behrwald, Ralf. "The Lykian League." *Federalism in Greek Antiquity*, edited by Hans Beck and Peter Funke, Cambridge University Press, 2015, pp. 403–418.

Bodin, Jean. *On Sovereignty*. 1576. Cambridge University Press, 1992.

Boone, Rebecca Ard. *Mercurino di Gattinara and the Creation of the Spanish Empire*. Routledge, 2014.

Bruni, Leonardo. *In Praise of Florence*. 1403–1404. Olive Press, 2005.

Campanella, Tomasso. *On the Spanish Monarchy*, translated by Edmund Chilmead, Philemon Stephens, 1654.

Cicero, Marcus Tullius. *The Republic and The Laws*, translated by Niall Rudd, Oxford University Press, 1998.

Dante Alighieri. *Monarchy*. 1312–1313. Edited and translated by Prue Shaw, Cambridge University Press, 2010.

Freeman, Edward. *History of Federal Government*. 1863. Ulan Press, 2012.

Gelderen, Martin van. "Universal Monarchy, the Rights of War and Peace and the Balance of Power." *Reflections on Europe: Defining a Political Order in Time and Space*, edited by Hans Åke Persson and Bo Stråth, Peter Lang, 2016, pp. 49–71.

Geuna, Marco. "The Tension between Law and Politics in the Modern Republican Tradition." *Republican Democracy: Liberty, Law and Politics*, edited by Andreas Niederberger and Philipp Schink, Edinburgh University Press, 2015, pp. 5–40.

Graeber, David, and David Wengrow. *The Dawn of Everything: A New History of Humanity*. Farrar, Straus, and Giroux, 2021.

Harvard Bodin Project. https://projects.iq.harvard.edu/bodinproject/. Accessed 6 March 2024.

Hexter, J. H. "Seyssel, Machiavelli, and Polybius VI: The Mystery of the Missing Translation." *Studies in the Renaissance*, vol. 3, 2019, pp. 75–96.

Hobbes, Thomas. *The Elements of Law*. 1640. *The Collected Political Works*, e-artnow, 2023.

Hobbes, Thomas. *Leviathan*. 1651. *The Collected Political Works*, e-artnow, 2023.

Hobbes, Thomas. *On the Citizen*. 1642. Edited and translated by Richard Tuck, Cambridge University Press, 1998.

Hörnqvist, Mikael. *Machiavelli and Empire*. Cambridge University Press, 2004.

Kavka, František, Vladimír Outrata, and Josef Polišenský. *The Universal Peace Organization of King George of Bohemia: A Fifteenth Century Peace Plan*. House of the Czechoslovak Academy of Sciences, 1964.

Lessafer, Randall. "Peace Treaties from Lodi to Westphalia." *Peace Treaties and International Law in European History, From the Late Middle Ages to World War One*, edited by Randall Lessager, Cambridge University Press, 2004, pp. 9–44.

Machiavelli, Niccoló. *The Discourses*. 1517. Edited with an introduction by Bernard Crick, using the translation of Leslie J. Walker, S. J., with revisions by Brian Richardson, Penguin Books, 1998.

Machiavelli, Niccoló. *Discursus about the Reforming of Florence*. 1520. *Collected Works*, Delphi Classics, 2017.

Machiavelli, Niccoló. *History of Florence and of the Affairs of Italy*. 1525. *Collected Works*, Delphi Classics, 2017.

Machiavelli, Niccoló. *The Prince*. 1513. Edited by Quentin Skinner and Russell Price, Cambridge University Press, 2000.

Machiavelli, Niccoló. *Report on the Affairs of Germany*. 1508. *Collected Works*, Delphi Classics, 2017.

Machiavelli, Niccoló. "Second Letter about the Mission to Emperor Maximilian I, January 17, 1508." *Collected Works of Niccoló Machiavelli*, e-book, Delphi Classics, 2017.

McCormick, John. *Reading Machiavelli: Scandalous Books, Suspect Engagements, and the Virtue of Populist Politics*. Princeton University Press, 2020.

Onuf, Nicholas. *The Republican Legacy in International Thought*. Cambridge University Press, 1998.

Plato. *The Republic*, translated with an introduction by Desmond Lee, Penguin Books, 1987.

Pocock, J. G. A. *The Machiavellian Moment: Florentine Political Thought in the Atlantic Republican Tradition*. Princeton University Press, 1975.

Polybius. *The Histories*, translated by Robin Waterfield, Oxford University Press, 2010.

Raimondi, Fabio. *Constituting Freedom: Machiavelli and Florence*. Oxford University Press, 2018.

Skinner, Quentin. *The Foundations of Modern Political Thought*. Cambridge University Press, 1978. 2 vols.

Skinner, Quentin. "Pre-Humanist Origins of Republican Ideas." *Machiavelli and Republicanism*, edited by Gisela Bock, Quentin Skinner, and Maurizio Viroli, Cambridge University Press, 1990, pp. 121–141.

Tuck, Richard. *The Rights of War and Peace: Political Thought and the International Order from Grotius to Kant*. Oxford University Press, 1999.

Wilson, Peter H. *The Holy Roman Empire: A Thousand Years of Europe's History*. Allen Lane, 2016.

2 A Taxonomy of Unions

Abstract

A number of practical experiments with leagues showed how thinkers and politicians in early modern composite states struggled to come up with answers to the three problems first defined by Machiavelli in his *Discourses*: its lack of a strong administrative centre, its inability to expand beyond a certain point, and its inability to maintain itself over time. On the theoretical level, there was a lively debate over how exactly to define this new type of regime. This debate would lead to the development of a new taxonomy of regimes, where federal union was one of the options.

Keywords: Swiss Confederacy, Polish-Lithuanian Commonwealth, Dutch United Provinces, Holy Roman Empire, Union of the Crowns, federal union

The Swiss Confederacy

Of one union we have an extensive description by Machiavelli himself. He wrote about the Swiss Confederacy in his main works as well as in diplomatic letters and memoranda to the Florentine Chancery. At times he referred to them as German (because they fell under the authority of the Holy Roman Empire), though this was mainly when he described certain traits that they had in common with the free German cities. When he discussed their individual traits and their constitutional regime, he referred to them clearly as Swiss.

Describing the Swiss as poor by Florentine standards but "completely independent" (Machiavelli, *The Prince* 44), in his "Second Letter about the Mission to Emperor Maximilian I" (17 January 1508) he sketched the Confederacy's organisation in the following terms: "[T]he main body of this country consists of twelve communities leagued together, and called Cantons. (...) These are united in such a manner that whatever is resolved upon in their Diet is always observed by all of them, and none of the Cantons will oppose it" (Machiavelli, *Collected Works* 5047). Apart from the twelve

Livestro, Joshua: *A More Perfect Union. Federal Union in Political Theory and Practice, 1500-1951.*
Amsterdam: Amsterdam University Press, 2024.
DOI: 10.5117/9789048563777_CH02

Cantons belonging to the Diet he mentioned two others who "are not so united to the other twelve" but were able to "take separate action in opposition to the others" (5052).

Machiavelli's assessment of the Diet's effectiveness was qualified somewhat by his observation that recently, French interference through bribery and propaganda had prevented "all action of the Diet in favour of the Emperor" (Machiavelli, *Collected Works* 5049). Perhaps as a result of that, "up to the time of my passing numerous meetings of the Diet have been held, but no resolutions passed" (5049). But, he assured his audience at the Chancery, these facts about the supposed authority and efficacy of the Diet he had "learned from various persons, but mainly from a gentleman at Fribourg, a very accurate man, who has commanded one of their companies" (5047).

Perhaps Machiavelli was speaking ironically when he praised the supposed efficacy of the Diet. Alternatively, he may have somewhat romanticised the image of the Swiss Confederacy as an effective union because he wanted to hold it up as an example to his political masters at home. In reality, it was probably no coincidence that he never got to witness the Diet passing a meaningful resolution, because it rarely did. Its twelve member cantons (soon to be thirteen, since Appenzell joined the original group of twelve in 1513, just five years after Machiavelli wrote his memorandum) each had one vote. To reach a decision, all cantons had to vote in agreement, and the decision would only be valid if all cantons then confirmed the vote in their own councils. The latter seemed a formality, because delegations in the Diet voted upon strict instructions from the home cantons, but in practice this wasn't always the case (Würgler 35).

This wasn't the only error Machiavelli made in interpreting the Swiss constitution. In his *Report on the Affairs of Germany* (1508) he claimed to have observed a fundamental difference between the German imperial or "free" cities and the Swiss cantons: "[T]he Swiss are not only hostile to the princes, the same as the free communities, but they are equally hostile to the gentlemen [*gentiluomini*; that is, landed gentry], for in their country there is no difference of rank; and all, with the exception only of those who sit as magistrates, enjoy without distinction an equal and entire liberty" (Machiavelli, *Collected Works* 6020). This was, if not a complete fabrication, then at least a terrible simplification. The original rural cantons may have fitted his description as being based on an "equal and entire liberty." The imperial cities of Luzern, Berne, Zug, and Zürich, however, were no less stratified than the German imperial cities. Like Florence, their governments were essentially merchant aristocracies or oligarchies, though they tended to see themselves as mixed regimes (Maissen 127).

It would be a mistake to look at the Swiss constitution through a modern prism and assume that because the Diet was the highest council in the Swiss constitutional framework, it must have been the most powerful one as well. In practice it was the other way round: all power rested with the individual cantons. The Diet had little power, either formal or informal. Nor, indeed, did the nominal sovereign of the Swiss cantons, the Holy Roman emperor. If Swiss commentators presented the emperor as "the sovereign" over Swiss politics and societies, that didn't mean that they were inclined to follow his lead. Internal laws and court rulings were said to be made in the name of the emperor, though they were always decisions by local magistrates. If the emperor himself presented the cantons with a request for troops in support of a campaign, he faced extensive negotiations to make them even consider it, let alone grant it.

In his "Second Letter" Machiavelli discussed one such case, in which the Swiss would not openly declare for the emperor because that would mean taking sides against France, but nor would they declare for France because that would mean taking sides against the emperor. But nor did they wish to remain neutral, "unless the king should give them special cause," because that would mean missing out on income as mercenaries (Machiavelli, *Collected Works* 5051). "These are the difficulties," Machiavelli concluded, "that have been the cause of so many meetings of the Diet and such few conclusions; and it is supposed that the present, like all the previous ones, will bring nothing but useless talk" (5051).

—

If there was some doubt about the nature of the Swiss Confederacy's constitutional status, that was based in part on its lack of a formal legal foundation. It relied instead on a patchwork of treaties between different groups of cantons signed at different times in the past. There was no single founding document, nor was there a clear sense of collective identity (Würgler 29–30). There were few duties and privileges linked to membership of the Confederacy, and those that there were, were not evenly distributed across all member cantons. There were a number of different groupings of full and restricted membership, depending on the issue.

Most complex was the relationship with the outside world. Here the individual cantons would basically operate their own policy, signing treaties either as single entities or as groups. Over time this would create overlapping networks of treaties where the Confederacy maintained a tie of some form with a neighbouring country (France, for example). But in most cases the treaties would only involve some, rather than all of the cantons. Prominent examples here were the treaties between the Catholic cantons and the kingdom of Spain, and of the Protestant cantons with the Republic of Venice (Würgler 32).

The most famous contemporary treatise on the nature of the Confederacy, written by the theologian Josias Simler (1530–1576), admitted that in classical regime terms, it clearly didn't meet the definition of a proper regime for lack of a confederal executive authority ("La Republique des Suisses n'a nuls Magistrats communs"). Bailiffs or governors were operating not on the instructions of the Confederation but on that of "chascun des Cantons, de chez soy" – every canton for itself (Simler 188). As for the Diet, individual Cantons would only send representatives if there were issues immediately relevant to themselves. With a few minor objections, discussions of all the Cantons combined tended to focus exclusively on issues of war and peace. On normal foreign relations, and on all internal affairs, the individual cantons had complete sovereignty.

Bodin's description of the Confederation as thirteen individual small republics was therefore less surprising than it seems. It also fitted with the self-image of the Swiss as essentially independent provinces and cities within the Holy Roman Empire. It wasn't until the end of the Empire, in the nineteenth century, that Swiss historians started reading back into Swiss history a sense of Swiss nationhood (Maissen 125–126).

This does raise the question how a confederacy that seemed to offer so little internal coherence – no common magistrates, each canton operating its own foreign policy – was still able to survive for so long. If we exclude "miracle" (Sir Francis Bacon, among others) and "divine providence" as explanations, that leaves two plausible theories. One is that it had existed mainly by the grace of its more powerful neighbours. The man who would formally end the independence of the Confederation in 1806, Napoleon Bonaparte, observed that Swiss unity would have ended long ago but for the protection provided by France. The other explanation is rooted in a quality much admired by Machiavelli, the martial prowess of the Swiss, who were "very well armed and completely independent" (Machiavelli, *The Prince* 44).

The fact that it was respected for its fighting spirit and its ability to endure where other states faltered does not necessarily make the Swiss Confederacy an example of federal virtue. It does, however, show how important a strong collective defence is for the continued existence of any federal union.

The Polish-Lithuanian Commonwealth

The Roman method of expansion was one where the larger power eventually imposed its will upon the smaller one. In such situations, incorporating union seemed the most plausible outcome of negotiations. A different result was only possible if there were a larger number of states, none of which was so powerful that it could dominate all the others, or if the negotiating states were more or less equal in terms of population size and territory – as was the case with the negotiations between Poland and Lithuania about the formation of a political union.

The Grand Duchy of Lithuania was not the modern Baltic state but a vast territory which at its zenith spanned modern day Lithuania, Latvia, and Belarus, as well as parts of Ukraine, Moldova, Estonia, Poland, and western Russia. The personal union between the two territories was the result of Grand Duke Jogaila adding the Polish crown to his Lithuanian title by marrying the Polish queen Jadwiga in 1386 – the founding moment of the Polish Jagiellonian dynasty.

In its relationship with Poland, Lithuania was the equal of its neighbour in every way but one: whereas Poland was a monarchy, Lithuania was a mere Grand Duchy. This hierarchical difference gave the Polish political class the confidence to treat the outcome as a foregone conclusion: Lithuania would merge with Poland, effectively becoming part of its territory. In reality, political union was anything but a foregone conclusion. The Poles had no way of forcing their preferred outcome on the Lithuanians, and the Jagiellonian kings were unwilling to push the case for union too far, for fear of creating a conflict between the two parts of their realm. This explains perhaps why the process of turning the Jagiellonian personal union into a political one was painfully slow, taking the better part of two centuries.

—

The political struggle between the two nations was obviously about power, but for the Poles it was also about expansion. Polish interests in eastward expansion first became a political issue in the late fifteenth century, as schemes involving access to Black Sea trade routes (no doubt inspired by Spanish and Portuguese colonial ventures) came onto the political agenda. Soon this idea was wedded to the Polish nobility's ambition to find new lands for settlement. These dreams of Polish expansion were projected mainly onto the Lithuanian border regions, and increasingly also onto Ukraine.

The late-sixteenth-century priest Piotr Grabowski wrote a number of treatises making the case for a Polish expansionist agenda. "Other peoples spread widely over the world and grow in strength," he argued, so why not Poland? (Grabowski, quoted in Grzybowksi 27). Since neither Western nor Northern Europe were serious options for territorial expansion, that left

Southeastern Europe. Obviously, that set the Poles up for a conflict with the Turkish rulers who at that point controlled the area, but that was a price worth paying. The chances of success were high, he thought, since the local populations would likely flock to their sides, as fellow Slavs: "The spirit of all the Slovaks will turn to us and wish to win fame with us" (35).

While politically, the debate about union was about Polish desire for expansion versus Lithuanian desire for security, legally speaking, it was about incorporating versus federal union: forming a single (Polish) nation versus forming a federation of two more or less equal parties. This debate boiled down to a difference of opinion about the interpretation of the agreement that formed the basis of the marriage between Jogaila and Jadwiega, the Union of Krewo (1386). This document confirmed that the "Lithuanian and Russian lands" were to be "permanently attached" (*applicare*) to the Kingdom of Poland. The Poles argued that the Latin term *applicare* meant "annexation" or "incorporation." The Lithuanians on the other hand interpreted it as a commitment to "voluntary association" (Dembowski 24).

In the centuries-long tug-of-war over the meaning of the word, the momentum would swing towards one side and then the other. In the fifteenth century, a series of further unions seemed to work to the advantage of the Lithuanians. The Union of Wilno (1401) described the union between the two territories as "free and personal"; the Union of Horodło (1413) talked about "joint meetings of the Poles and Lithuanians for settling matters of common interest" (Dembkowski 24–25). By 1446 the Lithuanians were so confident of their position that they even asked the new king, Kazimierz, to back their proposal for a full political union. The term *confederamus* was used to describe an equal relationship between the two nations, forming what was essentially a defensive alliance – which would obviously be of greater significance to the Lithuanians, since they faced constant threats of invasion from the Russians and the Tatars. In the end, no political union was agreed. The union would remain centred on the person of the Jagiellonian kings (Dembkowski 27–28).

The momentum shifted towards the Poles around the turn of the sixteenth century. This shift coincided with an important constitutional development within Poland. Around the middle of the fifteenth century, Kazimierz had granted the lower gentry (known collectively as the *szlachta*) the right of assembly in local councils (*Sejmiki*). By the end of the century, these local councils would eventually end up nominating representatives to a national *Sejm*, thereby introducing a third estate to counterbalance the existing two estates of monarchy and higher aristocracy, the latter meeting in the *Rada* or Senate (Dembkowski 28). The new mixed regime was formalised through a constitutional law introduced in 1505, which became known as the Nihil Novi principle (*Nihil novi sine omnium consensu* – nothing new adopted without the consent of all). It stipulated that from then on, any legislation required the consent of both houses of Parliament, including the newly formed Sejm (Opaliński 149).

Once established as the third constitutional power, the *szlachta* would quickly become the dominant force. It would use its newly found power to launch a reform campaign which became known as "The Execution of the Laws" (Jędrug 58). Most of the Executionist demands were focused on reform of Poland's internal political order: creating uniform legal standards, banning Catholic clergy from taking up certain political offices, and returning land distributed among the higher aristocracy to the Crown (this would not only weaken the economic power of the higher aristocracy in the Rada but would also provide the executive with much needed tax income). There was one demand, however, which had a clear external effect: the strengthening of the ties between the different territories of the Crown (Dembkowski 41–42). By framing the forming of a political union with Lithuania as a matter of mere "execution of the laws," in this case the various treaties signed by both territories since 1386, the Poles managed to give the idea of political unification an aspect of inevitability. Against this, all the Lithuanians could muster were the forces of time. Using delaying tactics and obstructionism, they would manage to postpone a final decision about political union by another seventy years.

—

Things came to a head during the rule of the last Jagiellonian king, Sigismund August (born 1520; reigned 1548–1572). His rule is generally remembered for two achievements: expanding his realm with Livonia (modern-day Latvia and Estonia), and turning the personal union of the two realms into a proper political union. It would take all his political talents to achieve it, and more than a little patience – another twenty years separated first attempt from final triumph.

The road to a compromise solution opened up when the leader of the Lithuanian resistance to closer union, Mikołaj Radziwiłł (known as Radziwiłł the Black), died in 1565. The pro-union camp was a coalition of the Polish *szlachta* and Sigismund August. The king had publicly embraced the reformist cause in dramatic fashion earlier that decade by entering a Sejm meeting in the dress of a common nobleman – dressing like a member of the *szlachta* to show them that their cause in the Execution of the Laws had now become his cause. Together they seized the moment in 1569, at a joint Polish-Lithuanian Sejm meeting in Lublin. When the Lithuanians again used their tried and tested tactic of returning home "for further consultations" – a transparent attempt to kill the momentum of the pro-Union side – the Polish delegates sprung a surprise. They demanded that the king agree to annexation by Poland of the Lithuanian western provinces of Podlasie and Volhynia. If the execution of the promise of "applicare" made during the Union of Krewo could not be achieved through consensus, then a dictate would do. To the shock of the Lithuanians, Sigismund August gave his consent to this naked land grab (Dembkowski 149). Before they could hurry back to Lublin to formally file their protest against it, the Poles had also annexed a significant part of central Ukraine, including Kiev. Utterly defeated by such a show of political force, the Grand Duchy delegation finally accepted political union.

Though the creation of the political union itself might have been based on a powerplay by one side which forced the other side to consent, in its details it was surprisingly even-handed Though the Lithuanians were given fewer seats in the joint national parliament, the fact that legislation required consensus for adoption made the number of delegates per territory less relevant. Lithuania was allowed to keep its title of Grand Duchy, its own government offices, its own taxation, its own army, and its own provincial assemblies. In the execution of joint offices, both territories were allowed to send one officer – to represent the commonwealth jointly in meetings with foreign dignitaries, or to represent their own territory during meetings of the Commonwealth parliament (Dembkowski 182–185).

Though it had some aspects of incorporation (an incorporated parliament for example), the union of Lublin was clearly a federal construct – a federal monarchical republic, to be precise. To its federal legislative and executive would eventually be added a federal judiciary in the form of the Crown Tribunal (Dembkowski 225). There was even a suggestion of separation of powers when parliament started insisting on excluding the monarch from its debates – though this seemed to be less a product of deliberate constitutional innovation than an expression of the Sejm's desire to establish political supremacy over the executive (Opaliński 153). As such, it made the constitution less balanced, not more.

The important thing to realise when assessing its constitutional features is that Polish authors considered the Polish-Lithuanian Commonwealth to be essentially a single state. Or more precisely: a *Polish* state. It seems that as far as they were concerned, Lithuania had simply become part of the Polish kingdom. It was an *incorporating* union – the fact that the constitutional details suggested otherwise was neither here nor there. This also explains why they saw no complications preventing them from analysing the union in classical regime theory terms, calling it a typical example of a mixed regime.

If they analysed the commonwealth in constitutional terms at all, that is. The sovereignty problem, for example, which according to Bodin made mixed regimes a practical impossibility (see xx above) was not recognised as such by Polish thinkers. In their view, sovereignty was not located in any one of the powers but in the *res publica* as a whole, the Rzeczpospolita (Pietrzyk-Reeves 199). A typical example of this approach was the humanist scholar Andrzej Frycz Modrzewski (1503–1572), who in his *De Republica Emendanda* defined the commonwealth as a "general principle" confirmed in "deep-rooted knowledge of what is right and honest" (Pietrzyk-Reeves 174). For Frycz and most other Polish thinkers at the time, the commonwealth was not so much a constitutional order as a moral one. To the extent that they did analyse the mixed regime, they therefore tended to describe it as an expression of a normative order rather than a legal-political one (179).[1]

———

The fact that they didn't recognise its federal aspects perhaps stopped Polish writers in the seventeenth and early eighteenth century from grasping the nature of one of the main flaws of their constitutional set-up: the *liberum veto*, the fact that all legislation required consensus or even outright unanimity. Polish Renaissance political thinkers tended to defend the practice as essential for the maintenance of concord in the commonwealth. They thought of it as a solution to, rather than a manifestation of, the problem of faction (Pietrzyk-Reeves 122).

The unanimity rule was interpreted as a kind of gentlemen's agreement: once a consensus position emerged, everyone accepted it and moved on. From the mid-1650s onwards, this was increasingly no longer the case. The first notable use of the veto as an instrument of obstruction happened in 1652, when a Lithuanian Sejm delegate, acting on instructions from the Lithuanian Hetman (highest military officer) Janusz Radziwiłł, blocked the ratification of a peace treaty with the Cossacks. Over the next 150 years,

---

1   Pietrzyk-Reeves suggests that this exclusive focus on the moral order rather than political reality was the reason there was hardly any serious reflection on constitutional issues: "Although they advocated the mixed form of government, they did not achieve very much in the way of vindicating it or giving a consistent explanation of how it was balanced. (...) Of course they did not entirely neglect the institutional aspect, since their fundamental principle of the rule of law was certainly an institutional issue. Yet they expected that once the ethical aspect was safely established, the institutional elements would fall into place" (178).

the veto would be used more and more freely, mainly by Lithuanian and Ukrainian representatives, and often at foreign request, leading to a sense of gridlock in the legislative process (Dembkowski 207). Eventually, the Sejm would develop a solution to it in the form of the *confederated* Sejm – a special unicameral session of parliament, usually dedicated to a single topic, in which majority rule applied. In the second half of the eighteenth century, most Sejm meetings would take place under these rules.

Though gridlock would remain a feature of Commonwealth politics, the *liberum veto* in and of itself did not fatally weaken the Polish constitutional framework. It did, however, show that it was based on a problematic assumption: that all sides would always be equally committed to its flourishing. By the middle part of the seventeenth century this was clearly no longer the case, especially in Ukraine. At one point the two founding powers came close to admitting it as a third member under the title of "Grand Ruthenian Duchy" (Treaty of Hadiach, 1658). But the treaty in which this was proposed was never implemented, and ten years later Ukraine was partitioned through an agreement between the Commonwealth and the Russian tsar, with its eastern part falling under Russian rule (Dembkowski 202–203).

The internal instability caused by the veto policy of rival factions might have been containable, if it hadn't been for the other main weakness of the Polish constitution: its elected kingship. This element, which had first been introduced after the death of the last Jagiellonian king, was intended to cement the Sejm's dominant position in its relationship with the monarch. The conditions imposed upon the first post-Jagiellonian elected monarch, Henry of Anjou (later King Henri III of France),[2] came to be seen as a kind of gold standard for the safeguarding of parliamentary powers and constitutional rights of the citizenry.

Eventually, however, the lack of dynastic continuity would end up weakening rather than strengthening the commonwealth's "golden liberties." After Henry's victory in the first open election, the other great powers of Europe quickly realised that the Commonwealth had opened itself up to outside interference through its monarchy. They would keep looking for ways to use the election process for their own purposes. In the early 1650s, a Ukrainian uprising opened the way for both Russia and Sweden to destabilise the monarchy by cultivating the internal opposition, even supporting alternative candidates for the throne. The subsequent Swedish

---

2   Henri would only rule the Commonwealth for thirteen months. He abandoned the Polish-Lithuanian throne when the French throne fell vacant after the sudden death of his brother, Charles IX.

and Russian invasions would force the king, Jan Kazimierz, to flee the capital. Order would eventually be restored through a combination of local resistance and outside interference (by the Dutch, the Danes, Brandenburg, and the Holy Roman Empire). However, peace came at a price, in the form of lost territories in the north, east, and west.

Much worse was to follow. The last quarter of the seventeenth century had seemingly produced a return of Poland's golden age, under the kingship of Jan Sobieski (born 1629; reigned 1674–1696). He tried to overcome the executive's lack of effective control over the levers of power by waging a series of foreign campaigns, culminating in his triumph over a Turkish army at the Battle of Vienna of 1683 at the head of an army of 36,000 Poles (Zamoyski 276). Yet this military success could not hide the fact that the Commonwealth's internal affairs were in a state of serious disorder. The full extent of the chaos was revealed after the death of King Jan.

Frederick Augustus Wettin, the Elector of Brandenburg, was nicknamed "The Strong" for his rumoured ability to break horseshoes with his bare hands. He had manifested this strength by imposing himself on an unwilling Polish-Lithuanian electorate through the barrel of a gun, using his Saxon troops to overturn the result of the final vote which had seen the crown handed to Louis XIV's preferred candidate François de Bourbon, the Prince de Conti (Zamoyski 321). Assuming the same forceful approach that had landed him the throne would also help him maintain a firm grip on his newly acquired kingdom, he got involved in a Danish-Russian coalition against the new young Swedish king Charles XII. Through this alliance, he hoped to be able to add a reconquered Livonia to his personal possessions.

In reality, the Great Northern War (1700–1721) would end up dramatically weakening his position. At one point, Augustus seemed to have been removed from the scene permanently when Charles XII invaded his native Saxony and forced him to abdicate. He was soon to find out, however, that there was something worse than not being in power. When Russian Tsar Peter I defeated Charles XII at the battle of Poltova in 1709, he put Augustus back on the Polish-Lithuanian throne – not as a sovereign, but as a puppet king. The Commonwealth was now effectively a Russian protectorate. This became most painfully obvious in 1717 when Peter sent an army to Warsaw to force the Sejm to accept a series of reforms dictated by him. The main measures were the disbanding of most of the Polish and Lithuanian armies, and the placement of Russian troops on Polish soil – "for protection" (Zamoyski, 328).

—

A number of critical assessments of the weaknesses of the Commonwealth's constitution were published in the second half of the eighteenth century. Ever since Peter I had developed a strategy of Divide and Rule, through bribery or threats of violence against individual members of the *szlachta*, Russian rulers had used the *liberum veto* to stop the Sejm from developing effective policy. Or indeed, any policy at all: during the reign of the last of the Saxon kings, Augustus III, only a single Sejm (that of 1736) had managed to conclude any business. In the rare cases where there was a semblance of effective decision-making, the Russian court would not hesitate to send troops to overturn the decision.[3]

The single most effective argument against the *liberum veto* was published in the period 1761 to 1763, under the title *On the Means to Successful Counsels*. Its author, Stanisław Konarski (1700–1772), was a Catholic educational theorist whose efforts were mainly focused on bringing the Commonwealth's ruling class into contact with Western ideas about education which he had studied during a tour of Europe's main centres of learning. The same travels had clearly also provided him with food for thought about the Commonwealth's political system and more importantly: its political class.

He lampooned the Polish-Lithuanian self-image as somehow more virtuous than the rest of Europe, declaring: "It is ridiculous to consider the human race one way and Poland another, to think otherwise of Poles alone, that they are, without a single exception, worthy and pious citizens" (Lubowski 440). Where his countrymen would draw from this premise the Ciceronian conclusion that they would simply have to work even harder at becoming virtuous, Konarski chose to make a Machiavellian point. It wasn't virtue, or the lack of it, that was the problem, but the *constitution*: "It is the form of our counsels which we need to correct, not people. (...) [I]t is the form of counsel, or rather, our lack of counsel and our anarchy which, with God's help, we can wholly improve, whenever we choose to do so" (Lubowski 441).

He focused most of his criticism on the *liberum veto*. Instead of being a means of protecting virtue and justice, it had become a tool for the spreading of chaos and licence: "All parliaments were always disrupted out of private motives and to the great harm of the Commonwealth" (Lubowski 442).

---

3   It was one such military intervention, the War of the Polish Succession (1733–1735) that had seen Augustus III placed on the backing. His opponent during the royal election, Stanisław Leszczyński, had won the throne of the overwhelming majority of the Polish and Lithuanian nobles. But as father-in-law of Louis XV he was seen as a French candidate, and therefore wholly unacceptable to the Court of St Petersburg.

Dismissing it as "unworthy, (...) incomprehensible, (...) destructive," he argued for its abolition and replacement with majority rule (*pluralitas*) (442–443).

—

Konarski wasn't the only writer to reflect critically on the effects of the veto. Two French thinkers who were approached by a delegation of the leading council of the Barist Revolt[4] to draft a new constitution for the Commonwealth both mentioned this power as one of the main weaknesses of the existing constitution. The Abbé de Mably argued for outright abolition, and a switch to qualified majority voting (Butterworth 112).

The other author, Jean-Jaques Rousseau, argued for a more measured approach. Observing that "[t]he *liberum veto* is not a destructive power in itself," he did acknowledge that "when it overshoots its target, it becomes the most dangerous of abuses" (Rousseau 107; my translation throughout). He suggested solving the problem by separating normal day-to-day decisions, for which majority voting was appropriate, with decisions about fundamental issues that affected the Commonwealth's political order: "The *liberum veto* would seem less unreasonable if it was applied to fundamental constitutional issues" (108).

In the end, though, Rousseau considered a reform of the veto power less relevant than a different change that fell outside the scope of constitutional reform. In his view it was not so much the existing constitution as the extended nature of the Commonwealth that was the cause of its lack of cohesion: "Your vast provinces will never support the strict administration of smaller republics." Somewhat in jest, he suggested that the Poles and Lithuanians should "[s]tart by drawing your borders tighter, if you want to reform your government. Perhaps your neighbours would be kind enough to do you a service here" (Rousseau 59).

—

As it turned out, the Commonwealth's neighbours Russia, Prussia, and Austria were only too willing to help redraw its boundaries. The First Polish Partition of 1772 significantly shrank its territory. The Second Partition of 1793 would effectively leave just a Polish rump state, most of the Lithuanian Grand Duchy

---

4   An uprising, starting in the spring of 1768. Though it had broader aims, some more religious than political, its main objective was to "end Russian domination in the Commonwealth." It was this revolt that would be used by the Russian Tsarina Catherine as a pretext for the first Partition of Poland, in 1772 (Butterworth 108).

having been incorporated into the Russian empire. This had been preceded by an attempt by the country's political class to refound the Commonwealth as a monarchical republic. On the third of May 1791, a new constitution was proposed which aimed to fix all of the Commonwealth's problems, both real and perceived, in a single move. The most meaningful changes were the switch to a hereditary kingship, the introduction at the constitutional level of a set of freedoms for the peasantry, and the abolition of the *liberum veto*. The latter, previously considered the cornerstone of the Commonwealth's constitutional order, was now described as "subversive of government, and destructive of society" (*Law on Government*, May 3, 1791, clause 6).

Catherine II's rejection of the new constitution was both immediate and definitive. She used the full range of Russian policies to block and reverse it. She sent out delegates to mobilise Austrian and Prussian support for punitive measures. She mobilised internal Polish resistance by getting its leaders to call a confederated Sejm in protest of the proposed changes, even promising them a restoration of the old republican form of government. Pride of place in this restorative exercise was given to those constitutional principles that had allowed her to keep the Commonwealth divided and weak: elected kingship and the *liberum veto* (Butterworth 311). To make sure that these proposals had every chance of being adopted, she also sent in her army.

The Polish resistance was unexpectedly fierce and effective, even leading to some battlefield victories. Yet before factors such as increased Polish morale and the potential mobilisation of more Polish troops, or the lack of ammunition and the absence of meaningful foreign support, could force a decision one way or the other, the war ended abruptly when King Stanisław August II inexplicably capitulated by joining the rebel confederated Sejm and accepting its demands. This decision had two dramatic consequences: a second Partition in 1793, and a revolt which would lead to the full and final partition in 1795.

—

The Polish-Lithuanian Commonwealth started out as a successful example of the transformation of a personal (royal) into a federal union. It ended as a byword for chaos, gridlock and weakness. It showed not only what happens when the idea of veto power as a way of protecting equality is taken to its logical conclusion, but also why a constitution's first task ought to be to safeguard the union against external interference.

Still, at its peak the Commonwealth was a shining example of the federal method's ability to create a union that could span a vast territory, and not just for a few years, but for centuries.

The Dutch United Provinces

In Machiavelli's *Discourses*, the discussion of the republic's expansion followed the discussion of its founding and constitutional development. This seemed a logical sequence. After all, only a commonwealth that had a sufficiently developed constitutional order would be capable of external action. But as the Dutch United Provinces would show, it was not the *only* possible sequence.

The Dutch Revolt started as a religious conflict. In 1566, Protestant nobles offered a petition to the Governess-General of the Dutch provinces of the Spanish empire, Charles V's daughter Margaret of Parma. In this petition, they demanded a degree of freedom of worship that the Spanish crown was unwilling to grant. A wave of iconoclastic furies rolled over the Dutch provinces, and a low-level rebellion grew into a full scale revolt when the Spanish king Philip II made the strategic mistake of replacing his conciliatory half-sister with the violently confrontational Duke of Alba.

By the middle of the 1570s it was clear that the revolt had produced an irreparable rift between Spain and the rebelling provinces. An ultimate attempt at peaceful settlement, during which the Dutch delegation demanded shared sovereignty in the form of limited monarchy and co-legislative powers for the States General, failed – not over these constitutional demands but over the same issue that had caused the revolt in the first place, namely the Dutch request for full equality for the Protestant faith. In the end, Philip was unwilling to make the kind of concessions that his father had made at Augsburg, even if it meant risking the loss of part of his realm (Israel 183).

For the Dutch, the failure to resolve the conflict peacefully raised the question of what could be the alternative to membership of the Spanish realm. The Union of Utrecht of 1579 was at first glance a purely defensive union. But to the individual provinces it was clear that signing the document would constitute a point of no return: it would *de facto*, if not *de jure*, confirm the severing of the ties with Spain, and would chain them to the explicitly Protestant core union of Holland and Zeeland. This made the ratification process far from plain sailing.[5]

The Stadtholder of the four Northern provinces, Rennenberg, tried to mobilise Catholic anti-Union support in an attempt to reject the treaty. His

---

5   In the seventeenth century, the Union of Utrecht would increasingly be interpreted as a kind of constitutional document. States would frequently appeal to its various articles, for example to justify the position of the Stadtholder (Art. 9), or to dispute the right of individual states to agree separate treaties with third parties, outside Union structures (Art. 10, 11). See Israel 707, 725.

attempt was eventually smothered by a combination of Holland troops and another wave of Protestant iconoclastic furies. Still he held out, keeping the province of Overijssel effectively out of the Union. It would mean that the province was the only one of the seven Northern provinces that did not initially sign the 1581 Act of Abjuration, which legally severed the ties with Spain (Israel 203–209).

It was this Act which established the United Provinces as a union. But it was a union without a clear constitutional structure, or indeed a sense of its own purpose beyond keeping the Spanish out. Having established a capacity for external action, the rebel provinces now had to start looking for a way to create some sense of internal order.

—

In the early 1580s, the United Provinces were, in reality, anything but united. One contemporary account described the provinces as "accustomed to seeking their own advantage and robbing one another of their navigation and trade (...) in order to aggrandize themselves. And while some are prepared to pay war-taxes, others are not" (Kossmann and Mellink 250). Others observed that partly "because of their jealousy for each other," the states were "slow in coming to decisions," instead "start[ing] to quarrel among themselves in total disorder." As a result, "discussions spun out from month to month," with "each of the individual provinces (...) successfully usurp[ing] control over affairs, which should be decided upon by the States General and their councillors appointed for this purpose" (Kossmann and Mellink 252–258).

This problem of every state being in it for itself increasingly frustrated the Stadtholder, the Prince of Orange. In a speech to the States General, he complained about the attitude of the states ("They act as if we had no enemy at all!") and summed up his predicament as commander in chief of the Dutch forces:

> Each province has its own council, almost every town and every province has its own army and its own money, with the result that resources which would in total be considerable are fragmented. It is true that a council has been established, but it has no power and if it has no authority, how could it supervise military discipline, finances, justice and everything else? (quoted in Kossmann and Mellink 235)

To solve this problem, the Prince encouraged the States General to find an external solution: someone who could both help to create a sense of internal order and act as a sponsor for their fight against Spain. They first approached the French king's brother, the Duke of Anjou. When a Dutch delegation met with Anjou, the latter demanded full sovereignty over the provinces, no doubt inspired by his political adviser Jean Bodin. In a conversation with the latter, the Dutch representative Marnix van Sint Aldegonde reaorted to rhetorical sleight of hand to escape the political consequences of Bodin's claim about the indivisibility of sovereignty, claiming that the term was of no use in the discussions because "[it] had no equivalent in the Dutch language" (Kossmann and Mellink 33). The best they could offer was the title of "highest lord," an elected lordship which, in keeping with the ancient customs of the provinces, could also be rescinded if the lord in question violated the conditions of good government on which his appointment would be based (Van Gelderen xxiv).

The French delegation was obviously less than impressed by the Dutch offer: it involved carrying most of the costs of the war operations with, at best, a share of the authority over the united provinces. In the end, the debate over shared versus full sovereignty was largely academic because Anjou died prematurely in 1584, aged just twenty-nine. The Dutch now turned to the English queen Elizabeth I. She was no more inclined to accept the Dutch offer than Anjou had been, but she did send her courtier the Duke of Leicester to The Hague, where the States General offered him the even grander title of "Governor and Captain General." His mission failed not so much because of Spanish incursions but because of internal opposition by the provinces, chiefly the States of Holland.

The fight between the two parties focused, again, on the issue of sovereignty. In his *Remonstrance to the States General and the States of Holland*, Leicester's councillor Thomas Wilkes introduced a concept that would at a later stage play an important role in the theoretical development of federalism: popular sovereignty. He claimed that it wasn't for the States General or the States of Holland to act against the instructions of the Governor General. It was "*the people* who through you as their officials and servants have committed this power, authority and government to His Excellency" (Kossmann and Mellink 273; my italics). It was therefore also through the people that they would have to receive authority to go against the original arrangement. Since no such authority had been granted, he declared, "you either do not understand what you have been doing and fail to see how extensive this power was or else you are guilty of the crime of disobedience" (273).

In his answer on behalf of the States of Holland, the pensionary of the town of Gouda, Francois Vranck, dismissed the idea of popular sovereignty as invoked by Wilkes: "[H]ow can the country survive, if the commonality lets itself be persuaded to take sides against the States, that is, against the nobles, magistrates and town-councillors, who are their protectors and lawful rulers?" (280). Against Wilkes's notion of popular sovereignty he invoked the medieval network of feudal arrangements and city rights out of which were selected the nobles, magistrates and councillors to make up the Provincial States: "On this foundation these countries have been founded for the last five, six or seven hundred years" (quoted in Kossmann and Mellink 279). It was with the nobility and the towns that sovereignty rested. This simply had to be true, according to Vranck, because if it didn't, "not only the validity of the treaties with Her Majesty and the commission and government of His Excellency but everything that the States have done for their defence these past fifteen years would be called into question." He concluded that "the authority of the States must be conserved as the keystone on which the commonwealth rests" (281).

—

The argument that sovereignty in the United Provinces rested exclusively with the Provincial States and towns would remain the dominant constitutional doctrine until the fall of the Dutch republic in the late eighteenth century. It meant the central authority suffered from a structural weakness, always vulnerable to the whims of its member provinces. Dutch political philosophy in the seventeenth century would discuss this problem without ever finding a solution for it.

The Dutch philosopher, historian, and legal scholar Hugo de Groot (or Grotius, 1583–1645) was a case in point. Like many of the great political thinkers of the age, Grotius had extensive practical experience in political affairs. He first accompanied the Holland State Pensionary Johan van Oldenbarnevelt on a diplomatic mission at the age of fifteen, when they visited the court of the new French king, Henri IV, to try to secure French support for the Dutch war effort against Spain. He would serve as legal counsel to the States of Holland and Zeeland, and as a personal adviser to Van Oldenbarnevelt, by then effectively the highest-ranked politician in the new union. After his arrest in 1618 and subsequent flight from captivity (famously smuggled out of prison in a book chest by his wife, Maria van Reigersbergh), he ended up in Paris, where he would serve for some time as the ambassador of the King of Sweden.

Grotius would produce a number of publications in which he reflected on the constitutional predicament of the United Provinces. The core problem with the Dutch constitution as he saw it was that the centre, embodied by the States General as a deliberative chamber and the Council of State as its executive body, had no real authority. The latter rested entirely with the states, who could ignore or veto federal decisions at will. The fact that the states enforced this through strict voting instructions to their delegates to the States General meant that the common good was rarely served by their deliberations:

> [W]hen dispatched to a convention, their main concern is not the common interest of the province but the interest of their particular township, indeed they are required to act that way by their office and by oath. And the same holds good to a large extent for those who are called delegates. This leads inevitably to protracted disagreement and concord is found only too rarely, thus leading to the neglect of the public interests.
> (Grotius, *De Republica Emendanda* 113)

The system of strict delegation in turn significantly weakened the federal executive authority: "The preponderance in the administration of those who are virtually held under obligation by directives from their own provinces makes itself felt to the detriment of the authority of the Council of State, the body that attends to what is the highest common interest" (Grotius, *De Republica Emendanda* 113). The federal administration also lacked the power to veto state laws or decisions that undermined the interests or cohesion of the federation. What was worse, the federal authority didn't even have the option of taking states to court if a conflict between the two administrative levels arose: "[T]he leaders of the confederate body have no authority themselves to reform provincial laws in the common interest and (...) if any point of controversy happens to arise between separate provinces there is no such thing as a permanent and constitutional court of justice to appeal to for a settlement" (113). The States, on the other hand, did have veto power over the decisions taken at federal level, and they were not shy about wielding it: "Indeed, if by chance they do decide on something of general applicability, then this decision is often overruled by the heads of the separate provinces" (115).

The distribution of powers, and checks upon them, between centre and states was completely unbalanced. Grotius therefore concluded, somewhat dramatically, that "not only is this not a united republic – since every province in itself clearly possesses the full rights of a republic – the confederacy is not firmly enough established to keep them together" (*De Republica Emendanda* 115). The only thing stopping the provinces from going their separate ways was the presence of a common enemy in the form of imperial Spain.

War may not have been desirable from a moral point of view, but to Grotius it had the virtue of forcing the states to focus on external agreements rather than internal disagreements: "[T]he only reason why they stick together at all is their fear of the enemy at this moment, and once this fear has gone the alliance will fall apart" (*De Republica* 113). This explains why, when Van Oldenbarnevelt started negotiating an extended truce with the Spanish crown, Grotius wrote an impassioned memorandum advising him against it: "When this urgency and danger would cease, and people thought peace was guaranteed, jealousy and weakheartedness would make this form of government collapse immediately in anarchy and confusion" (*Memorie* 43).

Grotius would turn out to be nearer the mark han even he might have thought likley when he wrote this warning. In the absence of a common enemy, the various religious communities would quickly renew their conflict, being first at each others' throats and eventually at Grotius's, too. The Stadtholder, Maurice of Orange, skilfully manipulated this conflict to outmanoeuvre Van Oldenbarnevelt, mobilising hard-line Calvinist support for a coup which saw the moderate Calvinist State Pensionary executed and his adviser Grotius imprisoned.[6]

In his *Verantwoordingh* (1622), in which he gave an account of his actions during his time on the (inter)national political stage, Grotius rather ironically turned the weakness of the federal authority into a weapon in his defence. He effectively denied that the States General, who had accused him of the crime of *lese majesté*, had the authority to do so. The actions for which he stood accused were also not done of his own volition, but on behalf of a higher authority than that of the States General, namely the States of Holland and the governors of Rotterdam. It was only to them, and not to the States General or anyone else, that he had to justify himself. He clearly thought himself innocent of the charges, but if he was to stand trial, it wasn't in front of a court nominated by the States General, but in front of "ordinarisse competente Rechters, volghens de Privilegien van de Landen ende Steden" – courts respecting the privileges of the sovereign province and city that he had served (10).

This use of the state sovereignty argument obviously smacked somewhat of opportunism. Grotius was nothing if not consistent though. In the book

---

6   Van Oldenbarnevelt's mistake was a carbon copy of the one made by the Habsburgs around the same time, when they signed a peace treaty with the common enemy of the various religious factions inside the German Empire. The 1606 Peace of Zsitvatorok would lead to a prolonged truce between the Christian West and the Ottoman Empire. Without a joint enemy, however, nothing would stop the escalation of the dispute between Protestant and Catholic factions, which would ultimately trigger the Thirty Years' War. See Asch, *The Thirty Years War* 28.

that is generally considered to be his magnum opus, *On the Law of War and Peace* (1625), he essentially made the same point. "It may happen," he observed, "that many states may be connected together by the closest union, which Strabo, in more places that one calls a system, and yet each retain the condition of a perfect, individual state" (219; ch. 3, § 7).

—

The Dutch would never really resolve the problem outlined by Grotius in his early works. In practice, the emphasis remained on the sovereignty of the individual states. One telling example came in 1652, when Pensionary Johan de Witt sharply rebuked the Dutch delegates discussing a potential peace settlement in the first Anglo-Dutch war. They had allowed the English Parliament to refer to the "respublica" (singular) of the United Provinces. He ordered them to point out to Parliament that the correct form was the plural *Respublicae Foederatae* – federated *republics* (Israel 719). If there was a unifying political doctrine, it wasn't a federal but a quasi-monarchical one, in support of the House of Orange. Against this Orangist idea, the States party stressed the sovereignty of the individual states. This may have been a "manifest fiction" given that majority voting was frequently used to break the deadlock in the States General (733), but it was a fiction that effectively blocked any theoretical development of a credible concept of federalism.

One of the few exceptions to this rule was Benedictus de Spinoza (1632–1677). His posthumously published *Tractatus Politicus*, which had strong Machiavellian overtones, took as its starting point the classical regime theory. Given its unfinished nature, it is impossible to draw any conclusions about the author's intentions; it did, however, offer an interesting contribution to the debate about federal unions. Within the aristocratic regime type, Spinoza made a distinction between an aristocracy which "takes its name from one city" and one "which is in the hands of more than one city." Declaring the latter type "preferable," even stressing its "superiority," he set out to describe its optimal constitution (Spinoza 73). Though it played no significant role in Dutch political discourse at the time and offered no solution to the sovereignty problem which had plagued the Dutch United Provinces in the previous one hundred years, his analysis did contain a number of suggestions which foreshadowed future discussions about federal constitutions.

One was his idea that thought needed to be given to the method of selecting a location of a capital city, because "if any city of the dominion were assigned for the meeting of this supreme council, it would in reality be the head of the dominion." He saw two options: "Either they would have to take turns, or a place would have to be assigned for this council that has not the right of citizenship and belongs equally to all" (Spinoza 75).[7] The other was the creation of a council of syndics which had one vital task: "[T]o see that the constitution is kept unbroken" (61). In a section in which he quoted directly from the passage in the *Discourses* where Machiavelli introduced his idea of *riddure ai principii*, he placed in this council the power to "bring back the dominion to that first principle, on which it was in the beginning established" (81–82). Excluding from this revision process "the absolutely fundamental laws of the dominion [which] may be everlasting" (any attempt to scrap them would in fact be punishable by death), he suggested that for "the other general rights of the dominion" a three-fourths or four-fifths majority of the supreme council would be required for any revision, provided the council of syndics had issued a recommendation of revision (62). The idea that a constitution needed protecting and that protection also meant the ability to mend its flaws – that the latter was, in fact, essential for the future wellbeing of the republic – would become an important theme in future discussions about federal union.

—

The lack of a clear solution at the theoretical level to the problem first identified by Grotius, namely the weakness of the federal institutions, created continued political and institutional gridlock. On two occasions, an extraordinary session of the States General was called to discuss proposals to reform the constitutional framework. The first time was in 1651, when the States of Holland used the unexpected death of Stadtholder William II to restore the federal form of government. The Great Assembly which gathered in the old Knight's Hall in The Hague offered an opportunity not just to reinstall the old federal form, but to improve on it. At the insistence of the States of Holland, the delegates suspended indefinitely the Stadtholder position, strongly associated with the House of Orange. They then made the States General and Raad van State jointly responsible for new military appointments (Israel 707–709). All other proposed changes foundered on the rock of states' interests.

The 1716 conference was the work of the later Pensionary of Holland, Simon van Slingelandt (1664–1736). While serving as Secretary of the Council

---

7   The latter option would eventually be taken by the American Founders in 1787. It would also resurface in the European discussions in the late 1940s and early 1950s.

of State he drafted an essay titled "Discourse on the Defects of the Present Constitution," in which he made the case for reform of the union's nearly bankrupt funding system, and its voting rules. The need for fiscal reform was the more urgent issue. Not only was the union drowning in war debts, it also had no means of paying them off. Since the revolt against Spain had been caused in part by Spanish taxes, the united provinces had no appetite for imposing a new tax on their populations on behalf of the collective. It meant that as United Provinces, the central authority relied for funding exclusively on a quota system that had been in place since the early sixteenth century – quotas that the individual provinces would not always decide to fulfil. Van Slingelandt's attempt to solve this by introducing an own resource for the union in the form of a tax earmarked for paying off the debt ended in failure. It meant the inadequate early sixteenth-century funding system would remain in place until the end of the eighteenth century, leaving what was arguably the wealthiest population in Europe with permanently bankrupt public finances (De Vries and Van der Woude 152–154).

On the voting rules, Van Slingelandt listed three main concerns. The most obvious was the fact that the members "could not outvote one another, which meant that they could never, or only very slowly, come to an agreement on issues of any significance" (Van Slingelandt I: 186; my translation). The second was that "when they do come to a decision, they cannot force one another to implement what they had voted on unanimously" (I: 187). And lastly, he pointed to the fact that the members of the States General acted "without an oath to the commonwealth" (I: 186). This mattered because a meeting of delegates who all acted on strict instructions from their home states would have needed some kind of binding sentiment to make them come to agreements – especially when the voting system required unanimity.

These obvious defects would not, however, persuade the delegates of the second Great Assembly to vote for fundamental reform, any more than they had persuaded the delegates of the first one. After nine months of talking, all they could agree on was a reduction of the size of the standing army, now that peace had made its maintenance less relevant (Israel 988).

Van Slingelandt's constitutional writings would remain unpublished until the mid-1780s, when the rise of the Patriot movement triggered a lively debate about the necessity of constitutional reform. The revolutionary fervour of the movement would peak in the summer of 1786, when large supportive crowds enabled its militias to seize control of the province of Holland, and the city of Utrecht (Israel 1107). The Patriot revolutionaries allowed the Prince of Orange, William V, to escape to the still loyal province of Gelderland. There his wife, Wilhelmina, asked for the help of his brother-in-law, the king of

Prussia. Nothing would have come of it if a Patriot militia had not blocked her from leaving the province to travel to The Hague, thereby indirectly insulting the Prussian king's honour. When the States of Holland refused to entertain a Prussian demand for restoration, a large Prussian army invaded the country, eventually succeeding in suppressing the Patriot revolt. They restored William to the Stadtholder position, but it was clear that his was only a nominal position of power. The United Provinces as a sovereign entity were no more.

—

Given its many constitutional and organisational defects, Van Slingelandt concluded that it was "more of a surprise that the Republic still exists than that it is in a state of collapse" (I: 187) It was certainly not easy for a union with such obvious flaws to function properly, let alone to survive for so long. The Dutch would, however, find a number of creative ways around the problem. One was delegating execution of crucial parts of foreign policy to corporations like the Vereenigde Oost-Indische Compagnie (VOC). The VOC was the first of a number of European corporations acting as quasi-sovereign powers in their own right on other continents. These corporations had their own armies, and sometimes held large territories under their own administration. Though formally they did not have the power to declare war or peace, they did have the delegated authority to stage military expeditions if these served company purposes.

At home, the seven provinces remained reasonably united because they were jointly involved in several wars. They kept the subject of internal division off the agenda by assertively maintaining the Dutch *respublicae*'s position in Europe, seeking advantage where they could for the Dutch merchant and fishing fleets. As long as they were fighting abroad, they stayed (somewhat) united at home.

The other political solution was more straightforward: simply ignore the unanimity rule. In moments of crisis, the states would find ways of manoeuvring around it. The lack of a written constitution undoubtedly helped here, but it was not so much the lack of a single founding document as the lack of an absolute status of ground rules, either written or unwritten, that allowed for their creative interpretation. In all the cases discussed so far – the Swiss Confederacy, the Polish-Lithuanian Commonwealth, the Dutch Republic – the federal regime form was, at heart, more a way of doing politics than a proper constitutional order. Flexibility was of the essence, because to the extent that there was a constitution, it gave powers to its constituent parts – chiefly the veto – that would have made normal functioning extremely difficult without a method to work round it.

A League of its Own: The German Holy Roman Empire

The first half of the seventeenth century was dominated by the Habsburg dynasty's ultimate attempt to re-establish some form of universal monarchy. It involved a war on two fronts: against the separatist Dutch provinces, and against rebelling Protestant principalities and cities in the Holy Roman Empire. The latter conflict, known as the Thirty Years' War, started in 1618 with the defenestration of three of the emperor's representatives by a crowd of Protestant assembly members in the Bohemian capital of Prague. The conflict would soon spread to other parts of the empire. Spain would use the truce with the Dutch United Provinces to join the fighting on the side of the emperor. Since the Protestant powers of England, Denmark, and the United Provinces all chose to stay out of what was essentially a German civil war, it looked like it was fizzling out when the main rebellious power centre of the Rhineland Palatinate was overrun by imperial forces.

Tragically for his subjects, emperor Ferdinand II managed to snatch defeat from the jaws of victory by passing the Edict of Restitution (1629). This edict was remarkable mainly for its ability to alienate everyone at once. Catholic princes could object to the way it was passed – in violation of centuries of constitutional convention, as a direct imperial decree, ignoring the customary consultative role of the Imperial Diet. Protestant princes found even more to dislike in it, since the Edict aimed to expropriate from them properties and lands they had claimed from the church during the Reformation. It also, at the stroke of a pen, outlawed an entire religious community by banning Calvinism.

Equally bad were Ferdinand's military mistakes: replacing his victorious commander Wallenstein and leaving his troops amassed in Northern Germany, thereby raising Swedish suspicions that they would be the next target of imperial aggression, practically inviting them to take preemptive action (Asch 94–95). Ferdinand's mistakes would end up prolonging the conflict by another twenty years, bringing first Sweden and then France into the war. By the time peace was finally restored, around one third of the German population had died from violence, hunger, or disease.

After the Second World War, the American Realist school in international relations saw in the Treaty of Westphalia of 1648, which finally ended the conflict, the confirmation of the rise of the sovereign state across Europe: "By the end of the Thirty Years' War, sovereignty as supreme power over a certain territory was a political fact" (Morgenthau 299). This Realist interpretation has been exposed to significant criticism in recent scholarship.[8] The core argument of this alternative interpretation is that, though the peace did end whatever chance remained of the Habsburgs establishing a universal monarchy, European politics after Westphalia continued to be dominated by the contest for continental supremacy. Another, no less significant objection is that Westphalia was, in essence, not a European peace treaty but a German constitutional settlement. The core objective of the negotiations was to regulate relations between the constituent parts of the Holy Roman Empire. For the latter, the treaty would therefore gain the force of a kind of constitution – of a political entity very different from the nation state.

—

The first sixty-three articles of the Treaty of Westphalia dealt with the consequences of the war, and focused on restitution of properties and rights, while recognising various changes in territorial and dynastic claims. The focus then switched to a discussion of the constitutional order of the newly restored Empire. It started with a confirmation of the continued validity of the various ancient rights and privileges that underpinned the Empire's political order: in order "to prevent for the future any Differences arising in the Politick State, all and every one of the Electors, Princes and States of the Roman Empire, are so establish'd and confirm'd in their antient Rights (...) that they never can or ought to be molested therein by any whomsoever upon any manner of pretence" (Art. 64). Article 65 dealt with the right of all members of the Diet to participate in deliberations on a range of subjects, from taxation to matters of peace and war. The article also confirmed that individual states had the right to enter into treaties with foreign powers, provided "those alliances do not go against the emperor, and the Empire." Further articles dealt with the powers of the Diet (Art. 67), the powers of the individual Electors, princes, and states within their own territories (Art. 68), and the regulation of tolls and customs in ports and on rivers (Art. 70). Article 120 confirmed the status of this treaty as "perpetual Law and establish'd Sanction of the Empire, to be inserted like other fundamental

8   See, for example, Durchard: "Historians are rather sceptical as far as the construct of the 'Westphalian order' is concerned. (...) [N]o durable political order of continental dimension was achieved in 1648, but only a peace order which was limited to the centre of the continent and, moreover, actually collapsed relatively quickly" ("From Westphalia to the Revolutionary Era" 45).

Laws and Constitutions of the Empire in the Acts of the next Diet of the Empire, and the Imperial Capitulation."

The question of what kind of regime had been established through this treaty would dominate German political-philosophical debate in the second half of the seventeenth century, involving all the greater (as well as many of the lesser) lights of the era. The main division within this debate was based on attempts to interpret the new constitution in traditional regime theory terms. One school, known as the *Caesarianer*, saw it as essentially a monarchy, with sovereignty resting with the emperor. Their opponents, the *Fürsterianer*, located it in the constituent states, and therefore saw the new constitution as a kind of aristocracy of local rulers.

Opposing both schools were two other interpretations that stressed the unique nature of the new constitution. One camp claimed the Empire wasn't a proper regime at all. Its champion was Samuel von Pufendorf (1632–1694). Pufendorf was a typical product of the German academy, a student of theology, law, and philosophy who made a living through both of the main options open to career academics at the time: tutoring the offspring of a prominent family and lecturing at a university. It wasn't until he was in his late thirties that he first became involved in practical politics, initially as a privy councillor to the Swedish king Charles XI, later serving in the same role to the Elector Frederick III of Brandenburg.[9]

In his *Two Books on the Elements of Jurisprudence*, published in 1660, Pufendorf laid the foundations for his analysis of the Empire by setting out his own regime theory. Following Bodin and Hobbes, he argued that there were basically only three different regime types: monarchy, aristocracy, and democracy. He dismissed the classical corrupted counterparts as mere reflections of the "dislike of the prince or of the present state of affairs" (Pufendorf, *Elements of Jurisprudence* 703). This in turn raised the question where in this classification the Empire should be placed. Pufendorf used his next study, *The Present State of Germany* (1667), to answer it.

Writing under the pseudonym Severinus de Monzambano, he presented his analysis of the Empire in the form of a fictional travel account. While describing its historical development and its present state, he introduced a new kind of classification of regime forms. Instead of the old distinction of perfect and corrupt regimes, he proposed a new pairing of *regular* and *irregular* regimes. By *regular*, he meant regimes where sovereignty resided

---

9   It was this same Frederick who, several years after Pufendorf's death, famously styled himself "King in Prussia," the word "in" reflecting the compromise between personal ambition and the constitutional reality that his realm covered only a part of historic Prussia.

fully with either the monarch, the aristocracy, or the people. Irregular regimes were those where sovereignty was divided. In his most famous work published a few years later, *On the Law of Nature and Nations*, he would flesh out this distinction. An irregular regime form was "one in which we do not find that unity which is the essence of the state so completely established" (Pufendorf, *On the Law of Nature and Nations* 144).

A third category of regimes was formed by what he called "systems of states." Here he distinguished between two different systems. The first was one in which different states had a king in common: "[W]hen several separate states have one and the same king, either by agreement or by reason of marriage, inheritance or conquest" (Pufendorf, *On the Law of Nature and Nations* 144). This was on the condition that "they are not amalgamated into one kingdom" – an incorporating union was, in his view, not a union but an enlarged monarchy. The other was what he called "alliances": "[W]here several neighbouring states are so connected by perpetual alliance that they renounce the intention of exercising some portions of their sovereign power" (144–145).[10]

———

The examples Pufendorf gave made it clear that any form of separation of powers was enough to make a regime fall into the irregular category. This classification was presented as a neutral analytical tool. There is no doubt, however, that in the case of the Empire, by *irregular* he meant not just unusual in form, but also dysfunctional in operation. The Empire, he stated, came "very near a System of [many Soveraign] States, in which one Prince or General [leader] of the League excels the rest of the Confederates, and is clothed with the [Ornaments of a Sovereign Prince]; but then this Body is attack'd by Furious Diseases" (Pufendorf, *The Present State of Germany* 299).

He recognised that the Empire had many potential strengths – the size and quality of its population made it the most significant military force in Europe, while its natural resources and river network made it an attractive trading partner for the rest of the continent. Still, it was relatively poor compared to its neighbours. Its lack of access to the high seas put it at a

---

10   In the section on alliances ("De foederibus") Pufendorf made a further distinction between *personal* and *real* treaties. The personal treaty was limited to the person of the king and could therefore expire upon his death; real treaties "are made not so much with the king or rulers of the people as such as with the country and the kingdom and persists despite the deaths of those who were the authors" (174).

disadvantage over the main trading centres of the later seventeenth century. It was in no position to look for expansion. Here, Pufendorf compared the Empire to the Polish-Lithuanian Commonwealth: "[T]he Interest of the Polish State is rather to defend what they have, than to [make any Conquests upon] their Neighbours. (...) [T]he Necessity of the German Affairs must needs teach them the selfsame modesty" (*The Present State of Germany* 315).

Its greatest weakness, though, was its constitution. The emperor had "nothing but a shadow of the Kingly Power (...) and seems liker [sic] the General of an Association than a King" (Pufendorf, *The Present State of Germany* 331). This set up a permanent conflict between emperor and States: "[F]or he, with might and main, by all waies, endeavoureth to regain the old Regal Power, and they, on the other side, are as solicitous to preserve the [Liberties and Wealth] they have got the possession of" (332). According to Pufendorf, the result of this internal conflict wasn't the kind of positive energy that Machiavelli attributed to it, but "Suspicions, Distrust, and underhand Contrivances to hinder each other's Designs, and break each other's Power" (332).

Not only were emperor and States pitted against each other, but the states were also internally divided. The different forms of government pitted them against each other, as did their different economies. The fact that some states – the Electors – were elevated in status above the others was a permanent cause of discontent. The religious schism caused by the Reformation had created multiple additional fault lines inside the Empire. Individual states, or leagues of states, regularly entered into alliances with foreign princes, significantly undermining its cohesion. There was no proper way of settling internal conflicts: the Chamber of the Spire took an eternity to produce its rulings, while the Chamber of Vienna was patently corrupt. Worst of all, the Empire didn't even have its own army, or its own Treasury. For both, it relied on contributions from the States. The Empire's constitution, in short, was fundamentally flawed: "Weakness and Diseases ever follow upon a loose Conjunction and an ill-combined and irregular Union" (Pufendorf, *The Present State of Germany* 329).

This pessimistic diagnosis was based on an analysis of the Empire's everyday political reality. There remained the challenge of defining its actual nature. Where in his taxonomy of regimes did Pufendorf think it should be placed? He looked for it first in the classical categories of monarchy, aristocracy, and democracy. The latter option was most easily dismissed: "I do not remember I ever saw one Author that did say, it was a *Democrasie*" (*The Present State of Germany* 274). The claim of some that the Empire was an aristocracy was dismissed, too. The essence of an aristocratic regime was its Council or Senate, "which has a Right to deliberate, consult on, and determine all the publick Concerns and Affairs" (279). But, he explained, "there is no such Senate in Germany" (279). The Chambers of Spire and Vienna were appeals courts, not legislative chambers. And the Diet was not a permanent body, it "has ever been call'd [only] upon [particular and emergent] Causes" (279). As for monarchy, "he that can think that the Emperor is an Absolute Monarch is wonderfully silly" (283). And it was no limited monarchy, either: "[T]he Emperor can exact nothing of [the States] against their will" (291).

He then looked at the system of states category. He noted that for a "System of many Cities [states] united by a League" to succeed, a number of exceptional circumstances were required: "[T]hat the Associated [Cities or] States have the same form of Government, and be not overmuch disproportioned in their Strength, and that the same or equal Advantages may from the Union arise to every one of them" (*The Present State of Germany* 329, 330).

Pufendorf concluded that none of the conditions for the formal recognition of a system of states were met by the Empire. It was, in fact, "neither a Kingdom, nor a System of States" but "something (without a name) that fluctuates between these two" (*The Present State of Germany* 331, 297). The result was "a most pernicious Convulsion in the Body of the Empire, whilst the Emperor and the States draw counter each to the other" (332). His final diagnosis was that the Empire was a "misshapen Monster" (296), and that "nothing similar to it, in my opinion, exists anywhere else on the whole globe" (296).

—

The gauntlet thrown down by Pufendorf was eventually picked up by the philosopher Gottfried Wilhelm Leibniz (1646–1716). In his anonymously published *Caesarinus Fürstenerius* (1677) Leibniz set out to prove that what Pufendorf saw as the Empire's main drawback – namely, its lack of a clear locus of sovereignty, owing to its divided nature – was in fact its main strength. Leibniz fully embraced the older, Machiavellian conception of any ruler's sovereignty as "sufficient jurisdiction to preserve his authority over his subjects" (116). He argued that it was essentially *because* sovereignty was omnipresent, divided over many layers of government, that the Empire functioned well.

The main public target of his book wasn't his compatriot Pufendorf but "the sharp-witted Englishman" Thomas Hobbes. "If we listen to Hobbes," he argued, "there will be nothing in our land but out-and-out anarchy" (Leibniz

118). Hobbes's error, Leibniz claimed, was the failure to recognize the way in which the Empire managed to function properly in spite of the supposed theoretical difficulty of a lack of unitary government. While accepting that "when the supreme power is divided, many dissensions can arise, (...) experience has shown that men usually hold to some middle road, so as not to commit everything to hazard by their obstinacy" (119). Here Leibniz specifically mentioned the tendency of the German, Polish-Lithuanian, and Dutch political classes to bend the constitutional rules when circumstances required them to do so. This "would seem anarchy to Hobbes," but "due to the prudence and moderation of those who preside over the whole, most matters are finished according to their wishes" (119).

In the course of making his argument, Leibniz introduced an important conceptual innovation: the distinction within the *genus* of leagues between the species of confederation and what he called "union." Both were collections of territories united in a league, but there was an essential difference between them: "A confederation is entered into by words alone and, if necessary, forces are joined. For a union, it is necessary that a certain administration be formed, with some power over the members. (...) Here I say there exists a state" (Leibniz 117). In other words: a confederation remained a mere collection of states, but a union was itself a kind of state, with administrative powers of its own. Crucially though, the latter came not at the expense of the sovereignty of the individual territories: "[I]t is clear that, the union notwithstanding, there still remains in each region that which I have defined as supremacy" (117). Where Pufendorf saw only monsters in the conceptual space between kingdoms and systems of states, Leibniz had found an entirely new category: a *union*, which was both a state *and* a collection of states.

He recognised that merely calling the Empire by a new name was not enough to refute Pufendorf's analysis of its many shortcomings. To solve this problem, he used a classic rhetorical ploy. Leibniz's answer to the objection by Hobbes and Pufendorf was to turn the flexibility required to prevent federal unions from collapsing into a kind of political virtue. It was in a letter to the Scottish nobleman Thomas Burnett, who in 1695 had been sent by William III to the court of Hanover to report on matters relating to the Hanoverian succession, that Leibniz fully developed his argument about the importance of the middle road and moderation as a constitutional method (Leibniz 193–194). He did it by praising the pragmatic decision-making processes of federal unions – referring explicitly to "the government of the United Provinces," though we know from his earlier writings that he placed the Empire and the Polish-Lithuanian

Commonwealth in the same category. In these regimes, he observed, "people align themselves with reason in important matters of state (...) because they do not follow [the principle of] the plurality of voices blindly there but mix it with what is called 'friendly coming to terms' ("*composition amiable*"). It is a matter of dealing with men in which someone tries to lead another to his end by force of persuasion only." It was this virtue of moderation and "friendly coming together" that was key to establishing an "empire of reason" (193–194).

—

As a political answer to Pufendorf's criticism it worked quite well, but theoretically Leibniz's approach of denying the relevance of sovereignty was somewhat unsatisfactory. Without a clear conception of sovereignty on which to base the federal union's constitutional settlement, it was always at risk of renewed political or even armed conflict between states and central authority. The most interesting attempt to solve the Empire's theoretical sovereignty challenge came from a legal theorist called Ludolf Hugo (1632–1704). Hugo was a student of the constitutional scholar Hermann Conring, one of the main proponents of the work of Machiavelli in the seventeenth-century Empire, and of the Leiden philosopher Marcus van Boxhorn. Through the latter, he also became acquainted with the work of Grotius, and with the constitutional structure of the Dutch United Provinces.

Hugo's main contribution to the debate about the Empire was his treatise *De Statu Regionum Germaniae* (1661). It contained two interesting conceptual innovations. The first was the idea of a kind of dual sovereignty structure. In the second chapter of his study, he described a classification of unions that would feature in more or less the same form in the work of Pufendorf: a loose confederation, an incorporated union, and something in between the two. In the first category, which contained unions like the Dutch United Provinces and the Swiss Confederacy, sovereignty was entirely with the member states. In the second, of which the Roman republic was the main representative, it rested completely with the centre. The situation was more complicated in the third category. Here he observed a kind of division of sovereignty on a practical basis: "Finally, the third category was interposed between the two previous ones; when the civil government of the republic is divided, in a manner, between the highest and the inferior, the former govern those things which belong to all in common, and the latter those which affect the safety of the individual regions" (ch. 2, § IIX; my translation).

In a subsequent chapter Hugo showed how this division of sovereignty led to a kind of double division of powers: not just horizontally in the form of an independent legislature, executive and judiciary, but also vertically through the division of powers in the execution of the key roles of government. In other words, not only did central authority and individual states each hold a different kind of sovereignty, but they also executed some of Bodin's marks of sovereignty separately and others jointly (what German constitutional scholars later called a *Kompetenzverteilung*; see Pfannenschmid 134). Coinage was a matter of the individual states, but as far as Hugo was concerned it should instead become the prerogative of the centre, to tackle the problem of forgeries (Hugo ch. 3, § 32). Other main powers like taxation, administration of the courts, and the conduct of foreign policy were a mixed competence.

Hugo's concept of a dual sovereignty and a division of labour between administrative centre and states in the execution of the marks of sovereignty would eventually be forgotten, as was much of the debate about the Holy Roman Empire's constitutional structure. His work would be revived in the late nineteenth century, but then mainly as a footnote to an entirely different constitutional debate (Pfannenschmid 218).

The union of the Crowns: a taxonomy of unions

Machiavelli's *Discourses* book II, chapter 4 would end up shaping the seventeenth- and early eighteenth-century British debate about the kind of union that could unite the English and Scottish crowns. Both monarchists and republicans would base their analysis on his overview of the three modes of expansion – perhaps not always agreeing with his conclusions, but always appreciative of the analysis that underpinned it.

This early modern debate about the modes of expansion in turn shaped the debate about the core concepts of union and federation as applied on a national and international scale. Eventually, the two concepts would merge into a single option: a *federal union*. This type of regime was part of a taxonomy of unions that also included the main systemic rivals of the league in this period, namely the composite monarchy – a monarchy spread out over various, not always contiguous territories, all united under a single crown. In its ultimate form, this option was known as *universal monarchy*.

It was the act of expansion that created the need for a new kind of classificatory system for the different types of relationship that it could create. The multiplicity of territories under a single ruler raised complicated constitutional questions about the relative status of the different territories, and about the relationship between them. This question was essentially one of union (Robertson 4–5).

Upon adding a new territory to the old one(s), the monarch became the embodiment of a *personal* union between them. This could cause obvious problems where constitutional regimes were not aligned. But even if they were reasonably similar, there were still a number of practical problems to be solved. Where was the monarch to reside? Would appointments reflect the priorities of the new territory, or of the old? Did a personal union mean that the new territory was expected to sign on to, and inevitably also pay for, the political priorities of the old territory? If so, would they have a vote in them? And by no means least: how was continuity of this union to be guaranteed beyond the life of the monarch? In the debate about these questions, all sides would base their analysis on Machiavelli's work.

The immediate cause of the debate was the death of the English monarch Elizabeth I in 1603. Following her death, the English parliament approached James VI to persuade him to add the English crown to his Scottish one. His acceptance created a union between the two countries, known as the Union of the Crowns. It was, however, strictly limited to the person of the king, not affecting the king's subjects in either country. James would repeatedly ask the English Parliament to find a way to turn this personal union into a *real* union by merging the two countries into a single constitutional unit, so that the union could survive his reign.

The king's request triggered a lively debate in both countries about the uses and modalities of a possible political union between the two realms. One of the main contributors was the statesman-philosopher Francis Bacon (1561–1626). In 1605 he published a pamphlet, *A Brief Discourse of the Happy Union Betwixt the two Kingdoms of Scotland and England*, in which he discussed the English-Scottish merger in the context of expansion of continental monarchies. This obviously raised the question what mechanism of expansion was the right one in this case. Closely following Machiavelli's argument in *Discourses* book II, chapter 4, he suggested there were three main modes of expansion. The first of these, expansion by conquest or as he called it "violent union" (Bacon 258), he dismissed out of hand. The remaining two, which Machiavelli had described as the way of Rome and the way of the Etruscans, Bacon called "mixed" and "composite" unions (256). Using arguments from nature, he rejected the latter option as "imperfect mixture," pointing to the fact that federations are usually "speedily dissolved" (259). Praising the successes of the Roman method, Bacon concluded by explicitly referring to the Florentine philosopher's work: "[T]he authority of Nicholas Machiavel seemeth not to be contemned; who inquiring the causes of the growth of the Roman empire, doth give judgment; there was not one greater than this, that the state did so easily compound and incorporate with strangers" (261).

It is clear that in this situation, to Bacon and his English contemporaries, England was Rome. Scotland's fate was to join as a junior partner in the realisation of English dreams of empire. Against this, Scottish contributors argued for equal status. The Scottish Reformation scholar Robert Pont (1524–1606), for example, while accepting the idea of an "incorporating" union, stressed the importance of equality between its member states: "[S]everal estats be drawn to a uniformity or equall mixture of all these points they ar perfectly incorporated" (Galloway 43).

—

Bacon's arguments in favour of a Roman style "incorporating union" of the two countries fell on deaf ears in the English parliament, which opted for the status quo of a union based on the person of the monarch. What remained was "confusion of sovereignty" (Robert Pont, quoted in Galloway 39). In the century that followed, it became clear that the way succeeding monarchs executed the personal prerogatives in both countries (what Bodin had called the "marks of sovereignty") worked to the disadvantage of Scotland. Appointments made in Scotland seemed to serve the court in London rather than Scotland itself. Taxes raised in Scotland helped to finance wars fought to further English causes – wars on which the Scottish parliament had no vote. The strict separation of the two realms meant that there were no clear economic benefits of the Union to compensate for these disadvantages. Scotland was not allowed to share in English trade and colonial ventures (Henderson Scott 238).

It was no surprise, therefore, that Scottish frustrations eventually boiled over. During a debate in the Scottish parliament in 1703, one member complained bitterly:

> All our affairs since the Union of the Crowns have been managed by the advice of English ministers, and the principal offices of the kingdom filled with such men, as the Court of England knew would be subservient to their designs. (...) We have from that time appeared to the rest of the world more like a conquered province than a free independent people. (Henderson Scott 359).

The immediate cause of this debate was the question of the succession of the childless queen regent Anne. To this was added the sensitive subject of the financing of English involvement in the great continental conflict known as the War of the Spanish Succession (1701–1713). When in the spring of 1703 the English court, through its representative the Duke of Queensberry, tabled a motion which was essentially seeking the Scottish parliament's support for the court's approach to both successions, it caused a four-year constitutional standoff that was only ended with the ratification of the Acts of Union of 1707.[11]

In this debate, the undisputed champion of the federal approach was Andrew Fletcher of Saltoun (1655–1716). Born into the Scottish aristocracy, he first entered the Scottish parliament in his early twenties, where he quickly established himself as an opponent of the court party loyal to Charles II. After becoming involved in a plot against Charles's successor, James II, he was forced to flee to the Dutch Republic. He would return several years later in the company of the Prince of Orange, later King William III, as part of the invading Dutch army. Fletcher's initial support for William gave way to increasing hostility when it turned out the new king was no more likely to respect Scottish rights than the previous one. For William the English throne was a means to a continental end: the countering of the expansionist agenda of the French king Louis XIV. Scottish taxes were expected to help finance military expeditions required to achieve that objective, even though Scottish parliamentarians had no vote in the decision to go to war.

To remedy this, Fletcher proposed a number of constitutional limits on the royal prerogative. The Scottish parliament would henceforth have a vote in all declarations of peace and war. It would choose its own president and appoint all officers of the king serving in Scotland. Royal assent would be granted automatically to any Scottish bill passed. And parliament would meet annually, with each parliament's composition based on new elections (Henderson Scott 363). The idea was that a shorter parliament would give the monarch's officers fewer opportunities to manipulate its proceedings or corrupt its members.

In subsequent parliamentary manoeuvring these demands were linked to a further condition: they would have to be settled in advance of any Scottish vote to agree to an English candidate for the royal succession. In other words, without these changes, there could no longer be a (personal) union linking the two countries. Though there would be some amendments to the list as proposed by Fletcher, it was eventually adopted as the Act of Security – security for Scotland in its relationship with England.

---

11   The motion tabled by the Queen's representative was a supply motion, which would have granted the Court political cover for additional taxes raised in Scotland. A vote in favour would, however, have been interpreted as a confidence vote in the general political course of the Court, including its handling of the succession issue. See Henderson Scott 345–346.

The effect of these limitations, if implemented, would have been to introduce a federal constitutional settlement for the two nations. In his political
writings, Fletcher would further expand on his proposal. He broadly accepted
Machiavelli's analysis about methods of expansion, but took issue with his
claim that the Roman option would under ideal circumstances be the best
method: "[I] am fully persuaded that all great governments, whether republicks
or monarchies, not only disturb the world in their rise and fall; but by bringing
together such numbers of men and immense riches into one city, inevitably
corrupt all good manners, and make them uncapable of order and discipline"
(Fletcher of Saltoun 202). His preferred option was "a considerable number
(...) united together for the common safety; by which union and league they
will be enabled to resist a powerful invasion, and yet remain uncapable of
conquest" (210). The Etruscan option, Fletcher seemed to suggest, wasn't just
the most workable in practice, it was also the best *in theory*.

—

The kind of union created through this proposal would come to be classed
by Fletcher's contemporaries as a *federal union*. The term was something
of an enigma, effectively meaning "concord-covenant" (Henderson Scott
634).[12] It featured, for example, in *The Rights and Interests of the Two British
Monarchies* (1703), a pamphlet by a London-based Presbyterian writer called
James Hodges: "A Confederate or federal union is that, whereby Distinct, Free
and Independent Kingdoms, Dominions or States, do unite their separate
interests into one common interest, (...) retaining in the meantime their
several Independencies, National Distinctions and the different Laws,
Customs and Governments of each" (quoted in Henderson Scott 640). In
the debate about the Act of Security and the later Acts of Union, the term
"federal union" came to be used as the alternative to the one proposed
a century earlier by Bacon: an *incorporating* union, integrating the two
countries into a single administrative structure.

The boundaries separating the two concepts, incorporating and federal
union, were not very well defined.[13] As Hodges would show in a later pam-

12   "Just as (...) '[U]nion' was a vague term meaning any form of agreement or concord, so 'federal',
according to the O.E.D., meant 'of or pertaining to a covenant, compact or treaty" (Henderson
Scott 634).

13   This wasn't just a particularly Scottish confusion. At the start of the seventeenth century,
the German legal philosopher Johannes Althusius had also described a (con)federation in
essentially incorporating union terms: "A complete confederation is one in which a foreign realm,
province, or any other universal association, together with its inhabitants, are fully and integrally

phlet entitled *Essay Upon the Union* (1706), in the early eighteenth century it was still possible to argue for one option while using the vocabulary of the other. He opened his argument by linking the conceptual pair to the familiar Machiavellian discussion about methods of expansion (though, significantly, he would not call it "expansion" but rather, "joining interest"; the former could be based on a unilateral decision by the expanding country, whereas the latter required consensus). The method of Rome he described as "Incorporating themselves under one and the same Head and Allegiance," that of the Etruscans as "Confederacies betwixt Nations abiding under distinct Heads and Allegiances." The third one was the method of conquest, "in which Case, the Conquered, Government and People both, are what the Conqueror thinks fit to make them" (Hodges, *Essay Upon the Union* 6).

Unlike Fletcher (and Machiavelli), Hodges dismissed the federal option as "exposed to the unstable Humours of distinct Powers and opposite Interests" (Hodges, *Essay Upon the Union* 8).[14] The risk of war in case of disagreement between the confederate partners would be a permanent threat. This left the incorporating Union option as the only practical solution. But in calling for a "United State," Hodges stressed that a new constitutional settlement would have to overcome one fundamental problem, namely the unequal treatment the Scots received within the existing union: "[T]he Scots [are] put under all manner of disadvantages in point of trade. (...) [T]he Amicable and United State of these two Nations hath been perverted from its natural Condition" (14–15).

In fact, Hodges's preferred version of an incorporating union looked remarkably similar to a federal union. The two nations would maintain their own municipal laws, their own court systems and civil services, their own revenue systems, their own trading companies, even their own national debts (Hodges *Essay Upon the Union*, 21). And though he allowed for the possibility that this system could be legislated for by a single ("incorporated") parliament, his preferred option was a system of two separate national

coopted and admitted into the right and communion of the realm by the communicating of its fundamental laws and right of sovereignty. To the extent that they coalesce and are united into one and the same body, they become members of that one and same body" (Althusius, *Politica* 242). He went on to describe a "partial confederation" in more or less the same terms later thinkers would use for a confederation, though with a twist (a limit in time): "[V]arious realms or provinces, while reserving their rights of sovereignty, solemnly obligate themselves one or the other by a treaty or covenant made preferably for a fixed period of time" (242).

14   George Mackenzie, Earl of Cromartie, an outspoken supporter of incorporating union, similarly dismissed federal union because of its supposed unstable character, describing it as "ambulatory and changeable, by the nature of treaties" (*Friendly Return Letter Fourth*, quoted in Robertson 221).

parliaments. It would offer the best guarantee against the potential problem of "Intrigues of Faction (...) by which the Scots may at one blow be cut off from all the Benefits which the Union can give them" (28).

The question was obviously how to make sure that this dual parliament system did not lead to a repeat of the situation in the 1690s and early 1700s, when the English parliament passed several laws specifically aimed at harming Scottish interests. In language that foreshadowed Montesquieu and the American Founders, Hodges described a system of checks that would allow either parliament to correct the excesses of the other and gave the monarch a separate "negative" (veto) power over the decisions of both. These checks gave both parliaments "a triple Security":

> they have their Proportion of Members to represent them in the united Committee, where they may do their best to prevent mistakes. If any thing is done amiss there, they may apply to the Parliament of their Neighbour Nation, and get the Mistake rectified. And if this Application does not prevail, the separate Parliament of that Nation, which is like to suffer, can interpose their Negative, and can thereby give Time and Opportunity to their Neighbours, to extricate themselves from the hurry and surprise of Faction.
> (Hodges, *Essay Upon the Union* 28)

—

The obvious problem with Hodges's plan was that it relied on the cooperation of the larger nation, a situation that tended more towards the Roman method. Hodges's only argument in favour of the dual parliament system was an appeal to the moral sense of the English political class: "[I]f either Nation does obstruct this intended Harmony, by refusing to enter into proper Terms, either in point of mutual *Benefit* or Security (...) they must answer to God and Man, for all these Troubles and Calamities which will attend an unnatural Separation" (Hodges, *Essay Upon the Union* 31).

In the end, neither God nor man could move the English to accept the idea of sharing power with the Scots on equal terms. The Queen's advisers managed the negotiations about the conditions for union carefully, packing the Scottish negotiating committee with loyalists. The inevitable end result of the brief federalist moment in Anglo-Scottish history was a single, incorporated parliament, based in Westminster, with a clear majority of English members in both the Commons and the Lords, and no Scottish veto in either House.

Though it left the Scots empty-handed, the century-long debate about the transformation of the Jacobean personal union of the two crowns into a political union between the two countries did provide political theory with an eminently workable taxonomy of the concept of union. This consisted of, first, the pairing of personal and real or political union, and further, within political union, the pairing of incorporating and federal union. As we will see, in the following centuries the latter concept would undergo further subdivisions.

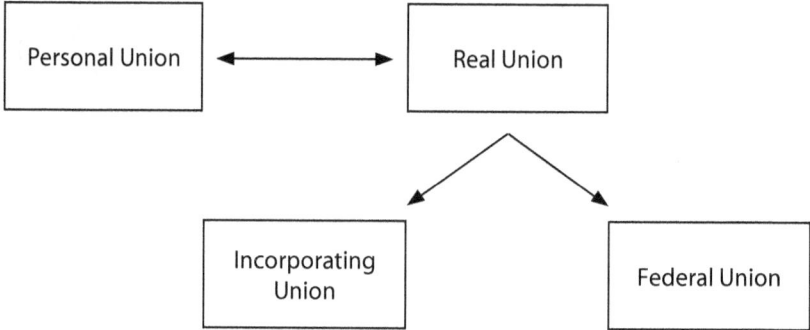

Figure 1: A taxonomy of unions

This taxonomy was based on Machiavelli's analysis of the three modes of expansion in *Discourses* (II, ch. 4). The Roman method formed the basis of the incorporating union, while the Etruscan method was now called federal union.

Bibliography

Althusius, Johannes. *Politica: An Abridged Translation of Politics Methodically Set Forth and Illustrated with Sacred and Profane Examples,* edited and translated with an introduction by Frederick S. Carney, foreword by Daniel J. Elezar, Liberty Fund, 2013.

Asch, Roland. *The Thirty Years War: The Holy Roman Empire and Europe, 1618–1648.* Palgrave, 1997.

Bacon, Francis. *A Brief Discourse of the Happy Union Betwixt the Two Kingdoms of Scotland and England.* 1605. *The Works of Francis Bacon,* vol. 3, C. & J. Rivington, 1826, pp. 254–264.

Butterworth, Richard. *The Polish-Lithuanian Commonwealth: Light and Flame.* Yale University Press, 2020.

Dembkowski, Harry. *The Union of Lublin: Polish Federalism in the Golden Age.* Columbia University Press, 1982.

Durchard, Heinz. "From Westphalia to the Revolutionary Era." *Peace Treaties and International Law in European History, From the Late Middle Ages to World War One*, edited by Randall Lessafer, Cambridge University Press, 2004, pp. 45–58.

Fletcher of Saltoun, Andrew. *Political Works*. Cambridge University Press, 1997.

Galloway, Bruce R., editor. *The Jacobean Union: Six Tracts of 1604*. Scottish History Society, 1985.

Gelderen, Martin van. *The Dutch Revolt*. Cambridge University Press, 2002.

Grotius, Hugo. *De Republica Emendanda: A Juvenile Tract by Hugo Grotius on the Emendation of the Dutch Polity*, edited by Arthur Eyffinger, Van Gorcum, 1984.

Grotius, Hugo. "Memorie 1607." *De Republica Emendanda: A Juvenile Tract by Hugo Grotius on the Emendation of the Dutch Polity*, edited by Arthur Eyffinger, Van Gorcum, 1984

Grotius, Hugo. *On the Law of War and Peace, Including the Law of Nature and of Nations*. 1625. Translated by Archibald Colin Campbell, B. Boothroyd, 1814.

Grotius, Hugo. *Verantwoordingh van de wettelijcke regiering van Hollant ende West Frieslant*. 1622.

Grzybowksi, Stanisław. "The Gentry and the Beginnings of Colonization." *Poland at the 14th International Congress of Historical Sciences in San Francisco*. Ossolineum, 1975, pp. 23–43.

Henderson Scott, Paul. *Andrew Fletcher and the Treaty of Union*. Birlinn, 2013.

Hodges, James. *Essay Upon the Union*. 1706. Hardpress Publishing, 2019.

Hodges, James. *The Rights and Interests of the Two British Monarchies*. 1706. Gale Ecco, 2010.

Hugo, Ludolf. *De Statu Regionum Germaniae*. Karger, 1689. (1661)

Israel, Jonathan. *The Dutch Republic: Its Rise, Greatness and Fall, 1477–1806*. Clarendon Press, 1998.

Jędrug, Jacek. *Constitutions, Elections and Legislatures of Poland, 1493–1993*. Hippocrene Books, 1998.

Kossmann, E. H., and A. E. Mellink. *Texts Concerning the Revolt of The Netherlands*. Cambridge University Press, 1975.

Leibniz, Gottfried Wilhelm. *Political Writings*, edited by Patrick Riley, Cambridge University Press, 2012.

Lessafer, Randall. "Peace Treaties from Lodi to Westphalia." *Peace Treaties and International Law in European History, From the Late Middle Ages to World War One*, edited by Randall Lessafer, Cambridge University Press, 2004, pp. 9–44.

Lubowski, Jerzy. "Stanisław Konarski (1700–1772): A Polish Machiavelli." *Enlightenment and Catholicism in Europe: A Transnational History*, edited by Jeffrey D. Burson and Ulrich Lehner, University of Notre Dame, 2014, pp. 433–454.

Machiavelli, Niccoló. *The Prince*. 1513. Edited by Quentin Skinner and Russell Price, Cambridge University Press, 2000.

Machiavelli, Niccoló. *Report on the Affairs of Germany*. 1508. *Collected Works of Niccoló Machiavelli*, Delphi Classics, 2017.

Machiavelli, Niccoló. "Second Letter about the Mission to Emperor Maximilian I, January 17, 1508." *Collected Works of Niccoló Machiavelli*, Delphi Classics, 2017.

Maissen, Thomas. "Inventing the Sovereign Republic." *The Republican Alternative: The Netherlands and Switzerland Compared*, edited by Andre Holenstein, Thomas Maissen, and Maarten Prak, Amsterdam University Press, 2008, pp. 125–150.

Morgenthau, Hans. *Politics Among Nations*. A. A. Knopf, 1948.

Opaliński, Edward. "Civic Humanism and Republican Citizenship in the Polish Renaissance." *Republicanism, A Shared European Heritage*, vol. 1, edited by Martin van Gelderen and Quentin Skinner, Cambridge University Press, 2005, pp. 147–168.

Pfannenschmid, Yvonne. *Ludolf Hugo, Früher Bundesstaattheoretiker und kurhannoverscher Staatsmann*. Nomos, 2005.

Pietrzyk-Reeves, Dorota. *Polish Republican Discourse in the Sixteenth Century*. Cambridge University Press, 2020.

Polish Law on Government, 1791. *Constitute Project*, https://www.constituteproject. org/constitution/Poland_1791. Accessed 6 March 2024.

Pufendorf, Samuel von. *On the Duty of Man and Citizen*. 1672. Cambridge University Press, 1991.

Pufendorf, Samuel von. *On the Present State of Germany*. 1667. Liberty Fund, 2007.

Pufendorf, Samuel von. *Two Books on the Elements of Jurisprudence*. 1660. Liberty Fund, 2009.

Robertson, John. *A Union for Empire: Political Thought and the Union of 1707*. Cambridge University Press, 2008.

Rousseau, Jean-Jacques. *Considérations sur la Gouvernement de Pologne*. 1782. Arvensa Editions, 2019.

Simler, Jozias. *La République des Suisses*. 1579. Nabu Press, 2010.

Slingelandt, Simon van. *Staatsrechtelijke Geschriften*. Petrus Schouten, 1784. 4 vols.

Spinoza, Benedictus. *A Political Treatise*. Jorge Pinto Books, 2018.

Treaty of Westphalia, 1648. *The Avalon Project*, https://avalon.law.yale.edu/17th_century/westphal.asp. Accessed 6 March 2024.

Vries, Jan de, and Ad van der Woude. *Nederland 1500–1815, De Eerste Ronde van Moderne Economische Groei*. 1995. Uitgeverij Balans, 2005.

Würgler, Andreas. "The League of Discordant Members, or How the Old Swiss Confederation Operated and How it Managed to Survive for so Long." *The Republican Alternative: The Netherlands and Switzerland Compared*, edited by Andre Holenstein, Thomas Maissen, and Maarten Prak Amsterdam University Press, 2008, pp. 29–50.

Zamoyski, Adam. *Poland, A History*. HCPA, 2015.

3   The European Republic

Abstract

Eighteenth-century European debate about continental order centred on
the issues of war and peace. The balance of power was enshrined in the
Peace of Utrecht (1713). As a system, it was based on war, which it regarded
as a mechanism for settling disputes and keeping the balance. The federal
model, on the other hand, was based on the idea of a peace pact between
all European countries. Such a pact would allow them to settle their differences through mediation, shifting the focus to economic development.
At the political-philosophical level, the Abbé de Saint-Pierre's plea for a
European Union, and fierce criticism of the Balance of Power method,
would provoke responses from many of the great thinkers of the age.

Keywords: European Republic, Balance of Power, Grand Design, raison
d'état, Perpetual Peace

Expansion and raison d'état

From around 1550 onwards, a number of factors pushed European countries
in the direction of raison d'état thinking. One of these was economic in
nature. Technological breakthroughs made warfare increasingly expensive.
Economic growth therefore became a political imperative. Since domestic
economies could only generate so much additional produce and commerce,
the focus almost naturally shifted towards expansion – which introduced inevitable new risks of conflict, as well as the practical challenges of managing
international commerce amid conflicts with rival powers. Maintaining one's
state in this vastly expanded game would consume a significant amount of
the Western intellectual resources of the age (Hont 11–17).

Another factor was early modern philosophy. In *The Passions and the
Interest*s, Albert Hirschman described the stages of theoretical development
in this period. First came the emancipation of the passions from classical
ethics. According to the Aristotelian moral scheme which had dominated

Livestro, Joshua: *A More Perfect Union. Federal Union in Political Theory and Practice, 1500-1951.*
Amsterdam: Amsterdam University Press, 2024.
DOI: 10.5117/9789048563777_CH03

European political thought for the previous two thousand years, politics was an ethical activity, linking knowledge of man as he was (ontology) through knowledge of his duties (deontology) to the ultimate aim of a good life, man's highest calling (teleology). Inspired in part by Machiavelli, early modern philosophy would move beyond this scheme by giving up the idea that ethics could serve as a link between man's nature and the ultimate ends of his existence. The new science of politics moved along different tracks. One would try to derive from the study of human nature knowledge about man's life in society, knowledge of his rights and duties. This would become known as the tradition of natural law. The other track would link the study of ends to the development of a concept of instrumental rationality. This pragmatic approach to politics focused chiefly on how to help the prince or republic survive the challenges of *fortuna*, and even to flourish and expand.

In this new scheme, passions were to be held in check by each other. This unchaining of the passions in turn led to the question how to help control those situations where certain passions became overwhelmingly powerful. The answer came in the form of the idea of "interest." What started life as a concept that applied only to the prince or the state, by the middle of the seventeenth century had become a notion that was widely applicable, including to the average economic calculations of individuals (Hirschman 34–37). The concept of interest gave individuals a chance to channel their passions by subjecting them to a rational check. A key precept of social contract theory was that any conception of enlightened self-interest would have to include an awareness of the importance of the continued existence of the state. This realisation, of the irreplaceable nature of the state, formed an ultimate external check on any pursuit of personal interests.

As Hobbes had claimed in his *Leviathan*, and subsequent natural law thinkers had not been able to refute, states did not have a similar external check. There seemed to be no escape from the law of nations. This meant that states pursuing their own interests would inevitably end up clashing, in commerce as in politics. "Jealousy of trade" would become an important cause of war in the early modern period – so much so, in fact, that the Scottish philosopher David Hume felt compelled to write an essay, "Of Jealousy of Trade" (published in 1759), trying to persuade rulers that an increase in riches in a neighbouring state wasn't a problem but a potential blessing, because it increased the chances of establishing lucrative local cross-border commerce.

Meanwhile, the ultimate prize of universal monarchy set off a fierce competition between the continent's main powers. They included a number of monarchies (the Habsburgs, the Bourbons, and the Stuarts chief among them, and from the early eighteenth century the Romanovs and the Hohen-zollern, as well) that combined what was, by the standards of the period, an extensive bureaucracy for the creation and maintenance of internal order with a large standing army for external security and conquest. Historians working within the intellectual framework of nineteenth-century nationalist romanticism would later claim that this kind of state had in fact always been the natural destination of European history – a theory that remained the dominant interpretation of modern Western political history until the turn of the twenty-first century (Van Caenegem 66).

Among its most celebrated proponents was the doyen of the Realism school in international relations, former US Secretary of State Henry Kissinger (1924–2023). In his magnum opus *Diplomacy* he presented the thesis that, out of the ashes of the medieval *Respublica Christiana* rose the state, pursuing its self-interest in a calculated way. This coincided with the birth of a new political idea: "With the concept of unity collapsing, the emerging states of Europe needed some principle to justify their heresy and to regulate their relations. They found it in the concept of *raison d'état...*" (Kissinger 58).

Kissinger's image of seventeenth-century post-Westphalia Europe as dominated by independent states is nowadays considered outdated.[1] But he was correct in linking the breakdown of the old order to the rise of reason of state thinking.

—

It was not the work of Machiavelli but that of his contemporary and friend Francesco Guicciardini (1483–1540) which informed the concept of raison d'état. In his *Dialogue on the Government of Florence* (1537) Guicciardini introduced it by referring to "the reason and customs of states," thereby suggesting that a state not only had its own identity but also its own reasons for acting, which he called "interests." Already a well-established concept by the middle of the sixteenth century, it became associated with late sixteenth-century authors like Giovanni Botero and Justus Lipsius, and the classical writers Tacitus and Seneca.[2]

1   As the historians Andrew Mackillop and Michael Ó Siochrú explained in their 2008 study *Forging the State: European State Formation and the Anglo-Scottish Union of 1707*, the dominant model in the early modern period was not the sovereign state but "the composite, conglomerate or multiple monarchy beneath which there existed a wide variety of provincial kingdoms, city states, republics, commonwealths and confederations" (13).

2   Lipsius was not only the author of a tract on the sceptical virtue of constancy, but also of a collection of aphorisms which showed how a ruler could and indeed should pursue his

An early definition of the "interests" that guided raison d'état thinking was produced by the Italian priest and diplomat Giovanni Botero (1544–1617). His *The Reason of State* (1589) seemed to be an attempt to rehabilitate the works of Machiavelli by showing how the latter's precepts could be made to work in a Christian moral setting – though he would significantly push out the boundaries of the latter. The subject of the book was the middle-sized monarchy looking for advantage.[3] The focus was therefore on the same concepts that also occupied Machiavelli: "Reason of state is knowledge of the means to found, conserve and expand dominion" (Botero 149).

The book's structure made it clear that Botero rated the act of the founding of a state (the ultimate form of *virtù* according to Machiavelli) as significantly less important than the other two objectives. Whereas the first six chapters were devoted to the study of maintaining the prince's state, and the last four to the expansion of his realm, the act of founding a commonwealth or kingdom barely got a mention. "The reason," he explained in his introduction, "is that reason of state presupposes a prince and a state which are not at all presupposed by foundation" (Botero 150). An alternative explanation is that he considered it unnecessary to devote separate chapters to founding since "the art of founding and expanding is the same, because the principles and the means are of the same nature" (269).

Botero's aim was to sketch the traits that would give a ruler a good reputation. This quality, which was assigned "only to those whom we have considered to have by their excellence and greatness surpassed the ordinary limits of virtue" (1075), served an important purpose in both the maintenance of internal order and the external defence of the state. Among its main traits were "subtlety of intellect and vigour of spirit," especially in the matters of peace and war, "because with the arts of peace he keeps his subjects quiet and with those of war he keeps his enemies at a distance" (1077).

Raison d'état was about more than just keeping enemies at a distance, though. Expansion was, in Botero's view, a natural and just aim of the state. Book VII was entirely devoted to the means of expansion. These boiled down to two main resources. One was people: "[F]or a nation that aspires to great undertakings nothing is of greater need than a numerous multitude of citizens" (Botero 693). The other was money – "the sinews of war," as

own interests. As the champion of self-interested rulers it seems entirely appropriate that the European Council building in the heart of the European quarter in Brussels was named after him.

3   In a next book, *The Universal Relations* (1596), Botero would touch on the subject of universal monarchy. The book was written from the perspective of, and with appreciation for, the Spanish empire, and offered an overview of the main regions of the world that were to be united in a single Christian kingdom under the Spanish Catholic monarchy.

Cicero had called it. To raise the latter princes had two options: taxation and borrowing. Neither was without dangers. Like Gattinara, he feared the potential of excessive taxation to lead to revolts. Botero's preferred option was to tax the rich, and with everyone else to follow the German model – also praised by Machiavelli in the *Discourses* (I, ch. 55) – in which people decided for themselves how much to pay: "Leave it to the conscience and oath of persons" (Botero 678). Loans were attractive because they allowed the prince to undertake his military campaigns without having to "[oppress] the people who were already worn out by previous contributions" (681). But he warned against taking out loans with interest, "the ruin of states" (680).

Of Machiavelli's three main methods of expansion, Botero basically only recognised two, since violent conquest followed by oppression of the conquered population didn't fit with his overall objective of boosting the prince's reputation in a morally acceptable way. That left, first of all, the Roman option of "attaching to themselves their conquered enemies" (Botero 754). This wasn't just a matter of conquest by military means. The Romans also used their citizenship as a strategic tool, liberally bestowing it when it could help to extend their territory. They would grant it to associated territories as well as to friendly states. One way they built these relationships was by offering protection against third party attacks. Botero pointed out that one prominent contemporary student of the Roman method was the Turkish sultan, who applied it with great success in his own campaigns of expansion: "[H]aving made himself protector of the Kurds, of the Tartars of Precop, and sometimes also of the Georgians, he has made use of their forces no less than of his own" (756).

War was not Botero's preferred means of expansion. He spent more time discussing the same soft power also discussed by Gattinara at the start of the century. These non-violent methods of expansion, like marriage, inheritance, purchase, and pledges (territory "pledged for money that has been loaned"; Botero 763) would become important tools in the great game of seventeenth- and eighteenth-century European dynastic politics.

Machiavelli's pragmatically preferred option for Florence, the league, was also recognised by Botero as a means of expanding territory. He discussed the idea in two places. It was listed among the means of expansion in *The Reason of State* (VII, ch. 14) under the heading "Alliances." An alliance would usually "make a prince stronger and more courageous (...) because [it] increases the satisfaction in success and diminishes the harm in failure" (Botero 770) – provided, that is, the alliance wasn't with a larger partner. In that case the weaker party would risk suffering the fate of the Latins, who in their alliance "were nothing but the servants of the Romans, and if they were also companions, they were so only in the labours and the danger of the war, without sharing at all in the glory or the acquisitions or the rule" (771). For the larger state, on the other hand, the upsides were clear. The ultimate example here was the Romans who "under the name of league and association (...) acquired with common resources the rule of the world for themselves alone" (772).

At the end of the chapter, Botero formulated a number of conditions for success of the league or alliance: "[P]erpetual alliances are better than temporary ones, the offensive and the defensive together better than the offensive or the defensive alone, and equality of the allies better than inequality" (Botero 778). The one example he could give of such an alliance, however, seemed to lack the kind of dynamism that would allow for expansion: "[A]lthough the Swiss have noteworthy opportunities to acquire rich states, they nevertheless have never done anything worthy of note" (779). Only an unequal alliance like that between Rome and the Latins, it seemed, was able to deliver that.

If (unequal) leagues were a powerful tool of expansion for the larger state, they could obviously pose a threat to rulers looking to preserve the internal order of a large kingdom or empire, too. In a section titled "How to Weaken their Union" (V, ch. 7), Botero reflected on the tools at the disposal of rulers who were faced with a revolt within their realm.[4] The most important was the sowing of dissent within the union's ranks: "You destroy their intent by fomenting suspicions and differences among them, so that no one risks to reveal himself and trust in another; to secure this effect, secret and trustworthy spies are very useful" (Botero 582–583).

———

In spite of this open embrace of the political dark arts, it is important not to mistake raison d'état for an overly cynical approach to politics. In normal circumstances, there was still the expectation that rulers would follow the established moral codes. The qualities writers in this tradition would come to stress above all were prudence and a stoic attitude towards life's problems (to the extent that they could not be avoided). They valued factual

---

4   Botero didn't mention the Dutch revolt in this chapter, though he did refer to Flanders and Brabant at the end of the previous chapter, where he mentioned the fact that "ordinary and extraordinary taxes now claim their money," which (as he warned in bk 7, ch. 7) had the potential to foment revolt. Instead of further discussing this, though, he thought it better to move on, since "unfortunately, princes already know all about this, so there is no need for me to expand on it" (Botero 581).

description above moral prescription – seeing things as they were, not as they ought to be. This combination of seeing things as they were and dealing in terms of political "musts" rather than moral "shoulds" formed the core of its approach, which was essentially a science of politics.

Raison d'état mainly applied to those situations where the normal code of law or morality was silent. These were extraordinary situations requiring extraordinary creativity in decision-making, based on the maxim *necessitas non habet legem* (necessity knows no law). In the period 1600–1800 there would be a lively debate about where exactly to draw the line between "fair" raison d'état and immoral abuse of the freedoms that this code provided. The rulers most successful in this abuse would come in for the fiercest criticism from political philosophers.

If one source of disagreement about raison d'état was where to draw the line between master stroke and cynical opportunism, another was what exactly constituted "reason" in any given situation. The pursuit of raison d'état would confront rulers with difficult dilemmas. Was it wiser to fight a war or to opt for peace? Would the state's interest be best served by joining a league or staying out of one? Political-philosophical debate in this period would sometimes boil down to fundamental disagreement about these issues.

Meanwhile, the initial strong emphasis on expansion as an objective of raison d'état would provoke a response that was equally calculating but devoted entirely to the opposite objective – that is, keeping states more or less in their place. The former courtier of Henri IV, the Duc de Rohan, would identify France's optimal strategic approach as blocking the rise to universal monarchy of the Spanish Habsburgs. Its very physical situation made it the likely counterweight against Spanish power: "France being seated between the Alpes and the Pyrenaen mountains, and flanked by two seas, seemes to be inuited by nature to oppose it selfe against the proceedings of this puissant Neighbourhood" (Rohan 13). Rohan's analysis of the importance of counterweights against the potential dominance of the Spanish monarchy was echoed by Francis Bacon in his essay "Of Empire," in which he observed about the relationship between France, England and the Holy Roman Empire in the first quarter of the sixteenth century, that "there was such a watch kept, that none of the three could win a palm of ground, but the other two would straightways balance it, either by confederation or, if need be, by a war. (...) And the like was done by that league which Guicciardini sayeth was the security of Italy" (Bacon 85). What both authors referred to would become known as the concept of *balance of power.*

The birth of the balance of power

The deeply pragmatic raison d'état approach to politics has generally been associated with two French figures above all: the royal councillor Cardinal Richelieu (1585–1642) and the French monarch *par excellence*, Louis XIV (whose rule stretched out over seven decades, from 1643 to 1715). Together, they oversaw the rise to prominence of the French state in continental European affairs during the seventeenth century.

Henry Kissinger attributed this rise entirely to the willingness of these two men to do whatever it took to further their country's interests, though he acknowledged that there were limits to the effectiveness of this approach: "[T]he nemesis of *raison d'etat* is overextension – except in the hands of a master, and it probably is even then" (*Diplomacy* 66). It was overextension – the expansion of his realm beyond its limits – that would eventually force all of Louis XIV's enemies to unite in a grand coalition. The century which saw France rise to European dominance ended with the entire might of Western and Central Europe combining against Louis XIV in the Nine Years' War (1688–1697). This war provided a classic example of the counterstrategy to raison d'état, applied in the quest for universal monarchy: the balance of power.

References to balance of power first emerged in the sixteenth century. Their origin was, again, the work of Guicciardini.[5] In his *History of Italy* (I, ch. 1), he sang the praises of the alliance of the main principalities and city states of Italy which was created to counterbalance the rising power of Venice. The peace treaty of Lodi (1454) would safeguard peace between them for a generation, maintained by the "eminent" Lorenzo de' Medici: "[H]e carefully saw to it that the Italian situation should be maintained in a state of balance, not leaning more toward one side than the other. This could not be achieved without preserving the peace and without being diligently on the watch against every incident, even the slightest" (Guicciardini, *History of Italy* 102).

By the end of the sixteenth century, the concept had found its way to Western Europe. In this early phase, balance mainly meant ad hoc coalitions

---

5   In his essay on the balance of power, Herbert Butterfield – historian and initiator of the British Committee on the Theory of International Politics – expressed his frustration about the fact that Machiavelli hadn't written anything of note on the subject when "his preoccupation ought to have drawn him to it" (quoted in Butterfield and Wight 156). Butterfield seemed to be missing the point: the reason Machiavelli didn't write about balance of power wasn't because he didn't recognise its existence but because it was contrary to his ultimate aim, which was the expansion of the *respublica*.

that could serve as a counterweight against the dominant power of the age. Around the turn of the seventeenth century, that dominant power was still very much the Spanish Habsburg empire. It was no surprise, therefore, that the countries producing the largest number of tracts on the idea of balance of power in this period were Spain's main strategic rivals – France and England.

—

By the middle of the seventeenth century the tables had turned. Spain's relative decline opened the way for other countries to claim the status of dominant power on the continent. Under the Pensionary of the States of Holland and West Friesland, Johan de Witt (1625–1672), it looked for a while as if this dominant power might become the Dutch Republic.

The Dutch approach to raison d'état was very much based on the original Machiavellian ideas of preservation and expansion as incorporated into the concept by Botero. As Pieter de la Court put it in his *Treatise on the Welfare of Leiden* (1659), this welfare was to be found in "the conservation and the increase of the republic" (De la Court 3). There was a twist, though. The Dutch Republic's strength was not in people but in money. And as the brothers De la Court, themselves wealthy merchants, concluded, money was made predominantly through trade. Dutch raison d'état was therefore thoroughly commercial. Its aim was to control Europe's main trade routes by sea.

The message was not lost on De Witt, who would wed the commercial interpretation of raison d'état as developed by the brothers De La Court with the concept of balance of power to design a highly successful foreign policy. He used it systematically to settle regional conflicts to the Dutch advantage. In the process, he also masterfully played the various Dutch provincial interests off against each other. Continuous success allowed him to give all things to all provinces – using an external balance of power policy to maintain an internal one, and vice versa (Israel 800).

When a Swedish army under King Charles X invaded Poland in 1655, starting the so-called Nordic War (1655–1660), the Dutch States General sent an expeditionary force to Gdansk to relieve the city – and secure Polish grain supplies. In 1658, an additional sea battle, in which the Swedish navy was decisively defeated, helped to reopen the Sound and the Baltic Sea to Dutch commercial shipping. After the peace treaty of 1660, the Dutch would initially remain closely aligned with Sweden's enemy Denmark. But when in 1668 a conflict between France and Spain threatened to destabilise the strategic situation on the continent – crucially, in the Strait of Gibraltar and the Mediterranean – De Witt pivoted to an alliance with Sweden. It also brought in England, with whom the Dutch had just fought the Second Anglo-Dutch War (1665–1667). The aim of this so-called Triple Alliance was to persuade the two belligerents to settle their differences, thereby securing the peace Dutch trade required to prosper.

For two decades, De Witt was a grandmaster of European politics, largely thanks to his expert use of balance of power as an offensive weapon. His end came, ironically, when the other main powers of Western Europe did what the balance of power doctrine by now dictated as a necessary move when faced with an increasingly dominant rival: they formed a coalition in an attempt to administer a crushing defeat to the Dutch Republic.

In Dutch history, 1672 is known as an *annus horribilis*, the "Rampjaar" (Year of Disasters). It was a disaster first and foremost for the Republic, which came close to collapse when a large French army rolled across the border, though it would eventually recover its position. The main price was paid by De Witt himself. Having failed to secure the peace and safety of the other provinces, he was forced to agree to the reinstatement of the young prince of Orange – William III – as Stadtholder. It was supposed to be a temporary appointment, for one campaign only, but once he was appointed William quickly seized complete control of the levers of power by disposing of State party rulers across the provinces and replacing them with his own men. A worse fate was reserved for Johan de Witt. Together with his brother Cornelis, he was violently murdered by a mob stirred up by William's agents.

—

If 1672 was an *annus horribilis* for the Dutch, it was an *annus mirabilis* for the French king Louis XIV. Having smashed the power of the Dutch Republic, he was now the undisputed candidate for universal monarch on the continent. Like De Witt, he would use balance of power as an offensive weapon. One of the ways he did this was by turning its logic on its head. In any given conflict, rulers or republics would normally support the weaker party in order to avoid a disturbance of the balance by the stronger party. Louis XIV used a more flexible interpretation of the concept, which was purely based on a personal interest calculation.

This somewhat cynical strategy worked very well for him, though eventually Kissinger's overextension problem would manifest itself. In an attempt further to weaken the power of the Austrian Habsburgs, in the early 1680s Louis made common cause with the other main enemy of the Holy Roman Empire – the Ottoman Sultan. His calculation was that a Turkish invasion of Eastern Europe would tie the Austrians up to such an extent that they wouldn't have the manpower to resist his own incursions into Habsburg territory in Western Europe.[6]

This ploy would have worked, but for the fact that the emperor had, by then, already secured Polish king Jan Sobieski's support. It led to the latter's famous intervention at the gates of Vienna, where he beat a large Ottoman army and forced it to retreat. In doing so, he bought the Austrians time to recover. They would use it to hand the Sultan a series of humiliating defeats, which enabled them to eventually conquer Hungary and parts of the Balkans. Louis XIV's "overextension" had led to the miraculous recovery and significant expansion of the Austrian Habsburg realm. Holy Roman Emperor Leopold I would thank him for it in 1688 by joining the coalition put together by the Dutch Stadtholder and later English and Scottish monarch William III, with the aim of doing to France what Louis XIV's coalition had done to the Dutch Republic fifteen years earlier.

—

The events in the final third of the seventeenth century would not leave political theory unaffected. One result was that they persuaded Europe's philosophers and statesmen that balance of power was not just a legitimate but a necessary aim of the strategy of European countries. In that context, Pufendorf spoke of "the publick good, which consists in preserving the ballance of *Europe*" (quoted in Tuck 163). The French archbishop François Fénelon (1651–1715) wrote in his *Examination of Conscience on the Duties of Kingship* (1711) about the balance of power as based on a "mutual duty of defence of common preservation, between neighbouring nations, against a neighbouring state that becomes too powerful" (Hanley 663).

It should be stressed that this would be taken to imply *any* neighbouring state. A disturbance of the equilibrium by one state would automatically impose a duty on the rest of them to restore what Fénelon called "the tranquillity and (...) the preservation of the universal republic" (Hanley 664). This was the second, more important effect of the continued attention paid to the concept. Through raison d'état theory, which dictated that relationships

---

6   This strategy was devised and first implemented by Louis's ancestor Francis I. It was during his capture in Madrid, after the Battle of Pavia in 1525, that his court had reached out to the court of the Sultan to discuss an anti-Habsburg alliance. The two would actually combine forces on a number of occasions, most notably at the siege of Nice in 1543. See Édith Garnier, *L'Alliance impie: François Ier et Soliman le Magnifique contre Charles V*. The use of Eastern allies to create a second front against the Holy Roman Empire, and later the German *Bund*/Reich, would remain part of French strategy until the outbreak of the Second World War.

between states ought not to be based on morality but on interests, the balance took on an almost mechanical character, becoming like an automated process whereby one side's growing dominance would inevitably force others to coalesce in order to restore the equilibrium (Sheehan 42).

In a supplement to *Examination of Conscience*, Fénelon formulated his theory of a European state system based on the balance of power as an organising principle. In the negative, it was a system for the prevention of a single scenario: universal monarchy. Here Fénelon maintained that even if the highest law seemed to give a king a rightful claim to the lands of another realm, it could still not be allowed because "everything that reverses the balance and gives the decisive blow for universal monarchy cannot be just" (Hanley 660). He held that in such a scenario it was both the right and the duty of all the others "to prevent this growth" (661). The permanent need for a correcting mechanism that maintained the equilibrium between them in effect created something like "a great body and a sort of community" where "all the members (...) are duty-bound to each other for the common good" (662).

This mechanistic conception of the balance of power would, over the course of the eighteenth century, come to be seen as the organising principle of a kind of secularised *Respublica Christiana* which went by the name of the "European Republic." However, this paradigm was not undisputed. In political theory, an alternative model for ordering European affairs was taking shape that would grow to become its great systemic rival. That alternative model's name was a continental federal union sometimes referred to as "European Union," though it would also be referred to as "the Grand Design."

The Grand Design

The concept of the continental federal union in early modern political theory is generally associated with the figure of the French late Renaissance king Henry IV. His *Grand Design*, which was never formally published but was described in the memoirs of his adviser the Duc de Sully (1560–1641), was the first of a number of blueprints for an integrated Europe that were to appear in the early modern period. Seemingly a mix comprising equal parts Christian unification plan, irenic utopia, and anti-Turkish defence league, the Grand Design was clearly a product of its age. Though it was never put to the test, it ended up casting a shadow over political debate in the next four centuries, with its core ideas eventually (though mostly indirectly) engaging all the great thinkers and politicians of the age.

Sully started his discussion of the plan with a reflection on the fall of the Roman empire, ascribing it to the same cause Machiavelli had also identified, namely a form of moral corruption which saw virtue give way to "luxury, avarice and ambition" (Sully 18). Unlike Machiavelli, though, he saw one other cause which was perhaps more than any other responsible for the decline of the empire: "[T]he irruptions of those vast bodies of barbarous peoples (...) from whom, both separately and united, the Roman empire received such violent shocks that it was at last overthrown by them" (Sully 18). The significance of this introduction wouldn't have been wasted on his contemporaries. Not only did he place the Grand Design squarely in the tradition of the Roman empire: he also observed that European unity wasn't just threatened by internal corruption but also by the external threat of invasion. If corruption made it weak, invasion would cause its actual downfall.

To prevent history repeating itself, now that the Ottoman empire had emerged as a credible threat on Europe's southeastern borders (following the fall of Constantinople in 1456), Henri IV had started speculating in his conversations with Sully about "a political system, by which all of Europe might be regulated and governed as one great family" (Sully 25). Sully was clearly persuaded of its benefits "to all Europe" but as the king's closest strategic adviser he was also a realist. He saw an insurmountable obstacle in the form of "the general situation of the affairs of Europe" which seemed to him "[in] every way contrary to the realisation of the project" (27). He therefore thought it best merely to make preparations for such time as conditions arose that would eventually facilitate its implementation.

However, waiting for the right conditions to arise wasn't merely a passive process. Sully described how he actively lobbied and planned for it, even undertaking a diplomatic mission to the court of the English queen Elizabeth I to secure her support (which she gave, albeit in a qualified manner). Nor was he necessarily averse to the use of violence in the implementation of his scheme. This became clearest when he discussed with Henri plans for the complete redrawing of the map of the Holy Roman Empire. The aim was to create a sense of balance on the continent by splitting the Empire into parts of roughly equal size, making some their own powers while attaching other parts to existing kingdoms. If that seemed ambitious, it had nothing on his plan for the military subjugation of bordering parts of Africa and Asia by a combined European army of "two hundred and seventy thousand foot, fifty thousand horse, two hundred cannons, and one hundred and twenty ships or galleys." It may have been an unusually large force, but it had the benefit of being to "the princes and states of Europe (...) inconsiderable (...) when compared with the forces which they usually keep on foot to awe their neighbours" (Sully 34).

In the end, all this planning came to nothing. First, the Grand Design's one external supporter, Elizabeth I, died. Then its main internal supporter, Henri IV, was assassinated. Even when Henri was still alive, it had remained "concealed from all without exception," and if it was referred to at all, then only as "a kind of general treaty of peace" (Sully 45). With so many different powers and denominations involved, the danger of some of them interpreting the plan as a conspiracy against themselves made it impossible to campaign for it openly. It was only towards the end of his life, thirty years after Henri's untimely death, that Sully thought it safe enough to make the existence of the scheme public.

The details of the plan as described by Sully suggest that the concept was in fact in an advanced stage of development (though his correspondence with Henri provides no convincing evidence that the latter was involved in its further development). The first thing to note was its reach. If previous centuries had left the concept of "Europe" undefined geographically, Sully's interpretation clearly approached the modern idea of it spanning not just Western and Southern Europe but also Scandinavia and Eastern Europe – the inclusion of the kingdoms of Sweden, Poland/Lithuania, Moravia, and Hungary in the plan confirmed that Europe's nations did indeed form one family, at least in Sully's eyes. Just as notable was his exclusion of the Ottoman empire – it was presented as a challenger, not a potential ally. Muscovy was offered the choice between joining the new European republic and a war with its combined powers.

As for its practical organisation: fifteen "powers" of various origins – hereditary monarchies, elected monarchies, confederations, and city states – were to send a total of sixty-six ambassadors or commissioners to a General Council. This council, which would meet in permanent assembly, would serve as a kind of European senate. Representation would be proportional, based on political relevance – more members for the more powerful ones, fewer for the less powerful. The Council would be able to issue binding decisions in the settlement of conflicts between its members. Sully's model came from classical antiquity: the Amphictyonic council, the confederal league for mutual defence purposes founded by Greek tribes before the era of Athenian democracy, as mentioned by Machiavelli in his *Discourses*.

—

It is tempting to think of the Grand Design as a direct response to the collapse of the *Respublica Christiana* – Sully even referred to the plan's aim as uniting "all the denominations of the christian republic." Alternatively, it's possible to interpret the scheme as a utopian experiment.[7] But both would probably be misreading Henri IV's intentions. His absolute priority was to find a way to prevent the Habsburgs establishing a universal monarchy on the continent. The planned Council was simply a way of placing limits on Spanish power. In fact, the plan's implementation would only become possible *after* "the humbling of the house of Austria" (Sully 27) which would consist of "divest[ing it] of its possessions in Germany, Italy and the Low Countries; in other words, to reduce it to the sole kingdom of Spain" (35). It was probably no coincidence that the only named supporter of the plan mentioned in Sully's memoirs was Elizabeth I, who was as preoccupied with the threat of Spanish hegemony as her French counterpart.

Henri's plan introduced several themes that would play an important role in political thought about intra-European relations. One was the idea of a "war to end all wars": the suggestion that a lasting peace on the continent could only be achieved through war – the ultimate just war. Another was the idea of a single, grand settlement between all the states of Europe, creating a new moral-political and, crucially, *institutional* framework to replace the old *Respublica Christiana*. Though it had relatively few organisational details, some would have a life well beyond that of Sully's scheme, especially the idea of a grand council in which all the member states could meet to discuss and settle their differences, and the concept of proportional representation in the selection of delegates.

The significance of the Grand Design was less in its details than in its impact on the political imagination of future generations of European statesmen and philosophers. Many better and lesser-known examples of similar grand designs would be produced in the next three centuries. These schemes in turn drew commentaries from the greatest political thinkers of the age, several of whom would write extensive commentaries on the idea of a great European settlement.

The new mixed regime: the division by powers

Of the various schemes written in the century following Henri IV's original plan, several stood out. One such scheme was produced by the English republican author James Harrington (1611–1677). In his *Oceana* (1656) he presented a plan for the conquest and colonisation of Europe by an agricultural English republic. His ultimate aim was the founding of a European "republican empire."

---

7   For a discussion of this concept, see Eliav-Feldon 51–76.

His proposal of a war of conquest aimed at establishing an essentially English republican empire across Europe was not born solely out of recognition of the natural urge of an agrarian republic like Oceana (England) to expand its realm. In a nod to raison d'état thinking, Harrington argued that it was also effectively a case of necessity. If England didn't make the first move, France was destined to become the dominant power on the continent, in which case England in turn was doomed to end up a province of France (Somos 34).

But if his motives were practical, his ideal of a European republican empire was very much a product of his study of political philosophy. Harrington's writings were profoundly influenced by Machiavelli, whom he quoted extensively and approvingly, describing him as "learned" and his writings as "excellent." When contemplating the means of founding the European republican empire, Harrington quoted at length from the passage about the three methods of expansion of the republic in Machiavelli's *Discourses* (II, ch. 4): subjugation, alliance, and confederation (Harrington I: 323). But where Machiavelli in the end opted for confederation because the method of Rome (government through alliances with conquered people) seemed to him not a realistic option for Renaissance Florence, Harrington had no hesitation in opting for enlargement through alliances, calling confederation as a method of enlargement "useless to the world" (Harrington I: 324).

Upon completing the conquest of Europe's continent, he recommended "taking the course of Rome: if you have subdued a nation that is capable of liberty, you shall make them a present of it" (Harrington I: 330). For those peoples that were incapable of liberty, the solution was to make them provinces of the realm. The former would be allowed republican citizenship and a form of self-government, even participation in deliberations in Westminster. The latter would be placed under control of the central republican (English) authority.

This central republican authority was itself based on the model of a mixed regime. Like Machiavelli, Harrington faithfully followed the classical regime theory. He did, however, introduce one important innovation which would later take on a life of its own. In *The Art of Lawgiving* (1657) he produced a second kind of mixed government, based not on a division by estates but by powers: "[T]he necessary definition of a commonwealth anything well ordered is that it is a government consisting of the senate proposing, the people resolving, and the magistracy executing" (Harrington II: 611). It was an incomplete *trias politica*, since it had no role for the judiciary, but it clearly did contain the contours of this role.

—

Referring mainly to the works of Harrington's successors Algernon Sydney and John Locke, the nineteenth-century German constitutional scholar Otto von Gierke observed that "the theory of the mixed constitution began to acquire a wholly new vigour when the doctrine of constitutionalism associated it with the principle of a *qualitative division of powers*" (157). The clearest explanation of the necessity of this new mixed constitution by powers came in Locke's essay published in 1689 on "The true original extent and end of civil government." Since legislation had "a *power always in being,*" there was a need for a second power "which should see to the *execution* of the laws that are made, and in force. And thus the *legislative* and *executive power* come often to be separated." Within the executive, he made a further distinction between "the *execution* of the municipal laws of the society *within* its self, upon all that are parts of it" and "the management of the *security and interest of the public without.*" The latter he called "the federative power" (Locke 77–78; original emphasis).

Power, reduced to a single dimension by Bodin, in this way underwent a new kind of subdivision. And as Von Gierke observed, it was this subdivision in the form of a new type of mixed constitution which, through the writings of Montesquieu, would come to be seen as the ultimate safeguard of political liberty (Von Gierke 158). Most of the first part of *Spirit of the Laws* was a reflection on the distribution and interaction of what he described as "the three powers": executive, legislative and judiciary. The most extensive discussion of this *trias* featured in Montesquieu's famous paean "On the Constitution of England" (XI, ch. 6). It is here that he made explicit the link between separation of powers and liberty: "When legislative power is united with executive power in a single person or in a single body of the magistracy, there is no liberty, because one can fear that the same monarch or senate that makes tyrannical laws will execute them tyrannically. Nor is there liberty if the power of judging is not separate from legislative power and from executive power" (Montesquieu 157).

For a constitution to function properly, it wasn't enough for the powers to be separated. They also needed to have checks upon each other, to make sure no single one of them could come to dominate the others. The aim, after all, was not to construct a mixed regime but to *maintain* one. He distinguished between two different forms of checks. One was "the faculty of enacting," by which he meant "to correct what has been ordered by another" (Montesquieu 161). The alternative was not to correct but to "render null" – the ability of the executive to block legislative proposals through the power of veto. "If the executive power does not have the right to check the enterprises of the legislative body," he observed, "the latter will be despotic, for it will wipe out all the other powers" (161). The legislative power should not have a reciprocal negative power, because the executive relied on an ability for "immediate action" to function properly (161). But its actions in their execution would be subject to examination by the legislature. The two bodies of the legislative power, the aristocratic and the democratic, also held checks against each other.[8]

—

The ultimate check within a mixed regime was the rule of law. As with most concepts used in this period, its roots were classical, going back to Aristotle. Its importance was restated by Harrington, who in the "Preliminaries" of his *Oceana* made the distinction between ancient and modern prudence, linking the former with "the empire of laws" and the latter with the empire of men. "The former," he observed, "is that which Machiavel (whose books are neglected) is the only politician that hath gone about to retrieve, and that Leviathan [by Thomas Hobbes] (...) goes about to destroy" (Harrington I: 161).

Making the law rather than the sovereign the supreme force within a constitutional order had several important advantages. It protected individuals, and the commonwealth as a whole, against arbitrary rule. As John Locke put it in his *Second Treatise*, the alternative of placing the ruler(s) above the law was an open invitation to tyranny: "As if when Men quitting the State of Nature entered into Society, they agreed that all of them but one, should be under the restraint of Laws, but that he should Still retain all the Liberty of the State of Nature, increased with Power, and made licentious with Impunity" (Locke 701; par. 93). By making sure individuals were "[not] being subjected to the Will or Authority of any other Man" (657), it also guaranteed a form of equality which was an essential element of citizenship. By claiming "[t]hat all Men by Nature are equal," Locke meant not that they were equal in "Age or Virtue, (...) Birth, (...) Alliance or Benefits" (657). It referred merely to "that equal Right that every Man hath, to his natural Freedom" (657).

The Peace of Utrecht

The War of the Spanish Succession (1701–1714) was the first of a series of European wars caused by dynastic succession crises during the first half

---

8   Montesquieu did not include the judiciary in his overview of checks, observing that it was "in some fashion null" (160). The key for him was in its proper establishment: "[T]he masterwork of legislation is to know where properly to place the power of judging" (169).

of the eighteenth century, along with the War of the Polish Succession (1733–1735) and the War of the Austrian Succession (1740–1748). The nature of the crisis was never quite the same. In the Polish case, it started over a French attempt to put Louis XV's father-in-law Stanisław Leszczyński on the throne, and ended with Russia succeeding in getting its own client-king (the son of Augustus II) recognised as the Commonwealth's legitimate ruler. The Austrian case was caused by a dispute about the so-called Pragmatic Sanction – the attempt by emperor Charles VI to circumvent the primogeniture principle so that his daughter Maria Theresa could inherit his titles. Upon his death in 1740, the kings of Bavaria and Prussia decided to contest the inheritance, leading to an eight-year war. It was eventually settled through a compromise where Maria Theresa was given the Habsburg inheritance (minus some territories conquered by Frederick II) while her husband was granted the right to use the title of Holy Roman Emperor.

The Spanish Succession crisis was the result of the last Spanish Habsburg king, Charles II, dying without leaving any offspring. Two candidates for the vacant throne emerged, one French, the other Austrian. Effectively, the two powers (and their allies) fought over not just the Spanish throne but also its vast possessions, which included parts of Italy and the Spanish Netherlands, as well as colonial territories in both Asia and the Americas.

At the end of thirteen years of conflict that seemingly ended in a stalemate, a peace conference was called to settle the issue. The choice for the peace negotiations fell on the medieval Dutch town of Utrecht, which in 1712 became the centre of the European political world. The opening session of the negotiations, on 29 January that year, was a spectacle of diplomatic splendour. The highlight was the joint entrance into the meeting room in the old town hall of the British and French ministers plenipotentiary. They entered at the same time through different doors, timing their steps to coincide with each other, regularly bowing in each other's direction, sitting down at the exact same moment, all to express perfect equality between the two monarchies they represented (Gerard 229).

It took fifteen months for negotiations to be concluded. The Peace of Utrecht (1713) initially seemed a misnomer, since the emperor Charles VI refused to acknowledge Louis XIV's final offer on the subject that had been the cause of the war – the rival claims to the Spanish throne. The war therefore continued, even after the treaties had been signed and ratified by the other participants. It would take further Austrian defeats at Landau and Freibourg before the emperor was finally ready to accept the other treaties negotiated at Utrecht (Treaty of Rastatt, 1714) and the French peace offer (Treaty of Baden, 1714). The latter treaty settled the issue of the

Spanish Succession to the advantage of the French, although the now legally confirmed king Philip V (formerly the Duke of Anjou) had to renounce his claim to the French throne to make sure the two countries could never form a personal or incorporating union. In return for its loss of its Spanish claim, the Empire was given compensation in the form of sovereignty over the Southern Netherlands and parts of Italy. The border with France would be guarded by a series of Dutch fortifications, a provision agreed in the Anglo-Dutch "Treaty of the Barrier" (the barrier in question being a safeguard against French incursions into the Low Countries – something that was as much an English as a Dutch interest).

The final result of the Utrecht negotiations was not a single treaty but a number of individual treaties settling affairs between pairs of belligerents or former allies. The main issues to be settled were always the same: territorial disputes (in these kinds of negotiations, land served as a form of currency), dynastic concerns, and clashing commercial ambitions. The treaty between France and England, for example, settled the sovereignty over a number of territories in North America. England accepted the Bourbon claim to the Spanish throne. In return, France recognised the legitimacy of the claim by the Elector of Hanover, later George I, to the right of succession to the British throne, and undertook to remove the Stuart crown prince from French territory, thereby confirming he no longer had its support (Gerard 285–286). A separate commercial treaty settled issues of navigation and confirmed the mutual granting of most favoured nation status.

For its willingness to accept a French candidate on the Spanish throne, the Dutch United Provinces received part of the province of Guelders, while the sovereignty of the other half was transferred from France to Prussia. The Duke of Savoy had all the territories taken by France restored to him, for him to possess "in the future as he had before the war." Finally the treaty between France, Prussia, and Spain confirmed the right of the Prussian ruler to use the formal title "king *of* Prussia," confirming his status as the equal of his fellow royals (Gerard 291).

The most sordid element of the negotiations took place once formal proceedings had been completed. The now confirmed Spanish king Philip V concluded a separate treaty with England. Under the heading of "Christian and universal peace," the two countries traded some territories, making Gibraltar a British outpost on the Iberian peninsula. The British negotiators then used the opportunity to acquire the right for a British trading company to deliver enslaved African people to the slave markets of the Spanish West Indies (Gerard 293).

For those willing to turn a blind eye to such obvious moral failures the peace negotiations did seem to offer hope for the future. It brought an end to what was effectively a period of nearly forty years of almost continuous warfare, starting with the French invasion of the Dutch United Provinces in 1672.[9] By settling conflicts on all continents at once, it aimed to create an opportunity for a period of prolonged peace. Its use of the method of a diplomatic conference seemed to offer a model for future conflict prevention. And its introduction of a network of treaties to regulate affairs between states led some to believe that they could serve as the basis for a rule-based "republic of states" to replace the previous system of monarchs fighting for the ultimate prize of universal monarchy (Ghervas 46).

—

The latter hope turned out to be somewhat optimistic. True, universal monarchy seemed to have lost some of its plausibility as an objective with the death of Louis XIV. But as a series of failed conferences in the 1720s proved, the balance of power mechanism was particularly ill-suited to the task of facilitating a system of conferences for the maintenance of order in Europe. It was one thing to organise a conference to settle a long-running, economically destructive war. It was quite another to expect the same willingness to agree to common priorities when there was no war to settle.

The organising principles of the conferences in this period were honour (of monarchs), and interests (of states). The latter might have offered some room for negotiation. The former however cut any such room down significantly. No monarch could accept a slight of their personal honour without significant compensation. Negotiations about any issue therefore automatically involved additional negotiations about a range of side-issues where potential compensation was to be obtained. It made the talks fiendishly complicated, always involving numerous files and parties.

Two further factors added to the complications. One was that more than one of the negotiating parties faced a parliament back home that had its own domestic agenda and could not always be counted on to support whatever outcome the monarch's representatives negotiated. It was one such split, between Augustus II and the Rada, that doomed the conference of Brunswick of 1720. The king had hoped to finalise a peace treaty with Sweden, but the Rada preferred to keep its options open, for fear of provoking Russia

---

9   Neither the Peace of Nijmegen (1678) nor the Peace of Rijswijk (1697) had managed to reconcile the belligerent parties to the idea of lasting peace. It is important to note, though, that not all conflicts were settled in Utrecht. The Great Northern War, which had started in the same year as the War of the Spanish Succession, would drag on for another eight years, finally being settled in 1721.

(Kosińska 43–44). In another case, the British Parliament repeatedly refused to schedule consideration of a Spanish request for the returning of Gibraltar, even though King George I had made a specific promise to arrange it. The growing frustration on the Spanish side about British intransigence would eventually boil over, leading to the Spanish-English war of 1727.[10]

The other was the factor of time. This was particularly relevant in dynastic disputes, where any decision could have dramatic consequences for the persons involved. Postponing a decision was often thought to be the most rational strategy. When the death of a number of potential successors of Louis XIV had suddenly made the Spanish Bourbon king Philip V next in line to the French throne, immediately after the five-year-old Louis XV, it became rational for him to refuse to commit to the promise made in Utrecht about never combining the two crowns. At the Congress of Cambrai of 1724, France and England tried to negotiate a final settlement of this and a range of other contested issues coming out of the Utrecht negotiations, to no avail. It was not until 1725, when it was increasingly clear that Louis XV was to remain monarch for the foreseeable future, that he would finally commit to the Utrecht provision by signing the Treaty of Vienna with his former rival to the Spanish throne, emperor Charles VI. The same treaty also saw Philip V recognise the Pragmatic Sanction as the legitimate solution to the Austrian succession issue.

By 1728 the number of issues that divided the main powers had grown to such an extent that another conference was considered necessary. Some were of a commercial nature, like the future of the Austrian-sanctioned Ostend Company, fiercely opposed by the Dutch, who were jealously guarding their monopoly of the overseas trade in the Low Countries. Others were of a dynastic nature, like the Spanish desire to see the crown prince Don Carlos wedded to the Austrian crown princess Maria Theresa. There were also, inevitably, a number of territorial disputes, including the future allegiance of the German duchies of Juliers and Bergh. Some of these, like the Spanish marriage proposal, would have obvious consequences for the overall balance of power on the continent. Others, like the Prussian attempt to obtain the sovereignty of the two smaller German duchies, would likely lead to a regional disturbance of the balance within the Holy Roman Empire (Goslinga 281–286).

The Congress of Soissons (1728) would be as ineffective as the previous great congresses of the decade, ending without an agreement. Writing several

---

10   In 1718, the new Spanish monarch Philip V had already contested the other main Spanish territorial concession by launching a war to reclaim his former possessions in Italy. It became known as the Quadruple Alliance, named for the alliance that countered this attempt: England, France, the Dutch United Provinces, and the Holy Roman Empire.

decades later, the Swiss legal philosopher Emer de Vattel would dismiss the efforts at Cambrai and Soissons as "tedious farces acted on the political theatre." According to him, "the principal performers were less desirous of coming to an accommodation than of appearing to desire it" (Vattel 835). This may be fair as an assessment of the outcome, but perhaps it did not give the negotiators enough credit. At least they tried to settle the main issues of their time diplomatically. By doing so, they allowed Europe's diplomats and political philosophers to learn an important lesson: for a congress to succeed, all participants needed to be willing to consider *the collective interest* as no less important than their private interests.

Against the balance of power: Saint-Pierre's Perpetual Peace

Harrington's would be one of the last of the grand designs to marry the idea of the founding of a European republic with the means of military conquest. Subsequent proposals would make the uniting of Europe an *alternative* to war, not the product of one. This had to do with the changing nature of warfare, which became increasingly violent and all-encompassing. In the words of the author of one such scheme, Andrew Fletcher of Saltoun:

> For matters are now brought to such a pass, that in every war almost all of Europe and America, with a great part of Asia and Africa become engaged. (...) [T]hese universal wars have continued for more than thirty years, have so distressed this part of the world, and occasioned such disorder in the affairs of men, that Europe is thought to be diminished a full fifth in value.
> (*Political Works* 205)

Taking his cue from Sully's scheme, Fletcher proposed dividing Europe into ten more or less equal regions, with each region having a number of "sovereign cities well fortified" within them (207). Given that "[t]he nature of human affairs is such (...) that a perpetual peace is not to be preserved among men" (205) the best that could be hoped for would be to construct a European map where "all such governments as are of a sufficient force to defend themselves, should be rendered either uncapable or unfit to make conquests" (206–207).

Fletcher's scheme was an attempt to limit the impact of war – making war less likely, not impossible. The first attempt to break with war altogether had come a decade earlier, in a plan published in 1693 under the grand title "An

Essay Towards the Present and Future Peace of Europe, by the Establishment of a European Diet, Parliament, or Estates." Its author was later revealed to be the English Quaker leader and founder of the colony of Pennsylvania, Willam Penn (1644–1718). His proposal was born out of desperation over the wars which by then had held Europe in their grip for many years already, with the fighting stretching from the Balkans in the east to Catalonia in the south and Northern Ireland in the west.

Penn's plan was remarkable for its detailed description of the proceedings of the proposed European Parliament – its method of representation (proportional, based on national wealth), its voting rules (three-quarter majorities were required for any proposal to pass), even its architecture (it should be housed in a round room, "to avoid quarrel for presidency" – a very Quaker solution to the traditional problem of power competition). But its true significance lay in its explicit presentation of European unification as an *alternative* to war. Penn rejected the idea, put forth by Sully and Harrington, that though the aim of European unification was lasting peace, it could only be achieved through war.

The fact that Penn chose diplomacy over war as the route to get to the desired end state of European unity made it the first *peace plan*, a concept that would have a significant role to play in political debate in the following century. One early adopter of the idea was a fellow Quaker, John Bellers (1654–1725). In a 1710 pamphlet titled *Some Reasons for an European State proposed to the Powers of Europe*, he discussed the preconditions for a "General Guarantee, for establishing the Universal Peace of Europe" (Bellers, *Some Reasons for an European State* 2). His solution was to extend the "Union of Scotland (which for several Ages had in vain been Attempted)" to the rest of the continent by "Uniting the Powers of Europe in one peaceable Settlement" (3). Using the language of raison d'état, he argued that the "Deluge of Christian Blood" that had been spilled in decades of warfare made it a "Necessity" to make the peace that by then had started to be negotiated "Perpetual if possible" (iii).

Bellers was clearly affected by the conceptual confusion around the term "federal union," which was born out of the debate about the same Acts of Union presented by him as a solution for Europe's problems (see pp. xxx–yyy above).[11] The rest of his pamphlet makes it clear he was not talking about an

---

11   Though Bellers did use the word "confederates" several times to refer to the participants in the formation of a union, he did not use the term "federal union" to describe any of the schemes he discussed in the text. This is perhaps an indication of the fact that, at this point, the term was still *in statu nascendi*.

incorporating union but a federal one as the future structure of Europe. He proposed a federal structure in the form of a European Supreme Court "to decide their future Disputes without Blood" (Bellers, *Some Reasons* iv). Citing the example of "the several Provinces of Holland, as well as the Cantons of Switzerland," he suggested Europe's countries should "consolidate and cement together, (...) by being United in Perilous Times" (v–vi).

In a separate address "To the Powers of Europe," he then proposed a further element of the federal scheme through the creation of "an Annual Congress, Senate, Dyet, or Parliament by all the Princes and States of Europe." Its aim would be "to Prevent any Disputes that might otherwise raise a New War in this Age, or the Ages to come" (Bellers, *To the Powers* 4). The evidence that such a union was possible he presented by referring to "[t]he several Methods used by the German Dyets, the Union of the Provinces of Holland, the Cantons of Switzerland, the Nature of Guarantees, with the Model of Henry the Fourth, and the *Foedus Sacrum* between the Emperor and Venice" (Bellers, *To the Powers* 4).

—

The idea of a Congress to organise Europe politically was given momentum by the Peace of Utrecht, whose success seemed a vindication of the organising principle of a "just equilibrium of power" (Treaty between Great Britain and Spain, 1713). It was this principle that triggered the imagination of the French author Charles Iréné Castel, abbé de Saint-Pierre (1658–1743). Saint-Pierre was known as a social reformer and a prolific writer, who cranked out his proposals in a sort of scattergun style, covering anything from women's rights to poverty. His contribution to the debate about Europe's political order came in the form of a book titled *Project pour Rendre la Paix Perpétuelle en Europe* (1713).

He started by observing that the system of commercial or peace treaties and mutual defence leagues of which Europe's countries had availed themselves seemed a manifestation of "the highest degree of prudence, with which the sovereigns of Europe and their ministers conducted their politics" (Saint-Pierre 10; my translation throughout). But since there was never sufficient security underpinning any of these treaties, in practice the system had led to the opposite of its stated objective: perpetual war, periodically interrupted by peace negotiations. What was needed was a different system, one that offered predictability and reliability to the continent's monarchs. That system was a European Union.

To sell his idea to what he assumed to be a sceptical audience, Saint-Pierre again made copious use of the dominant political language of the age, that of raison d'état. His argument was based on an appeal to the enlightened self-interest of the sovereigns he hoped to persuade. Time and again he stressed that his aim was to give them "sufficient security." He did this first of all by showing them that by any reasonable calculation his cooperative scheme was more financially lucrative than the alternative, which was permanent war of all against all. Given that several of the main powers were left close to bankruptcy by the loans that had allowed them to sustain decades of warfare, this argument would have sounded quite plausible to his contemporaries. In 1715, for example, the Dutch pay office that handled all state finances would be forced to close for nine months because of a lack of funds (Goslinga 42).[12]

Saint-Pierre also took on board their concern about possibly losing sovereignty by agreeing to participate in this plan. By promising any ruler that faced an internal threat of revolt "sufficient security" (Saint-Pierre 14) in the form of the assistance of all the other members, he wanted to make it clear that their personal sovereignty would not in any way be affected by his proposed Union. His aim was to safeguard stability both *within* and *between* the participating states. Still, it was clear Union membership would place certain limits on the freedom of manoeuvre of its members: wars between members were no longer an option, and if one member chose to ignore a collective decision it would face the combined condemnation of the others. By presenting his scheme as the rational choice given the circumstances, he hoped to persuade Europe's rulers that this sacrifice was worth it. And if they considered the end worth it, they would have to accept his means, because the alternative of uniting Europe through armed conquest was "a complete fantasy" (18).

—

If Saint-Pierre is today mainly remembered for what he was arguing *for* (a European Union), to his contemporaries he was also, and perhaps chiefly, known for what he was arguing against: the balance of power system. Its supporters presented war as a legitimate means for settling conflict. But as Saint-Pierre pointed out, as a rule war "does not in fact settle anything. (...) [Neither party] has abandoned its ambitions, it has only multiplied

---

12   In his addendum to the 1717 reprint, Saint-Pierre would refer explicitly to the Dutch financial crisis, observing that "[t]he Dutch are deeply indebted by the last two wars, forced to borrow large sums at high interest" and remarking that it would be "very advantageous for them to be able to repay these loans" through participation in his scheme (586).

them with the injuries sustained through the war" (Saint-Pierre 25). Peace treaties also settled nothing under the balance of power system, since there was "no security that one or the other of the Contracting Parties would not change its position, or that its offspring would not decide to ignore some old undertakings, or new ones, to implement what it had agreed to" (28–29).

The idea of balance itself he dismissed as unsustainable: "[T]he least interior or exterior cause suffices to create new movement, or sustain the one that existed before" (Saint-Pierre 38). In the same way the equilibrium between the two houses of Austria and France "might allow for some cessations of movement, some truces; but far from producing a solid break, an unalterable Peace, it gives every ambitious, impatient, restless sovereign the opportunity to restart the war, and even to make it last longer" (38–39). This "unhappy system," which according to him had existed "two hundred years," had produced nothing apart from "virtually perpetual wars. (...) This is the effect of this Balance that is so desired by all" (39).

Ultimately, the balance of power system did not even offer the monarchs the one thing they hoped to gain from it: glory. Here Saint-Pierre recycled an argument used by Gattinara and Botero: taxes cause trouble. Because it left them continuously involved in wars, they had great need of money to fund their armies. This in turn meant "they are often forced to squeeze their subjects for taxes," making them unloved at home (Saint-Pierre 133). If they decided instead to let their armies live off the land, this meant they were "under the necessity of ravaging and burning the provinces of their enemies," giving them "a strongly odious reputation for posterity" (133).

—

Against the balance of power, Saint-Pierre proposed a new system for the maintenance of order on the continent: the formation of a permanent association out of the eighteen sovereign European states through the signing of a "Treaty of Union" and the formation of a "perpetual congress" (Saint-Pierre 12). Like Bellers, he invoked not only Henri IV's grand Design but also the existing examples of federal unions to justify his proposal for a European equivalent: "[T]he seven sovereignties of Holland, (...) the thirteen sovereignties of the Swiss, (...) the sovereignties of Germany" (12). He claimed that "the same motives and the same means" that had led to the founding of these unions "will suffice for the formation of a much larger community" (52).

Though he acknowledged several weaknesses in the constitutional design of the Holy Roman Empire – the emperor had both too much power over the agenda of the Diet and not enough power over the Empire's army (*Perpetual Peace* 59) – Saint-Pierre thought its example was still instructive when it came to studying the potential advantages of a continental union. These were clearest in the case of the smaller states. Membership of the union offered them protection against external threats, allowing them "to preserve their territory" (64). For the larger states, this kind of external security was less important than the internal stability the union offered: "[T]o receive through the force and protection of the German Union a protection against (…) revolts and (…) civil wars" (64). Union membership thereby offered something that monarchs valued greatly: dynastic security.

It also offered security of another kind, namely for "the execution of reciprocal promises" stemming from any treaties they signed (Saint-Pierre 66). Union membership further offered the chance to limit the sizable costs of warfare, not just the expenses of maintaining large standing armies but also "the decrease in revenue, the destruction of frontiers, the loss of large numbers of good subjects" (66). Finally, it offered the participating sovereignties the chance "to maintain commerce with foreigners." It seemed clear to Saint-Pierre that "in an age in which navigation is thirty times as large and much easier than it was at the time, (…) today's sovereigns must have a motive thirty times as strong for maintaining foreign commerce by establishing a European Community" (67).

When assessing the relative significance of these obstacles for the two unions – the German and the European – his general conclusion was that if anything, the benefits of a European Union were clearer: "The (…) interests of Princes today are incomparably greater in themselves for forming a European Union than were those for Princes at the time for forming a German Union" (71).[13]

Having established that the formation of a European Union was in every sovereign's interests, he then dealt with some of the remaining practical obstacles to its establishment. Three of these would come to play a significant role in the centuries that followed. One was the question of how to get a large number of participants to sign a treaty. Here he introduced a distinction between two types of treaties. In one, the process involved all parties signing the final agreement at the same time. If one party refused to sign, or failed to make the signing ceremony, that would prevent all from entering into an agreement. The alternative was a treaty which became valid as soon as it was signed by "a small number, two, three, four," and which "left

---

13   This obviously was a gross misrepresentation of the founding of the Holy Roman Empire, which started out not as a union of kingdoms but as a single, unified monarchy.

space for those who wanted to enter and wanted to sign at a later time" (Saint-Pierre 71). Saint-Pierre seems to have meant this purely as a logistical suggestion, to allow for the kind of signing in stages that happened at the American Continental Congress with the Declaration of Independence. In the nineteenth century, European authors like Kant and Saint-Simon would give the idea a political twist.

The second was an issue that had not been a factor as a potential obstacle in the Holy Roman Empire but seemed an obvious problem for a European Union: the lack of a shared language. In his view, this was easily remedied by using delegates who were all able to communicate in a common language. To the extent that they were not able to speak the same language, "relief would be provided by interpreters," who would facilitate the smooth running of negotiations "without delegates being able to understand each other's language" (Saint-Pierre 76).

The third was an issue that would be discussed extensively by the American Founders and nineteenth-century European thinkers: the extent of the union. Machiavelli had identified it as one of the problematic aspects of a league, suggesting that there was a maximum size beyond which it could not grow without limiting its ability to function. Saint-Pierre used an argument that would return repeatedly in one form or another in the debate about federal union in centuries to come: technological development would help shrink distances, thereby making a larger union possible. In fact, compared to the time when the Holy Roman Empire was founded, Saint-Pierre claimed, roads were already "much better and shorter, through being paved, the construction of bridges, and the clearing of forests" (Saint-Pierre 76).

—-

Details of Saint-Pierre's constitutional design revealed just how radical an ambition it was to suggest a European society based on perpetual peace. It required, first of all, a complete elimination of the possibility of territorial expansion by any of the participating sovereignties. By making the map of Europe at the time of signing of the Treaty of Union a "fixed point" (Saint-Pierre 169), he forced the states involved into a kind of political straitjacket from which there was no escape. Article 4 of his proposed Fundamental Articles (which could only be rewritten on the basis of unanimous consent) stipulated that "Every sovereign will accept for themselves and their offspring the limits of the territory they currently possess" (169).

The draft constitution also ruled out the causes of war. This meant firstly a ban on the raison d'état endorsed dynastic schemes through which monarchs tended to aggrandise themselves and their realms. Article 4 of the Fundamental Articles banned enlargement through "Succession, Pacts between different Houses, Election, Donation, Cession, Sale, Conquest, Voluntary Submission or otherwise," and stated that no sovereign of one territory would be allowed to take on the title of another territory. It even ruled out any voluntary exchange of territory between sovereigns (Saint-Pierre 168–169). Article 5 banned personal unions: "No sovereign can possess two sovereignties, either hereditary or elective." If through succession the monarch was offered possession of a larger territory to add to his present one, the only way he could take possession of it would be by giving up his old realm (178).

Saint-Pierre also tried to rule out the possibility of trade acting as a cause of conflict between member states. Article 7 of the Fundamental Articles stated that the deputies would "work continually" to assure that the laws regulating commerce affected all countries equally, and were based on the principle of equity (Saint-Pierre 180). The only use of arms allowed inside the territory of the Union was to restore order. Article 8 of the Fundamental Articles provided for joint action against a sovereign who had violated the Treaty and had consequently been declared an "enemy of the Community" (182).

The institutional framework of the Union consisted of a single body: a Senate in which the various countries and territories were represented (Saint-Pierre 190). They were a selection of all the most important monarchies, elected monarchies, federal unions, and republics, as well as some of the most commercially successful city states. Decisions were taken by simple majority (193). The city of Utrecht was proposed as the location for the Senate (198). In a new edition published a few years later, he would add more articles to the original proposal. Among other things, they stipulated that senators would vote upon strict instruction of their sovereigns (Saint-Pierre 548), and that the capital city would become a kind of federal district, its sovereignty residing with the Senate (548–549).

In the 1717 reprint, Saint-Pierre would accompany the original text with a second part which was an extended appeal to the raison d'état tradition. Placing himself in the same camp as the Duc de Rohan, whose *Interest of Princes* of 1643 was seen as a standard text in the genre, he titled the addendum "Interest of Every Sovereign in Particular in Signing a Treaty of Lasting Polity and Permanent Arbitration." Adopting "the maxim of the Duc de Rohan," he claimed that "interest" commanded the sovereigns to "sign a treaty" that offered both a sense of public flourishing and arbitration for the prevention of conflicts, and that created "a perpetual compromise, and a social contract for reciprocal and perpetual protection" (Saint-Pierre 544).

His arguments here were tailored to the various national audiences that needed persuading. The Dutch were offered a stabilisation of their constitutional relations through the *de facto* abolition of the post of Stadthouder: "[S]uch a general, who is necessary in times of war becomes for them a very real danger once he has weapons in his hand" (Saint-Pierre 584). He also gave them the assurance that "treaties of commerce" on which they relied as a trading nation "will be executed" (590). In answer to the question by the Swiss what would happen to the income generated by its mercenary soldiers in foreign service, Saint-Pierre assured them that "the European League would maintain many troops on its borders" (617). King Augustus II of the Polish-Lithuanian Commonwealth, who had lost and regained his throne under Russian tutelage in the Great Northern War, was offered "sufficient security" of his rule. The proposed constitution would also allow his son to succeed him. The *szlachta* would be compensated for this loss of its electoral rights through the treaty's offer of "sufficient security" against all forms of warfare, both civil and foreign, and this "in perpetuity" (625).

After reviewing the many arguments in its favour, Saint Pierre's ended with a firm conclusion: "It is impossible that the Project of European Arbitration won't be executed" (Saint-Pierre 694). In the very long term, he would be proven right. His contemporaries, however, would see things rather differently.

The reception of Saint-Pierre's peace plan

All the great minds of the eighteenth century, from Leibniz to Voltaire, Rousseau, Vattel, and Kant, would reflect on Saint-Pierre's peace plan and take their own position on its central issue. If peace between Europe's nations was both more desirable and more lucrative than war, as he claimed it was, would it not make sense to create institutional safeguards for its maintenance?

The most sympathetic among Saint-Pierre's contemporaries was Leibniz. He is known to us today mainly as a mathematician and logician, but he was also, and to his contemporaries just as significantly, a political philosopher. Here he used his decades of experience as a privy counsellor to successive electors of Brunswick. In this capacity he not only corresponded with all the main political figures of his age, he also designed his own peace plan for Europe which he eventually presented, in bits and pieces, in a number of publications.

The scheme itself was essentially a plea for restoration of the pre-Reformation *Respublica Christiana*, with the Holy Roman Empire as its administrative structure and the Pope as its spiritual head. Leibniz even described his scheme as a Christian republic: "All Christendom forms a species of republic, in which Caesar has some authority" (Leibniz 111). Like the old *Respublica Christiana*, his Christian Republic had two heads, "the Emperor and a legitimate Pope" (112). He recognised that to make it work, there would have to be effectively a Counter-Reformation, not just politically but spiritually: "[I]t would be necessary at the same time that ecclesiastics resume their old authority (...) that an interdiction and an excommunication make kings and kingdoms tremble, as in the time of Nicholas I or Gregory VII" (184).

It was because he was familiar with these writings that Saint-Pierre had contacted Leibniz to seek his opinion about his own peace plan. While stressing the "great difficulties" involved with its implementation, Leibniz's response was broadly sympathetic, describing the plan as "on the whole feasible" and observing that "its execution would be one of the most useful things in the world" (178). While musing to Saint-Pierre that "men lack only the will to deliver themselves from an infinity of evils" and that all it would take to make his scheme a reality would be "five or six persons" of good will (177), he was less optimistic in discussions about the scheme with other correspondents. The core problem as he saw it was that, even if created, the new central administration would lack the authority to impose its rulings on member states ("the most powerful do not respect tribunals at all"), though he hoped that a solution for this problem could be found in the form of a deposit scheme, "so that the sentences of the tribunal could be executed on their money, in case they proved refractory" (183).

Leibniz was an exception, though. The consensus among eighteenth-century political philosophers seemed to be that while Saint-Pierre's aim of eternal peace may have sounded worthwhile, or indeed noble, the crucial problem was that there was no way of getting there, and that he was naive for thinking there was. Even a constructive critic like his biographer, Jean-Jacques Rousseau (1712–1778), felt compelled to stress its shortcomings in an extended discussion of the scheme.

—-

Rousseau was not unsympathetic to the idea of a European federal union. In his *Jugement sur la paix perpétuelle de l'abbé de Saint-Pierre* (1761) he went out of his way to present Saint-Pierre's scheme as essentially praiseworthy and deserving full attention: "Just as no greater, more beautiful, or more useful project ever occupied the human mind than that of perpetual peace among all the peoples of Europe, never did an author deserve more attention from the public than the one who proposes means to bring this project into execution" (Rousseau 51; my translation throughout).

It was, he observed, a subject that would inevitably force itself upon any thinker considering the means of perfecting a government: how to overcome those obstacles that "are born less of its constitution than of its external relations" (Rousseau 53). Recognising the influence of both Roman antiquity and Christianity, he observed that "all the powers of Europe form between them a sort of system that unites them" (56). But while Europe may have formed a cultural and political unity, the reality of European history was one of perpetual conflict. This was the central paradox of European politics: "Our beautiful discourse and our horrible proceedings, so much humanity in our maxims and so much cruelty in our actions, a religion so soft and an intolerance so bloody, a politics so wise in its writings and so harsh in its practice, such beneficial leaders and such miserable populations, such moderate governments and such cruel wars" (63). The powers of Europe were in a state of permanent war with each other, with peace treaties serving more like "ceasefires than like real periods of peace" (64).

To overcome this paradox was, however, easier said than done. One solution, universal monarchy, was impossible to achieve. The reason was the existence of the balance of power on the continent, which could never be fundamentally disturbed: "This balance exists, and only needs itself to sustain itself, without anyone's involvement; and if it is broken for a moment from one direction, it soon re-establishes itself in another direction" (Rousseau 69). Even alliances for domination would have no chance of achieving their goal: "The other half would certainly unite against them; they would therefore have to overcome others stronger than themselves" (71).

Nor was commerce the European peace mechanism that its proponents hoped it would be. In a reference to the jealousy of trade theory, Rousseau described its effects as producing "a space of political fanaticism" while giving some powers an "exclusive advantage" (Rousseau 75). The only way to overcome the "dangerous contradictions" at the heart of Europe's political constitution, he suggested, was through the formation of a "confederal government" (54). Here he mentioned the examples also mentioned by Machiavelli: the ancient Greek Amphictyonic council and Achaean league, the Etruscan league, the Swiss and German confederations.[14]

---

14 The fact that Rousseau mentioned the Etruscan League as one of his examples suggests he may have studied the chapters in Machiavelli's *Discourses* devoted to the league's historical antecedents.

Rousseau listed a number of criteria for the success of such a confederation. The first was that it needed to be broad in its composition, so no single
state or coalition of states could dominate proceedings (Rousseau 78). It
also needed to possess "a coactive and coercive power" – that is, a power
with and a power *over* – to make every member state submit to its joint
decisions (79). Without this power, any meeting of its representatives would
be like the congresses of the 1720s, "where they assembled to say nothing;
(...) where they discussed whether the table should be round or square, if
the room should have more or fewer doors, if a plenipotentiary should have
their face or their cheek turned towards the window, if someone should
move two inches closer or further away during a visit, and a thousand
other questions of similar importance" (93–94). To complete his sketch of
a functional confederation, he then proposed to implement the five clauses
of Saint-Pierre's plan.

He did not deny that Saint-Pierre's proposal would give rise to "a thousand
small difficulties" (Rousseau 84), but he thought those were not insurmountable in themselves. The more important question to ask was whether it
was possible in the first place to adopt the scheme. He split this question
into two halves: was the proposed confederation sufficient to give Europe
perpetual peace, and would the sovereigns involved be willing to pay the
price required to establish it?

The answer to the first one was a resounding *yes*: "I hold it to be sufficiently
demonstrated that the European diet, once established, would never have to
fear rebellion, and that, although some abuses may be introduced, they can
never go so far as to undermine the objective of the institution" (Rousseau 89).
In Rousseau's view, the advantages of this "European republic" (107) were so
clear that "all the so-called disadvantages of the state of confederation, when
properly considered, amount to nothing" (110). In fact, "to realise his European
republic even for a single day would be enough to make it last forever" (13).

If the sovereigns involved were to consult their "true interests" (Rousseau
115), the choice would be simple. And yet the scheme was, in Rousseau's view,
"evidently impossible" (12). Its core problem was that Saint-Pierre had failed
to take into account the fundamental difference between *real* and *apparent*
interests of sovereigns. Their real interest may well have been to adopt his
scheme. But their apparent interest seemed to be its rejection in favour of
the continued rule of fortune. This was clearly the less rational choice, but
it did at least offer them a chance to expand their territories (16). In the
contest between glory and reason, the latter was always going to come off
second best in the eyes of a monarch. In their eyes, the potential benefits
of war always outweighed its costs: "A prince who stakes his cause on the

chance of war is not unaware that he runs a risk; but he is less concerned about it than he is convinced of the advantages he promises himself" (19).

Saint-Pierre's problem, according to Rousseau, was that he fundamentally underestimated the difficulty of establishing a new system against this kind of royal resistance: "He reasoned like a child when considering the means to establish it" (Rousseau 24). By contrast, Rousseau had nothing but praise for the realism of Henri IV and his minister, the Duc de Sully. Facing the threat of universal monarchy from the Spanish empire (25), Henri formed a plan to break its stranglehold on Europe. He worked with the utmost secrecy (27) on a plan which each of the parties involved was able to embrace for its own selfish reasons (30). In the end, all that was required was some spark to set the scheme in motion: "The smallest pretext would have been enough to start that great revolution" (34). What would have followed would have been a war to end all wars: "A war that would have been the last war, would pave the way to an immortal peace" (34).

If Saint-Pierre's problem was that he paid no attention to the means of implementing his scheme, the problem with the scheme of Henri IV and Sully was the terrible price that had to be paid to see it established – "violent means, shocking to humanity" (Rousseau 35). Who in his right mind would argue for a scheme that came at such a terrible cost? As Rousseau asked: "Who among us would dare to say whether this European league is to be desired, or to be feared? It would perhaps do more harm in a single blow than it would prevent for centuries" (35).

The Balance of Power defended

Rousseau's sombre assessment was no doubt based in part on the scorn heaped on the plan by the likes of Frederick of Prussia and his philosophical adviser, Voltaire (1694–1778). The latter would, half a century after the publication of Saint-Pierre's plan, write a withering critique in which he called it, among other things, "absurd" and "a chimaera which will never subsist between princes any more than between elephants and rhinoceroses" (*De la Paix Perpetuelle*, 1769).

The intensity of Voltaire's rejection of Saint-Pierre's proposal was all the more remarkable given the amount of overlap between their views of the situation which Europe found itself in at the start of the eighteenth century. Like Saint-Pierre, Voltaire believed that with the Peace of Utrecht the continent had effectively buried the threat of universal monarchy. The new reality was that of a Europe of many fairly evenly matched states. Like

Saint-Pierre, he also dreamed up a scheme for their unification in a single overarching system, which he called a "great republic." And like Saint-Pierre, he believed that through this scheme, the beneficial effects of commerce could manifest themselves, to the betterment of all involved. The end state towards which it worked was even the same: perpetual peace. He claimed that this peace, which was essentially the complete absence of dogma and the establishment of toleration as official state doctrine in all its member states, "isn't a phantom; it exists among all honest men, from China to Quebec" (Voltaire 128; my translation).

In its organising principle, though, Voltaire's plan was very different. This principle was first discussed in a study published several decades earlier under the title *Anti-Machiavel*. It was originally authored by Frederick II of Prussia but then extensively rewritten by Voltaire. In it, the pair used the idea of balance of power as the organising principle of European politics. They presented it as a dynamic conception of power relations, informally regulating relationships between the participating states. Saint-Pierre had sought security in the development of a European administrative system which, through the collective effort of the participating states in a new transnational institutional set-up, was on a limited range of subjects also superior to them. Voltaire and Frederick instead sought it in permanent diplomatic relations between the states, and the development of a system of treaties between them (Nakhimovsky 61).

From a raison d'état perspective this proposal may have seemed more realistic than Saint-Pierre's. After all, it was easier to get the rulers of Europe to agree to a loosely organised quasi-confederation, within which they could all still defend their honour and pursue their selfish interests, than to the building of joint institutions. But measured in actual outcomes, perhaps Voltaire's was the less realistic option. Instead of providing a solution for the problem of war, it simply seemed to ignore it – not necessarily ruling it out, but pretending that its consequences would be beneficial enough not to disturb the overall balance of power ("A good war leads to, and secures, a good peace"; Frederick/Voltaire 407). This optimism became the main target of Saint-Pierre's in his own withering attack on Frederick/Voltaire's proposal, *Reflexions sur l'Antimachiavel*, published in 1742. Saint-Pierre observed that their plan did nothing to make war impossible and that therefore not diplomacy but "the superiority of force, skill, and treachery, remain the means for deciding the difference between sovereigns" (quoted in Nakhimovsky 70).

To Frederick/Voltaire, this argument would have seemed less cogent than it might seem to twenty-first-century readers. They had, after all, spent a good part of the *Anti-Machiavel* arguing that conditions in early eighteenth-century Europe had changed to such an extent that the old conception of raison d'état, which allowed for the pursuit of glory through military means in tactics of any kind, was no longer relevant. The rise of the commercial state made the prosperity and luxury of its citizens the new standard of national glory, and these were best pursued not through conflict but through commercial relations. In other words: Saint-Pierre was grossly exaggerating the threat of war, most likely in an effort to persuade states to join his utopian scheme. To the extent that war continued to play a role in European affairs, this was not necessarily a bad thing. A just war was considered a legitimate way of becoming the ruler of a country.

—

Frederick/Voltaire's idea of the European Republic would echo throughout the century.

Among its most important interpreters was Emer de Vattel. In his *Law of Nations,* published in 1758, he followed their lead in claiming that "Europe forms a political system, an integral body. (...) The continual attention of sovereigns to every occurrence, the constant residence of ministers, and the perpetual negotiations, make of modern Europe a kind of republic, of which the members – each independent, but all linked together by the ties of common interest – unite for the maintenance of order and liberty" (Vattel 891).

This "integral body" was based on "that famous scheme of the political balance, or the equilibrium of power" by which was meant the absence of the threat of universal monarchy: "[S]uch a disposition of things as that no one potentate is able absolutely to predominate, and prescribe laws to the others" (Vattel 892). The obvious question was how to maintain this balance, once established. Here Vattel dismissed "the surest means of preserving that equilibrium" (892), namely Henri IV's Grand Design: redrawing the map of Europe to create a collection of more or less equal commonwealths. It would be "impossible to carry it into execution without injustice and violence" and would be impossible to maintain because "commerce, industry, military pre-eminence, would soon put an end to it" (892). The tool proposed by the peace plan thinkers, of congresses in which the European states settled their differences, was dismissed based on the experience of similar gatherings earlier in the century (for Vattel, "tedious farces"; see xxx above).

Instead he suggested a more pragmatic solution: constantly shifting coalitions, where smaller states had the option of "forming confederations to oppose the more powerful potentate." By always choosing the side of the weaker party in a conflict between two dominant states, "like so many weights thrown into the lighter scale," they would help to "keep it in equilibrium with the other" (Vattel 892–893). Vattel was not naive about the prospects of smaller states always choosing the right option. There was a danger they would fall victim to their own moral weakness: "Dazzled by the glare of a present advantage, seduced by their avarice, deceived by faithless ministers – how many princes become the tools of a power which will once day swallow up either themselves or their successors." The only way to prevent this was to strike at the earliest opportunity in order to weaken "that potentate who destroys the equilibrium" (894).

It was no accident that Vattel's discussion of the European Republic featured in a part of his *Law of Nations* devoted to the topic of war. In his view, though undesirable in itself, war was a perfectly natural phenomenon. It was simply "that state in which we prosecute our right by force" (Vattel 841). He accepted that nature "gives men a right to employ force, when it is necessary for their defence, and for the preservation of their rights," though he stressed that this right fell "only to the sovereign power" (842). He therefore accepted that, under the right circumstances, both offensive and defensive wars could be just. It could be fought to avenge a harm to the sovereign's own state, or to prevent one, or indeed, to prevent harm in another state, or to punish a third one.

In reflecting on how to maintain the equilibrium of this "kind of" European republic, Vattel saw a clear role for warfare:

> In fine, there cannot exist a doubt that, if that formidable potentate certainly entertain designs of oppression and conquest – if he betray his views by his preparations and other proceedings – the other states have a right to anticipate him; and if the fate of war declares in their favour, they are justifiable in taking advantage of this happy opportunity to weaken and reduce a power to contrary to the equilibrium, and dangerous to the common liberty.
> (Vattel 895)

If there was to be a European republic, it would have to be based on the realisation that perpetual peace as an objective was unobtainable. The fact that peace treaties did talk about it didn't mean that previous generations disagreed. The concept was "not to be understood as if they promised never to make war on each other for any cause whatever" (Vattel 1186). It simply meant that the peace which was concluded made a permanent end to the war that had just been fought: "[I]t is in reality perpetual inasmuch as it does not allow them to revive the same war by taking up arms again for the same subject" (1186).

This raised an obvious question: how much internal warfare could the European republic as defined by Frederick/Voltaire and Vattel survive before its order broke down completely? The failure of the balance of power approach in the decades after Vattel's death showed that he had seriously underestimated the system's potential for all-out war and the destruction of sovereign states by their neighbours. A case in point was the fate of the Polish-Lithuanian Commonwealth. The same Frederick who in the *Anti-Machiavel* had solemnly declared that "[p]eace in Europe is founded (...) on the maintenance of that wise equilibrium through which the superior strength of one monarchy is counterbalanced by the combined power of various other sovereigns" (405), in 1772 was instrumental in building a coalition of other dominant states for the partial dismantling of his weaker republican neighbour. The Polish-Lithuanian Commonwealth was forced to part with large tracts of its territory to Russia, Prussia, and the Austrian empire. A few decades later, the same coalition of stronger states would divide what remained between them, effectively wiping what was until then the largest federal republic in European history off the map.

The balance of power system clearly didn't work for the Polish-Lithuanian Commonwealth.[15] It would soon break down violently for the rest of Europe as well through the French Revolutionary Wars. Even if it had somehow continued to work, by allowing for periodic limited wars to restore the balance, the question would have remained: how high a price was Europe prepared to pay for the unlimited sovereignty of its monarchs? Was there really no alternative to perpetual war? As the Austrian ambassador to Russia, Count Ludwig von Cobenzl, observed in a letter to his Foreign Secretary, what kind of system makes ever-bigger wars the most rational option to maintain the status quo?

> But, one will say to me, always more war, always more conquests! This language breathes the politics of the last 34 years. Do we not have enough with what we already possess? Must we run the risk inevitable in such enterprises, even when they are the best arranged and the most

---

15 Arguably the system didn't work for the dominant states either. In his book *The Transformation of European Politics, 1763–1848*, Paul W. Schroeder observes that the Austrian-French alliance, concluded in 1763 at the end of the Seven Years' War, "had worked to sustain the European system while doing little or nothing for the power and security of the two partners" (42).

advantageously formed? No doubt we could be content with what we
have, if all the other powers were willing to do likewise.
(Von Cobenzl to Kaunitz, August 1787, quoted in Schroeder 48)

Immanuel Kant: perpetual peace through federal union – eventually

The most consequential answer to the problem of war would come from
the Prussian philosopher Immanuel Kant (1724–1804). He first came to the
issue in his essay "Idea for a Universal History with a Cosmopolitan Purpose"
(1784). Here he defined his mission in rather ambitious terms. Just as nature
"produced a Kepler who found an expected means of reducing the eccentric
orbits of the planets to definite laws," and a Newton "who explained these
laws in terms of a universal natural cause," it was his ambition to discover
"a purpose in nature behind this senseless course of human events" (Kant
42). Unlike Kepler and Newton, though, Kant would formulate no laws of
historical development. His aim seemed to be merely to show the *possibility*
of history having certain guiding principles, and to describe by what means
these could bring mankind closer to its ultimate destination, if there was one.

Without ever overstating the possibility of defining this guiding principle
– he admitted that he could, at best, describe "a little" of it, because he, too,
was afflicted by mankind's "shortsightedness" in studying these issues – he
did try to define the contours of the historical process through the formulation of a series of logically linked propositions. The fourth proposition had
a distinctly Machiavellian flavour: "The means which nature employs to
bring about the development of innate capacities is that of antagonism
within society" (Kant 44). Conflict, in the form of "ungesellige Geselligkeit"
(unsocial sociability), was the driving force of human development.

After showing how this principle eventually led man to reconcile himself
to his fellow man in civil society (fifth proposition) through the acceptance of
a higher authority (sixth proposition), Kant then, in the seventh proposition,
formulated his constitutional hypothesis: "The problem of establishing a
perfect civil constitution is subordinate to the problem of a law-governed
external relationship with other states, and cannot be solved unless the
latter is also solved" (Kant 47). In other words, a constitution didn't just
involve the internal order of the state, but also the state's relations with other
states. Again, conflict played a crucial role in explaining how states would
eventually be driven towards a "great federation (*Foedus Amphictyonum*)"
driven by "united power and the law-governed decisions of a united will" (47).

Kant was aware he was entering dangerous territory here by defining European unification as the more or less inevitable outcome of a historical process – he even referred to the fact that the Abbé de Saint-Pierre had been ridiculed when he had proposed the same. The main conclusion he seemed to have drawn about the visceral response to this earlier proposal was that it had been provoked by the suggestion that its implementation was imminent. He therefore made a point of emphasising, both rhetorically and logically, that his final stage of historical development was still far off in time. It would take "many devastations, upheavals and even complete inner exhaustion of their powers" before mankind would "finally" reach this stage (Kant 48). It was also certainly not a given that it would get there. Kant accepted that there was a scenario in which nothing of value would ever emerge from this endless series of wars and calamities; however, he believed the balance of probability suggested that it would. Or rather, the "beneficial effect" of the "evils" of perpetual war would be that eventually it would induce mankind to discover a "law of equilibrium" which would then be reinforced through "a system of united power" (49).

Since mankind was currently only "a little beyond the half-way mark in its development" (Kant 49), the immediate political relevance of this analysis would be limited. Still, he thought it important enough to publish it, for two reasons. First, he wanted to make the point that it was definitely *possible* to produce a scheme like Saint-Pierre's on the basis of a philosophical analysis of historical processes. Second, and of greater practical importance: by publishing it, he could explain to the rulers of his age what would cause them to be remembered honourably in ages to come, namely their possible contributions to the reaching of this historical end stage of perpetual peace.

—

In this first sketch of the "logical" outcome of the historical process, the founding of a European confederation, Kant was eager to stress the speculative nature of his project. The aim seemed to be merely to show that a project like that of Saint-Pierre's was *not completely implausible*, given the forces that drove historical development. As a solution to the problem of war, however, it was far from satisfactory. Since Kant thought that lasting peace through the European balance of power was "a pure illusion" (Kant 92), he was under some obligation to show how mankind could solve this problem in the here and now.

This challenge would lead him to set out his proposal for a European federation. Before he could discuss this plan for perpetual peace, he would first bring its potential implementation forward in time by showing how most of the conditions for it had already been fulfilled in his lifetime. In an essay titled "On the Common Saying: This May Be True in Theory, but it does not Apply in Practice," published in 1793, he explained how frequent wars and the costs of maintaining standing armies would push up national debts. Since peace rarely lasted long enough to allow the economy to recover from the costs of the last war, the debt would prove to be an "ultimately self-defeating expedient" (Kant 90). It was in this situation, which would have sounded all too familiar to his contemporaries,[16] that Kant saw the start of the transformation away from a culture of war to one of peace – beginning with the transfer of the power to declare war from the sovereign to the people, since he assumed the latter would be much more hesitant to do so.

The title of the essay seemed an indirect reference to the criticism of Saint-Pierre's scheme as admirable theory but irrelevant to political practice. Kant's conclusion was that those who had objected to "the theory of Abbé de Saint-Pierre" on the grounds that it could never work in practice were wrong: "Whatever reason shows to be valid in theory, is also valid in practice" (Kant 90). If Saint-Pierre's proposal was right in theory, Kant concluded, it *had to* work in practice.

Though he didn't name Saint-Pierre at any point in his next essay, it is clear that "Perpetual Peace" was a tribute to the latter's peace plan. Unlike that plan, his own essay contained relatively few institutional details, short of indicating that a federation would have to be established through a single treaty rather than through a series of individual peace treaties. It did offer some important guiding principles for its establishment: no state could take over another by classical means like inheritance or marriage; all standing armies should gradually be abolished; national debts should no longer be allowed to be used as tools for foreign policymaking; and no state would be allowed to meddle in the constitutional affairs of another.

If war between two states within the proposed federation could not be avoided, it was important that they should at least respect certain fundamental rules of war. Only by refraining from "honourless stratagems" could states guarantee that any war would be followed by a restoration of peace. The inclusion of the latter principle was an acknowledgment by Kant that

---

16   On the American federation's struggle with the problem of national debt, see page 208 below. Also worth noting here is the fact that Kant's observations form an echo of David Hume's arguments in his essay "Of Public Credit," in which he portrayed Britain's large national debt as the most likely reason for a possible collapse of the European balance of power.

eternal peace wasn't an immediately reachable destination. Rather it was the eventual outcome of an "infinite process of gradual approximation" – ever closer union (Kant 130). Eternal peace was the phase that would follow that of "what have hitherto been wrongly called peace treaties (which are actually only truces)" (130).

Both the tools of war and the causes of war would eventually have to be outlawed under Kant's scheme, since "reason, as the highest legislative moral power, absolutely condemns war" (Kant 104). This kind of dramatic step could not come from a mere peace treaty, since it only "terminates one war." To "end all wars for good" required the founding of "a particular kind of league, which we may call a pacific federation (*foedus pacificum*)" (104). What Kant proposed wasn't so much a European Republic as a *federation* of European republics: "For if by good fortune one powerful and enlightened nation can form a republic (which is by its nature inclined to seek perpetual peace), this will provide a focal point for federal association among other states." This initial federal core would then "gradually spread further and further by a series of alliances of this kind" (104).

—

The Kantian interpretation of Saint-Pierre's peace plan was based on three fundamental adaptations that would have significant consequences for European political thought on the subject of federal union. The first was that he projected the end state of a federal union into the distant future. The objective was to depoliticise, to a certain extent at least, the process of moving towards it – a complete reversal of the logic of Machiavelli that constitutional development required internal conflict.

The second change introduced by Kant was a mechanism for bridging the gap between the here and now and the end state: the creation of a small advanced guard of states that would create a "pacific federation" that would eventually spread among all other states. This initial federation was a mere transition stage, an "enduring and gradually expanding federation" that was merely "likely to prevent war" (Kant 105). It would eventually become the dominant solution to the question of how to initiate the process of federalisation under the conditions that resulted from his first correction to Saint-Pierre's scheme.

These two innovations together had the effect of changing the formation of a federal union from immediately achieving a final state into a process of indefinite duration. It seemed as if Kant had solved the core problem of European theory on federation formation. Finally, an answer had been formulated to the question of how the first step towards a federal union could be taken. His solution would become a lasting part of European thinking on federation formation. However, over time, it would become clear that this solution also raised new questions. Was it too optimistic to think that the envisioned end goal would have the force of an Aristotelian telos – a natural endpoint of development towards which history would inevitably move? And if the end goal was not a telos but rather an ambition, did that not mean that the moment of political confrontation was at most postponed, rather than definitively avoided?

The third change was that, whereas Saint-Pierre had built his scheme around regimes of any kind, Kant restricted access to republics only. By "republic" he meant any state which met two binding conditions. The first was that it needed to be pure in its origin, that is, based on the principles of freedom and equality before the law. The other concerned its constitutional order. Here Kant used some familiar arguments to draw conclusions diametrically opposed to Bodin's. He accepted the latter's classification of regimes based on their locus of sovereignty: one (which he called autocracy), few (aristocracy), or many (democracy). He then suggested that each regime type had two forms: despotic and republican. The difference was in whether or not the regime had incorporated separation of powers in its constitutional set-up: "Republicanism is that political principle whereby the executive power (the government) is separated from the legislative power" (Kant 101). By contrast, "[d]espotism prevails in a state if the laws are made and arbitrarily executed by one and the same power" (101).

This distinction between republican and despotic regimes based on the presence or absence of separation of powers formed an echo of Montesquieu's argument in *Spirit of the Laws* (XI, ch. 6). This new idea, that legitimacy of a regime was linked to the separation of powers within it, would profoundly influence Western thinking about the nature of regimes, and would form the basis of the great ideological conflict between proponents of federal union (who argued in favour of separation of powers) and those who supported its counter-concepts: first caesarism (1851–1914), and then fascism, totalitarianism, or authoritarianism (1917 to the present), all of which argued for a unitary conception of state power.

To understand how federalism got wedded to the concepts of separation of powers, we have to turn to the late eighteenth-century United States of America. It was there that the various problematic aspects of the European federal tradition were first confronted in a systematic way. This would also be where the first solutions for these problematics were developed.

Bibliography

Bacon, Francis. "Of Empire." 1612. *The Essays of Francis Bacon*, edited, with introduction and notes by Mary Scott, Charles Scribner's Sons, 1908.

Bellers, John. *Some Reasons for an European State proposed to the Powers of Europe.* 1710. Gale Ecco, 2018.

Bellers, John. *To the Powers of Europe.* 1710. Gale Ecco, 2018.

Botero, Giovanni. *The Reason of State.* 1589. Translated by Robert Birley, Cambridge University Press, 2017.

Butterfield, Herbert, and Martin Wight, editors. *Diplomatic investigations: Essays in the Theory of International Politics.* 1966. Oxford University Press, 2019.

Caenegem, Raoul van. *An Historical Introduction to Western Constitutional Law.* Cambridge University Press, 1995.

Court, Pieter de la. *Treatise on the Welfare of Leiden.* 1659. Nijhoff, 1911.

Eliav-Feldon, Miriam. "Grand Designs, the Peace Plans of the Late Renaissance." *Vivarium*, vol. 27, no. 1, 1989, pp. 51–76.

Fletcher of Saltoun, Andrew. *Political Works.* Cambridge University Press, 1997.

Frederick of Prussia/Voltaire. *Antimachiavel. Frederick the Great's Philosophical Writings*, edited by Avi Lifschitz, translated by Angela Scholar, e-book, Princeton University Press, 2021.

Garnier, Édith. *L'Alliance impie: François Ier et Soliman le Magnifique contre Charles V.* Éditions du Félin, 2008.

Gerard, James W. *The Peace of Utrecht: Historical Review of the Great Treaty of 1713–14, and of the Principal Events of the War of the Spanish Succession.* G. Putnam and Sons, 1885.

Ghervas, Stella. *Conquering Peace, From the Enlightenment to the European Union.* Harvard University Press, 2021.

Gierke, Otto von. *Natural Law and the Theory of Society, 1500 to 1800.* 1913. The Lawbook Exchange, 2010.

Goslinga, Adriaan. *Slingelandt's Efforts towards European Peace.* Martinus Nijhoff, 1915.

Guicciardini, Francesco. *Dialogue on the Government of Florence.* 1527. Edited by Alison Brown, Cambridge University Press, 1994.

Guicciardini, Francesco. *The History of Italy.* 1537. With an introduction by Sidney Alexander, Princeton University Press, 1984.

Hanley, Ryan Patrick. *Fénelon: Moral and Political Writings.* E-book, Oxford University Press, 2020.

Harrington, James. *The Political Works of James Harrington*, edited by J. G. A. Pocock, Cambridge University Press, 2010. 2 vols.

Hirschman, Albert. *The Passions and The Interests: Political Arguments for Capitalism Before Its Triumph.* 1977. Princeton University Press, 2013.

Hont, Istvan. *Jealousy of Trade: International Competition and the Nation-State in Historical Perspective*, Harvard University Press, 2005

Hume, David. "Of Jealousy of Trade." 1759. *David Hume, Political Essays*, edited by Knud Haakonssen, Cambridge University Press, 2006, pp. 150–153.

Israel, Jonathan. *The Dutch Republic: Its Rise, Greatness and Fall, 1477–1806*. Clarendon Press, 1998.

Kant, Immanuel. *Political Writings*, edited by H. S. Reiss, Cambridge University Press, 1991.

Kissinger, Henry, *Diplomacy*. Pocket Books, 1995.

Kosińska, Urszula. "The Negotiations of Augustus II with Sweden in 1719–1720." *Kwartalnik Historyczny*, vol. 111, no. 3, 2004, pp. 23–44.

Leibniz, Gottfried Wilhelm. *Political Writings*, edited by Patrick Riley, Cambridge University Press, 2012.

Locke, John. *Two Treatises on Government*, edited with an introduction by Peter Laslett, Cambridge University Press, 1988.

Mackillop, Andrew, and Michael Ó Siochrú. *Forging the State: European State Formation and the Anglo-Scottish Union of 1707*. University of Aberdeen Press, 2008.

Montesquieu. *The Spirit of the Laws*. 1748. Translated and edited by Anne Cohler, Basia Carolyn Miller, and Harold Samuel Stone, Cambridge University Press, 1989.

Nakhimovsky, Isaac. "The Enlightened Prince and the Future of Europe." *Commerce and Peace in the Enlightenment*, edited by Béla Kapossy, Isaac Nakhimovsky, and Richard Whatmore, Cambridge University Press, 2018, pp. 44–77.

Peace and Friendship Treaty between Great Britain and Spain, 1713. *Wikisource*, https://en.wikisource.org/wiki/Peace_and_Friendship_Treaty_of_Utrecht_between_France_and_Great_Britain. Accessed 6 March 2024.

Penn, William. *An Essay Towards the Present and Future Peace of Europe, by the Establishment of a European Diet, Parliament, or Estates*. 1693.

Saint-Pierre, Abbé de (Charles Iréné Castel). *Project pour Rendre la Paix Perpétuelle en Europe*. 1713/1717. Fayard, 1986.

Rohan, Henri duc de. *A Treatise of the Interest of the Princes and States of Christendomme*, translated by Henry Hunt, Richard Hodgkinsonne, 1641.

Rousseau, Jean-Jacques. *Jugement sur la paix perpétuelle de l'abbé de Saint-Pierre*. 1761.

Schroeder, Paul W. *The Transformation of European Politics, 1763–1848*. Oxford University Press, 1996.

Segers, Mathieu. *The Origins of European Integration: The Pre-history of Today's European Union, 1937–1951*. Cambridge University Press, 2023.

Sheehan, Michael. *The Balance of Power: History and Theory*. Routledge, 1995.

Somos, Mark. "Harrington's Project: The Balance of Money, a Republican Constitution for Europe, and England's Patronage of the World." *Commerce and Peace
in the Enlightenment*, edited by Béla Kapossy, Isaac Nakhimovsky, and Richard
Whatmore, Cambridge University Press, 2018, pp. 20–43.

Sully, Duc de (Maximilian de Bethune). *Grand Design of Henri IV, from the Memoirs
of Maximilien de Bethune, Duc de Sully*, with an introduction by David Ogg,
Forgotten Books, 2015.

Tuck, Richard. *The Rights of War and Peace: Political Thought and the International
Order from Grotius to Kant*. Oxford University Press, 1999.

Vattel, Emer de. *Law of Nations, Or Principles of the Law of Nature, Applied to the
Conduct and Affairs of Nations and Sovereigns, with Three Early Essays on the
Origin and Nature of Natural Law and on Luxury*, edited and introduced by Bela
Kapossy and Richard Whatmore, Liberty Fund, 2008.

Voltaire. *De La Paix Perpétuelle*. 1769. Hachette 2016.

4   The American Moment

Abstract

The American Founders formed not one but two federal unions. The first, the Articles of Confederation, was based on the old European models. The second was based on a number of constitutional innovations. On sovereignty, they found a way of dividing it between the states and the centre. On representation, they managed to accommodate both the people and the states. This allowed them to create a federal union that could span a continent. Checks and balances were supposed to prevent any one of the new powers from overwhelming the others. Anti-federalists, however, warned about the possibility of them being directed instead against the people. They demanded, and received, an additional safeguard in the form of a Bill of Rights.

Keywords: federal union, constitution, sovereignty, representation, checks and balances, extended republic

A firm league of friendship: the Articles of Confederation[1]

The American Founders were influenced by many different intellectual traditions. Beyond Greek and Roman republicanism there were also the British political discourses of the Scottish Enlightenment (Hume, Smith), English radical Whiggism (Harrington, Algernon Sidney, Locke, and the Tacitus translator Thomas Gordon, among others), and British constitutionalism (Blackstone). There was a local American colonial tradition, of which arguably the most important representative was still very much active when the great debates of 1776–77 and 1787 took place (Benjamin Franklin).

There was also a highly visible native American tradition of federalism which served as a source of inspiration. Evidence suggests that the plan of

---

[1]   The letters, speeches, and pamphlets quoted in this chapter can be found in the Founders Online archive of the US National Archive: https://founders.archives.gov/, referred to throughout as FOA.

Livestro, Joshua: *A More Perfect Union. Federal Union in Political Theory and Practice, 1500-1951.* Amsterdam: Amsterdam University Press, 2024.
DOI: 10.5117/9789048563777_CH04

Union which Benjamin Franklin helped to draw up at the Albany Congress in 1754 was at least in part inspired by the example of the Iroquoi Confederacy.[2] During the debates in 1776 about the Articles of Confederation, Congressman James Wilson of Pennsylvania openly acknowledged the importance of this example: "Indians know the striking benefits of confederation; they have an example of it in the union of the Six Nations" (Adams II: 1159).

It would therefore be incorrect to suggest that the American constitution was entirely a product of European federal political thought and practice. But it is equally clear, both from their writings and from their public and private statements, that the Founders were deeply engaged with European theory and practice of federal unions. In 1776 this European tradition was quoted mainly uncritically in support of the American desire to form a union. A decade later, the European tradition served as a contrast with the new constitution drawn up in Philadelphia.

—

For the delegates of the Continental Congress who gathered in the summer of 1776 to discuss the next steps after the adoption of the Declaration of Independence, the easiest issue to settle was about what kind of union was to be formed. The consensus position was that, of the various options, the one most suited to American circumstances was the federal one. It was confirmed, for example, in the remarks by the New Jersey delegate John Witherspoon, a Scottish immigrant who served as president of the College of New Jersey (later called Princeton). In an intervention about the new Articles of Confederation he dismissed the example of the Scottish-English Acts of Union of 1707 as "an incorporating union, not a federal one" (Adams II: 1169). There had never been any serious proposal for the formation of a union of the thirteen colonies other than of a federal nature. Earlier schemes, like the 1697 plan by William Penn or the 1754 one by Benjamin Franklin,

---

2   The strongest evidence is this quote from a 1751 letter by Franklin: "It would be a very strange Thing, if Six Nations of ignorant Savages should be capable of forming a Scheme for such an Union, and be able to execute it in such a Manner, as that it has subsisted Ages, and appears indissoluble; and yet that a like Union should be impracticable for ten or a Dozen English Colonies, to whom it is more necessary, and must be more advantageous" (Benjamin Franklin to James Parker, postmaster of New York, 20 March 1751. Accessible at FOA). Note that Franklin uses the term "ignorant Savages" in an ironic sense, as is clear from a reading of his essay on native American affairs, *Remarks concerning the Savages of North-America*: "Savages we call them, because their manners differ from ours, which we think the perfection of civility; they think the same of theirs" (accessible at FOA).

were all based on the idea of a kind of federation, with a joint council and continued independent status for the individual states (though all equally subject to the British Crown).

If there was a debate about union, it was rather about whether to form one at all. There was some sentiment among the delegates to the Continental Congress that their union was merely a temporary one, and that it should be dissolved once the war was concluded. It was to counter that idea that Witherspoon rose to deliver a speech on 30 July 1776 (FOA). Stressing the "absolute necessity of union," he first attacked the idea of every state going it alone, arguing: "[W]e must, in the end, be subjected, the greatest part of us, to the power of one or more of the strongest or largest of the American states." He then proceeded to set out to make the case for a federal union.

Rather remarkably, he did it by referring to the example of the European Republic, "that enlarged system called the balance of power," which had transformed "the former disunited and hostile situation of kingdoms and states, to their present condition." By presenting this as a "step," he created the suggestion that the balance of power was actually a stage in a historical process which would eventually lead to "a state of more perfect and lasting union."

He then sketched a scenario where the American colonies followed the European example, creating a situation where "the states on one quarter of the globe [i.e., Europe and North America] may see it proper by some plan of union, to perpetuate security and peace." To show that it was possible for a group of states to build a lasting union, he also referred to the examples of "[t]he union of the seven provinces of the Low Countries," and "the Cantons of Switzerland."

Other delegates used European examples to argue for or against various technical aspects of the final settlement. Connecticut delegate Roger Sherman, for example, referred to the example of the "States of Holland" to justify his proposal for one vote per state (Adams, II: 1165). Stephen Hopkins of Delaware mentioned the "Germanic confederacy" and the "Helvetic confederacy" during a speech in support of the same idea (1168). Critical voices came chiefly from the Pennsylvania delegation which represented the large state perspective. They used the shortcomings of the Dutch United Provinces to show why one state, one vote would inevitably create gridlock. James Wilson observed that "the greatest imperfection in the constitution of the Belgic Confederacy is their voting by province" (Riker 501). Benjamin Rush added that the other weakness was the Dutch system of strict delegation: "[T]he members are obliged to consult their constituents upon all occasions" (Adams II: 1166). To counter the Dutch example, Rush pointed to the "confederation of Lycia," which Montesquieu had pronounced "the best that was ever made." There, "the cities had different weights in scale" (Adams II: 1167). On balance, the delegates of the Continental Congress mainly treated the European experience with federal union as an *exemplum virtutis*, worthy of emulation.

———

The first American federal union was formally established through the Articles of Confederation, drawn up in 1777 and ratified by 1781. In itself, that document had also created a more perfect Union, better at least than the first makeshift one created through the Declaration of Independence.[3] The Continental Congress that had drafted and signed the Declaration – the unilateral decision to "dissolve the political bands" connecting them with the British crown – had acted as a joint council of sorts, leading the united colonies through the early years of the war of independence.

That was by no means a small achievement. It took a remarkable amount of coordination to make "thirteen clocks strike together," as John Adams would later put it: moving as one on the key decisions of jointly declaring independence, setting out to create a Union of independent states, drafting constitutions for these states and for their common Union, and collectively establishing relations with the other powers of Europe (Hendrickson 124). But since this first Union had no constitutional standing whatsoever, its day-to-day decisions were mostly ignored by the individual colonies who remained "free and independent states" in every respect.

The Articles at least remedied this defect. They united the colonies in a pact for "their common defence, the security of their Liberties, and their mutual and general welfare, binding themselves to assist each other, against all force offered to, or attacks made upon them, or any of them" (Art. 3). The Union thus created, Article 13 solemnly declared, "shall be perpetual." Its title was lifted from the opening phrase of the Declaration of Independence: "The United States of America."

The joint drafting of these Articles was a political feat of the first order, but as a constitution-making exercise it was somewhat underwhelming. The final product of the deliberations of the Continental Congress was a document that was only the bare bones of a constitution. Still, it clearly had its merits. Colonies that had united in rebellion against the British Crown had found a way to continue acting together even while retaining full control

---

3   The Massachusetts senator Daniel Webster first formulated this idea of the Declaration of Independence creating a Union of sorts in a speech on 16 February 1833. See also Hendrickson 126.

over their own affairs. The latter was guaranteed through Article 2, which stated that "each state retains its sovereignty, freedom, and independence." On one important subject though, sovereignty had been pooled for a common purpose. Article 6 stated that the individual colonies no longer had the right to enter into treaties or alliances with foreign powers, or even establish diplomatic relations with them without the express permission of the other states. Nor were they allowed to enter into any kind of alliance with any other colonies without the permission of all of them. They were to operate jointly from now on, at least on the international stage.

A unicameral parliament and executive called Congress, in which the colonies were represented on an equal basis (one state, one vote), would meet to discuss common priorities and take joint decisions on a three-quarters majority basis. These common priorities were defined narrowly, in a list of enumerated powers set out in Article 9. The most important ones were the conduct of war and peace negotiations, the making of treaties with foreign powers, the offering of mediation in legal and border disputes between colonies, and the setting of common standards for coinage (though not for banknotes, which remained the preserve of the individual colonies). There was no court, so conflicts between states, or between states and the executive, would remain unresolved if Congressional mediation failed.

The Articles would quickly prove unequal to the challenges the newly created United States faced after the war with Great Britain was settled in the colonies' favour. Once the feeling set in that the job was done now that independence was won, Congress became increasingly irrelevant, often not even able to muster a quorum. Measures that it did manage to pass usually ended up being ignored by the states – inevitably so, since the Articles didn't contain any provision for making individual states respect collective decisions. Among the measures affected by this culture of neglect was the 1783 Peace Treaty with Great Britain. Several colonies chose to ignore its provisions – sufficient reason for the British government to hold onto its forts in the Ohio Valley that had been ceded to the United States.

—

From the moment they were finally ratified, it was clear the Articles caused as many problems as they were meant to solve. Perhaps no one grasped this earlier than the New York Congressman Alexander Hamilton (1755/1757–1804). Hamilton's personal story is too well known these days to require further introduction: born in poverty, he migrated to New York from the Caribbean island of St Croix as a teenager, and rose through the ranks of the Continental Army to become George Washington's aide de camp. His life – and the manner of his death – mark him out as one of the most remarkable characters of the American Founding, and indeed of the larger history of the concept of federal union. In this story, he managed to claim a unique place by being involved in both the most successful attempt to solve its problematics, and the most cogent theoretical defence of its characteristics.

As early as 1782, Hamilton had called for a Convention to "revise and amend the Confederation" ("Resolution of the New York Legislature calling for a Convention of the States to Revise and Amend the Articles of Confederation," 20 July 1782, FOA). A year later he drafted an extended motion to the same effect, this time also setting out the many defects that required amending ("Unsubmitted Resolution Calling for a Convention to Amend the Articles of Confederation," July 1783, FOA). The Articles, Hamilton argued in this second motion, had "confined the power of the Federal Government in too narrow a limit." It was guilty of "confounding legislative and executive powers in a single body." It was "in want of a Federal Judicature." It had vested in Congress the power of taxation, but had "rendered that power (...) nugatory, by withholding from them all control over either the imposition or the collection of the taxes for raising the sums required," and had authorised Congress to borrow money "without the power of establishing funds to secure the repayment of the money borrowed." Finally, and in the eyes of Hamilton as a military man, probably most worrying, it was guilty of "not making proper or competent provisions for interior or exterior defence."

More criticism of the Articles would emerge in the next few years. The Welsh Unitarian minister Richard Price (1723–1791) had won a reputation for himself in the American colonies for his decision to come out in support of the revolution, against his own government. His *Observations on the Nature of Civil Liberty, the Principles of Government, and the Justice and Policy of the War with America*, published in 1776, became an instant bestseller on both sides of the Atlantic, and led to him receiving an invitation from Congress to take up residence in the newly established United States. He declined the invitation, but through his writings he would maintain a connection with the former colonies.

In 1784 Price published *Observations on the Importance of the American Revolution and the Means of Rendering it a Benefit to the World*. In the section devoted to "the Means of promoting Human Improvement and Happiness in the United States" he identified what was in his view the most important challenge the states now faced: "It seems evident that what first requires the attention of the United States is the redemption of their debts" (Price

9). For this he suggested a solution used by the British government at the start of the century: "A sinking fund, guarded against misapplication, may soon extinguish them, and prove a resource in all events of the greatest importance" (12). In a subsequent section, titled "Of Peace, and the Means to Perpetuate It," he focused on what he considered the other main problem the American states were facing. The Articles of Confederation, he warned, had a fatal flaw: "No provision is made for enforcing the decisions of Congress; and this renders them inefficient and futile." "Without doubt," he concluded, "the powers of Congress must be enlarged" (14–16).

By 1786, a number of states had been won over to the reform cause. Delegates from Virginia, New York, Pennsylvania, New Jersey, and Delaware met in Annapolis (Maryland) to discuss the possibility of improving the Union. The lack of a quorum and the narrow focus of the meeting, which was only supposed to discuss the issue of commerce between the states, precluded it from proposing any major alterations to the Articles. The delegates did, however, use the opportunity to issue a joint call for a next convention, in Philadelphia, in the spring of 1787. That Convention, "with more enlarged powers," would be tasked with "taking into consideration the situation of the United States, to devise such further provisions as shall appear to them necessary to render the constitution of the Federal Government adequate to the exigencies of the Union." (quoted in *Federalist* 40)

The case for a more perfect union

The events of 1786 provided ample evidence for Hamilton's claim during the Annapolis Convention that "the situation of the United States [was] delicate and critical." A large-scale revolt against the state government's tax policy in Massachusetts – known as Shays' Rebellion – sent shockwaves through the other states. A series of skirmishes with native American tribes in the borderlands on the other side of the Appalachians threatened to plunge the Union into a new war it was unwilling to fight. Not least because it couldn't afford it: the Confederation was unable to repay its war debts, unable even to raise the import levies to finance the day-to-day running of the federal government. As the Massachusetts Congressman (and later New York senator) Rufus King explained in a letter to future American vice president Elbridge Gerry, the Union was facing almost certain bankruptcy, and the States were unwilling to do anything about it: "Resolves have been passed upon Resolves – and letter after letter has been sent to the deficient States, and all without the desired effect. We are without money or the prospect of it in the Federal Treasury; and the States, many of them, care so little about the Union, that they take no measures to keep a representation in Congress" (King to Gerry, 30 April 1786, FOA). The Union of the Articles of Confederation wasn't a state, but it had all the hallmarks of a failed one.

It was no surprise therefore, that the run-up to the Philadelphia Convention saw much speculation about the demise of the Union. Most of this speculation centred on the so-called Mississippi Navigation Crisis. It pitted North against South in a struggle for political and economic supremacy. The crisis started in early 1784, when Spain decided to enforce its rights to control the navigation on the Mississippi river by closing it to American trade. This posed a serious test for the United States. Negotiations between the American Secretary of State John Jay and Spanish chargé d'affaires Diego de Gardoqui eventually led to a provisional deal. A key element of the draft treaty was the acceptance of a twenty-five-year moratorium on American access to the Mississippi. In return for accepting the status quo on its Western border, the US would gain right of access for its merchant vessels to Spanish ports, both in Europe and in its West Indian colonies.

North and South were deeply divided over the outcome of the negotiations. Northern politicians, overwhelmingly concerned with Atlantic trade, had no problem with the faraway river being blocked. To them, the treaty merely acknowledged the status quo: the river was Spain's to do with as it pleased, the Union wouldn't be able to wrest control away from the Spanish even if it wanted to. In truth, many Northerners secretly welcomed the blockade. Refusing Western settlers access to the Mississippi and thereby cutting them off from markets further afield would inevitably decrease speculator and settler interest in Western lands, This would stop the North's own population from moving West, thereby securing Northern tax revenues and increasing the value of Northern land holdings. The deal would also offer compensation for the closure of the river in the form of increased access to Spanish markets, as well as lower tariffs – chiefly for goods in which the North held a near-monopoly. And by cutting off Southern access to the Mississippi, and therefore to the seaport of New Orleans, it would force Southern States to use the northern Atlantic ports to get their goods to the world markets. From a Northern perspective, the treaty was a win-win-win scenario. For those same reasons, the South fiercely opposed it. Its political class feared that the effects of ratifying it would be to "trade away the southern states' interests in unimpeded export of agriculture staples, western settlement and land speculation" (Merritt 118).

Virginia Congressman James Madison was in everything the opposite of Alexander Hamilton. Hamilton came from nothing; Madison's father was the richest landowner in the county. Hamilton was a man of action, who made his reputation as a soldier by leading the decisive bayonet charge at the Battle of Yorktown (the battle that effectively settled the outcome of the War of Independence). Madison was a scholar most at home in the quiet of his study. He was physically frail, and as understated as Hamilton was forceful. Though he showed no particular interest in it, Madison would probably have taken over his father's plantation, spending his free time reading and writing on general affairs, if he hadn't entered Virginian politics at a crucial time in the colony's history. His family's wealth and connections facilitated his election to Provincial Convention in the spring of 1776, at the very moment when it was to debate the issue of separation from England (Rakove, *James Madison* 11–12). Having found his calling, he would spend a lifetime participating in the political affairs of the newly founded United States. He would not retire from it until after his second term as president, in 1817.

By the mid-1780s, Madison's focus was fully on the Mississippi Navigation Crisis. He would dismiss the Jay–Gardoqui treaty as "a voluntary barter in time of profound peace of the rights of one part of the empire to the interests of another part" (Madison to Monroe, 21 June 1786, FOA). The crisis reached boiling point when, in a series of Congressional votes purely on regional lines, the Northern states imposed their will on the Southern states in a display of crude majoritarianism, even manipulating the voting rules by replacing the qualified three-quarters majority with a new simple majority one. In Madison's eyes, this was a clear attempt to establish "force as the measure of right." It confirmed his opinion that "[t]here is no maxim (...) which is more likely to be misapplied than the current one that the interest of the majority is the political standard of right and wrong" (Madison to Monroe, 5 October 1786, FOA).

At the height of the crisis, in August 1786, Virginia Congressman James Monroe wrote to his state's governor Patrick Henry to vent his frustration about the pursuit of naked self-interest by the Northern States. He thought their intentions were clear: "Break up the settlements on the western waters [the Mississippi], prevent any in future, and thereby keep the States southwards as they are now." The inevitable consequence, in his view, would be the breakup of the Union (Monroe to Henry, 12 August 1786, FOA). In a separate letter on the same subject to James Madison, Monroe went into the details of what a separation would look like, focusing his speculation on the state of Pennsylvania, even contemplating war to force it into a Southern Confederacy: "If a dismemberment takes place that State must not be added to the eastern scale. It were as well to use force to prevent it as to defend ourselves afterwards" (Monroe to Madison, 3 September 1786, FOA).

Madison, a cautious and studious character, wouldn't join in this kind of violent speculation, but he *was* worried about the effect the crisis could have on the chances of putting the Union on a more secure footing: "I am entirely convinced, from what I observe here, that unless the project of Congress can be reversed, the hopes of carrying this state into a proper federal system will be demolished" (Madison to Jefferson, 17 December 1786, FOA). The letter followed a unanimous vote by the Virginia legislature condemning the treaty with Spain that had caused the crisis as "a dishonorable violation of the basic principles of the Articles of Confederation" (Van Cleve, *We Have Not A Government* 595).

On the Northern side, sentiments were equally strong. Rufus King first started contemplating Northern secession by the end of 1785 (Van Cleve 578). His fellow Massachusetts Congressman Theodore Sedgewick also speculated about the possibility of life after the Union. In a letter to the later governor of Massachusetts Caleb Strong, he suggested that "it well becomes the eastern and middle states, who are in interest one, seriously to consider what advantages result to them from their connection with the Southern States. (...) Even the appearance of a union cannot in the way we now are long be preserved" (Sedgewick to Strong, 6 August 1786, FOA).

Beyond European federal examples

By early 1787 the appreciation of the Articles of Confederation had changed among America's political class, and with it also attitudes towards the European federal examples. This change in attitude would clearly manifest itself during the debates at the Philadelphia Convention and the subsequent state ratifying conventions. This is not to say that European federations were no longer used as positive examples; for instance, in *Federalist Paper* 14, the German and Polish examples were used to demonstrate that an extended republic could span a vast territory and yet maintain a functioning central Diet or congress. The overwhelming majority of references to European federal unions, however, served to warn of the shortcomings of traditional federal approaches.

The most often discussed example was that of the Dutch United Provinces, or "celebrated Belgic confederacy," as Madison mockingly called it in *Federalist Paper* 20 (Hamilton et al. 170). After that of Great Britain, the Dutch constitution was the single most referred to example in discussions in both Philadelphia and the state ratifying conventions (Riker 495). But whereas in 1776 it had been used mainly to discuss the merits and demerits of equal state representation, this time criticism of its record was much fiercer. Pennsylvania delegate James Wilson dismissed it as "held together not by any vital principle of energy but by the incumbent pressure of formidable neighbouring nations" (Madison 632). Madison saw the Dutch United Provinces as a typical example of "the tendency of the members to usurp on the [federal] authorities, and to bring confusion & ruin on the whole" (600).

In *Federalist* 20 he added to his critique in an extensive discussion of its main features. "The union," he stated, was "composed of seven coequal and sovereign states" (Hamilton et al. 169). At the federal level, "the sovereignty of the union" was "represented by the States-General" (169). Though it had certain powers, these were limited in two important ways: by the fact that all decisions required unanimity, and by the fact that in important cases not just the individual states but even the cities within them had a right of veto. The constitution, he concluded, had as its main characteristics "[i] mbicility in government, discord among the provinces" (170). It was, he continued, "long ago remarked by Grotius that nothing but the hatred of his countrymen to the House of Austria kept them from being ruined by the vices of their constitution" (170).

If the union did seem to function semi-competently, it was because the States-General were often "compelled to overleap their constitutional bounds" (171). This was not a praiseworthy quality though: "A weak constitution must necessarily terminate in dissolution for want of proper powers; or the usurpation of powers requisite for the public safety" (171). But for the periodic violent interventions by the Orange Stadtholders, "the cause of anarchy manifest in the confederacy would long ago have dissolved it" (171). A final, in Madison's view, fatal flaw was its inability to remedy its failings through a rewriting of its constitution. Several times attempts were made to do so, he claimed, and on all four occasions the reformers' "laudable zeal found it impossible to *unite the public councils* in reforming the known, the acknowledged, the fatal evils of the existing constitution" (172, emphasis in original). This inevitably led the United Provinces to "the crisis of their destiny" (172). By this he meant "popular convulsions," "dissensions among the states," and "the actual invasion of foreign arms" (172) – a clear reference to the Prussian invasion that had crushed the Dutch Patriot Revolt, and effectively ended Dutch sovereignty, just three months before the essay was written.

After the Dutch example, the ones most often discussed were those of the ancient Greek Amphictyonic and Achaean Councils and the Holy Roman Empire (generally referred to as "German Confederacy"). In his main speech at the Convention, Hamilton mentioned the Amphictyonic

Council as an example of a weak union whose internal divisions made it vulnerable to foreign interference: "Philip [of Macedon] at length taking advantage of their disunion, and insinuating himself into their councils, made himself master of their fortunes" (Madison 554). Madison repeated this charge, while extending it to the Achaean Council, who were targeted "first by Macedon, & afterwards by Rome" (603). When countering the argument by representatives from smaller states that their main concern was a coalition of the larger states dominating proceedings, he referred again to the Amphictyonic League, showing that its fatal weakness was the opposite: "The contentions, not the Coalitions of Sparta, Athens & Thebes, proved fatal to the smaller members of the Amphictyonic Confederacy" (728).

Madison would discuss the flaws of the Amphictyonic confederation at some length in *Federalist* 18. Here he concluded that internal dysfunction was linked to external vulnerability: "As a weak government when not at war is ever agitated by internal dissensions, so these never fail to bring on fresh calamities from abroad" (Hamilton et al. 161). The Achaean League seemed to possess fewer flaws. It had a relatively strong central executive, and single standards for laws, weights, and coinage. Madison regretted that relatively little was known about its functioning: "Could its interior structure and regular operation be ascertained, it is probable that more light would be thrown by it on the science of federal government than by any of the like experiments with which we are acquainted" (162).

Still, even the Achaean League was not without its flaws. Once the Macedonian kings fixed their gaze upon it, it too quickly fell to their machinations: "The arts of division were practised among the Achaeans; each city was seduced into a separate interest; the union was dissolved. Some of the cities fell under the tyranny of Macedonian garrisons, others under that of usurpers springing out of their own confusions" (Hamilton et al. 162–163). Clearly, its internal union wasn't strong enough to withstand external interventions. Through their shared fate, the Greek confederacies demonstrated what Hamilton in *Federalist* 15 had called the "eccentric tendency in the subordinate orbs, (...) a perpetual effort in each to fly off from the common centre" (150), what Madison in *Federalist* 18 described as "the tendency of federal bodies rather to anarchy among the members than to tyranny in the head" (164).

The Holy Roman Empire was mentioned no less than twenty times in the Convention. Most of these mentions were strongly critical. The Pennsylvania delegate Gouverneur Morris, sometimes referred to as the "Penman of the Constitution" for his role in styling the final text and drafting its preamble, saw in the German Confederacy an example of an important flaw shared by most historical examples of federal unions. It was the weakness of the centre, largely as a result of the desire of the states to hold onto their powers: "[T] here is no energy whatever in the General Government. Whence does this proceed? From the energy of the local authorities; from its being considered of more consequence to support the Prince of Hesse, than the Happiness of the people of Germany." In full rhetorical mode, he went on to ask: "Do Gentlemen wish this to be ye case here? Good God, Sir, is it possible they can so delude themselves?" (Madison 828).

In *Federalist* 19 Madison channelled the critique of Pufendorf's *The Present State of Germany*, which he didn't quote directly but certainly seemed to have read. We know that Madison was familiar with the book from the fact that he included it in his list of recommended works to be stocked by the first Library of Congress (Madison, "Report on Books for Congress," 23 January 1783, FOA). Referring to it as a "nerveless body" (Hamilton et al. 165), a "political monster" (166), and a "disjointed machine" (167), he summarised its main flaw as follows: "The fundamental principle on which it rests, that the Empire is a community of sovereigns, that the Diet is a representation of sovereigns, and that the laws are addressed to sovereigns, renders [it] (…) incapable of regulating its own members, insecure against external dangers, and agitated with unceasing fermentations in its own bowels" (165–166). If it did continue to exist as a union, it was mainly because of "[t]he weakness of most of the members, who are unwilling to expose themselves to the mercy of foreign powers" (167).

The harshest criticism was reserved for the Polish-Lithuanian and Swiss confederacies. Although, as observed in *Federalist* 14, Poland was mentioned as a positive example of an extended republic capable of maintaining a national Diet, in *Federalist* 19 Madison made it clear that to him its constitution seemed barely worth discussing, "[e]qually unfit for self-government and for self-defense" (Hamilton et al. 167). Most of the criticism during the Convention focused on its process for electing a new monarch. In summarising the arguments against an elected president, James Wilson observed that delegates had argued that the election of a new Polish monarch was "attended with the most dangerous commotions" (Madison 919–920). He dismissed this argument not because it was untrue but because it was irrelevant – the method of election in the United States would be an entirely different one. For Hamilton the main flaw of the Polish method of electing a new monarch wasn't its elective nature but the fact that the election was open to foreign princes, "with independent power, and ample means of raising commotion" (564). In *Federalist* 19 Madison would restate this argument, concluding that the weaknesses of the Polish constitution had left it "at the mercy of its powerful neighbors, who have lately had the mercy to disburden it of one third of its people and territories" (Hamilton et al. 168).

The Swiss Confederacy seemed unworthy even of criticism, so feeble was its constitution. As Hamilton observed during the Convention, "the Swiss cantons have scarce any union at all, and have been more than once at war with one another" (Madison 555). In *Federalist* 19, Madison expressed his agreement with this view: "The connection among the Swiss cantons scarcely amounts to a confederacy. (...) They have no common treasury; no common troops even in war; no common coin; no common judicatory; nor any other common mark of sovereignty" (Hamilton et al. 168). In *Federalist* 43 he went even further, claiming that the Swiss were "properly speaking (...) not under one government" (282).

Madison explained in *Federalist* 20 the relevance of these examples to their American audience. He made no apology for dwelling at length on European experiences with federal union: "Experience is the oracle of truth" (Hamilton et al. 172). It was essential to grasp the main lesson of these examples, namely "that a sovereignty over sovereigns, a government over governments, a legislation for communities, as contradistinguished from individuals, as it is a solecism in theory, so in practice it is subversive of the order and ends of civil polity" (172). The examples, derived from history and the present day – in 1787 the four European federal unions all still existed – showed that it was no accident that the first American federal experiment had failed. If the delegates of the Continental Congress in 1776 had studied these examples more closely, they would have seen that the kind of federation they were designing had never worked before and wouldn't work now. He therefore made "no apology for having dwelt so long on the contemplation of these federal precedents" (172).

The geopolitical context of the Philadelphia Convention

To understand the decisions made during the Philadelphia Convention, it is also important to look at the problems the states were facing collectively in 1787 – what we would nowadays call their geopolitical predicament.

The first thing to understand about this predicament is that the thirteen colonies feared themselves to be at very real risk of conflict with powerful neighbours. To the north lay British-controlled Canada, and to the south, Spanish Greater Florida, a territory that spanned modern-day Florida, Alabama, Mississippi, and Louisiana. In the nearby Caribbean, the French empire kept a foothold in the region. France and England controlled the high seas off the East Coast.

On the shores of the Mississippi River lay what remained of the settlements of New France, the French colony that until the end of the Seven Years' War in 1763 had included the lands between the river and the Appalachian mountain range. The American colonies laid claim to all the former French territories north of the Ohio River. The territory to the south of it, and north of Spanish Greater Florida, was granted as a reserve to the native American tribes. Their claim, based on the 1763 peace treaty between the British and the French, was however continually challenged by the southern colonies – and ignored by squatters and adventurers, who would start moving into the area almost as soon as the French pulled out. As John Adams had put it when contemplating the British presence in Canada, "It is not much to the honour of human nature, but the fact is certain that neighbouring nations are never friends in reality" (John Adams to Samuel Adams, 28 July 1778, FOA). In *Federalist* 3, John Jay would also warn of the risk created by the presence of European powers on their doorstep: "The bordering States (...) will be those who, under the impulse of sudden irritation (...) will be most likely, by direct violence, to excite war with these nations" (Hamilton et al. 96).

The borderlands posed the most immediate problem for the Founders. The Indian Confederacy that had chosen to fight on the side of the British during the War of Independence had been betrayed by their former ally at the negotiating table in Paris (1783). Instead of respecting their territorial sovereignty, as originally promised, the British negotiators granted colonial Americans sovereignty over the entire territory. This set up a first challenge: how to make the native American tribes accept the Union's claim to their lands? In the meantime, there was the militarily no less significant challenge of making the British give up their fortifications north of the Ohio River.

Finally, there was the question of how to control the ceaseless flow of speculators and settlers across the Appalachians, to prevent the growth of a lawless hinterland. Where no claim to state sovereignty was settled, the territories could even serve as a source of conflict between states. In 1784 one such conflict actually turned violent, when the Pennsylvanian government sent troops to force Connecticut squatters off land occupied in the Wyoming valley. Named the Third Yankee–Pennamite War, it would continue as low-level guerilla warfare well into the 1790s, when Pennsylvania was finally given sovereignty over the valley.

The challenge, in short, was to turn borderlands of an uncertain status into recognised and well-regulated border territories (Onuf xviii) – and ultimately, into *states*. Because what was clear from the moment the Union confirmed its independence in the Paris Peace Treaty, was that the newly won territories would have to end up as states in the Union. The Treaty had created the unique phenomenon of colonies-with-colonies: (former) colonies themselves laying claim to colonial territory beyond their borders. It was an unnatural situation, one that would have to end with the territories joining as new states. The challenge was to get North and South to agree to a regime for extending the United States that would be acceptable to both sides.

—

There were two main geopolitical issues that were of direct relevance to discussions on this topic. One was the Mississippi Navigation Crisis. The decision to cede control of the Mississippi to Spain did not only divide the colonies to the point of provoking talk on both sides of a dissolution of the union; it also had a direct impact on the territories west of the Appalachians. Settlers under attack from native American tribes who were fighting to retain control of their lands had already been left without protection from the states or Congress. To this injury was now added the insult of Congress seemingly abandoning the Mississippi to Spain, effectively cutting the territories off from access to the eastern seaboard – and the rest of the world.

Instead of linking East and West in an increasingly prosperous Union, there was a very real possibility of Europeanisation – several rival empires emerging on the same continent, vying for land and people, destined for war to settle their many border disputes. George Washington had identified this danger early on, writing to Virginia governor Benjamin Harrison that "The Western settlers (...) stand as it were upon a pivot – the touch of a feather, would turn them any way" (Washington to Harrison, 10 October 1784, FOA).

By 1787, the territories seemed to be pivoting away from the Union. The Kentucky-based general James Wilkinson made a trip to New Orleans to obtain both military protection and tariff-free access to the Mississippi for his territory in return for swearing allegiance to the Spanish crown (Merritt 119). The North Carolina Congressman James White would write soon after to Gardoqui that the territories were ready to secede and submit to Spanish rule. The territories' traders and adventurers were only too happy to swear allegiance to the Spanish king in return for getting access to the lucrative market towns along the Mississippi. Among them was a young lawyer who would later come back to the area as an American general: Andrew Jackson (Remini 9).

The fact that Western territories sought protection from the Spanish crown against native American attacks was somewhat ironic, given that it was the Spanish government that had encouraged the native American attacks in the first place. In an attempt to destabilise the territories, it had supplied the tribes with arms and ammunition. This strategic objective of dividing the American republic on its borders was most likely also why Spain insisted on banning Western commercial shipping from the Mississippi river. Keeping the river closed forced the territories to seek individual terms with the Spanish colonial government in New Orleans.

—

While Congress remained gridlocked on the Jay–Gardoqui Treaty, it had a second problem on its plate in the form of the territories north of the Ohio River. The Mississippi Navigation Crisis had made clear that their management offered a significant challenge to the young republic. But if they were a source of considerable problems, they clearly also offered opportunity, predominantly through vast commercial potential. Overcoming classical republican distrust of affluence, American writers predicted great bounties from the development of the agricultural possibilities of the territories. They waxed lyrical about their potential, describing them as "the garden of the world," "the seat of wealth," and "the parent of our manufactures" (Onuf 8–10).

The commercial potential of the territories didn't just start a foot race among settlers and speculators, it also triggered a competition among the colonies to establish the best infrastructure connections between themselves and the new settlements. Pennsylvania had the natural advantage of being connected to the West through the Ohio River. In New York plans were formed for an ambitious canal-building scheme that would connect the Hudson river to the eastern shore of Lake Erie. Meanwhile, in Virginia, Jefferson and Washington were involved in the setting up of the Patowmack Company. Its aim was the creation of a corridor for the Potomac river through the Allegheny mountains to connect the territories west of them, and ultimately the Ohio River, to Virginia's eastern seaboard. Though in the end the scheme would come to nothing, initial expectations for its economic potential were limitless. As Jefferson put it, "nature has declared in favor of the Patowmac and through that channel offers to pour into our lap the whole commerce of the Western world" (Onuf 11).

To the Union, the territories were an important source of potential revenues. When in 1784 the individual colonies ceded their claims to parts of it to the collective, Congress decided to use the sale of lands there to settle its war debts. Its ultimate ambition was to sell so much land that it would be able to finance its entire budget without having to hope for a breakthrough on the interminably gridlocked discussions on the confederation's ability to impose tariffs on incoming goods. Needless to say, the native American tribes who lived in these territories were not consulted on these plans. They would subsequently make their views known in diplomatic meetings between representatives of the various tribes on the one hand and Congress or state governments on the other, and less formally through violent attacks on the squatters who had invaded their lands.

But if the West offered prospects of great wealth, it also offered serious challenges. In the East, the fear was mainly that the promise of the West would prove to be a drain on its (human) resources, ultimately destabilising the Union, even endangering its continued existence. If its people headed West in too large numbers, it would leave the states' own economies dangerously underdeveloped. As Madison put it in a letter to Jefferson, a great migration could lead to the collapse of Eastern land prices. If that happened, the net effect of opening the West could ultimately be the "delay of that maritime strength which must be their only safety in times of war" (Madison to Jefferson, 20 August 1784, FOA).

Then again, too few settlers would also be problematic. If land sales were to provide a reliable source of income for the United States, it would need a steady stream of settlers to make the trek over the Appalachians to stop land prices there from falling. For that, more than anything it needed credible territorial governments able to offer protection of property claims and settle any boundary disputes. In the meantime, it also needed to offer the territories that had already been settled clarity on their prospects for statehood. But none of that would matter if the states couldn't settle a much more important question: did they actually want to form a Union?

A leap in the dark

It was clear that the Union in its current form worked neither in practice nor in theory. And it wasn't going to last much longer, in spite of its claim to eternal life. When they contemplated the purpose of the meeting in Philadelphia, the delegates therefore effectively faced a binary choice: either let the existing Union wither on the vine, or do what was required to form a more perfect one. Uncritically echoing European ideas and practices was no longer an option.

The option of continuing as independent states, or as a collection of smaller confederacies, was a constant theme in the early stages of discussions at the Convention. The Maryland delegate Luther Martin, for example, said he would "rather see partial confederacies take place than the plan on the table," and anyway, "in case a dissolution of the Union should take place, the smallest states would have nothing to fear from it" (Larson and

Winship 179). Massachusetts delegate Nathaniel Gorham also spoke about the "rupture of Union" theme by suggesting that though "[it] would be an unhappy event for all" it seemed plausible to him that "the large states would be least unable to care of themselves" (190–191).

A post-Union future of separate states or a number of confederacies coexisting peacefully had a theoretical foundation in the idea of peace through commerce. This idea, propagated by Scottish Enlightenment thinkers like David Hume and Adam Smith and embraced by European Republic theoreticians like Voltaire/Frederick and Vattel, was confirmed in Montesquieu's maxim that "[t]he natural effect of trade is to lead to peace. Two nations that trade with each other become reciprocally dependent. (...) All unions are founded on mutual needs" (Montesquieu 338). With trade links between the states already established, wouldn't peaceful coexistence be guaranteed – with or without a formal Union?

It was this theory that the proponents of a new Constitution set out to discredit first. James Madison implored "the gentlemen representing the small states" to "ponder well the consequences of suffering the confederacy to go to pieces. The same causes which have rendered the Old World the theatre of incessant wars and have banished liberty from the face of it would soon produce the same effect here." Madison tapped into the classical republican anxiety about the dictatorial potential of standing armies by suggesting that once the Union was broken up, either in separate states or various confederacies, these new nations "would quickly introduce some regular military force against sudden danger from their powerful neighbors. The example would be followed by others, and would soon become universal. The means of defense against foreign danger have been always the instruments of tyranny at home" (Larson and Winship 192–193).

Hamilton would revisit the argument in the *Federalist Papers*, where he would specifically focus on the "peace through commerce" thesis. He started out, in *Federalist* 6, by showing that republics were no less likely to engage in warfare than monarchies. There were, he observed, many historical examples of "dissensions, domestic factions and convulsions" that had caused republics to go to war: "Have republics in practice been less addicted to war than monarchies? Are not the former administered by men as well as the latter? Are there not aversions, predilections, rivalships, and desires of unjust acquisitions, that affect nations as well as kings?" (Hamilton et al. 106).

To this argument he then added another, namely the "jealousy of trade" theory that commerce offered no more of a guarantee for peace than a republican constitution:

Has commerce hitherto done anything more than change the object of war? (...) Have there not been as many wars founded upon commercial motives since that has become the prevailing system of nations, as were before occasioned by the cupidity of territory or dominion? Has not the spirit of commerce, in many instances, administered new incentives to the appetite, both for the one and for the other?
(Hamilton et al. 106)

In conclusion, neither their republican character nor the trade between them would offer the individual states any protection against the likelihood of war.

What Hamilton feared most, however, was not these internal divisions but the external intervention by Europe's main powers. As he explained in *Federalist* 7, this was no academic scenario. The independent colonies were hemmed in on all sides by the European great powers. With the states set against each other, it would be only too easy for their European neighbours to exploit these divisions: "By the destructive contentions of the parts into which she was divided, [she] would be likely to become a prey to the artifices and machinations of powers equally the enemies of them all" (Hamilton et al. 113).

—

In spite of continued speculation about possible alternatives, none of the delegates actually dared to argue in favour of breaking up the Union. The decision in favour of continuation of the Union was unanimous. What was less easy, however, was to define what the alternative of "perfecting" the Union was supposed to mean. As much as they wanted to create a more efficient executive within the existing federal structures and introduce measures to guarantee the smoother cooperation between the states, history offered no examples of federal unions that had managed to do this. If they really wanted a more perfect Union, they would have to come up with an entirely new constitutional mechanism.

The first puzzle: sharing sovereignty

Of the many challenges the delegates faced, by far the most complicated was the one that governed the relationship between the states and the new government to be created. Political theory and historical examples as known to them offered only two options: either the states would remain fully sovereign in a federal union, or they would surrender their sovereignty to a new, incorporating union. There was no third option, no possible compromise between the two. This constitutional principle, known to the participants as the impossibility of *imperia in imperio* ("a state within a state"), was a significant obstacle to any attempt to strengthen the Union. It had been introduced during a previous debate in the American colonies about the divisibility of sovereignty, in the decade before the Revolution. Of the authors writing about the subject at the time, John Joachim Zubly in his 1769 *Enquiry* came closest to an acknowledgement of the potential divisibility of sovereignty by suggesting about the various colonial parts of the empire that "the nature and degree of [their] dependence [upon Parliament] is not exactly alike," thereby introducing the idea of degrees and divisions of sovereignty (Bailyn, *Ideological Origins* 217–219). In the early 1770s the colonial leadership would, for a while, cling to this idea of a "line" separating the sovereignty of Parliament from that of the colonies, though without any ideological conviction. The British Parliament in turn continually stressed the indivisibility of sovereignty, and thereby its supremacy, through the *imperia in imperio* argument. This would eventually force the American colonists to conclude that only complete independence would suffice to protect their own claims to sovereignty.

   This, then, would be the first challenge for the reformers: to find a third way where theory offered none. As James Madison put it in a letter to Virginia governor Edmund Randolph, on the eve of the Convention:

> I hold it for a fundamental point that an individual independence of the States, is utterly irreconcilable with the idea of an aggregate sovereignty. I think at the same time that a consolidation of the States into one simple republic is not less unattainable than it would be inexpedient. Let it be tried then whether any middle ground can be taken...
> (Madison to Randolph, 8 April 1787, FOA)

—

During the Convention, the side that wanted to keep things broadly as they were, would march under the flag of federalism. To its supporters, federalism was merely another word for state sovereignty. The federal camp had a significant number of supporters at the Convention. Most were not in a mood to compromise. The New Jersey delegate William Paterson observed that "we are met here as the deputies of thirteen independent, sovereign states for federal purposes. (...) We have no power to go beyond the federal scheme" (Larson and Winship 114–115). Similarly, John Lansing of New York declared that his state "would never have concurred in sending deputies to the Convention if she had supposed the deliberations were to turn on a consolidation of the states and a national government" (130).

The other side saw the traditional states-focused interpretation of the concept of "sovereignty" as too limiting. In their view, the existing Congress, and the Articles of Confederation on which it was based, had already shown that a purely federal order couldn't work. The new Constitution was to serve as the birth certificate of a new *nation*, with its own governmental structures and its own claim to sovereignty, next to (and perhaps even superior to) that of the States. The question was, though, how to define this position. There were no historical examples they could turn to. And since they were unaware of the discussion about sovereignty in late seventeenth-century Germany (apart from Pufendorf's orthodox positions on its indivisibility), theory, such as they possessed it, wasn't much help either. How to go about claiming an option they didn't know how to define?

The answer was: by first creating rhetorical space for it, and then figuring out if they could somehow come up with a practical description and justification. The opening move came from one of the most eloquent (and radical) spokesmen for this position at the Convention: Alexander Hamilton. In a remarkable intervention, peppered with references to European federal experiences, Hamilton argued that the new constitution should basically not leave any room for the states at all. The central issue was that the States were "an overmatch for the General Government (...) render[ing] any confederacy, in its very nature precarious" (Madison 554). This would have to change radically if the union was to survive,

He started his argument by dismissing the option of continuing the present Confederation, suggesting that its failure mirrored the fatal flaws of previous European federal unions. In short order he dismissed the Amphictyonic Council ("disunion"), the Holy Roman Empire ("weakness"), the Swiss Cantons ("scarce any union at all"), and the Polish-Lithuanian Commonwealth (its method of election of the monarch gave foreign powers "ample means of raising commotion") (Madison 554–564). He went on to dismiss both the plans that were then on the table and made the case instead for an incorporating union, which would merge all the states and thereby create a new national union. What he proposed was nothing less than "a complete sovereignty in the general government. (...) The general power, whatever be its form, must swallow up the state powers. Otherwise it will be swallowed up by them" (Larson and Winship 143–144).

In the early 1820s, James Madison would write about negotiating tactics at the Convention, admitting that "in the course of discussions, where so much depended on compromise, the patrons of different opinions, often set out on negotiating grounds more remote from each other, than the real opinions of either were, from the point at which they finally met" (Madison to John Jackson, 28 December 1821, FOA). It is entirely possible that this was one such occasion. Hamilton's intervention may have seemed somewhat unusual to a neutral observer ("Brilliant, courageous, and, in retrospect, completely daft," is how one biographer described it; Chernow 650), but *strategically* the speech made perfect sense. Knowing full well that his contemporaries believed that, as he put it, "two sovereignties cannot coexist within the same limits," Hamilton may have decided to use this law to his advantage by spelling out to the state sovereignty supporters what the ultimate consequence would be of their continued unwillingness to compromise, through the use of a crude but effective syllogism. If the states were unable to survive without the Union, and the Union couldn't survive as a loose collection of sovereign states, then unless some kind of alternative solution was found, logically the only remaining option was the merging of the states into a single sovereign body.[4]

To make such a naked claim for a new, national government's right to take sovereignty away from the states was obviously a risky manoeuvre. After all, this very same idea was what had caused the colonial revolt against British rule – a fact of which the hero of the battle of Yorktown surely needed no reminding (Wood 528).[5] Still, if the national camp was to get anywhere with its plan of strengthening the Union, this was a debate it had to have. Unless its supporters managed to persuade the other side to accept that the new Constitution required a compromise over sovereignty, their project was destined to fall at the first hurdle.

Introducing a second absolute position had an important advantage: it created the logical space for such a compromise to appear. As Madison would summarise the situation after Hamilton's speech: "[T]he two extremes

4   The *imperia in imperio* argument would become the main line of attack by the Anti-Federalists during the ratification process. Wood gives an overview of their use of it in his *The Creation of the American Republic* (527–529).

5   Though the spark that lit the flame of the American Revolution is generally thought to have been the Boston Tea Party, a protest against the taxes imposed by the Townshend Acts, it was the Declaratory Act of 1766 that was the actual cause. Through this Act, the British Parliament had asserted *total sovereignty* over the American colonies, giving it a legal basis to introduce taxation there. See also Rakove, *Original Meanings* 715.

before us are a perfect separation & perfect incorporation, of the 13 states"
(Madison 730). If delegates didn't like either extreme, then they had no option
but to look for a third option, somewhere in between. The rest of the debate
would therefore take place within this space, between the two absolutes of
state sovereignty and national sovereignty. Or as the delegates themselves
came to call them: the *federal* and the *national* principle.

In the opening month of the convention, the national camp worked
diligently to win support for a shared sovereignty concept. Against the
federal assertion that "the separation from Great Britain placed the thirteen
states in a state of nature towards each other," delegates like Rufus King
claimed that the states were never fully sovereign to begin with: "They did
not possess the peculiar features of sovereignty; they could not make war,
nor peace, nor alliances, nor treaties" (Larson and Winship 155). James Wilson
went even further, stating that since independence had been a collective
decision by the states, not an act by individual states, their sovereignty could
also only be secured collectively, not individually: "They were independent
not individually, but unitedly" (156). In other words: though the states were
sovereign, they were never *individually* sovereign, and they had needed each
other from the start for the execution of the crucial federative power that
guaranteed their collective security.

The debate became increasingly heated. The day after Hamilton's intervention, Maryland delegate Luther Martin flatly stated that since "our
accession to the Union has been by states" he would "give it every opposition
(...) if any other principle is adopted by this convention" (Yates 151). But as is
often the case in negotiations, heat is a by-product of the kind of pressure
that eventually leads to a breakthrough. Though not spelled out in the
minutes, it is clear that some kind of discussion took place outside of the
Convention chamber. Whatever it was that was discussed there, it helped
to settle the issue. The day after his strident remarks, Martin confessed that
"I made use, on a former occasion, of expressions perhaps rather harsh."
He hadn't changed his position on where those powers came from (i.e., the
states, not the people), but he did accept that a stronger federal executive
was necessary: "I confess when the confederation was made, Congress should
have been invested with more extensive powers." The time had come, he
concluded, "that we can constitutionally grant them not only new powers,
but to modify their government, so that the State governments are not
endangered" (Yates 155–156).

In return for this concession, the national camp didn't object to the reference to "a national government," which had been adopted via a motion on the
first day of the Convention, getting replaced by "the government of the United

States." It seemed a retrograde step, but they clearly felt they had achieved their objective of staking a claim to at least partial sovereignty for a national government – whatever its name. A week later, Connecticut delegate Oliver Ellsworth's statement that the Union would be "partly national, partly federal" summarised the new consensus position (Larson and Winship 182). Though they never quite got round to explaining how this idea of shared sovereignty could be theoretically justified, most delegates seemed happy enough simply to accept it as a practical solution and move on to other problems.

—

In the Great Compromise that was subsequently negotiated, both the federal and the national idea would end up being included. States and the national government could both claim some form of sovereignty. The national government's sovereignty may have been of a limited nature (literally: its powers were enumerated), but the important thing was that the delegates had accepted that sovereignty could in fact be shared. It was the later Supreme Court Justice James Wilson who, during the Pennsylvania state ratification convention, provided the theoretical foundation for the new doctrine. He founded it in the concept of popular sovereignty, which had also served as one of the justifications for the revolution of 1776. For Wilson, it was in *the people,* and *only* in the people, that sovereignty resided. And since the people were the source and owners of sovereignty, it was also up to them to dispense as they saw fit: "They can delegate it in such proportions, to such bodies, on such terms, and under such limitations, as they think proper. (...) They can distribute one portion of power to the more contracted circle called State governments, they can also give another proportion to the government of the United States" (Wood 530–531).

Making this justification work had required a sleight of hand by the Founders. Strictly speaking there was no "American people" that could perform such acts of delegation – there were only "the People of the different states" mentioned in Article 4 of the Articles of Confederation (FOA). The original draft of the Preamble of the new Constitution recognised this fact by referring to the people of the thirteen individual states in geographical order, from North to South. It was only at the very end of the Convention, during the meeting of the Committee of Style and Arrangement that was tasked with producing the final draft, that the individual states were written out and the United States were written in, separating "We the People" from their native states. It would take an act of political transubstantiation to complete the process: the people of the different states, by ratifying the

Constitution each in their own states, somehow became a single people capable of delegating part of their sovereignty to the newly created government of an equally new nation.[6]

In *Federalist* 39, Madison would describe the final outcome of the negotiations as,

> in strictness, neither a national nor a federal Constitution, but a composition of both. In its foundation it is federal, not national; in the sources from which the ordinary powers of the government are drawn, it is partly federal and partly national; in the operation of these powers, it is national, not federal; in the extent of them, again, it is federal, not national; and, finally, in the authoritative mode of introducing amendments, it is neither wholly federal nor wholly national
> (Hamilton et al. 259)

This may in part have been a rhetorical exercise, aimed to confuse Anti-Federalist opponents who kept stressing the impossibility of *imperia in imperio*.[7] But it was also an honest assessment of the mixed nature of the concept of sovereignty underpinning the Constitution.

The second puzzle: representation

Having agreed that a compromise between the federal and the national idea on the core issue of sovereignty could work in theory, the next challenge was to show that such a compromise could also work in practice. This required the delegates to move onto another politically sensitive issue, namely that of representation.

The supporters of the national idea needed the new constitution to be based on the sovereignty of the people rather than on that of the states. It was the only way they could justify the national idea which formed the basis

---

6   It was no coincidence that this crucial change was introduced through the Committee of Style and Arrangement. Three of the five members were ardent nationalists: Hamilton, Madison, and Morris. It was Morris who suggested replacing the enumeration of the thirteen states with "of the United States." See Treanor, "The Framers' Intent" at *SCOTUSblog*.

7   Note the irony of the national camp appropriating the popular term "Federalist" for the Constitution they were going to defend, while labelling the defenders of what in the Convention had still been known as the federal position with the unpopular moniker *Anti-Federalists*. It's a reminder that, although we now see the process of writing and ratifying the Constitution as a kind of philosophical debate, to the men involved in it, it was first and foremost a political battle.

of their proposal for a stronger executive. It was also tactically important because without a direct appeal to the people, they ran the risk of having to submit the text for ratification to the states' legislatures instead – the very institutions whose power they wanted to curtail. Still, a national government based on an appeal to popular sovereignty was not without its problematic aspects.

One was what Hamilton called "the imprudence of democracy" (Larson and Winship 152).[8] This idea of the capricious nature of the people, its tendency to be led by emotions rather than by reason, was as old as Aristotle. In his *Politics*, he had listed democracy among the degenerate regime forms, saying that its main flaw was that it "[didn't] have the common good of all" in view (Aristotle 62). Democracy, in other words, wasn't just characterised by emotional or irrational decision-making, it was also likely to lead to the pursuit of selfish interests by the people. It needed a check to save the whole framework from becoming unbalanced.

Unfortunately for the Founders, their second problem was that the classical solution to the first problem, a mixed regime, wasn't available to them. The American colonies had neither an aristocracy nor a monarchy to throw into the constitutional mix. If they wanted a balanced constitution, they would either have to introduce American versions of aristocracy and monarchy, or come up with an entirely new concept on which to base their claims for a balance in their constitutional order.

———

Their eventual solution owed an intellectual debt to Montesquieu. In the late 1770s, his idea of the three constitutional powers balanced against each other through a system of reciprocal checks would form the basis for the state constitutions drafted by the American colonies. All would be based on clearly separated powers for legislative, executive, and judiciary. Most states would split the legislative into two separate chambers, copying the British example of the Houses of Commons and Lords. The idea was that in a republic, the legislature was the most powerful of the three institutions and would therefore have to be divided against itself to create an extra

8   At the end of the Convention, the Massachusetts delegate Elbridge Gerry stated the draft constitution would cause an even deeper division in his home state between "two parties, one devoted to democracy, the worst of all political evils, the one as violent in the opposite extreme" (quoted in Broadwater 205). The fact that he refused to sign it suggests that it was probably too democratic for his liking.

internal safeguard. All would also provide for some checks of every power on the others (Madison gave an overview of the most important examples per state in *Federalist* 47).

What was fundamentally different, though, was that these constitutions were drafted not for mixed regimes but for *republics*, with the sovereignty of all three branches of government derived fully from the people. By taking the idea of the three powers and separating them from their original regime forms, they recreated the idea of a balanced constitution *within* a republican regime. As Madison would put it in *Federalist* 14, while discussing "the great principle of representation": "If Europe has the merit of discovering this great mechanical power in government, by the simple agency of which the will of the largest political body may be concentred, and its force directed to any object which the public good requires, America can claim the merit of making the discovery the basis of unmixed (...) republics" (Hamilton et al. 141–142).

America's states were *unmixed* regimes, pure republics, who nevertheless incorporated the best elements of aristocracy and monarchy in their constitutional arrangements – their *powers*. Though there were discussions in the various state constitutional conventions about the need for an aristocracy of some description to make the upper chambers work, the debate would focus chiefly on ways of reproducing the *qualities* of an aristocracy in their membership rather than on the possibility of introducing an actual aristocracy in America. For the latter idea, there was virtually no support.

—

The mechanism for linking the various powers of government to the people, thereby rooting it in popular sovereignty, was that of representation. There was some disagreement about the optimal form this mechanism should take. Some argued in favour of mirroring: the representative assembly as a virtual likeness of the people it represented. John Adams for example thought that it "should be in miniature an exact portrait of the people at large. It should think, feel, reason and act like them" (Adams IV: 586). Others preferred a refining version of representation, with the delegates representing only the best qualities of their electorate. The two weren't necessarily incompatible: just before he set out his theory of representation as a mirror of the community, Adams stressed that "the first necessary step" in representation was to "depute power from the many to a few of the most good and wise" (585). The main thing, he observed, was that the *interests* of the people should be fairly represented: "It should be an equal representation, or, in other words, equal interests among the people should have equal interests in [the assembly]" (586).

What all sides certainly agreed on was that popular elections were the preferred way of establishing the link between the people and their representatives. In the legislature, that is, and usually only in the *democratic* chamber of the legislature. The idea of letting all people directly select all three branches of government, or even both chambers of the legislature, would risk unbalancing the constitutional framework by making the democratic element too powerful. To protect it from popular influence, the upper house or senate was usually elected indirectly. In most states, the members of the upper house would in turn cast a vote for the election of the governor, whose mandate was therefore twice removed from direct election. However indirect the representation may have been, though, in all states all three branches of government ultimately derived their authority from the people.

—

The same ideas would be discussed in Philadelphia. The debate in the Convention about separation of powers contained frequent references to the problems of pure democracy and the old regime theory solution. Even when they fundamentally disagreed about its place in the wider constitutional framework, both a supporter of the federal idea (like Maryland delegate John Dickinson) and an advocate of the national idea (like Pennsylvania delegate Gouverneur Morris) shared a tendency to speak about the upper chamber in aristocratic terms. Dickinson stressed that he "wished the Senate to consist of the most distinguished characters, distinguished for their rank in life and their weight of property, and bearing as strong a likeness to the House of Lords as possible" (Larson and Winship 104). Morris, in turn, when asking "what qualities are necessary" for this chamber, answered: "The [upper chamber] must have great personal property; it must have the aristocratic spirit. (...) The aristocratic body should be as independent and as firm as the democratic" (214–215). Like the state conventions ten years earlier, the Philadelphia delegates weren't looking for literal aristocracy and monarchy to add a sense of balance to their constitution. What they had in mind was an incorporation of the essential qualities of these regime forms – a *representation* of them, if you like – into the relevant branches of the new republican government.

Literal monarchy was seen as something to be avoided. Opponents of the idea of a presidential executive even used it as a straw man with which to burn down the idea of a president as a unitary executive. Edmund Randolph, who at the start of the Convention had introduced the idea of an executive council, saw in a unitary executive "a fetus of monarchy" (Larson and Winship 62). George Mason, the Virginia delegate who, like Randolph, would refuse to sign the final draft of the Constitution and ended up campaigning against its ratification, warned that "we are not constituting a British government, but a more dangerous monarchy, an elective one" (71), Against that, a supporter of the idea of a presidency like James Wilson argued that instead of threatening the sovereignty of the people, a presidential executive would help to protect it: "Unity in the executive instead of being the fetus of monarchy would be the best safeguard against tyranny" (63). Alexander Hamilton, a strong supporter of the idea of a unitary executive (and especially of George Washington as president), said he thought the attacks on it as a kind of monarchy in waiting were overblown: "Pray, what is a monarchy? May not the governors of the respective states be considered in that light?" (155).

—

Later democratic reform movements in other parts of the world would focus chiefly on the practical aspects of the conception of representation developed by the Founders. One element was the significantly wider franchise which was linked mainly to a qualifying age. Obviously, it still left whole sections of the population unrepresented – black men wouldn't get the vote for another seventy-five years; women, black or white, had to wait until 1919. Compared to the English system however, which allowed each district to set its own random criteria for qualification for the franchise, the American system was seen as a model of fairness and transparency.

Another widely admired characteristic was the creation of electoral districts of roughly equal numbers of voters. This avoided the problems of the British concept of *virtual* representation, with its so-called Rotten Boroughs (electoral districts with few, if any voters) and the complete exclusion of whole cities from Parliamentary representation. To guarantee that all districts would represent roughly the same number of voters, a mechanism was devised through which their size could be periodically readjusted to account for population changes.

Surprisingly enough, the Convention spent relatively little time on these organisational details of representation. An entirely different aspect of representation cropped up fairly early in the debate: the question whether representation should be based on *the people*, as the national camp suggested, or on *the states*, as the federal camp claimed. This debate, about *proportional* versus *equal* representation, would occupy delegates for most of the Convention. It would nearly derail proceedings, before the delegates would finally emerge with a compromise in the form of a hybrid concept of representation that matched the hybrid concept of sovereignty they had developed earlier. This hybrid concept of representation in turn would serve as the basis for a completely new, hybrid mixed regime form.

A Constitution takes shape

Delegates' positions on the issue of representation tended to be aligned with their positions on the sovereignty question. Those who favoured the national government option tended to back the proposal introduced by the Virginia delegation at the start of the Convention. The problem with the Confederation Congress as they saw it was that it was completely beholden to the States, and that this was blocking more vigorous action by the Congress as a national executive. A proportional formula for representation, linking the legislature directly to the people, was required to help break the stranglehold of the states on Congress.

The arguments against the Articles of Confederation, as set out by Virginia governor Edmund Randolph on the opening day of the Convention, were by now well-rehearsed:

> That the confederation produced no security against foreign invasion; (...) that the federal government could not check the quarrels between states nor a rebellion in any; (...) that the federal government could not defend itself against the encroachments from the states; that it was not even paramount to the state constitutions ratified, as it was, in the many states. (Larson and Winship 45–46)

To remedy these obvious shortcomings, his state's delegation had drawn up a list of resolutions that together would become known as the Virginia Plan. It constituted a radical break with the old Articles of Confederation. Where the 1777 document dealt mainly in negatives, the Virginia Plan was full of affirmatives. It claimed for example that it *was* possible for a federation to have a strong and active central government – and for this government to represent a joint *nation*, rather than the individual states.

By introducing the idea of proportional representation, attributing seats in both chambers of the legislature to states based on the size of their population, the Plan aimed to do justice to the larger states while also treating the smaller states fairly. Somewhat opportunistically, the concerns of the smaller states about possible dominance by the larger states were brushed aside with references to the Acts of Union of 1707. Benjamin Franklin observed that "[w]hen the Union was proposed of the two Kingdoms (...) the Scotch Patriots were full of fears, that unless they had an equal number of Representatives in Parliament, they should be ruined by the superiority of the English. (...) And yet to this day I do not recollect that any thing has been done in the Parliament of Great Britain to the prejudice of Scotland" (Madison 491). Similarly, Rufus King stated that "[w]hen that Union was in agitation, the same language of apprehension which has been heard from the smaller States, was in the mouths of the Scottish patriots. The articles however have not been violated and the Scotch have found an increase of prosperity & happiness" (776). In a letter to Jefferson, Madison predicted that the idea of proportional representation would get broad support in the Convention:

> This change is (...) just. I think also it will be practicable. A majority of the States conceive that they will be gainers by it. It is recommended to the Eastern States by the actual superiority of their populousness, and to the Southern by their expected superiority. And if a majority of the larger States concur, the fewer and smaller States must finally bend to them. (Madison to Jefferson, 19 March 1787, FOA)

Though the first chamber should be elected by "the people of the several States," and therefore beholden to them, the scales between national and federal could be evened out by giving this chamber a veto on all state laws which contravened the new constitution. On the whole, the Virginia Plan clearly favoured the national government over the states: it gave the legislature not just a negative on all state law, but also the right to "legislate in all cases to which the separate States are incompetent." Even more ambitiously, it gave the executive fairly open-ended "general authority to execute the national laws." If adopted, the Virginia Plan would not exactly have created a balanced constitution. Then again, this was only the opening move in what were likely to be protracted negotiations. The States camp was bound to counter with proposals of its own.

—

The counterproposal would eventually come from the New Jersey delegation, and was presented by future New Jersey governor and Supreme Court Justice William Paterson. It contained a few ideas that could help strengthen the existing confederation, like the creation of an independent executive with authority to "appoint all federal officers not otherwise provided for," the introduction of a federal judiciary, and most importantly, a supremacy clause: "All acts of the United States in Congress (...) and all treaties made and ratified under the authority of the United States, shall be the supreme law of the respective States" (Larson and Winship 551). But on the whole, it mainly read like a continuation of the Articles of Confederation. This showed most obviously in what was not in it: any language on reform of the legislature. By using the title created for it in the Articles of Confederation, "the United States in Congress," the plan confirmed the New Jersey delegation's commitment to the maintenance of a unicameral legislature, on an *equal* representation basis – one state, one vote. With that, the question was put: would delegates opt for proportional representation to link the legislative power directly to the people, or the old equal representation idea, which would effectively link it to the states?

By the time the New Jersey delegation tabled its proposal, there had already been some concrete steps taken towards the construction of a republican mixed regime similar to the ones in the state constitutions. The Convention had accepted the idea of a national government consisting of three branches. The delegates had settled provisionally on the idea of a unitary executive. They also agreed that this executive figure should have a conditional rather than an absolute negative over legislative proposals – a veto that could be overridden by a two-thirds majority of both houses. There was a clear majority for establishment of a federal judiciary based on lifetime appointments by the Senate. The same Senate also gained the "discretion" to establish lower federal courts.

Though sometimes treated as an afterthought in analyses of the constitutional negotiations, the introduction of a supreme court was one of the main priorities of the national camp. As Hamilton warned in *Federalist* 22:

> Laws are a dead letter without courts to expound and define their true meaning and operation. The treaties of the United States, to have any force at all, must be considered as part of the law of the land. (...) To produce uniformity in these determinations, they ought to be submitted, in the last resort, to one supreme tribunal. And this tribunal ought to be instituted under the same authority which forms the treaties themselves. (Hamilton et al. 182)

Without a federal Supreme Court, it would be impossible to sustain a federal body of laws: "If there is in each State a court of final jurisdiction, there may be as many different final determinations on the same point as there are courts" (Hamilton et al. 182). The lack of a Supreme Court was in his view "a circumstance which crowns the defects of the Confederation." Without it, it was "continually at the mercy of the prejudices, the passions, and the interests of every member of which it is composed" (183).

A Supreme Court wasn't just important for the development of clear and unambiguous jurisprudence about the interpretation of the Constitution. Through its rulings, the Court would also act as a guardian of the constitutional order. This meant that it could strike down acts of Congress or the Executive where they overstepped constitutional boundaries. As Hamilton explained in *Federalist* 78, in doing so, the court confirmed that the rule of law, not the rule of men, was the cornerstone of the constitutional order: "To deny this would be to affirm that the deputy is greater than his principal; that the servant is above his master; that the representatives of the people are superior to the people themselves; that men acting by virtue of powers may do not only what their powers do not authorize, but what they forbid" (Hamilton et al. 438).

To make sure it was able to produce such rulings, it was essential that the Court was set up as fully independent from the other two powers. Judges were appointed for life (the only qualification being that they held their posts "on good behavior"). Their pay was fixed without interference from Congress. The Court was also set up to be independent from the state supreme courts. Citizens had direct access to the federal courts and could ask for rulings not just on legal principles but on matters of substance. State supreme courts could not rule on matters of federal law, or indeed on where to draw the boundary between the competencies of state and federal courts.

To safeguard the Court's position, it was necessary to fix the status of the Constitution as inviolable. The key to this was the supremacy clause (Art. 6, par. 2). The wording here – "[t]his Constitution, and the Laws of the United States which shall be made in Pursuance thereof; and all Treaties made, or which shall be made, under the Authority of the United States, shall be the supreme Law of the Land" – was generally interpreted to mean that federal law came before state law. But the wording also fixed the order in which they were to be held. The Constitution came before the laws of the land and all treaties. In cases of conflict between these three, the Constitution came first – a supremacy clause within a supremacy clause. As Hamilton put it in *Federalist* 78: "A constitution is in fact, and must be regarded by the judges as, a fundamental law. (...) [T]he Constitution ought to be preferred to the statute, the intention of the people to the intention of their agents" (Hamilton et al. 439). This did not mean that the judiciary was superior to the legislative power. It merely meant that "the power of the people is superior to both" (439).

The Constitution was the ultimate guarantee that the new federal Union was to be an empire of laws, and not of men. Hamilton would explain this in his third letter published under the pseudonym Tully, in the summer of 1794:

> Government supposes controul. It is the Power by which individuals in society are kept from doing injury to each other and are bro't to co-operate to a common end. The instruments by which it must act are either the Authority of the Laws or Force. If the first be destroyed, the last must be substituted; and where this becomes the ordinary instrument of government there is an end to liberty.
> (Hamilton, "Tully No. III," 28 August 1794, FOA)

To make sure this didn't happen, he suggested that "the most sacred duty and the greatest source of security in a Republic" would be "[a]n inviolable respect for the Constitution and Laws" – the rule of law as embodied in the Constitution (Hamilton, "Tully III," FOA).

Having dealt with the executive and the judiciary, the debate then moved on to the legislature. Here there was early agreement on two issues: that the national legislature would consist of two houses, and that members of the first house would be elected by the people. When the debate turned to the second chamber, things ground to a halt.

—

The Virginia Plan had proposed to have members of the first house select those of the second. Against this, the Delaware delegate John Dickinson proposed that they should instead be chosen by the state legislatures, since "the preservation of the states in a certain degree of agency is indispensable" (Larson and Winship 109). Having made so much progress on the basic structure of the new constitution, the national camp suddenly faced the prospect of seeing the states re-establish themselves through the second chamber. The initial consensus seemed to be for establishing proportional representation as the electoral system for both houses, But the narrowness of the majority against equal representation and in favour of proportional representation as electoral system for the upper house (six to five in both cases) revealed the extent of the division.

It was at this moment that the New Jersey delegation tabled its own Plan. At first glance, it might seem somewhat strange that the plan proposed a unicameral legislature when the entire debate of the previous weeks had been based on a solid consensus that the new national government would have a bicameral system. After all, a resolution to establish that "the national legislature ought to consist of two branches" had been adopted unanimously, without any debate, two weeks earlier (Yates 104). Were the New Jersey delegates really looking to undo all the work of the first month for the sake of "an equal vote" for their state, as one of their opponents claimed (Larson and Winship 136)?

A more likely explanation is that it was a tactical move. In the debate about the bicameral system, two fronts had opened up: equal versus proportional on representation and federal versus national on the electoral system. By collapsing these two debates into one, the supporters of the federal approach could place themselves on the side of the smaller states who were trying to defend their equal status – after all, they stood to lose most by the abolition of the old unicameral system. This tactical manoeuvre in turn would allow them to build a majority for their own priority. The *real* New Jersey plan wasn't to continue the old unicameral legislature but to secure state representation in the upper chamber (Rakove, *Original Meanings* 233–234).

The introduction of the New Jersey Plan was followed by weeks of wrangling. It culminated in a motion by Connecticut delegate Oliver Ellsworth to introduce equal representation in the upper chamber. The vote on that motion resulted in a tie, but that was effectively a win for the state representation camp – by stopping the proportional representation side from getting a majority, they had created an opening for different solutions (Rakove, *Original Meanings* 235). Connecticut delegate Roger Sherman seized the opportunity: "We are now at a full stop, and nobody (…) meant that we should break up without doing something. A committee he thought most likely to hit on some expedient" (Larson and Winship 213). Madison, who had clearly miscalculated in his pre-Convention assessment that "the smaller states must surely bend" on the issue of proportional representation, launched an immediate protest against the idea ("He had rarely seen any other effect than delay from such committees in Congress") but the momentum for his side's proposal was gone (Larson and Winship 223). The Convention voted nine to two for establishing a committee to investigate if a way could be found to break the deadlock.

It was this committee that would later be credited with preparing a deal on representation. It is far from clear, though, if there was any immediate link between its recommendations and the final outcome. In a way, it didn't do much more than describe the current state of play in the gridlocked negotiations. It suggested basing the selection of delegates for the first house on proportional representation of the population, and that for the second chamber on equal representation of the states. To sugar the bitter pill somewhat for the national camp, it included the suggestion that the right to initiate appropriations bills should be granted exclusively to the first house. As one committee member put it, the idea was to give "the immediate representatives of the people" the right of "giving away the people's money" (Larson and Winship 228).

The proposal was treated almost as an insult by Madison. He stated he "could not regard [it] as any concession on the side of the small states." As far as he was concerned, the report had merely stated the obvious, namely that the debate was at an impasse: "The Convention was reduced to the alternative of either departing from justice in order to conciliate the smaller states and the minority of the people of the United States or of displeasing these by justly gratifying the larger states and the majority of the people" (Larson and Winship 220). Though a fair reflection of the main positions on the issue of representation at that point, it no longer reflected the *mood* of the Convention. Positions might not have changed, but attitudes had. There had been a significant shift towards a desire for a deal that did justice to both sides. The emerging majority for this position wasn't rock solid yet, but its commitment to getting a deal was. One delegate remarked he would "bury his bones in this city rather than expose his country to the consequences of a dissolution of the Convention without anything being done" (Larson and Winship 223). The time for debate about first principles was over; it was time to explore options for compromise.

—

The route to a deal on representation would run through the West: the territories between the Appalachian Mountains and the Mississippi. The Northern delegates had a number of anxieties about the idea of Western statehood. One was the fact that in the short term these future states were likely to be poorer relations to their Eastern cousins. This meant that they would get all of the benefits of membership of the Union without any of the costs – those would fall squarely on the richer members in the East. The Western states were also more exposed to native tribes and the European powers on the Union's doorstep. That fact, combined with their culture of lawlessness, made it likely that they would plunge the Union into costly wars – costs that would again have to be met mainly by Eastern states. For this reason the Pennsylvania delegate Morris suggested that "the rule of representation ought to be so fixed as to secure to the Atlantic states a prevalence in the national councils" (Larson and Winship 224).

If the East was going to end up paying for the West, then at least it should be offered compensation in the form of a permanent privileged position in the first chamber of the legislature. That would also deal with the *real* Northern anxiety about the West, namely that, as one Southern delegate put it, "in time they would be both more numerous and more wealthy than their Atlantic brethren" (Larson and Winship 254). Western economic and political priorities were unlikely to overlap with those of the North, so there was a real danger of the North being structurally outvoted – in the future, at least.

Southern delegates didn't share these Northern anxieties, not least because the territories most likely to apply for statehood first had been settled from the South. The new states were therefore bound to share their agenda (Rakove, *Original Meanings* 257). Southern delegates tried shifting the debate away from future considerations to the here and now. What was required, as far as they were concerned, was an agreement on the formula for the distribution of seats between the states currently in the Union. An additional mechanism would then be required to calculate the fair distribution of seats in the future, where new states would be treated on equal terms with the old ones.

A new committee was asked to come up with a proposal to deal with both sets of demands. Its report contained two suggestions: to accommodate the North, it proposed scrapping the formula for representation (one member per 40,000 inhabitants) and replacing it with a fixed number of seats per state in a distribution that favoured Northern states. To deal with the future distribution of seats, it proposed using a process of periodic reallocation based on "the principles of wealth and number of inhabitants" – a formula taken to favour the South (Larson and Winship 234). When asked what was meant by these terms, one of the committee members answered: "The number of blacks and whites with some regard to supposed wealth" (235). This brought the debate about proportional representation to the point where it had always been headed: what to do with the enslaved people living in the Southern states – should they be included or excluded in any representation calculation?

In a first intervention on this subject, on 30 June (several weeks before the standoff came to a head), Madison had already hinted at what in his view was the fundamental problem of representation for which a solution had to be found:

The states were divided into different interests not by their difference of size but by other circumstances, the most material of which resulted partly from climate but principally from the effects of their having or not

having slaves. These two causes concurred in forming the great division of interests in the United States. It did not lie between the large and the small states, it lay between the northern and southern.
(Larson and Winship 205)

This fundamental division – of North and South, free and slave – would come to dominate the debate going forward. Here both sides would make their stand; here a solution would have to be found.

—

Perhaps surprising was that it was the Northern states who would object to including enslaved people in any count for representation purposes, and the South which insisted on their inclusion. Paterson (New Jersey) declared his state would never vote for a deal that included them because "he could regard them in no light but as property" (Larson and Winship 237). Against that, South Carolina delegate Pierce Butler insisted that "the labor of a slave in South Carolina was as productive and as valuable as that of a freeman in Massachusetts" (256).

Northerners treating enslaved people like property, and Southerners stressing their equality with free people for representation purposes – it seemed like the world turned upside down. But seen from a negotiating perspective, it was quite plausible. Both sides were fighting to secure their interests in the future House of Representatives. In that fight, any argument, no matter how obscene, would do if it helped stake out a maximalist position for their side's interests. With one side now demanding full inclusion of enslaved people for representation purposes, and the other demanding their full exclusion, the seasoned negotiators and consensus politicians among the delegates started seeing the contours of a possible deal.

It involved a formula first used five years earlier in negotiations about an amendment to the taxation clause in the Articles of Confederation. That amendment had suggested a shift in the basis of taxation, away from wealth towards population. The new tax base would be formed by "all inhabitants" in a state ("excluding indians not paying tax"). Southern states at first refused, insisting instead that the formula should be changed to all *free* inhabitants. The North then suggested counting enslaved people for three-quarters of free ones, the South answered with half. The standoff that followed was eventually resolved when Madison brokered a compromise at three-fifths. The amendment was never ratified, but the idea would now get a second chance during the Convention.

The North Carolina delegate Hugh Williamson would introduce it as a way of bringing the two sides together. His resolution focused on the future rather than the present aspect of the last committee report, linking the three-fifths rule to the census instead of to the immediate distribution of seats in the first chamber. His resolution was rejected six to four, but it had the desired effect of putting the eventual compromise on the table. It was now just a matter of finding the right wording for it.

For the South, that meant attaching the compromise formula to the current distribution of seats. The compromise had to be valid here and now, not just at some point in the future. It was the only way the Southern states could trust that the North would respect the South's "peculiar tradition." Virginia governor Randolph urged Northern delegates that "express security ought to be provided for including slaves in the ratio of representation. He lamented that such a species of property existed. But as it did exist, the holders of it would require this security" (Larson and Winship 261). If that wasn't sufficiently clear for some Northern delegates, Butler was happy to spell it out for them: "The security the southern states want is that their negroes may not be taken from them" (264–265).

For the North, the right wording was less about the nature of the compromise than about the avoidance of the word "slave" in the final text. And if at all possible, they also wanted a formula that didn't link representation directly to slavery. The solution they came up with was that instead of linking the three-fifths formula directly to representation, the latter would now be linked to taxation – which would, in turn, be based on the three-fifths rule. This may seem hypocritical, but from a Northern perspective it was essential that the practice of slavery was not given official constitutional recognition.

Linking the three-fifths rule to representation, even indirectly, would create an additional issue that needed settling inside the Convention: the question of the future of the importation of enslaved people. After all, if the South was allowed to continue importing them without any kind of limit on their numbers, that could potentially end up having a distortive effect on the distribution of seats in the first chamber. The standoff over this issue would pit Northern abolitionists against Southern perpetualists, some of whom threatened to leave the Union unless they got their way. Randolph (Virginia) sketched the dilemma: "By agreeing to the clause, it would revolt the Quakers, the Methodists, and many others in the states having no slaves. On the other hand, two states might be lost to the Union" (Larson and Winship 405). Another committee was formed to help break the impasse – by now a tried and tested formula. The eventual compromise came in the form of a proposal that would give both sides some of what they wanted: the trade would be abolished, just not for another twenty years.

The fierceness of the debate about the formula for proportional representation in the first chamber formed a noticeable contrast with the lack of interest among delegates in further debating the issue of the second chamber. One logical explanation for this is that the issue had become irrelevant now that the South had already obtained through other means the required additional guarantees that slavery would be protected under the new constitution. Everything else was of lesser importance. An alternative explanation is that so much energy had been spent on obtaining a compromise on proportional representation that another fight on the method of selection of delegates for the second chamber was considered too risky. A new standoff could see the compromise unravel; in which case the Convention would almost certainly end in failure. Whatever the reason, it was decided without further debate that the second chamber would become an indirectly elected senate, whose members would be nominated by the state assemblies on an equal representation basis, each state getting two representatives – a clear victory for the smaller states.

—

The constitutional structure presented in September 1787 formed a remarkable hybrid construction. It combined two different forms of representation – proportional in the first chamber, equal in the second – to form a legislature that partly represented the people, and partly the states. The (indirect) presence of the states in the constitutional framework also created a rather unusual mixed regime, based on four powers rather than the usual three. Powers were separated not just horizontally, between legislative, executive, and judiciary, but also vertically, between the new central authority and the states.

It was clearly not what Madison had in mind when he set out for Philadelphia in the early spring of that year. Still, he was happy to defend its merits, such as they were. In *Federalist* 51, he would praise the new Constitution's ability to combine the various institutions in an intricate web of countervailing powers as an essential characteristic of the new federal union:

> In the compound republic of America, the power surrendered by the people is first divided between two distinct governments, and then the portion allotted to each subdivided among distinct and separate departments. Hence a double security arises to the rights of the people.

> The different governments will control each other, at the same time that
> each will be controlled by itself.
> (Hamilton et al. 321)

There were checks and balances everywhere in this representative democratic constitution: the people and their government would hold each other
in check, as would the national government and the states. Within the
latter two, the individual departments would also form checks on each
other's powers.

If there hadn't been a ratification fight to win, Madison would surely have
pointed out that the system was unbalanced in at least one critical sense:
the national government lacked an effective check on the powers of the
states. His suggestion of an absolute negative for the national executive on
all proposed state legislation was rejected by his fellow delegates. Instead,
they opted for giving the Supreme Court the power of constitutional review
of state legislation. But as he observed in a letter to Jefferson shortly after the
Convention, "[i]t is more convenient to prevent the passage of a law than to
declare it void after it passed" (Madison to Jefferson, 24 October 1787, FOA).
It would prove much more difficult to undo the damage of a state law that
violated the rights of the people through the courts. (Bailyn, *To Begin the
World Anew* 122).

To make sure this system of mutual checks performed its functions
perfectly, a number of additional qualities were required – what Madison
called "auxiliary precautions." One of these he had already discussed in
Federalist 48. Separation of powers was important, but it was essential
that this principle wasn't applied in an absolute way. Checks and balances
also required giving each department some role in the execution of the
powers of the other departments: "Unless these departments be so far
connected and blended as to give each a constitutional control over the
others, the degree of separation which the maxim requires, as essential to
a free government, can never in practice be duly maintained" (Hamilton et
al. 308). These concrete checks would take the form of a role in appointment
of each other's officers, of a (qualified) negative on each other's actions, and
of participation in each other's proceedings. Separation of powers wasn't an
absolute notion; it merely meant that one person or group shouldn't control
more than one power *completely*.

The other important quality that would help to secure the stability of the
new constitutional framework was the size of the territory it was to cover.
By solving Machiavelli's problem of the supposed limit on expansion of a
federation, the American founders turned the existing logic of republican

thinking about the optimal size of government on its head. To understand that we have to turn to the third puzzle in the box – that of the extended republic.

The extended republic

The national government camp's argument in favour of an extended republic was far from convincing. It simply asserted that an extended republic *could* work but left unresolved the question of exactly what kind of balance between states and national government would be required to protect it against the twin dangers of tyranny (too much power concentrated in central government) or fragmentation (too much power concentrated in the states). During the ratification debates, Anti-Federalists didn't hesitate to point this out. The author publishing under the pseudonym Centinel stated boldly that "[i]t would not be difficult to prove, that anything short of despotism, could not bind so great a country under one government." Using an argument later made famous by the classical liberal economist Friedrich Hayek, he claimed that it would be impossible for a central government to "attend to the various local concerns and wants, of every particular district, as well as the peculiar governments, who are nearer the scene, and possessed of superior means of information" (First Centinel letter, 5 October 1787, FOA).

The Anti-Federalist author "Brutus" observed that in large territories under "despotic rule," standing armies were essential for enforcing the decisions of the executive. Since free republics didn't have this option ("A free republic will never keep a standing army to execute its laws"), they would have to rely on the voluntary cooperation of its citizens. Here, he claimed, the extended nature of the republic would inevitably work against it:

> The different parts of so extensive a country could not possibly be made acquainted with the conduct of their representatives, nor be informed of the reasons upon which measures were founded. The consequence will be, they will have no confidence in their legislature, suspect them of ambitious views, be jealous of every measure they adopt, and will not support the laws they pass.
> (First Brutus letter, 18 October 1787, FOA)

The knowledge problem here worked the other way: the central government was so remote, and its acts so lacking in transparency, that citizens in the various states would never be able to relate to them, and therefore would be unwilling to accept them.

The Constitution clearly needed a better argument in favour of its extended territorial ambitions than the one provided during the Convention. Madison would take up this challenge in what would eventually become the most famous of the *Federalist Papers*, number 10.

—

The tenth paper formed a pair with Hamilton's ninth. Both essays were devoted to the subject of domestic faction and presented the Union as a safeguard against its undermining effects on the republic. Hamilton used the ninth paper to introduce the theme. He embedded it in a section in which he listed the advancements the modern "science of politics" had achieved over the ancients (Hamilton et al. 119). Among these "wholly new discoveries" (119) he listed the development of concepts like separation of powers, legislative checks and balances, lifetime appointments for judges, and the use of elected representatives – not coincidentally all characteristics of the new Constitutional settlement. To these four he then added a fifth: "The enlargement of the orbit within which such systems are to revolve, either in the dimensions of a single state, or to the consolidation of several smaller states into one great confederacy" (119). In other words: the extended republic.

Hamilton would spend the rest of his essay discussing the standard anti-Federalist objection to this invention, Montesquieu's observations about "the necessity of a contracted territory for a republican government" (Hamilton et al. 119). In earlier essays he had shown that it was, in fact, smaller republics that suffered most from the defects their supporters had attributed to the Union. Here, he used a different approach. He opened by pointing out that the kind of republic Montesquieu had in mind was much smaller than most of the existing states: "Neither Virginia, Massachusetts, Pennsylvania, New York, North Carolina nor Georgia can by any means be compared with the models from which he reasoned and to which the terms of his description apply." Strictly applying Montesquieu's norm would mean "splitting ourselves into an infinity of little, jealous, clashing, tumultuous commonwealths" (120).

Having dispatched with the "small republic" argument, he then turned it on its head by claiming that what Montesquieu had argued was that bigger was better. In quoting from the section in *The Spirit of the Laws* dealing with the idea of a federal republic Hamilton contended that "so far are the suggestions of Montesquieu from standing in opposition to a general Union of the states that he explicitly treats of a Confederate Republic as the expedient for extending the sphere of popular government and reconciling the advantages of monarchy with those of republicanism" (Hamilton et al. 120).

—

After Hamilton had used the Anti-Federalists' own favourite source to clear a path for the idea of the extended republic as most effective in dealing with the problem of faction, Madison then proceeded in *Federalist* 10 to set out the positive case for it. He began by defining the concept under discussion: "By a faction I understand a number of citizens, whether amounting to a majority or minority of the whole, who are united and actuated by some common impulse of passion, or interest, adverse to the rights of other citizens, or to the permanent and aggregate interests of the community" (Hamilton et al. 123). These common impulses or interests "introduced into the public council" the "dangerous vice" of "instability, injustice and confusion (...) the mortal dangers under which popular governments have everywhere perished" (122).

He praised the Constitution for its "valuable improvements (...) on the popular models, both ancient and modern" (Hamilton et al. 123). But, he warned, "it would be an unwarrantable partiality to contend that they have as effectually obviated the danger [of factions]" (123). In other words: something more than the constitutional system of separation of powers and checks and balances would be required. Nothing in it was an effective bulwark against the destabilising effect of factions.

If the American republic was to survive, some kind of additional check was required. Madison suggested two possible routes: either prevent factions from arising in the first place or mitigate their effects once they arise. On the effectiveness of the former, he was not very optimistic. Preventing factions from arising was in his view "impracticable" (Hamilton et al. 123). One reason was psychological: the inseparable connection between reason and self-love, opinions, and passions. Another was the "diversity in the faculties of men" (124), the uneven distribution of talents and preferences across society. Both factors would inevitably drive people towards different factions. Different talents and preferences would in turn lead to an uneven distribution of property across society. These material differences, and the accompanying differences in "sentiments and views of the respective proprietors" made "a division of the society into different interests and factions" practically inevitable (124).

The other way of preventing factions from arising, tyranny, was not worth discussing: "It could not be a less folly to abolish liberty, which is essential to political life, because it nourishes faction than it would be to wish the annihilation of air, which is essential to animal life, because it imparts to fire its destructive agency" (123). Since, Madison concluded, "the causes of faction cannot be removed" (125), the search for an effective remedy would therefore have to focus on "the means of controlling its *effects*" (125).

This mediating of its effects could be achieved in two different but complementary ways. One was through the mechanism of representation. Madison was clearly unconvinced by the standard argument in favour of representation, namely that it would result in a better class of men governing on behalf of the less virtuous. "It may well happen," he observed, "that the public voice, pronounced by the representatives of the people, will be more consonant to the public good than if pronounced by the people themselves" (Hamilton et al. 126). It was equally possible though to have the opposite effect: "Men of factious temper, of local prejudices, or of sinister designs may, by intrigue, by corruption, or by other means, first obtain the suffrages and then betray the interests of the people" (126).

The main benefit of representation, he claimed, was not the quality of the representatives but the fact that it was uniquely suited to an extended republic. In *Federalist* 14, which dealt with the subject of the extended republic ("Objections to the Proposed Constitution from Extent of Territory Answered"), Madison stressed the importance of the representative rather than democratic character of the American republic: "In a democracy, the people meet and exercise the government in person; in a republic, they assemble and administer it by their representatives and agents" (Hamilton et al. 141). The different modes of participation in the political process had a direct impact on the territorial potential of both: "A democracy (...) will be confined to a small spot. A republic may be extended over a large region" (141).

Obviously, a republic, too, would have a natural limit, "that distance from the centre which will barely allow the representatives to meet as often as may be necessary, for the administration of public affairs" (Hamilton et al. 142). But, Madison stressed, even if the republic were to extend its reach to the shores of the Mississippi it would be "not a great deal larger than Germany, where a diet representing the whole empire is continually assembled" (142). Just as Saint-Pierre had done half a century earlier, he argued that new infrastructure projects would help to shorten travel times and therefore make distance a less relevant factor: "Roads will everywhere be shortened and kept in better order. (...) The communication between the Western and Atlantic districts will be rendered more and more easy by numerous canals" (143).[9]

Provided the required technological advances materialised, representation as an organising principle could provide the basis for seemingly limitless expansion of the Union. This expansion was obviously primarily a territorial concept. In *Federalist* 51, Madison stressed that "the practicable sphere may be carried to a very great extent by a judicious modification and mixture of the *federal principle*" (Hamilton et al. 322, emphasis in original). But it also had an organisational aspect. The effective use of representation in a federal Union would allow the thirteen founding states to "add to them such other States as may arise in their own bosoms, or in their neighborhoods" (Hamilton et al. 143; *Federalist* 14). This was no mere footnote – out of the territory of the original thirteen states, another four states would be added to the Union in the next seventy-five years (Vermont, Kentucky, Maine, and West Virginia).

Having convincingly shown that representation would help to facilitate territorial and organisational expansion, Madison still had to prove that this would help in the tackling of the problem of faction. He did so by returning to the argument Hamilton had made in *Federalist* 6 when discussing Montesquieu's maxim about liberty requiring a small republic to flourish. On the contrary, Hamilton had argued: the larger the Union, the more likely its chances of survival. Madison would expand on this by claiming that the larger the political unit was, the greater the likely number of factions would be, and the smaller therefore the chance that any one of them could become dominant. By "extend[ing] the sphere and tak[ing] in a greater variety of parties" you could make it possible to "take in a greater variety of (...) interests," making it "less probable that a majority of the whole will have a common motive to invade the rights of other citizens, or if such a motive exists, it will be more difficult for all who feel it to discover their own strength and to act in unison with each other" (Hamilton et al. 127). In other words, it is "the extent and proper structure of the Union" which provides "a republican remedy for the diseases most incident to republican government" (128).

———

9   Given this acknowledgement of the importance of investment in infrastructure to strengthen the Union, it is all the more remarkable that Madison's last act as president would be to veto an infrastructure spending bill that would have provided exactly that.

The standard interpretation of *Federalist* 10 is to see it as announcing the advent of (classical) liberalism[10] or pluralism,[11] or as a systematic treatment of the problematics of political parties in republican government, a kind of foreshadowing of George Washington's argument on this subject in his Farewell Address. There is, however, another way to read this essay, one that perhaps gets closer to what Madison was trying to achieve at the political level and is more in line with his statements during the Convention.

The meaning of the entire section on the importance of mediating the effects of factions becomes clearer when we remember that what Madison had in mind with the terms *faction* and *property* was strongly influenced by his typically Southern political preoccupations. As we had seen above, the word "property" was a loaded term. It obviously referred first and foremost to property in general. In that sense the passage reads like an echo of Harringtonian arguments about the importance of equality of property for the health of the republic.[12] But Madison also tended to use the word "property" in another, typically Southern sense. See for example *Federalist* 54, devoted to a defence of the three-fifths rule which indirectly linked slavery to representation in the legislature: "They [enslaved persons] partake of both these qualities: being considered by our law, in some respects, as persons, and in other respects as property" (Hamilton et al. 332).

As he had explained in his intervention in the Convention's debate about representation on 30 June, the fundamental distinction in American society was that between slave states and free states. It seems plausible that by "uneven distribution of property across society," he meant chiefly having or not having slaves; and by "factions," the Southern states who did versus the Northern states who didn't. Madison's quest for a remedy for "the violence of faction" was directly inspired by the standoff between Northern and Southern states during the Mississippi Navigation Crisis. The kind of tyranny of the majority he wanted to prevent was that of Northern states manipulating Congressional voting rules to push through a contentious treaty that directly undermined Southern interests.

Here it is also important to understand that, in the eyes of Madison and his contemporaries, this was not necessarily a moral standoff. True, the Founders overwhelmingly rejected the slave *trade*, which they sketched

10   See for example Harvey Mansfield, "The Republican Form of Government in The Federalist."
11   For the liberal pluralist interpretation of Madison's thinking, see Paul Bourke, "The Pluralist Reading of James Madison's Tenth."
12   For a discussion of the Harringtonian influence on Madison's tenth, see David Schultz, "The Locke Republican Debate and the Paradox of Property Rights in Early American Jurisprudence" (especially 167).

as dehumanising to enslaved persons and traders alike (though not so overwhelmingly that they weren't prepared to let it continue for another twenty years). In the context of the discussion at the Convention, slavery was treated predominantly as a political issue rather than a moral one. It explains why no one pointed out the inconsistency when the South Carolina slaveholder Charles Pinckney at one point during the convention waxed lyrical about equality being "the leading feature of the United States," while at another giving a principled defence of the institution of slavery: "If slavery be wrong, it is justified by the example of all the world" (Larson and Winship 396).[13]

Even those who did see slavery as a morally troubling issue weren't overly burdened by it. The general view among its opponents was that slavery, though a "curse of heaven" (Larson and Winship 340), was a temporary phenomenon which was bound to disappear because of continued European immigration. As the Connecticut delegate Oliver Ellsworth put it: "As population increases, poor laborers will be so plenty as to render slaves useless. Slavery in time will not be a speck in this country." His suggestion in the meantime to let the South be the South ("Let us not intermeddle") neatly summarised the Northern consensus position at the Convention (380–381). Slavery was bad, but not so bad that it should be allowed to become a stumbling block on the road to a vital constitutional settlement between North and South. This also explains why, towards the end of the negotiations, the Convention decided unanimously to approve a clause that would compel any state to return runaway slaves "to the person justly claiming their service or labor" (393). If the new Union wanted to facilitate free commerce and movement of people between the states, Southern slaveholders needed assurances that their "property" couldn't claim asylum in states that didn't recognise slavery.

The real difference between North and South as Madison (and his fellow Founders) saw it was not about slavery as a moral issue, but about the competing economic and political priorities that the combination of differences in climate and possession or non-possession of slaves would inevitably generate ("from the influence of these on the sentiments and views of the respective proprietors ensues a division of the society into different interests and parties", Hamilton et al p. 124). The Mississippi Navigation Crisis

---

13 Clearly racism was also a factor in this partial blindness, an inability to see the enslaved people as proper human beings. For a more extensive discussion about the role of racism in American politics in the period discussed in this book, see for example Van Cleve, *A Slaveholders Union*, 797–800.

had shown that if the Northern and Southern factions were drawn into a confrontation about their core interests, there was a danger of escalation, with the accompanying temptation for the larger faction to impose its will on the smaller one through majoritarian rule.

What an expanded Union would bring, he hoped, would be a diminishing of the tension between North and South through the introduction of additional regional factions, each with their own economic and political priorities: Northwestern and Southwestern ones, perhaps eventually even factions from Spanish Florida and (parts of) Canada. Republican liberty was to be preserved by the formation of an American *empire*, using representation to facilitate its expansion.

The Bill of Rights

The Convention wound up with the adoption of a document that pleased almost all participants. Among those who rejected the final compromise text was the Virginia delegate George Mason (1725–1792), who tabled a motion to organise a second convention which was to vote on amendments to the constitution produced by the first one (Broadwater 204). In a pamphlet drafted in the immediate aftermath of the Convention in September 1787, he set out his thoughts about the document adopted in Philadelphia. Among his objections were the position of the federal court, which was "so constructed and extended, as to absorb and destroy the judiciaries of the several States," and the fact that the President had no "Constitutional Council" so that his only advice would come from "minions and favourites" (Mason, *Objections to This Constitution of Government*, FOA). He also warned about the weakness of the House of Representatives ("the shadow only of representation"), and the overbearing power of the Senate. The latter, he feared, was so powerful that it would end up "destroy[ing] any balance in the government." If that happened, it would "enable them to accomplish what usurpations they please upon the rights and liberties of the people" (Mason, *Objections*, FOA). It was for that reason that Mason ended up championing what would become the focus of the ratification debates in the several states: the addition of a Bill of Rights to the text of the proposed Constitution.

The authors of the *Federalist Papers* were not convinced of the need for such a bill. In *Federalist* 84, Hamilton set out his objections. Apart from a practical one – that "the Constitution proposed by the Convention contains (…) a number of such provisions" (Hamilton et al. 473) – his concerns were mainly of a principled nature. Previous bills of rights, like the British one adopted in 1689, offered protections not against lawful government but against arbitrary abuses of power by nobles of their underlings, or by the king of his nobles. Since the new constitution created no king, and explicitly ruled out the creation of a nobility ("No Title of Nobility shall be granted by the United States," Art. 1, section 9, clause 8), there was no need for a similar bill. Additionally, as he observed, "the people surrender nothing" in adopting the new Constitution (475). Their rights remained unalienable. In fact, a Bill of Rights could even be "dangerous" (476), by creating the impression that, since exceptions to certain undesirable powers had to be granted through certain amendments, these powers themselves must somehow be assumed to be part of the original text. Why else charge the text "with the absurdity of providing against the abuse of an authority which was not given" (476)?

James Madison formulated his own objections in the immediate aftermath of the Convention, in an exchange of letters with Thomas Jefferson. Jefferson had started the debate in a letter to Madison by observing that, though he liked the general structure of the Constitution and some of the elements contained in it, he also had several concerns. Chief of these was "the omission of a bill of rights providing clearly & without the aid of sophisms for freedom of religion, freedom of the press, protection against standing armies, restriction against monopolies, the eternal & unremitting force of the habeas corpus laws, and trials by jury in all matters of fact triable by the laws of the land" (Jefferson to Madison, 20 December 1787, FOA). He was not persuaded by the argument made by James Wilson that "all is reserved in the case of the general government which is not given" – Hamilton's argument that since the general government had not been given powers to regulate these matters, there was no need for clauses defining limits to those powers. He dismissed this argument by pointing to the fact that the new Constitution seemed to have left out deliberately the clause in the second of the Articles of Confederation which stated that the States retained "every Power, Jurisdiction and right, which is not by this confederation expressly delegated to the United States, in Congress assembled." But even if such a clause had been included in the text, it would still be logical to add a Bill of Rights, since it was "what the people are entitled to against every government on earth, general or particular, & what no just government should refuse or rest on inference" (Jefferson to Madison, 20 December 1787, FOA). In a letter drafted in March 1789, Jefferson would add one more argument to it by pointing to "the legal check which it puts into the hands of the judiciary. This is a body, which if rendered independent, and kept strictly to their own department merits great confidence for their learning and integrity" (Jefferson to Madison, 15 March 1789, FOA).

Madison's own thoughts were presented in a letter drafted in October 1788. He started it by claiming that, though he liked the idea of a Bill of Rights in principle, "I have never thought the omission a material defect, nor been anxious to supply it even by subsequent amendment." He argued that "the rights in question are reserved by the manner in which the federal powers are granted," and that "the limited powers of the federal Government and the jealousy of the subordinate Governments, afford a security which has not existed in the case of the State Governments, and exists in no other." Beyond that, he also thought the experience with State bills of rights showed their limited usefulness: "Repeated violations of these parchment barriers have been committed by overbearing majorities in every State." If he did end up supporting them, it was because "it is anxiously desired by others" (Madison to Jefferson, 17 October 1788, FOA).

—

In the fight between supporters and opponents of the new Constitution, the set of amendments that ended up forming the Bill of Rights would perform a crucial role. It provided enough cover for enough doubters to make ratification possible. The ratification process was far from smooth, however. True, it took only nine months for the required nine out of thirteen states to ratify, thereby making the Constitution binding. But it was far from certain that the last four states, among them the crucial states of Virginia and New York, would ratify (this was in part why Hamilton decided to undertake the project of publishing the *Federalist Papers*). The last of the holdouts, Rhode Island, would not ratify until May 1790.

By that time, Congress had already started debating the inclusion in the new Constitution of a Bill of Rights, consisting of several amendments. The Bill in its final form included a number of what, by now, had become well-established rights like those of freedom of religion, of speech, of assembly, and of petitioning the government (First Amendment), and the right to a trial by jury, and due process (Sixth Amendment). Not all these rights retained their relevance in subsequent centuries: the right not to have soldiers quartered in their houses was clearly relevant to a population that had suffered from that practice during the War of Independence, which was still very much in the memory then, but much less so to subsequent generations of American citizens. The most innovative one was the Second Amendment, which observed that "the right of the people to keep and bear Arms, shall not be infringed." It was the product of a classical republican debate about the dangers of standing armies as tools of oppression in the hands of an all-powerful central government (usually a monarch), and the right of the people to protect themselves against that threat by bearing arms. The British Bill of Rights of 1689 had focused on the former aspect by stipulating that "the raising or keeping a standing army within the kingdom in time of peace, unless it be with consent of Parliament, is against law."[14] The American version focused on the latter by stressing the need for "a well-regulated Militia, being necessary to the security of a free State."

—

Strictly speaking a mechanism to protect the people against a government that was supposed to be of, by, and for the people seemed somewhat superfluous. But the Founders accepted that any government, once created, had the ability (perhaps even the tendency) to seek powers beyond those attributed to it. After its adoption, the Bill of Rights became another check in the wider system of checks and balances – a check against the Constitution as a whole, by prohibiting any form of encroachment by the system of government it created upon the rights of the citizens it was supposed to serve.

Bibliography

Adams, John. *The Works of John Adams*. E-book, Verlag Jürgen Beck, 4 vols. 2021

Aristotle. *The Politics*, edited by Stephen Everson, Cambridge University Press, 1988.

Articles of Confederation, 1777. United States National Archives, https://www.archives.gov/milestone-documents/articles-of-confederation. Accessed 6 March 2024.

Bailyn, Bernard. *The Ideological Origins of the American Revolution*. 1967. Belknap Press, 1992.

Bailyn, Bernard. *To Begin The World Anew: The Genius and Ambiguities of the American Founders*. Vintage, 2004.

Bourke, Paul. "The Pluralist Reading of James Madison's Tenth." *Perspectives in American History*, vol. 9, 1975, pp. 271–295.

Broadwater, Jeff. *George Mason, Forgotten Founder*. University of North Carolina Press, 2006.

Chernow, Ron. *Alexander Hamilton*. 2005. E-book, Bloomsbury Publishing, 2020.

14   The text of the English Bill of Rights of 1689 can be found at https://www.legislation.gov.uk/aep/WillandMarSess2/1/2/introduction. The full text of the American Constitution, including the adopted amendments, is available at https://uscode.house.gov/static/constitution.pdf.

Cleve, George William van. *A Slaveholders' Union: Slavery, Politics, and the Constitution in the Early American Republic*. University of Chicago Press, 2010.

Cleve, George William van. *We Have Not a Government: The Articles of Confederation and the Road to the Constitution*. University of Chicago Press, 2017.

Constitution of the United States of America. *US House of Representatives*, https://uscode.house.gov/static/constitution.pdf. Accessed 6 March 2024.

English Bill of Rights, 1689. Legislation.gov.uk, https://www.legislation.gov.uk/aep/WillandMarSess2/1/2/introduction. Accessed 6 March 2024.

Hamilton, Alexander, James Madison, and John Jay. 1787. *The Federalist Papers*. Penguin, 1987.

Hendrickson, David. *Peace Pact: The Lost World of the American Founding*. University Press of Kansas, 2003.

Larson, Edward, and Michael Winship. *The Constitutional Convention: A Narrative History From the Notes of James Madison*. E-book, The Modern Library, 2005.

Madison, James. *Works of James Madison*. E-book, The Perfect Library, 2015.

Mansfield, Harvey. "The Republican Form of Government in The Federalist." *The Cambridge Companion to The Federalist*, edited by Jack Rakove and Colleen A. Sheehan, Cambridge University Press, 2020, pp. 557–586.

Mason, George. *Objections to this Constitution of Government*. 1787.

Merritt, Eli. "Sectional Conflict and Secret Compromise: The Mississippi River Question and the United States Constitution." *The American Journal of Legal History*, vol. 35, no. 2, 1991, pp. 117–171.

Montesquieu, *The Spirit of the Laws*. 1748. Translated and edited by Anne M. Cohler, Basia Carolyn Miller, and Harold Samuel Stone, Cambridge University Press, 1989.

Onuf, Peter. *Statehood and Union: A History of the Northwest Ordinance*. University of Notre Dame Press, 2019.

Price, Richard. *Observations on the Importance of the American Revolution and the Means of Rendering it a Benefit to the World*. 1784.

Rakove, Jack. *James Madison and the Creation of the American Republic*. Pearson Longman, 2007.

Rakove, Jack. *Original Meanings: Politics and Ideas in the Making of the Constitution*. 1996. Vintage Books, 1997.

Remini, Robert V. "Andrew Jackson Takes an Oath of Allegiance to Spain." *Tennessee Historical Quarterly*, vol. 54, no. 1, 1995, pp. 2–15.

Riker, William H. "Dutch and American Federalism." *Journal of the History of Ideas*, vol. 18, no. 4, 1957, pp. 495–521.

Schultz, David. "The Locke Republican Debate and the Paradox of Property Rights in Early American Jurisprudence." *Western New England Law Review*, vol. 13, no. 2, 1991, pp. 155–187.

Treanor, William. "The Framers' Intent: Gouverneur Morris, the Committee of Style and the Creation of a Federalist Constitution." *SCOTUSblog*, 5 August 2019, https://www.scotusblog.com/2019/08/the-framers-intent-gouverneur-morris-the-committee-of-style-and-the-creation-of-the-federalist-constitution/. Accessed 6 March 2024.

United States National Archive, *Founders Online*, https://founders.archives.gov/. Accessed 6 March 2024.

Wood, Gordon. *The Creation of the American Republic, 1776–1787.* 1969. Omohundro Institute and University of North Carolina Press, 1998.

Yates, Robert. *Secret Proceedings and Debates of the Convention Assembled at Philadelphia.* 1839. Bibliolife, 2021.

5   The Necessity of Compromise

Abstract
If the new Constitution was to survive, its cohesion needed to be actively maintained. To that end, in the final Federalist essay Alexander Hamilton presented a tool in the form of the necessity of compromise, which combined raison d'état thinking with the diplomatic tool of compromise. Over the next seventy years, it would be used on a number of occasions to settle a major crisis (usually on the topic of slavery): the first Great Compromise of 1890, the Missouri Compromise of 1820, the compromise of 1832 that settled the Nullification Crisis, and the last Great Compromise of 1850. When, in 1856, the Supreme Court made further compromises impossible through its notorious Dred Scott ruling, civil war followed shortly after.

Keywords: Compromise, raison d'état, federal union, Missouri Compromise, nullification, Dred Scott

How to keep a union[1]

The new American constitution had managed to solve two of the three problematics of federation as defined by Machiavelli: the inefficiency of its decision-making process, and the limits of its potential expansion. The third challenge was the one of duration. They had succeeded in creating a more perfect federal union. The question was: could it survive?

—

The Convention clearly hadn't been the kind of Socratic meeting of philosopher-kings that history has made it out to be. In reality, it was a clash

---

[1]   The letters, speeches, and pamphlets quoted in this chapter can be found in the Founders Online archive of the US National Archive: https://founders.archives.gov/, referred to throughout as FOA.

Livestro, Joshua: *A More Perfect Union. Federal Union in Political Theory and Practice, 1500-1951.*
Amsterdam: Amsterdam University Press, 2024.
DOI: 10.5117/9789048563777_CH05

between different factions of hard-nosed negotiators who fought each other over every clause and subclause – often to a standstill, and on one occasion to the point where it seemed like the Convention might actually end in failure. Negotiations could only be saved by a compromise over what even at the time was already seen as a patently immoral practice: slavery.[2] The text they finally agreed showed the scars of these battles. Its institutional framework was so unusual, and the consensus underpinning it so fragile, that most delegates doubted it could be made to work. Whatever it was, it clearly wasn't "the most wonderful work ever struck off by the brain of man," as the late nineteenth-century British Prime Minister William Gladstone would later claim (Gladstone 185).

Still, the fact that delegates had managed to reach agreement at all was a political feat of the first order. And the new constitution did contain a number of wholly original political concepts and mechanisms. Now that they had a republic, however, they inevitably faced the challenge of securing its continued existence. This in turn required a new political doctrine, one that made it possible to protect the union internally as well as externally. To put it in Machiavellian terms, the focus now shifted to *mantenere lo stato* – maintaining the union.

Surviving fortune's caprices was obviously why the delegates had settled on a system of institutional checks and balances. But ultimately, they recognised, this challenge was so great that at times it could be beyond the ability of institutions. It required an additional safeguard in the form of a kind of practical ability by the people running them to steer a course between the various dangers that were likely to threaten the Union's existence. The Founders distinguished two tools here, both typically associated with raison d'état thinking, to guide them.

The first was the concept of experience, "the best of all tests" as Benjamin Franklin called it (Larson and Winship 76). In the course of the Convention debates, experience would regularly be invoked to recommend certain courses of action. According to delegates, experience "suggested" and "satisfied," "confirmed," "proved" and "ratified," "showed," "taught" and "guided."

2   Remarkably enough, the most famous works on the intellectual history of the American constitution completely ignore this aspect. Gordon Wood's seminal *The Creation of the American Republic 1776–1787* doesn't contain a single mention of the words "slave" or "slavery." Neither does J. G. A. Pocock's *The Machiavellian Moment* in his discussion of the American Founding. Bailyn's *The Ideological Origins of the American Revolution* does have a short section on the issue, but it focuses mainly on the political use of the term as a condition of *white* colonists in their relationship with the British Crown and Parliament: "Slavery as a political concept had a specific meaning which a later generation would lose" (233).

Decisions about the handling of fortune's slings and arrows ought therefore to be inspired by practical knowledge of what had worked – and more importantly, given the reason for their meeting, *hadn't* worked – in the past.

The other tool wasn't so much a source of knowledge as a kind of mentality – a prudential attitude or willingness to be guided by practical reasonableness. In classical moral schemes this virtue was called *phronesis*. It was the type of wisdom most associated with politics. In the final essay of the *Federalist Papers*, number 85, Hamilton stated that maintenance of the Union required above all else the mastering of the art of compromise through an understanding of the necessities of the situation: "The intrinsic difficulty of governing thirteen states at any rate, independent of calculations upon an ordinary degree of public spirit and integrity, will, in my opinion constantly impose on the national rulers the necessity of a spirit of accommodation to the reasonable expectations of their constituents" (Hamilton et al. 485–486).

—

The concept of necessity dominated the discussions and the writings of the Founders. Their realism meant they would always keep a watchful eye on the requirements of the situation.[3] Edmund Randolph had introduced the Virginia Plan by stressing "the necessity of preventing the fulfilment of the prophecies of the American downfall" (Larson and Winship 42). At the most difficult point in the discussion, when failure seemed a serious option and Benjamin Franklin suggested "imploring the assistance of Heaven" (192) through a daily prayer at the start of proceedings – which Hamilton is supposed to have dismissed by remarking that the delegates didn't need "foreign aid" (193) – Delaware delegate Gunning Bedford tried to bring his fellow delegates back to the realisation that "all agree in the necessity of a more efficient government" (216). In the end, it was the awareness of what they perceived to be the needs of the situation which forced Northern delegates like James Wilson to let considerations of "the necessity of compromise" overrule objections to including enslaved people in the formula for proportional representation (262).

The term *necessity* featured prominently in the *Federalist Papers* (more than a hundred times in its eighty-five essays). Obviously, a concept of such

---

3   Most Founders gained their knowledge of the works of Tacitus through the annotated translation by the radical Whig historian Thomas Gordon. On the influence of Tacitism on the Founders, see for example Soll, "J. G. A. Pocock's Atlantic Republicanism Thesis Revisited," and Colbourn, "Thomas Jefferson's Use of the Past."

potentially unlimited rhetorical force was open to abuse and mistakes, as Hamilton acknowledged in *Federalist* 35: "Necessity, especially in politics, often occasions false hopes, false reasonings, and a system of measures correspondingly erroneous" (Hamilton et al. 232). The authors were fully aware of this. There were moments where they were clearly using it merely as a rhetorical instrument, to win an argument rather than grasp at a fundamental truth. By stressing "the necessity of the Union" (Madison, *Federalist* 14; Hamilton et al. 140), and within it "the necessity of a government at least equally energetic with the one proposed" (Hamilton, *Federalist* 23; Hamilton et al. 184), the authors undoubtedly hoped to persuade critical readers of the need to back the Constitution under discussion.

However, the term served other, more profound purposes, too. It was initially used as a raison d'état concept with which the Founders analysed geostrategic questions. In *Federalist* 20, for example, Madison observed of the Dutch Republic that "the surrounding powers impose an absolute necessity of union" (171). Later, in *Federalist* 22, Hamilton sketched a situation in which, to decide on an issue of war and peace, "the necessity of our situation" was juxtaposed with "the ambitions of our allies" (181).

It wasn't just external threats that forced the Founders to make calculations of necessity. The internal situation could do so as well. Creating a supreme court was "necessary" because "the laws of the whole" would otherwise be in danger of "being contravened by the laws of the part" (Hamilton et al. 182). And as we saw in the passage quoted above, the entire section in Madison's *Federalist* 51 on "instruments of prudence" dealt with "the necessity of auxiliary precautions" (320).

To the Founders, necessity was both a rhetorical and an analytical tool. In the form of the "necessity of compromise," it would become the guiding political doctrine of the Union they had helped to create. It was an interesting invention, as hybrid as the constitutional principles developed during the Convention. Whereas the political concept of necessity as used by raison d'état thinkers was generally associated with forceful action beyond the limits of the law (*necessitas non habet legem*), the diplomatic concept of compromise pointed to the opposite. It suggested if anything a willingness to hold back and refrain from decisive action. The new concept "necessity of compromise" somehow sought to reconcile these two ideas. "Actively maintaining the union's cohesion" is perhaps the best way to describe its objective or as Benjamin Franklin put it: "Keeping the Republic."

—

Maintaining the union's cohesion, it turned out, was easier said than done. If the continued existence of the American Union in its first seventy years looks plausible to us from our twenty-first-century vantage point, it certainly didn't to politicians at the time. At every turn, there were rumours of a split or threats of secession. Obviously, in some cases these threats mainly served a rhetorical function, putting opponents in the uncomfortable position of accepting responsibility for a potential break-up – unless they were willing to give up their position and make the first move towards an inevitable compromise.

There may also have been cases where the threat was more a lamentation than a statement of intent – the realisation that this Union they had joined hadn't turned out quite the way they had hoped. For example, in early 1794, Southern interests were pushing hard for President Washington to introduce a tariff as retaliation for a British tariff on US goods (thereby effectively giving up his neutral stance in the conflict between France and Great Britain). At the height of the crisis, New York senator Rufus King approached his Virginia colleague John Taylor to tell him that, in his view, the situation showed that "it was utterly impossible for the union to continue":

> That the southern and eastern people thought quite differently. That the former cloged [sic] and counteracted every operation of government. That the eastern would never submit to their politicks. And that under these circumstances, a dissolution of the union by mutual consent, was preferable to a certainty of the same thing, in a less desirable mode.
> (Memorandum from John Taylor addressed to James Madison, 11 May 1794, FOA)

Taylor clearly took the threat seriously, hence his decision to tell his Virginia colleague, then Congressman James Madison, that he was "thoroughly convinced that the design to break the union is contemplated."[4] (Taylor, Memorandum to Madison) It seems more likely, however, that King was venting his frustration about Southern proposals, rather than making an actual threat. With the two European superpowers now at war, and both parties maintaining a significant military presence in the Western hemisphere, it would make no sense for the North to split from the Union. New York's safety lay in the larger numbers that only the Union could provide.

Still, there is no doubt that at least in some cases, the threat of breaking the union was real. Most of those cases would involve the South, whose

---

4   For the background to this crisis, see Irwin, "Revenue or Reciprocity?"

political class became increasingly convinced that its "peculiar tradition" (slavery) could not survive inside a Union dominated by Northern interests. Secession wasn't an exclusively Southern preoccupation, however. During the War of 1812, Federalist Party opposition to Republican President Madison's decision to declare war on Great Britain reached such a state that around the time of the party's Hartford Convention, in the winter of 1814–15, rumours of secession were swirling across the New England region.

At the convention itself, a meeting of Federalist politicians from the Northern states, delegates stopped short of issuing a formal declaration about the breakup of the Union. They did, however, do the next best thing by demanding a complete rewrite of the Constitution, focusing their firepower chiefly on the three-fifths rule's link with representation. The first of the list of proposed Constitutional amendments up for debate at the Convention limited the basis for taxation and representation calculations to "the respective numbers of free persons, including those bound to serve for a term of years, and excluding Indians not taxed and all other persons." It dropped the "and three-fifths of all other persons" formula. As if to stress their intentions, "excluding (...) all other persons" was then added.

This Northern demand would almost certainly have spelled the end of the Union, but for the fact that the war had already been settled at the negotiating table. If it seems odd for the New England politicians to have missed this crucial fact, it's important to remember that news travelled slowly back then – it took two months for the news of the Treaty of Ghent to reach American shores. This also explains why the final battle of the War of 1812 took place more than six weeks after the peace treaty was signed (Walker Howe 15–16).

The fact the war was rounded off with a victory by American troops under general Andrew Jackson over a British invading force outside New Orleans was not without significance.[5] It left the New Englanders with no option but to withdraw their demands. With the nation in celebratory mood, tabling them would have looked churlish at best and treasonous at worst. It was too late, though, to save their reputation: the story of what was discussed in Hartford effectively ended the Federalist Party as a national political force.[6]

---

5   The very last military engagement of the war actually took place a full month later. The battle of Fort Bowyer, in the Alabama territory, ended in a British victory. It's probably for that reason that it ended up being ignored in the American narrative about the war.

6   Though the Federalists would continue as a regional party, with their power base in New England, the end of the War of 1812 is generally seen as the end of the First Party System. After a brief single-party system interlude, the Second Party System started with the rise of the Whig

Threats of secession, or speculation about the end of the Union, would be one of the constant themes during the period that separated the Founding from the start of the Civil War. The sense of feverish intensity that this tended to create meant every crisis had the potential to turn into an existential threat to the Union. The challenge for successive generations of politicians was therefore to maintain the compromise that the Constitution had helped to create.

—

Compromise is relatively easy when polarisation is not a factor. What is much less easy, though, is bridging the gap when parties seem far apart and unwilling to move. For those cases the Founders had, through their example, shown the use of another tool from the raison d'état tool kit, namely the *coup*. This concept was introduced by the French seventeenth-century author Gabriel Naudé (1600–1653) as part of his attempt to operationalise the concept of prudence.[7] In his *Considérations Politiques sur les Coups d'Estat* (eventually published in English under the title "Political Considerations upon Refined Politicks, and the Master-Strokes of State"), he distinguished two forms of prudence. The ordinary variety was sufficient to handle most political situations. The extraordinary form of prudence was reserved for situations that required "Bold and extraordinary Actions, which Princes are constrain'd to execute when their Affairs are difficult and almost to be despair'd of, contrary to the common Right, without observing any order or form of Justice, but hazarding particular Interest for the good of the Publick" (Naudé 61).

The extraordinary act of prudence, or *coup*, had three characteristics. Firstly, it was improvised. A successful coup was an act of pure creativity when the normal political rulebooks no longer offered any guidance. Secondly, it could not be judged by normal moral standards – necessity knew no law, either legal or moral. And thirdly, it often involved an element of dissimulation

Party under Kentucky senator Henry Clay as counterweight to the Democratic Party under Andrew Jackson and Martin van Buren. The collapse of the Second Party System, in the mid-1850s, would facilitate the rise of the anti-slavery Republican Party under Abraham Lincoln.

7   For the use of this concept as an analytical tool, I am indebted to Luuk van Middelaar. See his majestic *Passage naar Europa*, specifically 148–162 ("Coup in Milan"). For the operationalisation of it through the work of Naudé, I refer to the work of Van Middelaar's critic, Perry Anderson (see the latter's "The European Coup"). The reader will find that I don't share Anderson's uniformly negative assessment of the coup as an instrument of federal statecraft – or indeed of federalism itself.

or secrecy to pull it off. If the person performing the coup actually told those involved what they were up to, chances were that the coup would fail.

The Founders had handed their successors several examples of successful coups. The most important was obviously the Constitution itself, hinging as it did on a patently immoral but ultimately successful deal to bridge the gap between North and South through the indirect linking of representation to a compromise on slavery. The Congressional deal on the Northwest Ordinance offered another example of an amoral but extraordinarily creative statesman's ambiguous use of certain legal concepts allowed both North and South to come away feeling that their side had won the better deal, by pretending to have banned slavery when in fact leaving the door ajar for further settlement by slave owners.

This then, was how the Union would be held together: through a series of Great Compromises, each requiring acts of astonishing inventiveness and prudence by the politicians involved.

The first Great Compromise (1790)

The fact that the Convention had produced a new Constitution was a remarkable feat of political engineering. In a speech defending its merits at the New York ratifying convention one of the drafters of the Declaration of Independence, Robert Livingston, referring to "the last great plan of the illustrious Henry IV," claimed that "[i]t has pleased Heaven to afford the United States means for the attainment of this great object" (Elliot 2: 209). Similarly, at the Pennsylvania convention, James Wilson claimed that "now is accomplished what the great mind of Henry IV, of France, had in contemplation – a system of government for large and respectable dominions, united and bound together in peace, under a superintending head, by which all the differences may be accommodated." He explained the consequences of the Constitution in terms that made it sound like a realisation of the peace pact of Saint-Pierre:

> Let gentlemen turn their attention to the amazing consequences which this principle will have in this extended country. The several states cannot war with each other; the general government is the great arbiter in contentions between them; the whole force of the Union can be called forth to reduce an aggressor to reason. What a happy exchange for the disjointed, contentious state sovereignties!
> (Elliot 2: 509)

Still, the sense of accomplishment over the fact that they had managed to secure a compromise text did not lull the men who had helped to shape it into a false sense of security. The chances of it providing a lasting basis for the reconstituted federal union were considered small. After its signing, George Washington remarked that he didn't expect it to last more than twenty years. In a letter to Jefferson, Madison referred to the final text as "materially defective" (Madison to Jefferson, 24 October 1787, FOA). Jefferson suggested that Hamilton had described it to him as "a shilly-shally thing, mere milk and water, which could not last, and was only good as a step to something better" (Brodie 267). Hamilton clearly wasn't optimistic about the Constitution's ability to put the Union on a surer footing. In an assessment of the new constitution, written immediately after the Convention, he stated that "the most likely result" was that "in the course of a few years, contests about the boundaries of power between the particular governments and the general government and the *momentum* of the larger states in such contests will produce a dissolution of the Union" (Hamilton, "Conjectures about the New Constitution," 17–30 September 1787, FOA).

As Hamilton had predicted, the real test of the Constitution's durability came when the institutions it had helped to create started operating as a federal government. With both the executive and the legislature looking to test the limits of their powers, there was every chance of a significant conflict. After all, though the rules as set out in the Constitution created the suggestion of a carefully crafted balance between the institutions, the process of calibrating these powers into something approaching a dynamic equilibrium would take time. It was probably inevitable that the first real test, when it came, would be over an issue that affected the relationship between North and South.

—

In one of its first official acts, the newly installed House of Representatives had asked the freshly appointed Treasury Secretary Alexander Hamilton for a plan for putting the Union's finances on a more secure footing. He would submit it in early January 1791 in the form of the *First Report on the Public Credit*. Hamilton used the report to propose the national government taking over the debts of the states. Politically speaking, this move was almost as ambitious as the Declaration of Independence and the Constitution. As Hamilton surely intended, its adoption would permanently alter the relationship between national and state governments. In *Federalist* 34, he had pointed out that without debts to service, "the only call for revenue of any consequence, which the State governments will continue to experience, will be for the mere support of their respective civil list" (Hamilton et al. 229). This would leave the national government with a virtual monopoly on taxation, or as he would put it more neutrally in his *Report*, there would be no need for "competition for resources" (Hamilton, *First Report on the Further Provision Necessary for Establishing Public Credit*, December 1790, FOA). It would thereby significantly expand the national government's options for the generating of its own income – one of the main weaknesses of the old Confederation Congress.

In eighteenth-century political theory, the concept of debt was closely tied to that of sovereignty (hence the expression "*sovereign* debt"; Skinner 364). As Hamilton himself had stressed in the *Federalist Papers* and again in the *Report*, a government's ability to issue debt was closely linked with the most important activity of states: the waging of war (*Federalist* 30: "In the modern system of war, nations the most wealthy are obliged to have recourse to large loans"; Hamilton et al. 215). A proposal to centralise this power in the national government was therefore always likely to be contentious. Still, it would have come as an unpleasant surprise to Hamilton that it was Madison, of all people, who would lead the charge against it.

When the proposal came up for discussion in the House, Madison used it to draw a sharp distinction between the Secretary's position and his own. He started out by observing that he was obviously "not insensible that an assumption of the state debts is under certain aspects, a measure not unworthy of a favorable attention" (Madison, speech on the floor of the House of Representatives, 22 April 1790, FOA). However, on closer inspection he found the reasoning behind it to be flawed. If, as the supporters of the proposal argued, the states' debts were effectively already a collective debt, then why the need to bring them under the national heading? He feared the practical centralising effect of it, drawing scarce resources away from the state governments. He also suggested the size of the combined debt would, in practical terms, lead to the creation of a perpetual national debt. And by drawing a distinction between Virginia, which had faithfully paid off its war debt at great expense to its taxpayers, and Massachusetts, which had failed to do so, he opened a front between mostly debt-free Southern states and mostly debt-ridden Northern ones.

Madison's fundamental objection to Hamilton's proposal wasn't political but principled. It boiled down to a fundamental disagreement between the two about the meaning of the Constitution's "necessary & proper" clause. The clause was the result of a compromise between the old Articles of Confederation notion that the federal government only possessed those powers "expressly" granted by the States, and the proposal in the Virginia Plan to act in all cases in which "the separate States are incompetent." If the former was too narrow, the latter was seen by delegates as far too generous in its attribution of powers to the national government. In the end, the Convention agreed on an expanded list of enumerated powers to which was then added the power "to make all Laws which shall be necessary and proper for carrying into execution the foregoing Powers" (Article I, Section 8, Clause 8).

As a constitutional principle, it made perfect sense. After all, as Madison himself had admitted in *Federalist* 44, "No axiom is more clearly established in law, or in reason, than that wherever the end is required, the means are authorised" (Hamilton et al. 290). The problem was that it set up inevitable conflicts over its interpretation, pitting the two parts of the clause against each other. One side would claim that the government had the authority to act if they could show it was *necessary* to do so as part of the execution of its duties. The other side would refuse to accept any action that couldn't be proven to be constitutionally *proper*. To justify their position, supporters of expansive government policy would develop the doctrine of *implied powers*. Their opponents would resist any attempt to increase the role of the national government by insisting on a *strict construction* of the Constitution.

The disagreement would become manifest during a debate about another financial topic that same year. Hamilton introduced the concept of "implied powers" when presenting the bill to establish a Bank of the United States. In his "Opinion on the Constitutionality of a National Bank" (15 February 1791), he started out from the newly established constitutional principle of shared sovereignty, "the circumstance that the powers of sovereignty are in this country divided between the National and State governments" (Banning 299). The problem was that this "does not afford the distinction required" (299). The only thing we can conclude from it is that "each has sovereign power as to certain things, and not as to other things" (299). Where to draw the line in a case like this?

Hamilton answered this question in two stages. First, he showed that the national government's power to act, in general terms included the creation of new corporations: "It is unquestionably incident to sovereign power to erect corporations, and consequently to that of the United States, in relation to the objects intrusted [sic] to the management of the government" (Banning 300). Having shown that the government had the general power to create corporations, he then provided a legal basis for this specific corporation by identifying it as an example of the execution of powers implied in the "necessary and proper" clause: "As a power of erecting a corporation may as well be implied as any other thing, it may as well be employed as an instrument or mean of carrying into execution any of the specified powers" (302–303).

In an earlier speech, Madison had presented the alternative approach to this question of where to draw the line. After first excluding the possibility of the bank's creation being based on one of the enumerated powers in the Constitution, or on the "general welfare" clause in its preamble, he then took on the implied powers argument head-on by arguing that "the terms necessary and proper gave no additional powers to those enumerated" (Banning 285), citing a number of state ratification conventions in support of his claim that the Constitution excluded "every source of power not within The Constitution itself" (286). Hamilton's bill, he concluded, stood condemned "by the silence of the Constitution" and "by the rule of interpretation arising out of it" (287).

If Hamilton really wanted to introduce powers to create a national bank, Madison suggested, he should declare so openly and use the procedure provided for it in the Constitution: "There is no man more anxious for the success of the government than I am, and no one who will join more heartily in curing its defects; but I wish these defects to be remedied by additional constitutional powers, if they should be found necessary. This is the only proper, effectual, and permanent remedy" (Banning 287).

—

Through his arguments, and concerted action behind the scenes, Madison would build a wall of opposition against Hamilton's proposals. In the spring of 1790, Hamilton would run into it again and again. By June, the situation had become critical – both for Hamilton, who speculated about being forced to resign if his proposal for the assumption of state debts wasn't adopted, and for the Union as a whole. After all, a failure to agree on a major policy proposal like this would send the message that, in spite of the Constitution, politically speaking the new Union was still as imperfect as the old one.

When Hamilton was looking for a way out of the political quagmire on the assumption issue, he would eventually focus on a second major issue that divided Congress: the question of the location of the future capital of the Union. There was more than just pride at stake. The national government had committed to making a significant sum available for the purchase and development of a new autonomous government district. The decision had therefore resulted in intensive political lobbying by interested states. There were two prizes on the table. Second prize was to host the short-term transition capital. First prize was the permanent location. Winners of the second prize, though, could hold out the hope of turning a temporary status into a permanent one. This gave negotiations between states about who got which prize something of a Florentine aspect. Hamilton, for example, had secretly offered the permanent capital to both New Jersey and Pennsylvania – provided they would support his home state's continued hold on the temporary capital status, which he clearly intended to make permanent. Pennsylvania, meanwhile, was in secret negotiations with Virginia, offering it first prize in return for a prolonged temporary capital just outside Philadelphia.

The choice of a permanent location was a matter of some concern to Thomas Jefferson. He assumed the location would at least in part end up determining the national character. His preferred option was a city located on the Potomac, on the border of North and South (though strictly speaking more South than North). If at all possible, he wanted to avoid a Northern capital, where the local culture was insufficiently sympathetic to Southern priorities. His least favourite option was New York. Hamilton, for his part, had hoped to buy the votes for his assumption proposal from the Pennsylvania House delegation by lobbying for it to obtain the permanent capital. When this attempt failed, and it instead became clear that Virginia and Pennsylvania were close to a deal, he played his last trump card by getting his cabinet colleague Jefferson – then already a cabinet rival but not yet an enemy – to arrange a sit-down with Madison.

The dinner at Jefferson's temporary residence in New York has gone down in history as a decisive moment in this crisis. According to the host, who was the only person subsequently to give an account of what was discussed, Madison agreed to refrain from further agitating against assumption. He also promised to deliver two extra Virginia votes for the proposal, enough for it to pass the House. In return Hamilton would use his influence to persuade Northern members to back the Potomac as location for the permanent residence. Through this deal, the crisis would eventually be resolved.

—

Looking back on this episode, Hamilton expressed surprise about the intensity of Madison's opposition. It is certainly possible, as he claimed, that during the Philadelphia Convention Madison and he had been "perfectly agreed in the expediency and propriety" of the assumption by the federal government of state debts (Chernow 1102). It might even be a plausible hypothesis, given Madison's mission at that time of wresting control away from the States. Be that as it may, by 1790 the situation had changed in one fundamental way that made it more likely that Madison would oppose the idea.

It would be a misreading of Madison's thinking to see his idea of a balanced constitution as set out in *Federalist* 51, with its separation of powers and checks and balances, as a purely mechanical construction. To Madison, the Constitution wasn't simply a set of levers and scales to balance out the various powers. Their relations were organic and dynamic, open to development and constant change, not least because of the amount of overlap the system had allowed between them. Course corrections, where one part would have to be propped up or another hemmed in to prevent the whole from overbalancing, were an inevitable part of its functioning over time.

In the autumn of 1787, his main fear was still that the states would overpower the national government. In a letter to Thomas Jefferson (24 October 1787, FOA), he started by observing what he saw as the main gains of the Convention. One was that the United States had decided to stay united: "It appeared to be the sincere and unanimous wish of the Convention to cherish and preserve the Union of the States. No proposition was made, no suggestion was thrown out, in favor of a partition of the Empire into two or more Confederacies." The other was that "[i]t was generally agreed that the objects of the Union could not be secured by any system founded on the principle of a confederation of sovereign States. A voluntary observance of the federal law by all the members, could never be hoped for."

The main weakness he saw in the system that had emerged from the negotiations was the absence of a national government veto over state legislation. "Without such a check in the whole over the parts," he worried, "our system involves the evil of *imperia in imperio*." The risk continued to exist that "without the royal negative or some equivalent controul, the unity of the system would be destroyed." This was not just a theoretical risk. His study of historical examples of federal unions had shown him that "the want of some such provision seems to have been mortal to the antient Confederacies, and to be the disease of the modern" (Madison to Jefferson, 24 October 1787, FOA).

At this early stage, Madison still clearly leaned towards the national position. But when in 1789 the early interactions between the national government and the states showed that he had significantly underestimated the practical powers of the former, and overestimated the powers of the latter, it was inevitable that he would change his position. In the case of Hamilton's proposals, that meant defending the rights of the states against an attempted power grab by the central government. Going forward, securing states' rights would become one of Madison's main missions. Adding to this, he would develop two other "auxiliary precautions" against an overbearing national government. One was public opinion, which he would present as the natural check on any government claim of authority: "The censorial power is in the people over the government, and not in the government over the people" ("Who Are the Best Keepers of the People's Liberty?", *National Gazette*, 20 December 1792, FOA). The other was the Constitution, which through a strict construction of its powers would help to limit the national government's appetite for power.

—

If Madison's fear was an over-powerful national government, Hamilton's was that the national government would fail because of a *lack* of power. He had presented his own philosophical interpretation of the project underpinning the Constitution in *Federalist* 15. In it, he stressed that the graveyard of international relations was filled with projects where sovereign states had sought to create the preconditions for peace and prosperity by banding together "for defined purposes precisely stated in a treaty regulating all the details of time, place, circumstance, and quantity" (Hamilton et al. xxx). In what seemed a reference to the alliances under the balance of power system established through the Peace of Utrecht, he specifically referred to early eighteenth-century Europe, where there had been "an epidemical rage (...) for this species of compacts" (Hamilton et al. 148). The reason they failed, he observed, was the lack of a central authority that could force the individual members to abide by their regulations. Their failure contained "an instructive but afflicting lesson to mankind how little dependence is to be placed on treaties which have no other sanction than the obligations of good faith." (Hamilton et al, xxx) It was a lesson Hamilton had learned in person during the War of Independence, when the promises of Congress turned out to be worth not even the paper they were printed on, and when states would regularly refuse to come to the aid of the Union which was supposed to have served for their common defence.

To Hamilton, the central lesson of this failure was that an effective compact must deliver two things. First, it must "extend the authority of the Union to the persons of the citizens – the only proper objects of government" (Hamilton et al. 149). The second lesson was connected to the first. If the central government wanted to establish a direct relationship with the citizens of its territory, it would have to wrest power away from the states. If not, it would eventually, and inevitably, fall victim to "the eccentric tendency in the subordinate or inferior orbs by the operation of which there will be a perpetual effort in each to fly off from the common center" (150).

The states were the main obstacle to overcome. "Why has government been instituted at all?" he asked. Because "the passions of men will not conform to the dictates of reason and justice without restraint" (Hamilton et al. 149). What held for men also held for bodies of men, like the states. Even more so, in fact:

> Regard to reputation has a less active influence, when the infamy of a bad action is to be divided among a number than when it is to fall singly upon one. A spirit of faction, which is apt to mingle its poison in the deliberations of all bodies of men, will often hurry the persons of whom they are composed into improprieties and excesses, for which they would blush in a private capacity.
> (150)

The biggest danger threatening the Union would be the selfishness of the individual states: "Each State yielding to the persuasive voice of immediate interest or convenience has successively withdrawn its support, till the frail and tottering edifice seems ready to fall upon our heads and to crush us beneath its ruins" (151). The overwhelming priority of the national government would therefore be to establish its supremacy over the states, and break their stranglehold on the relationship with the citizenry.

—

The two Federalist authors had been able to unite in a common effort in the 1780s, when they had the shared objective of putting the Union on a surer footing. With the emphasis shifting to the implementation of the Constitution, their philosophical differences inevitably came to the fore – thereby bringing an end to one of the most extraordinary political-intellectual partnerships in history. The fact that they managed to settle them one last time in a grand bargain is a testament to their willingness to put the Union before their personal interests. In that sense, they provided the model for the Great Compromises that were to follow.

The Missouri Compromise on the issue of expansion (1820)

In theory, the Constitutional compromise of 1787 had solved Machiavelli's problem of expansion for federal unions. In practice, however, expansion was never greeted with universal acclaim. On a number of occasions, expansion would severely destabilise the union, almost causing its demise. Even the Louisiana Purchase, now generally seen as a political masterstroke, was greeted at the time by New England politicians as evidence of the fact that "our empire is growing unwieldy and must (...) ere long break in pieces" (Farnham 5). The loss of Northern control over the Union which expansion would inevitably bring in its wake, caused a growing rift between the Northern states and the federal government.[8] It would ultimately lead to a failed attempt to dissolve the Union at the Hartford Convention.

At the heart of the controversy that would greet every new attempt at expansion was the question of whose regime was to apply in the newly admitted states – that of the slave-owning South or the (largely) post-slavery North.[9] The first attempt to settle the issue had come in the summer of 1787, when Congress tried to conclude the long-running negotiations about the status of the territories the thirteen colonies had inherited from the British. Given the amount of political capital invested in the negotiations about the new constitutional settlement, it seemed North and South both had an incentive to resolve this side issue without too much fuss. As always, however, the devil was in the details. The Northern states, led by Massachusetts Congressman Rufus King, demanded a ban on slavery in the entire territory. In return they offered a fugitive slave clause, to persuade slaveholders that the territory would not become a safe haven for runaway slaves, the way that Spanish Florida already was on the Union's southern border (Van Cleve, *A Slaveholders' Union* 555). The Southern states rejected this proposal, seeing it as a transparent attempt to claim the territories for the Northern economic model. If Congress wanted to break this stalemate, it would have to come

---

8   The Massachusetts Congressman Manasseh Cutler summarised the New England objections to the purchase by stating that "the admission of the Province into the Union, must throw N. England quite into the background. Her influence in government, from the rapid [growth of] population at the southward and westward, is naturally declining, and this must be nearly a finishing stroke" (Farnham 11).

9   "Post-slavery" is a relative term here, referring to a political consensus rather than societal practice. As late as 1820, there were still nearly 20,000 enslaved persons living above the Mason–Dixon line, half of them in New York (Forbes 34). The standard for comparison were the more than 1.5 million enslaved people held in often abject conditions in the Southern states.

up with a solution that persuaded both sides that they had gotten enough out of the deal to make it possible to sell it to sceptical home audiences.

During his time as lead negotiator on this issue in 1784, Thomas Jefferson had tried solving it along the temporal axis. His proposal seemed radical: he called for the introduction of a ban on slavery in the entire territory. But by postponing the coming into effect of the ban until 1800, Jefferson effectively opened all of it to Southern settlement, including slavery. It was the kind of compromise that pleased neither side. Southern states saw in it an explicit rejection of their slavery-based economic model. Northern states feared the sixteen-year transition period with slavery – after all, nothing is more permanent than a temporary arrangement.

When he took over the file, Virginia Congressman James Monroe tried a different approach. He shifted the solution from the temporal to the spatial axis by using the Ohio river as a dividing line. All territory to the north of it would be off limits to slavery; all territory to the south would be opened to slaveholding settlement. By stipulating that the two territories that were thus created would produce roughly the same number of new states, he also introduced the idea of a mathematical balance between North and South.[10] To cement this new balance, the deal included the provision that had first been introduced by Jefferson, namely that the individual territories would be admitted "on equal footing" with existing states, "having the same rights of sovereignty, freedom and independence, as the other states" (Hall 60).

It seemed a generous offer to the Northern states. By ceding the territory south of the Ohio river they would merely be acknowledging the reality that these lands had already begun to be settled by Southern slaveholders. In return, they gained what they believed to be exclusive access to the rich lands north of the river. After all, no slaveholder would contemplate settling in a territory where slavery was forbidden. To Southern states however, Monroe's drafting skills still offered some hidden opportunities. Jefferson's original proposal had included the provision that while territories could legally (albeit temporarily) recognise slavery, slavery would be banned once they entered the Union. That meant there was no future for slavery in these territories once they obtained statehood. Monroe's draft deliberately left this issue open. While Article 6 of the proposed Ordinance clearly stipulated that slavery would be banned in the Northwest Territory, the "equal footing"

---

10   In the end, four states would be created out of the territory south of the Ohio River (Kentucky, Tennessee, Mississippi, and Alabama) and five out of the territory to the north of it (Ohio, Michigan, Indiana, Illinois, and Wisconsin). The state of Minnesota also contains a part of the territory covered by the Northwest Ordinance.

clause meant there would be no preconditions for entering the Union. If a territory upon gaining statehood chose to adopt a constitution legalising slavery, that was its own business (Hall 65).

Slavery would also not be completely banned. The draft text included a provision that all existing claims to *property* would be respected – a term that was acknowledged by all sides to include enslaved people. All existing slaveholder settlements in these territories would therefore be allowed to operate legally. Though the Ordinance didn't contain any language stating it openly, this additional compromise was reflected in the language on the procedure governing the application for statehood. Each stage in that process was linked to certain threshold population levels. These levels in turn were based on the number of "free male inhabitants." The trained Southern eye immediately identified this as an acknowledgement of the fact that there could also be *unfree* inhabitants. In short: some forms of slaveholding would continue to be allowed, and others might well be allowed once the territory had entered the Union as a new state.

Monroe's creative use of legal conceptual ambiguity opened up just enough space for a compromise between North and South to appear (Hall 69). The Northwest Ordinance, especially its Article 6, would end up playing a leading role in the negotiations to settle an unexpectedly intense crisis suddenly erupting in late 1819 over the statehood application of the Missouri territory.

—

When James Monroe took office as the Union's fifth president in 1817, the state of the Union seemed to be strong. With Napoleon defeated and the victors committed to restoring a sense of stability to the European continent's political set-up, transatlantic trade had picked up again, and so had the American economy. With the long-term relationship with Britain finally settled after the War of 1812, the last serious military threat on America's borders had evaporated. Militarily secure, and economically prosperous, the nation looked forward to the future with confidence.

Using his first inaugural address to refer to the United States as "one great family with a common interest," Monroe invoked the image of an age of Good Feeling (Walker-Howe 92). Unfortunately for Monroe, the good feeling was rudely disturbed shortly after by Speaker of the House Henry Clay. Instead of accepting the 1817 Illinois application for statehood on face value, he submitted it to the House for debate. This unravelled a crucial element of Monroe's old compromise on the Northwest Territory:

the fact that states, upon entering the Union, were free to adopt their own constitutions without interference from Washington, D.C. With Congress now looking to get involved in judging the validity of a territory's application to statehood, the content of its proposed constitution became the obvious focus. This, in turn, inevitably led to the reopening of a debate about an issue that had nearly derailed the 1787 Constitutional convention: slavery.

A constitutional crisis seemed sure to follow – sooner rather than later, as it turned out. A mere two years after Clay's intervention, in the winter of 1819, New York Congressman and committed abolitionist James Tallmadge (1778–1853) tabled an amendment to the enabling bill for the admission of the territory of Missouri as a new state in the Union. The amendment had two clauses. One asked for a ban on the importation of slaves from outside the territory (the "non-importation provision"), the other demanded the emancipation of all children of slaves when they reached the age of twenty-five (the "gradual emancipation provision"). Together they would have the effect of putting a time limit on Missouri's status as a slave state.

There was some concern in Northern circles that with the simultaneous admission of two slave states (Alabama had also put in an application), the balance in the union would tip from neutral to majority slave states (Hall 243). It is certainly possible this was what forced Tallmadge's hand. The eventual solution to the standoff caused by his amendment would in part focus on this issue. The final deal included a confirmation of the unwritten numerical rule, established during the adoption of the Northwest Ordinance, that any expansion of the Union should involve an equal number of slave and free states. It was achieved by linking Missouri's admission to the Union to that of Maine, a new state carved out of the northern part of the founding state of Massachusetts.

More likely, though, it was a combination of various reasons that forced Tallmadge's hand. One other likely important factor was that Missouri was the first territory on the other side of the Mississippi River to apply for statehood. All previous new state entries into the Union had been covered by arrangements made in the Northwest Ordinance (1787) and the Southwest Ordinance (1790). All territories above the Ohio River, up to the Mississippi, were set aside for "free" states, while slavery would be allowed in all states to be created below that line. Missouri proved a double headache in that regard: not only was it west of the Mississippi, it was also located partly above and partly below the line of settlement. If ever there was going to be a problem with a candidate-state seeking accession to the Union, Missouri was destined to be the one.

As Tallmadge made clear, in reply to fierce protests to his amendment from Southern members, if the fight about its status would lead to the undoing of the entire original Constitutional compromise between North and South, then that was a risk he was willing to take:

"[M]y purpose is fixed, (...) it is a great and glorious cause, setting bounds to a slavery the most cruel and debasing the world has ever witnessed. [I]t is the freedom of man. [I]f a dissolution of the Union must take place, let it be so! If civil war, which gentlemen so much threaten, must come, I can only say, let it come!"
(Hall 380)

He was far from alone in this sentiment. Speaker Henry Clay observed that "the Missouri question engrosses the whole thoughts of the members. (...) It is a most unhappy question, awakening sectional feelings, and exasperating them to the highest degree. The words 'civil war' and 'disunion' are uttered almost without emotion" (464–465).

Two anecdotes serve to show how febrile the atmosphere would eventually become. One was a resolution tabled by the New York Congressman Henry Meigs. After stating that "slavery in the United States is an evil of great and increasing magnitude," he proposed its outright abolition. Not gradually, as Tallmadge's amendment would have achieved, but instantly, by "emancipating the slaves" – and enslaved people in *all* states, not just in Missouri (Hall 486). In response to such Northern statements of intent, the Virginia senator James Barbour tried to garner support among his colleagues for the organising of a convention of the states at which the dissolution of the Union was to be settled through mutually agreeable terms of separation (527).

—

In this tempestuous debate, the newly admitted states from the Midwest would play a crucial mediating role. Indiana (admitted in 1816) and Illinois (1818) were geographically Northern states, but they were really slave states in all but name. Both allowed lifetime "ownership contracts" for enslaved people living in the territory at the time of accession to the Union – a creative interpretation of the anti-slavery Article 6 in the Northwest Ordinance. Illinois also set one part of the state aside as an area where "short-term" slavery was allowed in order to service the local salt mines. Its state constitution was effectively a mini version of the original Great Compromise between a southern part of the state settled by slave owning farmers from Indiana and Kentucky, and the northern part of the state settled by New England labour migrants.

It was an Illinois senator named Jesse Burgess Thomas (1777–1853) who ended up playing a leading role in the brokering of the compromise that saved the Union for another generation. Before moving to Illinois, Thomas had lived in what was then still the territory of Indiana, where he helped to draft its constitution – a precondition for statehood and admission to the Union. Since Indiana was included in the larger territory falling under the Northwest Ordinance, this meant that it was expected to respect Article 6, which explicitly banned slavery in the territories. Indiana, in other words, was expected to enter the Union as a free state. The problem was that the state was mainly colonised by settlers from the neighbouring slave state of Kentucky (the same route that would bring Abraham Lincoln's family to the Midwest, from slaveholding Kentucky through Indiana to Illinois). The slaveholders who dominated the state's embryonic political system were faced with a challenge: how to continue owning slaves while seemingly living in a free state?

Tackling this problem would give Thomas the kind of experience that would later stand him in good stead brokering the deal that unlocked the gridlocked negotiations about Missouri. He did it by a clever adaptation of the Northwest Ordinance's Article 6. The article's original political genius consisted in the fact that it seemingly offered both sides what they wanted without establishing a compromise between the two sides. But by 1820 attitudes about the clause's meaning had hardened to such an extent that it no longer offered a meaningful basis for a political settlement. Any compromise would have to somehow invoke the spirit of Article 6, without invoking the letter.

The solution in the end presented itself in the form of a word: *territory*. In the debate in which Thomas was intervening, it had two meanings. One was spatial: the land outside the United States proper that was placed under the control of Congress. The other was temporal. Here the word referred to the legal status of the future states. In fact, the temporal meaning came in two versions, one starting with a lowercase *t*, the other with an uppercase *T*. A *territory* was a stretch of land before the start of the process that would eventually lead to statehood, whereas a *Territory* was that same stretch of land halfway through the process, once it had met certain minimal criteria for political organisation. In his amendment, Thomas would play with these various meanings to produce a version of the old Article 6 – something that allowed all sides to read their own desired outcomes into the agreed wording.

The text he came up with read like this:

And be it further enacted, That in all that territory ceded by France to the United States, under the name of Louisiana, which lies north of thirty-six degrees and thirty minutes north latitude, excepting only such part thereof as is included within the limits of the state contemplated by this act, slavery and involuntary servitude, otherwise than in the punishment of crimes whereof the party shall have been duly convicted, shall be and is hereby forever prohibited; provided always, That any person escaping into the same, from whom labour or service is lawfully claimed in any State or Territory of the United States, such fugitive may be lawfully reclaimed and conveyed to the person claiming his or her labour or service as aforementioned. (Hall 502)

It had everything in it to please all sides. Abolitionists or restrictionists would interpret the clause geographically. In that case, it stated that in all territory to the West of the Mississippi, the same rules would be applied that had also been applied in the Northwest Territories – banning slavery "forever" above a line drawn by continuing the Ohio River on the other side of the Mississippi. Anti-restrictionist, pro-slavery politicians, however, would read it temporally. If they were free to interpret the word "territory" (with a lowercase *t*) as expressing a temporary status, the "forever" in the clause would end up being time limited.

Thomas's amendment would form the basis of the eventual compromise adopted in early March 1820. Before it could pass, though, Speaker Clay would have to use a parliamentary trick to get the whole package through. If the combined bill, which approved statehood for both Maine and Missouri, and set the administrative conditions to apply on the other side of the Mississippi, had been voted on as a single package, the opponents of the various parts of the bill may well have combined to vote it down. But by breaking it into three parts, and voting on all three individually, Clay managed to reduce the opposition to the bill sufficiently to guide it to final passage.

Once the dust had settled, one Southern newspaper complained that the bill had been adopted "by a sort of parliamentary coup de main" (Hall 353). If anything, this understated the creativity of the politicians involved. It had in fact been a double coup – procedural and textual.

The Nullification Crisis (1832)

The ratification of the constitution did not settle the debate about its meaning. Far from it, in fact. For the next seventy years, there would be a lively – and at times fiery – debate about its scope and meaning. There were, broadly speaking, two positions here: one federalist and the other anti-federalist. The latter found its ultimate expression in a concept that became a symbol of states' rights: nullification.

The idea first surfaced during the political crisis of 1798 over the Alien and Sedition Acts. It involved a package of legislative measures introduced by the Federalist Party in Congress and signed into law by President John Adams. The issues that led to the tabling of the proposals will be only too familiar to a twenty-first-century audience. One issue was immigration. At the start of the decade, the Federalists were still broadly in favour of the arrival of European immigrants, who had fled political persecution or economic deprivation to seek a better life in America. But when the numbers exceeded expectations, and the single largest group turned out to be *French* – America's enemy in all but name, according to the Federalists at least – opinions changed quickly.

By the summer of 1798, Adams was ready to sign several bills dealing with this issue. One was the Naturalization Act, which made it harder for immigrants to obtain citizenship and excluded from citizenship altogether people from countries with which the United States was at war. The other was the Alien Friends Act, which gave the government powers to arrest and repatriate immigrants it considered unwanted. The definition of unwanted was, well, whatever the administration decided it was. Mostly it was an anti-French measure. When one French emigré, who had come to America to escape Robespierre's Terror, demanded to know the reason his name was included in a list of persons selected for deportation, Adams is supposed to have answered: "Nothing in particular, but he's too French" (Wood, *Friends Divided* 877).

Any policy tends to have its own reasonable-sounding explanation. The Alien Friends Act was no different. There *were* a significant number of French immigrants living in the United States, especially in the temporary capital Philadelphia. It *was* true that the Directoire in Paris was actively fomenting pro-French rebellions in other countries – earlier in 1798 an Irish rebellion, supported by France, had attempted to end British rule and establish an Irish republic. The French navy *had* started acting in an increasingly hostile fashion towards US merchant vessels, even attacking them in American waters. Not long after the passing of the Alien Friends Act, Congress would vote to allow military force to be used in defence of commercial interests, even restoring the US Navy that had been abolished after the end of the Revolutionary War. Be that as it may, the fact that the measure seemed rational to President Adams and his allies in Congress didn't necessarily make it right. Certainly not in the eyes of his Vice President Thomas Jefferson, who denounced the Act as "a most detestable thing, worthy of the 8th or 9th century" (Wood, *Friends Divided* 876).

It was the Sedition Act, however, that would really raise the political temperature. Twenty-first-century social media full of unsubstantiated viral content ("Fake News") had their late eighteenth-century equivalent in fiercely partisan newspapers that traded mainly in libel and slander, or as Adams himself put it somewhat misogynistically, "the most envious malignity, the most base, vulgar, sordid, fishwoman scurrility, and the most palpable lies" (Wood, *Friends Divided* 879).

It raises the tough political question of what to do with publications that seemingly have only one purpose: namely, to foment dissent and sow division for the sake of destabilising the republic. In the US, the consensus nowadays is that the Constitution's First Amendment offers wide-ranging protection for all forms of speech, even the most contentious ones. But in 1798, that constitutional principle had not yet been established. Adams' contemporaries looked at the issue of free speech through the lens of English libel law: speech was free in the sense of not being controlled at the point of publication, but it was not unregulated. Statements that crossed the line were liable to prosecution. This is what the Act proposed to codify. In fact, it slightly tightened the criteria for prosecution compared to the British standard, making it more, not less, difficult to prosecute (Wood, *Friends Divided* 869).

Even Jefferson agreed with this approach. He just didn't think it was up to the national government to regulate this issue. And he certainly didn't accept the practical implication of it, namely that the law could be used to shut down his party's newspapers for criticising his opponent. He saw the ban as a sinister *political* move that required an immediate response. It came in the form of the Virginia and Kentucky Resolutions, the one drawn up by James Madison, the other by Jefferson himself. Though it seems unlikely the vice president of the United States would have been arrested for expressing his dissent on a policy by his own administration, it was an indication of how tense the situation had become that both authors felt their resolutions would best be published anonymously.

—

Of the two resolutions, the Virginia document drafted by Madison was the more moderate, though not by much. He began by stressing, once again, the importance of a strict construction of the Constitutional powers of the national government: "[T]he powers of the federal government, resulting from the compact to which the states are parties; limited by the plain sense and intention of the instrument constituting that compact" ("Virginia Resolutions," 21 December 1798, FOA).[11] Things took an unexpected turn when the former champion of the national idea then presented himself as a champion of the pre-1787 federal idea as he described the Constitution as "the Union of the States." It was on behalf of the states that he objected to the Acts, and it was through the states that he intended to deal with them.

After having accused the government of harbouring monarchical aspirations (a charge against which Adams was all too vulnerable, having expressed himself an admirer of Britain's constitutional monarchy), Madison then turned to the Alien and Sedition Acts, two "palpable and alarming infractions of the constitution." The first, he explained, by "exercising a power nowhere delegated to the federal government (...) subverts the general principles of free government, as well as the particular organization and positive provisions of the federal constitution." The latter did something even worse by exercising a power "expressly and positively forbidden by one of the amendments [the first amendment]." The Sedition Act was clearly the worse of the two according to Madison because it violated not just the letter but also the *spirit* of the Constitution, since it was "levelled against that right of freely examining public characters and measures, and of free communication among the people thereon, which has ever been justly deemed, the only effectual guardian of every other right."

It was a damning indictment, but Madison seemed unwilling to draw the obvious conclusion from it. He did point out that the states had "the right, and are in duty bound, to interpose for arresting the progress of the evil, and for maintaining within their respective limits, the authorities, rights and liberties appertaining to them." But authorities, rights, and liberties to do what, exactly? He refused to speculate, stating only that if the same states that argued forcefully for the first amendment now failed to defend it, it would be "a reproachful inconsistency and criminal degeneracy."[12]

---

11   Subsequent quotations from the Virginia Resolutions are from this source, unless otherwise stated.

12   Significantly, a passage inserted at the suggestion of Jefferson by House of Delegates member John Taylor of Caroline which stated that in such cases the acts ought to be declared "utterly null, void, and of no force or effect" was deleted before the motion was tabled for debate – most likely at the insistence of Madison himself. See Editorial Note to the Virginia Resolutions, *Founders Online*, https://founders.archives.gov/documents/Madison/01-17-02-0128.

Jefferson would have no such hesitation. In his Kentucky Resolutions, the solution would be given pride of place. Before he got to that point, though, he first gave his own interpretation of the Constitution:

> The several states composing the United States of America, are not united on the principle of unlimited submission to their General Government; but by compact under the style and title of a Constitution for the United States and of amendments thereto, they constituted a General Government for special purposes, delegated to that Government certain definite powers, reserving each state to itself, the residuary mass of right to their own self Government.
> ("Resolutions adopted by the Kentucky General Assembly," 10 November 1798, FOA)[13]

If Jefferson saw a difference between the Constitution and the Articles of Confederation, it was one of degree, not of kind. Power still rested with the states, even in this new, supposedly more perfect Union.

Note that he saw the *states* as having constituted a general government, not "We the People." Like Madison, Jefferson also thought of the states – not the federal Supreme Court – as the arbiters of what fell inside and outside the limits of the Constitution's enumerated powers of the executive. Whenever it acted beyond those limits, its acts would be "unauthoritative, void, and of no force."[14] And since, according to Jefferson, there was no higher authority or "common Judge" to establish such violations, each state has "an equal right to judge for itself, as well of infractions as of the mode and measure of redress."

This was an explosive suggestion, to say the least. It would make it virtually impossible for the national government to perform its functions if any state could decide on any given act that it wouldn't accept it. Even worse, he claimed that such a decision could be based merely on a state's own interpretation of the Constitution, leaving the process open to endless political manipulation by the states.

—

13   Subsequent quotations from the Kentucky Resolutions are from this source, unless otherwise stated.

14   The word "nullification" didn't feature in the version of the Resolutions adopted by the Kentucky legislature, but it was included in Jefferson's draft of the text: "[W]here powers are assumed which have not been delegated a nullification of the act is the rightful remedy."

At the time of publication of the two Resolutions, their call for Southern resistance against federal authority mainly caused shock and outrage. Even their home state Virginia overwhelmingly rejected Madison and Jefferson's seditious message. By the late 1820s, though, it seemed that one Southern state was ready to answer the call.

That South Carolina ended up being the first state to leave the Union, in 1860, was no coincidence. From the outset, the South Carolinian political elite turned out to be more militant in their defence of the institution of slavery than any other group of Southern politicians. No other state would produce more firebrand pro-slavery and anti-Union agitators. None would come closer in the decades before the Civil War to actually starting the process of secession.

The issue that triggered the standoff of 1832 was the federal tariff policy. In the first half of the nineteenth century, tariffs were a political fact of life. It wasn't until the repeal of the British Corn Laws in 1846, when the pro-tariff Tories were cast into the wilderness for a generation and were replaced by the pro-free-trade Liberals, that tariffs would lose some of their lustre. In late 1820s America, they were seen as a means of protecting domestic producers. For American policymakers, higher tariffs had an additional beneficial effect. It meant the federal government would have to rely less on land sales for its revenue streams. With demand for land for settlement thus outstripping supply, it could keep the price per acre higher.

The high tariffs pleased most producers, who saw in them a protection against foreign competition. One group, however, grew increasingly desperate about the protectionist policies of the federal government: Southern planters. Unlike Northern industrialists, who could sell their goods into domestic as well as foreign markets, they were completely dependent on foreign demand. The higher retaliatory tariffs that inevitably matched American ones meant that their export prospects took a serious hit.

In the febrile state of Southern politics, the negative impact of the tariffs was inevitably linked to Northern attitudes to slavery. One South Carolinian politician, Thomas T. Player, summed up this logic during a debate in the state legislature: "[T]he present measure [the tariff policy] is only preparatory to ulterior movements, destined by fanatics and abolitionists to subvert the institutions and established policies of the Southern country" (Freehling, *Prelude to Civil War* 174).

To protect itself from the Northern onslaught on its slaveholding "tradition," South Carolina's political class sought for remedies in the development of new constitutional concepts. They found it in Jefferson's Kentucky Resolution: "Mr. Jefferson's plain, practical and downright principle (...), our 'rightful remedy' – a nullification by the State (...) of the unauthorised act" (speech by Governor James Hamilton, October 1828, quoted in Freehling, *Prelude to Civil War* 152). Nullification became the buzzword of the South Carolinian revolt. By 1832, this revolt had a solid majority of the state legislature behind it.

—

The idea of a state veto of federal legislation had not been included in the Constitution of 1787 (nor had its counterpart of a federal veto of individual state legislation, a measure proposed by Madison – see page 212 above). For the idea to have any kind of political force, it would therefore need a legal justification outside of the Constitution. This is where South Carolina senator John Calhoun (1782–1850) came in.

As vice president to President John Quincy Adams, Calhoun had made a first attempt to justify the cancellation of the tariffs on constitutional ground, by arguing that though Article 1, section 8 (the Enumerated Powers clause) gave the federal government the right to lay and collect tariffs, these enumerated powers also had to be read as having enumerated *purposes*. Since trade policy wasn't explicitly mentioned as a purpose of government policy, it therefore had to be excluded as a "violation by perversion" of the Constitution (Calhoun, *Works* 439). When even his own supporters dismissed this argument as too far-fetched, he switched to the nullification cause.

Calhoun based his case for a state's veto right of federal legislation on a three-step reinterpretation of the act of the Founding. In the late 1820s, the standard interpretation of that act was that it had been performed by "We the People," which had given itself a constitutional government by adopting the text agreed in Philadelphia. The best-known defender of that interpretation in Calhoun's day was the Massachusetts senator Daniel Webster, who in 1830, in a debate with South Carolina senator Robert Hayne, had famously set out the theory that the People predated not just the union but the states themselves (the idea being that since rebellion against the British crown had been a collective act, it therefore made no sense to talk of separate states predating the union – an argument also made by James Wilson during the Philadelphia Convention). Federal legislation like the tariff act was therefore passed on behalf of the People, by the People's representatives. Calhoun's first step was to declare this interpretation to be fundamentally flawed. Like Jefferson in 1798, he claimed that the Founding was an act not of the People, but of the States (a theory that was known as the "Compact Theory").

The second step was to deny that the Constitution was based on a divided sovereignty. In fact, Calhoun declared the very idea of a divided sovereignty an impossibility: "We might as well speak of half a square, or of half a triangle, as of half a sovereign" (Freehling, *Prelude to Civil War* 163). This was obviously in complete denial of the truth as recorded in the historical records of the 1787 Convention, but for his argument on nullification to work, he *needed* it to be true. On this basis he then proceeded, in step three, to argue that since the states were the original founders, and since their sovereignty had remained undivided even in this act of the Founding, it had remained their sovereign right to pass judgement on any legislation adopted at the federal level – and to nullify it if it posed a threat to their sovereignty.

It was an interesting theoretical construct, even if it rested on shaky factual ground. There was a practical problem with it though: a three-quarters majority of the states could still override the veto of the individual state by embedding the idea behind the offending legislation in the Constitution itself (Freehling, *Prelude to Civil War* 166–167). Thus, any argument for nullification based on inviolable state sovereignty would sooner or later have to come to terms with the fact that there was really only one way to make the veto stick: secession. Though Calhoun would make nullification without secession his personal platform, others on both sides of the tariff debate were clearly aware of the incongruity of this position. From the start, President Jackson treated South Carolina's attempts at nullification as an existential threat to the Union, referring to it as an "act of intended treason," and vowing: "The union shall be preserved" (245). In his Nullification Proclamation of 10 December 1832, he would be even more explicit, declaring the South Carolinian nullification ordinance "contrary to the laws of their country, subversive of its Constitution, and having for its object the destruction of the Union" (245).

———

In the standoff that followed, Jackson would prove himself much the smarter politician. He started by moving several companies of federal soldiers to Fort Sumtrie at the entrance to the Charleston harbour. This not only served to send a strong signal to any South Carolinians contemplating revolt, but also made it possible for federal customs officers to levy tariffs on merchant ships before they could enter the port – thereby cutting the ground from under the South Carolina legislature initiatives to nullify the tariff act. At the same time, he offered the rebels an off-ramp in the form of concessions on the level of the tariffs. If this concession was an attempt to isolate the rebels rather than to soften them up, it clearly worked: no other Southern state would join South Carolina's campaign.

Increasingly outmanoeuvred, the nullifiers tried to regain the momentum by raising the state militia in a show of force against the federal government. Even this worked against them, though, when pro-union South Carolinians turned out their own force in support of the Union. It gave Jackson the opportunity to enforce federal law with South Carolinian troops, making the final nail in the nullifiers' coffin one of their own state's making.

It was Calhoun who would help settle the crisis by negotiating a Compromise Tariff. Its adoption reduced the chances of Southern support for South Carolina's rebellion to zero. It would be the last time a Southern state would take up arms against the Constitution until the start of the Civil War. In the decades that followed, it would in fact be Northern abolitionists who would attack the Constitution as a "pro-slavery compact" (the title of an 1845 book by abolitionist Wendell Phillips). They would increasingly turn to the "all men are created equal" creed of the Declaration of Independence as a higher standard by which to judge – and condemn – the outcome of the 1787 Convention. It allowed Calhoun to revert to his original stance of defender of the Constitution, a role he would play enthusiastically in the last of the great compromises, that of 1850.

The Last Compromise (1850)

In the next thirty years following the 1820 Missouri Compromise, it would be celebrated in unionist circles as a kind of second founding of the American republic. The United States' existence had been challenged, but at the last possible moment House and Senate had come up with a formula that allowed North and South, free states and slave states, to continue to coexist peacefully inside a single Union.

With every passing year, however, Southern discomfort about the 1820 settlement grew. Instead of feeling secure in their right to practise their "peculiar tradition" in their own states, they felt robbed of the right to settle freely in the new states above the line of partition. In a peculiar kind of mirroring act, they started seeing their relationship with the North through the prism of the relationship between slaveholder and enslaved person. Northerners, they claimed, were treating them like second-class citizens of the Union, denying them not just the full use of privileges and immunities that the Constitution was supposed to guarantee, but even their very right to exist *as slaveholders*. This feeling of discomfort would end up getting mixed with a sense of frustration about the original constitutional settlement. This sentiment would be most fully expressed by the later president of the

Confederacy Jefferson Davis, during the Senate debate leading to the 1850 Compromise. He stated that he feared the ultimate objective of Northern schemes was "that the South should be restricted from further growth – that around her should be drawn, as it were, a sanitary cordon to prevent the extension of a moral leprosy" (Freehling, *The Road to Disunion* 1119).

At the same time, in the North, feelings of unease about the continued existence of slavery within the Union grew in strength as the decades passed. In the early 1820s, abolition was still a marginal concern. By the 1830s, the call had inspired a movement. Though still a minority, and mostly ignored by Northern politicians, as its numbers grew, so did its impact. By the time the next significant crisis of the Union came around, in the late 1840s, abolitionism was sufficiently strong to shake the republic to its foundations.

—

If the crisis of 1850 was at its core about slavery, the immediate cause was once again the issue of expansion. Though the last of the remaining territories acquired in the Louisiana Purchase would not receive statehood for another half a century, by the early 1840s the question of further territorial expansion was firmly on the political agenda. Looking at it from a twenty-first-century perspective, a United States spanning the entire land mass between the Atlantic and the Pacific Ocean may look logical; yet it was far from logical to the American politicians of the early 1840s. Not just because the land in the West belonged to another country (Mexico), but also because part of the political class was not convinced of the wisdom of any further expansion.

This camp, chiefly consisting of Northern industrial states, emphasised the alternative strategy of deeper rather than wider union. As leader of the Whig Party, Henry Clay gave voice to this position. The main challenge the United States faced, as he saw it, was not expansion but internal improvements: "It is much more important that we unite, harmonize, and improve what we have than attempt to acquire more" (Walker Howe 706).[15] The pro-expansion camp was led by accidental president John Tyler, who moved into the White House in 1841 when its intended occupant, President William Henry Harrison, died of pneumonia after catching a cold at his inauguration. Tyler was nominally a Whig Party representative, but he was

15   In Southern eyes, the cause of internal improvement became so much associated with the North that the Confederate Constitution of 1861 expressly forbade the central government to sponsor any such projects. See Walker Howe 585.

in outlook more a Southern Democrat: a pro-slavery, pro-expansion strict
constructionist in the Thomas Jefferson mould.

After vetoing a signature Whig Party bill to (re)establish a national
bank, Tyler would receive the dubious honour of becoming the first sitting
president expelled by his own party. It was to prove an event of far-reaching
consequences. Following his expulsion, he purged the government of
all Whig appointments, replacing them with states' rights officials in
his own image. Even though they had lost the presidential election of
1840, the Democrats were thereby given the power to shape the national
agenda. An essential part of that agenda, as far as they were concerned,
was expansion.

The opportunity would present itself in the form of the independent Republic of Texas. Not only did this former Mexican province offer commercial
opportunities to Southern slaveholders, it also offered political opportunities
of extensive territorial gains to the United States. Tyler therefore made
inclusion of Texas in the Union his top priority. Though the majority Whig
Senate voted down a treaty of annexation, the 1844 election would help
settle the argument. Tyler's successor, the explicitly pro-expansionist James
Polk, defeated the anti-expansionist, Henry Clay. Even though the winning
margin was tight – a few thousand votes – the people's verdict was treated
as final. Tyler used the lame duck session to fix annexation without a new
vote on the treaty (Walker Howe 698).

With Texas included in the Union, focus immediately shifted to the
lands in the West. In an issue devoted to the Texas annexation debate, the
Democratic Review introduced a new doctrine that gave voice to the feeling
among expansionists. It was, the paper argued, "our manifest destiny to
overspread the continent allotted by Providence for the free development
of our yearly multiplying millions" (703). The only problem was that the
lands claimed in this way for the American Union were in fact legally the
property of its neighbour Mexico. Polk's mission therefore became finding
a way to loosen that country's grip on the territories. When negotiation
didn't produce the required result, he resorted to war.

The Mexican War of 1846 ended with a complete victory for the American
federal government. In the peace treaty that followed, Mexico was forced to
cede virtually half of its territory to the United States. Out of these newly
acquired lands, four states would be created: New Mexico, Nevada, Utah,
and California. A number of other states or territories already belonging
to the American Union would see their territory significantly expanded.

—

With the formal annexation of the former Mexican provinces of Alta California and Nuevo Mexico, expansionism's triumph seemed complete. In reality, the political crisis was only just beginning. With expansion a fait accompli, the debate turned to the *real* problem, the one the Whigs had tried to avoid having to debate by blocking the possibility of expansion: the issue of slavery in the new territories.

Just as in 1820, in 1846 a Northern Congressman – this time a Pennsylvania politician called David Wilmot – triggered the crisis by tabling an explosive amendment to seemingly innocuous legislation. It was an indication of how much the debate had moved on in the North that the amendment did not propose a gradual restriction (as Tallmadge had done in 1819) but an outright *ban* of slavery in the new territories.[16] Wilmot's amendment would go the same way as Tallmadge's in 1820: passing the majority anti-slavery House before dying in the majority pro-slavery Senate. But though the South managed to strangle the amendment in its crib, that did not make the debate about the underlying issue go away. "[T]here is no other subject claiming the deliberations of this house but slavery," one member complained in early 1848. "From morning to night, day after day, week after week, nothing is talked of here, nothing can get a hearing that will not afford an opportunity to lug in something about slavery" (Foner 123–124).

The cause of "no slavery in the territories" ended up dominating the remaining elections of the decade: first in the midterm elections of 1846, then in the presidential election of 1848. The latter saw the former president Martin van Buren, previously instrumental in delivering Northern Democratic votes for Southern attempts to stifle debate on slavery, accept the candidacy of the new Free Soil Party. His party platform was, in part, based on the Wilmot Proviso: no slavery in the new territories (Freehling, *The Road to Disunion* 1070). The party's success was greatest in New York and New England, where it drew substantial numbers of votes away from both established parties. The fact that this success came on the back of an explicit rejection of slavery fundamentally altered Northern political calculations. From now on, Northern politicians would have to add anti-slavery proposals to their platform if they wanted to be taken seriously by their voters (Foner 132).

---

16   Unlike Tallmadge, Wilmot was not an abolitionist out of concern over the treatment of enslaved people. He described his cause as that of "the white working man" and opposed slavery only as a form of unfair economic competition. Originally a Democrat, after the election of 1848 (which saw the Second Party System shattered) he would join the Free Soil Party – one of the forerunners of the later Republican Party.

It was the start of the collapse of the Second Party System that had sustained the post-1820 consensus. Before its eventual demise, the old order would right itself one last time to produce a final Compromise. It involved a complicated trade off over several issues that all involved slavery in one way or another. It banned the slave trade in the federal district of Washington, D.C. (though not slavery itself). It gave part of slave-owning Texas to the slavery-free New Mexico territory. And it introduced a new rule for letting states into the Union on the basis of "popular" or "squatter sovereignty" – basically taking them in as states without a final decision on the legal status of slavery, allowing the local population to settle that issue afterwards (Freehling, *The Road to Disunion* 1066). To compensate the South for what it feared would be a Northern-friendly deal, the North grudgingly accepted a new, much stricter Fugitive Slave Act.

If the Compromise of 1820 had secured the Union for another generation, the Compromise of 1850 did the opposite. The Fugitive Slave Act seemed not so much a piece of legislation as an attempt by the South to insult the North by forcing it to cooperate with a practice it had abolished. The North would inevitably take offence when the South started enforcing the law, requiring Northern states to hand over people who had lived among them freely – without a right of appeal.

For Southerners, it was compensation for being forced to watch California come into the union as a free state. Squatter sovereignty had worked against the South when the Gold Rush of 1849 brought large numbers of Northern adventurers and speculators to the state. Its entry gave the free states for the first time a numerical advantage in the Senate (Freehling, *The Road to Disunion* 1092). With the House already in the anti-slavery column, the pro-slavery South now felt itself an endangered minority. The fear expressed by some was that in due course, the remaining territories all coming in as free states would give the North the three-fourths majority required to write slavery out of the Constitution (1078). Further compromises would do nothing to help prevent that scenario. It was time, Southerners concluded, for more radical measures to protect their "peculiar tradition."

Beyond compromise: Dred Scott, Lincoln, and the slide into Civil War

It is in the speeches of Abraham Lincoln that the doctrine of the necessity of compromise would find its fullest expression. In a speech addressing the claims of his opponent in the 1858 Illinois Senate race, Stephen Douglas, he would summarise its significance for the American Founding:

It may be argued that there are certain conditions that make necessities and impose them upon us, and to the extent that a necessity is imposed upon a man, he must submit to it. I think that was the condition in which we found ourselves when we established this government. We had slaves among us; we could not get our Constitution unless we permitted them to remain in slavery; we could not secure the good we did secure, if we grasped for more; but, having by necessity submitted to that much, it does not destroy the principle that is the charter of our liberties. Let that charter stand as our standard. (Lincoln 294)

When Douglas in 1854 endeavoured to destroy the old consensus by stripping Congress of the right to regulate slavery in the remaining territories through the Kansas–Nebraska Act, Lincoln spoke out against him in a full-throated defence of the 1820 Compromise: "The Missouri Compromise ought to be restored. Slavery may or may not be established in Nebraska. But whether it be or not, we shall have repudiated (...) the spirit of compromise; for who, after this, will ever trust in a national compromise?" (Lincoln 83).

To defend the Union, and the Constitution on which it was based, Lincoln was willing to make the same immoral bargain the Founders had made seventy years earlier: "We allow slavery to exist in the slave States – not because slavery is right or good, but from the necessities of our Union. We grant a fugitive slave law because it is so 'nominated in the bond'; because our fathers so stipulated – had to – and we are bound to carry out this agreement." When someone in the audience shouted their objection to the idea of accepting the Fugitive Slave Act, Lincoln replied: "It was part of the bargain, and I'm for living up to it" (Lincoln 112).

In the run-up to the 1860 elections, Lincoln made restoration of the old Constitutional compromise his personal platform. Addressing Southerners, he stated that "[w]e mean to treat you, as near as we possibly can, as Washington, Jefferson, and Madison treated you. We mean to leave you alone, and in no way to interfere with your institution; to abide by all and every compromise of the Constitution." He even tried to address their growing feelings of anxiety about being treated as second-class citizens by making clear that his plea for the old Compromise approach was not just pragmatic but based on a feeling of kinship: "We mean to remember that you are as good as we; that there is no difference between us other than the difference of circumstances. We mean to recognise and bear in mind always, that you have as good hearts in your bosoms as other people" (Lincoln 264).

—

If Southerners had still been willing to compromise, they could not have found a better Northern champion of their right to hold slaves than Abraham Lincoln. But by the time he made his peace offering, compromise between slave states and free states had become virtually impossible – not least thanks to the Supreme Court. Its infamous 1857 Dred Scott ruling is mainly remembered for its shockingly racist language and reasoning. The racism was there for all to see in the answer to the central question as formulated by Chief Justice Taney. Could Scott, "whose ancestors were imported into this country, and sold as slaves, become a member of the political community formed and brought into existence by the Constitution of the United States?" In other words: were they potential citizens? The Court's answer was clear: "We think they are not" (United States Supreme Court, *Dred Scott* 20). That was not, however, what made the decision so controversial at the time. The language used was nothing out of the ordinary for 1850s America, nor was this particular conclusion (all slave state politicians would have agreed with it).[17] Its truly explosive aspect, to Lincoln and his contemporaries, was what it said about the Missouri Compromise.

To back up its decision to rule out citizenship for (formerly) "enslaved Africans," the Court had to twist itself – and the Constitution – into the logical equivalent of a pretzel. If some states at the moment of the Founding explicitly excluded "the African race" from citizenship while others did not, then which option did the Constitution support? If the Court was to be believed, it was that of the slave states. It denied that the Privileges and Immunity clause applied to Scott or any other (formerly) enslaved person: "They were at that time considered as a subordinate and inferior class of beings, who had been subjugated by the dominant race and, whether emancipated or not, yet remained subject to their authority, and had no rights and privileges which that instrument [the Constitution] provides for" (United States Supreme Court 23).

It wasn't a matter of the Constitution choosing the side of the slave states, though. Taney went on to claim that there had been no conflict because *all* states at the time of the Founding used the same definition of citizenship: "In the opinion of the court, the legislation and histories of the times, and the language used in the Declaration of Independence, show, that neither

---

17   Even Lincoln was not averse to pandering to the racism of 1850s audiences. He did it several times during his debates with Douglas, for example by observing that there was a "natural disgust ... at the idea of an indiscriminate amalgamation of the white and the black race" (*Speeches and Letters* 136). He did it again in a speech in 1859: "We mean to marry your girls when we have a chance – the white ones, I mean" (265).

the class of persons who had been imported as slaves, nor their descendants (...) were then acknowledged as part of the people" (United States Supreme Court 27–28). When asserting that the Declaration's famous dictum "that all men are created equal" could not possibly refer to enslaved Africans, he accepted that the actual behaviour of the men who drafted it may have seemed "utterly and flagrantly inconsistent with the principles they asserted" (33). But since these were "great men," they were "incapable of asserting principles inconsistent with those on which they were acting." There was therefore no real contradiction (33–34).

What remained to be explained away was the fact that Scott had visited free states north of the Ohio River line of partition. By the legal standard of the mid-1850s, his claim to have obtained his freedom there because of this fact would be sound – irrespective of whether he was an American citizen or not. The Court was determined to show that this couldn't be the case. It did it by focusing its fire power on the Missouri Compromise, specifically on the question of whether it had indeed "banned forever (...) slavery and involuntary servitude (...) in all that part of the territory ceded by France, which goes under the name of Louisiana, which lies north of thirty-six degrees thirty minutes latitude" (United States Supreme Court 76).

In 1820, Monroe had asked his cabinet if Congress had the power to regulate the process of incorporating new states into the Union. Yes, his ministers answered, referring to the Constitutional clause which stated that "Congress shall have Power to dispose of and make all needful Rules and Regulations respecting the Territory or other Property belonging to the United States" (Art. 4, section 3, clause 2). Taney now argued that this was an error of interpretation. Treating the Constitution as a kind of contract between the thirteen founding states, he claimed that it could only have covered the territory they already held in common at the time: "[T]he power there given, whatever it may be, is confined, and was intended to be confined, to the territory which at that time belonged to, or was claimed by, the United States" (United States Supreme Court 77). Since the Louisiana Territory was acquired *after* the drafting of the Constitution, it couldn't possibly be covered by this clause.

This inevitably led Taney to the incendiary conclusion that since Congress never had the power to regulate territories acquired after 1787, the Missouri Compromise had been based on a flawed interpretation of the Constitution: "Upon these considerations, it is the opinion of the court that the act of Congress which prohibited a citizen from holding and owning property of this kind in the territory of the United States north of the line therein mentioned, is not warranted by the Constitution" (United States Supreme

Court 115). This had two immediate consequences. One was that the 1820 Compromise was null and void. Regarding slavery, this meant that the territories were covered by Constitutional provisions which "distinctly and expressly affirmed" it as a legal right of property (114). *All* territory covered by the Louisiana purchase, including that above the 36 degrees 30 minutes parallel, was to be considered as always having been open to slavery. The other was that, at the stroke of a pen, the very idea of political compromise over slavery had been declared legally impossible.

—

Lincoln's attempt to preserve the Union through a restatement of the doctrine of "necessity of compromise," and a reinstatement of the Missouri Compromise, might with some justification be called the last act of the Founding. His approach was too clever by half, though – he was essentially trying to present as a status quo worth defending the growing conflict which was inexorably pushing his country towards civil war: between the Constitution that protected the institution of slavery, and the Declaration of Independence ("the charter of our liberties") that was used by anti-slavery campaigners as a weapon in their campaign to abolish that same institution.

As Lincoln himself recognised, without the possibility of compromise, the United States was facing an inevitable choice:

> 'A house divided against itself cannot stand'. I believe this government cannot endure permanently, half slave and half free. I do not expect the Union to be dissolved – I do not expect the house to fall; but I do expect it will cease to be divided. It will either become all one thing, or all the other. (Lincoln 143)

He would, of course, be right about this, though not in the way he expected when he spoke these words. In 1858 it was an "All Slave" future that he feared the most, at one point suggesting that the Union was just one more Supreme Court ruling away from making slavery lawful in *all* states. "Welcome or unwelcome," he warned his audience, "such a decision is probably coming" (154). All that stood between the Union as it was and that decision was the newly founded Republican Party: "If we stand firm, we cannot fail" (154).

It was profoundly ironic that the spark that caused the fire that would eventually help to end the original constitutional settlement came from the election of the one man still fully committed to the old compromise. The fact that Civil War followed shortly after showed the profound truth of

Hamilton's closing argument in *Federalist* 85: a Union without a doctrine of "necessity of compromise" could not survive the conflicts that changing circumstances would inevitably throw up.

—

Through the American debate, the taxonomy of unions had undergone a fundamental change. The concept of federal union as introduced in European debate (Pufendorf's "something in between") had become the genus for two different species of union. The Philadelphia Convention succeeded in creating a new kind of union, one that was clearly distinct from the one created through the Articles of Confederation. It was based on a double compromise: on sovereignty, and on representation. Whereas the European-style union established in 1777 had been based on complete state sovereignty and equal representation (one state, one vote), the 1787 union was founded on the idea of shared sovereignty between the centre and the states, and a mix of different concepts of representation (equal in the Senate, proportional in the House).

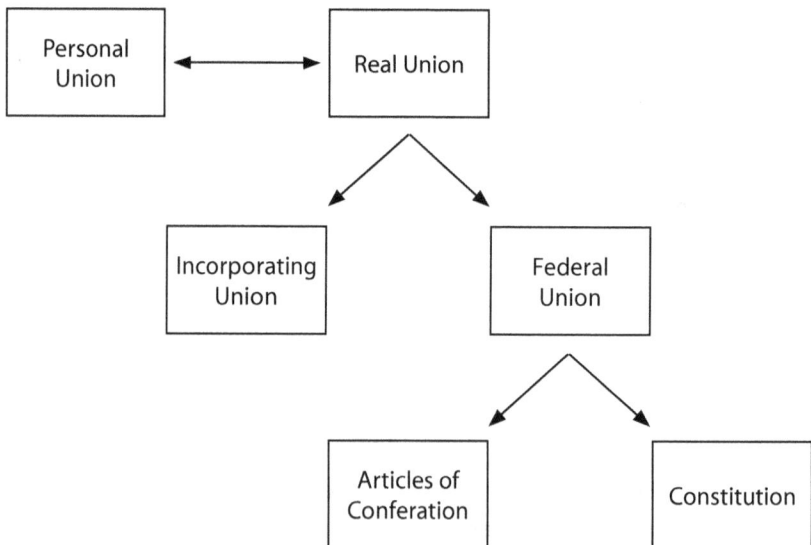

Figure 2: A taxonomy of unions, US

No attempt was made, however, to create a conceptual distinction between the two different types of union. At the Convention, Madison in one intervention used both "confederation" and "federal union" to refer to the same constitutional entity (Larson and Winship 151). On the same day, the Pennsylvania delegate James Wilson added to the conceptual confusion by remarking that he was "for a national government, though the idea of federal is, in my view, the same" (167). In common parlance, both unions were called "federal union," "confederal union," or simply "union." And though the union established through the 1777 Articles was regularly referred to as a "confederation," its executive was called the "federal government," and its powers "federal powers."

At the conceptual level, there remained a lot of confusion even after 1787. Perhaps this explains why three-quarters of a century later, politicians could still have widely varying interpretations of its meaning. If we look, for example, at Lincoln's view of the union in comparison with Calhoun's, we see two completely different stories about the same founding, and two equally different interpretations of the relationship between states and central government. Yet both were consistently referring to the same "federal union."

Afterthought: The Blood-Stained Gate

The preceding chapters talked about American constitutional politics as a kind of strategic challenge for the politicians involved, describing the deals that made and then saved the Union at various critical junctures, safeguarding the Constitutional Great Compromise for another generation.

The question needs to be asked: was this Union really worth saving? Was it worth it if, at least for another twenty years after the signing of the Constitution, it facilitated the transatlantic transportation of African men, women, and children in the most horrible circumstances? Was it worth it if it effectively legalised the treatment of enslaved Africans as less than human, mere property? The answer is most emphatically *no*. It took the United States nearly seventy-five years to reach that conclusion, and even then, only reluctantly.

There should be no doubt about it that the Constitution was a Faustian pact. The Founders bought stability and security for themselves at the expense of the ease, pleasures, and blood of millions of enslaved Africans. They knew this, and still they signed it. Lest there be any misunderstanding about the character of what Southern politicians called their "peculiar institution," some anecdotes will suffice. One category is representative of the immense cruelty of the practice known as the Triangular Trade, a trade that began in the middle of the seventeenth century and would last until the first part of the nineteenth century. European ships would load enslaved human cargo on the west coast of Africa, then transport them to Brazil, the West Indies, or North America, where those who survived the journey were offloaded for sale on the slave markets. The ships would then load up on local produce (sugar, tobacco) and make the journey back to Europe, where the cargo was offloaded before setting off to Africa again.

One such journey involved the Dutch slave ship the *Leusden*, which ran aground in a storm and capsized just off the coast of Surinam on New Year's Day, 1738. The captain ordered his crew to abandon ship, but not before boarding up all but a handful of the nearly 700 enslaved Africans inside the hull of the ship. By the time the storm had finally cleared, the people on board had all drowned. The captain and his crew were given a reward by the ship's owners, the Dutch West India Company, for saving the gold also carried on the ship.

Another infamous example is the slave ship *Zong*. On a voyage in 1781, it was carrying hundreds of enslaved Africans destined for the slave markets in Jamaica, which served as an important transport hub for enslaved people destined for the plantations of the Southern United States, when disease broke out on the ship. The captain ordered his crew to chain together the enslaved people who had fallen sick and throw them overboard. In three days, 132 people were murdered this way. By drowning them, he aimed to save his owners from commercial distress by giving them the chance to claim the insurance value of the "lost" human cargo.

It is estimated that of the 12.5 million men, women, and children who were forcibly transported along the Middle Passage, around 2 million died along the way – from sickness, from cruelty, and from cold, calculated murder.

Another type of evidence comes from the autobiography of an escaped slave who would end up becoming a leader of men and a giant of the abolitionist movement, Frederick Douglass (1817/1818–1895). His book contains vivid descriptions of the many everyday cruelties that made the life of the enslaved person a living nightmare. It started with being denied even the most basic marker of personal identity, the knowledge of his own birthday: "By far the larger part of the slaves know as little of their ages as horses know of theirs, and it is the wish of most masters within my knowledge to keep their slaves thus ignorant" (Douglass 33). When he asked his master – who, in a sick twist not uncommon in slaveholding circles, was most likely also his father – about his age, he was told that it was "improper, impertinent, and evidence of a restless spirit" (34).

When he was a mere infant, he was separated from his mother. Not by accident but by design: "It is a common custom, in the part of Maryland from which I ran away, to part children from their mothers at a very early age" (Douglass 35). In this case it meant his mother was sent away while he wasn't even a year old. Being the son of the slaveholder meant he himself would also be destined to be sold off at an early age. This, too, was common practice:

> cruel as the deed may strike any one to be, for a man to sell his own children to human flesh-mongers, it is often the dictate of humanity for him to do so; for unless he does this, he must not only whip them himself, but must stand by and see one white son tie up his brother, of but few shades darker complexion than himself, and ply the gory lash to his naked back (39)

This cruel, dehumanising system was sustained by violence. This was no mere by-product of the slave system but the very thing that held it together. Douglass describes it as "the blood-stained gate, the entrance to the hell of slavery," through which each enslaved person had to pass (Douglass 40). One of the many episodes of extreme physical cruelty that he witnessed involved an overseer, a woman, and her children. For reasons that he couldn't understand, the overseer decided to whip the woman to within an inch of her life, "causing the blood to run half an hour at the time; and this, too, in the midst of her crying children, pleading for their mother's release" (53). In another episode, an overseer whipped a man who went by the name of Demby. When the man went into the river to wash his wounds, the overseer ordered him to come out so he could continue the beating. When his command was not obeyed, he raised his gun and shot the enslaved man at point blank in the face: "[I]n an instant poor Demby was no more. His mangled body sank out of sight, and blood and brains marked the water where he had stood" (76).

———

The "Great Compromises" served to save a Constitution that sanctioned this cruel system. That Constitution died in the Civil War. It was replaced by a new, more perfect one, through the adoption of Lincoln's Thirteenth, Fourteenth and Fifteenth Amendment.[18] It raises an important question for the "necessity of compromise" doctrine: necessity may know no law, but should it not at least have a sense of good and evil?

18   In an interview with the Stanford News Service, the constitutional scholar Jack Rakove observed that "the Reconstruction amendments of 1865–1870 marked a second constitutional founding that rested on other premises. Together they made a broader definition of equality part of the constitutional order, and they gave the national government an effective basis for challenging racial inequalities within the states." See "When Thomas Jefferson Penned 'All Men Are Created Equal,' He Did Not Mean Individual Equality, Says Stanford Scholar," *Stanford News Service*, 1 July 2020.

Bibliography

Anderson, Perry. "The European Coup." *London Review of Books*, vol. 42, no. 24, 17 December 2020.

Bailyn, Bernard. *The Ideological Origins of the American Revolution*. 1967. Belknap Press, 1992.

Bailyn, Bernard. *To Begin The World Anew: The Genius and Ambiguities of the American Founders*. Vintage, 2004.

Banning, Lance. *Liberty and Order: The First American Party Struggle*. Liberty Fund, 2004.

Brodie, Fawn M. *Thomas Jefferson: An Intimate History*. W. W. Norton, 1974.

Calhoun, John. *South Carolina Exposition and Protest*. 1828. The Perfect Library, 2014.

Calhoun, John. *The Works of John Calhoun*. The Perfect Library, 2013.

Chernow, Ron. *Alexander Hamilton*. 2005. Bloomsbury Publishing, 2020.

Cleve, George William van. *A Slaveholders' Union: Slavery, Politics, and the Constitution in the Early American Republic*. University of Chicago Press, 2010.

Cleve, George William van. *We Have Not a Government: The Articles of Confederation and the Road to the Constitution*. University of Chicago Press, 2017.

Colbourn, H. Trevor. "Thomas Jefferson's Use of the Past." *William and Mary Quarterly*, vol. 1, 1958, pp. 56–70.

Constitution of the United States of America. *US House of Representatives*, https://uscode.house.gov/static/constitution.pdf. Accessed 6 March 2024.

Douglass, Frederick. *Narrative of the Life of Frederick Douglass*. 1845. OPU 2018 *History: The Journal of the Louisiana Historical Association*, vol. 6, no. 1, 1965, pp. 5–25.

Foner, Eric. *The Fiery Trial: Abraham Lincoln and American Slavery*. W. W. Norton, 2010.

Forbes, Robert Pierce. *The Missouri Compromise and Its Aftermath: Slavery and the Meaning of America*. University of North Carolina Press, 2009.

Freehling, William W. *Prelude to Civil War: The Nullification Controversy in South Carolina, 1816–1836*. Oxford University Press, 1991.

Freehling, William W. *The Road to Disunion: Secessionists at Bay, 1776–1854*. Oxford University Press, 1990.

Gladstone, William. "Kin Beyond Sea." *The North American Review*, Sept.–Oct. 1878, pp. 179–212.

Hall, Matthew. *Dividing the Union: Jesse Burgess Thomas and the Making of the Missouri Compromise*. Southern Illinois University Press, 2016.

Hamilton, Alexander, James Madison, and John Jay. *The Federalist Papers*. 1787. Penguin, 1987.

Irwin, Douglas. "Revenue or Reciprocity? Founding Feuds over Early U.S. Trade Policy." NBER Working Paper No. w15144, 21 July 2009, https://www.nber.org/papers/w15144. Accessed 6 March 2024.

Larson, Edward, and Michael Winship. *The Constitutional Convention: A Narrative History From the Notes of James Madison*. The Modern Library, 2005.

Lincoln, Abraham. *Speeches and Letters of Abraham Lincoln*. J. M. Dent & Sons, 1907.

Middelaar, Luuk van. *Passage naar Europa: Geschiedenis van een begin*. Historische Uitgeverij, 2009.

Naudé, Gabriel. *Political Considerations upon Refined Politicks, and the Master-Strokes of State*. 1667. Gale Ecco, 2010.

Pocock, J. G. A. *The Machiavellian Moment: Florentine Political Thought in the Atlantic Republican Tradition*. Princeton University Press, 1975.

Soll, Jacob. "J. G. A. Pocock's Atlantic Republicanism Thesis Revisited: The Case of John Adams's Tacitism." *Republics of Letters*, vol. 2, no. 1, 2010, pp. 21–37.

Skinner, Quentin. "A genealogy of the modern state." British Academy lecture, 13 May 2008, *Proceedings of the British Academy*, vol. 162, 2009, pp. 325–370.

United States National Archive, *Founders Online*, https://founders.archives.gov/. Accessed 6 March 2024.

United States Supreme Court. *Dred Scott, Plaintiff in Error v. John F. Sandford*. 1 December 1856, LawApp Publishers, 2019 .

Walker Howe, Daniel. *What Hath God Wrought: The Transformation of America, 1815–1848*. Oxford University Press, 2009.

"When Thomas Jefferson Penned 'All Men Are Created Equal,' He Did Not Mean Individual Equality, Says Stanford Scholar." *Stanford News Service*, 1 July 2020, https://news.stanford.edu/press-releases/2020/07/01/meaning-declaratnce-changed-time/. Accessed 6 March 2024.

Wood, Gordon. *The Creation of the American Republic 1776–1787*. 1969. Omohundro Institute and University of North Carolina Press, 1998.

Wood, Gordon. *Friends Divided: John Adams and Thomas Jefferson*. Penguin Books, 2017.

6   The European Congress as Peace Pact

Abstract

The negotiators at Vienna had to deal with the consequences of the end of the Holy Roman Empire. The result of their deliberations was the German Bund: an institutional framework for managing a political standoff between the Austrian Empire and Prussia. This standoff was in part also the product of a blockage at the theoretical level. There was a broadly shared understanding that a mere Staatenbund was not enough, but the alternative of a Bundesstaat was beyond reach. Until, that is, a theoretical breakthrough on the topic of sovereignty paved the way for the creation of a monarchical federal union. It would take a war to get there. That same war also settled the conflict with Austria in Prussia's favour.

Keywords: German *Bund*, German Reich, Staatenbund, Bundesstaat, Bismarck

The Napoleonic era and end of the balance of power

And then came Napoleon. "World spirit on horseback," according to Hegel. "A fool (...) aiming for world domination," according to the Prussian diplomat Karl August von Hardenberg (Dwyer 300).

—

It was probably inevitable that one of the many wars fought within the European framework of the balance of power would end up fundamentally disturbing the balance. Though it is difficult to say with accuracy which battle was the decisive one, one obvious candidate was that of January 1797 in Rivoli, in Northern Italy. The recently appointed commander of the French Army of Italy, Napoleon Bonaparte (1769–1821), defeated an Austrian army sent to reverse his conquest of the Piedmont region. Following this victory, Napoleon marched over the Alps and into the Habsburg heartland with

Livestro, Joshua: *A More Perfect Union. Federal Union in Political Theory and Practice, 1500-1951.*
Amsterdam: Amsterdam University Press, 2024.
DOI: 10.5117/9789048563777_CH06

the aim of conquering the capital Vienna. Though he didn't achieve that particular goal, the final result of his efforts was still an astounding victory in territorial and political terms. The peace treaty of Campo Formio at the end of the Italian Campaign gave France control of most of northern Italy, as well as of the Austrian Netherlands. The Austrians received compensation in the form of the Veneto, and of Venice itself – marking the end of a thousand years of independence for the *Serenissima*.

These first victories gave Napoleon the springboard he needed. He would go on to become the most prominent general in the French republican army, then the first consul in the republic, and eventually the supreme ruler of a newly founded empire. The monarchies allied against him abroad were as powerless to stop him as the republican factions at home. The coalition system which had been the mainstay of the balance of power doctrine no longer seemed to work. Over the next fifteen years, a number of different alliances would be formed to stop the French juggernaut, involving most of the other great powers at one point or another. But no matter what the composition of the coalition put into the field against him, Napoleon always came out on top. (On land, that is. At sea was another matter. There the French would regularly be outmanoeuvred and at crucial moments outfought by the British fleet.)

If his victories on the battlefield invoked the image of Alexander the Great, his conquests of countries and territories invoked those of Charlemagne. Once the conquests started piling up, fears among France's rivals grew that what Napoleon was after was more than the odd border correction. As early as 1803, the Austrian foreign minister Johann Ludwig von Cobenzl voiced the suspicion that he might in fact be intent on establishing a universal monarchy. The initial trickle of speculation became a flood after Napoleon crowned himself emperor in 1804; formally only "of France," but the Roman connotations of the title – and the fact that he insisted on using the same coronation oath as Charlemagne in 800 – left little room for doubt about the scale of his ambitions.

Of Napoleon's actual ambitions, we actually know surprisingly little. He produced no unambiguous statements about his intentions, though we can obviously deduce something from the record of his actions. A man who crowned himself emperor, who conquered (or at least, defeated) most of Western and Central Europe and then marched a large army into Russia could reasonably be suspected of harbouring aspirations on a Roman scale. Then again, for a man supposedly bent on establishing universal monarchy he had a surprisingly unambitious attitude when it came to actually estab-lishing one. He satisfied himself with mere territorial concessions instead of fundamentally redrawing the map of Europe. It seemed at times as if the wars he fought were more interesting to him than their aftermaths. The World Spirit on horseback that Hegel saw marching into Jena in 1806 marched right back out again in pursuit of other battles – battles virtually guaranteed by his own approach to peacemaking.[1]

—

While the great powers of Europe were struggling to find a way to overcome the Napoleonic challenge, Europe's political thinkers were trying to assess the causes and consequences of the war. The debate would focus on the role of the balance of power. There were, broadly speaking, two camps here. The first camp's main spokesman was the Comte D'Hauterive (1754–1830). Hauterive was a French diplomat who, in his *De l'État de la France à la Fin de l'An VIII* (published in 1800), argued that the "equilibrium" established by the Treaty of Westphalia, and enshrined in the "European public law" of subsequent treaties, had been rudely disturbed by three eighteenth-century developments that together had the effect of "introducing into the European political system a constant sense of unease, change and agitation" (Hauterive 26; my translation throughout).

The first was the rise of Russia, which went from being more or less insignificant in European affairs to "upsetting or at least modifying all existing relations" between the major and minor powers of Europe (Hauterive 4) The second was the rise of Prussia, which destabilised the internal relationships within the Holy Roman Empire and set off a "double mania" among the governments of Europe by its example of militarisation funded by a new, more efficient system of taxation (12). The third destabilising factor was the rise of the colonial systems, and specifically that of Great Britain. This triggered a new kind of competition which inevitably led to conflicts between states (Hauterive used the by now familiar term "jealousy of trade" to describe this process; 19). According to him, it also led to British governments from Cromwell onwards switching to a new kind of approach in their continental diplomatic strategy, focusing on "all motives of discord

---

1   As Frederick W. Kagan put it in *The End of the Old Order*, "Napoleon's diplomatic skills lay in getting the peace terms he wanted, not in designing a stable, durable peace. (...) In 1801 and 1802 Napoleon negotiated peace treaties based more on the transitory weaknesses and fears of his enemies than on the real correlation of forces in Europe. He did the same in 1805" (629). See also Paul Schroeder, *The Transformation of European Politics 1763–1848*: "He would always know his immediate goals, never his ultimate ones; he would be brilliant at playing roles, including that of peacemaker, but poor at sustaining them" (208).

that could disunite the states on the continent, and to use them to weaken them, (...) [t]o involve itself in all political arguments to stir them up, and to interfere in all federations in order to disrupt them" (22–23).

Hauterive concluded that, as a result of these developments, "there no longer existed in Europe a principle of government, a federal link or constant principle organising politics and behaviour." The new situation was one in which "the weak were at the mercy of the strong" (32), and where "the seeds of a political anarchy had been sown throughout Europe" (33), as a result of which "immediately before the Revolution the [European] public law only existed on paper" (34). Those commentators who had suggested the French Revolution had been the great disruptive force were wrong, he argued: "[It] had done nothing but clearly demonstrate the destruction [of the public law]" (34), chiefly by countries "blinded by a desire for expansion" (38–39).

The most important challenge as he saw it was to recreate "the European public law" (Hauterive, 46) He rejected the idea of recreating a balance of power to accompany it, not least because he thought the concept "somewhat chimerical," noting "the impossibility of establishing it with any hope of durability" (90). He did recognise the importance of establishing a new general equilibrium, but thought it would consist in practice of a series of smaller regional balances. If there was to be a form of coordination in this system, it was not to come from a council or from a balance of power like mechanism, but from the example and the leadership of the one country – France – that was already in the process of reintroducing the public law through its recently concluded treaties with "Holland, Spain, Switzerland and some of the states of Italy." In the "closer ties" which were the result of these treaties, he thought "one could already see the foundations of a new political code, which (...) could serve as a safeguard for some, a counterweight for others, and a rulebook for all" (46–47).

—

The most principled defender of the balance of power during the early years of the Napoleonic period was the Prussian political writer Friedrich von Gentz (1764–1832). Born into an exiled Huguenot family with a tradition of public service, he enrolled as a student at the University of Königsberg. There he was exposed to the thought of its most famous professor, Immanuel Kant. As befits a talented pupil, Von Gentz would strive to prove himself the opposite of his teacher. If Kant was an ascetic in every sense of the word, Von Gentz would gain fame for his drinking, gambling, and sexual prowess – his biographer Golo Mann described him as a "pleasure addict"

(Mann 29; my translation). And where Kant never left his hometown, Von Gentz would travel extensively, serving different countries and at one point the whole of Europe before eventually retiring in Vienna.

Philosophically, Von Gentz's urge to distinguish himself from Kant made it inevitable that he would take up the cause of defending the balance of power as the best system for preserving a sense of order on the continent. In a number of articles published in a periodical he founded in 1799, the *Historisches Journal*, he made the case in favour of the first and second methods of expansion as defined by Machiavelli, and against the one embraced by Kant: that of a European confederation to sustain perpetual peace. An essay on – or rather against – the latter idea ("On Perpetual Peace," 1800) offered a very different assessment of the chances of peace under a confederation that left room for hundreds of little principalities and republics: "Half of all the wars, that have torn Europe apart in the last three hundred years, arose from the existence of small states" (Von Gentz, "On Perpetual Peace," quoted in Stafford 76). Rather than securing perpetual peace, he claimed, Kant's European confederation would actually leave in place the conditions for perpetual war.

His solution was to create a new political map of Europe, where the smaller states were all incorporated into five or six larger entities. These remaining larger entities would then exist in a kind of Vattelian "imperfect civil constitution" under the balance of power system (Stafford 74). Von Gentz's perspective was obviously coloured by Prussian views on the three Polish Partitions. He described this kind of violent territorial expansion as not just "unavoidable" but also morally right, "a natural and beneficial tendency arising from the higher culture of nations" (81). In an essay on a similar process of territorial consolidation that led to the British incorporation of Ireland into the Union, he claimed that what the Irish lost in political liberty, they gained through participation in a higher culture and a global system of trade: "The true independence of citizens and the nation (...) will be increased, not reduced, through the combination of parliaments; this true independence hangs from the progress of culture, and the freedom of trade" ("Plan for a Closer Union," quoted in Stafford 90).

—

Von Gentz would use his reply to Hauterive, published under the title *On the State of Europe Before And After the French Revolution* (1801) to fully develop his theory of the balance of power, while portraying France as the cause of the entire destabilisation of the continental order. Hauterive's claim that the rise of Russia, Prussia, and the colonial system had disrupted the balance of power established in 1648 was in his view based on a flawed interpretation of events.

Russia's rise was of no consequence to France. Apart from their clashing interests regarding the fate of the Ottoman empire, the two had no real sources of rivalry. On the contrary, they actually had a shared interest in the "balance of Europe, which they mutually though tacitly concurred to support." They even cemented their relationship through a trade treaty, signed in 1787. And if Russia would ever threaten to destabilise the continental order, Austria and Prussia could be counted on to lead the resistance. "Thus," Von Gentz concluded, "the greatest danger which France could ever dread from Russia, was averted without any immediate effect of its own" (*On the State of Europe*, 111–112).

Rather than destabilising it, Prussia's rise also actually brought a greater sense of balance to relationships within the Holy Roman Empire, and to its relationship with France: "If Austria had attempted to aggrandize herself, Prussia would have been ready to oppose her; if Prussia had threatened France with hostility, the alliance of Austria was at hand" (Von Gentz, *On the State of Europe* 98). As for England and the colonial system, it never seriously threatened France's territorial security. And if there was a commercial rivalry, "the advantage was almost as often on the side of France as on that of England" (101). He considered it a gross mischaracterisation of England's intentions to suggest it had spent the hundred and fifty years since Westphalia plotting to destabilise the continent. In fact, in all the wars fought since then, it had only ever sought to maintain the balance of power: "In each of these wars, it was the constant plan and endeavour of England, to prevent any such revolution, to uphold existing relations, and to throw her weight into the scale from which France had withdrawn her own" (172).

If there was blame to be attributed for the destruction of Europe's federal order, it lay squarely with revolutionary France: "It was the revolution that produced this terrible war. The revolution, and that alone, overturned the political system (...); dissolved every federal obligation, subverted and demolished every pillar of the balance of power" (Von Gentz, *On the State of Europe* 209). Contrary to Hauterive's claims, Von Gentz pointed out that France waged wars not for the sake of self-defence but for territorial expansion: "[T]hey extended their territory on all sides by conquest, by forced alliance, or by compulsory treaties" (214). As a result, "[a]ll Europe bleeds at the wounds inflicted by the aggrandizement of France; and her dreadful preponderance still threatens, like an impending storm ready to burst over the heads of a trembling world" (280).

This "dreadful preponderance" resulting from a seemingly endless series of conquests obviously invoked the spectre of universal monarchy. Though he did refer to the French republic's expanded territory as an "empire" (Von Gentz, *On the State of Europe* 247), Von Gentz did not believe it was possible anymore to establish a universal monarchy in the early nineteenth century. The reason was an alternative version of the American anti-federalist argument about the centre's inability to govern the more remote regions: "[T]he business of government is become so much more difficult and intricate, that the most extravagant ambition will limit what it desires to rule" (284).[2] What France had obtained instead through the treaty of Lunéville of 1801 was an ability to rule Europe "indirectly and not immediately," as a kind of "feudal seigniory" (284–285).

This dominant French position, Von Gentz concluded, demanded a joint response by the other great powers. Though convinced of the necessity of such a coalition, he made his plea for a renewed coalition effort against France more in hope than expectation. The failure of the war of the Second Coalition (formally still ongoing when Von Gentz wrote his treatise but effectively already over when Austria was forced to sue for peace in 1800) was still an open wound for Europe's monarchs: "[T]he dreadful lesson is yet fresh in the memory of humbled Europe; and who now among the rulers of nations will venture to encounter a second?" (Von Gentz, *On the State of Europe* 246). But as Von Gentz saw it, France's seemingly unquenchable thirst for territorial expansion meant there was no alternative. If France, "not content with her present acquisitions," tried to impose its will on the rest of Europe, "a general league would be the only means of resisting the danger" (247–248).

—

Apart from taking issue with Hauterive's analysis of the situation in Europe before and after the French revolution, Von Gentz also disputed his interpretation of the Peace of Westphalia. In Von Gentz's view this was first and foremost a "constitution of the German Empire" (Von Gentz, *On the State of Europe* 13–14). "Only those can complain," he argued, "who consider the treaty of Westphalia as the foundation of a general [European]

---

2   Even though he had studied the American constitutional debate, Von Gentz seemed not to have been aware of Madison's argument in *Federalist* 14 that technological innovation and infrastructure investment in the form of new canals could help to expand the reach of central government.

constitution, which it never was, nor ever could be" (41). More importantly, Hauterive failed to grasp the essence of the balance of power system: "The federal constitution of nations can never be so completely organized, so carefully and exactly balanced, as to prevent every attempt to destroy the equilibrium and oppress the rest, on the part of powers invited by favourable circumstances, or impelled by enterprising princes" (54). In an echo of Machiavelli's arguments, he argued that the ambitions of rulers in the form of the "propensity to extend their limits" (35), and the constantly changing fortunes of states, meant that the balance needed to be a dynamic concept instead of a static one. In this interpretation, conflict through attempted expansion was a natural part of the system. The same changes that Hauterive saw as evidence of its decay – specifically the partition of Poland – were to Von Gentz signs of its continued proper functioning.

In a later study on the same subject, *Fragments Upon the Balance of Power in Europe* (1805), Von Gentz would expand on this idea by formulating the theory that the balance of power functioned essentially in the same way as a mixed regime:

> A system of political counterpoise has both in its structure and operations, a remarkable analogy with what, in the internal economy of states, is called a mixed constitution, or constitutional balance. (...) In precisely the same manner it is possible that the members of a great confederacy (...) should act as a counterpoise the one to the other.
> (Von Gentz, *Fragments* 72–73)

Unlike the American Founders, though, he would not take the next step of opening up the two axes of power – the one covering relations between states, the other the mix of powers within the states – to a form of integration within a single system. For Von Gentz, the kind of stability that the American federal constitution promised to provide was illusory, at least in a European context. He did consider the idea: "A law of nations, in the most extensive sense of the word, would be such a constitution as should establish all their several relations by immutable laws" (Von Gentz, *Fragments* 89). It would serve three useful functions: it would "assign to each the place it ought to hold in the general system," "guarantee the duration of this system" and "provide effectual means for preventing every undertaking of a nature to destroy that equilibrium" (89). But he concluded, with a reference to Kant's central idea, that it was a practical impossibility: "There never has been any law of nations in this sense of the word; and it would be in vain to expect it, until the project of perpetual peace be likewise realized" (89). Von Gentz's analysis on the location of a proper federation based on a law of nations in the realm of perpetual peace seemed to be overlapping with Kant's. But whereas for Kant the state of perpetual peace was a natural, or at least *plausible*, end point in historical development, for Von Gentz it was more like the historical equivalent of the mathematical concept of infinity: theoretically possible, practically unachievable.

That did not mean a European federal constitution as such was impossible. On the contrary, he thought it eminently achievable. But it was a different kind of federal constitution from the American one, much less perfect. "[T]he federal constitution of nations" in his view was not a fixed, or even fixable, single state, but a kind of continuum along which the balance of power moved, between periods of "no guaranty of public security" and "the most perfect federal system" which was in reality "at best only tolerable" (Von Gentz, *Fragments* 90).

Von Gentz reflected on what would be required for the "permanent amelioration of the political system" (Von Gentz, *Fragments* 101). Obviously, an essential precondition was "the successful progress of those arms which have been taken up in our great cause" (101). Once victory was achieved and order restored, two more conditions were essential to "the existence and preservation of a great political union" (104). One was that, though he admitted "a general code of laws cannot, in the proper sense of the word, be framed for the regulation of a state confederacy," it was essential that "no means should be left untried to procure for these maxims a common sanction" (102). The maintenance of this system further required a kind of active commitment on the part of its member states: "[T]he more perfect, harmonious and stable the federal system of the European states, the greater the sensibility each individual discovers to every violation of common rights, the stronger the tie which binds each member to the collective body, the more rarely wars occur" (107).

The ultimate aim of this "great political union" wasn't the creation of a "cosmo-political feeling" where "the Italian be united in affection with the German, the German with the Briton, the Briton with the Russian, and so forth." Enlightened self-interest in each of them was enough. "[T]o promote the glory, and above all the prosperity of his native land" the Italian, German, Briton and Russian should realise that "this first and most important of all objects cannot be attained as long as he remains indifferent whether others stand or fall." In other words, "[a] conviction of the necessity, and a sense of the excellence of the federal system, will always accompany the existence of true patriotism" (Von Gentz, *Fragments* 107–108).

The Congress of Vienna

While Von Gentz dreamed about the establishment of a new federal order based on the old Voltairean/Vattelian balance of power plus some unspeci- fied "common sanction" to give it greater coherence, Europe's nations would remain in a state of war for another decade. As late as the summer of 1812 the tide still seemed to be with Napoleon, but his decision to leave his defeated continental rivals with a semblance of independence would be his undoing. It gave them both time and motive to regroup and wait for the opportune moment to strike back. That moment came after the failure of his campaign to conquer Russia, in the autumn of 1812. First his Prussian generals deserted him, then eventually the Prussian government broke its oath and switched to supporting the victorious Tsar Alexander I. At the crucial moment, shortly before the battle that would determine Napoleon's fate (the Battle of the Nations, Leipzig, 1813), this new coalition was joined by the one party he had hoped would stay in his column until the end: Austria.

Napoleon had assumed that marrying an Austrian princess, and fathering a half-Habsburg son, would secure him, if not the support, then at least the neutrality of the Austrians in any conflict involving his empire. That, after all, was how dynastic politics had been done in previous centuries. But he had miscalculated. The man Napoleon had spent years cultivating as a close contact at the Austrian court planted the proverbial dagger in his back by persuading his own emperor to switch sides and join the anti-Napoleon coalition. By waiting till the very last moment before coming out against him, the Austrian Foreign Secretary Clemens von Metternich (1773–1859) not only increased the chances of success of his move, he also gave himself a place in the first rank of the anti-French Alliance. It was a position that he would use to great effect in the phase that was to follow: the rebuilding of Europe.

The first peace treaty of Paris, in 1814, was a conventional European affair. It did impose some conditions on the defeated French, most important of which was the removal of the now deposed emperor Napoleon to the island of Elba. But territorial concessions were limited to some border corrections (mainly in the Elzas region); more importantly, France, under the restored Bourbon monarchy, was allowed to retain its seat at the high table of European diplomacy.

The Congress of Vienna, a series of diplomatic meetings starting in Sep- tember 1814, was required as an addition to the Paris peace treaty because there were simply too many unresolved territorial and dynastic issues to be included in the treaty itself. The preceding twenty-five-year period had seen the end of three of the four federal unions on the continent: the Polish-Lithuanian Commonwealth, the Dutch United Provinces, and the Holy Roman Empire (the fourth, the Swiss Confederacy, had also seen its federal character abolished by Napoleon, but it would be restored by the Congress). It had also spelled the end of the republic of Venice, and several other minor territories and principalities – especially in the Holy Roman Empire, which in the Napoleonic era had seen a large number of minor principalities disappear. Some of the larger states had seen parts of their territories transferred to other principalities. Others had done rather well under Napoleonic rule – he had compensated them for their loyalty by adding to their titles and territories. The Congress had to decide in each of these cases whether to maintain the new borders and regimes or revert to the old ones.

Beyond that, it had to decide what to do with the territories of the former federal unions. The resurrected Polish territory going by the name of the Duchy of Warsaw (a strategic outpost created by Napoleon to serve as a buffer state against Russian aspirations) would almost entirely be linked to the Russian realm in a personal union, through the Tsar. Prussia was compensated for its loss of claims to Polish lands by an expansion of its German territories. The Dutch former United Provinces were to be grouped with the states of the former Austrian Netherlands, to form a monarchy under the house of Orange. This newly created kingdom was also to serve as a buffer state, this time against France.

The most complicated challenge of the three was that of the former Holy Roman Empire. A new kind of framework would have to be created which could bind Austria and newly enlarged Prussia to the "Third Germany" – the other German principalities and territories belonging to the former Empire. It was clear to all parties that the Empire itself, which had been formally disbanded in 1806, would not be restored. But what was to come in its place?

The German issue would be settled in the form of a new map, which replaced the pre-war constellation of hundreds of smaller and larger states with a new set of just thirty-nine consolidated states. These states were united under a new confederation, going under the name of *Deutsche Bund*.

It would take another five years, and several more conferences, to settle the final issues about a mutual defence clause, the state constitutions, and the rights of the smaller states. Most of the other matters, however, had been resolved by the time Napoleon briefly returned to power in the spring of 1815. His hundred-day campaign inevitably ended in defeat at Waterloo. With it died, at least temporarily, France's status as a first order power. The same allies who had been lenient in 1814 now opted for punitive measures. The second peace treaty of Paris (1815) was therefore much stricter than the first one. France not only lost its place among the highest ranked nations, having to suffer the indignity of a prolonged military occupation (for a maximum of five years), it would also have to give up all the lands conquered since the start of the Revolution, and pay a significant indemnity to the other powers. (The latter was standard practice under the balance of power system; Napoleon had forced Prussia to pay a similarly sizable indemnity after the end of the War of the Fourth Coalition, in the summer of 1807.[3])

—

Some of the participants in the negotiations might have been satisfied with merely settling these many territorial and dynastic issues, but not the Russian Tsar Alexander I (1777–1825). From the start, he had in mind a kind of settlement that didn't just conclude the last war, but also prevented the next one. Alexander's personal agenda was a curious mixture of orthodox mysticism and raison d'état. He had a strong sense of divine calling, which would lead him at times to embrace the causes of European fraternal unity and the abolition of both slavery abroad and serfdom at home – though never for long and certainly never consistently.

He was interested in doing the kind of work that Napoleon would fail to do: using the war as a springboard for a complete reordering of the European political constellation. His main guide here was his former Foreign Minister, the Polish prince Adam Czartoryski (1770–1861). In 1803, the latter had drafted secret instructions for negotiations with the British government about the aims with which the two could join a coalition against Napoleon. These instructions had two main elements. One was a redrawing of the map of Europe, strengthening some parts of it, while attaching others to one of the larger powers. Anticipating the demise of the Holy Roman Empire, it recommended the organisation of the smaller German states into "a sort of more concentrated federal government," separate from the two main German powers Austria and Prussia, "whose too unequal forces destroy all balance and patriotism" ("Secret Instructions to M. De Novosilitzoff," quoted in Gielgud II: 45).

Czartoryski also used the instructions to define a challenge that would come to dominate nineteenth-century European politics: the potentially destabilising effect of the disintegration of the Turkish empire. Its "weakness,"

---

3   Bismarck took his inspiration from this Napoleonic indemnity when devising the one imposed on the defeated French nation in 1871. See Taylor 133.

"anarchy," and "discontent" required "an intimate concert between Russia and England" to agree on "some arrangement (...) in conformity with the good of humanity and the precepts of sound policy" (49). Sound policy in this case meant staking out a Russian claim to the Balkans to guarantee "a more happy existence to the Christian populations which are suffering under the domination of the Porte" (50).

If the redrawing of the map and the dismemberment of the Holy Roman Empire and the Turkish empire brought to mind the Grand Design of Henri IV and Sully, this was even truer of the other element of the Secret Instructions.[4] The war was to be followed by the founding of a European federal union that would help to put relations between the continent's monarchies on a surer footing: "When peace is made, a new treaty should be drawn up as a basis for the reciprocal relations of the European States" (Gielgud II: 47). These relations were to take the form of "a league, formed under the auspices of Russia and England, which would be joined by all the second-class States and by all those who really wished to remain at peace" (50–51). The league's main objective was to keep the peace by making sure "the Powers who take part in it never (...) begin a war until after exhausting every means of mediation by a Third Power" (48). With peace secured, it could put the focus on "lay[ing] down a sort of new code of international law which, being sanction by the greater part of the European States, would, if violated by any of them, bind the others to turn against the offender and make good the evil he has committed" (48).

———

The ideas contained in the Secret Instructions, which were signed off by Alexander himself, were a mixture of cold calculation and Christian high idealism. The latter sentiment was more fully expressed in the Holy Alliance treaty (September 1815). In it, the leading continental monarchs (the British government had advised the Prince Regent not to sign) declared that "the sole principle of force, whether between the said Governments or between their Subjects, shall be that of doing each other reciprocal service, and of testifying by unalterable good will the mutual affection with which they ought to be animated, to consider themselves all as members of one and the same Christian nation" (Holy Alliance Treaty, article 2). Reciprocity, not

---

4   In his *Essay sur la Diplomatie*, written after Alexander's death in the mid-1820s, Czartoryski would reveal that the Grand Design had indeed been the source of inspiration for his Secret Instructions.

conflict, was to be the organising principle of the new continental order. It was a clear rejection of the logic behind the balance of power system. The use of Christianity as a cultural foundation introduced both a sense of community and a territorial limit – Islamic Turkey could clearly not be part of it.

The second treaty of Paris is remembered less for high ideals than for an important quasi-constitutional innovation that would move the European order decisively beyond the balance of power principle. In order to "consolidate the connections which at the present moment so closely unite the four Sovereigns for the happiness of the world," the four main powers (Russia, England, Austria, and Prussia, collectively referred to as the Quadruple Alliance) committed to meeting "at fixed periods, either under the immediate auspices of the sovereigns themselves or by their respective ministers." The aim of the meetings would be "consulting upon their interests or for the consideration of the measures which at each of these periods shall be considered the most salutary for the repose and prosperity of Nations, and for the maintenance of the peace of Europe" (article 6, second treaty of Paris, 20 November 1815).

The introduction of a permanent system of meetings for the settlement of conflicts and the arbitration of border disputes obviated the problem signalled by Vattel, namely that peace treaties only ever offered a kind of peace after the fact, and only perpetual "inasmuch as it does not allow them to revive the same war by taking up arms again for the same subject" (Vattel 1186). The second Paris treaty had bolder ambitions. Conflicts were no longer to be settled on the battlefield but at the negotiating table, and not after the fact but before they turned violent. The Great Powers were aiming for a Kantian perpetual peace, not a Vattelian one.

By basing the Congress system not on the people of the states involved but on their sovereigns, who were also pledged to protect each other's rule against internal dissent, the design closely followed the prescriptions of the Abbé de Saint-Pierre. The latter was explicitly referred to as a source of inspiration by Metternich in a letter to the Russian Foreign Minister Count Nesselrode. In it he expressed the hope that the system would at least "insure for a considerable time what the good Abbé de Saint-Pierre wished to establish forever" (Metternich to Nesselrode, 20 August 1817, quoted in Sofka 138).[5] To that end, Metternich was willing to accept the creation of

---

5   In *Conquering Peace: From the Enlightenment to the European Union*, Stella Ghervas suggests that, through his advisers, Tsar Alexander I might also have been familiar with the details of Saint-Pierre's proposal for a European union to achieve perpetual peace (111).

a system for the "regula[tion of] the social field of a broader area than that contained within the borders of a state" (135).

No doubt it would have doubly delighted Saint-Pierre to learn that the decision by Europe's early nineteenth-century leaders to embrace his idea was inspired not by idealism but by cynical calculation. The balance of power approach, which had already been severely tested in the previous decades, had proved to be wholly ineffective in helping to settle the issues that dominated the early peace negotiations: the future of the Polish rump state created by Napoleon, and of the princedom of Saxony. Traditional balance of power politics would have seen both issues eventually resolved through war, a scenario that none of the great powers apart from Russia could afford – and perhaps not even Russia, especially if its actions united the other powers against it (Schroeder 523–538). Raison d'état arguments persuaded the Great Powers to try perpetual peace instead of perpetual war as a method of maintaining the European equilibrium – just as Saint-Pierre had predicted.

—

Apart from Saint-Pierre, Metternich was also inspired by Kant, whose works he had studied closely while at university in Mainz (Siemann 77). But where Kant's federal scheme had an inescapable logic to it, Metternich's version had at its heart a kind of improvisation that was reminiscent of seventeenth-century raison d'état thinking. This improvisational quality was expressed in its organisation: conferences were not held according to a formal schedule, but called on an ad hoc basis, at moments when the Great Powers saw the need for one. This allowed them to solve problems as they arose – or preferably, *before* they arose (Sofka 144–145).

The mere commitment to a series of meetings did not in itself immediately produce a framework for European governance. That would have to be created, one congress at a time,[6] by hammering out agreements on a range of quasi-constitutional issues. It followed out of the initial battle over its structure, which had pitted the UK government, which thought of

---

6   I follow Paul W. Schroeder in using the term *congress* to describe all meetings which took place within this system. As he observed in *Metternich's Diplomacy at its Zenith, 1820–1823*, "Technically, only the Congress of Verona in this period was a congress, the meetings of Troppau and Laibach, lacking full representation of all the powers, were only conferences. (...) In practice, however, the diplomats often referred to the meetings of Troppau and Laibach as congresses. (...) For the sake of simplicity, I have followed their practice without attempting to maintain any nice distinctions" (xi).

the Congress system as limited in scope and time, against Tsar Alexander I, who aimed for it to become a permanent system with the widest possible remit, with Metternich preserving the balance between the two. Of the first few Congresses after the initial one in Vienna, a number would therefore be devoted to practical questions like the process of gradual inclusion of France in the congress system (Aix-la-Chapelle/Aachen, 1818), and the possibility of collective intervention in countries' internal affairs (Troppau 1820).

The other focus of the congress system was on tackling a range of practical political problems in different parts of Europe, sometimes of a dynastic nature but mainly stemming from local revolutionary movements (from Spain to Italy and Greece). The conferences of Troppau (1820) and Laibach (1821) focused on the issue of the revolutions in Naples and Piedmont. The meeting in Laibach also featured a preliminary discussion about an issue that would come to dominate discussions going forward: the Greek revolt against Ottoman rule. What made the issue extra-sensitive was the obvious link between the Orthodox Christian religion of the Greek rebels and that of the Russian Tsar. The links were not just religious but also personal. Alexander's close adviser, Count Ioannis Kapodistrias, was a Greek diplomat in Russian service who would later become the first governor of the newly independent Greek state. Metternich would spend a considerable amount of time and effort trying to persuade the Tsar to stick to the Congressional principles on collective (non-)intervention – and to ignore the counsel of his own adviser, Kapodistrias.

—

By the time the Congress assembled in Vienna, Von Gentz's career had taken a miraculous turn for the better. At the end of the first decade of the 1800s he was living as a pen for hire, spending his time in the casinos and salons of the Bohemian spa towns of Teplitz and Karlsbad, his exuberant lifestyle sponsored by the British government (Mann 195). His fortunes improved somewhat when he moved to Prague and fell into the company of Heinrich von Stein, the Prussian reformer who in 1808 had been banished from the Prussian court for expressing anti-Napoleon sentiments. In 1812 Von Stein would move to the Russian court, where Tsar Alexander selected him to lead the postwar reconstruction of the German federation (a plan that was eventually blocked by Metternich). It was to be the first of a number of fortuitous accidental meetings that would put Von Gentz, spider-like, at the centre of a web of connections of politicians of the highest rank who together would shape the future of post-Napoleonic Europe.[7] The most important of these new contacts was Metternich, with whom he would build strong personal ties after moving to Vienna. Metternich's rise would pave the way for his own, eventually taking him to the position of secretary of Europe's first Congress in the immediate aftermath of the war.

In the period after the establishment of the Congress system, Von Gentz would become one of its main philosophical backers. This might seem like a *volte face*, going from defending the old balance of power approach to the new dialogue-based system in a matter of years. The context, however, was that of peace after a long and bloody conflict – in relative terms, as a percentage of total population and gross domestic product, the Napoleonic wars were at least as destructive as the First World War (Siemann 413). During the war, Von Gentz's number one priority had been to mobilise the Great Powers to fight the Napoleonic threat. An appeal to the balance of power doctrine seemed the most effective way of doing so. With the war finally over, finding a way to avoid a renewed outbreak of the violence that had scarred the continent would be a logical new top priority.

It was therefore entirely plausible for him to conclude, in an essay titled "Considerations on the Political System Now Existing in Europe," that the old balance of power system which he had defended a decade earlier as essential to Europe's restoration had been superseded by a different idea, namely that of "general union, uniting all the states collectively, with a federative bond, under the guidance of the five principal Powers, four of which have equal share in that guidance" (quoted in Walker 71–72). The "cosmo-political feeling" that he had previously rejected as unachievable was now embraced out of a sense of shared destiny: "Europe really seems to form a grand political family, united under the auspices of a high tribunal of its own creation. (…) [T]he peace, the destinies, and the future existence of the peoples of Europe are directly and wholly bound up with it" (72–73). If it seemed superficially similar to the Kantian vision of a European confederation, it was different in two crucial aspects: it was a monarchical federation, not a republican one, and its main constituent parts were not the hundreds of smaller territorial units that had dominated the pre-war political map but the Five Great Powers that emerged from the conflict as the new hegemons of Europe.

---

7   In a letter to a former lover, Von Gentz boasted about this newly won position at the heart of European affairs: "I know everything; no person on earth knows of the current age what I know of it, because no one has been so intimate at once with so many prominent parties and personalities" (Mann 259).

He acknowledged the vulnerability of this system, a consequence of the "extreme fragility" of its institutional infrastructure. But he was not afraid of an imminent collapse: "[T]he situations of the principal Powers that compose it" convinced him that "no one of these Powers can safely, without risking imminent ruin, leave the circle of its present connections" (Walker 73). If raison d'état had brought the Great Powers together into this new union, it was raison d'état that would hold them there. And in his view the danger of a fundamental disruption by a change of heart among these leading powers could be summarised as significant but not likely, at least not in the short term. As for the minor countries, "[s]quabbles and changes among [them] could never have that effect" (73).

True, there was one among the main powers who could perhaps afford to go it alone: "The Emperor Alexander, despite all the zeal and enthusiasm he has consistently shown for the Grand Alliance, is the sovereign who could most easily get along without it" (Walker 80). Given his absolute power and the relative strength of Russia's army compared to that of the other monarchies in the Alliance, he was "the one sovereign fully in a position to undertake major enterprises at any time. (...) What he dreams of at night he can carry out in the morning" (80). He thought the chances of such Russian solo acts would remain limited, though, as long as Austria and Prussia remained united. The system would hold as long as "the *middle line*, formed by Powers whose only interest and whose only desire is peace, is not broken." Austria and Prussia were therefore, together with England, "the true rampart of the common security of Europe" (84).

Von Gentz saw one part of the map where Russia could potentially try to undertake a solo campaign, even against the expressed wishes of the others Powers: "It is certain that, given the present condition of the other Powers, Russian armies could have crossed the Danube and been in full march against Constantinople without bringing on the slightest hostile movement at their rear or on their flanks" (Walker 82). But, he concluded, "the Powers can never allow the Porte's territory to be invaded or dismembered by the Russians. Their opposition might be slow, but it need only be sure, to keep the Emperor from exposing himself to a reaction whose consequences might be quite as disastrous for him as those of a vain effort against Germany" (83).[8] Provided the other Powers stayed true to the purpose of the new union,

---

8   The Crimean War of 1853–1856, in which Russia was subdued by a coalition of France, Britain, Austria, and Turkey, could be seen as a vindication of Von Gentz's assessment, though the military situation in 1820 was obviously different from that of the mid-1850s.

"very great probabilities join in pointing to the maintenance of the general peace, and of the political system" (84).

—

It was the emphasis on the inviolability of the position of the sovereigns involved, more than the religious fervour with which the Holy Alliance of Austria, Russia, and Prussia had confirmed the ecumenical Christian nature of the new structure, which by the middle of the century would end up giving the Congress system (or as it was more frequently referred to, the Holy Alliance) the reputation of a reactionary institution. To the extent that the signatories rejected not just the practice but also the principles of the French Revolution, this is undoubtedly correct. But if we rejected the Congress as reactionary *tout court*, we would overlook the fact that it was the first sincere attempt to break with the war-based logic of the old balance of power system by establishing a lasting peace based on permanent dialogue between sovereigns: not just to settle the previous war but to prevent future ones. And we would be ignoring the fact that in its institutional details, it contained some interesting innovations within the context of the debate about the European Republic.

The four main signatories solved Machiavelli's first problematic of federations – that of the slowness of collective decision-making – by creating a kind of European executive in the form of a High Table at which only the foremost powers were represented. It didn't necessarily lead to instant breakthroughs (most conferences lasted months, and not all produced significant decisions), but bringing the main powers to the same town, at times even to the same room, would inevitably speed up deliberations. And more importantly: it institutionalised dialogue, setting it up as a permanent alternative to war.

Reducing the number of decision-makers to just the Great Powers obviously created a representation issue.[9] This was solved by the architects of the Congress system in an ingenious way. Several countries that were large but insufficiently large to merit a seat at the top table were offered a place

9   At the Congress of Vienna, the French foreign secretary Talleyrand would use the small-country argument of equal representation in an attempt to break open the decision-making process, which had seen France excluded from the head table. Metternich rejected the idea of submitting decisions to a vote by all the countries and territories present. Talleyrand's negotiating trick did work, however: in order to placate France (and thereby shut down the debate about representation), it was included in the group at the centre of the negotiations, consisting of the four Allied Powers. See Siemann 420.

at a second table, whose members were consulted on most matters. A third group consisted of countries that would be consulted only on matters that were of direct interest to them. A final group of the smallest states was given the right of petitioning the main powers.

While solving the problem of decision-making, the Congress also tackled the other problematic aspect of leagues raised by Machiavelli, namely their limited territorial reach. Just as in the case of the US constitution, once the decision-making process had been streamlined, the path had been cleared for the creation of a federal construct that could span a vast territory – in this case all of Europe, including Russia. The architects of the Congress had, it seemed, solved the problem of space. Unfortunately, as Von Gentz noted, they had not solved the problem of time. None of the parties involved treated the Congress system as anything other than a temporary arrangement. There was no formal constitutional framework that could serve as a foundation. This meant that membership would remain for most countries a matter of opportunity rather than principle.

The fact that it was not built to last, however, did not mean that it was without significance. "The treaty, such as it is," Von Gentz concluded,

> has the undeniable merit of having prepared the world for a more complete political structure. If ever the Powers should meet again to establish a political system by which wars of conquest would be rendered impossible, and the rights of all guaranteed, the Congress of Vienna as a preparatory assembly, will not have been without use. A number of vexatious issues have been settled, and the ground has been prepared for building up a better social structure.
> (Von Gentz, quoted in Phillips 119)

From Congress to Concert

In the end, it would take a mere change of personnel to trigger the Congress system's slow unravelling. When, in the summer of 1823, the British Foreign Secretary Lord Castlereagh committed suicide in a moment of madness by cutting his own throat, he was replaced by his rival, George Canning. The latter, described by Metternich as a "malevolent meteor," would gradually shift the British government's attitude towards the Congress system from obstructive cooperation to non-cooperative disengagement.

Meanwhile the appointment of François-René de Chateaubriand as French foreign minister would lead to that country steering a new, more assertive course in foreign affairs. At times he would encourage his government to go directly against the expressed wishes of the other Powers. This encouragement of diplomatic rule breaking would lead to a unilateral French armed intervention in Spain which helped to quell a liberal revolt and put the Bourbon king Ferdinand VII back on the throne. Most significantly, the death of Tsar Alexander I in 1825 saw the Congress system lose its cornerstone. Alexander's successor, his younger brother Nicholas I, was much less interested in esoteric concepts like peace and European unity. His decision to enter into a strategic alliance with Canning's Great Britain without involving Austria or Prussia effectively sealed the fate of the Congress system.

It would be unfair, however, to blame the failure of the Congress system on something as accidental as personnel issues. In essence, it failed because it was not built to last. Perhaps designing a proper constitution for their cooperative venture was also too much to expect from the parties involved. After all, they had just ended a bloody and costly twenty-five-year period of constant war, and were clearly focused on creating a just and lasting peace that would help prevent the next war. Constitutional issues would have been an afterthought at best, a distraction at worst. And though the Congress system showed that Saint-Pierre had been right that it was not impossible to get the monarchies of Europe to set up a joint council for the settlement of disputes and the prevention of war, it would almost certainly have been too great a challenge to get them to accept that this new congress should become an interest of its own, which at times could even trump their personal interests. In that respect, the Congress system clearly still fell short of his ideal peace pact.

The failure to create a proper constitutional framework for the Congress system meant that it lacked the means to project itself into the future. Its demise by the mid-1820s would open the way for the return of the balance of power doctrine as the organising principle of European inter-state relations. It wasn't the same kind of doctrine as before, however. If the overall goal was still the same – preserving the balance between the great powers – the means for achieving this had changed profoundly. Even if war again became acceptable, the memory of the unprecedented bloodshed of the Napoleonic Wars meant that a war of all against all like the ones fought in the eighteenth century (War of the Austrian Succession, Seven Years' War) was no longer an acceptable option. To prevent a new conflagration from breaking out, a number of diplomatic innovations were introduced that helped limit the potential disruption caused by individual conflicts.

—

One was the concept of neutrality. The roots of the concept lay in the thirteenth century, when Barcelona merchants developed the *Consolat de Mar*, a code for the handling of trade disputes which came to serve as a joint legal system for the Mediterranean. Among its rules were those covering the status of neutral vessels sailing in war zones – goods could only be confiscated if they belonged to, or were meant for, the warring party's enemy. (Abbenhuis, *An Age of Neutrals* 25). By 1625, when Grotius published his *On The Laws of War and Peace*, the maritime "right to avoid capture" had been significantly expanded to include certain rights and duties of territories not involved in a war between two other parties. In Chapter XVII, Grotius observed that "nothing short of extreme exigency can give one power a right over what belongs to another no way involved in the war" (Grotius 966). Neutral powers, for their part, had to accept that "it is the duty of those who profess neutrality in a war to do nothing towards increasing the strength of a party maintaining an unjust cause, nor to impede the measures of a power engaged in a just and righteous cause" (Grotius 967).

Up until the start of the Napoleonic Wars, few states used neutrality as a permanent status. Following the Congress of Vienna, that would change. Neutrality would become one of the main features of the nineteenth-century diplomatic system. Some states chose permanent neutrality; others, like post-independence Belgium, had it imposed upon them by the Great Powers. Even the Great Powers themselves would at times opt for strategic neutrality as a way of limiting the impact of a seemingly inevitable war involving one or more of the other Great Powers (Abbenhuis, *Age of Neutrals* 239).

A second feature of nineteenth century diplomacy was arbitration in case of conflicts between states. Already acknowledged as an option by Vattel, who distinguished mediation (where a third party helped two conflicting parties reach a compromise) from arbitration (where a third party passed a binding judgement in a conflict; Vattel 476–477), its use became more frequent in the nineteenth century. The presence of a *de facto* supreme authority in the form of the five Great Powers helped to create the preconditions for a more systematic application of the principle of arbitration.

Underpinning both ideas was the successor to the Congress system: the less formally organised European Concert. In a way, it was a product of the same fundamental trade-off that had also produced the Congress system: between a centrally organised common interest and the individual interests of the participating states. Whereas in 1815 the Four Powers opted for a strong(er) central organisation, after 1825 the five Great Powers would instead go for the most informal, loosely structured form of cooperation that could still be combined with some sense of common purpose.

As the series of wars that led to the founding of the unified Italian state and the German Reich showed, the Concert system would not prevent wars between Great Powers and smaller countries, or indeed between the Great Powers themselves. Even wars that pitted a few of them against one were possible within its framework, as the Crimean War demonstrated, when Britain and France combined with Turkey to deal a decisive defeat to the Russian Empire. Whatever the merits of the Concert system were supposed to be, eternal peace was certainly not one of them.

What it did provide was a framework for the pragmatic management of political crises that involved the Great Powers. The ninety years between the breakdown of the Congress system in 1825 and the start of the First World War in 1914 would see twenty-six major and minor European conferences take place, devoted to a range of issues. (Abbenhuis, *Age of Neutrals* 42). Sometimes a conference would be used to draft the peace articles for a freshly concluded war, as in the case of the Paris peace conference of 1856, when the victorious powers of the Crimean war dictated rather severe peace terms to the defeated Russians (among others things, Russia lost access to the Black Sea, a right that wouldn't be restored until Bismarck offered it back in return for Russian neutrality in the 1870 French-German war). Another was the Berlin conference of 1878, which settled the peace terms for the Russian-Turkish war in the Balkans. This war had nearly seen Russian troops march into Constantinople, but ended with Russia being forced to restore most of its conquests at the negotiating table. The Russian foreign minister Gorchakov would refer to the Berlin peace treaty as "the blackest page in my biography" (Radzinksy 271).[10]

———

On a number of occasions conferences did manage to help prevent a war. It may have been only because the parties involved didn't see the strategic necessity of fighting one. Still, in such circumstances the Concert system did at least provide a useful de-escalation route. One such case was the so-called Neuchâtel crisis. In 1856, an uprising by a local faction loyal to the Prussian king Frederick William IV would trigger an international crisis

---

10   The war would end up permanently dislodging the southern Balkans from the grip of the Turkish empire. The main winner was a party that hadn't even been involved in the fighting. Austria-Hungary was given the responsibility of administering Bosnia and Herzegovina. Its eventual decision to annex these territories would cause the Bosnian crisis of 1908–1909, the closest the Great Powers got to fighting a war before the outbreak of actual conflict five years later. See Abbenhuis et al., *War, Peace and International Order?* 22–26.

when the royalists were imprisoned and put on trial. The Prussian king threatened to intervene militarily, and when both the Prussian and the Swiss government mobilised tens of thousands of troops, a conference of the great powers was convened to prevent an outbreak of war. The final settlement saw Frederick William renounce his personal claim to sovereignty over the canton, and the royalist prisoners handed over to Prussia (Abbenhuis, *Age of Neutrals* 48–49).

Another example was the Luxembourg crisis of the mid-1860s, in which both France and Prussia were involved, as well as the Dutch monarch William III, who through a personal union served as head of state of the territory. This crisis, too, would be settled at the negotiating table during the London conference of 1867. Though the deal included the provision that Luxembourg would remain a member of the German customs union, France was satisfied with the final declaration stipulating that it was to become a neutral territory. (Darmstaedter 345).

Conferences would sometimes also be devoted to topics of common interest. Some, like the series of conferences on monetary issues from the late 1860s onwards, convened partly at the request of the US government, were destined to end up as historical footnotes. Others would turn out to have far-reaching consequences. The Berlin conference of 1884–85, for example, would determine the colonial fate of the African continent for the next seventy-five years.

—

Attitudes towards the Concert system that organised relations between the Five Great Powers would vary according to the situation. If it served a tactical purpose, the politicians involved were generally happy to accept the mediating role of the Concert to help prevent crises from developing into armed conflicts (Neuchâtel, Luxembourg). In other situations they would use a variety of strategies to make sure the system wouldn't rob them of their freedom of manoeuvre. The behaviour of the German Chancellor Bismarck was instructive here. His strategic neglect of the Congress system in his period as Prussian first minister is the main reason he has gone down in history as an outspoken enemy of the idea of European cooperation in any form. His opinion of the Concert system is generally reduced to his dismissive scribble in the margin of an 1876 memorandum in which his Russian counterpart Alexander Gorchakov mentioned the Balkans as "neither German nor Russian but European" problem: "Who speaks of Europe is wrong. Geographical notion" (quoted in Van Middelaar 31; my translation).

performed about as well as could be expected of a system that saw warfare as a legitimate way of settling disputes.

Its ultimate value must be measured by how it dealt with the fundamental challenges it faced. One was how to manage the decline of the Turkish sultanate in such a way that it did not fundamentally destabilise the balance of power on the continent. The other was how to keep some sense of peace and stability in the space between east and west, what eventually would become known as *Mitteleuropa*. Key here was the struggle for supremacy within the territory of the former Holy Roman Empire. This contest, which pitted the old Austrian Habsburg dynasty against the rising power of Hohenzollern Prussia, would eventually be decided via the unification of one of them with the remaining states. Given those challenges, some would argue that it performed remarkably well by postponing the final catastrophe for nearly a century. Others would point to that same catastrophe as the inevitable result of the balance of power method. Both camps are probably right.

The Holy Alliance of Peoples

In the twenty-first century, right-wing parties sometimes define nationalism as a kind of anti-federalism. For nineteenth-century national revolutionaries, however, there was no contradiction between the two ideas. They were federalists *because* they were nationalists.[11] Pragmatically, the best chance they had of securing an independent future for their nations was by embedding them in a European federation where their right to peaceful coexistence with others would be protected. But it was also a matter of principle: they believed in the brotherhood of nations, and in a shared European destiny.

In Poland, successive generations of nationalist writers and activists combined a longing for national liberation with a desire to secure this newfound freedom in a transnational federal union. Nostalgia drove some to reflect on the possibility of reviving the pre-Partition Polish-Lithuanian Commonwealth. Others took a broader view of things, looking to embed a new Polish state in a European federation, or indeed to combine the revival of the old Commonwealth with the formation of a similar scheme at the European level.

The latter camp was led by Adam Czartoryski, Alexander I's former Foreign Minister. Although he resigned his position in 1806, he would continue to play a prominent role, first as an informal adviser to the Tsar

---

11   In the twenty-first century, the older combination of nationalism and European federalism can still be found in progressive nationalist parties (in Scotland and Catalonia for example).

There is, however, more to the story than that. The confl
Gorchakov and Bismarck wasn't about the Concert system as su
whether it should be used in this particular case. A mere on
years later, the same Balkan crisis would see Bismarck volunt
host in Berlin to a new meeting of the European Powers. The di
that this time he expected that involving the other Great Power
settle the Russian-Turkish war, and by extension, the future of 1
on terms much more favourable to German interests. When a
this meeting his own diplomats congratulated him on its out
supposed to have remarked: "Now I drive Europe four-in-har
box" (Holbraad 99).

It was far from the only time Bismarck referred to Europe a:
rather than a geographical notion. In fact, just six months befc
ing Gorchakov's "European problem," he had used almost the
formulation that the Russian minister had used in a memoran
German ambassador in London when he observed that the Ba
leading to "[a] breach between England and Russia would be a grea
and a misfortune to Europe" (Bismarck to Count Munster, 6 Ju
Wilhelm I, *The Correspondence of William I and Bismarck* II: 1;
his memoirs, he looked back on an episode a year before his "ge
notion" remark, during the so-called "Is War in Sight?" crisis of 1
careless reporting in German pro-government newspapers nearl
outbreak of war with France. In the end, Bismarck managed to
the danger. He urged the German military command to take step
de-escalation, not least because, as he observed, "Europe would
in our action an abuse of the strength we had won" (Darmstaed1

In conversations between politicians of this era, the term "Eu
used interchangeably as referring to either the Concert system or
Powers that operated both inside and outside of this system. Th
of a political Europe was as much of an undisputed fact to Bism
was to any of his contemporaries. His strategic use combined wit.
neglect of the Concert system was nothing out of the ordinary. 1
merely acted as any European politician operating within this sys
Its loosely organised, informal character invited this kind of be
from the start.

The Concert system was a compromise between the old balance
system and the federal model propagated by the signatories of th
of Paris of 1815. Though it created little enthusiasm among smaller
representatives (the Dutch legal scholar Van Vollenhove later disn
as "international despotism"), given the strategic challenges of th

during the negotiations about the Vienna peace treaty, then as a leader of the Polish constructive opposition to the erratic Tsesarevich Konstantin, who had been tasked with governing the country on behalf of the Tsar.

Back in 1803, Czartoryski had defined the main strategic challenge as wresting from Napoleon "[t]he most powerful weapon hitherto used by the French: (...) the general opinion which France has managed to promulgate that her cause is the cause of national liberty and prosperity" (Gielgud II: 42). To placate the countries they tried to win over to the allied cause, Czartoryski recommended that, "far from attempting to re-establish old abuses," these countries should be "assured of liberties founded on a solid basis" (43).

In his *Notes on Diplomacy* (1826), Czartoryski would analyse the causes and consequences of the failure of this strategy. By the time the Congress of Vienna started, "[m]agnificent promises had been made to various nations" (Czartoryski 84; my translation throughout). At the negotiating table these promises turned out to be essentially worthless: "[A]fter the fall of Napoleon, the coalition partners, absolute masters of the situation, gave no further thought to honouring their pledges towards these nations" (84).

The only case that led to significant disagreement between the negotiating parties was the case of Poland. Alexander I spent a significant amount of political capital on an attempt to re-establish the old Commonwealth border as it was before the Second Partition. The aim was to establish a new Polish kingdom, based on the 1791 constitution. The new (old) country was to be tied to Russia through a personal union, with the Tsar wearing both the Russian and the Polish crowns. To buy Prussian support, he offered it compensation in the form of Saxony. This proposal was fiercely resisted by the other allies, first and foremost by the British Foreign Secretary Lord Castlereagh. The final result would be a compromise in the form of a much smaller country, commonly referred to as Congress Poland, constructed within the borders of the Napoleonic Grand Duchy of Warsaw.

As far as Czartoryski was concerned, there was little doubt that the Tsar's intentions were genuine. He described how he had witnessed Alexander's shock at his grandmother Catherine II's "iniquitous actions, without faith or law," leading to the Third Partition, and how he had sworn one day to "repair this odious injustice" (Czartoryski 86). In the end, though, it was never likely that the other powers would support this idea. What the Tsar proposed would have been seen by them as a significant land grab. It would have extended Russian power deep into Central Europe and would have also fundamentally disturbed the balance of power.

In Czartoryski's eyes, the failure to agree to Alexander's proposal was more than a missed opportunity for the Polish people – it was a missed opportunity for Europe as a whole. "If Poland had obtained (...) the more extensive and more suitable borders that Alexander wanted to give it," he explained, "a giant stride would have been made towards a state of normal justice and lasting security, of the kind that Europe had always pursued and never yet obtained" (Czartoryski 92). Given the distribution of powers on the continent, "Poland could have served as security for the long-term stability in the relationship between the North, East, and West" (92).

—

By the time Czartoryski wrote his *Essay*, it was clear that the attempt to organise the relationship between Europe's powers through a kind of informal confederation had failed. In an attempt to inspire the continent's rulers to revive and improve on it, he invoked the spirit of two former monarchs in the form of Henri IV and Elizabeth I, and the Grand Design of which he made the two the co-authors. Against "the House of Austria, which strove for (...) universal monarchy" (Czartoryski 263), he claimed, these two had proposed an alternative scheme for the government of Europe, based on "strict justice and the welfare of all nations" (264). Their aim was "to satisfy the wishes of nations, to assure their happiness, and to safeguard (...) the common good of Europe" (270).

In Czartoryski's view, a revived Grand Design would have some significant advantages over the kind of decision-making under the Viennese Congress system. One was representation: unlike the Congress, the European senate proposed by Henri IV and Elizabeth I didn't exclude any of Europe's sovereigns from deliberations. Another was the nature of its decisions. Those of the Congress were based on procedural improvisation, and were enforced mainly through fear. Those of the Grand Design, on the other hand, were the product of careful deliberation and therefore "a source of tranquillity" (Czartoryski 287).

In his concluding remarks, Czartoryski revealed why he had emphasised Elizabeth's co-authorship of the Grand Design. To get this scheme up and running "it would suffice if two sovereigns similar to Henri and Elizabeth" committed to its implementation (Czartoryski 323). Among the ones who could plausibly be called to fulfil such a role were, not coincidentally, the kings of England and France. One other Great Power could play a significant role in its establishment. To persuade that one, Czartoryski summoned a final spirit in the form of Alexander I: "If Russia was governed by a prince who was possessed of the same generous qualities as the emperor Alexander, and by the same noble thoughts that we suppose the latter to have been occupied with for such a long time, then that empire, instead of being the terror of mankind, would become its benefactor" (324–325). What the three Powers could achieve above all, apart from "preventing all oppression between nations," was "to repair ancient iniquities" – in other words: to restore Poland to its rightful place within the congress of nations (325). In the same way that Poland could become the guarantor of stability within a new European federation, that same federation could also become the guarantor of Poland's sovereignty.

Unfortunately for Czartoryski – and Poland – it turned out that the new Tsar Nicholas I had no intention of repairing ancient iniquities. Nor was he inclined to let others do so. When in 1830 a revolution in France threatened to trigger a series of similar uprisings against the new (old) order established in Vienna, he decided to act. But instead of settling things down, his decision to mobilise a Polish contingent for the purpose of crushing the French revolution would act as the trigger for a Polish uprising.[12] In the war that followed, Czartoryski could not persuade any of the Western Powers to come to Poland's aid. Even the new French regime decided to stay neutral, probably because it had concluded that the best way to stop Nicholas from considering a march on Paris was to make him focus on Warsaw instead. The lack of Western military aid meant that after some initial military successes, the Polish front eventually collapsed. The Russian army took Warsaw, and Czartoryski was forced to flee the country.

At the height of the Polish Uprising, an academic botanist called Wojciech Jastrzębowski (1799–1882) published a pamphlet titled "The Free Moments of a Polish Soldier, or Thoughts Concerning an Eternal Alliance Between Civilised Nations." In it, he reflected on the conditions for perpetual peace. His rhetoric at first suggested he was looking for peace to be secured through a kind of world state: "Henceforward let there be only two nations on earth: first, the civilised or those governing themselves according to law and, secondly, the barbarians or those governing themselves according to their passions" (Brock 70). But in the federal constitution he then went on to sketch, the individual nations of the European continent had a prominent place. Mind you: nations, not states. He expected the existing state boundaries to be redrawn based on national population clusters – a typical demand of national revolutionaries in this period (Brock 70–71).

---

12   In *Czartoryski and European Unity, 1770–1861*, the Polish historian Marian Kukiel explained that what tipped the scales towards an uprising was the feeling among Polish nationalists that they were made to march not just against the same ideals for which they had argued so passionately, but also against fellow revolutionaries with whom they had previously developed close personal ties (Kukiel, 169).

The most prominent among the Polish European federalists taking up the mantle after the failed uprising of 1830 was the poet Adam Mickiewicz (1798–1855). Where the monarchist Jastrzębowski had still used the old royal order as the basis for his federal European scheme, Mickiewicz's vision was explicitly republican. His poem "The Books of the Polish Nation" was first and foremost an ode to his home nation, but it also offered a vision of the future that was both national and European in scope.

Mickiewicz's interpretation of history seemed inspired by Rousseau. The beginning of mankind was one of freedom: "There were no laws, only the will of God, and there were no lords and slaves, only patriarchs and their children" (Mickiewicz, "The Books of the Polish Nation," quoted in Walker 151). Once men were corrupted, they seemed condemned to a state of perpetual slavery under the rule of emperors and monarchs who "desired to be like savage fathers dwelling in the forests, who yoke their children to carts like beasts and sell them to merchants for slaves" (Walker 154).

To play the peoples of Europe off against each other, the kings eventually took over the worship of "an idol goddess" called "*Political Balance of Power*" from the Italians, who "were the first to establish its worship among themselves." Having seen its effects, the kings "introduced her quickly into their kingdoms, and spread abroad her worship and bade men fight for her" (Walker 156). Among the "philosophers (...) who praised everything that the kings had devised," he singled out Machiavelli, "which signifieth in Greek a man *desirous of war*, in that his doctrine led to continual wars" (156).

Among the kings, three were mentioned specifically for their cynical use of the balance of power: "[T]he name of the first was *Frederick the Second* of Prussia, the name of the second was *Catherine the Second* of Russia, the name of the third was *Maria Theresa* of Austria." These three monarchs, who had devised the first partition of Poland in 1772, were described by him as "a Satanic trinity (...) in the manner of a mock and a derision of all that was holy. (...) The names of these three rulers (...) were thus three blasphemies, and their lives three crimes, and their memory three maledictions" (Walker 156–157).

Only one nation refused to play by these violent rules: Poland. God had rewarded it for its refusal to reduce itself to the pursuit of selfish national interests when "a great nation, Lithuania, united itself with Poland, as husband with wife, two souls in one body. (...) And God gave unto the Polish kings and knights freedom, that all might be called brothers, both the richest and the poorest" (Walker 158). This "union of nations" (158) was to become the destiny of all of Europe, though not before Poland was first "martyred," and "laid (...) in the grave" (160). This death, which the kings had planned as an attempt to "[slay] and [bury] freedom" (160), was not to be the end though. Christlike, Poland was destined for resurrection: "[O]n the third day the soul shall return to the body, and the Nation shall arise and free all the peoples of Europe from slavery. And as after the resurrection of Christ bloody offerings ceased in all the world, so after the resurrection of the Polish Nation wars shall cease in all Christendom" (160).

—

Thirty years later, general Józef Bossak-Hauke (1834–1871) was part of the new generation of revolutionaries that tried to turn Mickiewicz's prophecy into reality. He commanded Polish forces in the uprising of 1863–64, which had aimed to restore the Polish-Lithuanian Commonwealth. After its failure, he fled to Switzerland, where he used the platform of the European peace movement to argue for a Polish future inside a federal Europe. He was also closely linked to the wider European nationalist revolutionary movement. He died in 1871 while commanding one of the revolutionary army battalions in the Army of the Vosges, in defence of the newly formed French Third Republic.

The Army of the Vosges stood under the command of the great Italian revolutionary Giuseppe Garibaldi (1807–1882). Garibaldi was one of the larger-than-life characters who dominated the Risorgimento – the roughly forty-year period of Italian reawakening and revolution culminating in the creation of the Italian Kingdom under Victor Emmanuel, until then King of Sardinia. He fought in revolutionary wars on two continents, and in three campaigns to establish Italian sovereignty over Italian territories. Though not by any means a theoretician, over the course of his life he did commit to a number of ideological causes, including socialism, democracy and European federalism.

For the latter idea, he leaned heavily on the work of the other giant of the democratic faction of the Risorgimento, Giuseppe Mazzini (1805–1872). If Garibaldi was the greatest European revolutionary soldier of the nineteenth century, Mazzini was among its greatest revolutionary writers. Over a period of nearly half a century, he would produce a steady stream of pamphlets and newspaper articles to promote the twin causes of democratic national self-determination and European federation. He was not the only Risorgimento thinker to make the case for a European federal union. The Milanese philosopher-politician Carlo Cattaneo similarly argued for a "United States of Italy" embedded in a "United States of Europe."[13] Cattaneo claimed that

---

13 Cattaneo's federalism would have a profound impact on the generation of Italian thinkers and politicians who were active in the immediate aftermath of the Second World War. See

federalism, which in his eyes formed the ultimate embodiment of freedom and limited government, was the natural destination of the European state system.

Unlike Cattaneo, however, Mazzini was not primarily a political philosopher. His words were thought in action, aimed at furthering his causes and at persuading the particular audiences he addressed them to. His status as leader of the European democratic-nationalist revolutionary movement meant that they would always have an outsized impact on public debate across Europe. That impact was clearest for his anti-monarchical stance, and more importantly, his pro-democracy position. He broke with the 1820s post-Vienna revolutionaries (the so-called Carbonari) over their emphasis on an aristocratic, rather than a democratic structure for a unified Italy.

—

Mazzini's vision for Italy was essentially the same as that for Europe: opposition to the monarchies that sought to control the continent's populations. "We will raise up high the banner of the Italian people. (...) We will not attempt any alliance with the kings," he wrote in an 1832 essay on "the superiority of representative government" (Recchia and Urbinati 43). By the late 1840s, he would turn from merely opposing the Holy Alliance of Monarchs to proposing his own alternative: a Holy Alliance of the Peoples.

This Holy Alliance of the Peoples had a political destination: "Our goal is to create the United States of Europe" (Recchia and Urbinati 135). Like Kant and Saint-Simon, Mazzini made the goal more palatable to his readers by projecting it into the distant future: "We are far from having reached that final stage of development. Indeed, for most of the peoples their mission has not even been defined yet" (57). By keeping the final destination of the democratic "epoch" (56) on the horizon, he created space for the emergence of the nationalist movements whose task it was to defeat the monarchies of the old order. He thereby effectively merged the two ideas – what he called the "national" and the "cosmopolitan" – in a single vision of the European historical process. To ignore the cosmopolitan aspect would create a kind of false or selfish nationalism that was based on the idea that "a Nation could be constructed in the name of local interests, without establishing a brotherly bond with militant democracy throughout Europe" (133).

Mazzini's efforts would contribute to making democracy and national self-determination two central elements of European thinking about federal union. Any attempt at forming such a union would have to start as a union

Norberto Bobbio's remarks on his influence (Bobbio and Viroli 23–24).

of the peoples. But it would not have to end there. He did not exclude that in the longer term, as boundaries disappeared and the peaceful interactions between peoples increased, "the fusion of all members of Humanity" could be achieved: "We do not believe in the timelessness of races. We do not believe in the timelessness of languages" (Recchia and Urbinati 55). The main thing to recognise was that it could not be forced or sped up: "[A]ll this cannot be accomplished at once, by a single people, or even in a single epoch" (55). It was a plausible end state of a natural process.

It is a testament to Mazzini's influence that the French political philosopher Ernest Renan would incorporate his theory of nationalism's post-national future into the conclusion of his 1882 pamphlet *Qu'est-ce qu'une nation?* (What is a Nation?):

> Nations aren't eternal entities. They had a beginning, and they will end. The European Confederation will probably replace them. But not in the century we are currently living in. At the current time, the existence of nations is good, even necessary. Their existence is the safeguard of liberty, which would be lost if the world had only one law and one master.
> (Renan 25–26; my translation)

With this one paragraph, Renan demonstrated the lasting impact of the nationalist moment on European federalist thought. First of all, it made the republican notion of *liberty* rather than monarchical notions of order or stability the object of political organisation. It also made national sovereignty the starting point of any schemes for European unification. The construction would be based on the *peoples*, plural, not the people, singular. Finally, perhaps the most important effect was that it helped confirm the central position of the Kantian idea of European federation as a long-term process, where the final destination of full integration – and thereby the birth of a single European people – was always some way off.

Bibliography

Abbenhuis, Maartje. *An Age of Neutrals: Great Power Politics 1815–1914*, Cambridge University Press, 2014.

Abbenhuis, Maartje, Christopher Barber, and Annelise Higgins, editors. *War, Peace and International Order? The Legacies of the Hague Conferences of 1898 and 1907*. Routledge, 2017.

Bobbio, Norberto, and Maurizio Viroli. *The Idea of the Republic*. Polity, 2003.

Brock, Peter. "A Pacifist in Wartime: Wojciech Bogumił Jastrzębowski." *The Polish Review*, vol. 12, no. 2, 1967, pp. 68–77.

Czartoryski, Adam, *Essay sur la Diplomatie*. 1826. Hachette, 1864.

Darmstaedter, Friedrich. *Bismarck and the Creation of the Second Reich*. Routledge, 2008.

Dwyer, Philip. "Napoleon and the Universal Monarchy." *History*, vol. 95, no. 3, 2010, pp. 293–307.

Gentz, Friedrich von. *Fragments Upon the Balance of Power in Europe*. 1805. Andesite Press, 2017.

Gentz, Friedrich von. *On the State of Europe Before and After the French Revolution, Being an Answer to the Work Entitled "De L'État de la France a la Fin de l'An 8"*. 1803. Translated by John Charles Herries. Kessinger, 2008.

Ghervas, Stella. *Conquering Peace, From the Enlightenment to the European Union*. Harvard University Press, 2021.

Gielgud, Adam. *Memoirs of Prince Adam Czartoryski and his Correspondence with Alexander I*. 1832. Kessinger, 2010. 2 vols.

Grotius, Hugo. *The Rights of War and Peace, Including the Law of Nature and of Nations*. 1625. Translated by Archibald Colin Campbell. B. Boothroyd, 1814.

Hauterive, Comte d' (Alexander Maurice Blanc de Lanautte). *De l'État de la France à la Fin de l'An VIII*. Chez Henrics, 1800.

Holbraad, Carsten. *The Concert of Europe: A Study in German and British International Theory, 1815–1914*. Prentice Hall Press, 1970.

Holy Alliance Treaty, September 1815. *Napoleon Series Archive*, https://www.napoleon-series.org/research/government/diplomatic/c_alliance.html. Accessed 6 March 2024.

Kagan, Frederick. *The End of the Old Order: Napoleon and Europe, 1801–1805*. Da Capo Press, 2007.

Kukiel, Marian. *Czartoryski and European Unity, 1770–1861*. Greenwood Press, 1981.

Mann, Golo. *Friedrich von Gentz: Gegenspieler Napoleons, Vordenker Europas*. Fischer Taschenbuch, 2010.

Middelaar, Luuk van. *Passage naar Europa: Geschiedenis van een begin*. Historische Uitgeverij, 2009.

Phillips, Walter Alison. *The Confederation of Europe: A Study of the European Alliance, 1813–1823*. 1914. Kessinger, 2013.

Quadruple Alliance (Second Peace Treaty of Paris), November 1815. *Wikisource*, https://en.wikisource.org/wiki/Quadruple_Alliance. Accessed 6 March 2024.

Radzinksy, Edvard. *Alexander II: The Last Great Tsar*, translated by Antonina Bouis, Free Press, 2005.

Recchia, Stephano, and Nadia Urbinati. *A Cosmopolitanism of Nations: Giussepe Mazzini's Writings on Democracy, Nation Building, and International Relations*. Princeton University Press, 2010.

Renan, Ernest. *Qu'est-ce qu'une nation?* 1882. Éditions la Bibliothèque Digitale, 2013.

Schoeder, Paul W. *Metternich's Diplomacy at its Zenith, 1820–1823.* 1969. Library Licensing, 2011.

Siemann, Wolfram. *Metternich: Strategist and Visionary.* Belknap Press, 2019.

Schroeder, Paul W. *The Transformation of European Politics, 1763–1848.* Oxford University Press, 1996.

Sofka, James. "Metternich's Theory of European Order: A Plan for 'Perpetual Peace.'" *The Review of Politics*, vol. 60, no. 1, 1998, pp. 115–150.

Stafford, James. "The Alternative to Perpetual Peace: Britain, Ireland and the Case for Union in Friedrich Gentz's *Historisches Journal*, 1799–1800." *Modern Intellectual History*, vol. 13, no. 1, 2015, pp. 63–91.

Taylor, A. J. *Bismarck: The Man and the Statesman.* 1955. Penguin, 1995.

Vattel, Emer de. *Law of Nations, Or Principles of the Law of Nature, Applied to the Conduct and Affairs of Nations and Sovereigns, with Three Early Essays on the Origin and Nature of Natural Law and on Luxury,* edited and introduced by Bela Kapossy and Richard Whatmore. E-book, Liberty Fund, 2008.

Walker, Mack. *Metternich's Europe: Selected Documents.* Macmillan, 1968.

Wilhelm I of Prussia, *The Correspondence of William I and Bismarck: With Other Letters from and to Prince Bismarck.* Frederick A. Stokes, 1903. 2 vols.

7   Germany, from Staatenbund to Bundesstaat

Abstract

The negotiators at Vienna had to deal with the consequences of the end of the Holy Roman Empire. The result of their deliberations was the German *Bund*: an institutional framework for managing a political standoff between the Austrian Empire and Prussia. This standoff was in part also the product of a blockage at the theoretical level. There was a broadly shared understanding that a mere *Staatenbund* was not enough, but the alternative to a *Bundesstaat* was beyond reach. Until, that is, a theoretical breakthrough on the topic of sovereignty paved the way for the creation of a monarchical federal union. It would take a war to get there. That same war also settled the conflict with Austria in Prussia's favour.

Keywords: German *Bund*, German Reich, *Staatenbund*, *Bundesstaat*, Bismarck

Before unification: the Zollverein and the dividing of the German Bund

Not all nineteenth century nationalist movements would channel their energies into the construction of European federalist schemes. In the German case, the focus was instead chiefly on developing federal solutions on a *national* scale, not because they were anti-European, but because the more immediate challenge was to create a German union that would offer the states involved a double security: against each other (chiefly against the largest states), and against the great powers that surrounded them. Important to note is that in the German case, the distinction between European and national was one of degree. If the entire Austrian empire was included, the boundaries of this vast territory enclosed nearly half of continental Europe, running from the North Sea and the Baltic to the Mediterranean and the

Livestro, Joshua: *A More Perfect Union. Federal Union in Political Theory and Practice, 1500-1951.*
Amsterdam: Amsterdam University Press, 2024.
DOI: 10.5117/9789048563777_CH07

Adriatic, and from the Dutch border to Western Ukraine. Any German federation, therefore, was a European federation of sorts.

—

After his victory over the Russian-Austrian coalition at the Battle of Austerlitz, Napoleon had seized the opportunity to found the Confederation of the Rhine (1806). This move not only spelled the end of the Holy Roman Empire, but also of the formal connection within it between the two main German powers, Austria and Prussia, and of the connection of those two with what was called the "Third Germany," the collection of smaller German states.

If "divide and rule" was Napoleon's aim, it would work only temporarily. A mere seven years later the two main German powers reunited in an alliance with Russia and England to inflict a decisive defeat on him. Napoleon's decision to form a confederation out of the minor German states would, however, have an impact far beyond his reign. There was a direct line from the Confederation of the Rhine to the later German federal entities – via the German Bund (1815–1866), the North German Bund (1866–1871) and the federal constitution of the united German states under the Prussian Hohenzollern emperors (1871–1918), to the Weimar Republic (1918–1933), the postwar Federal Republic of West Germany (1948–1990) and the reunited German Federal Republic (1990 to the present day). The only interruption in this more or less continuous line was the Nazi-engineered Third Reich (1933--1945), which, as we will see, was explicitly anti-federalist in its founding principles.

The first Confederation period would leave a legacy in the form of a conceptual apparatus that eventually allowed a next generation of constitutional thinkers to come up with a solution to a much older German problem previously discussed by the likes of Leibniz and Pufendorf. In 1804 the legal scholar Karl Salomo Zachariae had already introduced the term "Staatenbund." This concept would quickly gain an undisputed status as the term with which to describe constitutional structures like that of the Confederation of the Rhine. Around the same time, circa 1806, the term "Bundesstaat" emerged. Initially it carried more or less the same meaning, the difference being one of degree of centralisation.[1] Over time, though, it would come to be used as the opposite of a Staatenbund. It was used to refer to a collective of states in which sovereignty rested not with the

1   For the etymology of the two concepts of Staatenbund and Bundesstaat, see Brie, 33 footnotes 3 and 4.

members but with the centre. Although quite how this kind of entity could be distinguished from a decentralised unitary state, and how its existence could be justified in the face of continued claims to sovereignty by the individual states, remained a matter of speculation.

Perhaps it was due to the lack of a workable definition that, for several decades, the term "Bundesstaat" would be largely ignored in German constitutional-philosophical debate (Brie 41--42). It wasn't until the late 1840s that the term would resurface, this time in the context of a debate about German unity.

—

When discussion at the Congress of Vienna turned to the future of the German states, the main question was how to recreate and maintain internal order within German territory in the absence of the old framework of the Holy Roman Empire, since the Austrian court was clear that the latter would not be resurrected. This was, first of all, a challenge for the individual states, many of whom had expanded their territories with formerly independent principalities and free cities. This was, again, a question of union. Recognising that simply extending their own constitutional framework might provoke a strong response from these formerly free territories, a number of states opted for the introduction of new constitutions. In doing so, they introduced a new concept: the constitutional monarchy. Inspired by the British constitution, it was based on a reconciliation of the old monarchical regime with the principle of popular sovereignty as embodied by the new middle class (Richter 96). This idea, of the mixing of old and new forms to create something acceptable to all, would form the basis of the debate about the need for a German constitution during the so-called Vormärz period, that is, in the decades before the events of March 1848.

At the level of the Bund, order would come before structure. The Carlsbad conference of 1819 would occupy itself with the question of what to do about the revolutionary nationalist climate at German universities. The immediate trigger for this discussion was the murder of the playwright August von Kotzebue, who had been revealed to have acted as a Russian agent, by a radicalised student named Karl Ludwig Sand (Hardtwig 15). The real reason for the discussion, however, was the rise of liberal nationalist ideology at German universities through the teaching of radical lecturers, the publishing of various magazines and most of all: the activities of the so-called *Burschenschaften*, the student fraternities that had become hotbeds of nationalist activism.

To quell the unrest, the Congress backed a series of measures proposed by Metternich, from the introduction of censorship laws to the disbanding of student societies. These measures would become known collectively as the Carlsbad Decrees. Metternich would use the same conference to fix the final details of the Bund's founding treaty, and to arrange all state constitutions on the same absolutist (*i.e.*, non-liberal) footing (Schroeder, *Metternich's Diplomacy* 15–19).

The final draft of the German confederal treaty would be presented at the next ministerial conference, in Vienna in 1820. In the opening article, it confirmed that "[t]he German Bund is a union under international law (...) for the maintenance of the domestic and external security of Germany." In Article 2, it would further specify that "[t]his union exists domestically as a community of independent states, none dominated by another, with mutual equal rights and obligations by treaty, but externally as a whole power bound in political unity." It was, in other words, to function as a confederation of fully sovereign states, with foreign policy determined collectively. In reality, Metternich anticipated that Austria would continue if not to prescribe then at least to influence the internal and external policies of the smaller "independent states" in the union.

If Metternich's Austria was the clear winner of the negotiations about the new confederal constitution, the loser was Prussia. It had tabled ambitious proposals in January 1815 for a kind of federal constitution, with a central committee of the five largest monarchies, a parliament, and a supreme court. The Prussian proposals were clearly intended to cement a place for the Prussian government at the top of the federal pyramid, jointly running the new federation with their Austrian rivals through an executive in which both countries played a leading role. But by claiming, and receiving, compensation for its loss of Polish lands in the form of expansion into Saxony, Prussia had fanned suspicions among the smaller states about its territorial ambitions. Metternich cleverly exploited that fear of Prussian intentions, using the carrot of equal representation of all states in the executive committee to create a majority for a much less ambitious form of confederation. It gave him what wanted: *"Einigkeit ohne Einheit"* – harmony without unity (Schroeder, *Transformation* 542–544).

—

Metternich may have hoped he had won a decisive victory for his emperor by blocking Prussia's proposals, but it would turn out rather differently in the long run. By not agreeing to joint rule together with Prussia, but instead attempting to set Austria up as the *de facto* leading state inside the Bund, he had put the two German superpowers on a path towards an inevitable collision. The defeat at the Congressional negotiating table forced the Prussian government to look for other ways to establish its claim to a share of the power inside the *Bund*. It found it in the form of the *Zollverein*, a network of customs unions formed in the 1820s which would eventually be united in a single customs union that spanned more than twenty German principalities, with Prussia at the centre. It was, as the late nineteenth century German historian Heinrich von Treitschke pointed out, an idea that set Prussia up for future conflicts with powerful neighbours: "Hanover still relied on England, Schleswig-Holstein on Denmark for political support, Luxembourg was still connected geographically to the unified Dutch state. How was an all-German customs law even thinkable while these foreign influences lingered?" (12; my translation throughout).

Metternich clearly grasped the political significance of the idea, noting "Within the larger confederation there now exists a smaller sub-federation, a *status in statu* in the truest sense of the word, which before too long will put the pursuit of its own goals with its own means first, those of the Confederation a distant second" (Krebs and Poloni 84). His instinct was that Austria would do well to join, if only to make sure it didn't develop in an unwanted (*i.e.*, pro-Prussian) direction (Siemann 680). The Austrian emperor, however, decided to stay out, giving greater weight to the lobby of domestic agricultural producers who feared the increased competition that lower tariffs would bring.

Over the next twenty years, the balance within the German Confederation would slowly shift away from Austria, just as Metternich had feared. In 1852, a customs officer noted that "as far as traffic with the other German states is concerned, Austria has become a foreign country" (Langewiesche 39). By the time the consequences of the emperor's decision fully manifested themselves, however, his long serving Chancellor was no longer in a position to do anything about it. Metternich was one of the most prominent victims of the revolution that broke out in early 1848. forced to resign, even to flee the country.

Federal union denied: the revolution of 1848 and the Frankfurt Parliament

The rise of German nationalism had coincided with the rise of the other great disruptive force of first half nineteenth century politics, liberalism.

Together, the two "isms" pushed the new middle class within the German *Bund* inexorably in the direction of a confrontation with the old monarchical order. The one force demanded the formation of a single German nation overriding the sovereignty claims of the individual principalities, while the other pushed for civil rights and a (moderately) democratic German parliament as an alternative to the reactionary, and often censorious, culture of the German royal courts.

In the second half of the 1840s, circumstances seemed ripe for a successful attempt at forcing change upon the unwilling German monarchs. Consecutive years of failed harvests across Western Europe led to the spread of famine (Richter 93). The one in Ireland, which was at least in part political in its causes, would kill one million people. In Germany, circumstances were only moderately better, with Prussia registering tens of thousands of deaths. The famines coincided with a series of worker revolts, the most famous of which had actually happened just prior to the first failed harvests, in Silesia. the part of modern day Poland annexed by Frederick II during the War of the Austrian Succession. The causes for which the Silesian weavers rioted were less about social progress than about keeping things as they were. They were mainly fighting to keep their old working practices and living standards. Still, they were included in the reformist narrative, where they became symbols of the popular demand for fundamental change (Richter 82).

There were also political stirrings, chiefly in Switzerland, where the canton of Neûchatel led the Catholic opposition against radical attempts to adopt a new constitution that would have paved the way for secularisation of the cloisters. When the radicals seemed poised to gain control of enough cantons to impose their will on the catholic minority through the Diet, the Catholic cantons launched a preemptive attack. What followed was the brief Sonderbund war of 1847, which resulted in a clear victory for the radical side (Schroeder, *Transformation* 794–796).

In Germany, things would come to a head in March 1848, when a bloody attempt by the Austrian court to disperse a demonstration by Viennese students, inspired by a similar outbreak of public anger in Paris, led to massive street protests. The revolution would quickly spread to other parts of Germany, all the while increasing in strength. It reached its peak when reformers called a special assembly in Frankfurt. Its aim was to draft a German constitution that would combine a strong central authority with respect for civil rights.

The clearest support came from the representatives of the smaller states. They felt that, in spite of their formal equality under the *Bund's* founding treaty, they effectively enjoyed second class status within it, regularly getting outmanoeuvred and ignored by the larger states. A new constitution, preferably under a German emperor as an independent arbiter, would guarantee that all states would have their concerns treated fairly. The other group of prominent supporters of a new constitution was the middle class, which had found itself permanently excluded from proceedings in the *Bund's* aristocratic parliament (*Bundestag*). In the declaration issued at the end of the Heidelberger meeting which preceded the convention in Frankfurt, representatives noted how "deeply saddening at this time the memory is of Germans being banned from addressing their [government]" (Krebs and Poloni 107). A new constitution was expected to solve all these problems.

—

The delegates elected to the Frankfurt parliament would draw inspiration from the new Swiss constitution, adopted in September 1848, which had created the first *Bundesstaat*. This new constitution was clearly inspired by the American example. Its institutional framework was based on an insight by the philosopher Ignaz Troxler (1780–1866). Troxler, a student of the German philosopher Schelling, had served as a Swiss emissary to the negotiations at the Congress of Vienna. It was the start of a life of involvement with the constitutional affairs of his country that would eventually see him deliver a crucial contribution to the debate in the constitutional Committee of Revision in the winter of 1846–47. When the two camps discussing alternatives for the old confederal order, representing the canton and the national idea, seemed gridlocked, his memorandum to one of its members showed how the two could be reconciled (Spiess 894).

In an essay titled "The Constitution of the United States as an example for Swiss federal reforms," Troxler praised the American Founders for providing the world with the definitive model for a federal union. It was through a study of its features that he realised that "only through the introduction of a *bicameral system*, as it exists in the republican Union, could the cantons be given an assurance of their continued existence and independence, while a central authority could be created for the union" (Spiess 893).

Troxler clearly understood the nature of the compromise over representation that lay at the heart of the American constitution, how it allowed "all members of the Union, great and small," to buy into it (893). But it seems he did not grasp the fact that this compromise, in turn, had been enabled by a prior compromise on sovereignty. Nor did the drafters of the constitution, for that matter. The new federation they created remained based on "twenty-two sovereign cantons" (893). As if to stress this continuity with what came before, it still went under the name of "Swiss Confederation."

—

The situation the Frankfurt Parliament found itself in seemed superficially similar to the one facing the American Founders at the Philadelphia Convention in 1787. There, too, frustration about the obvious weaknesses and failings of a founding treaty had caused delegates to look for a new kind of constitutional construct. Among both sets of delegates there were many for whom the new constitution was explicitly meant as an expression of national aspirations (in fact, among German delegates, the national idea was considered virtually identical with the ideal of a *Bundesstaat* (Nipperdey 356). The German delegates even saw the American constitution as an example of the kind of text they wanted to produce (Nipperdey 653). But unlike their American predecessors, the delegates in Frankfurt would fail to square the national–federal circle. A combination of obstacles would prove insurmountable.

One obstacle was of a practical–strategic nature: unlike the Philadelphia Convention, which focused exclusively on designing an institutional framework to create a properly functioning union, the Frankfurt delegates were also expected by public opinion to secure constitutional recognition for a set of civil and political rights. Many of these rights were lifted directly from the American Bill of Rights, including a version of the Second Amendment, which in the German setting would have given the citizenry a means of countering repressive actions by the monarchs' standing armies (Richter 99). If the German delegates had studied American constitutional history more closely, however, they would have noticed that the non-inclusion of a bill of rights in the draft constitution had one practical advantage: it had allowed for a relatively swift conclusion of the negotiations. Their inclusion in the Frankfurt agenda had the effect of substantially lengthening the duration of the negotiations, which would eventually lead to the cause of constitutional reform running out of steam (Nipperdey 652).

The second obstacle was geographical. The national cause was supposed to provide an exclamation mark for the reform movement's program, the one thing all delegates could unite around. Instead it became its biggest question mark. After all, which Germany was the union supposed to be based on? The convention was divided between a *Kleindeutsch* camp and a *Grossdeutsch* camp, the difference between them being the inclusion or exclusion of Austria in the new federation. For the Germans north of the

Alps, this may have seemed like a relatively straightforward question, though there would inevitably be some discussion about rights for non-German speaking minorities at regional level. For the Austrian government however, the question was potentially explosive. A German-only federal union would force it to choose between its German and non-German territories. And even if it found a way of avoiding that choice, in practice the second-class status of the non-German territories would, over time, make a separation inevitable. The Austrian general Count Johann Radetzky, whose victory over the northern Italian revolutionaries had elevated him to the status of national hero (celebrated in Strauss's famous Radetzky March) declared that though "a truly German heart beats in my breast" he would "force it to remain silent" if this was the cost of German unity (Rumpler 312).

Apart from imperial pride, there was also a geostrategic consideration that made the choice for a German-only union unacceptable. It was only their inclusion in the Austrian empire that stopped the Czar from attempting the incorporation of the non-German speaking territories into the Russian empire. A choice for German unity would therefore have introduced the risk of a significant Russian incursion into Central Europe (Rumpler 312).

With Austria thus unable to commit, and Prussia unwilling to force the issue for fear of provoking a conflict with its powerful rival, the situation remained deadlocked. Until delegates could agree on a single option, there could be no progress on drafting a new constitution. And by the time they finally did settle on a solution, the momentum for reform had gone.

The third complicating factor was a theoretical one. The Frankfurt delegates were facing the same dilemma that also confronted the American Founders: if they couldn't define what the alternative looked like, how could they ever hope to get there? Obviously, German scholars and politicians had the example of the Americans to guide them. But for some reason, they didn't quite grasp what the American constitution was really about. Some interpretations saw it as basically a Swiss Confederation by another name.[2] Even the ones that sensed it was something more didn't understand the kind of balance the final deal in Philadelphia had struck. As far as they were concerned, the American Founders had established a fully Hamiltonian framework, where the national government was superior to the states,

---

2   The republican delegate Gustav von Struve tabled a proposal for a constitution in which he referred to "the North American free states" as a model for a federal republic. But his proposed structure – states electing parliaments and presidents, who would then represent their states at the federal level – was a complete misrepresentation of the American constitution. See Krebs and Poloni 108–10, specifically Art. 15 on 110.

leaving them only those sovereign rights which hadn't been reserved for the national government. In other words: a *Bundesstaat*, as the term was then understood (Brie 78).

This dilemma had two important consequences. The first was that the Convention did not possess the conceptual apparatus to tackle the problem of the larger states. It was one thing for a small state to sacrifice sovereignty for the sake of security and a greater say in collective affairs. It was quite another thing for a large state to make that same sacrifice. A final settlement that did not respect their own claim to sovereignty seemed destined to alienate them. The other was that its inability to leave room for their own claims to sovereignty ended up alienating the monarchs that ruled the individual German states.

—

In the end, the delegates never came close to discovering a workable compromise on sovereignty. Without it, they lacked the means to persuade the larger states to sign on to the draft constitution that eventually emerged in late March 1849. known as the "Paulskirchen Constitution," after the place where the document was drafted.

The text was based on the same compromise on representation that was also included in the Swiss constitution of the previous year, between a House of the States (*Staatenhaus*) and a House of the People (*Volkshaus*). The latter was to be elected directly, the former appointed by the state governments and parliaments (Art. 86–94). The executive was to be formed by a hereditary monarch (Art. 69), who would adopt the title of "Emperor" (Art. 70) – at first elected, subsequently hereditary.

The dual representation structure seemed a fair solution to the concerns of the larger states. It might have worked, if the balance struck between empire and states had not been completely lopsided, clearly favouring the central authority. The final draft created something closer to a unitary state than a federal union (Nipperdey 653). It was granted exclusive competence on almost all of the marks of sovereignty identified by Bodin: war and peace (Paulskirche Constitution, Art. 10), coinage (Art. 46–48), the right of pardon (Art. 81), and of imposing oaths of loyalty on all persons serving in the army or navy (Art. 14). On top of these came the power to regulate customs (Art. 33), and taxation on production and consumption (Art. 34). The new empire was also given exclusive competence to represent the German people in all diplomatic matters (Art. 6). All the individual states were left with was the power to sign transport, policing, and private law treaties (Art. 8). Any treaties on other policies would be subject to a veto by the central executive (Art. 9). In an attempt to disentangle the *Bund* from the old ties with foreign monarchies that existed during the Holy Roman Empire, the treaty also robbed monarchs of the means to increase their status by banning them from entering into new personal unions with non-German territories (Art. 4).

If ratification had been up to the same citizens who successfully demanded the new constitution, it might just have been adopted. By the time the Convention finally produced a constitution however, counter-revolutionary efforts on behalf of the various German monarchies had more or less restored the order of the *Vormärz* period. It was the monarchs, therefore, who had to pass judgement on the draft text. The smaller ones were happy to sign. The larger ones… not so much. It might still have worked if the Prussian king had accepted the offer to become the new Reich's first emperor. Geopolitical considerations already made that unlikely: given its effect on the balance of power in central Europe, accepting the title would probably have triggered a war with Russia. And given that country's interests in maintaining an active role in German affairs, it would definitely have triggered one with Austria. None of this mattered though, because the king was never tempted to accept the title. He simply refused to be associated with the liberal revolutionaries who offered it, dismissing the imperial crown they offered him as "an imaginary hoop, baked of filth and clay" (Darmstaedter 91). Once Austria, Prussia, Bavaria, Hanover and Sachsen had all refused to accept the final text, and withdrew their delegates, the rump Convention dragged on for another few months before finally dissolving itself.

—

The Paulskirche Constitution would have a brief afterlife. Though never tempted to accept the offer of an imperial title based on mere popular sovereignty, Frederick Wilhelm IV's interest was sufficiently piqued to allow himself to be tempted by his adviser, Joseph von Radowitz, to consider attempting to form a similar Reich on the basis of monarchical sovereignty. The immediate product of this effort would remain limited to the Three Kings Union of Prussia, Saxony and Hanover (Nipperdey 670). Even in that limited form, the Union already formed a significant threat to Austria's position in the old *Bund*, especially when a number of smaller states joined it. The new Austrian chancellor, Prince Felix von Schwarzenberg – described by one historian as "clever and unscrupulous in his choice of means" (Darmstaedter 95) – did not hesitate to act. He first mobilised the other German states against the smaller Union by calling a meeting of the old *Bund's* Diet. Once he had secured his dominant position at the head of the German states, he then pressed his advantage by threatening military intervention against Prussia over the smaller state of Kur-Hesse. Given that the Czar had already come out on the side of Austria, Prussia had no choice but to back down.

The final settlement between the two powers, negotiated in the Moravian town of Olmütz (Olomouc), would see the constitutional settlement of the German states revert to the old *Bund* of 1815. This might have looked like a victory for Austria but given the continued existence of a desire for German unity, and the *Zollverein* that was pushing Austria away from its northern sister states, it was effectively only a matter of separation postponed. Schwarzenberg knew it, but, he stated, "a threadbare, torn skirt is better than no skirt at all" (Rumpler 319). He may have thought that he would solve future problems within the *Bund* in a similar forceful way, but history was to decide otherwise. The young new emperor he had helped to accede to the throne as part of his measures to settle the internal Austrian troubles, Franz Joseph I, decided that he did not need ministers to take political and military decisions for him. Schwarzenberg was spared the fate of seeing the results of this disastrous decision as they would manifest themselves over the next two decades. He died suddenly, of a brain aneurysm, in early 1852.

It is an open question as to what would have happened if Schwarzenberg had lived, and if the young monarch had decided to turn to him during his first crisis. As it was, his death cleared the way for a young Prussian Member of Parliament who first made his name on the German national stage by praising the outcome of the same deal that would later be used by Prussian propagandists as part of their *casus belli* against Austria. The MP's name: Otto von Bismarck.

—

Writing after the fact, the liberal revolutionary August Ludwig von Rochau (1810–1873) passed judgement on the failed Frankfurt convention. As a young man, Rochau's revolutionary elan had seen him support the Polish uprising of 1831, then get involved personally in the attempted German revolution of 1833 – the extremely badly thought through *Frankfurter Wachensturm*, in which a group of Burschenschaft members tried to seize control of the German *Bund's* parliament, situated in Frankfurt am Main, by first storming the local police headquarters. The attack ended in total failure, and, for Rochau himself, in a death sentence. After escaping from prison, he fled to Paris where he came into contact with the works of Auguste Comte. It is from the latter's positivist approach to politics that he developed his own concept of *Realpolitik*, combining socialist–liberal optimism with a fact-based approach to politics, a kind of new political science for the revolutionary age (Bew 25).

In *Grundsätze der Realpolitik*, Rochau observed that the Frankfurt proceedings fell far short of his new political-scientific standard. All the smart theoretical constructs proposed by the delegates had counted for nothing, he observed, because they had failed to grasp a fundamental truth about constitution building. The states on whose behalf they had been negotiating might have been willing to accept a joint constitution in theory, but "they would refuse to stick to the arrangement as soon as the obligations created through it clashed with their own state interests (Rochau 75; my translation throughout).

What the delegates had overlooked, was the fact that all politics – especially those involving claims of sovereignty – rested on power. Instead of focusing on constitutional constructs, Rochau claimed, they should have focused on constructing a state of sufficient "life force" (7). A liberal constitutional framework would have followed almost naturally if they had succeeded in uniting the nation first. Though he had no clear recipe for this "great task" ("An investigation of the question how this could be achieved goes beyond the objective of this publication," he remarked on one of the last pages of the book (224)), he was at least clear about what it required: "[N]either a principle nor an idea can contribute to the uniting of the scattered German forces, only a stronger power which pushes the others aside" (224). In pursuit of the liberal ideals which the delegates all shared, actions would speak louder than words.

Intermezzo: Tocqueville on divided sovereignty

In his *De La Democratie en Amerique* (1835), Alexis de Tocqueville (1805–1859) tried to achieve what his contemporaries seemed to him unable to do, stuck as they were "in the middle of a rapid stream, obstinately (...) fixing their eyes on the ruins which may still be descried upon the shore [they] have left, while the current hurries them away, and drags them backwards towards the abyss" (7). The river whose force he was describing was democracy, and his aim was to deal with it by disciplining its forces: "[T]o educate [it], to reawaken, if possible, its religious beliefs; to purify its morals, to mold its actions, to substitute a knowledge of statecraft for its inexperience, and an awareness of its true interest for its blind instincts" (7). It meant, in short, developing "[a] new science of politics (...) needed for a new world" (7).

The book offered an extensive meditation on the causes and effects of the inexorable rise of democracy. To understand the full significance of this "great social revolution," he had decided to study its functioning in the one country where it had "nearly reached its natural limits," the United States of America (Tocqueville 13). The aim was to draw lessons from it by discovering "the evils and the advantages which it brings" (14). As part of this study, he also aimed to discuss "the safeguards used by the Americans to direct it" (14). The latter effort took the form of a comprehensive discussion of the American constitution at both state and federal level.

Tocqueville presented himself as a supporter of the ideal of a federal constitution: "No one can be more inclined than I am to appreciate the advantages of the federal system, which I hold to be one of the most favour-able to the prosperity and freedom of man" (172). Its benefits, he claimed, were there for all to observe: "The union is as happy and as free as a small people, and glorious and strong as a great nation" (166) Still, it was clear to him that it was a far from perfect regime form. Its intricate system of checks and balances meant that it "rests upon a theory which is complicated at best, and which demands the daily exercise of a considerable share of discretion on the part of those who govern it" (166). Its foundation, a division of sovereignty between the federal centre and the states, also meant that it "must always be weaker than an entire [sovereignty]" (168).

The question was, then, what had made the American federation endure, in spite of these shortcomings. Previous confederacies (here he mentioned the Amphictyonic League, the Dutch Republic, and the Holy Roman Empire) had failed because they had been unable to maintain the balance between the states and the centre: "[E]ither the strongest of the allied states assumed the privileges of the federal authority and ruled all the others in its name; or the federal government was abandoned by its natural supporters, anarchy arose between the confederates, and the union lost all power of action" (Tocqueville 157–158). How did the American Constitution manage to avoid these twin threats?

In his discussion of the federal system, Tocqueville devoted the long-est section to the institution that formed, in his view, its cornerstone: the federal judiciary. This may, at first sight, have seemed like a strange choice to his contemporaries. After all, they would have remembered Hamilton's description of the judicial branch of the federal government in the *Federalist Papers* as "the weakest of the three" (Hamilton et al. 437). It had no arms or budget of its own to take on the other two branches. It could also only respond after the other two had acted, and then only if a complaint about these actions had been filed. In his view, though, the judiciary served two vital roles which made it the indispensable institution.

The first of these roles was the enforcement of the decisions of the federal authorities. "Governments," Tocqueville observed, "have generally but two means of overcoming the opposition of the governed: namely, the physical force that is at their own disposal, and the moral force that they derive from the decisions of the courts of justice" (139). The former was a means that a central government could really only use in moments of absolute necessity.[3] This fact, therefore, basically put the entire burden of enforcement onto the courts.

The Federal Courts were given a powerful tool in the form of the principle of constitutional review, "[T]he right of judges to found their decision on the *Constitution* rather than on the laws" (100). This gave them the authority "not to apply such laws as may appear to them to be unconstitutional" (100). Crucially, this power applied to both federal and state legislation. The Court existed as much to protect the states against encroachment by the federal government as the other way round. Its task was "to maintain the balance of power between the two rival governments as it had been established by the Constitution" (115).

This balancing task, in Tocqueville's view, had to be performed by the federal courts, not the state courts. To use the latter would be like "allow[ing] foreign judges to preside over the nation" (141). Not just foreign, in fact, but actively hostile – not out of evil intent, but because the logic of the situation would compel the state courts consistently to rule in favour of state interests. In this zero sum game, the result would be an erosion of the Union's foundation, "since whatever authority the Union loses turns to the advantage of the state" (141). Logically, the option of allowing the state courts to set judicial standards couldn't work: "To suppose that a state can exist when its fundamental laws are subjected to four-and-twenty different interpretations at the same time is to advance a proposition contrary alike to reason and to experience" (141).

Tocqueville also addressed the issue of boundaries between the two court systems. With two distinct systems of courts present within the same constitutional framework, the question would inevitably arise which of the two

---

3   One example from the early years of the federal republic was the Whiskey Rebellion of 1794, when settlers in Western Pennsylvania refused to pay a new excise tax on spirits imposed by the federal government. When federal tax collectors were attacked, even tarred and feathered the way British tax collectors had been in Boston twenty years earlier, Treasury Secretary Hamilton persuaded president Washington to send in federal troops to quell the rebellion. Washington rode out at the head of a nearly 15,000 strong army. There would be no confrontation – the rebellion simply evaporated – but the principle had been established that the central government was willing to use force of arms to enforce its decisions, including on taxation.

systems was allowed to determine who could arbitrate in cases where the two seemed to clash. Since an independent arbitrator wasn't an option, it had to be either the federal courts or the state courts. The latter was no option, though:

> The object of creating a Federal tribunal was to prevent the state courts from deciding, each after its own fashion, questions affecting the national interests (...) This end would not have been attained if the courts of the several states, even while they abstained from deciding cases avowedly Federal in their nature, had been able to decide them by pretending that they were not Federal.
> (Tocqueville 143)

It was therefore essential that the Federal Supreme Court was given the power to decide on whether cases fell within its jurisdiction. It had to have what German legal scholars would later call "Kompetenz Kompetenz."

—

The other important function the Federal Courts performed was to strengthen the relationship between the Union and the people. Whereas traditional confederations created only a relationship between the states and the union, the American Union also aimed to establish a direct relationship between the federal centre and the citizens. But as Tocqueville explained, this new relationship was not a secure one, being neither as solid in its foundation nor as profound in its attachment as the relationship between the states and the people:

> The sovereignty of the Union is an abstract being, which is connected with but few external objects; the sovereignty of the states is perceptible by the senses, easily understood, and constantly active. The former is of recent creation, the latter is coeval with the people itself. The sovereignty of the Union is factitious, that of the states is natural and self-evident. (...) The sovereignty of the nation affects a few of the chief interests of society; the authority of the states controls every individual citizen at every hour and in all circumstances.
> (Tocqueville 169)

The federal government therefore needed to find a means of cementing the ties between the centre and the citizen. The solution was to give every citizen the opportunity to seek the federal courts' protection against violation of their rights by either their state or the federal government. Through what Tocqueville called a "master-stroke of policy," the Founders had established that "the federal courts (...) should only take cognizance of parties in an individual capacity" (148). This confirmed that the measures taken by the federal government were understood by the Court to have a direct effect on the citizens.

As a result, he felt justified to conclude that whereas "[t]he old confederate governments presided over communities (...) that of the Union presides over individuals" (158). It may not have been a full sovereignty – "the comparative weakness of a restricted sovereignty is an evil inherent in the federal system" (158) – but it had its own claim to the people's loyalty. And thanks to the Federal courts, it had "the means of enforcing all it is empowered to demand" (158).

The *Bundesstaat* reconsidered

Tocqueville's analysis of the American constitution would help to unlock the mid-nineteenth century German federal debate. It finally solved the centuries old theoretical problem, first identified by Pufendorf, of the undefined nature in German constitutional theory of the regime type existing in the space between "kingdoms" and "systems of states."

The original American compromise lay undiscovered until it was addressed in the early 1850s by a German scholar called Georg Waitz (1813–1886). Waitz, a pupil of Von Ranke, was a medievalist and German constitutional historian, and briefly a politician in the Frankfurt Parliament that had tried, and failed, to establish a German monarchical federal union. In an essay in the *Allgemeinen (Kieler) Monatsschrift* (1853, later reprinted in his *Grundzüge der Politik*, 1862), Waitz started with a paean on "Tocqueville's sharp-minded description of the essence of the North American constitution" (Waitz, 158)[4] He then went on to describe the weaknesses of the German *Bund*, a system "so contrary to all political intelligence, that I will struggle to explain to future generations how it had ever been considered a possible construct" (158). Among its main weaknesses he listed the system of strict delegation which tied delegates to home state voting instructions, and the fact that the central authority had no powers to impose its decisions on unwilling states. A confederation like the German *Bund* was, therefore, in his view "an unsatisfactory form of constitutional organisation," at best "a transition stage leading to other constitutional forms" (159).

---

4   Translations from Waitz are my own, with key terms in German included for context.

Waitz saw two likely end stages of this developmental process: either the centre collapsed and the states became individual independent entities, or one state became so dominant that it incorporated all the others. He dismissed the Holy Roman Empire as a potential example of a functional and lasting confederation because it was, in his view, really just a slowly disintegrating feudal state. The process here was one of continued transfer of powers from the centre to the territories, until they had accumulated so many powers that they became states in their own right[5] (Waitz 160).

The American republic, which he described as a *"Bundesstaat,"* seemed to have overcome this problem. It was neither fully centralised nor completely decentralised, "as far from being like the old Empire as it is from a confederacy [Staatenbund]" (Waitz 161). The *Bundesstaat* was, "as the name suggests," a state (162). But it also remained a joint undertaking of sovereign states. "The People," which he equated with "the Nation," "stands in the same relationship to the member state and the collective state [*Gesammtstaat*]" (166) It solved the sovereignty problem by dividing its powers of execution between the two levels of government. Waitz also grasped where previous German interpretations of the US constitution had gone wrong. Their definition of the *Bundesstaat* as a construct in which the member states were fully subordinate to the new political centre failed to acknowledge that they had retained part of their sovereignty when creating the new central authority: "Only the reach, not the content of sovereignty had been limited" (166).

—

In the course of his discussion of the American example, Waitz made an interpretation error that would end up having a profound influence on German – and broader European – constitutional thinking about federal unions. Instead of sketching what really happened, namely that the constitution ended up *creating* an American people and nation (partly through a rhetorical sleight of hand: the "We The People" introduced by the Committee of Style), he claimed that the sequence was the other way round. Seemingly influenced by the idea of the *Volksgeist* developed by the thinkers of German Romanticism, a concept laden with notions of cultural and even ethnic unity,

5   Like the two scenarios of decline of the confederation, Weitz's description of the Holy Roman Empire as a slowly decaying feudal system seems derived from Pufendorf, who describes the long transition from the earliest feudal stage to the quasi-confederal period of the Westphalian period in his *Present State of Germany* (note though that Waitz doesn't cite Pufendorf anywhere). On the historical links between feudalism and federalism, see also Federalist 15 by Hamilton.

Waitz hypothesised that the state was, in fact, "the organisation of a people for the fulfilment of its higher objectives" (168). In other words: the people had created the state by willing it into existence through an "inner drive" (168).

To make his theory add up, Waitz had to resort to a rather implausible comparison: "Totally separate peoples won't easily submit to such a unification process, and if so only under exceptional circumstances like those in Switzerland; this process is more suited for a single, though tribally structured nation" (163). The American colonies, the product of many different forms of colonisation by people from different European countries, were suddenly reduced to tribes of a single nation.

On a positive note, this unusual (and historically incorrect) simile did allow Waitz to grasp the fact that, as Tocqueville had explained, and Hamilton had originally argued, in a *Bundesstaat* the people stand in a direct relationship to both member state and federal government. But the downsides of his interpretation error would prove to be more significant. It would, for one thing, reduce the reach of the *Bundesstaat* as a constitutional concept. Any federal experiment that spanned more than one people would from now on *by definition* have to be interpreted as a mere confederation.[6]

Other scholars would help to spread this flawed interpretation of the history of the American constitutional compact. The Swiss-German legal scholar Johann Bluntschli (1808–1881), for example, described the American constitution as "the People becoming an independent person which dominates the common life" (quoted in Seydel 188; my translation). In an 1881 essay titled "Die Organisation des Europäischen Staatenvereines" he was even more explicit: "The United States of America is a sovereign state (...) in which the North American people, united through nationality, language, culture, law, and interests, created a joint organisation" (Bluntschli 21; my translation throughout). Bluntschli thought no similar move was possible in Europe since:

[N]o European people exists. Europe consists of different nations that won't be united politically in a similar fashion, because geography,

6   This classification, which was based on the flawed interpretation of the American Founding as produced by Waitz, played an important role in the Maastricht ruling by the German *Bundesverfassungsgericht* dated 12 October 1993 (Decision in case 2 BvR 2134, 2159–2192), in which the Court claimed that the 1991 Treaty on European Union established a "*Staatenverbund* (confederation) for the establishment of an ever closer union between the peoples of Europe as organised in their respective states, not a new state resting on a European *Staatsvolk*." The Court clearly overlooked the historical evidence – from both American and German practice – that there was a third option, that a European people (singular) could also be the *result* of the formation of a union.

ethnicity, history, culture, interests and law have kept them separate from each other. (...) European constitutional unity without a European people is a contradiction in terms. There is no European people, therefore there can be no state called Europe.
(Bluntschli 21, 27)

Another influential scholar who engaged with Waitz's interpretation of the American founding was the Austrian-German constitutional lawyer Georg Jellinek (1851–1911). Jellinek was born into the Viennese intellectual establishment and became a professor of constitutional law at the University of Vienna by the age of 32. This was after he had published a book that would cement his reputation as a prominent thinker on constitutional legal issues in the late 19th century German language area.

His *Die Lehre von den Staatenverbindungen* (1882) was a remarkable work. It introduced a taxonomy of unions, distinguishing personal from real unions, and informal unions from treaty-based legal communities. Apart from alliances, he also discussed the category of composite states (*Staatenstaate*), in which one state governed a number of other states or territories, and federal unions, in which the states were admitted on an equal footing. Within the category of federal unions, he further distinguished the confederation (*Staatenbund*) from an American-style federal union (*Bundesstaat*).

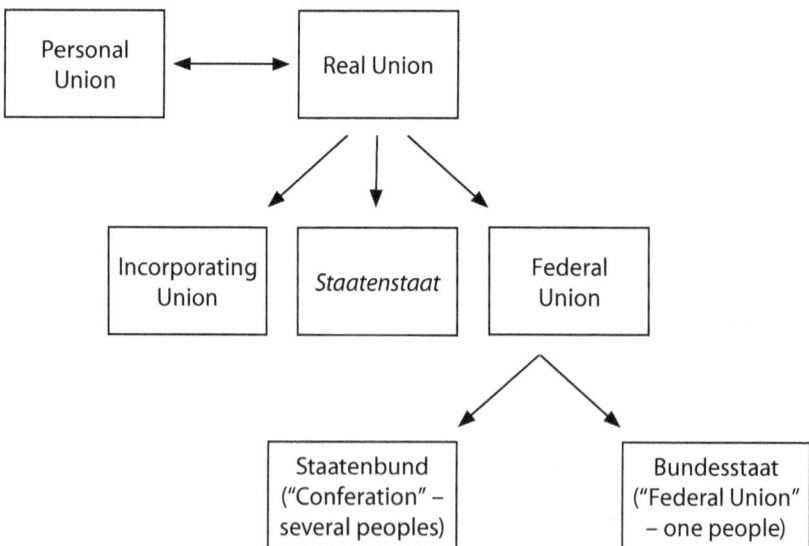

Figure 3: Taxonomy of unions III (Jellinek's classification)

Though Jellinek's taxonomy was fairly comprehensive, the analysis that underpinned it was based on the problematic assumption that sovereignty was indivisible, as Bodin had claimed and the Bavarian legal scholar Max Von Seydel had reaffirmed in an 1872 essay on the concept of the *Bundesstaat*. This assumption ended up creating a practical political dilemma. In the conflict between the States' Rights camp (Jefferson, Calhoun) and the Federalists (Hamilton, Lincoln), Jellinek's political sympathies clearly lay with the latter. But since, in his view, sovereignty was indivisible, he could also not deny the logic of Calhoun that a union of fully sovereign states could never have created a new sovereign entity to which the states were in any way subservient. The historically accurate interpretation of the US constitution, that it was a union created by several independent peoples who thereby became a new people with a new national government, was to him therefore "logically impossible," since "a state can't create a new state personality separate from itself" (Jellinek 266). How, then, to explain the nature of the United States?

He solved this problem by making a further distinction between traditional and modern states. In the traditional category, all the classical mechanisms for state formation and expansion already discussed by early-modern raison d'état theorists – "incorporation, cession, debellation, personal and real union" (Jellinek 263; my translation throughout) – were at the disposal of an already existing state. Modern states, however, were entirely new creations, the product of "a people, which feels and knows itself to be a unit, expressing this sense of unity by organising and thereby constituting itself as a state" (263). It was the fundamental logic which Waitz had also assumed to have applied in the case of a *Bundesstaat*, "a nation organising itself as a state" (Jellinek 263).

If this was true for the United States, then it logically had to follow that the nation had always had a higher claim to sovereignty than the states to which Jefferson and Calhoun had appealed, even before the creation of the new American federal union. Jellink found the justification for this position in Abraham Lincoln's 1861 speech to both Houses of Congress.[7] In this speech, Lincoln, who was looking for reasons to deny the validity of secessionism, argued that "[o]ur states have neither more nor less power than that reserved to them in the Union by the Constitution – *no one of*

---

7   In his first speech as president, Lincoln made the political and legal case against secession. As part of his case, he recycled the argument used by nationalists like Rufus King and James Wilson during the Philadelphia Convention that since the states had declared independence collectively, their sovereignty could also only be exercised collectively. See page 166 above.

them ever having been a state out of the Union – The Union is older than any of the states, and, in fact, it created them as states"[8] (quoted in Jellinek 291 fn 35; my emphasis). In other words: if the situation in 1787 had been one of independent states forming a new union, Calhoun may have had a point. But since such a scenario was, according to Jellinek, both "logically impossible" and historically incorrect, he was clearly wrong.[9]

German unification in practice: Bismarck's federalism of conquest

In the early nineteenth century, there was a revival of interest in the works of Machiavelli in the German speaking countries.[10] The authors involved in this revival seemed less interested in his theory of expansion through empire or federation as set out in his *Discourses* than in his call for liberation from foreign oppression in the final chapter of *The Prince*. This preoccupation is probably explained by the fact that, since the start of the War of the First Coalition (1792–1797), the French republic had repeatedly overrun the German border territories, even incorporating some of them, specifically the Saarland, which, like Elzas and Lotharingia, would spend the next 150 years periodically getting annexed by either Germany or France. To German observers, the start of the nineteenth century may well have felt like a moment of rupture not unlike that which Machiavelli experienced in early fifteenth century Florence.

Georg Wilhem Friedrich Hegel would use his study of the German constitution (1802), in which he praised "the genius of Machiavelli's works" (83) and pointed to his "basic aim of raising Italy to statehood" (80), to describe the double challenge faced by the German lands of his time. In a passage reminiscent of Machiavelli's sketch of a deeply divided Italy, he observed that "It has been the fate of Italy to come for the most part under the authority of foreign powers. (...) If Germany is not to suffer the same fate as this after a

---

8   Jellinek's argument seems a conscious attempt to prove that it was entirely possible to take the starting position defined by Von Seydel, namely that sovereignty is indivisible, and end up with a justification of the *Bundesstaat* – something Von Seydel had categorically ruled out (his treatise was based on a particularly Bavarian preoccupation with the idea of state sovereignty).
9   It seems ironic that to refute Calhoun's states' rights theory, Jellinek borrowed an argument about the American Founding first put forward by the Massachusetts senator Daniel Webster in the early 1830s in a debate with Calhoun about the subject of nullification. Calhoun was generally considered to have won that debate, not least because he destroyed the Webster thesis about the nation somehow being prior to the states in the story of the Founding. NB: it was Calhoun who in that debate had defended the position that sovereignty was indivisible.
10   On the early 19th century revival of German interest in Machiavelli, see Robertson 58–77.

few wars, it should re-organise itself as a state" (98). To this end, two things were necessary, according to Hegel. One was "organising a political power (...) by amalgamating the whole military strength of Germany into a single army," with the emperor as supreme commander; the other was that the emperor would again be placed at the head of the German empire (98–99).

In his 1807 essay "On Machiavelli, as an author," Johann Gottlieb Fichte gave expression to this same sense of disruption. What Machiavelli's "book on the prince" offered most of all was "stability and constancy to the incessantly fluctuating relations among the states in Italy" (Fichte 763). The methods discussed in *The Prince* were less important than this ultimate objective. The points on which Machiavelli recommended Cesare Borgia as a model, Fichte observed, were exactly those through which the latter had introduced "tranquillity, order, and public security in a province that had become completely wild" (764). The changing circumstances made Machiavelli accept that it was "no longer a matter of Florence alone, but rather of all of Italy," and that for unification to happen "it must be united under the rule of a single native [Italian]" (765). According to Fichte, the book could be read as an attempt to find a prince to unite the country. He thought Machiavelli found "this united sovereign authority" (766) in the figure to whom the book was dedicated, Lorenzo de' Medici. "His book on the prince," Fichte asserted, "emerged from this, as well as his moving appeal for the liberation of Italy with which it closes" (766). It is tempting to read this whole passage as referring not only to Machiavelli's sixteenth century Italy, but also to Fichte's own early nineteenth century Germany (and perhaps even justified since he would shortly afterwards repeat the call in his *Lectures to the German People*).

—

Achieving the unity of Germany through the development of answers to the double challenge defined by Hegel was to become the life's work of the eventual first German Chancellor, Otto von Bismarck (1815–1898). Not literally, of course. Bismarck had read some of Hegel's theoretical works but dismissed them as "not understood" (Darmstaedter 39). It is clear, however, that the same two ideas that Hegel had identified also occupied his mind. In an 1858 memorandum to the Prussian King Friedrich Wilhem IV, he formulated the objectives that he would ruthlessly pursue over the course of the next fifteen years: "The leadership of Prussia from the Prussian standpoint, the unification of Germany from a national standpoint" (159). In his view, the two aims were one and the same ("The two ends coincide"):

German reunification could only be achieved through Prussian leadership, with the Prussian king as its undisputed head (quoted in Darmstaedter 159–160). And, as he observed in a notorious speech to the Prussian Chamber of Deputies shortly after becoming chief minister, "Germany doesn't look to the liberalism of Prussia, but to the might of Prussia. (...) The great questions of the time will not be resolved by speeches and majority decisions – that was the great mistake of 1848 and 1849 – but by iron and blood" (197).

Though he never used the term himself and disapproved completely of the liberal aspirations connected with it, Bismarck's policies would become associated with the term *Realpolitik* propagated by Von Rochau to the point that commentators treated him like its living embodiment. He was certainly not shy of the actions advocated by Von Rochau. Any measure that helped further his double objective of German unity under Prussian leadership was ruthlessly implemented, including warfare.

War wasn't just a question of necessity. There were also benefits attached to achieving German unification under Prussian rule through war, according to Bismarck: "I [felt] convinced that the gulf which diverse dynastic and family influences and different habits of life had in the course of history created between the south and north of the Fatherland, could not be more effectually bridged over than by (...) joint national war" (Bismarck, 99). The shared experience of war would, so he hoped, "foster a consciousness" among the various German states which would "blot out" any memories of previous divisions (Bismarck 100). In other words: war could work as a great unifying force, helping the German nation overcome its historic divisions.

In his ten years at the head of the Prussian government, from 1862 to 1871, Bismarck would plunge his country into a series of increasingly ambitious wars. The first was caused by an ongoing border dispute with the kingdom of Denmark over the administration of the principalities of Schleswig and Holstein in 1864. Here he got Austria to agree to act as an ally at the head of the German *Bund*. Jointly with the "Third Germany" (the smaller states), they first crushed the Danish army and then dismissed the claims to sovereignty of the local ruling family (although the Austrians had some misgivings about the latter action). Once he had positioned Prussia to effectively incorporate the two states, he then used a *fait accompli* strategy to cause a significant conflict with Austria. This conflict would grow into the Seven Weeks War of 1866, through which Prussia would push Austria out of the *Bund*.

The Prussian win in 1866, in turn, would set up the war for dominance of continental Europe in which an army of the united German states would defeat a French army under emperor Napoleon III (1870–1871). The latter war was the result of another Spanish succession crisis. When the Spanish parliament, the Cortes, took informal soundings with a lesser Hohenzollern prince about him taking the Spanish throne which had been vacant since the Bourbon queen Isabella II was deposed in 1868, French authorities soon found out about it. Napoleon III, keen to avoid a repeat of the sixteenth century scenario where his country would find itself wedged between two large monarchies controlled by the same powerful royal family, felt forced to issue a quasi-veto. Out of the wording of the French request, or to be more precise, the Prussian royal response to this request, Bismarck then skilfully managed to distil his desired *casus belli*.

—

The series of Prussian victories raised the question as to what kind of constitutional order Prussia would like to use to strengthen its grip on German territories. Theoretical arguments about the new interpretation of the concept of the *Bundesstaat*, and the principles that underpinned it, were largely wasted on Bismarck, not because he was incapable of grasping their content, obviously – though not an academic, Bismarck was undoubtedly among the smartest political minds of his age – but rather that he had no use for principles of any kind, unless they could be used as tactical weapons in the quest to achieve his ultimate objectives: a united Germany under Prussian rule.[11]

In the early 1860s, his preferred option had been incorporation of any territories conquered in war. The reason for this was obvious. Prussia started the post-Napoleonic period as the smallest of the Great Powers in terms of both territory and population. If it was to become the dominant force among the European Great Powers, it needed to expand. Following the annexation of Schleswig and Holstein in 1865, Bismarck would use the settlement of the war with Austria to execute the annexation of the northern German principalities of Hanover, Hesse, and Nassau, as well as the free city of Frankfurt, supposedly as a nod to "the principle of retribution" but in reality mainly to add their nearly five million inhabitants and 25,000 square kilometres to the Prussian scale (Darmstaedter 302–304).

If Bismarck ever used federal arguments, it was mainly in a tactical way. In the early 1860s he torpedoed an Austrian proposal for a second federal

11   Perhaps the most famous example of Bismarck's creative (ab)use of constitutional principles was his claim to have discovered "a gap" in the Prussian constitution. This supposed gap allowed him to circumvent the objections of the Prussian parliament in continuing to finance the reorganisation of the Prussian army. He did it by prolonging the old budget when the parliament proposed cutting defence spending in a new one, a manoeuvre the English diplomat Sir Robert Morier described as "devilish sophistry." See Darmstaedter 196.

chamber in the German Bund by outfederalising his opponent. Whereas the Austrians had suggested selecting delegates from the state parliaments, Bismarck proposed a directly elected second chamber, not because he believed in the idea, but because he knew that the Austrians would feel forced to veto any move in that direction. By cornering them in this way, he managed to kill the broader attempt at reform of the *Bund* which may well have locked in Austrian membership for the long term (Darmstaedter 209).

This kind of cynical use of federal stratagems to kill federal outcomes did not, however, mean that Bismarck was a principled opponent of federalism. As with most matters of principle, he fundamentally didn't care enough to be either for or against it. There was no inconsistency, therefore, when in 1871, he used federalism as a solution to the problem of how to unify the different parts of Germany that only five years earlier had faced each other across the battlefield. Bismarck wanted the German people – and their rulers – to come together under a Prussian emperor. Preferably they'd do so in a spirit of unity, an aim that could never have been squared with the use of the kind of violence that would have been required to force an unwilling southern Germany to submit to Prussian rule. Or, indeed, even with open claims of Prussian superiority within a federal structure. When, at the signing of the Versailles peace treaty, the Prussian monarch Friedrich Wilhelm IV insisted on being introduced as "emperor *of* Germany," not merely "German emperor," Bismarck feared that this would be interpreted by the other German states as a violation of their sovereignty. He solved it by introducing him instead as "Emperor Wilhelm" (Darmstaedter 394).

In defending the federal constitution, he also came up with a politically expedient solution to the old German sovereignty problem. Contemporary German theorists had followed Waitz in adopting the American solution of a division of sovereignty between the federal centre and the member states. Bismarck would use a different concept to help sell his constitution to potentially obstructive states, no doubt anticipating the kind of objections to the idea of federal (read: Prussian) sovereignty as formulated by the Bavarian legal scholar Seydel (to make his claim of full states' sovereignty add up, Seydel ended up arguing that the Reich was in fact not a *Bundesstaat* but a *Staatenbund*). In a monarchical federation like Germany, Bismarck claimed in a debate in the new Reichstag in April 1871, sovereignty was not derived from the people, the way it was in republican federations. Instead "the united states are the empire, and the empire consists of the united states" (364). In other words: the empire may have been a *Bundesstaat*, but sovereignty remained undivided. It rested fully with the states and their monarchs: "[S]overeignty rests not with the emperor but with the collective of the united states" (365. It was a political fiction, a *Gute Nacht Geschichte* to send the lesser monarchs off to sleep. In practice, Prussia would end up completely dominating the federation, just as Bismarck had planned it.

Eventually, theory would catch up with practice. A number of constitutional scholars decided that in truth, sovereignty rested with the empire rather than the states. Key spokespersons for this camp were Albert Haenel (1833–1918) and Paul Laband (1838–1918). The former was instrumental in the development of the concept of *Kompetenz-Kompetenz* as a criterion for judging where sovereignty lay. The authority that had the power to decide on new competences was the one that could claim to have sovereignty. In the case of the new constitution, it was the Reich: "[T]hrough the sovereign decision on its own competence, it rules decisively on the competence of the individual states, who are therefore not sovereign" (Hänel 240; my translation).

In his seminal work, *Das Staatsrecht des Deutschen Reiches* (1876), Paul Laband (1838–1918) argued that by definition, in a *Bundesstaat* "the central authority is sovereign" (52; my translation throughout). Though he recognised the Reich possessed a "double structure" (53), involving both the central power and the states, this did not mean sovereignty could be divided between the two layers. "A shared sovereignty would be a limited sovereignty," which in his view was a logical impossibility since sovereignty was supposed to be *un*limited (57). To justify the continued existence of states when they had lost their claim to sovereignty, he explained that statehood was not just a product of sovereignty but also of dominion (*Herrschaft*): "Dominion is the right to issue orders to free persons (and collectives of persons), and to force them to obey" (62). It meant that the states were still fully states, even though they were no longer sovereign: "The member state is a ruler facing down, and a subject facing up" (53).

The brief embrace of the idea of shared sovereignty, led by Waitz, had allowed for the theoretical breakthrough that made the *Bundesstaat* possible as a political solution. Once an actual *Bundestaat* was created however, the debate reverted to the old state versus empire division. It was Fürsterianer versus Caesarianer all over again.

—

Bismarck's 1871 constitution would adopt the external form of a rudimentary division of powers, with only two out of three parts of the usual trias (an independent federal judiciary would be introduced six years later, in 1877). It had an executive in the form of an emperor served by a Chancellor and cabinet, and a divided legislative power with a lower chamber (*Reichstag*) and upper chamber (*Bundesrat*), the latter representing the states and the former representing the German people. Hegel's challenge of "amalgamating the whole military strength of Germany into a single army" (99) was solved by making the power to declare war and peace the exclusive preserve of the Prussian emperor. At a stroke, Kaiser Wilhelm thereby became commander in chief of all armies in the German empire (to confirm this, soldiers would henceforth be asked to swear allegiance to him instead of to their local rulers). The remaining powers underwent a further separation, with the *Reichstag* and *Bundesrat* getting the powers affecting domestic policy while Bismarck gave himself as Chancellor the exclusive right to determine foreign policy (Locke's "federative power" – in Bismarck's view more important than any power affecting domestic policy. In this, Bismarck was a typical product of his time. The "primacy of foreign policy" was a maxim in Russian, French, Austrian and British as much as in German politics).

On the vertical axis, certain powers were to remain with the individual states (defence in peacetime for example). States were also at liberty to sign their own treaties with third parties. To confirm that, on paper at least, sovereignty remained as much with the states as with the centre, Bismarck gave them the right to veto any offensive wars proposed by the executive (no doubt trusting in his ability to frame any proposed war as purely defensive).

Though propagated by Kant in his *Eternal Peace*, separation of powers was not deeply rooted in German constitutional practice. The 1850 Prussian constitution was still essentially a unitary monarchical construction, though it did have the suggestion of separation by introducing courts who were said to be subject only to "the law," not the monarch (Windhorst 906). In that sense, the 1871 constitution contained an important innovation, at least in the German context.

The way Bismarck chose to implement the principle, though, was fundamentally different from the way it had been described by Montesquieu and subsequently enacted by the American Founders. He had no desire to make his German federation a liberal one. He therefore designed the separated powers in such a way that they had no effective checks on each other. This meant that the Reichstag had no influence on the key policy areas of foreign affairs and war and peace, or indeed on any issue that was brought under those two broad headings. Ministers were appointed by the crown without any scrutiny from the legislature. The latter also had no way of forcing individual ministers (or the cabinet as a whole) to account for their actions. The net result of this system of separated powers without checks and balances was a dominant executive and a powerless parliament.

Bismarckian federalism's fatal flaw

Bismarck's constitution, and the Reich it helped to create, would only survive for four decades. This failure to project itself further into the future was undoubtedly a product of many factors. One was the only clear strategic miscalculation of Bismarck's career: his decision to tie Germany into strategic partnerships with Austria-Hungary (1879) and Italy (1882) to form the Triple Alliance. On paper, the formation of a permanent axis at the centre of Europe to counter the strategic threat from Russia in the east and France and Great Britain in the west may have seemed sensible. In practice, however, the Triple Alliance robbed Europe's diplomatic system of its ability to deal with shifts in the equilibrium through the construction of *ad hoc* coalitions. Worse, Bismarck's move would eventually end up driving Russia into the arms of France (Dual Alliance, 1894) and Great Britain (Anglo-Russian Entente, 1907), turning what was previously a flexible system into a rigid opposition of two heavily armed power blocks. In the end, it would only take a minor incident to bring these two blocks to blows.

—

The main reason Bismarck's constitution failed was the very reason why it was introduced in the first place. It was a constitution created for a single purpose: the ability to wage war. The division of powers in the 1871 constitution which made the Prussian monarch the commander-in-chief created a giant German war machine that could be put into action at short notice whenever he saw fit. In practice, though, he never would. Bismarck was aware that after the war of 1870–1871, the German Reich's position as dominant Great Power at the centre of the European continent meant that it had little room for further expansion. The inner logic of the balance of power system was such that any German attempt in that direction could lead to the other four Great Powers (five, if Italy was included) combining against it to deal it a crushing defeat.

It put Germany in an uncomfortable position: a society geared towards war, in a European state system based on war, forced by political realities to adopt a diplomatic strategy of maintaining peace at all cosst. It was clear that Germany's political class didn't much like this forced passivity – not in practice, and certainly not in theory. The supreme commander of the Prussian armed forces, General Helmut von Moltke, caused a stir in 1880 when, in answer to a letter from Johann Bluntschli, he publicly dismissed the idea of eternal peace as "a dream, and not even a nice one," while claiming that war was "part of God's world order (...) [t]hrough whom the noblest virtues of man are manifested" (194). He expressed the hope that progress would make war less cruel but claimed that the laws of war proposed by Bluntschli's fellow international law professors would in fact do the opposite, making it more cruel by making it less effective. "The greatest blessing of war," he observed, "is the quick ending of it, and to that end all not completely reprehensible means must remain at our disposal" (Moltke 195–96; my translation throughout).

Moltke dismissed both the recently developed laws of war and the concept of international arbitration, which he described as "a permanent assembly of members unelected by the peoples" (200). Instead of this "Areopagus," he rather trusted in direct negotiations between the governments involved. While stressing it was a misunderstanding to assume he wanted war "merely because I don't consider it an evil to be avoided" (206), he reaffirmed his commitment to what was by then the orthodox German position on the subject of war. It was effectively a restatement of the Roman maxim *Si vis pacem, para bellum:* if you want peace, prepare for war. "Germany has achieved its goal of reunion; it has no reason whatsoever to launch itself into new warlike adventures, but it can always be forced to defend itself and must be fully prepared for that" (201).

This warlike spirit would seep into the pores of German debate. Even Bluntschli himself seemed infected with it. In his pamphlet on the European society of states, published shortly after his correspondence with Moltke, he included a withering attack on the peace plan of the Abbé de Saint-Pierre, dismissing his proposal as based on "the utopia of 'eternal peace'" (15) Saint-Pierre, he claimed, clearly failed to grasp the merits of war:

> The unchangeable nature of public life and the general decadence and decay would be a much worse fate for humanity than war (...) which while bringing misery on many fronts also wakes dormant ambitions, fosters manly virtues, cleanses the political atmosphere like a thunderstorm, and brings new forms of development to society.
> (Bluntschli 15–16; my translation)

—

No German thinker would go further in celebrating the idea of war than Heinrich von Treitschke (1834–1896). A historian and a parliamentarian, he was known mainly for his outspoken nationalism. In a series of lectures delivered as professor at Berlin University, he would deal with the main issues of his age, incorporating them all in a single systematic analysis which had warfare at its core.

The lectures were remarkable for two reasons. First, they made Machiavelli the cornerstone of all modern thinking about the state's power: "It will ever remain Machiavelli's glory that he set the State upon its own feet and freed it in its morality from the Church; and also, above all, that he declared clearly for the first time: 'The State is power'" (Treitschke 27). The "gifted Florentine" was not above reproach, though: "That the power acquired must justify itself by employing itself for the highest moral good of mankind, of that we find no trace in his teaching" (28).

The main reason the lectures are remembered is their Clausewitzian embrace of war as a means of conducting state policy. The purpose of war, in turn, was the Machiavellian maxim of *mantenere lo stato*: "The state is power for this reason only, that it may maintain itself alongside other equally independent powers" (9). This created two core challenges for any state: "War and the administration of justice are the first tasks of even the rudest barbaric State" (9) And since warfare was a core task of any state, this meant the existence of other states was a prerequisite: "These tasks are only conceivable in a plurality of States permanently existing alongside one another" (Treitschke 9). He therefore dismissed the "barren uniformity of a world empire" (11). "[I]n this everlasting for and against of different States," he explained, "lies the beauty of history; to wish to abolish this rivalry is simply unreason" (11).

The "sacredness of war" (Treitschke 16) demanded not just the continued existence of individual states able to meet each other in combat. It also meant that states could not accept any authority higher than themselves which could limit their right to wage war (14). States could voluntarily limit their sovereignty through the signing of treaties. But, Treitschke observed, "that does not invalidate the rule, for every treaty is a voluntary limitation of the individual power, and all international treaties are written with the stipulation: *rebus sic stantibus*" ['Things thus standing', implying that a change in circumstances could justify withdrawal from a treaty. Treitschke 15]. For a state to subject itself to the verdict of another state through arbitration was unthinkable. Not just because he knew of "no impartial foreign power in existence," but mainly because it was "a matter of honour for a State to determine such a question itself" (16).

This absolutist interpretation of the position of the state did not mean that all states were equal in his eyes. On the contrary, he thought it entirely reasonable that the Great Powers claimed the right to decide matters between themselves, likening their joint rule of Europe to an aristocracy (Treitschke 16). And not just of Europe, as the "partitioning of the non-European world among the European powers" was a logical extension of the mission of this "aristocratic" regime (17), or even an essential one, for as he observed, "[a] time may come when States without oversea possessions will no longer count among the great States at all" (19).

Treitschke's observations about the essential functions of the state were mainly meant as a warning against the "blind worshippers of perpetual peace," who "dream of a World-State, which we have already recognised as something irrational" (20). In his aristocratic society of Great Powers, war wasn't just a way for individual states to maintain themselves. It was, in fact, a great organising principle. It served as " a lawsuit by which the claims of states are enforced" (20). It also offered states a way of growing closer to each other. They "learn through it to know and respect one another in their particular idiosyncrasies" (21). Civilizational progress may well result in making wars rarer. But, he concluded, "it is a fallacy to infer from that that they could ever cease altogether. They cannot and should not cease, so long as the State is sovereign and confronts other sovereign States" (26).

—

The turn of the twentieth century found the German Reich in a nervous mood. Its military class seemed determined to seize the earliest opportunity to plunge the country into a war that would help to give it the world power status they thought it deserved. On the other hand the civil political class was deeply divided about the need for war, not least because of growing scepticism about its usefulness, or indeed its moral legitimacy. Military concerns became profound worries when the moral confusion started to affect the Kaiser himself: in the Moroccan crisis of early 1911, he prevaricated, eventually deciding to do nothing to counter a French landing of troops in the country, in spite of earlier German pledges to safeguard Moroccan sovereignty (the aim obviously being to make it a German protectorate). It was clear to them that something had to be done.

Into the breach stepped the military historian Friedrich von Bernhardi (1849–1930). In his *Germany and the Next War* (1912) he would use a simple two-step argument to make the case for war. First he warned his audience about the consequences of taking the peace message seriously. "The aspirations for peace," he argued, "threaten to poison the soul of the German people"; they "fettered" the nation's political power, "fritter[ing] itself away in fruitless bickerings and doctrinaire disputes" (Bernhardi v). Against those "theorists and fanatics" who waxed lyrical about "perpetual peace," he restated the principled case for war (vii). Not any kind of war, mind you:

following Moltke, he was willing to accept the argument that it would be "a most desirable consummation if wars for trivial reasons should be rendered impossible" (vii). But some wars remained definitely necessary. His mission was "to try to prove that war is not merely a necessary element in the life of nations, but an indispensable factor of cultures in which a true civilised nation finds the highest expression of strength and vitality" (v).

The commercial success of the book – it would go through five editions in its first year of publication alone – may well have helped to firm up German pro-war sentiments in the runup to the events of the First World War. It was this desire for war among parts of its political and military establishment that would eventually push the country towards it when an opportunity presented itself in the summer of 1914. What followed was the kind of war its constitution was created for. It turned out that it was also the very thing that caused its demise.

Bibliography

Bew, John. *Realpolitik: A History*. Oxford University Press, 2015.

Bernhardi, Friedrich von. *Germany and the Next War*. 1911. Createspace Independent Publishing Platform, 2015.

Bismarck, Otto von. *Bismarck, the Man the Statesman, Vol. 2: Being the Reflections and Reminiscences of Otto, Prince Von Bismarck*. 1898. Forgotten Books, 2018.

Bluntschli, Johann Caspar. *Die Organisation des Europäischen Staatenvereins*. 1878. Wissenschaflichte Buchgesellschaft, 1962.

Brie, Siegfried. *Der Bundesstaat: Eine historisch-dogmatische Untersuchung. Erster Abteilung: Geschichte der Lehre vom Bundesstaate*. 1874. Palala Press, 2016.

Darmstaedter, Friedrich. *Bismarck and the Creation of the Second Reich*. Routledge, 2008.

"Decision of the German Federal Constitutional Court, October 12, 1993: In re Maastricht Treaty." Case 2 BvR 2134, 2159/92. *European University Institute*, https://iow.eui.eu/wp-content/uploads/sites/18/2013/04/06-Von-Bogdandy-German-Federal-Constitutional-Court.pdf. Accessed 6 March 2024.

Fichte, Johann Gottlieb. "On Machiavelli, as an Author, and Passages from His Writings." Translated by Ian Alexander Moore and Christopher Turner, *Philosophy Today*, vol. 60, no. 3, 2016, pp. 761–788.

Hänel, Albert. *Studien zum Deutschen Staatsrechte. Erste Studie: Die vertragsmässigen Elemente der Deutschen Reichsverfassung*. H. Haessel, 1873.

Hamilton, Alexander, James Madison and John Jay. *The Federalist Papers*. 1787. Penguin, 1987.

Hardtwig, Wolfgang. *Vormärz: Der Monarchische Staat und das Bürgertum.* 1985. Deutscher Taschenbuch Verlag, 1998.

Hegel, Georg Wilhelm Friedrich. *Political Writings.* Edited by Lawrence Dickey, Cambridge University Press, 2012.

Jellinek, Georg. *Die Lehre von den Staatenverbindungen.* 1882. Hansebooks, 2017.

Krebs, Gilbert and Bernard Poloni, editors. *Volk, Reich und Nation: Texte zur Einheit Deutschlands in Staat, Wirtschaft und Gesellschaft 1806–1918.* Université de La Sorbonne Nouvelle, 1994.

Laband, Paul. *Das Staatsrecht des Deutschen Reiches.* 1876. Von Mohr, 1895.

Langewiesche, Dieter. *Vom Vielstaatlichen Reich zum Föderativen Bundesstaat.* Heidelberger Akademische Bibliothek, 2020.

Mayer, Otto. ”Republikanischer und monarchischer Bundesstaat.” *Archiv des öffentlichen Rechts*, vol. 18, no. 3,1903, pp. 337–372.

Moltke, Helmuth von. *Gesammelte Schriften und Denkwürdigkeiten.* 1891.Hansebooks, 2017.

Nipperdey, Thomas, *Deutsche Geschichte 1800–1866: Bürgerwelt und Starker Staat.* 1983. Verlag C. H. Beck, 2017.

Paulskirche Constitution, 28 March 1849. Verfassungen.de, https://www.verfassungen.de/de06-66/verfassung48-i.htm. Accessed 6 March 2024.

Richter, Hedwig, *Demokratie: Eine Deutsche Affäre, Vom 18. Jahrhundert bis zur Gegenwart.* C. H. Beck, 2020.

Robertson, Ritchie. ”The Rediscovery of Machiavelli in Napoleon's Germany. Heinrich von Kleist and Contemporaries.” *Etica & Politica / Ethics & Politics*, vol. XVII, no. 3, 2015, pp. 58–77.

Rochau, August Ludwig von. *Grundsätze der Realpolitik, Angewendet auf die Staatlichen Zustände Deutschlands.* 1853. Forgotten Books, 2018.

Rumpler, Helmut. *Österreichische Geschichte, 1804–1914: Eine Chance für Mitteleuropa: Bürgerliche Emanzipation and Staatsverfall in der Habsburgermonarchie.* Ueberreuter, 1997.

Schroeder, Paul W. *The Transformation of European Politics, 1763–1848.* Oxford University Press, 1996.

Schroeder, Paul W. *Metternich's Diplomacy at its Zenith, 1820–1823.* 1969. Library Licensing LLC, 2011.

Seydel, Max von, ”Der Bundesstaatbegriff, eine staatsrechtliche Untersuchung.” *Zeitschrift für die gesamte Staatswissenschaft*, vol. 28, 1872, pp. 185–256.

Siemann, Wolfram. *Metternich: Strategist and Visionary.* Belknap Press, an imprint of Harvard University Press, 2019.

Spiess, Emil. *Ignaz Paul Vital Troxler.* Francke, 1967.

Taylor, A. J. P. *Bismarck: The Man and the Statesman.* 1955. Penguin, 1995.

Tocqueville, Alexis de. *Democracy in America.* 1835. Everyman, 1994.

Treaty of Vienna (constitution of the German *Bund*), 15 May 1820. "Final Act of the Viennese Ministerial Conferences." *German History in Documents and Images*, https://germanhistorydocs.org/en/from-vormaerz-to-prussian-dominance-1815-1866/ghdi:document-234 . Accessed 6 March 2024.

Treitschke, Heinrich von. *Der Deutsche Zollverein und seine Geschichte*. 1913. Europäischer Hochschulverlag, 2009.

Treitschke, Heinrich von. *Selections from Treitschke's Lectures on Politics*. Gowans and Gray, 1914.

Waitz, Georg. *Grundzüge der Politik, nebst Einzelnen Ausführungen*. 1862. Nabu Press, 2010.

Windhorst, Kay. "Separation of Power from the German Perspective." *Duquesne Law Review*, vol. 47, no. 4, 2009, pp. 905–919.

8   The Peace Movement's Federal Utopianism

Abstract

In post-Holy Alliance Europe, the concept of federal union developed along two different tracks. One was that of international law, which used the canons of peace schemes and practical experiences with federal union to propose an international federal quasi-government to justify international law. The other was the peace movement, which promoted federation as a means of establishing perpetual peace. Writers within this tradition introduced several conceptual innovations. They made federalism a process rather than an end state and suggested the use of a vanguard of committed states and economic cooperation as levers for the establishment of continental political union. By discussing these ideas in a trans-Atlantic setting, they made the idea of trans-Atlantic union part of the agenda going forward.

Keywords: Federal union, international law, peace movement, United States of Europe

International law and the problem of sovereignty

The fact that Bernhardi's book had to be written at all was an indication that, on the eve of Armageddon, the idea of perpetual peace was very much an active force in European political thought and debate. This was in large part due to two nineteenth century developments: one academic, the other political.

Academically, the idea of European federation would play a role in the development of the new discipline of international law. Its rise was an answer to the demise of the natural law tradition, specifically of the law of nations. The latter was born in the seventeenth century out of the Scholastic tradition. Two events had led to its emergence. One was the discovery of

---

Livestro, Joshua: *A More Perfect Union. Federal Union in Political Theory and Practice, 1500-1951.*
Amsterdam: Amsterdam University Press, 2024.
DOI: 10.5117/9789048563777_CH08

the new world, which stimulated the development of new theories about relationships between peoples. To this tradition was attached, above all, the name of the School of Salamanca, with authors like Francisco de Vitoria and Francisco Suárez. The other was the end of the *Respublica Christiana* which created the need for a new set of rules to coordinate the relationship between Europe's various monarchies, republics, and federations.

For three hundred years, the concepts of the law of nations tradition developed by authors like Gentili and Grotius, Hobbes, Pufendorf, and Vattel would form the basis of all Western thought about inter-state or international relations. By the middle of the nineteenth century however, this tradition was in terminal decline. The failure of the Enlightenment project to establish a credible empirical foundation for the natural law – or as Hume put it, its inability to draw "ought" conclusions from "is" premises – led to a crisis in thinking about international relations. Out of this crisis came the new discipline of legal positivism, which tried to find a justification for law inside the law itself. The study of custom, jurisprudence, and legal history, it was hoped, would provide a foundation for the study of law, grounding it in facts rather than ideals.

In the second half of the nineteenth century, a number of lawyers who reflected on inter-state aspects of law from a legal positivist perspective founded the new academic discipline of international law (Holbraad 186). One of them, the Master of Trinity College, Cambridge, William Whewell (1794–1866), explained its central problem as follows:

> [I]nasmuch as there exists no single definitive seat of authority, from which (...) International Law can be promulgated, in the way in which the National Law is promulgated by the National Government (...) how can International Rights and Obligations exist? And how can the Morality which assumes their existence be real? (Whewell 250)

The problem as Whewell saw it was this: if, as Bodin claimed, "law was the command of the sovereign", how could international law be law, given the absence of an international sovereign?

Of the various answers to this question that were developed in the second half of the nineteenth century,[1] one was formulated by the co-founder of the first journal devoted to the study of international law, the *Revue de Droit International et de Législation Comparée*, the Belgian lawyer Gustave

---

1   For a discussion of this founding period of international law, see the opening chapter "The Legal Conscience of the Civilized World" in Koskenniemi 11–97.

Rolin-Jaequemyns (1835–1902).[2] In the journal's opening issue, he used an article titled "*De l'Étude du Droit International*" to reflect on the question of what gives international law its authority. He rejected the political philosophical tradition that had argued for the creation of a kind of federal authority that could act as lawgiver and judge in disputes between the states of Europe (here he discussed, among others, Henri IV/Sully, St Pierre, Rousseau and Kant). He noted, given that states were sovereign, and that they were unlikely to hand over any part of this sovereignty willingly, "to get to perpetual peace we'd have to start a perpetual war" (236; my translation throughout). Rejecting this option, he observed, left only one serious alternative source of authority: public opinion. By this he meant not the whims of the public or the prejudices of the moment, but a "serious and calm" public opinion, "based on the application of certain principles of universal justice" (225). This public opinion was "truly and rightly the queen and legislator of the world" (225). While admitting that it was "far from fixed on certain issues," he still thought it provided a relatively solid basis on "a great number of questions" (225). The task of the study of international law was to explore both the settled issues and the open questions (238).

An alternative approach would try to rehabilitate the same federal tradition rejected by Rolin-Jaequemyns. If law required the command of a sovereign to be accepted as law, and no such sovereign existed at international level, then perhaps the solution was to create one. The question, as always, was how. The two most prominent attempts to answer this question represented the two main strands in the debate. One was written by Johann Bluntschli. His proposal was a plea for a European confederation, which, in his view, was only thinkable if "the sovereignty of the united states was fundamentally and factually fully secured" (Bluntschli 27; my translation throughout).

Bluntschli's scheme had some interesting details. For sensitive decisions a double qualified majority of the entire *Bundesrat* of member state delegations and of the large member states was required. His union was built on economic integration, leaving the sensitive issues of taxation and defence as exclusive member state competencies. His reasoning was that aiming for low hanging political fruit would be the safest way of building a durable union: "It is much easier to create international institutions that deal with minor administrative and process issues, than to create organs tasked with deciding on matters of political life and death" (Bluntschli 34).

---

2   The other founding editors were the British social reformer John Westlake, a one-time MP and eventual member of the International Court of Arbitration at The Hague, and the Dutch lawyer and later Nobel Peace Price winner Tobias Asser.

In his concluding remarks, he claimed that his proposal for a European constitution may have seemed ambitious but was in fact "sober and modest" (39). If it resembled anything in the past, it was not "the Utopia of the Abbé de Saint-Pierre" but the "original plan of Henri IV and Sully" (39–40). Still, if it was sober in its details, it was also optimistic in its reasoning. Bluntschli somehow seemed convinced that full member state sovereignty could be squared with (qualified) majority voting in both houses of his proposed European legislature, and that the member states would then uncritically accept and implement these decisions. He clearly didn't believe that the kind of economic issues with which he wanted to task the union could ever lead to inter-state conflicts, let alone war. The latter option he thought "not completely impossible" but still "rare" and in the case of wars of conquest even "actually impossible" (38).

—

Bluntschli's short treatise would trigger the production of a more extensive study of the same subject by the Scottish Regius professor of public law, James Lorimer (1818–1890). In his two volume study *The Institutes of the Law of Nations*, he sought to formulate an answer to the central challenge of international law, "the vindication of national freedom of action, not apart from, but in and through the recognition of international dependence" (Lorimer, I: 11). But how to give structure to this international dependence? Though recognizing that there had been examples in history of international laws that had emerged without any involvement from legislators, like "the famous sea laws of the middle ages, the *consolate del mare*" (I: 29), the problem remained: "How to find international equivalents for the factors known to national law as legislation, jurisdiction, and execution? (...) Is the development of such a system within the domain of the international relations humanly possible? [And if so] by what arrangements?" (II: 186–187).

As far as Lorimer was concerned, the answer to the question about the possibility of such a system was yes: "The problem is not insoluble" (II: 193). But though a solution was possible, the experience of previous centuries showed that developing a durable one was far from straightforward. He dismissed the balance of power method as having "done little to mitigate the egotism of separate states," eventually becoming "a permanent '*casus belli*'" (II: 199, 201). He also dismissed its most recent incarnation, the Concert system, as insufficient as a source of international legislation, since its interventions were "essentially retrospective and special. (...) [I]t formulates no general rule whatsoever" (II: 204). If the balance of power method suffered from an excess of violent force, the weakness of its main alternative, voluntary international arbitration, was a clear shortage of violent power to enforce its decisions. It made it useless as a source of international legislation: "Positive law is a dead letter which force alone will bring to life" (II: 208).

Lorimer next turned to various non-institutional methods for the informal organisation of the system of states, such as trade and education, dismissing them as logically insufficient for the purpose of creating an international legal framework. This left only one possible solution:

> Conscious of the imperfections of the doctrine of the balance of power, and of all other attempts to give a positive character to international law (...) speculative jurists have long been occupied with schemes for the creation of an international government which should embrace the functions of legislation, jurisdiction and execution.
> (Lorimer II: 216)

After an extensive review of what was by now a well-established canon of European peace plans – he discussed, among others, Henri IV/Sully, Leibniz, Penn, St Pierre, Rousseau, Kant and Bluntschli – he concluded that they all suffered from one or both of the two main failings of the peace plan tradition: "In aiming at finality of relations and equality of states, they violated laws of nature which are unchangeable" (II: 240). This insight, that the constitutional arrangement needed to possess a degree of openness to allow for natural development and that an "end state" was therefore undesirable, was perhaps Lorimer's most original contribution. His most creative suggestion was his idea of introducing a radical separation between the international level and the national governments that created them. By cutting the vertical umbilical cord that connected states and their collective government in a federal set-up, he created institutions that were "exclusively international" in their functions (i.e., no overlap with national competencies) and possessed "a separate freedom of their own" (no national influence on its decision-making) (II: 273).

Lorimer was not blind to the practical difficulties entailed in making such institutions work. "A separate central executive may be a rope of sand," he admitted, "but the 'European Concert' is a handful of sand, and though its advantage may be but in form, I must still prefer the rope" (II: 275). The reason was that his purely international construct, on paper at least, seemed capable of avoiding what he considered the central weakness of federations: "[T]he conflict between the centrifugal and centripetal forces, which I have elsewhere pointed out as the source of weakness in composite states, could scarcely arise in a body which neither possessed the characteristics nor aimed at the objects of State existence" (II: 276).

What remained was for him to explain what "force" could help compel states to follow the international rules and rulings produced by these new institutions. Here he came up with an alternative for the more *ad hoc* method of intervention used by the Great Powers during the Congress and Concert phase: a small international standing army, with a supreme commander whose position would be "substantially that of a superintendent of international police" (Lorimer, II: 278). To make sure they were beyond the influence of individual states, "[a]ll officers of the international force above the rank of colonel [would] be commissioned by the International Bureau, and (...) be responsible to the International Government alone" (II: 286). To justify military action by the International Government against a member state, Lorimer suggested the creation of an offence called "international rebellion" (II: 287). This could be invoked if a state either committed an act of war without the consent of the International Government, or if a state interfered with the discharging of international duties of the International Legislature or the International Tribunals. For such crises, the president of the International Government would be given the power to call out the international contingents of member states' armies.

The weaknesses of Lorimer's scheme were clear. The fact that under his system, it was possible for decisions to adversely affect individual member states was clearly a fundamental flaw. If such contentious decisions were possible in principle, states would seek ways of making sure they could either influence them or prevent them from being taken, thereby creating exactly the kind of "conflict between centrifugal and centripetal forces" that he hoped to avoid. The idea that the individual states would help create an international army that could be used to impose international law upon them was also somewhat naive. But the greatest weakness of his scheme was probably his inability to grasp that without a compromise on sovereignty on the part of the states, no international law would ever succeed in binding them. Still, for all its weaknesses, it did contribute to the growth of a new school in international-legal thinking, which focused on international institution building.

The nineteenth century peace movement and the rise of public opinion

The ideas of Bluntschli and Lorimer would end up influencing the debate about the post–First World War international architecture by providing both a canon of foundational texts and a framework of concepts that diplomats could work with. The fact that they decided to reach for this particular solution, however, had everything to do with the second of the two nineteenth century phenomena mentioned above: the rise of the international peace movement.

Intellectually and morally, the roots of the peace movement were in the Christian irenic tradition. It is, therefore, no surprise that the earliest forms of nineteenth century peace activism, in the UK and the United States, had an explicitly Christian (chiefly Quaker) background. Fairly early on though, different political communities also became involved in this new movement. By the 1840s, the peace movement consisted of an eclectic mix of Christian activists, free market economists, radical politicians and nation-building federalist revolutionaries.

With that many different ideologies represented, there were obviously always going to be disagreements. Some, like Mazzini, refused the label of pacifism because they still saw a use for war in certain circumstances. Others disagreed with the idea of decolonisation as a necessary condition for the creation of a truly equal global community. But on the whole, the peace movement was remarkably coherent in its approach to what it perceived as its core priorities. One was the replacement of war by arbitration as a means of settling conflicts between nations. The second was disarmament, to reduce the chances of violence erupting. And last, but by no means least, was the idea of forming a congress of nations to prevent conflicts from arising in the first place.

The 1840s would see a wave of proposals for the formation of such a congress or league.[3] The inspiration for these proposals was in part the older tradition of Henri IV, Saint-Pierre, Rousseau and Kant. But there were also references to more recent schemes, such as the Holy Alliance and the plan produced by the French political thinker Claude de Saint-Simon, duc de Rouvroy (1760–1825).

---

3   In her PhD thesis *Organizing International Society: The French Peace Movement and the Origins of Reformist Internationalism*, Vanessa Lincoln speaks of a "confederation mania" in French and broader European political society in the 1840s (72). Similarly, in the introduction to *Vision Europa: Deutsche und polnische Föderationspläne des 19. und frühen 20. Jahrhunderts*, Heinz Duchhardt and Małgorata Morawiec observe that "There is no question that the post-Napoleonic era saw an 'explosion' in the Europe discourse." Compared to the pre-Napoleonic era, the nineteenth century saw an increase of around 250 percent in the number of peace schemes (x; my translation).

Saint-Simon had published his own blueprint for "The reorganisation of European society" in 1815. In it, he observed that after the collapse of the old Roman–Christian order, "[t]he treaty of Westphalia established a new order through a political mechanism called *balance of power*. (...) Since [then] war has been the habitual state of affairs in Europe" (Saint-Simon II: 351; my translation throughout). To get beyond it, he proposed "common institutions" of the sort first proposed by "two men who saw the problem and proposed a remedy for it (...) Henri IV and the abbé de Saint Pierre" (II: 360–361). In its details though, he thought Saint-Pierre's plan was "absolutely impracticable" (II: 363). He suggested that when it came to its actual operation, even the old order of the *Respublica Christiana* was "infinitely superior" (II: 365). The reason was that, whereas in Saint-Pierre's scheme it was inevitable that every delegate to the joint council would vote on strict instructions of their monarch or ruling body, in the old order, the general government had been "completely independent of national governments," while its functionaries "devote[d] themselves specifically to the general interest" (II: 366).

To remedy this defect in Saint-Pierre's scheme would require adopting a constitution that bound both the general (European) and national governments. The best model Saint-Simon could think of was the same model that formed part of the inspiration for the American Founders: the British constitution. The ideal scenario, as he envisaged it, saw a similar constitution based on a division of powers created at the European level, complete with a hereditary monarchical figure. It also had a Kantian republican element to it: "Europe would have the best possible organisation if all its nations were governed by a parliament, while recognising the supremacy of a general parliament placed over the national governments and possessing the powers to settle their differences" (Saint-Simon, II: 382–383).

Unfortunately not all European nations were currently governed that way, or rather, nearly all were not. Saint-Simon therefore had to come up with a strategy for helping the continent make the transition to his desired end state. He suggested starting with just two member states: France and the United Kingdom. Once they had established a common parliament, "the principal goal of this association would be to enlarge itself by drawing towards itself all the other peoples" (II: 393).

If this was an attempt at correcting the perceived lack of realism in Saint-Pierre's plan, it was a most peculiar one. After all, as the negotiations in Vienna showed, no Great Power was less inclined to join a federal scheme than Great Britain, let alone one as ambitious as the one he proposed (quite another matter is that the soon to be created Congress system would show that perhaps Saint-Pierre's proposal hadn't been completely unrealistic after all). Saint-Simon's main strength, however, was not his realism but his idealism. It was his ability to sketch a future that was more peaceful, more prosperous, and more just that made him attractive to his followers.

He would set out his vision for the future of Europe most specifically in a pamphlet published ten years later, under the title "To the Europeans," in which he predicted the arrival of a new age in which "Europe will witness the formation of a free society (...) with entirely new political principles" (Saint-Simon, IV: 154). In this new age, the power to set policy ought to be handed over to "those who have achieved the greatest success in culture, production and commerce," while the spiritual power of education must be handed to "those who study the sciences and mathematics, (...) those who have distinguished themselves in observation and calculation" (IV: 155). The adoption of this scheme would mean that "the Europeans, thanks to their revolution, enjoy life in a calm and stable order, an order which offers them the greatest sum of social wellbeing that people can hope to achieve" (IV: 156).

—

The Saint-Simonians would become evangelists for his theory of peace and social well-being through the transformative power of technological innovations, and through federation. During the nineteenth century, several of them would publish peace plans of their own, including plans for a European federation. Among his immediate followers, the most prominent proponent of a European federal scheme for the promotion of peace was the socialist economist Constantin Pecquer. Pecquer made his reputation through a winning contribution to an essay contest issued by the London Peace Society and the *Société de la Morale Chrétienne*.

These kinds of essay contests were one of the many publicity tools used by the nineteenth century peace movement. Whatever the tool, the aim was always the same: to mobilise the increasingly relevant power of public opinion. Making maximum use of new technologies like the railway and the newspaper, they devised highly visible publicity campaigns in support of their objectives. This strategy was described by one nineteenth century commentator as "the silent enginery of invisible activities concentrating the individual wills of communities upon the minds of statesmen (...) and turning them to the bias of ideas which they had perhaps ridiculed and resisted" (Northend 63–64).

A typical example was the organised effort to create public support for a motion proposing binding international arbitration as an international dispute resolution mechanism, tabled in the British House of Commons in early 1848 by Richard Cobden, a radical MP who became one of the main spokesmen of the British peace movement. The campaign consisted of 150 public meetings (one a day in different parts of the country during a six month period); one thousand petitions, some carrying as many as ten thousand signatures; the sending of around fifty thousand letters to MPs, Lords and local dignitaries across the country; and the distribution of hundreds of thousands of leaflets at factory gates and in town centres. In the end, the motion was not adopted. But the fact that as many as 70 MPs backed it was still greeted as a significant success since it "clearly indicat[ed] that the idea of stipulated arbitration had taken strong hold upon the public mind and could not fail of being resorted to, sooner or later, by all the governments of Christendom" (Northend 74).

One of the most important tools in the public outreach campaign in support of the peace movement's objectives was the international conference. In the period 1848 to 1853, annual conferences would take place in different European countries, always extensively covered by the growing number of newspapers, and watched with some curiosity by the political classes in the various host countries. The most celebrated of these conferences was the one of 1849, in the French capital Paris, where several hundred delegates gathered at the invitation of the French Foreign Secretary, Alexis de Tocqueville. Among them were Christian pacifists, anti-war economists, free trade radicals, revolutionary dreamers about the brotherhood of man, and members of various national parliaments.

—

The stated aim of the conference was to discuss the promotion of the three core demands of the movement: arbitration, disarmament, and (con)federation. The latter formed the main theme of the opening speech of the conference's president, the French novelist and parliamentarian Victor Hugo (1802–1885). Hugo, who had started his life as a romantic conservative but had gradually converted to reformist radicalism, had first found common cause with the same people who made up the peace movement when he published a novel against the death penalty, titled *Le Dernier Jour d'un Condamné* (1829). Though he would pay lip service to the Christian motives of many of his fellow activists, his own peace activism was rooted in a (politically) secular radicalism.

The common Enlightenment belief that the two positions, faith and rationality, were not necessarily fully aligned, could have caused a rift in the movement if it had been left unanswered. Hugo therefore made a special point of tackling it early on in his speech on the opening day of the conference, on 21 August 1849

Gentlemen, this religious thinking, the universal peace, all nations linked with each other through a common bond, the Gospel as the supreme law, mediation replacing war, this religious thinking, is it a practical one? (...) Many positive spirits, as we are used to say today, many political men, experienced in the field of business, say No. As for me, I say Yes and I say it with you and without hesitation.
(Hugo)[4]

He then launched into a quasi-Kantian discourse in which he argued first from principle, and then from history, that humanity's ultimate destiny was a realm of perpetual peace. Making a comparison with the formerly independent regions of France and the United States, he predicted that in Europe, too, "[a] day will come when war shall appear as impossible (...) between Paris and London, between St Petersburg and Berlin, between Vienna and Turin, as it is now between Rouen and Amiens, between Boston and Philadelphia" (Hugo). Not content with predicting the arrival of perpetual peace, he also predicted the unavoidable fate of Europe as being that of union: "A day will come when you, (...) nations of the continent, shall, without losing your distinctive qualities and your glorious individuality, be blended into a superior unity, and shall constitute a European fraternity" (Hugo). This "superior unity" would be dominated by commerce and freedom of thought. "Bullets and shells" would be replaced by "universal suffrage of nations," and the "venerable arbitration of a sovereign Senate, which shall be to Europe what the Parliament is to England" (Hugo).

Emphasising the importance of technological development for the realisation of his utopian vision of a European federal union, he used arguments familiar from Saint-Pierre, Madison, and Saint-Simon to describe how "[t]hanks to railroads, Europe will soon be no more extent than France was in the Middle Ages. Thanks to steamships, we traverse the mighty ocean more cosily than the Mediterranean was formerly crossed" (Hugo). Predicting that the globe would soon be encircled by an "electric wire of concord," he concluded: "How people so separated from each other so lately, now almost touch! How distances become less and less; and this rapid approach, what is it but the commencement of fraternity?" (Hugo).

—

4   This and all subsequent references to Hugo are taken from a transcript of the speech published later that hear in the *Sydney Morning Herald*.

In calling for the three key priorities of arbitration, disarmament and a congress of nations, the conference's final declaration was addressed to "the governments and people of Christendom" (Jay, 145). It was, in fact, a clever way of solving another problem that could have divided the delegates, one of a geographical nature. The presence of American delegates made it impossible to define the movement in purely European terms. By reaching back to the older concept of the *Respublica Christiana*, and adapting it to new geographical realities, Hugo was able to find a common cultural foundation for what seemed to be two communities destined for separate existences, divided by 3000 miles of ocean. In his Paris conference speech, he described his ultimate vision as being one of "two immense groups, the United States of America, and the United States of Europe" who would be "seen placed in the presence of each other, extending the hand of fellowship across the ocean – exchanging their produce, their commerce, their industries, their arts, their genius" (Hugo).

The Peace Movement's Utopia: the United States of Europe

The first peace movement collapsed at the start of the Crimean War. Its next iteration would spring to life in the aftermath of the Luxembourg crisis of 1867. It would have the same objectives as the first movement, and would pursue them with the same means. Of the various organisations that together made up the second wave of international peace activism, two stood out. One was founded in Paris under the title *Ligue International et Permanente de la Paix*. The most prominent figure in this organisation was the future winner of the inaugural Nobel Peace Prize (1901), the French economist Frédéric Passy (1822–1912). Passy combined free trade views, inspired by Cobden and Bastiat (both prominent members of the first peace movement), with the social justice agenda of the socialist movement. Though he had published a call for the forming of a European federation in the late 1850s, his main efforts would focus on furthering the cause of arbitration, and of fostering understanding between nations. The latter cause would inspire him to help set up the Inter-Parliamentary Conference (later: Union), together with the British MP William Randal Cremer.

Meanwhile in Geneva, peace activists founded the *Ligue International de la Paix et de la Liberté*. Their efforts culminated in a new international peace congress, held in Geneva in September 1867. The conference's central committee counted the Russian anarchist Michail Bakunin among its members. Among those expressing support for the conference's efforts were John Stuart Mill and the Russian exiled writer Alexander Herzen. Also offering words of support was Victor Hugo, who at the time was living in self-imposed exile on the island of Guernsey, just off the French coast.

The honour of opening the conference was given to the great revolutionary general Giuseppe Garibaldi. Where Hugo had shown a diplomatic touch in 1849, using his opening speech to bring the various constituencies in the audience together and uniting them for the common cause, the never knowingly understated Garibaldi used his to pick a fight with the Catholics in the room by insulting his arch enemy, the Pope. More constructively, he used his speech to embrace the idea of a European confederation, where all democratic nations would be represented on an equal basis.

The fact that one of Europe's most famous nationalists had come out in favour of a European federal union should have been a headline-grabbing event. All people talked about afterwards, though, was his verbal attack on the Vatican. It was a somewhat sensitive issue in a country that, twenty years earlier, had fought a civil war over its religious divisions, with the Protestant majority ending up imposing its will on the Catholic minority. By the second day his statements turned into an official row, complete with a Catholic riot threatening to disturb the conference. Not that the great revolutionary himself would have noticed though. By the time his words had filtered through to the outside world, he had already left town. Whether he left in order to escape a Catholic backlash or not is unclear, but it was certainly a case of fortunate timing (Campanella 468).

If Garibaldi was the guest of honour, it was the spirit of Victor Hugo that hovered over the conference. The main idea of his 1849 opening speech, the forming of a United States of Europe, was made the central plank of the 1867 conference program. Two of the three questions on which the programme was based were explicitly devoted to it:

> 1st Question: (...) Isn't the essential condition for a perpetual peace between the nations for each people liberty, and in their international relations the establishment of a confederation of free democracies constituting the United States of Europe? 2nd Question: What are the means by which we can prepare and hasten the arrival of this confederation of free peoples?" (International League 127;. my translation).

The idea of a "United States of Europe" would come to dominate the short lifespan of the second peace movement. At the 1869 congress in Lausanne, under the honorary presidency of Victor Hugo himself, the delegates adopted a resolution stating that "the only means of founding peace in Europe is the formation of a federation of peoples under the style of United States of Europe," and that "the government of this union must be republican and federal, which means resting on the sovereignty of the people, while respecting the autonomy and independence of each of the members of the confederation" (quoted in Lemonnier 99–100; my translation). The fact that both "people" and "peoples," "federal" and "confederation," were used in the same section to discuss one and the same union was indicative of the level of conceptual and philosophical confusion on the European side of the Atlantic about the idea of federal union. The intention was clear though: to overcome the challenge of war, Europe had to unite.

—

The Second Peace Movement's official newspaper was called *Les Etats-Unis d'Europe/Die Vereinigten Staaten von Europa*, a bilingual paper which would go on to appear on a weekly basis until 1914. It thereby significantly outlived the second peace movement, which ground to a halt in the wake of the Franco-German war of 1871. Through its longevity, the newspaper helped the concept of the "United States of Europe" take root in European, and especially in French, public debate.

Another relevant contribution to that process was the eponymous book by the newspaper's co-founder, Charles Lemonnier (1806–1891). Lemonnier was the editor of the collected works of Saint-Simon, and a typical product of the Saint-Simonian school, combining a sense of technological optimism with a commitment to social justice and a belief in the need for European unification. In his book, he used a discussion of strengths and shortcomings of the main peace plans (Henri IV/Sully, Saint-Pierre, Kant, and Saint-Simon) to construct his own blueprint for a more perfect European union.

Of the various schemes, he was least impressed by that of Henri IV/ Sully, which he dismissed as "at its core nothing more than a conspiracy of princes against the universal monarchy aspirations of the house of Austria" (Lemonnier 23). Equally unappealing to him was the fact that the scheme was run by, and for, princes. It meant that what was "born out of the intrigue of kings and princes, could also be undone in the same way" (25). Here Lemonnier effectively corrected Rousseau, who had claimed that Saint-Pierre's scheme would last forever if it could only be tried for a single day. The kind of founders involved in setting up the federal union, he argued, were at least as important as the quality of the federal scheme agreed to. With too many different kinds of regime types involved in the founding, the end result would be "a juxtaposition, not a real union" (32). One essential condition of a successful federal union was therefore "homogeneity of interests and organisation." More specifically: only *republics* could found a successful federal union. Following the schemes of Kant and Saint-Simon, he explained that only a federation of republics would have "the homogeneity without which there can be no solidity" (47).

The other precondition for success was the disarmament of the individual states, and the transfer of decisions of war and peace to the federal centre. On this issue, he criticised Saint-Simon for being too pragmatic in his concessions to the "diplomats gathered in Vienna," leaving crucial issues of disarmament and war powers deliberately unaddressed so as not to offend them (Lemonnier 66). His preferred scheme was Kant's, "who didn't have to spare a Holy Alliance" and could therefore afford complete clarity in both principles and details on these issues (64).

As for his own scheme, he was quite explicit that it was modelled on the US constitution: "In place of the particular states which form the union of the United States of America, let us place the main nations of Europe" (Lemonnier 127–128). As a thought experiment, he suggested that either all these nations, or a small vanguard of "two or three only" (following Saint-Simon), could establish a similar federation to the American one. It would have "a single military organisation," based on a militia system similar to that of the Swiss Confederation (129). There would be no customs checks between the member states, free exchange of goods, "economic and social union as well as a political one" (130). And, he stressed, a certain amount of homogeneity among the constitutions of the member states: "[T]here cannot be a contradiction of principle between the federal constitution and the constitutions of the individual states. (...) [I]t would inevitably form a cause of conflict and dissolution" (134). A final, essential quality of the union's constitution was that it would be perfectible, and therefore amendable.

While being aware that there were powerful vested interests that would have to be overcome for the establishment of the union, he thought that as an ideal it was only as distant as his audience would want it to be: "It is up to each of us to turn this utopia into a reality" (Lemonnier 181). Then again, maybe it was happening already. The establishment of a federal republic in Switzerland meant it would only take one more European republic to create the preconditions for the founding of a union that would "provide the first foundation for the United States of Europe" (186). It was through continued striving for it by people of good will that Europe would get closer and closer to it: "We have to know how to remain patient while working and know how to work without getting tired. Every day will bring the horizon a little closer" (189). This kind of voluntarism dressed up as strategy was characteristic of the second peace movement's thinking about federal union: long on ambition, short on details. Partly as a result, by the late nineteenth century, European federalism came to be seen as a utopian objective – important in principle but meaningless in practice.

—

Its utopian character didn't mean that the second peace movement was without its own very real political opponents. If it was enthusiastically in favour of a European federal union, it was just as outspoken in what it opposed: the nineteenth century regime form called "Caesarism" or "Bona-partism." Its main representative was the French emperor Charles-Louis Napoleon Bonaparte (1808–1873). He had put an end to the second republic through a *coup d'état* on 2 December 1851,[5] a date no doubt chosen for its strong Bonapartist overtones: it was the date of Napoleon's coronation in 1804, and of one of his greatest military triumphs at the battle of Austerlitz (Strauss-Schom 145).

Caesarism had two defining characteristics. One was a claim to democratic legitimacy through the use of periodic (manipulated) plebiscites (Baehr and Richter 2). Louis Napoleon would use democracy as a political tool to further his own ambitions. After two somewhat farcical failed coup attempts, both of which ended up with him fleeing to London, it was through a democratic election in 1848 that he finally rose to the highest office in the land, in this case the presidency of the Second Republic. After this first success, he would follow the example of his uncle Napoleon Bonaparte by using plebiscites to justify and strengthen his rule. (The elder Napoleon had asked, and received, confirmation of the people's support for both his elevation to First Consul in 1800, his receiving that same title for life in 1802, and his coronation as emperor in 1804 through heavily manipulated plebiscites).

In 1851, Louis Napoleon successfully used a referendum to confirm the results of the coup that gave him indefinite power. The words on the ballot left no room for doubt. In fact, it wasn't even a question that voters were asked to decide on, rather more a communication of a decision that had effectively already been taken by the man himself: "The French people

---

5   In the short period of resistance to the coup, Victor Hugo tried to rally a defence of the constitutional order through the mobilisation of supporters and the erecting of barricades in the streets of central Paris. The army, which was on the side of the president/soon-to-be emperor, moved to crush the resistance, leaving 400 dead. Hugo would go into exile, not returning to France until the republic's restoration in 1871. See Strauss-Schom 162.

want Louis Napoleon Bonaparte to maintain all authority, and transfer to him such powers as are required to establish a constitution on the basis of his proclamation of the 2nd of December 1851."[6] In 1852, he would again ask for the people's support, this time on the question of whether he should be crowned emperor. And in 1860, he would organise two referendums on the issue of the proposed annexation of Nice and Savoy, territories he had obtained in exchange for supporting the Italian independence movement in its war against Austria. Unsurprisingly, in each of these cases the people voted overwhelmingly to grant him his requests.

The use of referendums with manipulated questions was, in itself, a recognition of the fact that the people had, since the American and French Revolutions, become a significant constitutional factor. Unlike the Ancien Régime, whose attempts to suppress popular opinion had led to the Revolution of 1848, Caesarism supported giving the people a role of some sort in the constitutional set-up. What it did not support, however, was using popular opinion as a *check* on the ruling power. Like traditional monarchy, Caesarism rejected any suggestion of separation of powers in favour of what the French anarchist philosopher Pierre-Joseph Proudhon (1809–1865) disapprovingly described as the idea of "indivisibility of power" in his 1863 publication *Du Principe Fédérative*:

> The prince is at one and the same time legislator, administrator, judge, ge-
> neral and pontiff. He has eminent domain over the soil and all its produce;
> he is the master of arts and professions, of commerce, of agriculture, of
> shipping, of public education, invested with all right and all authority. In
> other words, the prince is the representative of society, its embodiment;
> the state, that is he.
> (Proudhon 3203)

This came to be seen as Caesarism's other defining characteristic: a unitary government based on an executive with near-absolute powers. Its undivided powers were to be used in the pursuit of the typical objectives of empire: national glory and territorial expansion (Baehr and Richter 6).

On the first day of the 1867 Geneva peace conference, the exiled French philosopher Jules Barni (1818–1878), translator of the works of Immanuel Kant and later a parliamentarian in the newly established Third Republic, made the case for the incompatibility of Caesarism with the objectives of the peace movement:

---

6   Source: https://mjp.univ-perp.fr/france/ref1851.htm. Accessed 6 March 2024.

> I wish to speak of the development of Caesarism, which means that regime of monarchical militarism which sacrifices the liberty of all for the power of the leader of the army, measures the power of the state by the size of the army it can maintain, and searches incessantly for agglomerations of men it can bring under its rule. (*International League* 119)

Its triumph, he warned, would be "the ruin of all that remains in Europe of constitutional or republican liberty, making peace forever impossible, unless it is the peace of the grave" (119). The challenge for the delegates was, therefore, "to counter the Caesarian spirit with the spirit of republicanism, the military spirit with the civil one, and the spirit of centralisation with the spirit of federalism" (120). If Caesarism was the problem, federalism was the solution. Only through the formation of a federal union could Europe's peace and freedom be secured.

Peace through law: the 1899 The Hague Peace Conference

The third and final iteration of the peace movement, which lasted from the 1880s until the outbreak of the First World War, was arguably the most consequential one on the institutional level. It led to the creation of a number of international organisations that are still with us today: the Red Cross, the Olympic movement, the Inter-Parliamentary Union, and, though it's not a formal institution, the annually awarded Nobel Peace Prize. It also saw the agenda of the peace movement finally being discussed at the level of the European Concert, during the peace conferences of 1899 and 1907.

The fact that a Concert meeting was called to discuss the issue of disarmament, was down to the Russian tsar Nicholas II (1868–1918). In August 1898 he issued a declaration which took his Western counterparts by surprise. For the sake of "[t]he preservation of universal peace and a possible reduction of the excessive armaments that weigh heavily upon all nations" he had ordered his Foreign Minister, Count Mikhail Muraviev, to "propose to all governments whose representatives are accredited to the Imperial Court to convene a conference for the purpose of discussing this grave problem" (quoted in Oldenburg 104–105).

A positive explanation for his call for a summit could be that he was trying to cement his place in history by picking up the mantle of his reformist ancestors Alexander I ('the peacemaker') and II ('the abolitionist'). It was certainly the explanation most often quoted at the time. In his opening speech, the president of the Conference, Dutch Foreign Secretary Willem

Hendrik de Beaufort, speculated that the Tsar's motive must have been "to realise the wish of one of his most illustrious predecessors, Emperor Alexander I – that all the sovereigns and all the nations of Europe might agree to live together like brothers and help each other in their mutual needs" (Scott 14). Speculation was fed by the fact that the release of the Circular coincided with the dedication by Nicholas II of a new monument to his grandfather, Alexander II (Abbenhuis, *1913* 43).

Raison d'état explanations also abounded. Having just committed to a strengthening of Russia's grip on the far eastern territories bordering the Pacific Ocean, in part through the construction of the Trans-Siberian railway, the Tsar wanted to safeguard stability on his western flank by pacifying all of Europe (if this was indeed Nicholas II's strategy, Japan's victory at Port Arthur in 1905 would put paid to it). There was also speculation that Russia's depleted treasury meant it was no longer able to keep up an arms race with the West, and so had no choice but to press for multilateral talks on disarmament.[7]

—

Whatever the reason, the conference would provide a unique opportunity for the one party that came to the table with a fully developed agenda: the peace movement. Successfully mobilising Western public opinion for the Tsar's proposal, they managed to persuade the invited governments to send a delegation. They even succeeded in getting the agenda extended to two of their main priorities: disarmament and international arbitration. To these was added a third in the form of a rewriting of the laws of warfare.

The peace movement would use all the tools in its arsenal to mobilise public support for the conference's objectives: thousands of public petitions, countless media articles, sermons and speeches, and large national manifestations (Abbenhuis et al, *War, Peace and International Order* 146–147). The conference itself was turned into a public spectacle, complete with lectures, public receptions and even a daily newspaper. A horrified German delegate, Count Münster, described it in typically antisemitic and sexist terms as a gathering of "the political riffraff of the entire world, (...) journalists of the worst type (...), baptised Jews (...) and female peace fanatics" (Tuchman 287).

—

7   The latter seems an unlikely reason, since Russia had just committed to a doubling of the size of its fleet, committing 90 million Rubles to the project (Oldenburg 99).

Political enthusiasm for the conference was decidedly more limited than that of the public. The Prince of Wales described it as "the greatest nonsense and rubbish I ever heard of" (Tuchman 266). The German Kaiser Wilhelm II was less annoyed about the idea behind the conference, which he dismissed as a plan for "handing over his towns to Anarchists and Democracy," than about the fact that it was Nicholas II who had proposed it: "He simply can't stand someone else coming to the front of the stage," one of his friends explained (268–269). Though the pressure of European public opinion forced him to relent, the delegation he selected for the conference showed how little regard he had for his "cousin's" proposal. One of the German delegates, professor Karl von Stengel, had recently published a blistering critique of the Kantian idea of perpetual peace, along the lines of Moltke and Treitschke (Stengel 1899). Another, the legal scholar Philipp Zorn, saw international relations as defined by the acts of sovereign states, not by a non-existing international community (Koskenniemi 211). In France, Clemenceau treated the idea of a peace conference as an irrelevance, predicting that "nothing would come of [it]" (Tuchman 276).

The fact that something, however minimal, did come of it was largely down to the other group that had steadfastly worked to further some of the same causes that also motivated the peace movement: the community of international lawyers. The Hague offered them a chance to prove to the world that their ideas were ready to be tested on the highest stage, and they worked hard to make the most of the unexpected opportunity.

Without losing themselves in an internal debate about what the source of legitimacy for international law was to be, the various camps within the international legal community agreed that the conference presented an excellent opportunity to push for the creation of a system of rules that could bring the practice of warfare into line with the enlightened consensus of the late nineteenth century. The aim was not to ban war, but to civilise it somewhat by introducing rules for its conduct and by creating a framework for the avoidance of it if at all possible.

—

The policy achievements of the first conference were limited to a "Convention with Respect to the Laws and Customs of War on Land," which codified a number of rules about the treatment of prisoners and occupied territories. The institution builders among the international lawyers achieved their objective through the establishment of a court of arbitration in The Hague. It was a list of possible arbitrators that countries could call on rather than an actual court, and it operated only on a voluntary basis. The original proposal for a formal court had been watered down to increase its chances of being adopted. Even then, it was still nearly vetoed by the German Kaiser Wilhelm II. He objected to the whole idea of arbitration, but in the end he relented to the compromise brokered by his own delegation with the statement: "So that he [Tsar Nicholas II] will not appear the fool before the whole of Europe, I agree to that nonsense! But in practice I will continue to rely and depend only on God and my own sharp sword" (quoted in Oldenburg 114).

Even without an actual court building though, the creation of the first international institution with a remit to prevent conflicts between nations was still a significant event. But as the German international legal scholar Walther Schücking would later argue, perhaps its true significance was not to be found in its outcomes but in the fact that countries had gathered to discuss and, if possible, settle international legal problems: "[I]n the year 1899 the Hague Conference, although not *expressis verbis*, yet *implicit* and *ipso facto*, created a World Confederation [*Weltstaatenbund*]" (quoted in Koskenniemi 217).

The peace movement would certainly treat it as such. It saw in the mere fact of the meeting in The Hague evidence that its ideal of a European or transatlantic federation for the establishment of perpetual peace was very much a realisable goal. The century that had started with all-out war thereby ended with a clarion call for peace through union. It seemed to give the cause of federal union a new lease of life. The movement would start the new century more energised than ever, ready to realise its goal of the formation of an international federation to pass and enforce international regulations that would help make war a thing of the past. But as events in the first half of the next century would show, progress in European history is rarely linear...

Bibliography

Abbenhuis, Maartje, Christopher Barber, Annelise Higgins, editors. *War, Peace and International Order? The Legacies of the Hague Conferences of 1898 and 1907.* Routledge, 2017.

Abbenhuis, Maartje, Christopher Barber, Annelise Higgins, editors. *1913: The Hague Conferences and International Politics 1898–1915.* Bloomsbury Academic, 2020.

Baehr Peter and Melvin Richter. *Dictatorship in History and Theory: Bonapartism, Caesarism, and Totalitarianism.* Cambridge University Press, 2004.

Bluntschli, Johann Caspar. *Die Organisation des Europäischen Staatenvereins.* 1878. Wissenschaftliche Buchgesellschaft, 1962.

Campanella A. "Garibaldi and the First Peace Congress in Geneva in 1867." *International Review of Social History*, vol. 5, issue 3, Dec. 1960, pp. 456–486.

Duchhardt, Heinz and Małgorata Morawiec. *Vision Europa: Deutsche und polnische Föderationspläne des 19. und frühen 20. Jahrhunderts.* Vandenhoeck and Ruprecht, 2009.

Holbraad, Carsten. *The Concert of Europe: A Study in German and British International Theory, 1815–1914.* Prentice Hall Press, 1970.

Hugo, Victor. "Speech of Victor Hugo to the Peace Congress at Paris." [21 August 211849.] Opening Speech as published on in the Sydney Morning Herald, 26 December 1849. https://trove.nla.gov.au/newspaper/article/12914658. Accessed 6 March 2024.

International League of Peace and Liberty. *Annales du Congres de Geneve, 9–12 Septembre 1867.* Chez Vérésoff & Garrigues, 1868

Jay, William, Brooks, Charles, Beckwith, Geo C, Brown, William C, Goodwin, B, 'The Peace Congress of 1849', *Advocate of Peace*, Vol. 8, No. 12/13, November/December 1849, pp. 133-153.

Koskenniemi, Martti. *The Gentle Civilizer of Nations: The Rise and Fall of International Law 1870–1960 (Hersch Lauterpacht Memorial Lectures).* Cambridge University Press, 2009.

Lemonnier, Charles. *Les États Unis d'Europe.* 1872. Manucius, 2011.

Lincoln, Vanessa. *Organizing International Society: The French Peace Movement and the Origins of Reformist Internationalism.* 2013. University of California, Berkeley, PhD dissertation.

Lorimer, James. *The Institutes of the Law of Nations.* 1883–1884. Adamant Media Corporation, 2001. 2 vols.

Northend, Charles. *Elihu Burritt: A Memorial Volume Containing a Sketch of His Life and Labours, with Selections from His Writings and Lectures, and Extracts from His Private Journals in Europe and America.* 1879. Legare Street Press, 2022.

Oldenburg, Sergei. *Last Tsar: Nicholas II, His Reign & His Russia, Vol. I The Autocracy 1894–1900.* Academic International Press, 1977.

Proudhon, Pierre-Joseph. *Oeuvres de Proudhon.* Editions La Bibliotheque Digitale, 2012.

Rolin-Jaequemyns, Gustave. "De l'Étude du Droit International." *Revue de Droit International et de Législation Comparée*, vol. I, 1869, pp. 225–243.

Saint-Simon, Henri. *Oeuvres Complètes, Édition critique présentée, établie et annotée par Juliette Grange, Pierre Musso, Philippe Régnier et Franck Yonnet.* Presses Universitaires de France, 2012. 4 vols.

Scott, James Brown, *The Proceedings of The Hague Peace Conferences: The Conference of 1899*, Oxford University Press, 1920

Stengel, Karl Michael Joseph Leopold Freiherr von, *Der Ewige Friede*, C Haushalter, 1899

Strauss-Schom, Alan. *The Shadow Emperor: A Biography of Napoléon III*, Amberley Publishing, 2018

Tuchman, Barbara. *The Proud Tower: A Portrait of the World Before the War 1890 1914*. 1966. Random House, 1996.

Whewell, William. *The Elements of Morality, Including Polity*, vol. 2. 1856. Kessinger Publishing, 2010.

9   Peace through Union

Abstract

The international peace movement's finest hour arrived after the First World War, when its century-old priorities of arbitration, disarmament, and a European or trans-Atlantic league of nations formed the platform for the negotiations at Versailles. The League delivered on part of its promise by uniting the majority of Europe's states in an international peace union. But the exclusion of Germany and Soviet Russia, and the American decision to stay out, would significantly limit its impact. Meanwhile, in Germany, a second postwar federal union was created in the form of the Weimar Republic. It, too, seemed to deliver on a promise first formulated in Frankfurt in 1848 by constructing a democratic constitution that tied the states and the federal centre together.

Keywords: Federal union, peace movement, League of Nations, Weimar

Federal union in the Third Peace Movement

In his address to the Banquet of the 1904 World Peace Congress in Boston, the American philosopher William James warned his audience to be under no illusion about the challenge they faced. Peace may have seemed the reasonable option, but "[r]eason is one of the feeblest of nature's forces," especially in confrontation with "[o]ur noted enemy (...) the bellicosity of human nature" (James, 845 "The plain truth," he observed despondently, "is that people want war. (...) War, they feel, is human nature at its uttermost. It is a sacrament. Society would rot, they think, without the mystical blood payment" (846) Warning that "[w]e do ill (...) to talk much of a universal peace or of a general disarmament," he called on the delegates instead to "organise in every conceivable way the practical machinery for making each successive chance of war abortive. Seize every pretext, no matter how small, for arbitration methods, and multiply the precedents" (847)

Livestro, Joshua: *A More Perfect Union. Federal Union in Political Theory and Practice, 1500-1951.*
Amsterdam: Amsterdam University Press, 2024.
DOI: 10.5117/9789048563777_CH09

For a movement that had spent much of the nineteenth century formulating seemingly impossible aspirations, the switch to a pragmatic approach
was clearly a challenge. Still, of its three overarching goals, arbitration was
the area where most progress was likely to be achieved. Not only had the
1899 Peace Conference created the first international court of arbitration
(even if it was on a voluntary basis, and the "court" itself was only a list of
potential arbitrators), since that first conference, attention for the subject of
arbitration had grown significantly, especially thanks to the United States
government, which, under presidents Roosevelt and Taft, would take an
active interest in promoting it as a tool for international conflict resolution.

The second priority, disarmament, was given a lift by the election victory in 1906 of the British Liberal Party. It had fought the campaign on an
explicit promise to reduce military expenditure, a promise that had proven
popular with the electorate in the aftermath of the Boer War. In Sir Henry
Campbell-Bannerman it also had a Prime Minister who seemed comfortable
with the idea of disarmament. Undoubtedly to the consternation of the
British diplomatic and military establishment, he used his first public
speaking engagement as newly elected Prime Minister to commit his cabinet
to actually delivering on his election pledge. In that same speech, he also
hinted at his support for the peace movement's third priority, the formation
of a Congress of Nations: "What nobler role could this great country assume
than to place itself at the head of a League of Peace?" (quoted in Tuchman,
Proud Tower 308).

The idea of a European federal union had enjoyed mixed fortunes since
the 1840s. Given a big lift by Victor Hugo's intervention at the 1849 Paris
Peace Congress, it became the official chief objective of the second European
peace movement in the late 1860s in the form of a call for a "United States of
Europe." With the demise of the second peace movement, the momentum
shifted to the other two priorities, with arbitration getting most of the
political focus and disarmament gaining most public support. But even if
it was, for a while, the least successful of the three main priorities, the idea
of a European federal union as a means to achieve perpetual peace always
remained part of the platform of the peace movement, and, by extension,
of political debate.

The 1892 Peace Conference in Berne, for example, adopted a resolution
stating that:

Whereas the federal union of Europe, which is demanded by the commercial interests of all countries, would put an end to this condition of
anarchy by the constitution of a European juridic state (...) therefore the

Congress invites the European Peace Societies and their adherents to make a union of the European states, based upon the solidarity of their interests, the supreme aim of their propaganda.

(Casano 231)

And at the 1896 Peace Conference in Budapest, another one of Europe's generation of nineteenth century revolutionary soldiers, the Hungarian general István Türr (1825–1908), declared rather optimistically that "[w]e have today six Great Powers, and these have united themselves, some in a Triple Alliance, the other in an *Entente Cordiale*. If these groups would unite, the smaller states would attach themselves, and the union of the European Powers would be an accomplished fact"[1] (quoted in Phillips 11).

The turn of the twentieth century would see the topic regain its prominent place on the political agenda, through events and through the efforts of a number of prominent advocates.[2]

———

The British newspaper man William Thomas Stead (1849–1912) was widely credited with reinventing British journalism in the 1880s. He was also one of the most effective campaigners of the age, who ended up being nominated for the Nobel Peace Prize more than once for his efforts on behalf of the peace movement. Possessing an incredible drive and creativity, he combined the ability to publish a ceaseless stream of articles and letters in support of the ideals of the peace movement with a hectic travel schedule that took him to all parts of the globe. The purpose of these trips was always the same: to evangelise for world peace, and to organise for it. It was one of these trips that would cause his untimely death. On his way to New York to attend a peace conference in the spring of 1912, he ended up drowning when the ship he was on, the Titanic, sank in the mid-Atlantic.[3]

---

1   Türr ended up serving under Garibaldi, and joined him as his *aide de camp* during the famous Expedition of the Thousand that saw the Bourbon kingdom of the Two Sicilies incorporated into the new Italian kingdom under Victor Emmanuel (March 1861). For his services to the Italian cause in this campaign, the king promoted him to the rank of general. In later life, he would distinguish himself as a water engineer, and a campaigner for the creation of the Panama Canal as a stimulus for global trade.

2   For this idea as discussed in the following section, I am indebted to Prof. Maartje Abbenhuis.

3   Stead was mentioned in James Joyce's 1916 *Portrait of the Artist as a Young Man* as the force behind a public petition in the run-up to the 1899 peace conference. See Higgins in Abbenhuis et.al. pp.138–39.

Stead's enthusiasm for a European federal future was expressed not only in his newspaper articles and his speeches, but also in a book titled *The United States of Europe*. Written in the run-up to the 1899 Peace Conference, it was typical for the kind of pro-federation publications of that period: long on aspiration, short on method.

On the question of how to bridge the gap between vision and reality, he used two rhetorical ploys. One was the argument of self-evidence: it was pointless to question federalisation because it was already happening. Here anything from the introduction of new technologies which had helped to shrink distances (locomotion, telegraphy) to the Concert system ("the germ of the United States of Europe") (Stead 39) was used as an indication that the establishment of a European federal union was only a matter of time. The other was the Kantian ploy of pushing its arrival into a more distant, undefined future. This had the benefit of depoliticising what could otherwise become an intensely political debate triggered by those who insisted on defending state sovereignty.

If the simultaneous use of both strategies could at times be somewhat confusing – at one point Stead declared that "The United States of Europe (...) may be much nearer than even the most sanguine amongst us venture at present to hope" (7) while at another claimed that the "ultimate ideal (...) lies far ahead, [and] will not be attained until the United States of Europe have come into formal and juridical existence" (40) – the overall effect of their use was to leave the reader enthusiastic about the future without being overly concerned about the possible costs of getting there. About these costs, Stead was remarkably relaxed. "[W]e need not be surprised," he observed, "if the United States of Europe only gets itself into material existence after considerable bloodshed" (46) This however, he asserted, was "a detail. (...) [I]t is a thousand times better that men should be killed in order that their corpses should pave the way to the reign of law, than that they should be slaughtered merely to perpetuate the existing anarchy" (46). If there was to be war, he seemed to suggest, best if it was a war to establish perpetual peace.

Preferably, though, war was to be avoided. To that end, Stead suggested that the Great Powers combine military efforts to create a kind of "international police" whose task it was "to execute the decisions of the Federal Government" (39). Smaller states didn't really feature in Stead's calculations. "Space fails me," he stated at one point in his 500-page tome, "to do more than cast a rapid glance at the smaller states" (77). When he suggested that even in the federal future there would still remain "a sovereign right to go to war to enforce its protest," he granted this right only to the Great Powers; and in his sketch of "the European Council Chamber," the only states participating in deliberations and decision-making were the same Great Powers (42–43).

To facilitate the kind of decision-making that would make the international police an effective force, he also suggested a move away from the *"liberum veto"* which like in "the old Polish kingdom" had created a situation where "any one member of the Assembly could defeat any proposition by simply uttering his protest" (Stead 41). On these issues, Stead's position reflected the pre-war consensus among peace activists. If the proposed league was to survive and flourish, it should be granted real powers – powers to decide efficiently, and powers to enforce effectively. Intervention served the purpose of restoring peace and imposing a just outcome in a conflict. To that end, some schemes even proposed a joint army or police force to keep recalcitrant states in line.

This idea was less radical than it seemed: the consensus underpinning the Concert system, after all, had been that military intervention by a coalition of the Great Powers was acceptable, provided none of them saw a reason to veto it. Stead was able to justify his proposal by pointing to a recent example in the form of Crete, where in 1897–1898 an international squadron consisting of war ships from several of the Great Powers had helped to impose a peace settlement on the Ottoman empire, effectively forcing it to withdraw.

Stead's most interesting contribution to the broader debate about federal union was his suggestion that gradual progress towards the ultimate objective could be made through an ongoing process of essentially technical, mostly economic, policymaking. Here he referred to an 1897 speech by the head of the International Railway Bureau, the former Swiss president Numa Droz, in which the latter had explained the work of the international agencies as "partly technical and partly diplomatic" (Stead 30). Describing these agencies as "ice crystals which form on the surface of the water before the cold is sufficiently intense to freeze the whole surface into one solid sheet," he suggested their work was paving the way for the final unification of the continent: "an embodied prophecy of the coming of the United States of Europe" (26).

The idea of an essentially technical, predominantly economic union serving as a vehicle for political unification was not new in itself; that, after all, was what the German Customs Union had turned out to be. What was new, however, was deliberately using this kind of mechanism as a means of building a more perfect union. In the decades that followed, this idea would take on a life of its own.

—

One person who would pick it up was one of Stead's closest contacts in the peace movement, the German-British industrialist Max Waechter (1837–1924). During a business visit to his native Germany in 1906, he was shocked to find "a strong war-like feeling apparently pervading the whole nation," with the

nation's media "entirely dominated by the War Party" (607). Concluding that
he must "do all I can to prevent it," he set out to write a memo to the German
emperor and the British king, advocating the formation of a United States
of Europe as the best way of guaranteeing perpetual peace (Waechter 607).

Like Saint-Pierre two centuries earlier, Waechter would use *raison d'état*
arguments to sell his idea of a European federal union to potentially sceptical
monarchs. He did it by basing his memorandum on an issue he knew they
cared about: a comparison of the relative strengths of the American and
European economies. He observed that the many internal obstacles to trade
in Europe made it almost inevitable that it would fall behind its American
counterpart, pointing to the high costs to industry of intra-European customs
tariffs and the high costs to taxpayers of the large standing armies required
to keep each other at bay (Waechter 609).

Not content with lobbying the heads of state of the Great Powers, Waechter
would use his considerable resources to finance a public relations campaign
and the building of a European organisation. The aim of both was to help
spread the ideas he had discussed in his pamphlet. His efforts generated a
stream of newspaper coverage, not just in Europe but across the globe. They
also led to the organisation of the Congress of the European Federation,
which held its first meeting in May 1909 in the Italian capital, Rome.

In 1913, he would intensify his efforts for peace by launching the European
Unity League. It was meant "as a means of promoting the federation of
Europe in the United Kingdom and throughout the continent" (Waechter
607). By the summer of 1914, he had built an impressive British organisation,
with a membership of more than 20,000 people and a General Council
that by his own account included "48 peers, 51 admirals, 52 generals, and
162 members of Parliament," including the future Labour Prime Minister
Ramsay MacDonald (608). But before he could expand the movement by
building similar organisations on the continent, events in Sarajevo threw
a definitive spanner in his works.

———

Baroness Bertha von Suttner (1843–1914) had gained global fame following
the publication in 1889 of her anti-war novel *Nieder die Waffen* ("Lay Down
Your Arms"). When her family rejected her choice of marriage partner she
was forced to take whatever work she could find to provide for herself. One
such engagement, working as a company secretary, introduced her to the
Swedish industrialist Alfred Nobel, with whom she would maintain a lifelong
friendship (there is some suggestion that she was instrumental in persuading

him to create the Nobel Peace Prize, of which she herself became one of the first recipients in 1905). She would eventually have an independent career as a journalist and writer. Her success in these professions allowed her to build up a wide network of contacts across European literary and journalistic circles which she would later mobilise for her work as a peace activist.

A year after the 1899 peace conference, Suttner would reflect on the status of the peace movement following the relative failure of the meeting in The Hague, and the subsequent outbreak of the Boer War (a few months after the end of the conference). While acknowledging the setback, she insisted peace was not just an idea whose time had come, but also an ideal that inspired a movement willing to take the difficult decisions to secure it. When challenged how perpetual peace could be possible, given that "conditions may at any time arise which will force upon men a resort to arms," she answered that it would come through the creation of an international executive with full policing powers: "As a well-ordered State maintains a police force to execute the decrees of its judges (...) so would an alliance of Culture-States [German: *Kulturstaten;* my translation], such as we contemplate, require an armed force to serve international right as an executive power" (Suttner, "Present Status" 658).

In her 1906 Nobel Peace Prize acceptance speech, she would again touch upon the idea of an "alliance of culture-states" (Suttner).[4] Styling it "a peace union between nations," she suggested the resistance encountered by the peace movement's pursuit of it was part of a wider struggle between a new world waiting to be born and an old one refusing to die:

> Quite apart from the peace movement, which is a symptom rather than a cause of actual change, there is taking place in the world a process of internationalisation and unification. Factors contributing to the development of this process are technical inventions, improved communications, economic interdependence, and closer international relations.

The counterforce was the party of war, with its "constantly refined methods of annihilation," whose ultimate outcome could be "the destruction of humanity." To prevent that outcome, she called again for the formation of "[a]n international body with strength to maintain law between nations, as between the States of North America, (...) through which the need for recourse to war may be abolished."

While admitting this vision was regarded by some as a "utopian dream," she thought that a sufficient awareness of what would be gained by its

---

4   All subsequent quotes in this section come from this source unless otherwise attributed.

implementation would motivate its supporters to see it through: "On the solution of this problem depends whether our Europe will become a showpiece of ruins and failure, or whether we can avoid this danger and so enter sooner the coming era of secure peace and law in which a civilization of unimagined glory will develop."

———

American president Theodore Roosevelt (1858–1919), was probably the peace movement's unlikeliest champion. The war hero of the Battle of San Juan Hill had been a staunch supporter of American expansionism. He would oversee a massive build-up of American naval capacity, which helped to confirm his country's status as a first order military power gained after victory in the Spanish American war of 1898. But if he equipped his country with a big stick in the military sense, he combined it with the diplomatic habit of walking softly where possible. His role as mediator, through which he helped to bring an end to the 1904–1905 Russian–Japanese war, earned him the 1906 Nobel Peace Prize.

He backed up his practical efforts on behalf of peace with calls for international steps to make peace more sustainable. One such step would be the creation of a permanent court of arbitration. In his 1905 Message to Congress, Roosevelt explained why he had called for a second peace conference. His hope was that the countries there assembled would "devise some way to make arbitration between nations the customary way of settling international disputes in all save a few classes of cases" (Roosevelt, Fifth Annual Message). Another measure he consistently supported, both in and out of office, was the idea of an "organization of the civilized nations"; he noted that "as the world becomes more highly organized the need for navies and armies will diminish" (Roosevelt, Fifth Annual Message).

In his 1910 delayed acceptance lecture for the 1906 Nobel Peace Prize, he gave some details of his ideas for what by now he had styled the "League of Peace" (Roosevelt, Nobel Lecture).[5] The leading role in its establishment would be reserved for "some combination between those great nations which sincerely desire peace and have no thought themselves of committing aggressions." While acknowledging certain "fundamental differences," the model he held up was the United States Constitution, which "in the establishment of the Supreme Court and in the methods adopted for securing peace and good relations among and between the different states, offers certain valuable analogies to what should be striven for in order to secure,

5   All subsequent quotes in this section come from this source unless otherwise attributed.

through the Hague courts and conferences, a species of world federation for international peace and justice." The scope of the proposed league would likely be limited geographically, at least in its initial stage, but "the ruler or statesman who should bring about such a combination would have earned his place in history for all time and his title to the gratitude of all mankind."

The aim of his scheme was to make the one proposed new international institution the guarantor of the rulings of the other. Recognising that an international court would likely suffer from the unwillingness of countries to adhere to its rulings, by 1914 Roosevelt was ready to commit to the idea of an international quasi-constitution, complete with powers of enforcement. This would put him in the same camp as the League to Enforce Peace, co-founded a year later in 1915 by his bitter rival for the presidency, Howard Taft (it was Roosevelt's controversial decision to run as an independent against his fellow Republican Taft that had handed the 1912 presidential election to the Democrat Woodrow Wilson). The league's stated aim was "that the signatory powers shall forthwith use their economic and military forces against any member that goes to war before taking its case either to the court or council" (Holt 68). No less significantly, the league also proposed that nations would meet at regular intervals to create international legislation, thereby completing the *trias politica* at international level.

As the war progressed, Roosevelt's position became increasingly aligned with that of the other camp in the internal peace movement debate. This camp stressed the use of strictly legal means to enforce decisions made by a league council. What it rejected above all was equipping the league with its own military force. What use would a Peace League be if maintaining peace in practice meant fighting wars? This conflict at the heart of the American peace movement would play a significant role during the negotiations at Versailles, and during the ratification fight in the US Senate.[6]

———

6   In "The League That Wasn't: American Designs for a Legalist-Sanctionist League of Nations and the Intellectual Origins of International Organization, 1914–1920," American historian Stephen Wertheim suggests that this failure to agree on a joint position on the use of force might also be the product of the inability of the leading men of the "legalist-sanctionist" approach – Roosevelt, Taft, and former Secretary of State Elihu Root – to agree on common positions on what were essentially a range of constitutional questions: would the new international organisations powers be limited or unlimited, and who should decide on matters of competence (league or states)? Though plausible, this analysis overlooks the possibility that Roosevelt's opposition may well have been the product of political calculation rather than principled objections. He very much intended to run again for the presidency in 1920, and he hoped to win by making opposition to Wilson's League of Nations one of the focal points of his campaign. See Wertheim, pp. 819-821.

Roosevelt's 1905 Message to Congress would eventually lead to the gathering of the Second The Hague Peace Conference in 1907. Attended by government delegations from 44 countries, it adopted 13 conventions on a range of topics, mostly to do with the laws of war (Tuchman, *Proud Tower* 315). Its main achievement, however, was not its output but the fact that it managed to keep the top priorities of the peace movement – arbitration, disarmament, and federation – on the global political agenda.

One of the conference's participants was the French delegate Leon Bourgeois (1851–1925). In the course of a long career in service of the Third Republic, Bourgeois had risen to cabinet rank, eventually becoming first minister and minister of Foreign Affairs. A committed radical reformer, he was the originator of the concept of solidarism, a theory of social justice that became the central doctrine of Third Republic politics.[7] To Bourgeois, it expressed most of all a desire to put peace and justice at the heart of relations between classes as well as nations (Hayward 20). His efforts on behalf of the cause of international peace flowed naturally from this. In the late 1890s, they made him an obvious candidate to represent the French government at the first Peace Conference in The Hague.

At the Second Peace Conference of 1907, he tried – and failed – to get delegates to sign up to a new system of international arbitration. In the aftermath of that event, in November 1907, he addressed a gathering of French and American delegates in the Palais du Luxembourg in Paris. In his address, he made it clear he did not share the negative assessment of some newspaper commentaries: "In 1907, the rule of law has spread across the world" (Bourgeois 176; my translation throughout). He pointed to concrete achievements like the fact that, for the first time in history, the delegates had been able to establish a formal procedure for the declaration of war (178), and that the commission on arbitration (which he had chaired) had proposed, though not adopted, a procedure that was both simpler and more precise than the 1899 version (181).

According to Bourgeois, by showing up in unprecedented numbers, by discussing issues on the basis of perfect equality between all delegations, and then deciding for the common good, the forty-four participating countries had done something much more important than merely adopting a number of conventions. They had, in fact, helped to establish the ground rules for the functioning of a "League of Nations." And through their meeting, they

---

7   Though the concept had been around for longer, with roots in the ideal of fraternity as propagated in the 1789 Revolutionary period, Bourgeois would become associated with it following publication of his 1895 book *Solidarité*.

had also helped to give birth to "the organs of that League of Nations, the legal institutions that will regulate its existence" (190). True, its full and final establishment would likely take time, but "patience and faith" would see it happen.

A year later, in a lecture to the Parisian École des Sciences Politiques, Bourgeois would go even further by claiming that "[t]he League of Nations has been created – it is fully alive" (209). This assertion may seem somewhat optimistic, but it was a sentiment shared by those delegates who had argued at the end of the conference for a third Peace Conference to be organised "within a period analogous to that which had elapsed since the previous conference" (Tuchman, *Proud Tower* 322). The aim was to use the process of organising regular conferences to create a permanent organisation, preferably with its own secretariat. The absence of one was generally felt to have been a stumbling block to the achievement of more meaningful progress during the first two conferences. The fact the motion was passed was considered a significant achievement. The year chosen for its organisation, 1915, also seemed perfectly acceptable.

The Grand Design canon in pre-Versailles debate about the League of Nations

In the summer of 1917, Bourgeois would be called on one more time to serve the cause of peace on behalf of his country. He was asked to head a committee tasked with preparing a French position on the issue of the possible formation of a league of nations. The report that came out of that work would form the basis of the French government's position during the peace conference of 1919. During that conference, he would participate as lead French negotiator in the talks leading to the founding of the League of Nations.

The French were not the only ones to use a committee to prepare for the upcoming negotiations about the likely formation of a League of Nations. On the British side, a committee was founded at the suggestion of the Assistant Secretary of State for Foreign Affairs, Lord Robert Cecil. The committee was placed under the leadership of the Court of Appeal Judge and international law expert, Lord Walter Phillimore (1845–1929). Its final report was accompanied by a handbook for the British delegates to the peace conference. The booklet contained a comprehensive overview of schemes for European unification, from Dante's plea for universal monarchy to the federal plans of Henri IV and the Abbé de Saint Pierre, via Penn and Kant to Bluntschli and Sir Max Waechter. It also presented an overview of more recent "schemes of federation," noting that they came in three different categories: "Some writers lay stress upon recourse to Arbitration, others upon a European or World Federation or League" (Phillimore 23).

In breaking down the details of the various federal schemes published since the turn of the century, Phillimore's overview showed that, though there were variations between them, most authors had by now fully internalised the logic of separation of powers: a Council representing the member states as a kind of executive, a Court for arbitration of disputes between states, and a Parliament to produce international legislation (Phillimore 23–25). There were also several fundamental differences of opinion, for example about the role of the smaller states; some wanted to include them on a one state, one vote basis, others wanted the executive to exclude all but the largest states (24). Enforcement was another source of division: whether or not to accept military power as a form of enforcement (25),[8] and if so, whether there could be such a thing as a binding duty to enforce, or indeed to protect fellow League members against attacks by a non-member country (26).

—

Phillimore's overview of peace schemes was one of a number of documents published in the pre-Versailles period that placed the discussion about the League of Nations in the context of the Grand Design tradition. To underline both possibility and plausibility of their federal schemes, authors regularly referred to the canon of peace schemes that had been established in the second half of the nineteenth century. William Stead, for example, started his *The United States of Europe* with a discussion of the ancient Greek Amphictyonic Council, the "great designs" of Henri IV, William Penn and Immanuel Kant, as well as the constitutions of the United States of America and the recently established Germany federal empire. In his 1904 study of international tribunals, William Evans Darby gave a similar overview of historical examples, in which he included the peace plans of Henri IV, Penn, St Pierre, Bentham, and Kant, as well as various nineteenth century arbitration treaties. The American historian John Spencer Bassett

8   One of the most outspoken opponents of the use of force was the British legal scholar and secretary of the British Peace Society William Evans Darby. Darby was quoted by Phillimore as being against the very concept of "enforcement of peace," stating that it would effectively accept that "peace cannot be enforced without war or the threat of war." This idea was unacceptable to him, since "the Federation of the World cannot be secured by an International Army" (Darby 51).

included a complete overview of the canon, from Henri IV and Sully to the The Hague Peace Conferences of 1899 and 1907, in a study of the Congress System as a source of inspiration for the coming negotiations about the League of Nations.[9] His compatriot, the scientist E. B. Copeland, produced a pamphlet in 1918 in which he invoked virtually the entire canon and all of Western history, from the Holy Roman Empire to the United States and the Congress of Vienna, and from Henri IV to Abraham Lincoln ("The nations of the World cannot live together, half monarchical-aristocratic and half free" Copeland 12–13).

Most studies were somewhat superficial in their use of the historical examples, using them mainly as props in political arguments that might just as easily have been constructed without them. There were some notable exceptions though. Two studies in particular stood out, for clearly adding to the accumulated knowledge and insight about the European federal tradition. One was a study of the development of the concept of international organisation in the period 1300–1889, probably the most comprehensive study of the subject published until then. Its author was the Dutch peace activist and later director of the library of the Peace Palace in The Hague, Jacob ter Meulen (1884–1962). He was a pupil of the Swiss 1907 Peace Conference delegate Max Huber, who, in the mid 1920s, would serve as president of the Permanent Court of International Justice.

Meulen's study was the first attempt to offer a systematic analysis of the many plans for the creation of a European-level political order that together made up the canon as it had been established in the second half of the nineteenth century. However, his analysis still was somewhat incomplete in its systematisation. It grouped together more straightforward *organisational characteristics* like the location and frequency of meetings with *issues of principle* like whether, and if so in what form, the collective organisation should have a capacity for enforcement, and the fundamental *problematics of federation* like the optimal size of the federation. It also failed to grasp what had proven to be the biggest problem in federal union theory, namely the distribution of sovereignty between unions and their member states. What was important though was that it showed that all schemes engaged with most of these issues to a certain extent.

The study was systematic as well in its attempt to develop a theory of history to explain, and justify, federal union. Seemingly taking his cue from the nineteenth century predictions about the twentieth century as the "era of federation" (among others Proudhon and Renan), Meulen described a

9   Basset, *The Lost Fruits of Waterloo*, 1918.

"developmental process" towards federalism which would be delayed, but not blocked indefinitely, by "the necessary ordering of peoples in national territorial states" (Meulen 361; my translation throughout). In the end, though, these "egotistical partial communities" would not prove to be insurmountable obstacles. Instead, they would serve as a "foundation" for the development of "substantial positive international law" (361). Nation states were to remain an essential part of the international federal organisation that was to come. Whether that new organisation was to be European or international in character was left open.

The other historical study that helped to shed a new light on the continental federal tradition was a publication by the British historian Walter Allison Phillips (1864–1950) of the record of the Congress system established in Vienna. In this book, which was based on a series of lectures delivered at Oxford University in the spring of 1913, Philips described the Vienna Congress system as an "experiment in international government" which "represented (...) an attempt to solve the problem of reconciling central and general control by a 'European confederation' with the maintenance of the liberties of its constituent states, and thus to establish a juridical system" (7). While acknowledging its eventual failure, he thought it was still worth studying "in order to see what light it throws on those modern peace projects to the promulgation of which so great an impulse was given by the Hague Conferences of 1899 and 1907" (8).

In his conclusion, Philips reflected on the central problem faced by the Holy Alliance in the post-1815 period: the tension between territory and nationality, the need to protect borders that were to a large extent artificially drawn against the revolutionary strivings of national movements. He feared the same would happen to a new iteration of the Holy Alliance in the early twentieth century: "The attempt would be even less likely to succeed now, when the spirit of nationalism is strong, than a hundred years ago, when it was in its weak beginnings" (297). The logic of these nationalist movements would be the same as that of the earlier Polish and Italian nationalists: "Thus (...) Mazzini had dreamed of perpetual peace; but first Italy must be united under a republican government and the other 'oppressed nationalities' of Europe secured in their rights" (298). The inevitable consequence of this was that "the new Holy Alliance (...) would find itself face to face with revolutionary forces which it would have to repress, save in the very improbable event of its being willing to conciliate them by conceding their extreme demands" (298). The issue of national rights versus territorial jurisdiction would be one of the dilemmas at the heart of the post-war negotiations about the reordering of the continent.

Expansionism of the eve of the First World War

Peaceful, voluntary federation was not the only kind of expansion discussed on the eve of the First World War, or indeed even the most prominent one. Though it had a lot of moral force behind it, the momentum seemed to be with the other methods of expansion.

In the United States of America, the issue of expansion dominated public debate in the late 1890s and the early 1900s. With the westward conquest of the continent completed, the idea of Manifest Destiny was projected on the world beyond its continental borders. On the Atlantic side, this meant trying to get a foothold in the Caribbean and gaining control over a stretch of Central America in order to build a canal there linking the Atlantic with the Pacific. thereby connecting the two coastal economies of the US. More ambitious still was the plan for the Pacific Ocean. Here, the American republic was to engage with the other Great Powers in a struggle for supremacy. This was partly a fight for colonial territory, but it was mainly about control of shipping lanes for American goods and troops.

The great prophet of American sea power, Alfred Thayer Mahan (1840–1914)[10], had used a study titled *The Influence of Sea Power Upon History, 1660–1783* to explain the crucial influence of control of the high seas over the outcome of military conflicts on land. Most instructive was the example of Roman naval dominance. Using the example of Hannibal's famous march around the Mediterranean, he asked his audience to imagine that it had not been a sea but a desert, and that this desert territory had been so firmly under control of a Roman army that its opponents were "therefore compelled to a great circuit in order to concentrate their troops" (Mahan 2276). In that case "the military situation would have been at once recognised, and no words would have been too strong to express the value and effect of that peculiar force" (2276). The moral of his story: wars on land were often won at sea, even if no actual battle took place there. The power that controlled the high seas had a significant advantage over ones that were reduced to land power only.

Mahan's writings would have an extraordinary influence on American policy. The nation that had always defined foreign affairs in Washingtonian terms as something to be avoided suddenly became extremely

10   Mahan would be invited by the McKinley administration to attend the first The Hague Peace Conference as a member of the American delegation. He ended up vetoing all proposals for reform of the laws of war on sea, casting the sole vote against the banning of the use of poison gas as a weapon of war. See Tuchman, Proud Tower, pp. 290–91

interested in the world beyond its borders. The most enthusiastic supporters of the Mahanian agenda were two young Republican politicians: Theodore Roosevelt and Henry Cabot Lodge. They were supported by the New York newspaper magnate William Randolph Hearst, who also made the switch from continental to Pacific and Atlantic expansion, though probably more out of calculation than out of conviction. (When asked what helped sell his papers, he answered with a single word: "War" (Tuchman, *Proud Tower* 161).

Initially Roosevelt and Cabot Lodge were outnumbered in the Republican Party. The Party's leader, House Speaker Thomas B. Reed, was implacably opposed to the idea of expansion beyond the country's continental borders, dismissing it as "a policy no Republican ought to excuse much less adopt" (Reed 157). Their fortunes would turn, however, with the nomination and subsequent election as president of William McKinley. In his first (and as fate would have it, only) term, McKinley would start the process for the building of an American-controlled canal in Central America. He would also initiate wars with Spain over the control of Cuba and the Philippines. Like a European monarch operating within the balance of power system, he would claim – and receive – a prize for victory in the Cuban war in the form of Puerto Rico. Before that, he had already successfully pushed a treaty for the annexation of Hawaii through the Senate, defending this step by suggesting it was a case of "Manifest Destiny" (Tuchman, *Proud Tower* 172).

—

Serbia used the two Balkan wars of 1912–1913 virtually to double its territory. This expansion was no accident. The wars had been fueled by a Slavic nationalist ideology that pushed for the establishment of a Greater Serbia within a wider Slavic community. The natural limits of Serb expansionism were defined by the Yugoslav ideology, the ideal of all Slav peoples united in a single union: Serbs, Slovenes, and Croats. That brought it inevitably into conflict with the Great Power to its north, the Austro-Hungarian Empire.

Fog surrounds much of what happened in the immediate run-up to the murder of the Austrian crown prince Franz Ferdinand and his wife Sophie in the Bosnian capital Sarajevo. What we do know is that the murderer, Gavrilo Princip, was part of a terror group consisting mostly of teenagers who seemed to have been groomed for this purpose by an organisation called the Black Hand, which had contacts in the Serbian security establishment. We also know that the same Serbian security establishment had developed the theory that the Austro-Hungarian Empire's weakness made it a target for a Serbian expansionist campaign (Clark 47–56).

The assassination of the Empire's crown prince provoked exactly the kind of response the Black Hand members had hoped for. One month later, on 28 July, the Austrian government handed a declaration of war to its Serbian counterpart. Much has been written about what happened after. The most relevant thing to highlight here is the fact that, when the Serbian government published its war aims on 7 December 1914, it was entirely based on the expansionist agenda of the Greater Serbia movement. The Niš Declaration talked about the freeing of "unliberated brothers" and the uniting of the "three tribes of one people" (by which it meant Serbs, Croats, and Slovenes) (Lampe, 102) It also included in this scheme the Ottoman province of Macedonia and the Austro-Hungarian province of Bosnia-Herzegovina.

—

Perhaps the best known example of pre-war expansionist thinking came from Germany. Here, academia and political praxis combined to create an agenda that would push the country inexorably towards war – a war that was very much meant as one of conquest, with (continental) European hegemony as its ultimate objective.

By 1914, the German Reich had become an entirely different entity from the one created by Bismarck. Its population had expanded dramatically, from 41 million people in 1871 to 68 million at the start of the war. With one third of its population under fifteen years of age, it was a young country. It was also an economically expanding country, with a massively growing industrial sector (Fischer 11–13). In the eyes of German commentators, these developments forced the Reich's government to make some significant adjustments to its priorities. The objective need for more imports of raw materials and new markets to sell its end products made colonial expansion overseas a top priority. The perceived need for more land to settle its surplus population would also lead to a reopening of the debate about Germany's "natural borders."

Both forms of expansionism – economic and geographical – were extensively discussed in a new academic discipline that took its name from a concept introduced in one of the works of the Swedish political scientist and geographer Rudolf Kjellén (1864–1922): "Geopolitics is the doctrine of the state as geographical organism, existing in space: in other words the state as land, territory, region or, in its most advanced form, empire" (Kjellén 46; my translation throughout)

This idea, of the state as a kind of living organism existing in a physical space, had its roots in the work of the late nineteenth century German scholar Friedrich Ratzel (1844–1904). What distinguished organisms like states from a mere aggregate of factors, he explained, was "the variety of their territories and the spread of their populations" (Ratzel, *Politische Geographie* 15; my translation) This variety and spread, over which the state could only have a limited influence, was crucial for its "organ formation." By the latter he meant its "periphery and central provinces, coastal and inland areas, mountains and plains, cities and countryside" (15–16). Once developed, a state could also grow. This stage of growth (*Wachstum*) could be achieved through conquest and colonisation. For growth to work, the two mechanisms ideally had to be combined (Ratzel 115–118). In an essay, published in 1901 as "a biogeographical study," he would introduce a term to describe this kind of territorial expansion: the quest for *Lebensraum* (Ratzel, *Lebensraum*, 59)

"No one," Kjellén observed about Ratzel, "has so clearly recognised the close relationship between the state and its territory as he did" (Kjellén 21). But, he concluded, though *Politische Geographie* was an insightful work, its one-sided focus on geographical aspects made it ultimately less valuable as an analytical framework. What Kjellén was looking for was a theory that married the old constitutional theory of the state with the new discipline of geography. A theory, in other words, that recognised that the state "like Janus has two faces, one directed inward, the other to the outside world" (20). This required a new science that combined geopolitics with constitutional politics, and in between these two a third pillar in the form of what he called "ethno- or demopolitics, (...) the academic discipline that studies the people in its working life, or the state as an economic entity" – what we would now call political economy (43).

The core idea of geopolitics – the state as a living entity existing in geographical space – was in turn based on two other presuppositions. One was that the state was tied to a territory, without which it could not exist (Kjellén 48). The other was that the state was the embodiment of a people or *Volk*, whose ultimate constitutional expression it formed (49). These two factors worked to restrict the operational space of the state to a certain extent. After all, unlike a human being, a state couldn't physically move itself from A to B. It remained tied to its original territory, and to its *Volk*.

What the state could do, though, was expand. When Henry Kissinger rehabilitated geopolitics in the late 1970s, he attempted to claim it for his own preferred diplomatic doctrine, the balance of power: "[B]y geopolitical I mean an approach that pays attention to the requirements of equilibrium" (quoted in Gray and Sloan 1). Though in itself a perfectly legitimate interpretation of the concept of geopolitics, equilibrium was most definitely not on the minds of its earliest exponents. The natural purpose of the state as they saw it was not to live in balance with other states, but to conquer and grow. "*Kampf um den Raum*," the struggle for space, was "a historical *Leitmotiv*" (Kjellén 65). In the eyes of Kjellén, expansion wasn't just a natural phenomenon, it was an existential need: "States full of life force existing within limited space obey the categorial political imperative (…) of expanding their territory" (81).

He considered small states, in their "vegetative state" (Kjellén 83), as essentially doomed. Their fate was to fall under the dominion of larger neighbours, whose "gaze was on the horizon, whetting their conquering appetite for distant lands" (83). Conquest could not be infinite though. There were limits to expansion: organisational, physical, and perhaps even moral, when "expansion exceeds the measure of genuine existential demand" (83). He warned that there were even risks involved in excessive expansion: overly expanded states could suffer from a "weakness of form" (85).

Kjellén never mentioned Machiavelli, and there is no evidence that he was familiar with the latter's discussion of the topic of expansion in the *Discourses*. That makes it all the more remarkable that he essentially described the same taxonomy of forms of expansion: conquest, colonisation, and federation: "[T]he image of a cluster or block of states built to meet the need for space" (Kjellén 82). He considered federal union a mere "transition stage," less stable and therefore less perfect than an empire under a single ruling nation (59–60), but like Machiavelli, he ended up settling for this imperfect option as the most practical one for the German Reich, given the circumstances. The presence of the World Powers of England, Russia and the United States demanded a *Mitteleuropa*, "either in the smaller form of Germany-Austria-Hungary (…) or in the larger form including the Levant" (82). He called its formation a "political necessity" (82).

—

The pre-war period would see the publication of a number of German expansion plans. Bernhardi for example proposed both "a vigorous colonial policy" and "alliances or ententes" to help the country prepare for "the next war" (Bernhardi cxxxix). The aim of that war would be to move beyond "notions (…) opposed to our weightiest interests" (lv-lvi). By that he meant most of all moving beyond the nineteenth century rules of the European Great Powers system: "[I]t becomes essential that we do not allow ourselves to be cramped in our freedom of action by considerations, devoid of any inherent political necessity" (lvii). The balance of power system "which has, since the Congress of Vienna, led an almost sacrosanct but entirely unjustifiable existence, must be entirely disregarded" (lv).

The war aims as formulated by Chancellor Theobald von Bethmann Hollweg (1856–1921) in his "September Program" of 1914 started from a similar ambition to move beyond the Concert system. His memorandum, which seemed to reflect the consensus position among the German political and military establishment (Fischer 106), rested on three main pillars. One was the ambition to humble France, effectively eliminating it as a factor in continental Great Power politics. This was to be achieved through a combination of annexations (the memorandum specifically mentions the western slopes of the Vosges mountain range and a coastal strip, "from Dunkirk to Boulogne"), a war indemnity that was so large that it would "prevent France from spending any considerable sum on armaments in the next 15–20 years," and a trade treaty that "makes France economically dependent on Germany" (Bethmann Hollweg).

If this sounded harsh, it was a better fate than the one in store for Belgium ("must be reduced to a vassal state") and Luxembourg ("Will become a German federal state") (Bethmann Hollweg). It was exactly this scenario that one month earlier had made the British government decide to enter the war on the side of the French. In his speech to the House of Commons in which he explained the decision, Viscount Edward Grey invoked the logic of the balance of power to counter the spectre of France, Belgium, Holland and Denmark "falling under the domination of a single power," noting that this kind of "unmeasured aggrandisement" was against "British interests" (Tuchman, *Guns of August* 129).

A second war aim as described by Bethman Hollweg was the strengthening of Germany's position as dominant Great Power on the continent through a quasi-federal scheme (obviously in combination with the abovementioned incorporation of conquered territories). The aim was to build an economic union that would span virtually all of Europe apart from the Greek and Iberian peninsulas, the Baltic States and the Grand Duchy of Finland (then still part of the Russian empire): "A central European economic association is to be constructed through common customs agreements, to comprise France, Belgium, Holland, Denmark, Austria-Hungary, Poland and possibly Italy, Sweden and Norway."[11] (Bethmann Hollweg).

The German-Finnish peace and commercial treaties, including its secret clauses, of March 1918, give a glimpse of what the reality of this scheme would have been like for other participating states. Finland was banned

---

11   It is important to remember that at this time the Austrian-Hungarian empire spanned not just these two countries but also modern day Czechia, Slovakia, Slovenia, Croatia, Bosnia-Herzegovina, as well as parts of Romania, Ukraine, Moldova and Poland.

from signing treaties of alliance with third countries without German permission, and from letting troops from other countries be stationed on its territory. It also had to grant German products and investments access to its market on the same footing as domestic Finnish products and investments, without levying any import duties. Germany, on the other hand, was free to levy import duties on Finnish products entering its market. It was also granted the right to establish naval bases and a telegraph post on Finnish territory (Fischer 512–513).

—-

The third objective, meanwhile, focused on Africa. It proposed a campaign of colonisation that would help to confirm Germany's status as a World Power on a par with England, Russia, and the United States (Fischer 103–106). This objective would eventually go under the name of *Mittelafrika*. It was a reference not just to the geopolitical objective of German control of a broad swath of land in the middle of the African continent, running from the Belgian-controlled Congo to the Cameroons on the Gulf of Guinea, but also to the equivalent European objective of *Mitteleuropa*. Having been around since the early 1800s, the term would be popularised during the war by Friedrich Naumann (1860–1919).

Naumann, a preacher who had become a member of the Reichstag in the middle of the first decade of the new century, had built a reputation as a spokesman for a nationalist version of social liberalism, combining social activism with outspoken support for German expansionism. His book, *Mitteleuropa*, was an intervention in an ongoing debate about the German war aims and Germany's place in the world. Some argued in favour of a campaign of German expansion into Eastern Europe. Incorporation of conquered Polish territories into the German Reich was to be followed by internal colonisation through resettlement there of part of the German population.

The accompanying objective of Germanification (*Germanisierung*) of these territories obviously raised the issue of the fate of the local population, both Polish and Jewish. At a government conference devoted to the issue, the consensus was that they would have to be removed from the territory to the remaining rump of Congress Poland, the territory established at the negotiating table in Vienna a century earlier (Geiss 93–94). The same issue would be revisited a few decades later by Nazi strategists during the Wannsee conference of January 1942, this time with genocidal consequences.

Against this new Blood and Iron approach, others argued in favour of a more diplomatic form of expansion. The run-up to the war saw the

publication of a number of tracts embracing the idea of a (Middle) European customs union (*Zollverein*). Ignoring Treitschke's warning that "the
political effects of the Customs Union (...) had not manifested themselves
anywhere near as fast or as clearly as many clever minds now seem to think"
(Treitschke 231), they projected on it their hopes of establishing German
political dominance over central Europe by economic means.

The most prominent of these authors was the German industrialist and
later Foreign Minister, Walther Rathenau. In 1913 and 1914, he produced
a series of opinion articles and memorandums in support of the creation
of a "Middle-European customs union" (Rathenau 276); my translation
throughout). The idea was that, after Germany and Austria–Hungary had
formed the core of this new economic union, the surrounding smaller
countries would join too, if not out of conviction, then to avoid "economic
isolation" (274). The ultimate aim of this union was "not world peace or
disarmament (...) but a softening of conflicts, a saving of forces and [the
building of] a civilisation based on solidarity" (278).

In the hands of Naumann, the concept of *Mitteleuropa* became more
general in its objectives. It remained predominantly an economic concept,
but, like Treitschke, he was wary of putting too much faith in a customs
union alone:

> It must not be forgotten that the Prussian Customs Union with Hanover,
> Bavaria and Württemberg did not prevent these States from taking up
> arms against each other in 1866. (...) Therefore if today we wish to establish
> a future Mid-European political unity, the history of this old Prusso-
> German Customs Union shows that (...) [it] will not in itself be sufficient.
> (Naumann 224–225)

While admitting that it was a "most convenient step towards the great
object" (225), something else was required to put the proposed union on a
secure footing.

Those who expected him to define what the "great object" was towards
which a Middle European Customs Union was just a first step, or what
this "something else" was that was required to establish it, would end up
disappointed. True, he stressed "a considerable adjustment of the transition"
to make sure the customs union ended up working equally well for all parties
(Naumann 239) and addressed in passing some additional economic issues
like the treatment for tax purposes of cross-border syndicates (244). But such
details were only a distraction from what Naumann considered to be his
real mission: to exhort European states to seize this historic opportunity.

Anyone could "borrow a few quite general ideas out of the treasury of existing conceptions of State rights, and (…) apply them to the subject to be dealt with" (253). What was required was "poetry and prose" in which the idea of Middle Europe was "exalted," not "draft[ing] upon paper an ideal Mid-European construction" (252–253).

To ask too much, too soon of the new cooperative venture would be a strategic mistake: "It is very important at this stage that the content of the problem should not be increased, but on the contrary decreased as far as possible, since an overladen boat cannot be pushed off from the bank at all" (Naumann 253). Better to start small, focusing on a Customs Union involving "just" Germany and Austria-Hungary: "The discussion of many European States at once destroys businesslike progress from the outset" (253–254). It might not have seemed exciting, but "what is wanted here is restrained and disciplined political imagination, no universal, boldly arbitrary spirit of prophecy leaping over whole decades" (254).

The pragmatic federal tradition of gradualism, which dated back to Kant and Saint-Simon, found one its most effective early twentieth century spokespeople in Naumann. His thesis that a federal union was not created at once but was instead the product of many decades of incremental changes accompanied by "an endless number of debates and discussions about States' rights" (Nauman, 254) foreshadowed the discussion about the method of European integration chosen in the early 1950s.

The war that will end war

As *The Economist* explained in an editorial comment on 12 October 1907, the European federal union aspired to by peace activists like Sir Max Waechter might well have been noble in its intentions, but the practical obstacles were significant: "[T]he vested interests obstructing the project are stupendous" (quoted in: Tiedau, 137) Even if these could somehow be overcome, one fundamental problem remained: "[S]eeing that Federation implies an external danger, what is it that Europe is to federalise against?" (137).

Until August 1914, no convincing answers were available. Right up to the start of the war, it was assumed that the same Concert system that had prevented a great conflagration for the past one hundred years would do so again this time. Both the United States and Great Britain repeatedly offered mediation or a congress to settle the issues involved in the conflict between Austria-Hungary and Serbia, and the French government indicated that it was willing to participate. But for reasons known only to itself, the

German government encouraged its Austrian counterpart not to take up these offers. The war that nobody thought was possible thereby suddenly became inevitable (Fischer 69–72).

The First World War was, in reality, not the first world-wide war. The theme of global war had been around in European political thought since the late seventeenth century. Fletcher of Saltoun had already described the Nine Years War of 1688–1697 in those terms, and the series of conflicts starting with the War of the Austrian Succession and ending with the Seven Years War of 1756–1763 were widely acknowledged to have been global military conflicts.

In a lecture series at Cambridge University in 1883, the historian John Robert Seeley (1834–1895) incorporated all these conflicts in what he described as the "Second Hundred Years War" between France and England, "the great and decisive duel between England and France for the possession of the New World" (Seeley 16). This century-long conflict was triggered by France's settlement of Louisiana in 1683 and did not end properly until 1815 with the final defeat of Napoleon. The Napoleonic Wars were triggered by a conflict over Malta, which would grant the possessor control over the Eastern Mediterranean – the gateway to India and the Far East (Seeley 20). They were equally global in their scope, involving battles on land and at sea on four different continents. In that respect, there was nothing unique about the First World War. And though it was particularly bloody in terms of the number of lives lost, it wasn't *categorically* more destructive than, for example, the Napoleonic wars.

In one aspect, though, the conflict that started in 1914 was truly different. It was the first war to be associated by its contemporaries with the idea introduced by Henri IV and the Duc de Sully: the final war, the one that would open the way to perpetual peace. There had, of course, been extensive political–philosophical speculation about the use for, and inevitability of, such a war. Rousseau had concluded despondently that only a war of unimaginable destruction could create the preconditions for the creation of a league uniting all the powers of Europe. Victor Hugo had used his speech as chairman of the 1869 Lausanne peace conference to warn his audience that establishing a union of perpetual peace might require a terrible sacrifice: "The first condition of peace is liberation. For this liberation, a revolution is needed, which shall be a great one, and perhaps, alas a war which shall be the last one. Then all will be accomplished. Peace (...) shall be eternal" (quoted in Cooper 42). And as recently as 1899, William Stead had spoken grimly of the "foundations" of the "temple" that was "[t]he Federation of Europe" being formed by the bones of the dead (Stead 81).

In the autumn of 1914 the British writer Herbert George (H. G.) Wells (1866–1946) introduced the idea in the context of the new war, in a newspaper column titled "The War That Will End War': "[T]his is now a war for peace. It aims straight at disarmament. It aims at a settlement that shall stop this sort of thing for ever. (…) This, the greatest of all wars, is not just another war – it is the last war" (Wells 14).

—

Though it was Wells who introduced the idea of the "war to end war," it was the American president Woodrow Wilson who became associated with it. The speech in early April 1917, in which he asked Congressional approval for his decision to declare war on Germany, was used not just to make the case for war but also to define its objective (Wilson, Joint Address to Congress).[12] It was to be a war *for*, rather than against, international order: "Our motive will not be revenge or the victorious assertion of the physical might of the nation, but only the vindication of right, of human right, of which we are only a single champion." This was not in itself a new idea – more than a few monarchs had in centuries past claimed to be fighting for "the tranquillity of Europe." What was new was the rejection of any kind of spoils in the aftermath of the conflict: "We desire no conquest, no dominion. We seek no indemnities for ourselves, no material compensation for the sacrifices we shall freely make."[13] The only reward he sought was the restoration of international justice. Justice was defined by Wilson as "the ultimate peace of the world." An essential precondition for this "ultimate peace" was "the liberation of its peoples, the German peoples included," and "the rights of nations great and small, and the privilege of men everywhere to choose their way of life and of obedience."

In this fight for justice, neutrality – the preferred American approach in all conflicts between European states since the Founding in 1787 – was no longer an option. In cases "where the peace of the world is involved and the freedom of its peoples, and the menace to that peace and freedom lies in the existence of autocratic governments backed by organized force," the United States had no choice but to act: "We have seen the

---

12   All subsequent quotes in this section are to this source unless stated otherwise.
13   In August 1941, Roosevelt and Churchill would make a similar pledge the cornerstone of their *Atlantic Charter*: "First, their countries seek no aggrandisement, territorial or other." *Declaration of Principles issued by the President of the United States and the Prime Minister of the United Kingdom*, 14 August 1941. See also Segers, *The Origins of European Integration* 58.

last of neutrality in such circumstances. We are at the beginning of an age in which it will be insisted that the same standards of conduct and of responsibility for wrong done shall be observed among nations and their governments that are observed among the individual citizens of civilized states."

If he had been relatively late at picking up the idea – there is no evidence that Wilson was a supporter of the forming of a league of nations before the start of the war[14] – by the spring of 1917 he had become its leading advocate, even making it one of the central planks of his war manifesto. He used the idea to round off his Fourteen Points speech: "A steadfast concert for peace can never be maintained except by a partnership of democratic nations" (Wilson, President Woodrow Wilson's 14 Points).[15] The inclusion of the additional criterion of legitimacy ("*democratic* nations") would have the obvious effect of excluding the Axis powers from the postwar order, at least until they had undergone regime change: "No autocratic government could be trusted to keep faith within it or observe its covenants." Making the world safe for democracy meant taking on autocracy, and banning it from the community of nations.

As if to underline that he did not want this democracy criterion to be interpreted as an anti-German measure, Wilson concluded his address with a long message of goodwill to the German people. America, he stressed, had "no jealousy of German greatness." Indeed, the fighting would stop once she showed herself "willing to associate herself with us and the other peace-loving nations of the world in covenants of justice and law and fair dealing." All he wanted was for her to "accept a place of equality among the peoples of the world (...) instead of a place of mastery."

—

If Wilson wanted to end war, he also had to end the system through which Europe had arranged its political relations in the prewar period: the balance of power. In a speech in January 1917, when the US had not yet entered the war, he had already rejected the idea that the postwar period could see a return to the old approach: "There must be, not a balance of power, but a

14   The earliest recorded expression of Wilson's support for the idea of a league of nations dates from the autumn of 1914. In a private conversation with his brother-in-law, Dr. Stockton Axson, Wilson is supposed to have remarked that upon conclusion of the war "all nations must be absorbed into some great association of nations whereby all shall guarantee the integrity of each other" (Fleming, *The United States and the League of Nations* 7).

15   All subsequent quotes in this section are to this source unless stated otherwise.

community of power; not organised rivalries, but an organised common peace" (Wilson, Address to the Senate).

In the immediate aftermath of the war, Wilson gave a number of speeches in which he was even more explicit in his renunciation of the balance of power idea. On 28 December 1918, he addressed a British crowd of politicians in the Guildhall, at a reception hosted by the Lord Mayor of London. He used the occasion to describe an old order based on "that unstable thing which we used to call the 'balance of power' – a thing in which the balance was determined by the sword which was thrown in one side or the other" (Fleming 100). The war, Wilson concluded, had been fought to end not just all wars but also the Balance of Power system that had used war to maintain order: "The men who have fought in this war have been the men from free nations, who were determined that that sort of thing should end now and forever" (100).

In an address to the Italian Parliament, on the third of January 1919, Wilson categorically ruled out a return to the balance of power system because it had been proven to be incapable of delivering the very thing it was supposed to guarantee: "[It] has been tried and found wanting, for the best of all reasons that it does not stay balanced inside itself, and a weight which does not hold together can not constitute a makeweight in the affairs of men" (Fleming 101).

With the rejection of the balance of power came a rejection of its method for peacemaking. The idea of the winner claiming spoils in the form of land formerly belonging to their opponents was anathema to Wilson. Hence his description of the 1871 German annexation of Alsace Lorraine, which under the old method had been a perfectly acceptable practice, as a "wrong done to France by Prussia" (Wilson, Joint Address to Congress point VIII). Hence also the plea for the righting of an even older wrong through the restoration of "an independent Polish state" (point XIII). If there was to be a reorganisation of borders, it was to be done not on the basis of winners taking spoils but on the basis of nationality and justice (points IX, XI).

On the fourth of July 1918, Wilson would bring the various strands of his thinking together in a speech about the Allied war aims. At its heart was the idea of "[t]he establishment of an organization of peace" whose aim was to guarantee that "the combined power of free nations will check every invasion of right" and to establish "a definitive tribunal of opinion to which all must submit" (Fleming 20). "What we seek," he concluded, "is the reign of law based on the consent of the governed and sustained by the organized opinion of mankind" (21). Delivery of this agenda became a *conditio sine qua non* for him during the peace negotiations.

The League of Nations established

The summer offensive of 1918 had seen a combined force of French, British, Greek and Serbian troops break through the Bulgarian and German defensive lines in the southern Balkans. Bulgaria's subsequent capitulation freed the British forces to march on Constantinople, where the Ottoman government was forced to sue for peace in late October. One week later the Austrian–Hungarian empire followed suit.

By then the empire had already started falling apart. Having lost the war, it seemed to have no energy left to fight its own implosion. When an emissary of the Slovene, Croat and Serb Council met the new Austrian emperor Charles I, he greeted the news of their impending declaration of South Slav independence with a shrug: "Do as you please" (Djokic 36).

The disintegration of the empire opened the door for a complete political rearrangement of Central Europe, as foreseen by Wilson in his Fourteen Points: "The peoples of Austria-Hungary, whose place among the nations we wish to see safeguarded and assured, should be accorded the freest opportunity to autonomous development" (Wilson, Joint address to Congress, point X). The Bohemian political leaders Tomáš Masaryk and Edvard Beneš used essentially the same arguments they had previously used for political independence *within* the Empire to make the case for independence *from* the Empire. Incorporating Moravia, Slovakia (which broke away from the Kingdom of Hungary) and formerly Polish southern Silesia, in late October 1918 they formed the new fully independent state of Czechoslovakia.

Inevitably, the new state inherited not only around one third of the Empire's lands and population but also a good part of its political problems. The most important of these was the dilemma as to what to use as the foundation of the state: territory or nationality. Wilson's promise had been one of *national* self-determination or, as the historian Henri Brugmans would later call it, "the monstrous doctrine of *cuius regio, ejus lingua*" (Brugmans 131). But of the states created at the end of the war and in its immediate aftermath, none were nationally homogenous – they were independent states, but not *nation*–states.

—

The nineteenth and early twentieth century peace movement had failed to prevent the great conflicts of the previous seventy-five years – the Crimean War, the Franco–German War of 1870, and the First World War. Once the fighting was over however, it was offered an unexpected opportunity to win the peace. The agenda for the Versailles negotiations would be based on its three, by now almost a century old, priorities: arbitration, disarmament, and the formation of a League of Nations.

The Commission that was to negotiate the formation of the League was stacked with supporters of the idea. The British delegation consisted of Lord Cecil and the later South African prime minister Jan Christian Smuts, who had expressed his personal support for the idea of a league in a memorandum to his Imperial War Cabinet colleagues. The French delegation was led by Leon Bourgeois. In the chair sat the man who had invested so much political capital in the idea and who was now determined to see it made a reality: Woodrow Wilson. No wonder that to a supporter of the league idea like Wilson's predecessor in the White House, Howard Taft, it seemed as if "the stars in their courses" were aliging for its realisation (Kuehl 260). By the time the delegates met in Paris, the formation of a league seemed a foregone conclusion. What was not settled, however, was what kind of league it would be.

—

If Wilson thought the Peace Conference was about constituting a clean break with the old Balance of Power logic, he was disabused of that notion on the opening day. The first item on the agenda as far as the European powers were concerned was a traditional Balance of Power topic: the division of the spoils in the form of the former German colonies in the Pacific and East Africa. After a prolonged disagreement between the American and European delegations, Wilson suggested parking the issue on the agenda of the Commission that was set up to negotiate the structure and remit of the League.

One other early stumbling block was a Japanese request for the addition of a further objective: securing racial equality. The idea divided the delegates, with both Wilson and the British government firmly against it. At one point, Colonel House had tried solving the impasse by drafting an article based on the "all men are created equal" passage in the American Declaration of Independence. In informal discussions with the British Foreign Secretary, Lord Balfour, the latter dismissed this idea as "an eighteenth century proposition" which he thought was true only in part: "[T]rue in a certain sense that all men of a particular nation were created equal, but not that a man in Central Africa was created equal to a European" (Miller 183). Wilson, whose party's power base was in the former Confederacy, and who had won re-election in a closely fought race in 1916 thanks to victory in the state of California, where the issue of Japanese immigration had led to deadly race riots, tenaciously fought to keep the idea off the agenda. In the end, he used his power as chair of the Commission to declare the amendment "not carried" – even though a clear majority of delegates present had voted in favour (Henig 34).

These anecdotes are not meant to discredit the end result of the negotiations. It should be clear, though, that the Covenant of the League was, in its own way, no less tainted by immoral concepts and compromises than the 1787 US Constitution. This double character – immoral machinations mixed with, or perhaps veiled by, high minded rhetoric – expressed itself most clearly in proclamations that the League was to be an association of "civilised" nations. The development of international law was a matter of "organised peoples" only (Covenant of the League of Nations, Preamble), not of "peoples not yet able to stand by themselves under the strenuous conditions of the modern world." These peoples were to be held in "sacred trust" by "civilization" (Covenant, Art. 22).

If it is easy to overstate the high mindedness of the Covenant, the same goes for its supposed *naivité*. Neither Wilson nor any of the other negotiators were in the least bit naive in their assessment of the causes of the war, or of the challenges facing them in developing a plan for construction of a new world order. The peace talks were all about fixing the manifest shortcomings of the old political-strategic architecture of continental Europe. The Balance of Power system had – not for the first time – led to warfare on a catastrophic scale. To observe that a new approach was needed wasn't idealism but realism.

Though some of its negotiators, like Bourgeois, were also ideologically committed to the idea of a league of nations for the establishment of an international rule of law, it was *raison d'état* that persuaded the French government to support the idea of the League. It saw in it one possible avenue for building a defensive union against future German aggression. Germany may have been defeated, and Bismarck's Reich may have disappeared, but the fundamental reality remained that it had a significantly larger population and economy than France. It would therefore remain an existential threat, even in the new era of "post" war politics. Hence the French proposal to create a permanent military command structure within the League, and to grant the League real *military* powers of enforcement.

The same objective explained the French demand that any candidate–member of the league would have to meet certain minimal standards of democratic legitimacy. Like the necessity of military powers of enforcement, this too was a well established idea within the peace movement, but in the hands of the French it became a tool for excluding Germany rather than a way of safeguarding the League's internal cohesion. It meant the French negotiating position was based on a fundamental tension. Either the League was an anti-German defence pact, or it was a peace league – it could not be both.

It was also *raison d'état* that had made the British government propose a league in the first place. The feeling in Whitehall was that the war could have been prevented if there had been a diplomatic mechanism in place that could have forced all parties round the table in July 1914 (Henig 9). Since the country was in no position to fight another war any time soon, the creation of this mechanism became a priority of the first order. But it would have to be a league with legal rather than military powers of enforcement. Just as in 1815, the British government supported the idea of closer cooperation between the Great Powers, provided it didn't lead to strategic (military) entanglement in continental affairs.

In the search for an alternative to military enforcement, it proposed the creation of a Court. This caused a disagreement with President Wilson, who seems to have feared that discussions about the remit and composition of the Court would lead to significant delay in the negotiations[16] (Kuehl 261). The British negotiators managed to persuade him by explaining that their government's reason for proposing the addition of a Court was that without military policing powers of its own, a Court would become essential to the League's chances of enforcing its decisions. Though Wilson still refused to devote any of the scarce time reserved for the negotiations to the subject of an international court, he did accept a compromise in the form of a clause which announced that its formation would be settled separately. The latter was provided for through Article 14, which left it to the Council to "formulate and submit to the Members of the League for adoption plans for the establishment of a Permanent Court of International Justice" (Covenant).

In subsequent negotiations about the formation of the Permanent Court, the British government would refuse to heed the advice of its own negotiator, Lord Phillimore, to make adjudication compulsory rather than voluntary – thereby robbing the Court of much of its enforcement power (Spiermann 10). The British negotiating position too seemed to be based on a fundamental tension. Its objective was the formation of a league, but it refused to provide

---

16   Wilson was most likely unaware of this, but there were good grounds for fearing a delay. At the 1907 The Hague Peace Conference, attempts to create a Court of Arbitral Justice had failed because of a dispute between delegates over the method of selection of the judges. See Spiermann, *International Legal Argument* 7.

that league with credible powers of enforcement – legal or military. It seemed that whereas the French government wanted the means but not the end of a peace league, the British government wanted the end but not the means. It was up to the American delegation, led by Wilson himself, somehow to reconcile these two positions.

—

To the frustration of those around him, Wilson had at best a vague idea of what the league's structure and purpose should be. Smuts had called his statements about the League "rather nebulous" (Henig 23), while Wilson's chief adviser Colonel House regularly complained about the president's insufficient command of the details of the subject. On his way over to Europe for the start of the peace talks, Wilson confirmed to fellow passengers that he didn't have any fixed ideas about the structure of the proposed league. His aim was to negotiate only the outlines of one, and then allow "experience to guide subsequent action" (Kuehl 266). During the second plenary session of the Conference, on 25 January, he would summarise his approach as a quest for "permanent processes (...) not (...) permanent decisions" (Fleming 107). Perhaps this preference for gradualism also explains Wilson's choice for the term "Covenant" as title for the treaty to establish the league. What mattered to him was a solemn promise on the part of the participating states to commit to perpetual peace. The actual details of the peacekeeping architecture on which peace was to be based were less important to him.

This kind of vagueness wasn't necessarily a disadvantage, especially when faced with the challenge of bridging the gap between two seemingly irreconcilable positions (French and British). Nor was Wilson's pragmatic approach to league building completely out of step with the international consensus. The general use of the older, more limited term "league" rather than the more ambitious "union," for example, suggested that the aim of most participating states was to take only the first tentative steps on the road to international association rather than jump straight to the construction of a (con)federal union (Kuehl 231).

Still, at times, the feeling was that more could have been achieved if the President and his team had done more to lay the groundwork for the talks about the Covenant. As a result of this lack of preparation on the American side, the draft Covenant as adopted by the League Commission on 13 February 1919 seemed to lean heavily on British ideas outlined in the Phillimore and Smuts plans. It proposed the kind of scheme that had become the standard in the course of the nineteenth century, with an assembly, an executive and a judiciary, as well as a Council and a secretariat.

Like the Court, the Council was originally not planned for by Wilson. It was only included at the last moment after he was persuaded to do so by Smuts. The latter had suggested a traditional Great Power approach by making the Council the preserve of the main Allies: the US, UK, France, Italy and Japan, with Germany to be added at a later stage (Henig 21). Wilson, who had stated publicly that he wanted to provide "some kind of protection" for small nations, had been confronted by the practical consequences of this promise during the opening session of the Commission, when the smaller states fought to increase their representation (29). It was a foretaste of the battle that was to follow about the composition of the Council.

The British position on that issue was stated by Cecil, who claimed that the Council could only be effective if it was controlled by the Great Powers: "Our purpose (...) is to make the League a success, and that demands the support of the Great Powers. Two representatives of the lesser powers should suffice" (Henig 31). The Belgian Foreign Secretary Paul Hymans countered by observing that what was proposed was "a revival of the Holy Alliance of unhallowed memory" (31). With French and Italian support, the small powers' argument won out: their number on the Council would be increased from two to four. Even with that, the Great Powers still had a special status on the Council. They had permanent seats, whereas the seats of the Smaller Powers would be held on a rotating basis.

Significantly, the final draft of the Covenant included a permanent secretariat. thereby tackling one of the perceived shortcomings of the 1899 and 1907 The Hague Peace Conferences. This Secretariat was also to have a permanent home in Geneva. Switzerland was already home to a number of international organisations, including the International Telecommunication Union, the Universal Postal Union, and the Intergovernmental Organization for International Carriage by Rail. These organisations were now placed under the direction of the League of Nations. The League was also entrusted with the setting of international labour standards, and the general supervision of the trade in arms and ammunition, and of the execution of agreements to tackle anti-trafficking measures for the traffic in women, children, and "opium and other dangerous drugs" (Covenant, Art. 23).

—

The inclusion of clauses on arbitration, judicial settlement and conciliation met with surprisingly little opposition. Twelve years earlier delegates had achieved no progress on these issues at the second Peace Conference in The Hague. This time, however, the main disagreement was not about their inclusion, but about their nature. Wilson's original proposal had suggested making arbitration for all non-justiciable disputes obligatory, but that was scrapped at the British delegation's insistence. In its place came a clause which gave each member of the League the power to decide in their own case whether arbitration was a relevant option ("... whenever any dispute shall arise between them which they recognise to be suitable for submission to arbitration" (Covenant, Art. 13, clause 1)).

Similarly in Article 14, which provided for the establishment of a Permanent Court of International Justice, the only cases it could hear were "dispute[s] of an international character which the parties thereto submit to it" (Covenant). In other words: it could only rule in cases where both parties had decided in advance to accept its jurisdiction, and then only if they themselves had brought the case. In cases referred by the Council or the Assembly all it could do was publish an "advisory opinion." The practical consequence of all this watering down was that war had merely been made less likely, not banned altogether. The Covenant, it was clear, was not a Peace Plan.

If anything, this made the discussion about the issues covered by Articles 10 and 11, and by extension Article 16 on the subject of sanctions, more important. It was in these articles that the League's ability to prevent future wars was to be determined. Here the French delegation made its stance in favour of military powers for the League. Bourgeois warned that "[w]ithout military backing in some force, and always ready to act, our League and our Covenant will be filed away, not as a solemn treaty, but simply as a rather ornate piece of literature" (Henig 32). Throughout the negotiations, he would continue to argue for their inclusion, against equally committed British opposition.

Wilson's advisers aimed for a compromise between the two positions by bringing the English language into play. A casual reading of clause 10 suggested that the League was committing itself to a defence of the "territorial integrity" and "political independence" of its members in cases of "external aggression" (Covenant). The second part of the clause, however, contained what could be read as an important qualification: "In case of any such aggression (...) the Council shall advise upon the means by which this obligation shall be fulfilled" (Covenant). Where the French were free to read Article 10 as containing a mutual defence principle, the British could interpret it as a conditional mechanism. As a piece of draughtsmanship it was probably not quite in the same class as Monroe's NorthWest Ordinance or Jesse Thomas' 1820 Missouri Compromise, but it was sufficiently flexible to bridge the gap between the two sides.

The nature of the League

During the Third Plenary Session of the Peace Conference, on 14 February 1919, President Wilson had presented the draft text of the Covenant with the claim that "a living thing is born." But what kind of thing was it? The question would stir the imagination of constitutional and international legal scholars.

Either for their own strategic purposes or because they genuinely believed it, American opponents of the League argued that it was a federal union in the American sense. In their eyes, the fact that all three of Montesquieu's powers and the states seemed present in the League's structure, and that through the mandate territories it also had its own claim to sovereignty, meant that it met all the formal criteria for it.

The German international legal scholars Walter Schücking and Hans Wehberg used Jellinek's taxonomy of unions to analyse and categorise the League. Their conclusion: "All of Jellinek's list of characteristics of a *Staatenbund* can be found in the League of Nations" (Schücking and Wehberg 103; my translation throughout). One important characteristic was its permanent nature. According to Schücking and Wehberg, the fact that the Covenant offered the possibility of an exit by an individual member state presupposed the continuation of the League by its other members. Another characteristic was its dual objective, which was typical for a confederation: the maintenance of internal peace and external security. What made the League more than an alliance was its additional economic and social objectives. In spite of this, it was not a *Bundesstaat*, since "it lacks a necessary criterion of statehood, the 'original power to govern'" (105). The fact that the member states remained fully sovereign was, according to them, also reflected in the fact that "as a rule any binding decisions can only be adopted by unanimity" (104). Based on these findings, they put the League in the same category as the Dutch United Provinces, the American Confederal United States of 1776–1787, the Swiss Confederation, the German Confederation of the Rhine and the German Bund of 1815–1866 (105).

To the other French member of the committee that had negotiated the League's structure, Ferdinand Larnaude (1853–1942), this kind of categorisation made no sense. It was clear to him that the League was "not a society of states similar to a federal state, nor a confederation of states, nor a Union [a personal union like the former Austrian Empire], nor any other kind of non-unitary state" (Larnaude 5; my translation throughout). It was in fact "a formation of a completely new type, before all else, or perhaps one should say exclusively, contractual in nature, in which the states assume certain obligations, though these obligations do leave their sovereignty fully intact" (Larnaude 5). The League was, in his eyes, a political rather than a legal entity: "The League of Nations is nothing but a new form of international political life. The law is of course not entirely absent. But (...) [t]he law is rigid, here it is flexibility which rules" (8).

Larnaude's interpretation of the League's character seemed closest to that of President Wilson himself. The latter had commented on the question of the nature of the League during a discussion about an amendment tabled by Larnaude's colleague Leon Bourgeois. The French delegation had suggested giving Article 8, which dealt with the issue of decommissioning, teeth by giving the League a right of inspection and control of national arms stockpiles. He answered that to him this did not seem a good idea: "If we had made a union of states with a common legislature, we could have envisaged such a mechanism; but our constant guiding principle has been to dismiss the concept of a Super-State, and in those conditions it seems difficult to perform inspections inside the member countries" (Miller 320).

This academic discussion showed two things. The first was that the participants were far from united on the constitutional character of the League. The other was that though by the mid 1920s there seemed to be an emerging consensus about the need to make a categorical distinction between confederation and federation, there was still a lot of uncertainty about the practical application of these concepts.

—

The confusion also extended to the structure and functions of the League. As the Austrian legal scholar Hans Kelsen (1881–1973) pointed out, the fact that Montesquieu's powers seemed to be included in the League's structure did not mean that they actually served the functions the French philosopher had attributed to them. The Assembly, for one, was not a proper legislature. Kelsen was also critical of the fact that not the Court but the Council had been placed in charge of decisions about sanctions. He warned that this would politicise these decisions, making their imposition less likely and their enforcement more complicated (Rub 278–79; my translation).

During the Paris negotiations, delegates had rejected the suggestion by Smuts to create a second, representative assembly. In his overview of the negotiations, Wilson's legal adviser David Hunter Miller would dismiss the term "League of Peoples" as "a meaningless form of words" (Miller 272). Smuts had intended it to serve as a way of establishing a direct link between the League and the peoples of the member countries. This rejection would have an important consequence. It meant the League would remain an association of *governments*, not of nations in the way that word had been used in the nineteenth century by writers like Mazzini, as representing the European peoples rather than their rulers (274–275).

The Dutch international legal scholar Cornelis van Vollenhoven pointed out the consequences of this absence of the people(s) from the Covenant:

> [T]he members of all judicial and executive councils of a league should be disengaged from national desires to as great an extent as are the members of the Supreme Court of the United States from the interests of the individual states. The Paris draft of the League of Nations provides for quite the contrary. Its Executive Council is a combination of egoistic power, a combination of representatives of nations who will be instructed by, removable by and dependent upon their respective governments, and who will bring the clashing jealousies of their governments into this council. (Vollenhoven 205)

What he feared most was a repeat of the European Concert system. For smaller states, the arbitrary use of power by the larger states had turned it into "an international despotism" (Vollenhove 204). The solution, he argued, was the creation of a system characterised by "impartiality and disinterestedness" (205). Impartiality "needed first of all in the organisation of judicial and executive international boards. All of these should be entirely free from national and egotistic influences" (205). The Assembly and Council should not be staffed by "representatives of special nations" but by "'international minded' individuals, chosen from the citizens of any country (large or small) with a view to their personal abilities and trustworthiness in the eyes of all the nations together" (205).

—

In his reflection on the nature of the League, the German constitutional scholar Carl Schmitt (1888–1985) cast doubt on the desirability of the idea of an impartial, disinterested Council: "A League of Nations can only exists if at least one Great Power has a political interest in it, or if the smaller or medium-sized powers that constitute its membership through it become a significant political force" (Schmitt 6–7; my translation throughout). In other words: "It is doubtful if the League would continue to exist if the Great Powers no longer saw a political advantage in it" (6).

The Philadelphia Convention's solution to this dilemma had, of course, been to create a union that did both. Through the Court and the Executive, it created institutions that represented the interests of the whole union rather than those of the individual states. The other kind of representation, based on states' interests, was reserved for the legislative powers assembled in Congress, where the larger states also received a larger number of delegates (in the House of Representatives, that is). Schmitt did not rule out that this is where the League could end up. At the end of his inquiry into its nature, he concluded that "up to now the question of the League's nature has intentionally been left open, its federal character left undefined" (Schmitt 82).

Schmitt recognised that one plausible interpretation of the League saw it as nothing more than a "permanent international office" that undertook "interesting and valuable administrative activities" (Schmitt 12). Another interpretation however was to see the League as definitely capable of meaningful action. In fact, "nobody would deny that (…) since 1920 [it] has achieved successes in a number of different areas" (6). The problem with the League was that it was not clear which way the organisation was going to develop over time.

There were two scenarios here. One was that the two different characters of the League would take on an institutionalised character: "That way it would have two faces, one facing West and the other East. To the Western powers it could present itself as an obedient, modest organisation which acted only carefully and in a non-binding way, while showing weak and disarmed states its powerful face" (Schmitt 81). The other was that "the loose structure of international relations" could turn overnight into "a tightly organised system" with "all the consequences of membership of a real federation" (82). In either case League membership could end up costing Germany dearly. Unless it was guaranteed an "equal status" in decision-making (meaning equal to the other Great Powers), membership would effectively mean "the immortalisation of its defeat," making inevitable the "horrendous and unprecedented surrender of its arms" (82).

The same systemic ambiguity that Schmitt defined as a potential threat was described by the French international legal scholar Georges Scelle (1878–1961) as essential for the League's long-term survival. In his *Le Pacte des Nations Et Sa Liaison Avec le Traité de Paix* ("The Covenant between Nations and its Relation with the Peace Treaty," 1919) he posited that the best way to define the League was a "negative solution," by observing that it was "neither a universal monarchy, nor a federation, nor an administrative board" (Scelle 148; my translation throughout).

A brief excursion into the history of the Holy Alliance had taught him that the chief cause of its failure was a lack of flexibility in the application of its solutions: "[It] had looked for perfection and peace in the immutability of social conditions, and of the map it had given Europe" (Scelle 148). If the League was to avoid making the same mistake, it needed to create "an organism that is flexible enough to adapt to political change" (148). Interestingly, he suggested that the demand for flexibility might even apply to "the principles for whose triumph it was founded" (148). Without this kind of fundamental flexibility there was "no hope of surviving long, or of remaining a work of peace" (148).

The Weimar moment

The formation of the League of Nations was not the only federal moment in the immediate post-war period, or even the most significant. In terms of impact on European history, the formation of the federal Weimar Republic was undoubtedly more important. The old constitution, which had created the institutional framework for a monarchical federal union, became instantly worthless when the German princes collectively abdicated in the final days of the war. With the proclamation of the republic that replaced the old empire, the question arose what a republican constitution should look like. A special committee was tasked with making recommendations.

One prominent member of this committee was the sociologist and political economist Max Weber (1864–1920). In *Parliament and Government in Germany under a New Political Order* (1918) he had dissected the old constitution in a chapter titled "Federalism and the introduction of parliamentary government." According to Weber, the most important problem with the Bismarckian constitution was the complete dominance of Prussia, "a special position which is entirely divergent, privileged and exceptional in relation to *all* other parliaments and authorities of individual states" (Weber 234). Not only could no change of legislation in the field of defence, commerce, and trade policy be introduced without Prussia's support, it even had a special negative power: "Prussia has the right to veto (...) even if *all* other governments in the Federation *and* the entire Reichstag decide unanimously in favour of the change" (235).

The lack of a reciprocal check of the Reich on affairs in Prussia was not in itself a problem: "Prussia's internal questions are of course the concern of this state alone, and there cannot be any question that (...) other states of the federation should interfere in internal Prussian affairs" (Weber 257). There was one important exception to this rule however: Prussia's own constitutional order was very much a concern of the Reich. In a strong Kantian echo, he argued that:

> [i]n every federal state in the world the principle holds true that certain, quite fundamental structural foundations must exist in each of the member states for the sake of the federation. For that reason, these foundations are regarded as a federal matter, notwithstanding the very extensive autonomy and division of competences between federation and individual state.
> (Weber 257)

Democratisation of Prussia's constitution would therefore have to take place in close coordination with the other states and the federal centre. After all, for the future functioning of the Reich, it mattered very much what kind of suffrage system the Prussians adopted: ""If equal suffrage is established – in reality and not just in appearance – the composition of the Reichstag and of the Prussian Diet will grow increasingly similar in future, whatever else happens" (259).

Of the other flaws, the lack of effective parliamentary oversight was the most important. The biggest obstacle here was "the concept, undefined in its scope, of the Kaiser's 'power of command', (...) a prerogative which parliament may not violate and behind which everything can be hidden that is to be withheld from parliamentary scrutiny" (Weber 243). This lack of executive accountability at the federal level was mirrored by a similar absence of parliamentary oversight at the state level, where an effective appeal to "princely prerogative" had allowed local executives to operate virtually unchecked (245).

Even where it did get a say, parliament was generally not able effectively to check the executive. Votes in the Bundesrat, the second chamber of the Reich's parliament which gathered representatives of national government ministries and the several state governments within it, were hampered not just by Prussian veto power but also by strict voting instructions from the delegates' home administrations. The lack of incentive for serious debate meant that, as Weber put it, it "led a comfortable and harmonious 'still life' on the whole" (246). In the exceptional cases where the Bundesrat did actually take a significant position on a political issue, Bismarck just ignored it: "[H]e simply passed over resolutions of the Bundesrat in silence and proceeded with the agenda, without anyone from the Bundesrat daring to appeal to the constitution of the Reich" (Weber 247).

—

Weber made the case for reform by arguing for a relaxation of the strict separation of powers which had prevented the legislative power from acting as a check on the executive. By allowing the main parties' political leaders in the Reichstag to assume some form of responsibility for the Reich's policies in the Bundesrat, he aimed to improve democratic accountability within the system by "placing the burden of responsibility on their *party* in the Reichstag" (Weber 248).

By strengthening parliament's position, he also hoped to adjust the federal balance within the system – the trade-off between "freedom *from* the Reich" and "influence *in* the Reich" (Weber 250). This trade-off would work just as well under a revised system in which party leaders had a greater say because of the essential quality all federal systems had in common: "[T]he course of politics in the Reich will still rest on compromise" (258). It was *compromise* "between Reich interests and those of individual states" (256) that had kept a flawed system from collapsing so far. And it was a similar ability to compromise, "to strike a balance between hegemonial power [of Prussia] and the Reichstag" that would guarantee its continued existence in future[17] (258).

Strengthening the position of parliament would serve not just a constitutional purpose but also a broader political one. Weber's embrace of democratisation would extend to the newly created position of president of the Reich. In an essay titled "The President of the Reich," written in February 1919 when the process of constitutional revision was still ongoing, he explained that without a directly elected presidency, the fundamental weakness of the old constitution would inevitably resurface: "A President of the Reich who had not been elected by the whole people would (...) play a pitiful role *vis-à-vis* the Prussian head of state, so that the predominance of Prussia in Berlin, and thus in the Reich, would again emerge in a highly dangerous, which is to say particularist form" (Weber 308).

In what was perhaps his most famous essay, *Politik als Beruf* ("The Profession and Vocation of Politics," based on a lecture given in Munich in

17   Weber's argument, that federal union requires a willingness to compromise, of course was strikingly similar to that made by Leibniz two centuries earlier. At no point in his work, however, did Weber refer to Leibniz's writings.

January 1919), Weber explained that the greatest flaw of the old constitution wasn't any one of its clauses but the effect of their sum total. The "impotence of our parliaments" (note the plural, both federal ànd state) meant that "no one with leadership qualities went into parliament for any length of time" (Weber 348). Political parties became *"gesinnungspolitische"* organisations (348), focused on principles rather than outcomes. The country was run by the civil service, making political debate a sideshow at best, "unspeakably boring" at worst (348).

Weber's ultimate vision of a more effective constitution was inspired by Machiavelli. It relied less on structures than on the people operating within it and the culture that underpinned it. Referring to the Florentine thinker throughout the closing section of his essay, he sketched a political system peopled by a different kind of politician, not the testifying ones of the old constitution (whom he dismissed as "windbags") but ones fully aware of the inherently problematic, violent nature of politics. This type of politician would focus not so much on intentions as on the effects of their actions: "Machiavelli had such situations in mind when, in a beautiful passage in his Florentine histories (…) he has one of his heroes praise those citizens who placed the greatness of their native city above the salvation of their soul" (Weber 366).

In the end, though, he stressed that a *Verantwortungsethik* alone was not enough. It could potentially leave the politician "inwardly dead" if it wasn't combined with a greater purpose. The ideal politician combined a goal greater than themselves with a willingness to be judged on the outcome of their actions, a new kind of *virtù*: "[O]nly in combination do they [the ethics of conviction and the ethics of responsibility] produce the true human being who is *capable* of having a 'vocation in politics'" (Weber 368).

—

The committee tasked with discussing the fundamental principles of the new constitution for the Weimar republic was chaired by the constitutional scholar Hugo Preuss (1860–1925). Preuss, a pupil of Otto von Gierke, had gained a reputation for being one of the most astute critics of the old Reich constitution. Given that his politics also lined up with those of the revolutionary regime, the leader of the provisional government (and later first president of the republic) Friedrich Ebert had no hesitation in selecting him for the job of drafting the new constitution.

In his scholarly work, Preuss had identified a number of weaknesses of German federal theory. The most significant flaw in his view concerned

its use of the concept of sovereignty. Unlike his colleagues in the constitutional–legal community, who had looked for it either in the Reich or in the
states, he thought the idea of sovereignty, a remnant of an older monarchical
period, was "incompatible" with the concept of federalism (Neumann 33). He
solved the problem by moving it outside the realm of politics, stressing that
"the German people in its entirety is the bearer of sovereignty" (Preuss 32).

This idea, in turn, allowed him to develop an entirely new conception of
federalism, based on the idea of *Genossenschaft*'(associations) as developed
by his teacher Gierke. His was a bottom-up conception of federalism, where
each layer of political administration had its own claim to *Selbstverwaltung*
(self-government) (Preuss 48). The upper layer of this organic construction
was not formed by the federal state, but by the international community,
whose legal standards he considered to be binding on the German federal
state (56). This principle would be included in the new constitution in the
form of Article 4: "The generally accepted rules of international law are to
be considered as binding integral parts of the law of the German Reich"
(Weimar Constitution). It logically followed from this that he was more
willing than previous generations of German constitutional scholars to
accept the concept of separation of powers, though not so much horizontally
as vertically – he considered the latter one of the essential characteristics
of federalism (Neumann 34).

—

These ideas formed part of his agenda for the Committee meetings. In
drafting the new constitution, he was also motivated by a desire to resolve
two issues that had plagued the old constitutional order. The first was the
one highlighted by Weber, namely the status of Prussia. Its monarch may be
gone, but how could a democratic federal constitution be made to function
properly if one member state represented more than sixty percent of the
union's total population? Neither a proportional nor an equal representation
formula made much sense in this setting. Preuss therefore argued strongly
in favour of cutting the state up into a number of smaller subsections. In the
end he would not get his way on this. Prussia would enter the new federation
with its territory more or less intact, apart from the border corrections later
confirmed at Versailles. Through Article 61, the Weimar Constitution did
introduce a new stipulation that in the new Reichsrat, "no Land may be
represented by more than two-fifths of the vote" – no longer a majority, but
still a large plurality that made it a factor that was impossible to ignore in
daily political life (Weimar Constitution). The topic of Prussian dominance

would therefore continue to occupy the minds of German constitutional scholars and politicians. The issue was eventually used as a pretext in 1932 by the reactionary Von Papen government to take control of the social democrat governed Prussian state apparatus, in a coup known as the *Preussenschlag*.

The other challenge, as Preuss saw it, was to strengthen the constitution's democratic nature. In his view, the key here was not so much, as Weber claimed, the direct election of the republic's president, as to increase the people's influence in all parts of the constitutional framework. What form that influence would take was less important to him. Though Weber's idea would, in the end, win out, Preuss would have been happy to settle for an indirectly elected president appointed by Parliament. The one option he wanted to avoid was a Swiss style rotating presidency where "each of the larger states would claim a seat in the directorate" (Stirk 513). The main change he wanted to make was to the old *Reichsrat*, whose Prussian dominance and mix of state and national government representatives he had dismissed as "fake federalism" (Neumann 147). He proposed a clearer separation of powers in this body by removing the executive representatives. Inspired by the Swiss and American models of double representation, he then suggested making it a house of state representatives (*Staatenhaus*, House of the States), to accompany the lower chamber which was to be elected by the whole German people. Members of the new upper chamber would be nominated by their state parliaments on the basis of proportional representation (Neumann 147).

—

In early February 1919, Preuss presented his draft text to the National Assembly with a reference to the 1849 Paulskirche document, stressing that in spite of the apparent "wonderful repeat of the phenomena," there was a crucial difference between the two assemblies that made success this time round a virtual guarantee: "Then the question was if it was really the task of the national assembly, as carrier of the sovereignty of the people, to create a new reality all on its own. (...) Today there can be no doubt about the remit of this assembly which, resting on democratic foundations, represents the will of the people" (Deutscher Reichstag 12).

In the extensive revision process that took place once he had tabled his first draft, more than a few of his ideas would end up on the cutting room floor, while others were grafted onto it. The final text created a federal structure that seemed more like a decentralised unitary state than a federal one, though as Preuss remarked, "the difference between these two options is greater in theory than in practice" (Preuss 22). The central government was given exclusive control over all of Bodin's old marks of sovereignty, from war and peace to coinage (Weimar Constitution Art. 6). It was also given a range of modern government powers, from regulating citizenship and poor relief to industrial policy and public culture (Art. 7). Significantly, the federal government received powers of direct taxation (Art. 8). This meant that, unlike under previous German federations, the central government was no longer reliant on state funding for the financing of its running costs, which seemed a significant strengthening of its position.

The final text contained a number of innovations, at least in a German context. The newly introduced President and their Chancellor on the one hand, and the lower house of Parliament (the *Reichstag*) on the other, were given substantive checks on each others' powers. The President could disband the *Reichstag* (Weimar Constitution Art. 25), while he also possessed the power of a suspensive veto on any bills adopted by the Reichstag. The suspended bill was then submitted to the people, who could overturn the President's veto in a referendum (Art. 73). The *Reichstag*, for its part, could impeach the President through a motion to suspend which, if supported by two-thirds of members, was then put to the German people for approval (Art. 43). The Chancellor and cabinet ministers required the confidence of the *Reichstag*, and would have to leave if they lost it (Art. 54). Though limited to certain economic matters listed under Article 7, Section 13, the federal government was also given a power Madison had greatly desired as part of the American Constitution: a veto of state legislation (Art. 12). The second chapter delivered on Preuss' promise to carry on where the Paulskirche constitution had left off by presenting a bill of rights, both the classic ones and more recently developed social ones.

The House of the States idea was implemented, though under the old name of *Reichsrat*, and not based on nomination of delegates by the State parliaments. The state governments would instead select delegates to represent them. The *Reichsrat* thereby remained a mix of legislative and executive authority. He was philosophical about this defeat: "When you have been working on German constitutional history for thirty years, you don't have any particular illusions about your first draft of a new German constitution" (Preuss 27).

In spite of the many changes, his contemporaries would refer to Preuss as "The Father of the Constitution." In view of subsequent events, this would prove to be a dubious honour (his reputation would take the better part of a century to recover from it). The failure of the Weimar constitution was to be of great significance for the future of European unification – greater even than that of the League of Nations. Much has been made of its design flaws; some of them will be discussed in chapters to come (specifically Art. 48.2 and 76). Preuss himself had warned that its main weakness was not in any of its articles but in the society it served. He feared that the German revolution had not really settled anything on the political level. The reformist element was currently in control, but, he warned, "the reaction which was not showing its head now would emerge sooner or later." When it did, it would "emphasise any lack of success in any field" to discredit and destabilise the new order (Preuss 16).

The political reception of the League

As we have seen, *coups* are essential in establishing and maintaining successful federal unions. The birth or survival of a union sometimes came down to inspired draughtsmanship that allowed all sides to read their own version of the truth into a founding document or a crucial piece of legislation. The Covenant that established the League of Nations showed what happened if this political conjuring trick failed to work. Instead of producing a solution that satisfied all sides, the vagueness of the language in Article 10 allowed all sides to read their own worst fears into it.

—

After the publication of the first draft of the agreement, Wilson had gone back to Washington, DC to talk to potential supporters and detractors in the Senate. Out of these conversations, and various submissions that were sent to his office in the immediate aftermath of its publication, he distilled a number of topics for amendment. He wanted to find language that made it clear that the Monroe Doctrine would not be affected by American League membership. He also wanted to include a clause that created a right of member countries to exit the League, and provide for a right of refusal when asked to administer a mandate territory.

The proposed exit clause was an intervention in an ongoing debate about the nature of treaties. They were obviously supposed to be binding on their signatories – *pacta sunt servanda*. But were there limits to this binding nature, especially limits in time? At the 1871 London meeting under the Concert system, the participating countries adopted a declaration that basically answered this question in the negative. Or at least: in the negative for individual signatories. They remained bound to it, unless and until all parties agreed jointly to bring the treaty to an end.

The London declaration was greeted with near-universal derision. At the theoretical level, it led to the cultivation of a counter-idea in the form of the principle of *Rebus Sic Stantibus*: the idea that a treaty could no longer remain binding if the circumstances under which it was signed were materially changed. This idea would become increasingly prominent in German political debate, where it would feature in the work of Treitschke and Bernhardi before being elevated to the status of dogma through the work of the international legal scholar Erich Kaufmann (*Das Wesen des Völkerrechts und die Clausula Rebus Sic Stantibus*, 1911).

During the negotiations about the drafting of the Covenant, Wilson (who was a constitutional scholar rather than an international legal scholar) said he was under the impression that a state could denounce any treaty it had signed. His legal adviser, David Hunter Miller, answered that "except under the doctrine of changed circumstances, which was known as the doctrine of *rebus sic stantibus*, my opinion was that a State did not have the right to withdraw from a treaty" (Miller 293). The only possibility in law for the termination of a treaty lay in the treaty itself, if it had been "drawn to continue for a certain period, with a clause permitting termination thereafter" (293).

Miller therefore proposed an amendment which gave any member of the League the right to withdraw from the organisation, "[a]fter the expiration of ten years from the ratification of the Treaty of Peace of which the Covenant forms a part, (...) after one year's notice, provided all its international obligations and all its obligations under this Covenant shall have been fulfilled at the time of its withdrawal" (Miller 342). The Italian Prime Minister Vittorio Orlando pointed out that the inclusion of the ten year reference introduced the possibility of collective withdrawal by all members at the end of that period. The League would then be considered to have been created for ten years only. His suggestion was to scrap the time limit: "If the States are satisfied that it will be enough merely to announce their intention to leave to make an exit from the League possible, it is likely that they won't use the option" (343) What mattered, he concluded, "is not to be free but to believe oneself to be free" (343). In its commentary on the final text, the British Foreign Office agreed with Orlando: "It is believed that the concession of the right of withdrawal will, in fact, remove all likelihood of a wish for it, by freeing States from any sense of restraint, and so tending to their more whole-hearted acceptance of membership" (quoted in Magliveras 29).

—

In a memorandum to Wilson, Secretary of State Robert Lansing suggested that instead of formulating Article 10 as a positive duty to support, it might be better to draft it as a negative duty to refrain from interference. Not only would it make the clause more palatable to participating governments, it would have the added benefit of "remov[ing] the argument of unconstitutionality, of infringement of the Monroe doctrine and Pan-Americanism, and of any abandonment of abstention from foreign alliances" (Miller 30). Perhaps Lansing's suggestion would have done something to cut the ground out from under the Covenant's opponents. But it's far from clear whether any single amendment would have done enough to win the Senate's backing by the two-thirds margin required for treaty ratifications, especially given the determination of its opponents to block ratification by all means possible.

The Covenant's most outspoken opponents presented its potential ratification as an existential threat to the United States. One such critic was the Republican senator for New Mexico, Albert Fall. Fall, who would later, as Secretary for the Interior under president Harding, be convicted for bribery in the Teapot Dome scandal, presented the argument against the League as a kind of moral crusade. He warned that joining the League would "[destroy] the government of our fathers" and thereby "retard more than a thousand years that reign of Christ which we all hope will eventually bring the people of the earth together" (Fleming 302).

Fall's colleague from South Dakota, Senator Thomas Sterling, observed that though the White House had indeed secured adoption of an amendment that allowed for withdrawal from the League, the stipulation that withdrawal could only take place "provided that all its international obligations and all its obligations under this Covenant shall have been fulfilled" (Covenant Art. 1, clause 3) meant that the US would be expected to fulfil in full "any covenants that we have entered into in the long years since we became a sovereign nation (...) before we can withdraw from this supreme covenant – this lord over all" (Fleming, 303). The suggestion was that League membership was like a prison from which it would be impossible to escape once entered.

An essential part of the Republican Senate majority's campaign against the Covenant was to paint the League as a full-fledged global federal union that would inevitably demand the obedience of the American federal Union. The most devastating version of this argument was presented by the Senate Majority Leader, Henry Cabot Lodge (1850–1924). It came in a speech at the end of February 1919, when the Senate was offered the chance to discuss the first draft that had just been produced in Paris. By consistently referring to the Covenant as a constitution, he made sure his audience understood what the stakes were. Its constitutional nature meant that, once signed and ratified by the United States, the country would be absolutely bound to it: "[I]t must carry out the provisions of that instrument to the last jot and tittle, and observe it absolutely both in letter and in spirit" (Cabot Lodge,).[18]

The binding nature of the Covenant obviously made its content all the more potentially dangerous. Cabot Lodge warned that under its terms the Monroe doctrine, "our cherished guide and guard for nearly a century, (…) that doctrine (…) that American questions shall be settled by Americans alone," would disappear. Joining the League, he suggested, would mean "reject[ing] the policies of Washington and Monroe, which have been in our foreign relations the Palladium of the Republic." These "cardinal principles of American government" were "as vital as on the day when Washington addressed the people of the United States for the last time." To treat them as "suddenly valueless" and as "injurious obstacles to be cast out upon the dust heaps of history" would, he suggested, be a grave mistake.

Equally bad, he warned, would be the effect on US immigration policy. Once signed, the Covenant would transfer control of the country's borders to other countries. "Are we ready," he asked rhetorically (and with more than a hint of racism), "to leave to other nations to determine whether we shall admit to the United States a flood of Japanese, Chinese and Hindu labour?" Ratifying the Covenant would mean "to give up in part our sovereignty and our independence, (…) to substitute (…) an American state for pure Americanism."

Cabot Lodge reserved his fiercest criticism for Article 10. Through it, he claimed, the United States would "ultimately guarantee the independence and the boundaries (…) of every nation on earth." He warned that it was "a very grave, a very perilous promise to make," because the only way it could be delivered on was "the way of force." This meant that the United States would be forced to commit "the sons, brothers and husbands of the people of America" to the defence of foreign nations. Worse: to commit them not at the request of the US government, but "forced into war by other nations against her own will." Never mind the fact that Congress had the sole right to declare war and peace on behalf of the United States – "that is a detail," he declared, "which we may decide later." His more fundamental objection was that the signing of the Covenant meant that in order to protect the world's peace, the United States would have to make "preparations for war."

It would probably have been impossible to win over such critics with mere amendments. But Wilson was also not inclined to make further compromises over a clause that in his view already contained the kind of language his opponents were asking for, especially because he was convinced that Article 10 was

---

18   All subsequent quotes in this section come from this source unless otherwise indicated.

the only article that the French considered non-negotiable (Miller 289). In the end, defeat came in two stages. First the Covenant ended up seven votes short during the final vote about its ratification. Then the idea of the League was convincingly defeated at the ballot box during the presidential elections of 1920. It meant that the League would be launched without American involvement.

—

Meanwhile in Germany, the initial response to the proposed League was overwhelmingly positive. The German government had concluded that membership would solve two problems at once: it would restore German standing as a Great Power, and would send a message to the German people that its government was able to re-establish the country's connection to the world community, and thereby also to the world markets on which it relied for its food supplies and its exports (Kimmich 12–13). To ensure the German population's enthusiasm for League membership did not go unnoticed in Paris, the government sponsored a German Society for the League of Nations. At its peak, it had around ten million members, including the leaders of all the main parties, as well as prominent academics, employers, and trade union leaders (15).

In the spring of 1919, the German government also commissioned the international legal scholar Walter Schücking to produce a German proposal for a League as a contribution to the discussion in Paris. Schücking, a future member of the Permanent Court of International Justice, suggested a structure whereby not only the arbitration of conflicts themselves would be made compulsory, but also the adherence to the two mediating bodies' decisions. A sliding scale of sanctions could even see the League use military measures to enforce its decisions (Kimmich 20). His calculation was that by outfederalising the League's negotiators, Germany could demonstrate its commitment to the League as an ideal, and thereby its suitability as a member (20).

It would all be to no avail. In June 1919, the Great Powers decided not to allow Germany to join the League at the start. In fact, they didn't even offer a clear path to membership in the near future. All they did was formulate a number of rather strict demands to be met before membership could be contemplated: the country must disarm and accept the territorial provisions of the Versailles treaty in full. Irrespective of membership it was also banned from seeking to form a union with Austria (referred to in both countries as the *Anschluss*; Article 61 of the Weimar constitution referred to the idea as a likely scenario) unless it was given explicit and unanimous permission by the League's Council.

The French were most outspoken in their opposition to the idea of German membership. It would rob them of the opportunity to turn the League into a tool for the enforcement of the various restorative or retributive provisions in the Versailles Treaty. Wilson, for his part, simply did not believe that Germany had made a lasting transition to parliamentary democracy yet, though this lack of faith also conveniently gave him the opportunity to offer the French some compensation for not getting their way on the military sanctions issue.

With the possibility of membership pushed into the distant future, German attitudes to the League turned one hundred and eighty degrees. The League became just another part of the detested Versailles Treaty. When it first received the terms, the German cabinet declared a week of national mourning, dismissing them as "unbearable" and "unrealisable." It would eventually resign rather than ratify the treaty (Mayer 765).

Whether this German response was entirely reasonable was an open question. The leftwing opposition Independents pointed out that in terms of population and territory, the losses amounted to little of significance, especially since the industrial base in the Ruhr, which also had the most important coal reserves, remained firmly in German hands. The repayment schedule was harsh but not significantly harsher than the ones the French had accepted without complaint in 1871, while the terms would likely be subject to revision in due course (Mayer 766). Perhaps the fierceness of the German rejection of Versailles had more to do with its loss of status than with the actual justice of the terms.[19]

Reasonable or not, German refusal to abide by the terms was a political fact that would have a significant impact on developments in the next decade and beyond, especially because the French would doggedly stick to the letter of the Versailles treaty.

—

The decision to exclude Germany from membership was not without its critics. Most outspoken was neighbouring Switzerland. In a memorandum about the first draft of the Covenant, it warned about the potential consequences: "Switzerland considers the exclusion of any States, especially of those depending by their geographic position and the needs of their economic life on their intercourse with members of the League, as apt to provoke counter-alliances and thereby to endanger peace" (Miller 303).

19   Christoph Kimmich's explanation seems a plausible one: "In attacking Versailles, the Germans vented deeper passions. For behind the frustration over Versailles lay an unwillingness to accept the collapse of the extravagant expectations which Germany's prewar stature had seemed to warrant" (Kimmich 28).

This danger, of a counter-League that would institutionalise rather than solve the problem of war, had been pointed out two years earlier by the Norwegian economist Thorstein Veblen in a pamphlet titled *An Inquiry into the Nature of Peace and the Terms of its Perpetuation*:

> A Pacific League not including [Germany and Russia], or not extending its jurisdiction and surveillance to them and their conduct, would come to the same thing as a coalition of nations in two hostile groups, (...) both groups bidding for the favour of those minor Powers whose traditions and current aspirations run to national (dynastic) aggrandisement by way of political intrigue.
> (Veblen 149)

In practice, a coalition between Germany and Russia was unlikely to become a full alternative to the League. The 1922 Rapallo treaty between the two states seemed motivated more by a desire to upset Western strategy than to form an actual alliance. For Soviet Russia, its significance was its prevention of a European anti-Soviet coalition. For Germany, it banished the spectre of "encirclement." What it mainly showed was that the two remaining Great Powers in Central and Eastern Europe were entirely capable of agreeing to disagree for mutual benefit, something that would come back to hurt the region – and the world at large – in 1939 (Taylor 76–77).

Rapallo did confirm the fears of those in the West who had suggested that the decision to exclude Germany from League membership would leave them with no option but to form a counter-league with Soviet Russia. It was perhaps not entirely coincidental that shortly after the news of its signing was broadcast to the world, the British Prime Minister Lloyd George first started hinting at the possibility of German membership.[20]

———

In the end, German membership came only once France had fully exhausted the option of military containment.[21] The path to membership would present

---

20   The Rapallo Treaty was signed in April 1922. Two months later, Lloyd George answered what clearly seemed to be a planted question by Robert Cecil that "we would support a proposal to admit Germany to the League of Nations" (Hansard, House of Commons, 26 June 1922).

21   Germany's demand for permanent Council membership caused the first serious membership crisis in the League's existence. When its own demand for a permanent Council seat was turned down, Brazil announced in June 1926 that it would not just relinquish its non-permanent seat but also leave the League (Magliveras 50). In total, sixteen states would use the exit clause to

itself in the form of the treaty of Locarno (1925), which not only cleared the way for German entry into the League but also created a setting for European cooperation within the framework of the League.

The decision by the US Senate not to ratify the Covenant, and the collapse of its hoped-for military alliance with the United States, had caused the French government to seek an alliance with the British government instead. This new objective was to prove as elusive as the old one. The British Foreign Secretary Arthur Balfour at one point dismissed the French "obsession with security" as "intolerably foolish" (Jacobson 15). This statement of exasperation masked a deliberate British policy of non-commitment as far as continental military affairs were concerned. The one thing the British government wanted to avoid at all cost was to be dragged into another European war. It feared that the French would abuse a new alliance to launch a war of conquest across the Rhine.

German failure to repay its war debts would indeed lead the French government to occupy the Ruhr area – first partly (1921), later completely (1923). This dramatic step, initiated by the man who would dominate French foreign politics in the 1920s, the eleven times Prime Minister Aristide Briand (1862–1932), served not only as a way of crippling any potential German war effort, but also as a convenient means of feeding the French steel industry with German coal.

The cost of maintaining an occupying force in the Rhineland and the Ruhr was in no way compensated by German reparations even before the US government imposed a significant reduction of these reparations on its European counterparts through the Dawes Plan (1924). The economic fallout from this decision, combined with strategic concerns about a potential German rapprochement with London, caused a French rethink. Again, Briand was the moving force behind the switch, this time arguing for reconciliation with Germany.

The opportunity for a change in approach had presented itself in the form of a proposal for a tripartite non-aggression treaty by the German government under Gustav Stresemann (1878–1929). It was a case of the right proposal at the right time. The new Conservative British government was looking for an excuse not to support the much more ambitious Geneva Protocol presented by the Czechoslovak Foreign Secretary Edvard Beneš, which proposed the introduction of binding arbitration by the Permanent Court of International Justice for all disputes involving League of Nations member states anywhere

cancel their League membership, including Axis members Germany, Italy, Japan, Hungary, and Romania (29).

in the world. A more modest regional pact between the British, French, Belgian and German government clearly fit the bill (Jacobson 14),

For the Germans, Locarno solved a number of problems at once. It opened the way for a discussion about the evacuation of occupied German territory in the Western part of the country, restoring German sovereignty over German territory (Jacobson 9). It also reduced the threat to its Western flank, by limiting the risk of Britain and France uniting in an alliance against it.

Locarno would help to settle affairs in Western Europe, at least for a while. It also led to some interesting diplomatic initiatives, the most consequential of which was the International Steel Cartel founded by France and Germany in September 1926, together with Belgium, Luxemburg and the Saar region. The Cartel, which chiefly consisted of a system of export quotas, was greeted by supporters of European federalisation as "a completely new political and economic alignment in Europe" (Tower). It would later be quoted by Jean Monnet as a source of inspiration for his plan to form a European Coal and Steel Community.

Things were rather different in Eastern Europe. By making any League intervention in Eastern border conflicts conditional upon Council agreement, a Council of which Germany would soon become a permanent member (1926), it effectively gave the German government a free hand in its relations with countries there; especially because France would no longer be able to march through Germany in support of its Eastern allies Poland and Czechoslovakia (Jacobson 41). Germany itself had signed arbitration treaties with both countries, but it refused to give security guarantees to them, or to recognise the new borders. It even refused to rule out the use of force to correct them (29). The Eastern Question was therefore set up to pose a threat to Europe's hard-won peace.

Bibliography

Abbenhuis, Maartje, Christopher Barber, Annelise Higgins, editors. *War, Peace and International Order? The Legacies of the Hague Conferences of 1898 and 1907.* Routledge, 2017.

Bassett, John Spencer. *The Lost Fruits of Waterloo.* Macmillan, 1918.

Bernhardi, Friedrich von. *Germany and the Next War.* 1911. Createspace Independent Publishing Platform, 2015.

Bethmann Hollweg, Theobald von. "September Memorandum." 9 September 1914. https://ghdi.ghi-dc.org/sub_document.cfm?document_id=980. Accessed 6 March 2024.

Bourgeois, Leon. *Pour la Société des Nations.* Hachette Livre BnF, 2013.

Brugmans, Henri. *Panorama de la Pensée Fédéraliste*. La Colombe, 1956.

Cabot Lodge, Henry. "Senate Speech Opposing the League of Nations." 28 February 1919, Floor of the US Senate. https://web.mit.edu/21h.102/www/Lodge,%20Opposition%20to%20the%20League%20of%20Nations.html. Accessed 6 March 2024.

Casano, The Prince of. "Address at the opening of the conference on European federation." *The Advocate of Peace*, vol. 71, no. 10, Nov. 1909, pp. 229–232.

Clark, Christopher. *The Sleepwalkers: How Europe Went to War in 1914*. Penguin Books, 2012.

Cooper, Sandi. *Patriotic Pacifism: Waging War on War, 1815–1914*. Oxford University Press, 1991.

Copeland, Edwin Bingham. *The Sole Condition of Permanent Peace*. 1919. Palala Press, 2016.

Covenant of the League of Nations. 28 June 1919. https://www.ungeneva.org/en/about/league-of-nations/covenant. Accessed 6 March 2024.

Darby, William Evans. *International Arbitration. International Tribunals: A Collection of the Various Schemes Which Have Been Propounded; and of Instances in the Nineteenth Century*. 1904. Legare Street Press, 2023.

Djokić, Dejan. *Yugoslavism, Histories of a Failed Idea, 1918–1992*. University of Wisconsin Press, 2003.

Deutsche Reichstag. *Reichsprotokolle*. 8 February 1919.

Fischer, Fritz. *Germany's Aims in the First World War*. W. W. Norton, 1968.

Frank Fleming, Denna. *The United States and the League of Nations, 1918–1920*. G. Putnam, 1932.

Geiss, Imanuel. *Der Polnische Grenzstreifen 1914–1918: Ein Beitrag zur deutschen Kriegszielpolitik im Ersten Weltkrieg*. Matthiesen, 1960.

Gray, Colin and Geoffrey Sloan, editors. *Geopolitics: Geography and Strategy*. Frank Cass, 1999.

Hansard, House of Commons debate, June 26, 1922, cc 1638-39

Hayward, J. E. S. "The official social philosophy of the French Third Republic: Léon Bourgeois and solidarism." *International Review of Social History*, vol. 6, no. 1. 1961, pp. 19–48.

Henig, Ruth. *The Peace That Never Was: A History of the League of Nations*. University of Chicago Press, 2010.

Holt, Hamilton. "The League to Enforce Peace." *Proceedings of the Academy of Political Science in the City of New York*, vol. 7, no. 2, July 1917, pp. 65–69.

Jacobson, Jon. *Locarno Diplomacy: Germany and the West, 1925–1929*. 1972. Princeton University Press, 2016.

James, William. "Remarks at the Peace Banquet." *The Atlantic*, December 1904, pp. 845–847.

Kimmich, Christoph M, *Germany and the League of Nations*. 1976. University of Chicago Press, 1995.

Kjellén, Rudolf. *Der Staat als Lebensform*. 1917. Leopold Classic Library, 2015.

Kuehl, Warren F.. *Seeking World Order: The United States and International Organization to 1920*. Vanderbilt University Press, 1969

Lampe, John R, *Yugoslavia as History: Twice There Was a Country*, Cambridge University Press, 1996:

Larnaude, Ferdinand. *La Societé des Nations*. Imprimerie Nationale, 1920.

Magliveras, Konstantin D, "The Withdrawal From the League of Nations Revisited." *Dickinson Journal of International Law*, vol. 10, no. 1, Jan. 1991, pp. 25–71.

Mahan, Alfred Thayer. *Works*. The Perfect Library, 2013.

Mayer, Arno J, *Politics and Diplomacy of Peacemaking: Containment and Counter-revolution at Versailles, 1918–1919*. Alfred A. Knopf, 1967.

Meulen, Jacob ter. *Der Gedanke der Internationalen Organisation in seiner Entwicklung*, vol. I, Springer, 1929.

Miller, David Hunter. *The Drafting of the Covenant, with an introduction by Nicholas Murray Butler*, G. P. Putnam's Sons, vol. 1, 1928.

Naumann, Friedrich. *Central Europe.Translated by Christabel M. Meredith*, P. S. King and Son, 1916.

Neumann, Almut. *Preussen zwischen Hegemonie und "Preussenschlag": Beiträge zur Rechtsgeschichte des 20. Jahrhundert*. Mohr Siebeck, 2019.

Phillimore, Walter. *Schemes for Maintaining General Peace*. H. M. Stationery Office, 1920.

Phillips, Walter Alison. *The Confederation of Europe, A Study of the European Alliance, 1813–1823*. 1914. Kessinger Publishing, 2013.

Preuss, Hugo. *Das Verfassungswerk von Weimar*. Mohr Siebeck, 2015.

Rathenau, Walther. *Gesammelte Schriften*, vol. I, Fischer Verlag, 1918.

Ratzel, Friedrich. *Politische Geographie*. 1897. Hansebooks, 2016.

Ratzel, Friedrich, 'Lebensraum: A Biographical Study, translated into English by Tul'si (Tuesday) Bhambry', *Journal of Historical Geography*, Elsevier, vol. 61, July 2018 (1901), pp. 59-80

Roosevelt, Theodore. Fifth Annual Message to Congress. 5 December 1905. https://www.presidency.ucsb.edu/documents/fifth-annual-message-4. Accessed 6 March 2024.

Roosevelt, Theodore. Nobel Lecture. Oslo, 5 May 1910. https://www.nobelprize.org/prizes/peace/1906/roosevelt/lecture/. Accessed 6 March 2024.

Rub Alfred. *Hans Kelsens Völkerrechtslehre: Versuch einer Würdigung*. Schulthess Juristische Medien, 1995.

Scelle, Georges. *Le Pacte des Nations Et Sa Liaison Avec le Traité de Paix*. 1919. Forgotten Books, 2018.

Schmitt, Carl. *Die Kernfrage des Völkerbundes*. Ferdinand Dümmler Verlag, 1926.

Schücking, Walter and Hans Wehberg. *Die Satzung des Volkerbundes* 1931. Gale, 2013.

Seeley, John Robert. *The Expansion of England, Two Courses of Lectures*. 1883. Elibron Classics, 2006.

Segers, Mathieu. *The Origins of European Integration: The Prehistory of Today's European Union, 1937–1951*. Cambridge University Press, 2023.

Spiermann, Ole. *International Legal Argument in the Permanent Court of International Justice: The Rise of the International Judiciary*. Cambridge University Press, 2009.

Stead, William Thomas. *The United States of Europe, on the Eve of the Parliament of Peace*. 1899. Kessinger Publishing, 2008.

Stirk, Peter. "Hugo Preuss, German Political Thought and the Weimar Constitution." *History of Political Thought*, vol. 23, no.3, 2002, pp. 497–516.

Suttner, Bertha von. Nobel Peace Prize Acceptance Lecture, 1906. https://www.nobelprize.org/prizes/peace/1905/suttner/lecture/. Accessed 6 March 2024.

Suttner, Bertha von. "Present Status and Prospects of the Peace Movement." *The North American Review*, vol. 171, no. 528, Nov. 1900, pp. 653–663

Taylor, A. J. P. *The Origins of the Second World War*. 1961. Penguin, 2001.

Tiedau, Ulrich. "Max Waechter, Anglo-German rapprochement and the European Unity League." *Visions and Ideas of Europe During the First World War,* edited by Matthew D'Auria and Jan Vermeiren, Routledge, 2019, pp. 112–149

Tower, Walter S, "The New Steel Cartel." *Foreign Affairs*, Vvol. 5, no. 2, 1 Jan. 1927, pp. 249–266.

Treitschke, Heinrich von. *Der Deutsche Zollverein und seine Geschichte*. 1913. Europäischer Hochschulverlag, 2009.

Tuchman, Barbara. *The Guns of August*. 1962. Penguin Group, 2014.

Tuchman, Barbara. *The Proud Tower: A Portrait of the World Before the War 1890 1914*. 1966. Random House, 1996.

Veblen, Thorstein. *An Inquiry into the Nature of Peace and the Terms of its Perpetuation*. 1917. Echo Library, 2008.

Vollenhoven, Cornelis van. "Holland's International Policy." *Political Science Quarterly*, vol. 34, no. 2, June 1919, pp. 193–209.

Waechter, Max. "The United States of Europe." *Advocate of Peace through Justice*, vol. 86, no. 11, Nov. 1924, pp. 607–611.

Weber, Max. *Political Writings*. Edited by Peter Lassman, translated by Ronald Speirs. Cambridge University Press, 1994.

Weimar Constitution. 11 August 1919. https://germanhistorydocs.ghi-dc.org/pdf/eng/ghi_wr_weimarconstitution_Eng.pdf. Accessed 6 March 2024.

Wells, H. G, *The War That Will End War*. 1914. Kessinger Publishing, 2010.

Wertheim, Stephen. "The League That Wasn't: American Designs for a Legalist-Sanctionist League of Nations and the Intellectual Origins of International Organization, 1914–1920." *Diplomatic History*, vol. 35, no. 5, Nov. 2011, pp. 797–836.

Wilson, Woodrow. "A World League for Peace." Address to the Senate, 22 January 1917.
    https://www.presidency.ucsb.edu/documents/address-the-senate-the-united-
    states-world-league-for-peace. Accessed 6 March 2024.
Wilson, Woodrow. Joint Address to Congress Leading to a Declaration of War Against
    Germany, 2 April 1917. https://www.archives.gov/milestone-documents/address-
    to-congress-declaration-of-war-against-germany. Accessed 6 March 2024.
Wilson, Woodrow. "President Woodrow Wilson's 14 Points." Address to Congress,
    8 January 1918. https://www.archives.gov/milestone-documents/president-
    woodrow-wilsons-14-points. Accessed 6 March 2024.

10   Europe's Anti-Federalist Moment

Abstract

The Interbellum saw the idea of federal union come under sustained
attack from universal monarchy's latest incarnation, totalitarianism.
Both Stalin and Hitler dismissed federalism as an outdated idea, a mere
stage on the way to a continent-wide incorporating union. At the practical
level, totalitarianism set about dismantling the separated powers and
checks and balances on which federalism relied. It was supported in
this effort by the legal philosopher Carl Schmitt, who worked to destroy
federalism from within by giving the executive powers that completely
unbalanced the constitutional system. Federal theorists would eventually
launch a counter-offensive along two lines. They worked to outlaw one of
Machiavelli's other methods of expansion, and to discredit the concept
on which totalitarianism was built: national sovereignty.

Keywords: Federal union, anti-federalism, separation of powers,
totalitarianism

The Eastern Question

The world after the war was very different from the world before it. All the
continental empires had disappeared, either overthrown in a revolution or
simply disintegrated under the pressures of various nationalist movements.
The demise of the Ottoman empire had been anticipated for a long time.
Ever since Alexander I's foreign minister Adam Czartoryski first speculated
about it at the turn of the nineteenth century, European politics had faced
the challenge of managing this decline in an orderly way. The outbreak of
war in 1914 made its implosion a foregone conclusion.

The Austrian empire's dissolution was treated as equally inevitable.
After all, even the Empire's own legal scholars had been unable to prove
it even constituted a state in the first place. Or rather: that it constituted
one state. The settlement of 1867 between Hungary and Cisleithania had

Livestro, Joshua: *A More Perfect Union. Federal Union in Political Theory and Practice, 1500-1951.*
Amsterdam: Amsterdam University Press, 2024.
DOI: 10.5117/9789048563777_CH10

created a kind of personal union that was more familiar from early modern times. The conflict centred on the question which element of it, if any, was the bearer of sovereignty. The Austrian side argued that the union was represented through the person of the emperor. The Hungarians denied that the emperor had any say in Hungarian matters. All the two countries had in common was "the physical person of the ruler, in whom two different governing persons were united" (Rumpler 411). In other words: where the Austrians saw a political union, the Hungarians saw only a personal one.

This lack of agreement about what constituted the common element in the relationship between the two halves was symbolised by a fundamental disagreement about foreign and defence policy. The Austrian law that confirmed the 1867 agreement talked about a *"gemeinsam"* policy in this area. The Austrians interpreted this term as "single." The Hungarian translation on the other hand had used the term *"együttes,"* which carried the meaning of "acting together" (Wheatley 69–70). In their eyes, there was no *single* foreign and defence policy, only a *common* one. Though Austrian commentators angrily dismissed this logic as "witch's arithmetic" which claimed that "1+1=1+1," they had no way of demonstrating the answer was wrong (72). This conflict would remain unresolved until the Empire's collapse in 1918.

For an entity that was supposedly so clearly destined for disintegration, the Empire did feature remarkably often in the plans for the future of its constituent parts in the pre-First World War period. For the Hungarians, who in 1849 had looked for a complete break with the Empire (an ambition that was eventually blocked on the battlefield, in part thanks to a Russian intervention), the settlement of 1867 may have been the best option short of actual independence. For the Bohemians and Moravians, however, the same kind of quasi-independent status *inside* the Empire would quickly become a constitutional ideal. Initially they demanded a status similar to that of Hungary: independent from the Empire, though not from the Emperor. When that proved too great an ask, they shifted their attention to federal solutions inside the Cisleithanian part of the empire. Around the turn of the century a number of proposals would be published which all aimed to turn the Empire – or, at least, the non-Hungarian part of it – into a federal union in which the states and other entities resorting under the crown would have their own claim to sovereignty fully recognised (Wheatley 129).

The same kind of solutions were also discussed by representatives from the Slovene, Croat and Serb communities living under the Hungarian Monarchy (whose monarch was also the emperor). Having been denied the sort of independence that the Hungarians had eagerly accepted for themselves in 1867 – consistency was never a virtue in the Empire's internal politics – these three nations spent the last years of the war looking for a joint way forward. The most plausible scenario they could come up with was for the various South Slav nations to be united in a greater Jugoslav entity. Deputies from the various Slav groups represented in the Austrian *Reichsrat* decided to form a single Jugoslav parliamentary group in the spring of 1917. The aim was unification in a separate constitutional entity under Habsburg rule, with a constitutional status similar to Hungary's (Djokić 32).

—

The Kingdom of Romania had joined the Allied war effort against the Central Powers. It claimed a reward for its sacrifices in the form of a Union with Bessarabia, Bukinova and the former Empire lands of Transylvania (1 December 1919). Bulgaria lost territory to both Greece and Romania. It was also forced to cede territory to a newly created country in the Southern Balkans: the Kingdom of Serbs, Croats and Slovenes.

While the three communities living on the Hungarian side of the border had initially looked for a solution within the framework of the Empire, the communities on the other side, led by the Serbian government in exile, proposed a more radical solution. What they wanted was a complete break with Habsburg rule, and the formation of a Yugoslav union under the Serbian monarchy (Djokić 34). The course of events in the final month of the war settled this argument in favour of the Serbs. It raised a new question: where within this new union was power to lie? The provisional Slovenian-Croatian governing council pushed for a federal solution. Against this, the Serbian government made the case for a more integrated structure with the Serbian monarch as head of state. Given the strength of republican sentiments on the Croatian side, the negotiations would almost certainly have ended in a stalemate if the facts on the ground had not forced a change of mind (Lampe 111).

The Italian government had decided to use the collapse of Austrian authority in the region to expand its territory in the direction of Slovenia and Croatia. In keeping with the old Balance of Power logic, it claimed these territories as a reward for its decision to switch to the winning side at the start of the war. Facing overwhelming military odds, the Croatians were forced to call upon Serbia's military for aid. The Serbian forces that turned back the Italian army then chose to stay in Croatian and Slovenian territory, ostensibly to protect the peace, but really to secure the implementation of the Serbian Yugoslav scheme (Lampe 112). The eventual union that was created was not quite a Serbian *diktat*, but with the Serbian king as monarch,

Belgrade as its capital city, and the location of its incorporated parliament, it was clear that the Croats and Slovenes had not joined as equal partners – a fact that would place a significant mortgage on the country's future.

In Poland, the political class had used the collapse of the three empires that 125 years earlier had carved up what remained of its country to re-establish an independent state. Debate inevitably touched on the question of the country's borders: Poland, but which Poland? There were, after all, many different historical Polands to reach back to. The most ambitious among the Polish leadership made the case for the restoration of the Commonwealth before the First Partition of 1772. Among them was General Józef Piłsudski (1867–1935), the later president of the independent Polish state. Even though he was born and raised in modern-day Lithuania, Piłsudski's political instincts and cultural outlook were thoroughly Polish. As leader of the pre-war Socialist Party, he had stood on a platform of the formation of a Polish federal state that included not just Poland itself but also Lithuania, Belarus, and Ukraine. In 1919, he presented a plan for the securing of Poland's newly regained independence which included the formation of a federation tying the country to a number of border states. The motivation for this plan seemed a mix of Commonwealth nostalgia and *raison d'état* considerations. The border states were to be welcomed into the union as fellow Poles, but they were also expected to form a buffer against Bolshevik intrusion. In a speech to the parliament of the independent Ukrainian republic, he described his country's aim as "to reject all that threatens it as far as possible from its borders" (Zimmerman 354). This required some form of organisation of these border states, either as part of a federation or as independent states (335).

When, in the summer of 1919, Polish armies conquered first Minsk and then Kyiv, both part of the ancient Polish–Lithuanian Commonwealth, Piłsudski presented these moves as acts of liberation: "I am a son of the same lands you are. (...) Poland marches everywhere with the slogan of freedom. Poland marches not with the desire to oppress under the brutal boot of her soldiers nor with the desire to impose on anybody adherence to her laws" (Zimmerman 348). For a while, it seemed as if the federation idea he had praised in countless speeches would come to fruition. In the end, though, Polish ambitions would collide with the growing desire for national self-determination in the border countries, where the old cultural ties to Poland were no match for the new nationalisms.

Poland's armies also clashed with the Bolshevik army, which fought to keep as much of the Russian empire as possible under its control. For a while it looked as if the Bolsheviks would reoccupy not just the newly independent republics of Ukraine and Belarus but even Poland itself. Plans were presented for a Polish Soviet Republic to be ruled by the architect of the Red Terror, Felix Dzerzhinsky. But after an unexpectedly clear victory in the battle of Warsaw by Polish forces under Piłsudski's command, a kind of status quo was established that would last until 1939.

—

The establishment of a belt of border states to shield Europe from Russian aggression was not just a Polish ambition. It was described in early 1919 as a "vital necessity" by the British geopolitical theorist Sir Halford Mackinder (Mackinder 126). An essential part of "mak[ing] the world a safe place for democracy" was to prevent the possibility of the "Great Continent," by which he meant Europe, Asia, and Africa (the "World Island") falling under the rule of a single power, "the great ultimate threat to the World's liberty" (58). The task as he saw it was "to provide against it in our new political system" (58). This wasn't just a matter of designing the right constitutional framework. It was also, and predominantly, a matter of the strategic use of "geographical realities": "If we are to realise our ideal of a League of Nations which shall prevent war in the future, we must recognise these geographical realities and take steps to counter their influence" (4).

One of the chief geographical realities was that "[w]ho rules East Europe commands the Heartland; who rules the Heartland commands the World Island; who commands the World Island commands the World"[1] (Mackinder 121). It was therefore "essential that we should focus our thoughts on the stable resettlement of the affairs of East Europe" (124). He warned against the idea of a direct border between East and West, such as the one "contemplated by Naumann in his *Central Europe*," because "no lasting stability would have ensued" (136). A better option, in Mackinder's view, was the construction of "a Middle Tier of really independent States between Germany and Russia"

---

1   By the Heartland, Mackinder meant "Western Siberia, Turkestan, and the Volga basin of Europe," which left "a broad gateway from Siberia into Europe," bordering in the south on the mountain ridges of "Persia, Afghanistan and Baluchistan" (Mackinder 61). Its strategic significance was that it was unassailable from the sea, and provided secure "landways into China, India, Arabia, and the African heartland." With the arrival of rail and air transport that connected these regions, he imagined that sea power would lose its significance for trade purposes, and therefore also its strategic purpose (91).

(136). Referring to the "idealists" who proposed the formation of a League of Nations, he stated bluntly: "With [a Middle Tier] they will achieve their end, and without it they will not" (136).

What was required, in short, was the creation of a significant number of independent states out of the former empires in the region: "Poles, Bohemians, Hungarians, Rumanians, Serbs, Bulgarians, and Greeks" (137) These new States would be "too unlike to federate for any purpose apart from defence, yet they are all so different from both Germans and Russians that they may be trusted to resist any new organisation (...) towards the Empire of East Europe" (137).

The new countries in the region did eventually organise themselves into a defensive union. Not against the new threats of Germany or Soviet Russia though, but against their old overlord Hungary. The Little Entente of Czechoslovakia, Romania, and the Kingdom of Serbia, Croatia, and Slovenia would do little to help secure long-term peace in the region. It merely demonstrated that in Eastern Europe the Empire remained a living presence. Its issues would continue to dominate the region's political debate for many decades to come.

From *war* against war to *law* against war: the Briand-Kellogg Pact

In discussions about the nature of the League, the focus was inevitably on Article 10. Since the Covenant's introduction, the article had become remarkably popular among French legal scholars, who, in spite of their government's protestations to the contrary, saw in it exactly the kind of guarantee of collective security that Wilson had claimed it was. The question was of course: what was it a guarantee against? According to Schmitt, by the mid-1920s the consensus position was that it was exclusively interpreted as "a guarantee against violent changes of ownership" of territory (Schmitt, *Die Kernfrage des Völkerbundes* 35; my translation throughout). In other words: against Machiavelli's first method of expansion, violent conquest, or as it was called by Schmitt's contemporaries: "[T]he Prussian method, bringing about changes of territory through armed violence and military force" (35).

There was, as Schmitt did not hesitate to point out, something opportunistic about the Western embrace of this idea. While it banned the Prussian method, it did not ban the building of empires as such, provided they were commercial rather than territorial. Nor did it ban war, provided it wasn't a war of conquest. Even territorial expansion remained possible, as long as it was achieved by non-violent means. "In that sense," Schmitt concluded,

"Article 10 of the League's statute is an expression of modern imperialism, which after all is characterised by the fact that it has substituted economic for military means of power" (35–36).

In the late 1930s, Schmitt would argue in favour of retaining Machiavelli's first method of expansion, the violent one associated with the Athenians and the Spartans. He had hinted at the development of this idea already in his pamphlet on the League, when he remarked that the political independence of many states, especially the smaller ones, was merely a paper reality. The trend was "for their number to decrease so that through several 'Monroe Doctrines' eventually only entire continents or other giant constructs would remain as true carriers of sovereignty" (Schmitt, *Kernfrage* 11). He was willing to accept in theory that these continental sovereign entities could be federations. In *The Turn to the Discriminating Concept of War* (1937) he even acknowledged "Proudhon's astounding prediction regarding international jurisprudence (...): that the twentieth century would be as federalistic as the nineteenth century had been constitutionalist" (Schmitt, *Discriminating Concept of War* 38). But in practice, he tended more towards the Roman option of a continental entirely under the leadership of the Reich.

Though conquest did not necessarily form the core of its method of expansion, as far as he was concerned it could not and, as a matter of principle, should not be excluded. More important was that other great powers would not have a right to intervene in German/continental affairs. His embrace of the principle of non-intervention underpinning the Monroe Doctrine was meant specifically as a rebuke of Anglo-Saxon universalism. Hence the inclusion in the title of the 1939 publication in which he presented his *Grossraum* theory of a reference to "a ban on intervention by outside powers" (*Völkerrechtliche Grossraumordnung mit Interventionsverbot für raumfremde Mächte: Ein Beitrag zum Reichsbegriff im Völkerrecht*).

———

Schmitt's most principled case for war came in arguably his most (in)famous work, *The Concept of the Political*. Placing himself in the tradition of Moltke, Treitschke and Bernhardi, he offered a defence of the right to wage war against a two-pronged attack that he saw taking place in his time. The one front had been opened up philosophically by the Kantian pursuit of perpetual peace, as expressed in the League of Nations' Covenant. In Schmitt's view society was based on a fundamental distinction between friend and enemy. This enemy was "existentially something different and alien, so that in the extreme case conflicts with him are possible" (Schmitt,

Concept of the Political 127–128). He rejected the possibility of mediation or
arbitration to settle these existential conflicts because he thought that "(o)
nly the actual participants can correctly recognize, understand, and judge
the concrete situation and settle the extreme case of conflict" (128). *In ultimo*,
this settlement would have to take the form of "war or revolution" (135).

He warned his liberal democratic audience that it had to be careful what
it wished for. To abolish war would not just be a sin against man's nature.
It could have a further unintended, undesirable consequence, namely the
death of politics: "A world in which the possibility of war is utterly eliminated,
a completely pacified globe, would be a world without the distinction of
friend and enemy and hence a world without politics" (Schmitt, *Concept of
the Political* 143–144). Even if politics as a whole did not disappear, the group
that denounced the idea of war could still run the risk of negating itself:
"A human group which renounces these consequences of a political entity
ceases to be a political group, because it thereby renounces the possibility of
deciding whom it considers to be the enemy and how he should be treated"
(170). Even worse, it would end up helping the other side: "If a part of the
population declares that it no longer recognizes enemies, then, depending
on the circumstances, it joins their side and aids them" (178–179).

A world without politics or group identity in which those who rejected the
idea of war could end up being permanently dominated by their opponents
obviously would have sounded to this liberal democratic audience like a
scenario to avoid. But, he consoled them, though it was possible to imagine
such a world, it could never actually come about: "Nothing can escape this
logical conclusion of the political" (Schmitt, *Concept of the Political* 146).
Even a war against war such as the one that had just been fought proved
his point: "The feasibility of such war is particularly illustrative of the fact
that war as a real possibility is still present today" (147).

—

This philosophical attack on the idea of war would have been irrelevant if
it had not also been given legal status through the Briand-Kellogg pact of
1928. That treaty was born out of a desire on the part of the French political
establishment and the American pro-League camp to find a way to tie the
US to the Covenant (and thereby to France's security). At its core was a
restatement of Article 10 of the Covenant. Instead of focusing on the states
however – the threats to some and the possible duty of others to protect
them – the treaty focused on the force behind the threat: war. By specifically
"condemn[ing]" and "renounc[ing]" Clausewitz's famous dictum that "war is

an instrument of policy," it allowed the signatory states to make a principled statement against war, seemingly without creating any kind of obligations of enforcement (Hathaway and Shapiro 120–121).

In his *Concept of the Political*, Schmitt had limited himself to pointing out the supposed futility of a "solemn declaration of outlawing war" since "it does not abolish the friend-enemy distinction, but, on the contrary, opens new possibilities by giving an international *hostis* declaration new content and vigour" (178). By 1937 he had changed his mind on the issue. He realised that this new "friend–enemy" distinction was fundamentally different from older ones. The "war on war" had become the "just war," which had its counterpart in the "unjust war" – the war started for mere territorial gain, a war *against peace*. The suggestion was that countries might, in due course, create international structures to prosecute those accused of waging unjust war, thus making the merely unjust actually *illegal*. If not all wars, then at least some – those fought for territorial gain – would from now on be banned. He presented the 1935–1936 efforts to impose sanctions on Italy after its invasion of Abyssinia as a "pathognomic moment; a moment, in other words, that makes the critical stage of the progressive or regressive 'institutionalisation' or 'concretisation' of the League of Nations and international law clear for all the world to see" (Schmitt, *Writings on War* 34).

The man Schmitt identified as one of the driving forces behind this transformation of the concept of the just war, the British international legal scholar Hersch Lauterpacht, would in 1945 make the Briand-Kellogg pact part of the legal basis for the case against the Nazi government at the Nuremberg trial. Just as Schmitt had predicted (or feared), the Nazi regime's defendants stood trial not just on the basis of charges of war crimes and crimes against humanity but also for "crimes against peace."[2] In the process, one of Machiavelli's methods of expansion had been declared permanently off limits.

Briand's gamble: the United States of Europe

France had tried for the better part of a decade to get some form of security guarantee from the other allied powers. An initial attempt to win president Wilson for an Entente had failed in 1919. Successive British governments

---

2   Of the twenty-two main defendants at the tribunal, twelve were convicted of crimes against peace. On the central place of the ban on aggressive war in the post–Second World War international order, see Hathaway and Shapiro's *The Internationalists*, specifically chapter 13 "The End of Conquest."

then kept the French at arm's length, most creatively at Locarno by giving the same security guarantee to both France and its perceived main threat, Germany, thus effectively cancelling the two commitments out against each other.[3] A renewed request in 1927 for an alliance with the United States was equally unsuccessful. The eventual Briand-Kellogg Pact was granted by Kellogg more as a consolation prize for French efforts than as an actual commitment (Schuker 385).

The Locarno system, which followed the signing of the pact in 1925, could have created the climate for a real breakthrough in the quest for peace on the continent. The regular meetings of the three main powers, through their foreign ministers Aristide Briand, Austin Chamberlain, and Gustav Stresemann, at times did serve as a kind of informal European Council. Fundamentally though, it suffered from the same problems as the Congress system a century earlier. The lack of permanent structures and a proper constitutional framework meant its success depended entirely on the three men involved, while the lack of common long term objectives made a real rapprochement virtually impossible.

By 1929 the last of the issues that kept the three countries around the table – the withdrawal of French troops from the Rhineland and the repayment schedule of German and Allied war debts – were about to be settled. Without any means of limiting German ambitions for rearmament, and with completion of the defensive Maginot Line still years away, Briand seems to have decided that something new had to be tried to keep Berlin constructively engaged. He ultimately settled on an idea that had been pushed from several sides: a move towards a European federal union.

Industrialists from different countries had been arguing since the early 1920s for a kind of federal European economic pact. The most concrete form this idea would take was that of a Europe-wide customs union. In 1924 a group of economists, led by the Frenchman Charles Gide and the Hungarian Ernö Bleier, published a manifesto arguing that a customs union was the best remedy against a possible slide of the continent into "anarchy" and "chaos" (Pegg 33). One commentator praised its potential by making the obvious historical comparison: "The *Zollverein* created the German Empire. A European customs union will create a United States of Europe and put an end to war among the states of Europe" (51). The publication led to the

---

3   This double bind created the remarkable situation where the British military leadership would have been required to plan with its French counterpart for a campaign against Germany while planning with the German military leadership for a campaign against France. In the end, no planning meetings ever took place.

creation, in 1925, of an organisation called the European Customs Union, which would lobby for the adoption of the idea by European governments.

In the second half of the 1920s, a number of conferences were organised within the League of Nations framework to explore the idea. The need for progress on this issue was clear. The collapse of the old empires, and the subsequent creation of new states in Eastern Europe, had created around 20,000 kilometres of new internal borders on the continent (Fleury and Jílek 571). This massive expansion of the network of internal custom barriers coincided with a gradual but seemingly unstoppable increase in Europe's trade deficit with the rest of the world. By 1928, the deficit amounted to around £5 billion, nearly the same as the entire sum of German war debt payments (Herriot 95). In the words of one commentator who summarised the trade situation on the continent: "Europe, from being a creditor, has become a debtor" (90).

The response of participating government delegations, however, was typical for the general approach to federal schemes in the Interbellum: there was widespread recognition of the (significant) gains that could be achieved through their implementation, but the practical complications were always considered too great to take any concrete steps at that stage. The Belgian Foreign Secretary Hymans, who in 1921 had signed the regional customs union between Belgium and Luxembourg (itself a former member of the German *Zollverein*), compared the conference to a theatre audience: "[It] glows with pleasure at the representation of all the virtues, but does not commit itself to adopt them" (Herriot 86).

In the case of a European customs union, the best participating governments could come up with was a temporary freeze on further tariff increases – in itself an important signal against the protectionism of the age, but nowhere near enough to make a significant difference for the economic development of the countries involved, given the levels of existing tariffs (the average national rate was nearly 50 percent, with rates on some goods as high as 70 percent). The final recommendations of the Paris Conference of 1930 also included an idea that had its roots in Saint-Simon's writings: the creation of an *avantgarde* of France, Germany and their most immediate neighbouring countries in Western Europe to form a Western European Customs Union (Pegg 148).

—

The objective of perpetual peace through economic integration was given a further boost through the campaigning of a number of political organisations whose aim was the formation of a European federal union. Some of these organisations had been around for a long time – the International League for Peace and Freedom, that had staged its opening congress with Garibaldi in 1867, was still organising for European unity in the late 1920s. The 1920s also saw the birth of a number of new platforms dedicated to the idea of European unification, many of which also had national chapters. Of these new organisations the most high profile was undoubtedly the Pan-European Union, founded in 1923 by the Austrian count Richard Coudenhove-Kalerghi (1894–1972). In the bestselling book through which he launched his movement, *Pan-Europe,* he argued for a European federal union chiefly on geopolitical grounds. Europe had lost its global hegemony. It was divided into many smaller and larger states, and was therefore unable to meet the challenge of the new age of large power blocks. There was an answer, though: "The solution is called Pan-Europe: the political and economic integration of all states, from Poland to Portugal, in a confederation (*"Staatenbund"*) (Coudenhove-Kalerghi 27). If Russia was the most immediate military threat, Pan-America was both "Europe's greatest threat, and its greatest hope" (76).

Armed with this message, he would build an organisation whose aim was to form a separate European league, if necessary outside of the League of Nations. "The Genevan League of Nations," he argued, "has made Europe into an object of global politics, a playground for intrigue" (Coudenhove-Kalerghi 85). Against this, he argued for "Europe for the Europeans" – a separate European league to deal with European problems.

Coudenhove-Kalerghi's anti-League message created room for an alternative movement, especially in Poland, where the League was considered the cornerstone of regional security policy (Fleury and Jílek 61). The answer came in the form of the Federation of European Entente, founded by the Polish-Austrian artist Alfred Nossig (1864–1943). Though he had a better starting position than his rival in terms of government backing, the fact that he overreached by trying and failing to bridge the gap in positions between Germany and France, and between Germany and Poland (over the issue of Germany's eastern borders), eventually left him politically isolated. The first international conference of his organisation in 1926 would have no significant political representation. The second was cancelled, and no further attempts to organise one would take place (Fleury and Jílek 68).

In his effort to position himself as a champion of the European federal idea, Briand would cultivate both Coudenhove-Kalerghi and Nossig, as well as a number of other individuals and organisations working in support of the spread of the ideal of a European federal union. When he rose on 5 September 1929 to address the 10th Assembly of the League of Nations on the topic of European federation, he started by acknowledging their efforts, and his personal link to them: "Propagandists have united to spread it abroad, to establish it more firmly in the minds of the nations, and among these propagandists I stand confessed" (Herriot 50).

The speech's preannouncement over the summer had created expectations that Briand would use it to call for a European federal union. In reality, he knew his audience well enough to understand that he had to avoid overly romantic language if he wanted to win them for his scheme. The day's most poetic speech in fact came from his German colleague Stresemann, who speculated about a European currency and European stamps, and who seemed to echo Victor Hugo's 1849 speech when he compared Europe's situation in 1929 to the German situation sixty years earlier, when the German economy was also hampered by a lack of integration (Pegg 120).

The most memorable part of Briand's speech was his rather prosaic announcement of the French government's intention to launch a discussion about the possibility of establishing "some kind of federal bond" between "the peoples of Europe," which would be "[o]bviously (...) primarily economic" but also "political and social," while stressing that this would happen "without affecting the sovereignty of any of the nations belonging to such an association" (Pegg 50–51). The speech was followed by an invitation for a behind closed doors lunch with participation of all twenty-seven European countries existing at the time (referred to at the time as "The Banquet of Europe"). At this meeting, the French government was invited by the other governments present to produce a memorandum to set out the main objectives of the federal scheme, as well as the practical obstacles to be overcome in its implementation. The document was then to be discussed at the 11th Assembly of the League a year later.

The text published in May 1930 ("Memorandum on the organisation of a regime of federal European union") tried to thread the needle on presenting a proposal without actually presenting a proposal.

The memorandum opened with the claim that the mere fact that it was based on a unanimous request from all participating countries already created a kind of "moral European Union" (Fleury and Jílek 570) It then reminded its audience of the main obstacle to the formation of an actual union: a "dispersal of forces (...) limits significantly the possibilities for the formation of a larger economic market, attempts to intensify and improve industrial production, and all guarantees against a crisis in the labour market" (570).

In a first response to the idea in the immediate aftermath of his September 1929 speech, governments had expressed concerns about the impact of the initiative on the integrity of the League of Nations. The memorandum therefore set out to prove that a federal European union would "in no sense constitute a European group outside of the League of Nations but would in fact harmonise European interests under the auspices of, and in the spirit of, the League" (Fleury and Jílek 571). As if to stress that fact, it suggested that membership should initially be limited to European League members only, and meetings of the proposed Conference of member countries and the executive Committee would take place in Geneva, in the margins of the annual Assembly. Once the workload made its formation necessary, the Union's permanent secretariat would be embedded within the League's secretariat.

Governments had also observed that they would be forced to block any initiative that sought to impose limits on their sovereignty. When addressing this issue, the authors stressed that "in no case and to no extent will the federal institution searched for between European governments affect in any way the sovereign rights of the member states of such an organisation" (Fleury and Jílek 573). If there was to be a union, it would be based on "the absolute sovereignty and total independence" of the governments involved (573)

If there was to be any substantive integration, it was projected into the more distant future. The gap between present and future was to be bridged by a "general pact (...) for the affirmation of the principle of moral European union, and for the consecration of the factual solidarity between the European states" (Fleury and Jílek 573). Institutionally, it would take the somewhat minimal form of periodic or special meetings to discuss any issues of common interest. One of the tasks of these periodic meetings would be to study the objectives of a future union, and to discuss the means for achieving these objectives.

Though it formally left the selection of both objectives and means open to the governments involved, the memorandum did try to provide some input for that discussion. A future union was to be based chiefly on economic integration through the creation of a common market and a customs union, though there would also be a political element in the form of a system of arbitration and a joint security policy. The authors warned though that if there was to be any progress on economic integration (an idea for which there was at least some support), there would have to be progress on security first. And for there to be any progress on security, "it is at the political level that a constructive effort should first of all be made, giving Europe its organic structure" (Fleury and Jílek 577). This political structure was to be "a federation based on the concept of union, not unity" (578) For the avoidance of doubt, the authors stressed that by this they meant an organisation based on the complete sovereignty of the member states (578).

—

In a newspaper interview given after publication of the memorandum, Briand stated that what mattered to him was "the idea of a European federation. As for the details, like whether it's to be an actual organisation or merely a political platform, and as for procedural issues, I'm less interested in that. The essential thing is to unite to face the crisis of the moment" (Fleury and Jílek, 249) He was also not asking for any concrete steps at this stage: "For me, it would be enough to see the problem assigned to a committee for further study. The essential thing is that it isn't buried" (Fleury and Jílek 249).

The problem for Briand was for the governments involved, the devil was very much in the details. The colonial powers among the European states were concerned that committing to a continental Union would limit their options for conducting independent policy outside Europe. Some countries thought the Union would be an instrument to prevent border corrections. Others feared the exact opposite: that the Union could force them to accept changes to the postwar territorial settlement. Placing the proposed union inside the League's structures also created a whole host of technical problems. How would it work if, as suggested by the Memorandum, the same people represented both the European and the League's Assembly and secretariat? Legally the only basis for action was the Covenant as embedded in the Versailles Treaty. How could that be squared with the idea of separate European action? If the Union's expenses were to be paid for out of the League's budget, would that not mean that the non-European states were effectively paying for European union costs without having a vote on how it was spent?

In the end, Briand's proposed committee became the plan's burial ground. It would meet once more, under the leadership of his successor Edouard Herriot, never to feature again on the League's agenda.[4] Perhaps it was the universal lack of government commitment that killed it, or perhaps a change of personnel – the premature death of Stresemann shortly after the proposal's presentation in late 1929 probably did not help its cause. Briand's statement when he heard the news that "[I]t is all over now" seemed like an accurate prediction of what was to follow (Schuker 387).

---

4   Herriot would go down in history as the committed European federalist who in August 1954 as opposition spokesman in the Assemblée Nationale killed European political and defence integration out of fear of German rearmament.

More important than these personnel changes was probably the election triumph by the Nazi Party in September 1930, when it went from just 8 to 107 seats in the *Reichstag*. The NSDAP represented a new kind of nationalism, one that saw European federalism not as a means to a national end but as inimical to its objective of national greatness.

Who is the guardian of the federal constitution?

Protecting the right to wage wars of conquest from liberal-democratic efforts to outlaw it was only part of Schmitt's mission in the Weimar period. The other main task, as he saw it, was to save the liberal–democratic constitution from itself, and especially (or so he claimed) from the threat of the anti-constitutional elements on the extremes of the party system.

He pursued this mission in part through a reinvention of the concept of sovereignty. In its founding period, the Weimar republic suffered from a chronic lack of stability. Economically, the country was reeling from the aftershocks of the war. German GDP had shrunk twenty-five percent compared to pre-war levels. Supplies were still scarce because of the Allied blockades, which were only slowly being lifted. The economic instability in turn led to political instability. Militant forces on the right tried to supplant the bourgeois regime through military coups. On the left, marxist organisations tried to achieve the same objective through revolution.

Schmitt had experienced some of this instability up close in early 1919. He was still based in Munich, serving in the Army's general staff, when Marxist revolutionaries there announced the creation of a Bavarian Soviet republic. It was eventually overturned by the army, but the event clearly made an impact. It caused him, for one, to write a study titled *Dictatorship from the Origin of the Modern Concept of Sovereignty to Proletarian Class Struggle*. Through it he sought to answer a basic question: in the federal Weimar constitution, where if anywhere did sovereignty lie?

The new constitution did not immediately answer this question. Nor could it, as he would later explain in his 1928 study *Constitutional Theory*: "The bourgeois *Rechtsstaat* takes its point of departure from the idea of being able to comprehend and to limit the entire exercise of all state power without exceptions in written laws" (Schmitt 154). The consequence of this was that "political action of any given subject, (...) even sovereignty itself, is no longer possible. (...) [T]here is no longer any sovereignty at all, or, what is the same thing, (...) 'the constitution', more precisely constitutional norms are sovereign" (Schmitt 154–155).

In the case of the Weimar republic, this effect was compounded by the nature of federal unions. In every federation, Schmitt explained, "two types of political existence" will be found side by side: "[T]he collective existence of the federation and the individual existence of the federation members" (*Constitutional Theory* 388). The nature of their relationship is one of permanent rivalry: "Such an intermediary condition necessarily leads to tensions" (389). It was the fate of federations that this tension could not be resolved: "It is part of the essence of the federation (...) that the question of sovereignty between federation and member states always remains open as long as the federation as such exists along the member states as such" (390).

Without a clear answer to the question of where if anywhere sovereignty resided, it was difficult to see how the federal Weimar republic could save itself in a crisis situation such as the one that it found itself in. Decisions had to be taken without recourse to normal constitutional procedures, in order to save the constitution itself. To answer the question, Schmitt revisited a classical solution: dictatorship. Here he referred specifically to Machiavelli, whose "remarks on dictatorship display a profound and genuine interest in politics and a remarkable capacity for discernment" (Schmitt, *Dictatorship* 88). The essence of dictatorship as Machiavelli had defined it was that, though dictators were independent from the governing institutions and could act outside the law if required, they "cannot change the laws; neither can [they] suspend the constitution or the organisation of office" (90). In other words, "dictatorship was a constitutional instrument for the Republic" (90).

There was a problem with this classic definition though. As Bodin had explained in his *Six Books on the Republic*, just as a sovereign could never be a dictator because he could not serve as his own commissar in the execution of dictatorial powers, dictators could never be sovereign because though as commissars their remits were unlimited in power and function, they *were* limited in time (Schmitt, *Dictatorship* 26). Schmitt therefore set out to prove that the concept had undergone a fundamental transformation in the modern era, changing from commissary dictatorship, where the dictator was licensed merely to restore the old order, to sovereign dictatorship, where the dictator was licensed to innovate, either by filling gaps in the fundamental law or by creating an entirely new fundamental law.

Having thus reintroduced sovereignty outside the constitutional system, the final step was to relocate it within the system. This was done by equalling sovereignty with the power to decide on when dictatorial powers had to be used: "Sovereign is the one who decides on the state of exception" (Schmitt, *Political Theology* 3). He argued that in the Weimar Constitution, this power

rested with the *Reich's* president, based on Article 48.2 of the Constitution:
"If public security and order are seriously disturbed or endangered within
the German *Reich*, the president of the *Reich* may take measures necessary
for their restoration".

Was the presidency therefore really the sovereign power within the Weimar
republic? All Schmitt's earlier observations about the absence of sovereignty
in the *Rechtsstaat*, especially in a federal republic, still applied in full. He
would only be sovereign in the state of exception – moments in which the law
alone was not enough to help save the republic. Schmitt would never give an
adequate definition of these moments.[5] This may have seemed like a weakness
at the theoretical level, but it had a practical advantage. The absence of a clear
definition gave the president a lot of freedom in invoking Article 48.2 without
having to fear getting stuck in legal debates. As president, Paul von Hindenburg
would do so with increased frequency in the late twenties and early thirties,
always with Schmitt's full support, and frequently at his instigation.

One problem remained to be solved: the constitution itself could prove an
obstacle in the execution of dictatorial powers. As Schmitt saw it, "[t]he fact
that *the* constitution is inalienable (...) means that every particular legislation of
the constitution is, for the dictator, an unbridgeable obstacle in the fulfilment
of his duty. In this way the meaning and purpose of dictatorship (...) will be
violated and turned into its opposite" (Schmitt, *Dictatorship* 57). If the dictator
was to have the freedom required successfully to defend the constitution's
founding ideals, he could not be bound by its individual clauses: if they were
to save the constitution, they should be free to destroy parts of it if that was
what the situation required. To secure this freedom for the *Reich's* president
would become Schmitt's mission in the last years of the Weimar republic. It
would trigger a debate about which institution was best placed to defend the
constitution. Making the case for the alternative solution was Hans Kelsen.

———

The exact identity of the Habsburg empire had always been a mystery. At
its peak, it constituted a patchwork of hundreds of countries, territories,

---

5   In *The Guardian of the Constitution* he did distinguish three different kinds of state of
exception: "[T]he jurisdictional state employs martial law (...) i.e. summary justice; the state
as executive relies, above all, on the concentration of executive power, which is coupled, if
necessary, with a suspension of basic rights; the legislative state, finally, uses decrees to govern
the emergency or state of exception. It relies on a summary procedure of legislation" (128). But
none of these three different states of exception were further defined, which meant that the
decision to invoke them would always remain a political rather than a legal act.

and free cities. They all tied together through a series of personal unions involving the Emperor, who also doubled up as King, Archduke, Grand Duke, Duke, Margrave, Prince, Princely Count, Count, Lord, and Grand Vojvod.[6]

In the course of its history, there would be several attempts to integrate the various parts of the empire into a simplified structure by turning the patchwork of personal unions into a single political one. Once she had secured her right to rule, the Empress Maria Theresia used a codification of the empire's various legal traditions to push through a certain degree of centralisation (Wheatley 9). And shortly after he had taken the throne, in 1850 the ministers of the young Emperor Franz Joseph pushed through a new imperial administrative system that all but abolished the old territorial administrations. Following the defeat in 1859 in the Italian war of independence, these measures would be partly overturned in the two constitutional reforms of 1860 and 1861, before finally being rolled back completely in 1867, in the aftermath of the Austrian-Prussian war (53–54).

This unique system would have to wait until the final years of its existence for a convincing theoretical explanation and justification. It presented itself in the form of the Pure Theory of Law. Kelsen had introduced it as "general legal theory, not an interpretation of particular national or international legal norms" (Kelsen, *Introduction to the Problems of Legal Theory* 7). This may have been true at the theoretical level, but it was also, as he later admitted, very much a response to an Empire problem.

No legal philosopher was more rooted in the living experience of the Empire than Kelsen: born in Prague, educated in Vienna, a pupil of Jellinek, a friend of Sigmund Freud, a typical product of early twentieth century Viennese intellectual society. It made Kelsen eminently qualified to attempt to answer a question that had plagued political and legal philosophers since the seventeenth century: how to justify the Empire's existence at the theoretical level, especially since "theories that tried to base the unity of the state on some sort of social-psychological or social-biological connection" were "fictions"? (quoted in Wheatley 169–170).

Kelsen started by drawing a clear dividing line between the world of facts and the world of law, or as he put it: the world of *is* and that of *ought*. "Ought" was not a moral concept here, but a strictly legal one, "express[ing] the unique sense in which the material facts belonging to the system of law are posited in their reciprocal relation" (Kelsen, *Introduction* 24).

---

6   Personal unions of this kind still exist even in the Twenty-first century. During his coronation, the British king Charles III also became the head of state of several otherwise independent countries and territories.

In a next step, he stripped legal analysis of all metaphors that obscured rather than revealed the true nature of this system of law. What was referred to as society or community was in fact "the actual coexistence of human beings or a normative system of their reciprocal behaviour" (Kelsen, "Sovereignty" 526 – not some mystical collective entity but a collection of individuals. The same went for the concept of the state. Kelsen rejected the Hobbesian idea of the state as an artificial person: "There is no such superman or superhuman in society, whose sole reality is the individual human being" (Kelsen, "Sovereignty" 526). With it, he also rejected the idea that law and state were somehow different entities, that "the law can justify the state, which creates and subjects itself to the law" (Kelsen, *Introduction* 98). Dismissing the dualism propagated by his tutor Jellinek as a product of "ideology, (...) metaphysics and mysticism," he posited that all that could be said was that "the state (...) is a legal system" (99).

After thus reducing the state to a mere system of law and separating it from any political notions of the state as a person with its own will and interests, Kelsen finally also did away with the concept of sovereignty. He rejected the idea of the state's sovereign legal system, of it having "the capacity, unrestricted by any higher legal system, to extend its validity territorially as well as materially" (Kelsen, *Introduction* 100). The existence of an international legal system which "rises above the legal systems of the individual states" meant that the state was "only the highest system relatively speaking" (100). And since sovereignty was supposed to "represent the presupposition of a normative system qua highest system," it meant the state could never be considered sovereign (Kelsen, "Sovereignty" 528).

This destruction of the concept of sovereignty, which he described as "the principal instrument of imperialistic ideology against international law," was in Kelsen's eyes "one of the most substantial achievements of the Pure Theory of Law" (Kelsen, *Introduction* 114). It is not difficult to see why. Not only did it allow him to formulate an elegant answer to the question of the justification of the old Empire's structure, it also created room for the construction of a federal constitution for the new post-Empire Austria – a constitution of which Kelsen was not coincidentally the main author (hence his honorific title in Austrian modern history of "Father of the Constitution').

The Austrian post–First World War constitution, adopted in 1920, announced in Article 2 that Austria was to be a *"Bundesstaat"* formed out of "independent lands" (Austrian Constitution). An essential element of the new constitution was the Supreme Court. Kelsen, who would himself serve as a Justice on the court, had argued successfully for the inclusion of a number of clauses that made the Court the arbiter about conflicts involving the constitution's provisions. Clause 138 gave it the power to decide not just on conflicts of law between lower and higher courts, but also between Lands or between one or more Lands and the federal government. Clause 139 meanwhile gave it powers to review the constitutional propriety of both Land and Federal legislative acts and executive actions.

—

It was against this idea that Schmitt would take aim in his 1932 publication *The Guardian of the Constitution*. His argument was based on a seemingly rather narrow procedural concern. Once the constitution was amended, he observed, "every opportunity for judicial review end[ed], according to the reasoning of the *Reichsgericht*," in spite of "the possibility of an obvious abuse of Article 76," the article that stipulated the proper process for the passing of constitutional amendments (Vinx 83). By ignoring this possibility, the Court would also ignore "the question of whether there are illicit breaches of the constitution that could not be legalised through the employment of article 76, as well as the question of whether this article customarily allows for 'apocryphal acts of sovereignty'" (83)

The Court clearly was not capable of intervening in such cases. As far as Schmitt was concerned, that was also how it should remain. The reason was that "the authoritative determination of a constitutional law that is doubtful in its content is in substance constitutional legislation, not adjudication" (Vinx 107). Since "the bourgeois rule-of-law state (…) rests on a material distinction between different powers," it would be impossible to "give [a judge] the power of political decision, without changing a judge's constitutional position" (107). Only a political power could rule in these quintessentially political cases. And since "[f]rom a democratic point of view, it will hardly be possible to transfer such powers to an aristocracy of the robe" (168), that ruled out the option of the Court as guardian of the constitution.

In Schmitt's view, the only plausible political power that could take up that role was the president. There was of course another political power, namely the *Reichstag*. But as Schmitt had already set out a decade earlier in *The Crisis of Parliamentary Democracy*, it was too much to expect the latter to rise to the level of responsibility that was required of a proper constitutional guardian. In the nineteenth century, it might still have been able to fulfil this role. Back then, Parliament, as "the representative of the people," faced "a strong monarchical administrative state that [was] independent of it" (130) The two formed a kind of "constitutional pact" in which parliament, "in so far as it is a representative of the people (...) turn[ed] into the true guardian and guarantee of the constitution" (Vinx 130–131). Around the turn of the twentieth century, however, the rise of a new kind of state, "the economic state" (135), and with it a new kind of party politics focused on the control of the economy, had caused parliament to turn into "an entity divided within itself" (136). The end result of this process was that, "by virtue of the great number of parties and parliamentary parties that are necessary to reach a majority, the ascent from the egoistic will of the party to a responsible will of the state is prevented again and again" (142).

Their position as *pouvoir neutre* (neutral power, a concept traced back by Schmitt to the Napoleonic era philosopher Benjamin Constant), and the fact that they were "elected by the people as a whole" (Vinx 157), favourably positioned the *Reich's* president to fulfil the role of constitutional guardian. The fact that they were also "equipped, in the case of necessity, with effective competences for the active protection of the constitution" (157) provided the closing argument. The ideal solution, as Schmitt saw it, was to "give to the authority of the president of the Reich the opportunity to connect itself immediately with this unified will of the German people and to act, on that basis, as the guardian and the preserver of the constitutional unity and wholeness of the German people" (172). In an implicit reference to the dangerously unstable political situation in early 1930's Weimar, he warned that "[t]he existence and permanence of today's German state depends on whether this effort will succeed" (172).

—

Kelsen's answer came in the form of a review of Schmitt's publication. In "Who Ought to be the Guardian of the Constitution" (1932), he took issue with several of Schmitt's arguments. He first of all dismissed the use of the "neutral power" argument as "the dustiest prop from the storeroom of the constitutional theatre" (Vinx 177). He pointed to the monarchist ideological roots of the concept and expressed surprise about the fact that Schmitt had aimed to "transfer it without any restriction to the republican head of state" (178). The surprise stemmed from the fact that it was Schmitt himself who, in his *Constitutional Theory*, had rejected the use of "many traditional forms and concepts" as "not even old bottles for new wine" but "only outdated and mistaken labels" (quoted by Kelsen in Vinx 178). He pointed out that Schmitt's approach seemed to be to accept that the nineteenth century constitutional monarchical framework no longer existed, but then to try to make the president the new monarchical figure of the Weimar Republic

– "and this according to the constitution now in force, not according to a constitutional reform that is yet to take place" (179). And worse: to ignore his own observation that in the nineteenth century structure it was parliament that had served as guardian of the constitution since "the danger of a violation of the constitution, in a constitutional monarchy, emanated from (...) the sphere of the 'executive'" (180).

This transfer of monarchical powers to the president was "especially dubious" according to Kelsen if it "occurs together with the tendency to enlarge the powers of this organ" (Vinx 180). Schmitt's proposal to "extend the competence of the president, through a more than extensive interpretation of article 48" would end up turning the president "into a sovereign ruler of the state" with powers that were "incompatible with the function of a guardian of the constitution" (180).

Kelsen further accused Schmitt of an error of interpretation. The latter's case rested "on the erroneous assumption that there is an essential difference between the function of adjudication and 'political' functions, and in particular on the assumption that the decision on the constitutionality of a statute and the annulment of an unconstitutional statute are 'political' acts, from which it is inferred that such acts are no longer adjudicative" (Vinx 183). Schmitt, in short, was guilty of an overly strict interpretation of the idea of separation of powers by suggesting that judges could *never* take political decisions.[7]

In a 1929 essay titled *Wesen und Entwicklung der Staatsgerichtsbarkeit* ("On the Nature and Development of Constitutional Adjudication") Kelsen had concluded that there was no absolute separation between the three powers as far as their functions were concerned. They were "not opposed to each other in the sense that there is an absolute contrast between the creation and the application of law; rather, each of them, on closer inspection, turns out to be both creation as well as application. (...) Legislation and execution are not two co-ordinate functions of the state, but only two different levels of the process of the creation of law" (quoted in Vinx 23). The difference in function between parliament and the courts was one of degree, not category. Judges may have only possessed "negative" powers of legislation – the power to annul a statute, not the power to replace it with a new one – but that did

---

7   The idea of a strict separation between legal and political powers was first introduced in Napoleonic France. Article 107 of the Napoleonic Penal Code stated that "judges shall be guilty of an abuse of their authority and punished with loss of their civil rights" for interfering with the legislature or administration "by issuing regulations containing legislative provisions, by suspending application of one or several laws, or by deliberating on whether or not a law will be published or applied" (quoted in Sweet 2746 fn 7).

not make the act of annulment any less political: "If one conceives of 'the political' as the authoritative resolution of conflicts of interest, i.e. if one conceives of it, to use C.S.'s terminology, as 'the decision', then one should admit that every court contains, to a higher or less degree, an element of decision, an element of an exercise of power" (Vinx 184).

As for a constitutional court, its "function is political in character to a much higher degree than the function of other courts" (Vinx 185). Schmitt's attempt to argue that constitutional adjudication could never be a legal kind of adjudication *because* it involved a political verdict therefore did not make sense. To create a constitutional court and vest it with the power of acting as guardian of the constitution was entirely possible. Not just possible: necessary. Kelsen reminded his audience that "[n]o legal–technical principle commands a more universal assent than the demand that no person ought to be judge in his own cause" (175). Not only would this clearly rule out the president, as head of the executive power or indeed parliament; it would even rule out any part of the established judiciary. Only a newly created, fully independent court could serve as the ultimate arbiter in conflicts between the different powers of the federal government, or between the *Reich* and the Lands.

—

After the Second World War, it was Kelsen's solution that would win out. His idea of a separate court that would rule or advise on the constitutionality of statutes was adopted in most European member states (Sweet 2765–2766). Schmitt's alternative would come in for sustained criticism, with most reviewers pointing to the all too seamless continuity between his proposal to elevate the presidency to a kind of quasi-monarchical position while investing it with dictatorial powers, and the constitutional practice of Hitler's Third Reich. The fact that Schmitt joined the Nazi Party once it had come to power, and then actively supported the dismantling of the federal system of checks and balances, even contributing to it by advising the Nazi government on how to achieve it, provided additional evidence for their case.

The man Carl Schmitt certainly deserves no sympathy. His collaboration with the Nazi regime after January 1933, his legal justification of the murders of the Night of the Long Knives and the Nuremberg Race Laws, and his willing embrace of antisemitic theory and practice remain an insurmountable obstacle to any form of personal rehabilitation. But the thinker Carl Schmitt cannot be dismissed so easily. As one of the most systematic critics of federal theory in the twentieth century, he raised a question to which even Kelsen could not provide a convincing answer: what if enemies of liberal democracy use provisions *within* the constitution to destroy it?

In the end, Weimar's death came not through the temporary dictatorship declared under Article 48.2, but through a constitutional amendment passed under Article 76. There was no constitutional court to which to appeal, but it's doubtful that it would have been able to do anything to overturn what was presented as a legal use of the procedure.

The authors of the *Federalist Papers* warned against external efforts to destabilise the American federal union. What they overlooked, though, was that destabilisation could also come from internal sources, through abuse of the very constitutional provisions they had created to safeguard its existence. Kelsen was right that Schmitt's overly strict interpretation of the concept of separation of powers prevented him from accepting a court as a possible guardian of the constitution. But Kelsen, for his part, was guilty of reducing all challenges to the constitution to mere legal issues. Guardianship was, for him, a matter of "constitutional control" (Vinx 211): managing legal conflicts within the broader constitutional framework, not defending the constitution itself against explicitly *political* attacks of the kind that would eventually bring it down.

His sentiment of "not allow[ing oneself] to be drawn into a fatal contradiction and reach for the method of dictatorship in order to save democracy" but instead to "stay loyal to one's flag even if the ship is sinking" is undoubtedly noble (Vinx 19). But the lesson of 1933 was that allowing the ship to sink is not an option in the face of a totalitarian challenge.

Stalin, Hitler and the anti-federalist moment in Interbellum political theory

If the international legal community focused its efforts during the Interbellum on the outlawing of Machiavelli's first method of expansion (violent conquest), the authoritarian regimes that were spawned in this period tried instead to do away with the third method: federation. The authoritarian anti-federalist movement launched an attack on two fronts against the concept of federal union: the one theoretical, the other practical.

—

In the immediate aftermath of the Russian Revolution, there was a debate inside the Bolshevik camp about the country's future constitutional order.

Lenin had rejected the idea of federalism as incompatible with the Marxist revolutionary ideal of a centralised state (Aspaturian 20). Before the war he had declared: "We are opposed to federation in principle, it loosens economic ties, and is unsuitable for a single state. You want to secede? All right, go to the devil. You don't want to secede? In that case, excuse me, but don't decide *for* me; don't think that you have a *"right"* to federation" (Lenin).

The debate would not die down however. Some members were arguing that the idea that best suited the ideals of the movement was federalism. One such contribution, by Iosif Okulich made the case for a Russian federation similar to the American one:

> Let there be instituted a single Russian army, a single currency, a single foreign policy, a single supreme court. But let the various regions of the single state be free to build their new life independently. If already in 1776 the Americans (...) created a "United States" by means of a treaty of union, why should we in 1917 be incapable of creating a firm union of regions? (quoted in Stalin 12)

In this debate Stalin would mark his position through an article published in *Pravda* in March 1917 in which he came out firmly against these federal proposals. Dismissing Okulich's proposal as "a peculiar piece of muddle headedness" (12) he sketched a kind of historical law through which every federation eventually turned into a unitary state. He started his argument with a brief historical excursion:

> In 1776, the United States was not a federation, but a confederation of what until then were independent colonies, or states. That is, there were independent colonies, but later, in order to protect their common interests against their enemies, chiefly external, they concluded an alliance (*con-federation*), without, however, ceasing to be fully independent state units. (Stalin 12)

Placing the moment of transition from confederation to federation around the time of the Civil War, he suggested that "[f]ederation proved to be as much a transitional measure as confederation" (12) Eventually, "dual govern-ment became intolerable, and in the course of its further evolution the United States was transformed from a federation into a *unitary* (integral) state. (...) The name "federation" as applied to the United States became an empty word, a relic of the past which had long since ceased to correspond to the actual state of affairs" (12).

Observing that the same shift from federalisation to centralisation took place in Switzerland and Canada, he concluded that history pointed not in the direction of federalism but away from it, towards the unitary state: "[T]he trend of development is not in favour of federation, but *against* it. Federation is a transitional form." "[I]t follows from this," he concluded, "that in Russia it would be unwise to work for a federation, which is doomed by the very realities of life to disappear" (Stalin 12). Russia's constitutional future lay not in "quixotic attempts to turn back the wheel of history," but in "[p]olitical autonomy within the framework of the single (integral) state, with uniform constitutional provisions, for the regions which have a specific national composition and which remain within the integral framework" (12).

Stalin would not, however, win this particular battle. Or at least, not at the theoretical level. The 1919 party congress embraced federalism as a transitional arrangement, and in 1922 a Treaty of Union between the existing Soviet Republics and the reoccupied states of Ukraine and Belarus formally established federalism as the organising principle of the USSR. It was not a type of federalism that Western scholars would have recognised though. All power was vested in the Communist Party, and there were no effective checks and balances within the constitutional framework, let alone a rule of law. Neither the federal legislature and judiciary, nor the states, had any means of checking the power of the federal executive. But on paper at least the structure did vaguely resemble its American counterpart.

By the mid-twenties Stalin had moved away from his earlier outspoken criticism of the idea of federal union, dismissing debates about its constitutional significance as "scholastic questions" (Aspaturian 27). What mattered to him was that the Party, not the constitution, was the ultimate source of legitimacy. The Party's centralising *modus operandi* overrode any federal elements in the Soviet constitutional framework (Forestier-Peyrat 531). The fact that the 1936 USSR constitution created a federal union was therefore of little practical significance. During Stalin's lifetime, the Soviet Union's *real* constitutional structure would remain that of the rule of one man who was both legislator, executive and judge, and whose past pronouncements could never be taken as a basis for expectations about future decisions.

—

A similar theoretical rejection of the federal idea was produced by Adolf Hitler. In a chapter of *Mein Kampf* dripping with antisemitism titled "Federalism as a mask," he explained that it was "[t]he controversy over federation and unification, so cunningly propagandized by the Jews in 1919–1920 and onwards" which had "forced National Socialism (...) to take up a definite stand in relation to the essential problem concerned in it" (Hitler 1518). The choice as framed in the debate was: "Ought Germany to be a confederacy or a military state?" (Hitler 1518). The latter was the *Militärstaat* as propagated by authors like Carl Schmitt. In this debate, Hitler came down firmly against the former.

He used the same argument as Stalin for rejecting the idea of a federal constitutional order for Germany: "[E]very State in the world has to face the question of unification in its internal organisation" (Hitler 1536) In this world-historical process, he observed, "Germany is no exception" (1536). This ongoing process of centralisation meant that it had become "an absurdity to speak of 'state sovereignty' of individual provinces" (1536).

In a variation on the theme of Madison's 14th *Federalist Paper*, Hitler suggested that "[M]odern means of communication and mechanical progress have been increasingly restricting distance and space. What was one a State is to-day only a province and the territory covered by a modern State had once the importance of a continent" (Hitler 1536). But whereas Madison had claimed that technological progress would make federal government over an extended territory more feasible, Hitler argued that it would, in fact, end up making it surplus to requirement: "The purely technical difficulty of administering a State like Germany is not greater than that of governing a province like Brandenburg a hundred years ago" (1537–1538).

The consequences of this development for National Socialist constitutional thinking were clear. The movement needed to "claim the right to impose its principles on the whole German nation, without regard for what were hitherto the confines of federal states" (Hitler 1550). In this effort, it "must imperatively demand the right to overstep boundaries that have been traced by a political development which we repudiate" (1551). As events would prove, by "boundaries" Hitler meant not just internal borders. The ideological conflict was destined to become an armed one.

—

Before he dealt with the outside world though, he would first settle constitutional affairs in Germany itself. His inspiration here came from the Italian dictator Benito Mussolini. Of the three main representatives of totalitarianism in the post-1918 period, Mussolini's Fascist regime in Italy had the least to say about federalism. It would not have made sense for him to spend any time on refuting it on the theoretical level, since federalism had stopped being a significant factor in Italian politics after the 1861 unification settled the debate in favour of an incorporating union. He focused instead on dismantling the institutional checks on his power as appointed dictator. The first step came in 1923 with the adoption of the Acerbo law, which replaced a system of proportional representation for parliamentary elections with a system that gave the largest party an automatic two thirds majority of the seats, provided it had gained at least 25 percent of the votes (Paxton 109). The elections the year after, which were neither free nor fair, gave Mussolini the majority he needed to suspend the democratic process indefinitely; no more parliamentary elections would be held until after the end of the war. Or at least: no *free* elections. In 1934, voters were presented with a list of candidates from the National Fascist Party and asked whether they approved of it – a typical manipulated plebiscite in the Caesarist tradition.

A series of laws passed in 1925 and early 1926 then effectively abolished the constitutional system of separation of powers. One abolished the collegial cabinet system, investing all powers of decision-making instead in the "Capo del Governo." Another allowed this leader figure to bypass parliament by legislating by decree (Velez 70–71). Since the judiciary had already been, to a certain extent at least, under control of the executive under the old monarchical constitution, the three powers were thereby effectively united in a single office (Paxton 134).

In its earliest form, as presented in a program published in the spring of 1919, fascism was a collection of seemingly unconnected ambitions – some nationalist or expansionist, others more radical in nature. What tied them together was a fascination with the concepts of action and violence, and a virulent dislike of socialism and intellectualism (Paxton 5). By 1932, Mussolini had been dictator for almost a decade, using the unified powers of his office to exercise total control over society. In an essay published that year, he presented a full-fledged fascist doctrine to justify the new, all-embracing concept of state power. Fascism, which had started life as a theory of action, had become a theory of organisation. *Total* organisation, in fact: "The Fascist conception of the State is all embracing; outside it no spiritual or human values can exist, much less have value. Thus understood, Fascism is totalitarian" (Mussolini and Gentile 2).

Under fascism, only the state had rights. The individual life was one of duty towards the state: "The Fascist State is an inwardly accepted standard and rule of conduct, a discipline of the whole person; it permeates the will no less than the intellect" (Mussolini and Gentile 3). If it rejected individualism, fascism also rejected the egalitarian premise of the rule of law: "In rejecting democracy Fascism rejects the absurd conventional lie of political equalitarianism" (6). Instead Mussolini asserted "the irremediable and fertile and beneficent inequality of men who cannot be levelled by any such mechanical and extrinsic device as universal suffrage" (5). Procedural democracy was therefore rejected: "Fascism is (...) opposed to that form of democracy which equates a nation to the majority, lowering it to the level of the largest number" (2). If the fascist state was a democracy at all, then it was "an organized, centralized, authoritarian democracy" (6).

—

Hitler would copy Mussolini's constitutional agenda. He too used the idea of manipulating constitutional processes to give himself the powers required to abolish the Weimar Republic's federal structures of separated powers and checks and balances. The February 1933 *Reichstag* fire was used to persuade Hindenburg to suspend a number of constitutional provisions indefinitely, including Articles 114 (on the inviolability of personal liberty), 118 (freedom of expression), and 123 (freedom of assembly). The Enabling Act, passed shortly afterwards under Article 76 of the Constitution, gave the government the right to bypass the constitution when passing legislation. The Reconstruction Act and the Acts for the Unification of the States with the *Reich*, both passed by decree in the first months of 1934, gave the *Reich's* government full control over the state-level governments. In August 1934, the Act for the Abolition of the *Reichsrat*, passed on the advice of the Third *Reich's* new *Kronjurist* Carl Schmitt, completed the dismantling of the old federal structures (Wilson 490–491). Decision by majority was replaced by decision by authority – the authority of one man, to whom all cabinet ministers and civil servants were to swear obedience (Wilson 492).

Of the three powers, the judiciary proved the most difficult to bring under control. In the end, the Nazi government achieved it through a combination of policies: rewriting of the standards of judicial interpretation, purging the courts and replacing its personnel with judges and clerks loyal to the party line, and the creation of a number of new courts specifically empowered to enforce Nazi laws.

The re-emergence of Balance of Power politics and the slide into war

Among the League's more outspoken supporters during the American ratification debate was the 1920 vice-presidential candidate Franklin Delano Roosevelt (1882–1945). At one of his campaign stops, he warned of the effect of American isolationism on Europe's chances of making the transition to democracy: "Unless the United States entered the League of Nations, it would become a new form of the Holy Alliance of Europe" (Roosevelt). He also made it clear that in his view, American membership of the League would have seen it transformed into a defence league for democracy: "If America had been a member of the League of Nations, the Polish nation would not be today fighting Bolshevism with its back to the wall" (Roosevelt).

During the 1920s, Roosevelt would prove himself a faithful friend of the concept of the League, though with an open eye to its shortcomings. In a 1923 anonymous submission to a newly created peace prize, he pleaded for a reconstituted League with qualified majority voting to replace the existing unanimity rule: "Common sense cannot defend a procedure by which one or two recalcitrant nations could block the will of the great majority" (quoted in Schabas 245 fn 33).

As newly elected president, Roosevelt would attempt to tie the United States more closely to the League, but as in 1919 the Senate's isolationism proved too strong a force to overcome. Roosevelt's attempt to make his country a member of the Permanent Court of International Justice failed in January 1935 by the same seven vote margin that had killed the Covenant's ratification attempt. The American decision to stay out definitively was one in a series of setbacks for the League in the middle part of the 1930s. A number of security crises (Manchuria and Ethiopia) created the impression that the Covenant was not worth much in practice. By then however, a much greater problem had presented itself in the person of the new German Chancellor, Adolf Hitler.

—

By the time he finished dismantling the structures of the old Weimar federal republic, Hitler had already taken the country out of the League of Nations. In October 1933 he triggered the Covenant's exit clause, suggesting it was an existential issue – Nazi propaganda claimed that "Germany's right to exist is now a question of to be or not to be" ("All Germans rounded up to vote"). He then had this decision rubber stamped by the German people in a referendum. The question was as leading as any of the plebiscites organised by Louis Napoleon 75 years earlier: "Do you, German man, and you, German woman, approve this policy of your Reich's government, and are you willing to accept it as the expression of your own opinion and your own will, and solemnly declare it?" (Referendum, November 12, 1933) Forty million Germans turned up to vote, or rather, were harassed to do so. Of those, more than 90% voted yes. With that, Hitler was free to pursue his expansionist policies without further League interference.

Forced to solve its security issues with Germany outside the structures of the League, France and the United Kingdom reverted to the old Balance of Power approach. While the methods were those of the nineteenth century – using the Concert system of summits, usually involving Mussolini as a go-between, to prevent military conflict as far as possible – the solutions were at times closer to those of the eighteenth century. Like Frederick II, Hitler used the logic of the balance system to his advantage in a rolling campaign of German territorial expansion, first by forcing through the reclaiming of German sovereignty over the Rhineland and the *Anschluss* with Austria. Both were greeted by Britain and France with indifference since they did not seem to impact the Balance. The carving up of Czechoslovakia during the Munich summit of 1938 was reminiscent of the Polish Partition in its methodology. The country involved had no vote, or even a voice, in the decisions that eventually led to it being forced to surrender a sizable part of its territory to Germany and Hungary.

It wasn't until the subsequent occupation of the remaining Czechoslovak rump state in March 1939 that the two Western European powers finally decided to plan for armed conflict. They did so in part in response to public opinion in both countries. British and French voters had greeted the outcome of the Munich negotiations not as a triumph for the Balance system ("Peace for our time") but as a violation of their national honour. The annexation of the remaining part of Czechoslovakia led to a decisive shift in public opinion. The general consensus was that Hitler could not be trusted, and that war was inevitable (Taylor 51). Another factor pushing the British government into an anti-German alliance with the French was an assessment by British intelligence that Germany was actively preparing military action against Romania and Poland (Williams 55).

The fact that Poland was the next object of Hitler's territorial desires also made further negotiations pointless. Given the country's historical experience with partition, no Polish government was ever going to accept the idea of territorial concessions in return for Western security guarantees, irrespective of what had happened to Czechoslovakia. Nor was it likely to accept Russian offers of military assistance; experience had taught the Poles that the Russians tended to come as friends and stay as conquerors. The British government therefore faced a simple choice: either it signed a full defensive pact with Poland, or there would be no pact at all. Given the logic of the Balance of Power system, it was inevitable that it chose the former option.

France's commitment to Polish security predated the 1939 crisis. In keeping with the French strategy that had been in place since Francis I of maintaining a *barrière de l'Est* as a way of creating a second front against the Holy Roman Empire, after the First World War the French government had invested in alliances with the newly created Eastern European states. The idea was that these countries could be mobilised to attack Germany from the east in case of a new war. Given this strategic commitment, like Britain it now had no option but to tie its fate to that of Poland.

—

The war that followed may not have been inevitable, but it was certainly no accident. Anyone who had read Hitler's statements in opposition knew that his expansionist agenda would eventually put Germany in conflict with the other major powers on the continent. In *Mein Kampf,* he stated quite clearly that he saw Germany's future as one of eastward expansion: "We put an end to the perpetual Germanic march towards the South and West of Europe and turn our eyes towards the lands of the East. We finally put a stop to the colonial and trade policy of the pre-War times and pass over to the territorial policy of the future" (Hitler 1759). His description of a German policy of Eastern conquest and colonisation suggested that he had internalised the lessons of the German geopolitical writer Karl Haushofer (1869–1946).

Haushofer, a former military attaché to the Japanese imperial court who, upon his return to Germany, had served on the Western Front, was an extreme German nationalist whose views made him a suitable companion for the NSDAP's number two, Rudolf Hess.

He paid regular visits to him and his fellow inmate, the party's leader Adolf Hitler, while both were serving a prison sentence for the failed Bierkeller Putsch of 1923. During those visits, which would take place over a space of six months (June to November 1924), Hitler received a kind of personal tutorial in geopolitical analysis. He would be introduced to the work of Ratzel, Kjellén and Haushofer himself, and to the concept of *Lebensraum* (Herwig 225).

Hitler's interpretation of Haushofer's teachings wasn't necessarily a faithful one. Unlike Haushofer, Hitler had no interest in constructing a "Eurafrica "axis as counterbalance against the Asian Heartland (Herwig 221). His thinking was much more racist than his teacher's. The *Lebensraum* Hitler had in mind wasn't just intended to create more space for the German people, but also – and mainly – to create the preconditions for the flourishing of a racially pure *Volk*. His explicitly racist description in *Mein Kampf* of France's formation of a colonial empire that stretched "from the Rhine to the Congo" as "inhabited by an inferior race which had developed through a slow and steady process of bastardisation" (1670) was intended as a warning of what would happen to Germany if expansion happened at the expense of racial purity. There is no doubt though that it is through Haushofer that he became familiar with the geopolitical way of analysing world politics, and that he shared his objective of making Germany an *Autarkie* (a self-sufficient economic entity).

Of all its concepts, the one geopolitical principle that most fundamentally influenced Hitler was that of expansion. Unlike Bismarck, Hitler was not willing to accept that territorial ambitions should stop at Germany's borders as established in 1871. As he put it in the second volume of *Mein Kampf,* in a chapter on Germany's policy towards Eastern Europe, "[t]o demand that the 1914 frontiers should be restored is a glaring political absurdity (...). The confines of the *Reich* as they existed in 1914 were thoroughly illogical. (...) [T]hey were temporary frontiers established in virtue of a political struggle that had not been brought to a finish" (Hitler 1745).

Echoing both Bernhardi and the geopolitical writers, Hitler claimed that "the German nation could assure its own future only by being a World Power" (1727). It was abundantly clear to him that Germany in the 1920s was anything but that: "What importance on earth has a State in which the proportion between the size of the population and the territorial area is so miserable as in the present German *Reich*?" (1729). The aim of German foreign policy would therefore have to be "[w]ithout respect for 'tradition' and without any preconceived notions, to find the courage to organise our national forces and set them on the path which will lead them away from that territorial restriction which is the bane of our national life today, and win new territory for them" (1735).

It was this belief in what Kjellén had called the "categorical imperative' of expansion that would lead Hitler ultimately to plunge his country into war on a scale the world had never witnessed before.

Hannah Arendt and the ideological conflict at the heart of the Second World War

In the aftermath of the First World War, the nation–state had been identified as the answer to a European problem. The old empires of Germany, Austria–Hungary and Turkey, seen by many as the cause of the great conflagration that had nearly destroyed the continent, were dismantled. In their place came states based on claims to national self-determination. By offering each people its own national home, the peace negotiators at Versailles hoped to restore a sense of stability to European politics. However, what had been presented as the answer after the First World War turned out to be a problem in the run-up to the Second World War.

The Versailles peace negotiators who redrew the map of the old continent were confronted with a number of situations in which different communities were living so closely together that there was no way of creating a state without creating a minority problem. Of the newly created states, none were "nation states" in the true sense of the word.

The minorities issue was one of a number of problems with which the Council of the League of Nations was confronted after the various peace treaties had been signed. Another problem presented itself in the form of different states claiming full sovereignty over disputed territory. Some problems, like the future status of the Saar, were resolved through diplomatic means. In other cases the Council was less successful. One of these intractable problems, the status of the Danzig corridor, would eventually serve as the immediate cause of the Second World War.

—

There were many interpretations of the nature of this war. One saw it as a clash between the regime forms of democracy and tyranny. Another portrayed it as a conflict between the societal organisational principles of freedom and order. Both interpretations can be found in the work of the German philosopher Hannah Arendt (1906–1975). There was another interpretation that also featured prominently in her work: the war as an inevitable consequence of the embrace by Europeans of the concept of national sovereignty. The only way to break out of the endless cycle of violence that it brought with it was the construction of a European federation.[8]

According to Arendt, the war had made it abundantly clear that the European crisis was a crisis of the nation-state, and of the concept of sovereignty with which it had become associated. In a 1944 essay titled "Foreign Affairs in the Foreign-Language Press," she observed that "it has dawned upon most of the smaller nations that sovereignty and independence alone will give neither national security nor economic prosperity" (Arendt, *Thinking Without A Banister* 131). In fact, as she remarked in a book review titled "Power Politics Triumphs," the situation was even worse, affecting not just smaller nations but *all* nations: "[T]he whole continent is likely to collapse because of the principle of national sovereignty" (188). She described a "new feeling" among "European peoples" that "the national state is neither capable of protecting the existence of the nation nor able to guarantee the

8   On the recent rediscovery of the federalist element in Arendt's work, see Klusmeyer, "Hannah Arendt's Case for Federalism."

sovereignty of the people. The national border lines (...) have proved to be no longer of any real avail" (Arendt, *The Jewish Writings* 371).

It wasn't just that the idea of national sovereignty, whose roots she traced to the writings of the early French Revolutionaries and the Declaration of the Rights of Man and the Citizen, had failed to deliver on its promise of keeping people safe and free. National sovereignty was not a failed answer to a problem: it *was* the problem. The identification of the nation with sovereignty in the late eighteenth century was "the first step transforming the state into an instrument of the nation, which finally has ended in those totalitarian forms of nationalism in which all laws and the legal institutions of the state as such are interpreted as a means for the welfare of the nation" (*The Jewish Writings* 240). "The evil of our times," she stated plainly, was not the "deification of the state" but that of the nation: "[I] is the nation which has usurped the traditional place of God and religion" (240).

In her postwar writings she would expand on this theory. In a 1970 interview with the German writer Adelbert Reif, she stressed the link between sovereignty and war: "Sovereignty means, among other things, that conflicts of an international nature can only be settled by war; there is no other last resort" (Arendt, *Crises of the Republic* 229). The coupling of the concept of the nation to sovereignty also linked it to a concept whose very core was the suppression of individual rights. She feared sovereignty above all because it legitimised the regime form based on "the extreme of violence (...): one against all" (Arendt, *Thinking Without A Banister* 469).

Inevitably, Arendt rejected not only the concept of national sovereignty but also the Balance of Power system through which sovereign states had tried to manage their relationships. She dismissed the thoughts of those who saw in the great conflagrations of 1914–1918 and 1939–1945 mere "accidents" which required the restoration of the old order by referring to Kant's dismissal of the Balance of Power method: "The balance achieved by the system of nation-states was not a mere phantasm, but it did collapse exactly as Kant predicted. In the words of a modern historian: "The iron test of the balance of power lies in the very thing it is designed to stave off—war" (Holborn quoted in Arendt, *Essays in Understanding* 361).

Her rejection of sovereignty as a founding concept of political order led her to an exploration of the counter-tradition, which according to her led from Machiavelli via Montesquieu to the American Founders.[9] One such

---

9   In "Hannah Arendt on Hannah Arendt," she was asked by the Marxist professor of political economy C. B. Macpherson how she squared her rejection of the tradition of Hobbes and Rousseau with her acceptance of the tradition of Montesquieu and the Federalists, given that both were

historical excursion led her to a confrontation with the writings and acts of Friedrich von Gentz, to mark the one hundredth anniversary of his death, in 1932. His embrace of the lost cause of European order had led to him being "thoroughly forgotten" (Arendt, *Essays in Understanding* 84), a fact that she also put down to his being neither liberal nor conservative, and therefore without allies with an interest in keeping his memory alive. And though his "mode of life was early Romantic," his "mode of argumentation was drawn from the Enlightenment" (Arendt, 'Review' 247). Here too, his seeming lack of consistency did not win him any friends on either side. His worst sin in the eyes of those who would subsequently condemn his memory was that he had gone squarely against "the spirit of the age," which was "nothing else than the growing nationalism of the 19th century which destroyed the unity of Europe" (Arendt, "Review: A Believer in European Unity" 247). Even during the Congress of Vienna, when all the other participants defended their national interests, she claimed, "Gentz laboured to defend the interest of Europe" against an increasingly "violent chauvinism" (247).

A few years before her death, at a 1972 conference about the meaning of her work, she would confess that her mission had been to do "something like Montesquieu did with the English constitution in that I construed out of the American Constitution a certain ideal type" (Arendt, *Thinking Without A Banister* 466). What she admired above all about it was the way it balanced private interests and public opinions through a carefully calibrated institutional framework that owed much of its inspiration to the Romans:

> This distinction is between the notion of group interests (...) and opinions (...). You have it in the Constitution itself: the legislature was supposed to represent the interests of the inhabitants; the Senate on the contrary, was supposed to filter these interests and to reach impartial opinions which relate to the common weal. (...) It follows the Roman *potestas in populo, auctoritas in senatu.*
> (469)

In her postwar works she tried to identify a theoretical pathway for the development of a federal alternative to the violence-based sovereign state

---

based on a "model of man as a calculating individual seeking to maximise his own interest." She answered that "[t]he tradition of Montesquieu that you mentioned could really go back to Machiavelli and Montaigne, and so on. They ransacked the archives of antiquity precisely to find a different model of man. And this man is not bourgeois, but the citizen" (Arendt, *Thinking Without A Banister* 467).

system. Hope came, ironically, in the form of the concept of mutually assured destruction through atomic weapons: "Between sovereign states there can be no last resort except war; if war no longer serves that purpose, that fact alone proves that we must have a new concept of the state" (Arendt, *Crises of the Republic* 230). It could not be a mere copy of the League of Nations though, "since the same conflicts between sovereign governments can only be played out there all over again" (230). A new state concept could only be found in "the federal system, whose advantage it is that power moves neither from above nor from below but is horizontally directed so that the federated units mutually check and control their powers" (230). At the pinnacle of this new system would stand the council, the kind of organisation that had emerged in every revolution, "entirely spontaneously, each time as though there had never been anything of the sort before" (231). This, then, was the ultimate objective of her new science of politics: "In this direction, I think, there must be something to be found, a completely different principle of organisation, which begins from below, continues upward, and finally leads to a parliament" (232.)

—

All this lay in the future – both the "people's Utopia" of her federal vision (231) and her more systematic reflections on the nature and potential of federal union. During the Second World War, her writings had a more urgent character. She wrote chiefly to persuade that the failings of the pre-war national sovereignty-based states system were not accidental but systematic. She rejected not just the nation state and its concept of sovereignty, but also the attempt to manage its conflicts through the League of Nations, which she dismissed as "a club that one could resign from whenever one wanted" (Arendt, *The Jewish Writings* 127). To the extent that she did look forward, she painted a kind of federal vision: "There may soon come a time when the idea of belonging to a territory is replaced by the idea of belonging to a commonwealth of nations whose politics are determined solely by the commonwealth as a whole. That means European politics – while at the same time all nationalities are maintained" (130).

Her source of inspiration here was twofold. In part it was the past as she reconstructed it, partly through her own studies and partly through the work of other academics. About Paul Sweet's 1941 biography of Gentz for example she wrote that his book was "of a strange and exciting timeliness, since, again, the question of European unity presents itself as one of the most important political tasks" (Arendt, 'Review' 247). The other source of inspiration was the European resistance movement.

Strictly speaking there was no single "European" resistance, only a number of national resistance movements. The individual movements usually operated without knowledge of each other's publications or positions.[10] That made it even more remarkable in her eyes that they tended to converge around the same ideological position: the fight was not against Germany but against fascism. "Those who emerged to wage war," she observed, "fought against fascism and nothing else" (Arendt, *Essays in Understanding* 144). This may not have been surprising, though the willingness to separate the German people from the crimes committed in its name was remarkable enough. What was surprising, she continued, was that the fight was also in favour of a positive idea: a new constitutional idea and a new geographical reality. It was "precisely because of its strict, almost logical, consequence (...) that all of these movements at once found a positive political slogan which plainly indicated the non-national though very popular character of the new struggle. That slogan was simply *Europe*" (Arendt, *Essays in Understanding* 144).

The embrace of federal union by European resistance movements

Given the outspoken rejection of the idea and its constituent elements by totalitarian leaders, it should perhaps not come as a surprise that federalism would emerge as the political creed of anti-fascist movements across Europe during the interbellum and the war years. It didn't always have the same geographical objective – among Eastern European writers there seemed to be as much interest in a regional federation (either a *Mitteleuropa* or a "great Yugoslavia') as in a European one. Indeed, some even speculated about a North Atlantic union or a transcontinental one between Europe and Africa. And perhaps as a result of a lack of access to historical sources, the debate seemed to take place without reference to the federalist canon. There were a few notable exceptions though. One was on the third canon of practical experiences with federation. Here the authors uniformly rejected the option of returning to a League of Nations style construction in the

10   In the spring and summer of 1944, representatives of various national resistance movements met in Geneva to discuss Europe's postwar future. The joint declaration, largely based on the writings of Spinelli, stressed the importance of forming a "federal Union" with "[a] government responsible not to the governments of the various member States but to the peoples, who must be under its direct jurisdiction in the spheres to which its powers extend." *Draft declaration of the European resistance movements, Geneva*, 20 May 1944.

postwar period.[11] As early as 1918, the economist Luigi Einaudi (1874–1961) had already rejected the League of Nations as equivalent to the American Articles of Confederation – doomed to fail because of "the diabolical power of the *idée fixe* of sovereignty" ("Il dogma della sovranità e l'idea della società delle nazioni") (Einaudi; my translation). In 1943 Einaudi, who after the war would serve as finance minister, deputy prime minister and ultimately as the second president of the Italian Republic, renewed his criticism of the League. He claimed those who formed it had been ignorant of all historical experience. Referring to "the failure of all past attempts at federation, from the Hellenic Amphictyonic League to the Holy Roman Empire, and the American Confederation of 1776 to the Holy Alliance," he concluded that "mere leagues of peoples always ended in trouble" (Lipgens 71; my translation throughout) The reasons for their failure were "no own resources (...), no own army (...), no own decision-making powers, and no executive authority" (Lipgens 71). He preferred even the "old European balance of power between the Alliance and the Entente" to the "union of all, which because of the veto of every member was entirely devoid of power" (71).

The French pre-war (and briefly post-war) Prime Minister Léon Blum (1872–1950) had made similar observations about the League in writings smuggled from his prison cell. It had undoubtedly been "a generous and great creation," but its shortcomings had doomed it from the start. The founders of the League had failed "to give it the necessary institutions and powers" (Lipgens 188). It had not been created as an autonomous authority, "independent from the sovereign nations" (188–189) nor had it been given the "political authority or material powers" necessary to impose its decisions on those same sovereign nations (189).

Still, as critical as they were of the League of Nations, the various non-communist resistance movements seemed to agree that some form of federal union was required after the war. The editor of one of the main French resistance newspapers, Jean-Daniel Jurgensen of *Défense de la France*, published an article in 1943 in which he observed that, "whether we want it or not (...) an experiment of a similar nature [to the League] will have to be repeated, while avoiding the errors of the past" (Lipgens 210). Among the errors he counted not just the structural flaws mentioned by Blum and Einaudi, and the unwillingness of the founding states to compromise over sovereignty, but also what he called the "anarchical universality" of the League: "[T]he

---

11   For this point, I am indebted to Walter Lipgens. See his introduction in *Europa-Föderationspläne der Widerstandsbewegungen 1940–1945*, where he pointed out that the question of the reasons for the failure of the League was one that occupied resistance writers all over Europe (2–6).

fact that all states (...) were grouped together in an unstructured, colourful collective led to an anarchical and artificial situation" (201).

A similar point was made by the Dutch historian Jan Romein. In an essay for the Dutch resistance newspaper *Het Parool* published around the same time as Jurgensen's contribution, he observed that in spite of the "bitter disappoint[ment]" over the League's pre-war record, "the thought of an 'organ that is superior to the States' still lives in the hearts and heads of twentieth century people" (Lipgens 279). He too, though, stressed the importance of avoiding the mistakes made by the founders of the League: "[I]t needs to be stated (...) that the League overreached. Wilson attempted to create a global organisation while Europe was still in chaos" (279). Like Jurgensen, Romein proposed an organic system of local and regional federations of which a new League could then form the highest level of organisation. "Continental communities" would have the additional benefit of being "better able to know and assess the interests of individual countries (...). They would be able to create a much tighter sense of community than a global organisation" (280).

—

Arguably the most famous wartime resistance publication was published in Italy in the summer of 1941. A number of opposition politicians, journalists and academics had been imprisoned by the Fascist regime on the island of Ventotene, off the coast of Naples. One of the prisoners, the journalist and later politician Altiero Spinelli (1907–1986), described in his autobiography how, almost by accident, he and one of his fellow prisoners, Ernesto Rossi, stumbled across Einaudi's 1918 opinion piece in which he criticised the League of Nations. As an economist, Rossi was allowed to write to his fellow economist Einaudi, supposedly on matters of shared academic interest, but in reality, to discuss federalism. During this correspondence, Einaudi sent him a small stack of English-language books. Among them was *The Economic Causes of War* by the British economist Lionel Robbins (1898–1984), in which the author dismissed "the dreary spectacle of power politics (...) with which the history of unhappy Europe has made us so depressingly familiar," blaming it on "the existence of sovereign independent states" (Robbins 103). As an alternative, he praised the American constitution, which had been created "deliberately to avoid such a state of chaos" (104). Robbins concluded that "the remedy is plain. Independent sovereignty must be limited. (...) We do not need a unitary world state. (...) We do need a federal organisation" (104–105).

Like Briand earlier that decade, Robbins had called for a United States of Europe. But unlike Briand, he meant by this "not a mere confederation of sovereign states as was the League of Nations," whose history he considered "one long demonstration of the truth of the proposition long ago set forth by Hamilton and Madison, that there is no safety in confederations. Unless we destroy the sovereign state, the sovereign state will destroy us." Instead he argued for the formation of a genuine federation which takes over from the states of which it is composed, those powers which engender conflict" (Robbins 105).

Spinelli described the impact of these ideas on him and his fellow prisoners as "revelatory." "As I was seeking clarity and precision of thought," he continued, "my attention went not to the nebulous and convoluted ideological federalism of the Proudhonian or Mazzinian type, but to the clean and precise thought of these Anglo-Saxon federalists" (Vanni 425; my translation). He would discuss these issues extensively with Rossi, as well as with the philosopher Eugenio Colorni and his wife, the economist Ursula Hirschmann.[12] Rejecting the European tradition of gradualism, they would take the American Founding, and the *Federalist Papers*, as inspiration for a pamphlet that would become known as the *Ventotene Manifesto* (Lipgens 36).

The *Manifesto* started with a discussion of the political and social processes that led to the eventual outbreak of war. It sketched a historical process in which nations "secured the right to turn themselves into states" (Lipgens 37). Previously merely "a historical product of human cohabitation," the nation had more recently taken on the status of "a divine entity," an "organism" that was "allowed to think of its own development only" (37). Linking the concept of "absolute sovereignty" to geopolitics, the authors then described a situation in which every state was "striving for dominance," seeing "ever larger areas" as its "*Lebensraum*"; this ever-larger area would allow the state to "move freely, and secure for itself the means of existence without being dependent on anyone else" (37). [The reference is clearly to Haushofer's concept of "Autarkie"] The desire to gear everything towards the building of ever more efficient war machines almost naturally pushed the state towards totalitarianism.

The authors presented themselves as part of a countermovement against totalitarianism, a movement of "all those (...) who out of an innate sense of self-worth were incapable of bending their spines in humiliating servitude"

---

12   Ursula Hirschmann was the sister of the economist Albert O. Hirschmann. She would later marry Spinelli, after Colorni was murdered in Rome when he tried to escape from a roadside ambush by a fascist brigade. Albert Hirschmann would dedicate his 1970 study *Exit, Voice, and Loyalty* to the memory of Colorni. Ursula Hirschmann recorded her own life as a refugee in *Nous Sans Patrie*.

(Lipgens 39). It was this movement that they wanted to address, calling on it to prepare for "the challenges of the post-war era" (39). The defeat of Nazi Germany would not automatically lead to the founding of a better world. Certain powers would be comfortable with the thought of simply restoring the old national systems (40), perhaps in combination with the creation of "useless, or even harmful, institutions of the League of Nations variety" (41). The new post-war cleavage would therefore be between "those whose most important objective would remain the conquest of national power" and "those who see as their central task the creation of a solidly grounded international state" (42).

In a supplementary essay published a month later under the title "The United States of Europe and the main political trends," Spinelli then sketched the outlines of the constitutional framework that the European federal union was to receive. Apart from the usual three separated powers, a second, vertical division of powers between the centre and the states, and a not quite enumerated list of federal competencies (defence and foreign policy, the regulation of interstate commerce and the mutual recognition of privileges and immunities, the issuing of federal coinage, and the administration of mandate territories), he also suggested the introduction of a federal power to decide on issues of jurisdiction between states, and between the federal centre and the states (Lipgens 50). Clearly having studied Hamilton's arguments from *Federalist Paper* 15, he stressed the importance of the right of the federal union to raise taxes "directly from the citizens," and to create "legislative and control powers based on the direct involvement of the citizens, and not on the representation of the states" (50).

Spinelli also dealt with what was likely to be the national sovereignty camp's main objection to his scheme: that the establishment of a link between a government and its citizens had to be based on a pre-existing shared national bond. This, he observed, would be "to put the cart before the horse" (Lipgens 51) The work of constructing "a new tradition and a new popular myth of European unity" could logically only start *after* the creation of the union (51). Worth noting here is that the same idea of a "myth' of a European community arising out of the act of federating was also referred to by the Dutch historian Jan Romein. He linked it to the introduction of a directly elected executive: "This type of election creates a direct tie between the peoples of the continental community. In this and other ways this tie will have to be strengthened, so that the myth of a supranational community can gain strength" (Romein 281).

—

The wartime writings of the resistance movement had led to the creation of not one but two lines of division within the European federalist debate. The first was between those who defined the idea of a United States of Europe as being based on full sovereignty of the member states versus those who thought it had to be based on some form of divided sovereignty between the states and the federal centre. The other was between those who favoured the traditional Kantian/Saint-Simonian approach of gradual union building (chiefly through economic integration) and those who thought it required a bolder approach through the immediate creation of a proper political union.

Across these two dividing lines ran the issue of the transatlantic relationship. Ever since the idea was first raised as a possibility by Victor Hugo and his contemporaries, American involvement had both energised and complicated the European debate about federal union.

The absence of a single, clearly defined concept of federal union would lead to a lively debate in the years after 1945 about the optimal structure of both European and transatlantic cooperation. This debate would lead to several attempts to form federal schemes of a more limited or ambitious nature, either regional, Europe-wide or transatlantic in scope. For a while it seemed that, instead of settling on a single conception of federal union, Europe's postwar politicians were happy to try them all.

Bibliography

"'All Germans rounded up to vote." *The Manchester Guardian*, 13 Nov. 1933, p. 9.

Ancinelli, Robert D, "The Roosevelt Administration and the World Court Defeat, 1935." *The Historian*, vol. 40, no. 3, May 1978, pp. 463–78.

Arendt, Hannah. "Review: A Believer in European Unity." *The Review of Politics*, vol. 4, no. 2, 1942, pp. 245–247.

Arendt, Hannah. *Crises of the Republic*. Harcourt Brace and Company, 1972.

Arendt, Hannah. *Essays in Understanding 1930–1954: Formation, Exile, and Totalitarianism*. Schocken Books, 2005.

Arendt, Hannah. *The Jewish Writings. Edited by Jerome Kohn and Ron H. Feldman*, Schocken Books, 2008.

Arendt, Hannah. *Thinking Without a Banister: Essays in Understanding, 1953–1975. Edited and with an introduction by Jerome Kohn*, Schocken Books, 2018.

Aspaturian, Vernon. "The Theory and Practice of Soviet Federalism." *The Journal of Politics*, vol. 12, no. 1, February 1950, pp. 20–51.

Austrian constitution. 1920. https://www.constituteproject.org/constitution/Austria_2009. Accessed 6 March 2024.

Coudenhove-Kalerghi, Richard. *Pan-Europa*. 1923. Pan-Europa Verlag,1982.

Djokić, Dejan. *Yugoslavism, Histories of a Failed Idea, 1918–1992*. University of Wisconsin Press, 2003.

Draft declaration of the European resistance movements., Geneva, 20 May 1944. https://www.cvce.eu/content/publication/1997/10/13/d68ca0ad-c24b-4906-8235-96b82814133a/publishable_en.pdf. Accessed 6 March 2024.

Einaudi, Luigi. "Il dogma della sovranità e l'idea della società delle nazioni." *Corriere della Sera*, 28Dec. 1918. https://www.luigieinaudi.it/doc/lettera-undicesima-il-dogma-della-sovranita-e-lidea-della-societa-delle-nazioni/. Accessed 6 March 2024.

Fleury, Antoine and Lubor Jílek. *Le Plan Briand d'Union fédérale européenne*. Verlag Peter Lang, 1999.

Hathaway, Oona and Scott Shapiro. *The Internationalists: How a Radical Plan to Outlaw War Remade the World*. Penguin, 2018.

Forestier-Peyrat, Etienne. "Soviet Federalism at Work: Lessons from the History of the Trans-Caucasian Federation, 1922–1936." *JGO Jahrbücher für Geschichte Osteuropas*, vol. 65, , issue 4, Dec. 2017, pp. 529–59.

Herriot, Edouard. *The United States of Europe*. Translated by Reginald Herriot, The Viking Press, 1930.

Herwig, Holger H, "Geopolitik: Haushofer, Hitler and Lebensraum." *Geopolitics: Geography and Strategy*, edited by Colin Gray and Geoffrey Sloan, Frank Cass, 1999, pp. 218–241.

Hitler, Adolf. *Mein Kampf.* 1925–26. Translated into English by James Murphy, 1938. Liber Electronicus, 2018.

Kelsen, Hans. *Introduction to the Problems of Legal Theory*. Translated by Bonnie Litschewski Paulson and Stanley L. Paulson, Clarendon Press, 1997.

Kelsen, Hans. "Sovereignty." *Normativity and Norms: Critical Perspectives on Kelsenian Themes*. Edited with an Introduction by Stanley L. Paulson and Bonnie Litschewski-Paulson, Clarendon Press, 1999, pp. 524–536.

Klusmeyer, Douglas. "Hannah Arendt's Case for Federalism." *Publius, the Journal of Federalism*. 2010, pp. 31–58

Lampe, John R, *Yugoslavia as History. Twice There was a Country*. Cambridge University Press, 1996.

Lenin, Vladimir. Letter to Stepan Shaumian. 6 December 1913. https://www.marxists.org/archive/lenin/works/1913/nov/23.htm. Accessed 6 March 2024.

Lipgens, Walter. *Europa-Föderationspläne der Widerstandsbewegungen 1940–1945*. Oldenbourg, 1968.

Mackinder, Halford. *Democratic Ideals and Reality: The Geographical Pivot of History*. 1919. Origami Books, 2018.

Mussolini, Benito and Giovanni Gentile. *The Doctrine of Fascism.* 1932. https://sjsu. edu/faculty/wooda/2B-HUM/Readings/The-Doctrine-of-Fascism.pdf. Accessed 6 March 2024.

Paxton, Robert O, *The Anatomy of Fascism.* 2004. Penguins Books, 2005.

Pegg, Carl H, *Evolution of the European Idea, 1914–1932.* University of North Carolina Press, 1983.

Robbins, Lionel. *The Economic Causes of War.* 1939. Howard Fertig, 1968.Roosevelt, Franklin D.. Campaign Speech.Milwaukee, 12 August 1920. http://www.fdrlibrary. marist.edu/_resources/images/msf/msf00137. Accessed 6 March 2024.

Rumpler, Helmut. *Österreichische Geschichte 1804–1914. Eine Chance für Mitteleuropa: Bürgerliche Emanzipation and Staatsverfall in der Habsburgermonarchie.* Ueberreuter, 1997.

Schabas, William. *The Cambridge Companion to International Criminal Law.* Cambridge University Press, 2016.

Schmitt, Carl. *The Concept of the Political.* 1932. Translation, introduction and notes by Charles Schwab, University of Chicago Press, 2007.

Schmitt, Carl. *Constitutional Theory.* 1928. Translated and edited by Jeffrey Seitzer, Duke University Press, 2008.

Schmitt, Carl. *Dictatorship: From the Origins of the Modern Concept of Sovereignty to Proletarian Class Struggle.* 1921. Translated by Michael Hoelzl and Graham Ward, Polity Press, 2014.

Schmitt, Carl. *Die Kernfrage des Völkerbundes.* Ferdinand Dümmler Verlag, 1926.

Schmitt, Carl. *Political Theology: Four Chapters on the Concept of Sovereignty.* 1922. Translated by George Schwab, University of Chicago Press, 2006.

Schmitt, Carl. *Völkerrechtliche Grossraumordnung mit Interventionsverbot für raumfremde Mächte: Ein Beitrag zum Reichsbegriff im Völkerrecht.* 1939. Duncker & Humblot, 1991.

Schmitt, Carl. *Writings on War.* Translated and edited by Timothy Nunan, Polity, 2011.

Schuker, Stephen. "Les États Unis, la France et l'Europe." *Aristide Briand, la Société des Nations et l'Europe.* Edited by Jacques Bariéty, Presses Universitaires de Strasbourg, 2007, pp. 383–96.

Stalin, Josef. "Against Federalism." *Pravda,* no. 19, 29 Mar. 1917. Marxist Internet Archive. https://www.marxists.org/reference/archive/stalin/works/1917/03/28. htm. Accessed 6 March 2024.

Sweet, Alec S., "Why Europe Rejected American Judicial Review – And Why It May Not Matter." *Michigan Law Review,* Aug. 2003, pp. 2744–2780.

Taylor, A. J. P, *The Origins of the Second World War,* Penguin, 2001 (1961)

Vanni, Giuseppe, *Il Federalismo Europeo in Italia: Dal Risorgimento a Ventotene,* Giuseppe Vanni/Streetlib.com, 2019

Velez, Pedro. "On the constitutional order in/of Fascist Italy." Janus.net, *eJournal of International Relations*, vol. 7, no. 2, Nov. 2016, pp. 65–89.

Vinx, Lars. *The Guardian of the Constitution: Hans Kelsen and Carl Schmitt on the Limits of Constitutional Law.* Cambridge University Press, 2015.

Weimar Constitution. 11 August 1919. https://germanhistorydocs.ghi-dc.org/pdf/eng/ghi_wr_weimarconstitution_Eng.pdf. Accessed 6 March 2024.

Wheatley, Natasha. *The Life and Death of States: Central Europe and the Transformation of Modern Sovereignty.* Princeton University Press, 2023.

Williams, T. D. "The Balance of Power and the Second World War." *University Review*, vol. 1, No. 3, 1954–55, pp. 50–61.

Wilson, Charles H.. "The Separation of Powers under Democracy and Fascism." *Political Science Quarterly*, vol. 52, no. 4, 1937, pp. 481–504.

Zimmerman, Joshua D. *Jozef Pilsudksi, Founding Father of Modern Poland.* Harvard University Press, 2022.

11   The Hour for Union

Abstract
The immediate postwar years were a period of federal institution building.
Initially the objective was to create the preconditions for perpetual peace
through the establishment of the United Nations. It was to serve not just
as a platform for managing relations with the Soviet Union, but also as
a framework for the creation of regional leagues, the most important of
which would be a European federal union. When it became clear that the
strategic relationship with the Soviet Union was broken beyond repair,
Western European countries organised themselves in a federal union
for their mutual defence called the Brussels Pact. An effort to extend the
pact to North America would eventually lead to the founding of NATO.

Keywords: Federal union, United Nations, NATO, Atlanticism, European
Movement

Two roads

Through his post–First World War novels, Ernst Jünger (1895–1998) had
become known as a glorifier of military violence and an exponent of German nationalism. Though his ideological stance during the Interbellum
was close to fascism, he was no Nazi party sympathiser. Like Schmitt, he
rejected the Nazis for their vulgarity, and unlike Schmitt their coming to
power did nothing to change his stance. Not that he was an outspoken critic
of the regime – before the start of the Second World War, his distancing
from the Hitler government was more of a social than a political nature. In
1941 however, he started work on a pamphlet that would be adopted as the
unofficial platform for hoped-for negotiations with the Allied Powers by a
group of his admirers: the men behind the so-called Stauffenberg plot (1944).

Published in 1948 in an English translation under the title *The Peace*, it
was an essay in two parts. In the first section, "The Seed," he sketched the
full scale of the horrors of the Nazi regime, "of unconcealed despotism and

Livestro, Joshua: *A More Perfect Union. Federal Union in Political Theory and Practice, 1500-1951.*
Amsterdam: Amsterdam University Press, 2024.
DOI: 10.5117/9789048563777_CH11

(...) naked bestiality" (Jünger 32). One aspect of it was the hollowing out of ordinary life under totalitarian rule: "Things lost their cheerful hue and with each new morning came the question: Would evening find the family united round the table or torn apart, its members dragged away? And when at night the light was extinguished, the ear strained to catch the whispering of the police agents without" (Jünger 32–33).

Even more terrible was the reality of enormous numbers of "Golgothas where the disenfranchised were slaughtered" as "disseminators of their faith, which laws invented overnight had decreed to be a moral taint" (Jünger 34). "Dark rumours passed from mouth to mouth" told of "hordes driven like cattle to the graveyards and cremation ovens where the executioners waited. There they were stripped of their rags and slaughtered like shorn sheeThey were forced even to dig their own graves, if their murderers did not fill the quarries and pit-shafts with the corpses which piled up too fast" (35). The day would come, he warned, when "[t]hese scenes of horror (...) will be brought to light," when "the lost souls who played the hangman there, together with their superiors, are forced to break silence before the court" (35).

It would, he stated, be an essential part of the work of postwar reconstruction to grasp the full scale of the suffering. If people wanted to understand the enormity of the change to come, they had to acknowledge the enormity of what it was that had to be overcome. Whereas in the First World War the suffering was mainly military, embodied by the Unknown Soldier, in this Second World War "the suffering was more widely spread, more obscure and complex. (...) It was closer to the great religious images. For that reason it will form the base of structures towering higher into the light" (Jünger 40).

In part two, "The Fruit," he went on to describe the nature and purpose of these towering structures. He first sketched their foundation, which was the complete and utter defeat of the Nazi regime. This was necessary not only because it had to rob "those who recognise no other arguments" (Jünger 45) of the illusion of "if only," but also because it was essential that there was to be no suggestion of a possible return to the *status quo ante*. Using rhetoric like that used by Stead half a century earlier, he argued that "it is better for man to suffer longer than to postpone part of the process and return to the old world. (...) [T]here is no compromise in the race towards the goal" (45–56)

But if the path to this new world was one of bloody violence, its final establishment could only be achieved through justice: "The peace cannot be a peace of compromise. But just as little may the peace be one of violence" (Jünger 47). It was to be an entirely different peace from the one that settled the last war, avoiding not only its sense of victors' justice but also its embrace of "national democracies" as successors to the old empires (47). The new era, he proclaimed, was to be one of "synthesis" and "coalition." The end of the war would bring "the hour for union," which was to be "the hour when Europe, founding itself on the union of its peoples, attains sovereignty and constitutional form" (49).

This then was the choice that Europe would face after war's end: "Two roads are opening up before the nations. One is the road of hatred and retribution. (…) The true road, on the contrary, leads to unity; the forces which consumed each other in deadly opposition must unite for the new shape of things, the new life. Here alone are the sources of true peace, of prosperity, security and strength" (Jünger 50).

—

The Western Powers would eventually choose the second road, but not before contemplating taking the first. The French government in exile under Charles de Gaulle had advocated a strategy of neutralising the German threat by de-federalising the old constituent states. A version of this idea, essentially a version of Henri IV's strategy of dealing with the Habsburg empire by dividing it into more manageable parts, would become the official Allied approach in the immediate postwar period. At the Potsdam conference in the summer of 1945, Germany was first stripped of its eastern Prussian lands (they became part of a newly reconstituted Poland, while Russia claimed Kant's old hometown of Königsberg) and then divided into four zones of occupation.

Towards the end of the war, there was also some momentum for a radical strategy of de-industrialisation first set out in a 1944 memorandum by the US Treasury Secretary Henry Morgenthau Jr. Its objective was to reduce Germany to an agricultural society, leaving it without the means of ever becoming an economic or military powerhouse again. Morgenthau used a leaders' meeting in Quebec in September 1944 to gain support for his approach from Roosevelt and Churchill (Hathaway and Shapiro 255).

Against this "denuding" strategy, another group of American policymakers led by Roosevelt's former Secretary of State, Cordell Hull, argued that the best way of pacifying Germany would be to integrate it fully in a transatlantic free market. Hull's successor as Secretary of State, Henry Stimson, fully agreed: "The essential basis of enduring peace must be economic" (Isaacson and Thomas 235).

A third, more pragmatic position combined the two ideas. It accepted German economic reconstruction as a main objective, but suggested building in certain safeguards by putting its industrial heartland – traditionally the engine of the German war machine – beyond German control. The latter idea would eventually take the form of the International Authority for the Ruhr, which put the area under joint control of a Council with representatives from the US, UK, France, and the Benelux countries (a Western European regional customs union involving Belgium, The Netherlands and Luxembourg, founded in 1944 by the governments in exile of the three countries). Meanwhile the German coal reserves in the Saar region were placed under French authority, a decision that would prove to be of great significance for Europe's future.

—

Reconstruction was far from an easy objective, given the scale of the destruction. The damage caused by six years of warfare was enormous. Tens of millions of people dead, tens of millions of houses and public buildings destroyed. Countless bridges, roads, railroads, canals, harbours, and airports wrecked or deliberately demolished. In some parts of Eastern Europe, the fighting had taken on such a nihilistic character that whole regions were simply destroyed rather than left to the advancing enemy: forests hacked down, fields and villages burned, plains flooded. In German towns, the Allied bombings had reduced anywhere between fifty and seventy percent of the housing stock to rubble. In Poland and parts of the Soviet Union (especially Ukraine), the damage was even worse. By the time the Nazis were finally ready to leave Warsaw to the advancing Soviet troops, they had destroyed more than ninety percent of all buildings. The Royal Castle, St John's Cathedral, the National Library, the whole old town: everything was razed to the ground in a deliberate campaign of destruction (Lowe 3–4).

A second challenge was that of hunger. Allied trade blockades and Axis military requisitioning of scarce civilian resources had led to a dramatic drop in daily caloric intakes during the war. A whole continent had slowly starved itself to death (Lowe 36). Even after the fighting stopped, food production and food distribution networks remained a fraction of the pre-war capacity, making the fight against mass starvation a serious policy challenge in the immediate aftermath of the war. In most countries rationing would remain in place until the early 1950s.

A third challenge was the displacement of tens of millions of people. In part this was the result of Nazi measures to sustain the war effort. By the end of the war, Germany held approximately eight million forced labourers within its borders, from all parts of Europe (Lowe 27). Conversely, millions of German and Austrian men were still being held as prisoners of war. Germany was also home to millions of refugees who had fled Eastern Europe ahead of the advancing Soviet army. Millions more would follow because of deliberate policies of ethnic cleansing or de-Germanification, for example through the decrees passed by the Czechoslovak government in exile under Edvard Beneš. The aim of these decrees had been to undo the consequences of 1918 by creating a nationally homogenous Czechoslovak state. It led to the forced expulsion of numerous German and Hungarian citizens in the immediate aftermath of the second World War, and to the expropriation of houses, shops, farms, and factories.[1] According to an official early 1950s estimate by the German Statistical Office, in October 1946 Germany was home to 5.6 million refugees from former German communities in Eastern Europe (Statistisches Bundesamt 33).

—

In early February 1946 Stalin fired the opening shot in what was to become known as the Cold War. In a section of a speech devoted to the assessment of the causes of the two world wars, he made an observation that contained an unmistakable warning to the West: "Perhaps catastrophic wars could be avoided if it were possible periodically to redistribute raw materials and markets among the respective countries in conformity with their economic weight by means of concerted and peaceful decisions. But this is impossible under the present capitalist conditions of world economic development" (Stalin). In other words: another war was unavoidable.

Two weeks later, George Kennan produced his famous Long Telegram, a missive sent from the US Embassy in Moscow. It marked the start of a gradual process of reorientation inside the American foreign policy establishment. Kennan stressed that the Soviets didn't believe cooperation with the West was sustainable: "USSR still lives in antagonistic 'capitalist encirclement' with which in the long run there can be no permanent peaceful coexistence" (Kennan). He concluded that this premise would lead the Soviet leadership to seek to advance its own strength and weaken that of the Western powers.

As evidence mounted that Stalin was indeed tempted to suspend cooperation with the West, other key foreign policy advisers to Truman came round to the position that the West needed a policy of containment of Soviet power. Not only did they reject domestic pleas for a return to the isolationism of the

1   The decrees would resurface during the Czech and Slovak EU accession talks, when Germany, Austria and Hungary suggested making their repeal a condition for entry.

pre-war period, but they also actively encouraged Truman to seek a leading role for the United States in shaping and executing the required policy.

The American president would announce his doctrine to that effect on 12 March 1947. In a speech to a joint session of Congress, he sketched a scene of European countries on the brink, with several already having fallen to Soviet intervention:

> The peoples of a number of countries of the world have recently had totalitarian regimes forced upon them against their will. The Government of the United States has made frequent protests against coercion and intimidation, in violation of the Yalta agreement, in Poland, Rumania, and Bulgaria. I must also state that in a number of other countries there have been similar developments.
> (Truman)[2]

His proposal had two main elements: provide the kind of aid that would "assist free peoples to work out their destinies in their own way," while taking a stand against "changes in the status quo (...) by such methods as coercion, or such subterfuges as political infiltration." The strategy he proposed was based on the linking of economic development to military security: the more affluent the Western economies would get, the more secure they would be against Russian infiltration. It would start with aid packages for Greece and Turkey, but it was clear it wouldn't end there. For this strategy to work, the entire Western European coalition of states that had been involved in the defeat of Germany would need to be provided with the kind of support that would allow them to prevent the flowering of "the seeds of totalitarian regimes" (by which he clearly meant Soviet totalitarianism, though he never mentioned the USSR by name during his speech).

For Truman, this was a "whatever it takes" moment: "If further funds, or further authority, should be needed for purposes indicated in this message, I shall not hesitate to bring the situation before the Congress." It would fall to his Secretary of State George Marshall to make the actual request, which he first announced in a speech at Harvard University, in June 1947. His audience knew Marshall wasn't the kind of man to use dramatic language in his public statements, which made his warning of impending European doom all the more impressive: "The truth of the matter is that Europe's requirements for the next three or four years of foreign food and other essential products – principally from America – are so much greater than

---

2   All subsequent quotes in this section come from this speech unless indicated otherwise.

her present ability to pay that she must have substantial additional help or face economic, social, and political deterioration of a very grave character" (Marshall).

The aid program that followed this speech would considerably help Europe's economic recovery. No less significant was its political impact. By forcing European countries to come to an agreement about the distribution of available resources through the Organisation for European Economic Co-operation (OEEC), the Truman administration made Europe's governments for the first time work on solving economic problems jointly – not as part of an international Bretton Woods style programme, but in Europe, as Europeans.

A New League

As significant as the economic damage caused by the war was the moral damage wrecked by the Holocaust. As foretold by Jünger, the end of the war and the liberation of the death camps revealed the full scale of the horror. The images had a big impact on Western policymakers, adding a sense of moral urgency to their deliberations. To the economic reconstruction mission was added the task of dealing with the moral consequences of the Holocaust and five years of totalitarian rule.

The moral restoration project had to be on a significant scale if it was to match the size of the damage done to the rule of law. First came the reckoning with the crimes committed during the war. This required a dramatic gesture, in the true sense of the word: theatrical, though of a profoundly serious nature, with an element of katharsis. Churchill's preferred solution of simply rounding up and shooting the main culprits would not do – it might have been acceptable as retributive justice, but not as a public act of moral restoration. The death of the main Nazi leadership – Hitler, Goebbels, and Himmler – gave the British Prime Minister sufficient cover to accept the alternative solution of a public trial. The Nuremberg tribunal created two important forms of jurisprudence. Not only did it produce the first ever convictions for the waging of a war of aggression (confirming Schmitt's prediction), it also saw the conviction of a number of defendants on the charge of crimes against humanity – a new type of charge introduced by the British prosecution team on the advice of Hersch Lauterpacht.

During its first session, in New York in December 1946, the United Nations General Assembly would affirm as international law the entire Nuremburg Charter, including the prohibitions on wars of aggression and crimes against humanity (Sands 954). The session in New York was actually the second half of the first meeting. The first half had taken place at the start of the year, in London. There, the Economic and Social Council had charged a special commission with drawing up a report on the tasks of the Permanent Commission on Human Rights. It was this special commission that, under the leadership of Eleanor Roosevelt, would produce the Universal Declaration of Human Rights.

The many abhorrent abuses of people's rights, both before and during the war, made a restatement of their fundamental importance necessary. As the Belgian UN delegate Count Henry Carton de Wiart put it, it was vital once more "to emphasise the high dignity of the human person after the outrages to which men and women had been exposed during the last war" (Morsink 37). The Declaration was to serve as more than just a restatement of this fundamental truth, though. It was also, and more importantly, enshrining in law the commitment of "Never Again" that echoed through Western societies after war's end.[3] Some of the rights introduced through the Universal Declaration specifically refuted elements of Nazi doctrine, like the non-discrimination clause (Art. 2), the clause guaranteeing the individual's "life, liberty and security" (Art. 3) and the call for an independent judiciary (Art. 10). Others focused on preventing a repeat of Nazi practices like slavery (Art. 4), torture (Art. 5) and arbitrary arrest (Art. 9) (Morsink 38–43).

By making these rights actionable through regional Declarations with their own courts, the Universal Declaration would become one of the cornerstones of the postwar rule of law. It would form a legally enforceable external check against the powers of the state.

—

The war had also created a strategic challenge of the first order for Western policymakers. On the one hand, they considered continued strong ties with the Soviet leadership essential for world peace and security. On the other, it was clear that a vast ideological gulf separated the two sides. The reality of Soviet totalitarianism was impossible to ignore. Finding a way to manage this tension became a core mission.

Peace seemed to have been safeguarded when the victorious parties signed the treaty to establish the United Nations in San Francisco, in June 1945.

---

3   In his analysis of the Universal Declaration on 37, Morsink states that "[t]he motif that runs throughout these adoptions and rejections [of the various draft articles] is that the Universal Declaration was adopted to avoid another Holocaust or similar abomination."

Just like in 1919, the defeated Axis coalition countries had been excluded from the negotiations ("The United Nations" was the term with which the Allied coalition had described itself during the war, making an invitation for Axis coalition countries unlikely), but this time there was no claim of victor's justice, let alone a "stab in the back" legend to feed new grievances.

The League of Nations had generally been dismissed as a failure by wartime commentators and resistance writers. In President Roosevelt's plans for a "new order" to be established after the end of the war, however, the formation of "a friendly, civilised society" of "free countries, working together" was an essential element (Roosevelt). Creation of a new version of the old League was therefore part of the American war aims before the country had even entered the war.

The United Nations managed to achieve one thing that the League had not: secure American membership. The Roosevelt administration had agonised for a while over the best strategy to achieve a speedy ratification in the Senate. In the end it opted for the method of full cooptation of the Republican opposition. What made this choice more remarkable was the fact that it involved extending an invitation to join the negotiating team to the Michigan senator Arthur Vandenberg (1884–1951), who had been one of the leading voices of Republican isolationism in the prewar years.

There were solid reasons though for assuming Vandenberg would not abuse the occasion for a renewal of his old isolationist campaign. Not only had isolationism suffered a shattering blow on 7 December 1941 (the attack on Pearl Harbor), Vandenberg himself had earlier in 1945 publicly confessed his changed attitude on international engagement in a speech on the Senate floor that was hailed by the progressive political magazine *The New Republic* as "a turning point in world affairs" (Kaplan, *The Conversion of Senator Arthur H. Vandenberg* 109). His involvement in the UN Treaty negotiations would further strengthen his newfound faith in the cause of multilateralism – a fact that would later play a decisive role in negotiations about the formation of a transatlantic union.

No less remarkable than America's enthusiastic involvement in the UN was the speed with which the new organisation was created. It was negotiated and signed before the Japanese government had even surrendered. There had, of course, been negotiations before the end of the war to deal with the main potential stumbling blocks. In a working conference held in the second half of 1944 in the former residence of Vice President John Calhoun (the Dumbarton Oaks estate in Georgetown, Washington DC), the Great Powers had settled on a structure that resembled that of the League of Nations. Like the old League, this "new League," as Senator Vandenberg called it (Kaplan 101) would have an assembly, a court, and a permanent secretariat. The Council was rechristened the "Security Council," as if to underline the importance of its task of managing relations between the Great Powers. Among the permanent members, the US and China would take the seats once occupied by Germany and Japan.

Dumbarton Oaks, and the subsequent discussion at Yalta, left two main issues unresolved: the question of the veto, and the Soviet demand to have not one but three votes in the general assembly. During the San Francisco negotiations, the latter issue would be resolved in the Kremlin's favour: Ukraine and Belarus were both made members with full voting rights.[4] On the veto the Great Powers eventually agreed to disagree. The American delegation was not of a mind to abolish it altogether, but it had been willing to contemplate an arrangement where the permanent members of the Security Council would give up the right to veto cases involving their own acts of aggression. "I am opposed to any such immunity. In my view it would represent a new imperialism," Senator Vandenberg had declared in the run-up to the conference.[5] (Kaplan, *Vandenberg* 109). But the Russian negotiator, the later Foreign Secretary Andrei Gromyko, would not budge. He even demanded that the veto power be extended to cover not just the final vote but even the opening of an initial investigation.

In the end, a Russian signature under the Charter was more important to the American government than a compromise on the veto issue. As events would show, the compromise that was struck would quickly make the Security Council unworkable. In the first five years after its creation, the Soviet delegation would make liberal use of its veto power, blocking a number of membership applications, recommendations on conventional and nuclear arms control, and most contentiously, reports on its own involvement in attempted regime change in Greece and Czechoslovakia.

The latter veto, cast in the aftermath of the communist coup of February 1948, confirmed what was by then already generally feared to be the case: when it came to Eastern Europe, the Western Powers were effectively powerless to deliver the Charter's promise to "reaffirm faith in fundamental human rights of men and women and of nations large and small" (United Nations Charter preamble). After May 1945, the Soviet sphere of influence agreed to in the Moscow summit of 1944, and confirmed at Yalta in early

---

4   I use the current name "Ukraine" for the sake of historical continuity, though it is important to note that the Soviet name at the time was "the Ukraine."

5   This did not stop Vandenberg from demanding that the US government should under all circumstances retain the veto when it came to the Monroe doctrine. See Kaplan 134.

1945, quickly became a solid power block under Russian control. In some countries (Czechoslovakia, Hungary), the initial focus of local communist parties was on gaining power through the ballot box. When this yielded insufficient results, other parties were systematically purged from the political system until only pro-communist parties remained. In other countries (Poland, Romania, Yugoslavia) violence was employed early on to establish communist dominance (Rady 468–469). Although until the end of the decade attempts were made from both parts of Europe to give collaborative projects a joint aspect, it was clear that a European union for the near future would be based solely on Western Europe.

Servants of the Grand Design: Winston Churchill and the European Movement

Every movement needs a prophet. The cause of European union found its own in the person of the British wartime Prime Minister, Sir Winston Churchill (1874–1965). On 19 September 1946 he gave a speech at the University of Zurich which, according to the Belgian politician Paul-Henri Spaak (1899–1972), served as a clarion call for European unification: "The Zurich speech galvanised all those who believed in the necessity of a new Europe" (Spaak 22).

Churchill started his speech by sketching the seemingly hopeless state of the continent, invoking images of a new Dark Age: "[O]ver wide areas are a vast, quivering mass of tormented, hungry, careworn and bewildered human beings, who wait in the ruins of their cities and homes and scan the dark horizons for the approach of some new form of tyranny or terror" (Churchill, Speech at the University of Zurich).[6] There was, however, a way forward:

> [T]here is a remedy which, if it were generally and spontaneously adopted by the great majority of people in many lands, would as by a miracle transform the whole scene and would in a few years make all Europe, or the greater part of it, as free and happy as Switzerland is today. What is this sovereign remedy? It is to recreate the European fabric, or as much of it as we can, and to provide it with a structure under which it can dwell in peace, safety and freedom. We must build a kind of United States of Europe.

He went on to identify two different sources of inspiration for this unification plan. One was the various prewar schemes for unification which provided

---

6   All subsequent quotes in this section come from this speech unless indicated otherwise.

a kind of canon from which ideas could be lifted. Here he referred specifically to "the famous French patriot and statesman Aristide Briand," and to Coudenhove-Kalerghi's pan-Europe scheme. The other was the practical example of the League of Nations. The latter reference may have surprised his audience, given its reputation as a failed experiment. But, he explained, it was still worth studying: "The League did not fail because of its principles or conceptions. It failed because those principles were deserted by those states which brought it into being, because the governments of those states feared to face the facts and act while time remained."

—

Though the Zurich speech was the first time since the end of the war that Churchill had openly reflected on the topic of European unification, the message itself was not new for him. There were, in fact, several constants in Churchill's thinking about European order, confirmed over a period of decades. He would touch on them in his Zurich speech. One was his view that perpetual peace on the continent could only be achieved through reconciliation between France and Germany: "In this way only can France recover the moral and cultural leadership of Europe. There can be no revival of Europe without a spiritually great France and a spiritually great Germany" (Churchill, Speech at the University of Zurich). In his postwar memoirs published in 1948, Churchill wrote that he first came to this idea in the context of the negotiations leading to the Locarno Pact, when he served as Chancellor of the Exchequer under the Conservative Prime Minister Stanley Baldwin. He noted that the British Dominion governments seemed mostly unenthusiastic about the idea of a pact that tied the British government – and therefore indirectly their own countries – to the continent. In the end, though, the government did decide to enter the Locarno negotiations, with Churchill's wholehearted support: "To me the aim of ending the thousand-year strife between France and Germany seemed a supreme objective." "This," he concluded, "is still my view today" (Churchill, *The Gathering Storm* 90–91).

The second constant element in his thinking was the need for a European federation. In an American newspaper article published in 1930, he first called for a federal Europe as a pillar next to Russia, the British Commonwealth and the United States. It would, he observed, inevitably constitute a power equal to these three:

> Let Russia slide back, as Count Calergi proposes, and as is already so largely a fact, into Asia. Let the British Empire, excluded in his plan,

realise its own world-spread ideal; even so, the mass of Europe, once united, once federalised or partially federalised, once continentally self-conscious—Europe, with its African and Asiatic possessions and plantations— would constitute an organism beyond compare.
(Churchill, "'The United States of Europe")

It's worth noting here that he did not have a clear idea of the constitutional shape this "organism" should take. Like Woodrow Wilson, he seemed to think that the act of unification was more important than the immediate working out of a constitutional arrangement. Contained in this second constant element was the third: the idea that a European federal union was something that Britain should support wholeheartedly but not necessarily participate in: "We are with Europe, but not of it. We are linked but not comprised. We are interested and associated, but not absorbed." The reason was the British Empire: "We belong to no single continent, but to all. Not to one hemisphere, but to both; as well to the New World as to the Old" (Churchill, "The United States of Europe").

In a debate about the British government's decision not to accept an invitation to participate in the negotiations that would eventually lead to the formation of the European Coal and Steel Community, Churchill stressed that in considering any issue, "first in all our thoughts" would always be "the Empire and Commonwealth; secondly, the fraternal association of the English-speaking world; and thirdly, not in rank or status but in order, the revival of united Europe as a vast factor in the preserving of what is left of the civilisation and culture of the free world" (Hansard, Debate on the Schuman Plan).

—

To these three elements was added a fourth in the form of the establishment of a permanent platform for transatlantic cooperation. European unification alone was not enough. An effort was also required to create the preconditions for permanent American engagement in European affairs. He would address this idea on a number of occasions, most prominently in a speech on 5 March 1946 at Westminster College in Fulton, Missouri (Churchill, "Address at Westminster College").[7] It would become known as his "Iron Curtain" speech, where he acknowledged that from Poland to Yugoslavia, "all are subject in one form or another, not only to Soviet influence but to a

7   All subsequent quotes in this section come from this speech unless indicated otherwise.

very high and, in some cases, increasing measure of control from Moscow." The purpose of his speech was not just to warn of the descending of an iron curtain across the continent though. It was also a reflection on the preconditions for lasting peace – if not in perpetuity then at least for "many peaceful years."

Having formulated the two main threats to this peaceful scenario – war and tyranny – he came to what he described as "the crux of what I have travelled here to say." He went on to describe what he called "the sinews of peace," the kind of institutions that would help to guarantee that peace would be allowed to endure. He mentioned three of them specifically. The first was the newly created "temple of peace" called the United Nations, "the successor of the League of Nations, with the decisive addition of the United States and all that that means."

Within that international league setting he proposed the creation of further regional leagues. Contrary to the pre-war consensus that such regional organisations would undermine the cohesion of the League of Nations, he argued that they could actually help to strengthen the new UN: "Special associations between members of the United Nations which have no aggressive point against any other country, which harbour no design incompatible with the Charter of the United Nations, far from being harmful, are beneficial and, as I believe, indispensable." One example of this was the establishment of "a new unity in Europe." "We should," he proposed, "work with conscious purpose for a grand pacification of Europe, within the structure of the United Nations and in accordance with its Charter. That I feel is an open cause of policy of very great importance."

The final one of his proposed institutions was the one he specifically wanted to recommend to his Fulton audience, which included President Truman. As its basis it had "the fraternal association of the English-speaking peoples," more specifically the "special relationship between the British Commonwealth and Empire and the United States."[8] Though based on "growing friendship and mutual understanding," it could not end there. What was required was a close and lasting cooperation, especially in military affairs, through "common study of potential dangers, the similarity of weapons and manuals of instructions, and to the interchange of officers and

---

8   This wasn't the first time Churchill addressed the theme of a closer relationship between the UK and US. In a speech in Westchester, New York, delivered the day after the death of Aristide Briand, he had observed that the US and UK must develop a joint position if Europe were to unify: "Let us have no fear of the United States of Europe, as long as the United States and England grow closer together" ("Churchill warns of United Europe," *New York Times*, 9 March 1932).

cadets at technical colleges," and through "the continuance of the present facilities for mutual security by the joint use of all Naval and Air Force bases in the possession of either country all over the world."

This military union, which would be based on the kind of Permanent Defence Agreement already in place between the United States and Canada, could over time grow into something more: "Eventually there may come – I feel eventually there will come – the principle of common citizenship." That however he was "content to leave to destiny, whose outstretched arm many of us can already clearly see."

—

These four themes would serve as the building blocks of Churchill's postwar international political message, though he would at times vary the details, depending on his audience. Always, though, he would draw the contrast between the old era of "nationalist quarrels" (Churchill, Zurich) or "nationalistic feuds" (Churchill, Speech at the meeting of the United Europe Committee). In that latter speech, he talked off a new era in which "the people of Europe come together and work together for mutual advantage." In this "hour of choice" he saw it as Britain's duty to "be a prime mover" in "the cause of United Europe" (Churchill, United Europe Committee).

It was a mission that he clearly took personally. Not only did he help to found the British United Europe Movement, serving as its chairman, he was also instrumental in gathering the various pro-Union movements across the continent and uniting them in a single organisation. Out of this merger, which apart from the United Europe Movement also involved groups like the *Conseil Français Pour l'Europe Unie*, the *Nouvelles Equipes Internationales*, the *Movement Socialiste pour les États Unis d'Europe*, the European Union of Federalists, and the Economic League for European Cooperation, was born the European Movement (Zurcher 21–22).

The first meaningful act of this new movement was the organisation of a conference in the old Knight's Hall of the Dutch Parliament, in The Hague in May 1948. Much like the Paris Peace Conference of a century earlier, this was a gathering of the great and the good of the European unification movement. Leading the British delegation was a trio of past and future prime ministers: Winston Churchill, Anthony Eden and Harold Macmillan. Among the German delegation were future Chancellor Konrad Adenauer and future European Commission President Walter Hallstein. France sent both former Prime Ministers like Paul Reynaud and Edouard Daladier, and a future president in the person of François Mitterand (then already a cabinet minister). Also present were noted propagandists for a federal Europe like Richard Coudenhove-Kalergi, Altiero Spinelli and Józef Retinger[9], exiled political figures like the former Spanish Republican minister Salvador de Madariaga and the Polish former government minister Jan Piłsudski (brother of the former president Józef Piłsudski), and a large number of current and former cabinet ministers, senators, MPs, as well as representatives of employers federations, universities and churches. There was even a contingent of intellectual leaders like the Dutch future Nobel Prize winning economist Jan Tinbergen, the Swiss novelist and philosopher Denis de Rougemont and the French philosopher Raymond Aron.

As Honorary President, it was up to Churchill to deliver the main address (Churchill, "Address to the Congress of Europe").[10] He started by defining the new movement. It was first of all a movement of peoples. It could not be otherwise, in fact. Any attempt to reduce it to one particular ideological movement, to make it the ownership of one particular party or group of parties, would see it fail: "Europe can only be united by the heart-felt wish and vehement expression of the great majority of all the peoples in all the parties in all the freedom-loving countries, no matter where they dwell or how they vote."[11] And it was a movement with a history: "There are many famous names associated with the revival and presentation of this idea, but we may all, I think, yield our pretensions to Henry Navarre, King of France, who, with his great Minister Sully, between the years 1600 and 1607, laboured to set up a permanent committee representing the fifteen – now we are sixteen – leading Christian States of Europe." Placing his movement firmly in that tradition, he declared: "We are the servants of the Grand Design."

He then went on to check all of his familiar themes. The call for European unity was most obvious, forming the very reason his audience was assembled. It was in every section of his speech, from the opening praise for "great governments" who had "associated for economic purposes" under the Marshall Plan to the Lincoln-like exhortation at the end to "here and

---

9   On May 7 1946, Retinger had given a lecture at the Royal Institute of International Affairs in which he sketched how, during the war, the Polish Prime Minister in exile, General Wladyslaw Sikorski, had argued that "European states ought to relinquish part of their sovereignty for the common interest." The inspiration for this had come from "a precedent for such a federal block of nations in the past history of Poland herself. In the 15th century she concluded a union with Lithuania (incorporating the White Russians), which worked most successfully for all concerned until the downfall of Poland."

10   All subsequent quotes in this section come from this speech unless indicated otherwise.

11   A veiled reference to the notable absence of the Labour government. It had in fact issued orders to its MPs not to attend the conference.

now resolve that in one form or another a European Assembly shall be constituted which will enable that voice to make itself continuously heard."

There was also the theme of Franco-German reconciliation:

> Some time ago I stated that it was the proud mission of the victor nations to take the Germans by the hand and lead them back into the European family, and I rejoice that some of the most eminent and powerful Frenchmen have spoken in this sense. To rebuild Europe from its ruins and make its light shine forth again upon the world, we must first of all conquer ourselves.

As for Britain's committed but separate position, it was one of those occasions where Churchill tailored his words to fit his purpose. In contrast to the Fulton speech, where he told his American audience that the core of the new world order must be formed by the special relationship between the United States and the British Commonwealth and Empire, he now chose to place that same British Commonwealth and Empire squarely in the European camp. He did it in a section devoted to the global security architecture, which he described as consisting of three pillars of the new world order, all resting under "the permanent authority of a world organisation of the United Nations."[12] The first pillar was "the vast Soviet Union." In a hat tip to the Monroe Doctrine, he described the second as "the United States and her sister republics in the Western Hemisphere with all their great spheres of interest and influence." The third was "the Council of Europe, *including Great Britain linked with her Empire and Commonwealth*" (my emphasis).

—

As Churchill himself knew when he spoke these words, the global house of security was in the process of dividing against itself. In his Fulton speech, he had already hinted at the answer: to create the preconditions for the strongest possible Western alliance. What was required was not "the old doctrine of a balance of power," which he dismissed as "unsound," but a clear Western preponderance – an unbalance, as it were. It was in his view the only way to get the Soviet Union to stay true to the principles of the UN Charter: "If the Western Democracies stand together (...) their influence

---

12   A year earlier, he had spoken of "four main pillars of the temple of peace," one of which was "the British Empire and Commonwealth." But then that was an address to a British audience, and this was a speech to a room full of continental European politicians…

for furthering those principles will be immense and no one is likely to molest them" (Churchill, Fulton). But this would require the Americans to contemplate something even president Wilson had categorically ruled out in 1919: a permanent military commitment to safeguard European peace and security.

Pax Atlantica

On the American side of the Atlantic, the postwar years saw a keen interest in the issue of European unification. This was in part a product of *raison d'état* considerations. The amount of economic devastation, and the threat posed by Soviet troops and propaganda to the remaining free parts of Europe, meant that in American eyes nothing short of European federal union would do to revive and protect it. Writing in 1948, the founder of the postwar Realist school of International Relations, Hans Morgenthau, prescribed federalism as the only possible solution for Western Europe's predicament: "[I]n Western Europe at least, the nation state is an obsolescent principle of political organisation which, far from assuring the security and power of its members, condemns them to impotence and ultimate extinction either by each other or by their more powerful neighbours" (Morgenthau 122).

It was not all a matter of calculation though. Equally important was the American commitment to the idea of federal union. The man who a few years later would become President Eisenhower's Secretary of State, John Foster Dulles (1888–1959), would regularly touch on this theme, both as a senior adviser to the Republican Party leadership and, briefly, as a Senator. Dulles was the closest thing the US has had to State Department aristocracy: his maternal grandfather, John W. Foster, was Secretary of State under President Harrison, while his wife's uncle was Robert Lansing, Secretary of State under Woodrow Wilson. Dulles himself started his diplomatic career at the age of eighteen, serving as secretary to the Chinese delegation for the 1907 The Hague Peace Conference. He was subsequently involved in virtually every major US peace negotiation, serving in the US delegation for the Versailles peace talks and the San Francisco conference that led to the signing of the UN Treaty, as well as the 1951 San Francisco treaty that finally created peace with Japan (Kaplan, *NATO 1948* 18).

In a speech delivered in New York in January 1947 titled "Europe Must Federate or Perish," Dulles presented the US Constitution as a model for European development: "Americans ought to give them precious assistance. (...) We have, more than any other people, experience in using the federal formula" (quoted in Kaplan, *NATO 1948* 18). At times he would mix *raison d'état* and ideological commitment, for example in an article published in *Collier's* in June 1948, where he presented the idea of European federation as a plausible end goal for American foreign policy. It would, he explained, solve two problems at once. By enabling the Europeans "to stand alone" financially and militarily, it would allow the American government to stop "bolstering up peoples who have the possibility of standing independently on their own feet" (Dulles 75). And by helping to create a "great sister federation," it would also "bring to an end the considerable risk of war" (76).

Around the same time that Dulles first went public with his support for the idea of a European federal union, Congress passed a motion calling for the establishment of a United States of Europe. The great supporter of this idea was Senator J. William Fulbright (1905–1995). In speeches on the Senate floor, as well as in numerous articles, he would make the case that "now is the time" for a European federal union, for example in an article in the *Annals of the American Academy of Political and Social Science* of May 1948 (Fulbright, "A United States of Europe?" 151). He pointed out that the idea of European federation did not just have "a long and respected history" (here he referred to, among others, Henry IV, William Penn, and Kant, to the "kind of unity achieved under the Holy Alliance," and to twentieth century advocates of the idea like Briand, Herriot and Churchill), it also had a relevance, and even an urgency, in the here and now. "[I]f unification of Europe is to be achieved," he claimed, "it must be started without delay" unless "the reassertion of nationalistic individualism will appear" (Fulbright 151).

The same message was put out by newspaper editorial boards across the US. "Europe must federate or perish," declared the *New York Times*. The *Wall Street Journal* warned that "Europe's unification is Europe's last chance." The *St Louis Post-Dispatch* put it in American Revolutionary terms: "[F]or Europe it is a case of join – or die" (Beugel 461).

—

Support for *European* federation was probably the most prominent form in which American postwar federal enthusiasm manifested itself. It was by no means the only form though. Two other ideas also gained a significant following. One, which was particularly popular in the immediate aftermath of the war, was the idea of using the United Nations as a starting point for the construction of a global federation. This so-called "One World" idea had been launched in 1943 by the 1940 Republican Party's presidential nominee, Wendell Wilkie (1892–1944). His book *One World*, part travel diary and part political pamphlet, was a remarkable success, topping the bestsellers' charts for several months. It derived its impact from the messianic final chapter, in which he called for active American involvement in "the creation of a world in which there shall be an equality of opportunity for every race and every nation" (Wilkie 144). Wilkie himself did not present any ideas for the creation of a world federation, but this gap was soon filled by a number of world federalist organisations, some of whom would succeed in getting endorsements from prominent public figures like Albert Einstein and Mahatma Gandhi.

One prominent American spokesman for this idea was the Harvard based political scientist Arthur N. Holcombe (1884–1977), who had introduced the teaching of political theory and philosophy within the Harvard study of government and politics curriculum, and counted Henry Kissinger and the later president John F. Kennedy among his students. Holcombe used a study titled *Our More Perfect Union: From Eighteenth Century Principles to Twentieth Century Practice* to develop the theme, also touched on by Dulles, of the United States founding and constitution serving as a source of inspiration, in this case for world federation. "We are in the midst of a period of revolutionary change," he declared in the preface. The reality of Hiroshima meant that "even in the best organised parts of the world there was need to reexamine the established processes of government with a view to reappraising their value under the strenuous conditions of modern times" (Holcombe v). At the global level, this meant developing "plans which moderate and conciliatory politicians are capable of making. Such plans should be based upon the principles of government which American experience has demonstrated to be sound. The principles of the separation of powers and of federalism seem well suited to the task of forming a more perfect Union of the Nations" (428–429).

In *The Great Rehearsal,* the Benjamin Franklin biographer and ghostwriter of Wendell Wilkie's bestseller, Carl van Doren (1885–1950), used the same theme. Though he admitted that "the parallel between 1787 and 1948 is naturally not exact," it was "impossible to read the story of the making and ratifying of the Constitution of the United States without finding there all the arguments in favour of a general government for the United Nations, as well as all the arguments now raised in opposition to it" (Doren viii). It was, moreover, entirely legitimate to use the debate of 1787 to enlighten that of 1948: "The supporters of the Constitution of 1787 knew that they were planning a government only for the United States, but they believed their experiment would instruct and benefit all mankind. Their undertaking might be, though of course no one of them ever used the term, a rehearsal for the federal governments of the future" (x).

The One World idea would dominate American public debate and political discourse in the immediate aftermath of the war, but by 1946 enthusiasm for it had begun to wane (Segers 22). Attention from US policymakers would shift to another form of international federalism.

—

The third idea was only slightly less ambitious: the formation of a transatlantic federal union. Politically this took the form of a campaign for the organisation of a constitutional convention involving the United States, Canada, the United Kingdom, France, and the Benelux countries (Belgium, The Netherlands and Luxembourg). It was pushed by an organisation called the Atlantic Union, which was chaired by the former Supreme Court Justice Owen J. Roberts, and counted among its board members a former Secretary of War, Robert Patterson, and a former Under Secretary of State for Economic Affairs, Will L. Clayton. Among its most prominent political supporters were a group of Senators and Congressmen of both parties who actively campaigned for the idea. It included the man who would serve as Democratic Vice Presidential nominee in the 1956 elections, Senator Estes Kefauver. Another notable supporter, first from the Senate, later from the State Department, was John Foster Dulles.

Dulles' support for the Atlantic Union's campaign was most likely a consequence of his personal ties with the chief intellectual propagandist for Atlantic unity, the journalist Clarence Streit (1896–1986). Streit, a former League of Nations correspondent for the *New York Times*, had shot to fame in 1939 when he published *Union Now: A Proposal for an Atlantic Federal Union of the Free*. The book was based on the same idea also used by Doren and Holcombe: using the American founding as a source of inspiration for the creation of an international union. He went one better though by essentially redrafting the US Constitution to serve as the founding document for a transatlantic union.

The book's aim was to persuade his American audience of the need for an international union involving the US. His core argument was somewhat counter-intuitive: it was precisely because it was so affluent and seemingly unassailable, both economically and militarily, that it needed to look at the world beyond its borders. "[T]he richer, the stronger, the faster in communications and generally the more developed mechanically and the more educated and civilised a people is," he explained, "the higher the ratio of its external to its internal problems and the more urgent its need of world government" (Streit 34). This logic pushed the US inexorably in the direction of a union with what was by far its largest partner in economic and political terms: Europe. Quoting Herbert Hoover, he pointed out that "[o]ur expansion overseas has entangled us for good or ill" which required the US to commit to "an honest attempt to join with Europe's better spirits to prevent these entanglements from involving us in war" (42).

If the case for transatlantic cooperation was obvious, it was less obvious what form it should take. Streit used a process of elimination to reach his answer. What was clear was that any cooperative scheme should break with what in his view was the core problem of the international system, "the heresy of absolute sovereignty" (Streit 6). He rejected any kind of League of Nations style patching, by which he meant "any change, in law or fact, which however reached and however great, leaves intact the existing world machinery based on the principle of national sovereignty" (53). Without a concession on the issue of sovereignty, it would leave the international system "no means of enforcing any peace agreements" (54). This, in turn, meant that "each nation must depend entirely on its own arms, alliances, and secret diplomacy. No system of law and government has ever yet succeeded without having overwhelming force behind it" (54–55).

Because of the need for "overwhelming" force to guarantee peace, Streit also dismissed the Balance of Power as an organising principle for world affairs: "[W]hen the scales do hang in perfect balance it takes but a breath, only the wind that goes with a word spoken or shrieked in the Hitlerian manner, to end at once the stability, the peace that was achieved" (22). He argued instead for an "*unbalance* of power": "We get it by putting so much weight surely on the side of law that the strongest lawbreaker cannot possibly offset it, (...) by having one side of the balance safely on the ground and the other high in the air" (22).

This left three options: alliances, leagues, and federal unions. After dismissing alliances as the less durable and less organised version of leagues ("all the faults of a league with some of its own added"), he then dismissed the latter as "thoroughly undemocratic, untrustworthy, unsound, unable either to make or to enforce its laws in time" (Streit 17). He pointed to the record of failure of the league as a form of international organisation, "a method which has just failed in the League of Nations, which before that led the original thirteen American democracies to a similar failure, and failed the Swiss democracies, and the Dutch democracies, and the democracies of ancient Greece" (17). Any democracy worthy of the name would have to choose the democratic option, which he called a "union."[13] He summed up his

---

13   Streit avoided the use of the word "federal" in his book. He clearly seems to have intended the two words to be used interchangeably though. The most obvious proof of that is in the index: under the heading "federation," he put "see union."

argument with use of a Hamiltonian distinction: "[A] league is a government for governments or states. (...) A union is a government for the people" (9).

The rest of the book was devoted to explaining what this transatlantic union should look like. He first of all stressed the need for the creation of a direct tie between the union and the citizens. Invoking the Federalist principle, he stressed that "[t]he inter-state government where it governs must govern people, never states." This meant that "all the organs of the Union government, legislative, executive, judicial, and the machinery for amending the Union constitution, must be based directly on the people" (Streit 133–134). In his illustrative constitution, which was otherwise in every way modelled on the US Constitution, the federal government would be given five core tasks which were slightly different from the enumerated powers of the American version: to supervise citizenship, to make peace and war, to regulate both interstate and international commerce, to issue coinage and fix weights and measurements, and to facilitate communication within the union (Art. 3; Streit 204–205). The other main differences with the constitution of 1787 were the fact that even the Senate would have a degree of proportional representation (whereas most states would get two senators, the UK and France would get four, and the US ten), and that the executive would have a council (or "board") as its leadership, rather than a unitary power in the form of a president (Art. 4 and 5; Streit 205).

The book turned out to be a commercial and political success. Streit used the first wave of publicity surrounding it to cultivate Washington's political class. Through people like Dulles and Justice Roberts, the Atlantic Union's first chairman, he managed to make the book's topic part of conversation in policymaking circles (Imlay 79). Through them, he would turn out to have an outsized impact on his country's destiny. In part through his writing and campaigning, it was persuaded to ditch a maxim which it had considered the cornerstone of its foreign policy since the Founding.

An entangling trans-Atlantic alliance

For their part, the Europeans seemed less concerned about the modalities of a potential transatlantic association than about the actual creation of one. The war had left their countries' resources depleted and their armed forces exhausted. As much as they needed American money and American arms, they also needed an American security guarantee. Fearing the presence of Russian divisions on their doorstep, and large and growing Communist Parties actively working to destabilise their political systems, obtaining a permanent American commitment to the defence of Western Europe became a top priority.

The first move was made by the British Defence Secretary, Ernest Bevin (1881–1951). Bevin was a self-taught individual who, after a long career in the trade union movement, ended up in the House of Commons on behalf of the Labour Party. He was a committed anti-fascist and a member of the Federal Union, a British organisation founded in 1938 to promote the cause of a federal European union. Other prominent individuals involved in this organisation included Lionel Robbins, the social reformer William Beveridge, and Friedrich Hayek (Segers 72).

In January 1948, Bevin used a speech in the House of Commons to call for closer cooperation between the countries of Western Europe, preferably involving the US in some form.[14] The setting of the speech was formed by the final breakdown of the Four Power talks about the future of Germany one month earlier in London. Without dialogue as an option for managing relations with the Soviets, the question was how to avoid the scenario of a gradual communist takeover of the entire continent. This was not an academic question, as far as Bevin was concerned. He highlighted the cases of Poland, Hungary, Bulgaria, and Romania where the local communist parties had taken control of their countries' main institutions. He also pointed to Greece, where a struggle was taking place to prevent a similar communist takeover and warned of further such communist efforts to come. Given that "[n]o one disputes the idea of European unity," the issue became "whether European unity cannot be achieved without the domination and control of one great Power [the Soviet Union]" (Bevin, speech in the House of Commons, 22 January 1948). In other words, the choice as he saw it was between the two old mechanisms for managing continental unity: universal monarchy and federal union.

Though Bevin would remain somewhat vague in his embrace of the latter option, he did set out three criteria for its functioning: "The first is that no one nation should dominate Europe. The second is that the old-fashioned conception of the balance of power as an aim should be discarded if possible. The third is that there should be substituted Four-Power co-operation and assistance to all the States of Europe." Given that four had effectively become three, what he was really proposing was the formation of some kind of

14   All subsequent quotes in this section come from this speech unless indicated otherwise.

federation with Britain and France at its heart, and unspecified American involvement. He had no concrete idea of how this cooperation should take shape. He thought that "treaties will be needed," but what he had in mind was more of a "brotherhood" than a "rigid system."

To appeal to American policymakers, he concluded with a promise and an invitation. The promise was a British commitment to European integration: "[A]ll these developments which I have been describing, point to the conclusion that the free nations of Western Europe must now draw closely together. (...) I believe the time is ripe for a consolidation of Western Europe." The invitation, even if worded rather indirectly, was to the decision-makers in Washington DC. When describing "the organisation in respect of a Western Union," he emphasised that he was "not concerned only with Europe as a geographical conception."

—

Shortly after Bevin's speech, the Czechoslovak Communist Party staged a coup (February 1948) which saw non-communist parties purged from government and hundreds of people arrested. These events pushed the previously wavering French, Dutch, Belgian, and Luxembourgeois governments into negotiations leading to the Brussels Treaty (17 March 1948). Through this treaty, the UK, France, and the Benelux countries committed to closer cooperation in a number of areas. Article 1 couched the reasons for the formation of the organisation entirely in Saint-Pierre like *raison d'état* terms. Based on "the close community of their interests" and "the *necessity of uniting* in order to promote the economic recovery of Europe" (my emphasis), the participating countries undertook to "organise and coordinate their economic activities as to produce the best possible results, by the elimination of conflict in their economic policies, the coordination of production and the development of commercial exchanges." Its real significance, though, was its military paragraph. The signatories promised that in case one of them was attacked, the others would "afford the Party so attacked all the military and other aid and assistance in the power" (Art. 4).

The fact that this clause took the form of an automatic trigger of mutual assistance seemed a significant victory for French diplomacy, which had spent the years after the First World War fruitlessly trying to get the British government to give a similar commitment. In the specific case of a renewed German threat however, the other governments were not willing to commit to more than a 1919-style fudge, promising "to take such steps as may be held to be necessary" (Preamble). This was less a case of continued British unwillingness to commit to French security than of a growing divergence between Britain and France in their views of Germany's future. In the spring of 1948, the French government still saw a divided and demilitarised Germany as the only effective way of guaranteeing its own security, whereas the British government was increasingly convinced that only a reconstituted Germany could help to keep the Soviet Union at bay.

In the end, the British perspective would win out: at the London Six Power Conference involving the US, British, French and Benelux governments in June 1948, which would also see the creation of an international authority for the control of the Ruhr area, the three Western occupying powers agreed on forming a single administration for their zones. With this decision, they agreed to put the newly reunited western part of Germany on the path to independence.[15] In spite of serious misgivings, the French parliament voted by a small majority to accept the decisions of the London Conference. The anger over the German return to the international community did lead to the fall of the French government. Eventually a new cabinet was formed. In it, the Foreign Secretary George Bidault, who had negotiated the Treaty of Brussels, was replaced by the outgoing Prime Minister, Robert Schuman.[16]

—

The Truman administration initially did not seem inclined to take the British government up on its invitation to enter into discussions about joining the new security organisation. The Senate was dominated by the Republican Party under the leadership of the isolationist Majority Leader Robert Taft (son of the former president). This meant that even if the White House had wanted to move forward with the idea, the scope for doing so was limited. Even more limiting was the fact that President Truman was gearing up for his re-election campaign – rarely the best time for potentially risky political experiments.

At the diplomatic level, however, there was some movement. In Washington DC, representatives of the American, Canadian, and British governments met in March 1948 to talk behind closed doors about preconditions for a transatlantic security treaty similar to the Brussels Pact. The talks were inspired in part by rumours of an impending Norwegian–Soviet security

15   The West-German constitution, adopted in May 1949, would recommit Germany to the principle of federal union.
16   In the chaotic days of the IVth Republic, this kind of change of post was quite normal. In the first five years after the war, France had 11 Prime Ministers. Two of them – Bidault and Schuman – held the post twice.

pact along the lines of the Soviet–Finnish treaty that had just been concluded. Bevin stated that if realised, it would effectively be a "repeat of our
experience with Hitler," when the British government was forced to "witness
helplessly the slow deterioration of our position," forcing it in the end "to
resort to war in order to defend our lives and liberty" (Sayle 21). The Truman
administration agreed that urgent action was required to prevent Western
European countries from "being intimidated by the Soviet colossus" to such
an extent that they ended up "losing the will to resist" (Sayle 21). A dramatic
gesture was needed to strengthen their resolve. The only thing that would
do was a show of America's lasting commitment to Europe's security.

The meeting concluded with the outlines of a treaty, though without a
timetable for its negotiation and adoption. First the White House had to find
a way to steer the treaty past the Republican Senate majority. This obstacle
was eventually removed through the kind of coup through which federal
unions were usually created or sustained. It involved a Senate resolution
which had the effect of splitting the Republican opposition, thereby isolating
the isolationists. The remarkable thing was that it came from the Republican
chair of the Senate Foreign Relations Committee, Senator Vandenberg.
In what was effectively a rerun of the United Nations playbook aimed at
avoiding Wilson's 1919 mistake, the White House succeeded in bringing the
leading Republican internationalist into its coalition, even allowing him to
lead the charge for a transatlantic alliance.

The resolution itself was a thing of parliamentary beauty (US Senate
Resolution 239).[17] It was clearly intended to pave the way for an Atlantic
alliance, but the text conspicuously avoided any mention of the words
"Atlantic" or "Europe." It merely committed the United States to associate
itself, within the confines of the UN Charter, "with such regional and other
collective arrangements as are based on continuous and effective self-help
and mutual aid, and as affect its national security." To clear the potential
hurdle of a Soviet Security Council veto, it stressed that such "arrangements"
would be covered by Article 51 of the UN Charter which covered actions
that did not fall under the Security Council's veto rule.[18]) It also affirmed
that any US involvement would be based on "a constitutional process." The
resolution thereby ticked all the boxes for potentially wavering colleagues: it

---

17 All subsequent quotes in this section come from this document unless indicated otherwise.
18 "Nothing in the present Charter shall impair the inherent right of individual or collective
self-defence if an armed attack occurs against a Member of the United Nations, until the Security
Council has taken measures necessary to maintain international peace and security" (United
Nations Charter).

respected the UN Charter, pointed to a way around the Soviet veto, stressed the importance of European self-help and American national security, and confirmed that any decision to commit American troops would still have to be approved by the Senate first ("constitutional"). It passed the Senate by 82 votes to 13, giving Truman the freedom to negotiate a transatlantic treaty.

—

The negotiations that followed were effectively a drama in two parts. In one room the various US government factions and institutions were trying to settle on a single position for the talks in the other room, where US and Canadian diplomats sat with government representatives from the five Brussels Pact countries. The internal American debate was eventually settled in favour of the faction that had initiated the talks. Its main actors were the State Department's Europe director John Hickerson (1898–1989) and his colleague Theodore Achilles (1905–1986). Both men were committed to the idea of a transatlantic union in some form. In an interview conducted in the early 1970s, Achilles revealed the extent to which NATO for them had been an ideological project: "Jack Hickerson and I had both read Clarence Streit's *Union Now*, and had been deeply impressed by it. We shared enthusiasm for negotiating a military alliance and getting it ratified as a basis for further progress towards unity" (Achilles). This obviously did not mean that the American government was equally committed ideologically, but the idea that Hickerson and Achilles were pushing – some form of alliance with its own institutions, whether "as a basis for further progress towards unity" or not – did become the official US government objective.

On the losing side of the argument was George Kennan (1904–2005). He dismissed the idea of an entangling alliance with Western Europe as both unnecessary ("What in the world did they think we were doing in Europe these four or five years?" (Kaplan, *NATO 1948* 96)) and possibly even counterproductive. Given that he considered the Soviet Union more a political than a military threat to the countries of Western Europe, he thought that they would be much better served by programmes that helped them with their economic recovery than with a military alliance. He also confessed himself sceptical of the effectiveness of military alliances on the European continent: "European history has shown only too clearly the weakness of multilateral defensive alliances between complete sovereign nations" (US State Department, *Report by the Policy Planning Staff*, 24 February 1948).

With a reference to Streit's bestseller, he hinted at a possible alternative in the form of the kind of Anglo-Saxon pillar that Churchill had spoken about in his Fulton speech: "If we were to take Britain into our own U.S.-Canadian orbits according to some formula of "Union now," this would probably solve Britain's long term economic problem and create a natural political entity of great strength"[19] (US State Department, *Report by the Policy Planning Staff*). He would keep pushing for this idea of a Western community resting on two pillars – one European, the other Anglo-Saxon – practically up to the day of the signing of the NATO Treaty.

—

The formula for "Union Now" that the American government eventually settled on had three objectives. It wanted to bring in as many countries as was feasible, provided they served a strategic purpose. It aimed to limit the alliance to military matters only. And it wanted it to be based on a clear understanding that any American commitment for mutual defence would always be conditional, because subject to Senate approval.

Of these three, the issue of the geographical extent of the alliance proved the most complicated. One problem took the form of Scandinavian involvement. The Danish and Norwegian governments felt the pull of a Swedish counteroffer, but in the end decided that only American military assistance offered sufficient safeguards. The US government, for its part, wanted the two countries in mainly for military–strategic reasons. It wanted to prevent the Norwegian coastline, with its access to the Atlantic, falling into Soviet hands, and it needed Danish-controlled Greenland as a potential mid-Atlantic air and naval base.

For the same reason, it pushed for the inclusion of Portugal in the alliance. When European governments objected to the inclusion of a fascist government in an organisation of democratic states, the American government pointed to the importance of the Azores as a mid-Atlantic stage post for its airforce and navy. It justified the ditching of the rule formulated by Wilson in 1919 ("democratic governments only") by explaining that the Portuguese government was "authoritarian, (...) not totalitarian" (Kaplan, *NATO 1948* 210). In other words: it may not have been a Western-style democracy, but at least it was anti-Soviet, and that was good enough as far as the White House was concerned (210).

The last question mark was formed by Italy. Most Western European countries saw no need for the inclusion of a country that was clearly not

---

19   In 1941, Streit had in fact published an alternative version of his book titled *Union Now With Britain*, which made the case for an Anglo-Saxon union, now that the continental European countries he had hoped to include in his original plan had all fallen under Nazi occupation.

attached to the Atlantic. It was France that insisted on Italian membership. Italy's inclusion served as a way of justifying its own demand for including its North African colony Algeria within the scope of the treaty. The American government was generally dismissive of European attempts to have their colonies protected by American military means. But since it was keen to prevent Italy from falling into communist hands (it had barely survived a failed communist coup at the end of 1947), it was, in the end, included in the group of founder members. Achilles solved the French colonial problem by using a version of Monroe's solution to the Northwest Territory issue. Simply including Algerian territory was impossible given the strong anti-colonial sentiments among Senators of both parties. But by suggesting the Tropic of Cancer circle of latitude as the alliance's southern border, he drew the line in such a way that Algeria happened to fall just inside NATO's territorial boundaries (Kaplan, *NATO 1948* 221).

The American attempt to limit the alliance to military issues was a product of the counter-pressure applied by the Senate on the White House's trade agenda. The Havana Charter of 1948 which had established the International Trade Organisation had run into considerable difficulty in the Senate, with both employers and trade unions coming out against it. If the American negotiators tried to limit the NATO treaty to military matters only, it was because they felt that this was already a difficult issue to get through the Senate, and it would therefore not serve any strategic purpose to ask for more than that at this stage.

In the end, it was the Canadian government that insisted on a more ambitious proposal. "A true Atlantic community" would need a cultural and economic component, as well as a military one (Kaplan, *NATO 1948* 121). Some of the suggested language triggered a strong negative response in American political circles, especially the suggestion of the inclusion of a reference to the promotion of "general welfare." Pointing out that these two words in the US Constitution had led to a mountain of litigation, Senate Majority Leader Tom Connally insisted: "Get it the hell out of this treaty!" (221).

In the end, the Canadians succeeded in securing the inclusion of what became Article 2, which talked about "strengthening free institutions" and "promoting conditions of stability and wellbeing"; it also formulated the goals of "eliminat[ing] conflict in their international economic policies" and "encourag[ing] economic collaboration between any or all of them" (The North Atlantic Treaty, Art. 2). As the Canadian Deputy Under-Secretary for External Affairs, Escott Reid (1905–1999), observed in his memoirs about NATO's founding, the fact that article 2 was included was not all his country's doing: "Canada's efforts would probably have failed if, within the State

Department, two of the principal United States negotiators, Hickerson and Achilles, had not, as they themselves have said, strongly favoured [its] inclusion" (Reid, 135). Quoting a diplomatic cable which summarised their position, he claimed that they saw it "as the basis upon which a true Atlantic Community, going far beyond the military field, could be built" (135).

In the Senate debate about the draft treaty, the biggest stumbling block turned out to be Article 5, the mutual defence clause. This should not have come as a surprise. It was essentially the same type of clause (Art. 10) that had derailed American ratification of the Covenant. Then, as now, at stake were the Senate's own constitutional prerogatives on the issue of declarations of war. What it feared was that the draft text would commit the country to automatic military action if the article was invoked. It therefore insisted on a conditionality mechanism whereby the US government wouldn't commit to more than a promise to consider acting – effectively the kind of compromise the negotiators came up with in 1919. This kind of conditionality was completely unacceptable to the European negotiators. Having experienced the reality of Article 10 in the League of Nations period, they insisted on an automatic triggering of the assistance of all in case of an attack on one, like Article 4 in the Brussels Treaty. Anything less than what had already been discussed publicly would also be seen by their own populations as a sign of weakness of the alliance and give unwanted encouragement to the communist parties in their countries (Sayle 26).

The solution was the inserting of a single word in the draft text. The revised article promised that any action by individual governments after an attack on one of them would be taken "forthwith"[20] (Kaplan, *NATO 1948* 205). The Europeans felt that this offered sufficient guarantee that the American government would at least act immediately – even though the treaty left undefined what this action would consist of. After all, it would still be up to the Senate to decide what "such action as it deems necessary" meant in every individual case.

—

NATO fell far short of Streit's call for "common citizenship, army, market, money and stamp" (Streit 212). Since it was based on the undivided

---

20   Probably not coincidentally the same word was also used in the military assistance clause in the list of principles of the League to Enforce Peace as reported by Hamilton Holt in 1917: "[T] he signatory powers shall *forthwith* use their economic and military forces against any member that goes to war..." (my emphasis). See page 349 above.

sovereignty of its member states, it was clearly not a union. In fact it was not even a league, but an alliance – the kind of cooperative venture Streit had dismissed as wholly insufficient. On the institutional side, the treaty text offered little beyond the establishment of a council where all were represented on an equal basis. The Council, in turn, could set up "such subsidiary bodies as may be necessary" (The North Atlantic Treaty, Art. 9). The Treaty also provided for an expansion clause which applied to "any other European State in a position to further the principles of this Treaty and to contribute to the security of the North Atlantic area," subject to a veto by the individual existing members (Art. 10).

Still, even the mere creation of an Atlantic alliance was evidence of the fact that his idea was treated as a serious option by America's governing class. It would remain part of the political conversation about future scenarios for transatlantic relationships for quite some time after NATO's founding. In July 1955, Senator Kefauver, when addressing the Senate Foreign Relations committee to explain his resolution calling for a transatlantic convention, claimed it would "electrify free men everywhere" ("Kefauver Explains Atlantic Union Idea"). Eventually, it electrified enough of his colleagues (or at least their voters) to allow the motion to pass. In 1960, the same year it was signed into law by President Eisenhower (Imlay 169), the Director of the Harvard International Seminar, Henry Kissinger, also came out as a supporter of the idea.

In an essay titled "The United States and Europe" he explained what was at stake for the US: "If the states bordering the North Atlantic were to split into a congeries of squabbling sovereignties, it would be final proof to all uncommitted nations of the bankruptcy of the liberal values of the West. The United States would find itself isolated not only physically but also spiritually"[21] (Kissinger, *The Necessity for Choice* 99). Since it was "beyond the capacity of either the United States or our European allies" to deal with the many revolutionary changes of the age, what was required was "the closest cooperation between North America – indeed the entire Western hemisphere – and Europe" (99–100).

This close cooperation could take two forms. One was European integration, chiefly in the form of a European Atomic Force that would enable Europe to withstand Russian nuclear pressure (Kissinger 125). However, he admitted this option involved "great complexities," being "extremely costly and technically difficult" (126). The alternative was for "the North Atlantic Community [to] increase its political cohesion so that it approaches a federal system" (121).

---

21   Note the echo in the words "split into a congeries of squabbling sovereignties" of Hamilton's 9th *Federalist Paper*, where he talks about "splitting ourselves into an infinity of little, jealous, clashing, tumultuous commonwealths."

"The minimum condition," he stated, "is to move in the direction of a North Atlantic Confederation." If this seemed ambitious, he pointed out that "[s]ome steps towards confederation can be taken even within the existing NATO framework" (121–122). His conclusion contained the closest the *Realpolitiker* Kissinger would come to an an emotional exhortation: "We of the West, who bequeathed the concept of nationalism to others, must summon the initiative and imagination to show the way to a new international order"[22] (168).

Bibliography

Achilles, Theodore. Oral History Interview with Richard D. McKinzie. 13 November and 18 December 1972, Washington, DC. https://www.trumanlibrary.gov/library/oral-histories/achilles. Accessed 6 March 2024.

Beugel, Ernst van den. "An Act Without Peer: The Marshall Plan in American-Dutch Relations." *Bijdragen en Mededelingen Betreffende de Geschiedenis der Nederlanden*, vol. 97, 1982, pp. 456–469.

Bevin, Ernest, speech to the House of Commons, January 22, 1948 Address given by Ernest Bevin to the House of Commons (22 January 1948) (cvce.eu)

The Brussels Treaty. 1948. https://www.cvce.eu/en/obj/the_brussels_treaty_17_march_1948-en-3467de5e-9802-4b65-8076-778bc7d164d3.html. Accessed 6 March 2024.

"Churchill warns of United Europe." *New York Times*, 9 Mar. 1932.

Churchill, Winston. "The United States of Europe." *The Saturday Evening Post*, 15 Feb. 1930.

Churchill, Winston. Address given by Winston Churchill at Westminster College. Fulton, Missouri, 5 March 1946. https://www.cvce.eu/en/obj/address_given_by_winston_churchill_fulton_5_march_1946-en-5bd9a782-e0ee-4ab9-9a8a-2a8cace3cfb8.html. Accessed 6 March 2024.

Churchill, Winston. Speech delivered at the University of Zurich. 19 September 1946. https://rm.coe.int/16806981f3. Accessed 6 March 2024.

Churchill, Winston. "On a United Europe." Speech at the meeting of the United Europe Committee, Royal Albert Hall, London, 14 May 1947. https://archive.org/stream/W.S.ChurchillOnAUnitedEurope1947/W.S.%20Churchill%20-%20

---

22 As late as January 1963, Kissinger referred to President Kennedy's 1962 Fourth of July speech, in which he had presented a vision of two unions working closely together ("The Declaration of Interdependence") as a "Grand Design" whose objective of "a vital Atlantic system" was in his view "one of the great opportunities of our time." But by then he had come to recognise that there was nothing inevitable about such an outcome, and that the Western Alliance was in fact facing "serious internal division." See Henry Kissinger, "Strains on the Alliance," *Foreign Affairs*, vol. 41, no. 2, p. 261.

%27%27On%20a%20United%20Europe%27%27%20%5B1947%5D_djvu.txt.
Accessed 6 March 2024.

Churchill, Winston. *The Gathering Storm*. 1948. Rosetta Books, 2013.

Doren, Carl van. *The Great Rehearsal: The Story of the Making and Ratifying of the Constitution of the United States*. Viking Press, 1948.

Dulles, John Foster. "Can We Guarantee a Free Europe?" *Collier's*, CXXI, 12 June 1948, pp. 74–76.

Fulbright, J. William. "A United States of Europe?" *Annals of the American Academy of Political and Social Science*, vol. 257, issue 1, pp. 151–156.

Hamilton, Alexander, James Madison and John Jay. *The Federalist Papers*. 1787. Penguin, 1987.

Hansard, House of Commons debate, June 27, 1950, Vol. 476, column 2155

Hathaway, Oona and Scott Shapiro. *The Internationalists: How a Radical Plan to Outlaw War Remade the World*. Penguin, 2018.

Holcombe, Arthur N, *Our More Perfect Union: From Eighteenth Century Principles to Twentieth Century Practice*. Harvard University Press, 1950.

Holt, Hamilton. "The League to Enforce Peace." *Proceedings of the Academy of Political Science in the City of New York*, vol. 7, no. 2, The Foreign Relations of the United States: Part I, Jul. 1917, pp. 65–69.

Imlay, Talbot C, *Clarence Streit and Twentieth Century American Internationalism*. Cambridge University Press, 2023.

Isaacson, Walter and Evan Thomas. *The Wise Men: Six Friends and the World They Made*. 1986. Simon & Schuster, 1997.

Jünger, Ernst. *The Peace*. Henry Regnery Company, 1948.

Kaplan, Lawrence S. *The Conversion of Senator Arthur H. Vandenberg: From Isolation to Engagement*. University Press of Kentucky, 2015.

Kaplan, Lawrence S. *NATO 1948: The Birth of the Transatlantic Alliance*. Rowman & Littlefield, 2007.

Kennan, George. The Long Telegram [original], from George Kennan in Moscow to the Secretary of State. 22 February 1946. https://nsarchive.gwu.edu/document/21042-long-telegram-original. Accessed 6 March 2024.

"Kefauver Explains Atlantic Union Idea." *New York Times*. 25 July 1955.

Kissinger, Henry. *The Necessity for Choice: Prospects of American Foreign Policy* Harper Collins, 1961.

Kissinger, Henry. "Strains on the Alliance." *Foreign Affairs*, vol. 41, no. 2, pp. 261–285.

Lowe, Keith. *Savage Continent: Europe in the Aftermath of World War II*. 2012. Penguin Books, 2013.

Marshall, George. The Marshall Plan Speech to the Harvard Alumni Association, 5 June 5 1947. https://www.marshallfoundation.org/the-marshall-plan/speech/. Accessed 6 March 2024.

Morgenthau, Hans. *Politics Among Nations*. A. A. Knopf, 1948.

Morsink, Johannes. *The Universal Declaration of Human Rights: Origins, Drafting and Intent*. University of Pennsylvania Press, 2000.

The North Atlantic Treaty. Washington, DC. 4 April 1949. https://www.nato.int/cps/en/natolive/official_texts_17120.htm. Accessed 6 March 2024.

Rady, Martyn. *The Middle Kingdoms: A New History of Central Europe*. Allen Lane, 2023.

Reid, Escott. *Time of Hope and Fear: The Making of the North Atlantic Treaty, 1947–1949*. McClelland & Stewart, 1977.

Roosevelt, Franklin D, "The Four Freedoms." Annual Address to Congress. 6 January 1941. http://docs.fdrlibrary.marist.edu/od4frees.html. Accessed 6 March 2024.

Sands, Philippe. *East West Street: On the Origins of Genocide and Crimes Against Humanity*. Weidenfeld & Nicolson, 2016.

Sayle, Timothy Andrews. *Enduring Alliance: A History of NATO and the Postwar Global Order*. Cornell University Press, 2019.

Segers, Mathieu. *The Origins of European Integration: The Prehistory of Today's European Union, 1937–1951*. Cambridge University Press, 2023.

Spaak, Paul-Henri. *Combats Inachevées Vol. II: De l'Espoir aux Déceptions*. Fayard, 1969.

Stalin, Josef. Speech at a Meeting of Voters of the Stalin Electoral Area. Moscow, 9 February 1946 Stalin Election Speech – Seventeen Moments in Soviet History (msu.edu)

US State Department, *Report by the Policy Planning Staff*, 24 February 1948 Foreign Relations of the United States, 1948, General; the United Nations, Volume I, Part 2 – Office of the Historian

Statistisches Bundesamt. *Die Deutschen Vertreibungsverluste: Bevölkerungsbilanzen für die Deutschen Vertreibungsgebiete*. 1958.

Streit, Clarence. *Union Now: A Proposal for an Atlantic Federal Union of the Free*. 1939. Harper & Brothers, 1948.

Truman, Harry S, "Truman Doctrine." Address to a Joint Session of Congress. 12 March 1947. https://www.archives.gov/milestone-documents/truman-doctrine. Accessed 6 March 2024.

United Nations Charter. https://www.un.org/en/about-us/un-charter/full-text. Accessed 6 March 2024.

Universal Declaration of Human Rights. https://www.un.org/en/about-us/universal-declaration-of-human-rights. Accessed 6 March 2024.

US Senate Resolution 239. "The Vandenberg Resolution."Wendell. *One World*. Cassell and Company, 1943.

Zurcher, Arnold. *The Struggle to Unite Europe: 1940–1958*. Greenwood Press, 1958.

12   Europe's Federalist Moment

Abstract

It is a common misconception that the European Founding lacked a con-
stitutional moment comparable to the American Philadelphia Convention.
In reality, there was a lively debate about constitutional first principles, in
which different interpretations of the concept of federal union competed
for public and political support. This debate started at the European
Movement's great conference in The Hague in 1948 and continued at the
Council of Europe in Strasbourg in 1949 and 1950. Through it, Western
European politicians eventually settled on the same approach that had
been identified in the European federal tradition since Kant: using a
vanguard of committed countries and an economic cooperative project
to take the first steps on the path to federal union.

Keywords: Federal union, supranationalism, functionalism, Council of
Europe, ECSC, United States of Europe

Europe Divided: the Council of Europe

The debates at the 1948 The Hague conference showed how difficult it would
be to find a formula that could unite the different strands of European
unionism. It was in the Political Committee, which convened the day after
the plenary at which Churchill gave his keynote speech, that the motions
that would define the legacy of the conference would be discussed. The
debate revealed how deeply divided the participating countries were on
the key issues of sovereignty and representation.

On sovereignty the main division was that between the French and the
British delegations. The French aim was for the conference to propose a
directly elected deliberative assembly, with its own mandate separate from
that of the member states. The main thing was to act fast, so as not to lose
momentum. As the Dutch president of the Union of European Federalists
Henri Brugmans observed, acting fast and decisively also had a tactical use.

Livestro, Joshua: *A More Perfect Union. Federal Union in Political Theory and Practice, 1500-1951.*
Amsterdam: Amsterdam University Press, 2024.
DOI: 10.5117/9789048563777_CH12

It served as a "psychological choc," and created a *"fait accompli"* (Council of Europe 103).

The man who had assembled the French delegation for the conference, the economist René Courtin, explained how a European Assembly could become a sovereign institution in its own right. Once established, the Assembly would "gain authority bit by bit, acquiring at first a little, subsequently a larger amount of sovereignty" (Council of Europe 49). Eventually it would "transform itself (...) in the great European Assembly that would represent the common order on this continent" (49). A French member of the Union of European Federalists, Leon van Vassenhove, pointed out that the mere "exercising in common of the rights of sovereignty" was not a sufficient way to define a "European union" because "it leaves the possibility of the exercise of the right of veto intact" (76). If the assembly was to function properly, some transfer of sovereignty to the new federal authority would therefore be unavoidable.

Against this idea the British delegation spoke up first to point out the many practical difficulties involved with the French proposal. The later British Prime Minister Harold MacMillan used an intervention to ask a series of pointed questions:

> We are asked to carry a series of amendments which will bring into being, within this year, as I understand it, a universal European assembly, elected upon a suffrage with one member for every million voters, throughout the whole of Europe. But who is to do this? (...) By what machineries, by what legislative actions? (...) Who is to make the list of voters, how is the voting to be? Is it to be on proportional representation? Who is to be the returning officer? Under whose authority are the elections to be held? What is to be its juridical basis? (Council of Europe 97).

In what the French would undoubtedly have recognised as a rebuke of their approach, he concluded by calling for less haste, and a more considered approach: "It is quite easy to write constitutions. What is difficult is to make them effective and durable"[1] (97).

The National Liberal MP James Henderson-Stewart turned the logic of the French proposal on its head. If urgency required dramatic action, creating an

---

1   Note that none of these practical difficulties had stopped the German states a century earlier from organising elections at very short notice to select delegates for the Frankfurt Convention. Elections took place across Germany in May 1848, only one month after they had been called for by the Bundestag. See Richter, *Demokratie, Eine Deutsche Affäre* 115–117.

Assembly first would be the wrong option: "According to the definition of the powers of the assembly, the assembly is prohibited from taking immediate action. (…) It is required to represent public opinion, to advise upon such matters, to examine some other matters, to prepare plans, but nowhere in all that list is there any power to take immediate action upon anything" (106). What was first of all required therefore was the creation of an executive "with the power to take action for the immediate rule of Europe" (106). Claiming that this approach "enjoyed the general approval of the House of Commons," he called on the conference "forthwith" to establish "an emergency council of Europe" (106). There was no need to invent a new structure, as it already existed in the form of the council of the Brussels Pact. As a first step, "[a]ll the other free countries of Europe should at once be invited to accede" (106).

The conference would split over this issue. The Scandinavian delegates would choose the British side, opting for less haste and a council of governments as the preferred structure. Though in theory delegates in this camp recognised the importance of sharing sovereignty, in practice they were unwilling to commit to any immediate steps in that direction. Most Benelux and Italian delegates ended up supporting the French approach. Some sovereignty needed to be transferred to the European level, and the only body that it could be transferred to would be a democratic one.

—

Another issue that would come back with some venom during the negotiations about the European Coal and Steel Community was that of representation. As in Philadelphia, so too in The Hague the larger states had assumed that there would be broad support for a formula that gave them a larger share of the seats in a proposed Assembly based on proportional representation (as we saw, the French delegation had proposed a basic formula of one seat per one million inhabitants).

The rival concept of equal representation had been put forward at the Philadelphia Convention by the New Jersey delegation. In The Hague, it was introduced by the Dutch Socialist MP Corry Tendeloo (1887–1956). Having served on the Amsterdam town council before the war, in 1945 she was elected as an MP for the socialist/progressive liberal merger party PvdA. In parliament, she would use her mandate to work for the advancement of women's rights, both in The Netherlands (where she managed to persuade a majority of her fellow MPs to back abolition of the law that forced female civil servants to resign once they got married) and in the Dutch colonies (where she fought successfully for the introduction of the female franchise).

Tendeloo was also a committed federalist, listed by the Dutch World Federalist Movement chapter as one of its representatives in Parliament (Dammen 19). As such, her presence at the conference in The Hague was a plausible one. But if she was there out of ideological commitment, she had also come to defend her country's interests. In the section of the resolution devoted to the establishment of a European assembly, she suggested a short but politically explosive amendment: "[T]o put in Article 3 after the words 'some portion of their sovereignty' the words 'on a basis of equality'" (Council of Europe 73). She claimed it was "of the utmost importance for the public here in Holland" that the new union was founded on the idea "that everybody has got the same vote." Failure to do so was in her view one of the "great mistakes" of the UN Charter (73)

Though the British delegates were generally not inclined to support the idea of an assembly, what they supported even less was an assembly where their country's vote had the same weight as that of the smaller countries. This explains perhaps why a British delegate, in response to Tendeloo's amendment, emphasised federalism's inherent link to proportional representation: "I think she doesn't realise what federation means. If you have an elected European authority, it does not represent the states, it represents the people" (Council of Europe 74). In the end, there was no reconciliation of the two positions. That was all the more remarkable because it was essentially a repeat of the debate about representation at the OEEC, where a compromise had been found. At its first meeting in March 1948, a group of smaller states, led by the Benelux trio, had argued successfully that the larger states (France and the UK) should not become overly dominant in the central decision-making committee. Through this Benelux intervention, the smaller states had obtained a seat on the central committee (Price 80–81).

Perhaps the lack of agreement in The Hague was predictable. In the OEEC governments had a strong incentive to work out their differences because it was the only way to unlock American funding. Any compromise would do. At the conference in The Hague, delegates were talking about competing visions for the future of the continent. Here, compromise was hard. And as events at the Council of Europe would show, it would only get harder.

—

In the final vote on the political declaration, the French delegation got its way on the general principle. The political motion as adopted called for "the gathering, with a sense of urgency, of a European assembly" (Congress of Europe 411). But the delegates had taken some of the sting out of it by eliminating the idea of direct election of Assembly members, making it instead a gathering of delegations from the various national parliaments.

The British Labour government was still far from pleased with the result. Politically it was put in a difficult position, first by the media coverage in the immediate aftermath of the conference in The Hague which had raised expectations about the creation of an Assembly, then by the Belgian government's decision to actively embrace the idea (Zurcher 37). The strategy the Attlee government settled on was to kill the plan by going along with it, on one condition: that the assembly was replaced by a council of ministers. A committee under the former French Prime Minister, and former head of Briand's study committee, Edouard Herriot, came up with what seemed like a workable compromise: the institutional framework would consist of a Council of Ministers and an Assembly, supported by a secretariat[2] (Spaak, *Combats Inachevées* 27).

In a speech in the future seat of the Council, the Alsace town of Strasbourg, the French Foreign Secretary Robert Schuman welcomed the creation of the new "supranational association" (Schuman, "The Coming Century of Supranational Communities").[3] "We are," he observed, "carrying out a great experiment, the fulfilment of the same recurring dream that for ten centuries has revisited the peoples of Europe: creating between them an organisation putting an end to war and guaranteeing an eternal peace." He placed the new experiment in the same tradition in which "audacious minds, such as Dante, Erasmus, Abbé de Saint-Pierre, Rousseau, Kant and Proudhon, had created in the abstract the framework for systems that were both ingenious and generous." As such, it was the complete opposite of the other tradition which had sought to unify the continent, "that of a world empire constituted under the auspices of German emperors (...) [relying] on the unacceptable pretensions of a '*Führertum*' (domination by dictatorship) whose 'charms' we have all experienced."

If after such promises of greatness the initial result seemed somewhat underwhelming, he asked for the audience's understanding: "We are still at the start of things. We would do well to bridle our impatience. If not, we are likely to make the doubters more distrustful and what is more serious, endanger not only the experiment but also the whole idea of a united Europe."

2   Herriot would get one more rather remarkable footnote in the history of European federal union when he led the French parliamentary opposition against the proposed European Defence Community. The committed European federalist thereby helped to kill the idea of a European political union, for fear of facilitating German rearmament (the latter would happen anyway).

3   All subsequent quotes in this section come from this speech unless indicated otherwise.

Failure of this "supreme attempt to save our Continent and preserve the world from suicide" was not an option.

—

The Statutes adopted by the ten founder member states of the Council of Europe created an organisation that offered considerably less than what the French participants in The Hague would have hoped for. Its membership, as defined in Article 4 of its founding treaty, consisted of European states (Statute of the Council of Europe). It was through the parliaments of these states that the joint Assembly was selected. And it was through their governments that ministers were delegated to the Committee of Ministers.

The Assembly had a consultative function only (Art. 22). Worse was that it was not even allowed to determine its own agenda. It was for the Council of Ministers to decide what it wanted to be consulted on, and even then, it could choose to ignore the Assembly's advice (Art. 23). Not that the Council had any real powers. All it could do was send recommendations to the member state governments, who could then either act on them or ignore them (Art. 15). There was no sanction for noncompliance; in fact, compliance was not even a formal requirement. This was mostly a theoretical problem though. Nothing happened without the consent of the states and therefore, usually, nothing happened. The unanimity requirement under Article 20 killed all but the most anodyne of resolutions. As Spaak put it in his memoirs, "[t]his acceptance of the total sovereignty of the states would once more show its paralysing and detestable effect" (Spaak, *Combats Inachevées* 28).

In spite of this paralysis – or perhaps because of it – the British government seemed pleased with the result. In a Foreign Office document, the Council of Europe was described as a "nongovernmental body." The same document also stressed that there were "no limitations of the sovereignty of the participating countries" (Zurcher 42). This anti-federalism was not solely down to a British unwillingness to put European interests before Commonwealth ones, though that undoubtedly determined Britain's stance in the negotiations. The fact that it had just lost an empire through the independence of India and Pakistan in 1947 seemed not to have impacted the British self-image as the central power of a global commonwealth.

There was also some concern in British circles – and indeed American ones – that the French intended to establish a European union as a "third power' in between the US and Russia, thereby dividing instead of uniting the West. Even if that could be avoided, the British government feared an overly ambitious project for the establishment of a federal style union could still cause a split inside the

Western European block, at a time when unity in the face of the Soviet threat was critically important. Given the fact that subsequent French proposals would indeed cause such a split, this was a not entirely unfair argument.

—

In their urge to accommodate the British government and thereby protect Western European unity, the participating governments had created a union that, as one contemporary commentator described it "scarcely qualified as a confederal organisation" (Zurcher 41). What the British had not accounted for though, was the fact that the assembly, for lack of a substantive agenda of its own, would fill the void with a principled discussion about the future of Europe.

Spaak, who served as the Assembly's first president, later described the debate as "federalists versus wait-and-seers" (Spaak, *Combats Inachevés* 30). Though as president he did not intervene in this debate, there was little doubt where his sympathies lay. In an article in *Foreign Affairs*, he nailed his federalist colours to the mast: "[A] profound transformation of Europe certainly is necessary, and I am one of those who believe that such a transformation must include not only organisation of Europe's resources but eventually the union of the European countries" (Spaak, "The Integration of Europe, Dreams and Realities" 94). To that end, he also accepted that a compromise on sovereignty was required: "The organised international life for which we are working cannot be realised unless we destroy the dogma of the absolute sovereignty of states" (97)

In the Assembly itself, the federalists – mainly French, though with some Dutch and Italian support – hoped that a debate about first principles would eventually lead to an emerging consensus in favour of a federal union. To that end, they scheduled a number of debates on the topic of "necessary changes to the structure of Europe to achieve a greater unity" (Walton 379). The French participants were clear about what they wanted: "[T]he creation of a political authority of a supranational character" (Walton 379).

—

The pushback by British and Scandinavian antifederalists caused the federal camp to look for new, more veiled concepts through which to sell their federal scheme. When the term "'supranationalism," a less specific alternative for the words "'federal union," still proved too divisive, they settled instead for the vague description proposed by the Greek delegate Grégoire Cassimatis: a "European authority with limited functions but real powers" (Walton 380).

Even this was unacceptable to the British delegation. But if it wanted to win the debate, it needed a persuasive counterproposal of its own. It came in the form of a new concept, "functionalism," a term coined during the war by the British–Romanian political scientist David Mitrany (1888–1975). In a 1943 pamphlet titled *A Working Peace System*, he had firmly rejected federation as an option for Europe: "None of the elements of neighbourhood, of kinship, of history, are there to serve as steps" (Mitrany 6). He equally rejected the idea of a transatlantic union, "Mr Streit's first proposal for the federation of fifteen democracies" (13) Not only would it "lack unity of outlook," it would also "abandon to their fate democratic sections in the states excluded" (13). Worse than that, it would actively antagonise those countries not included in the union: "The first effect of any such sectional grouping (...) must be to force those left outside to join together in some counter-group" (17). Such regional unions would, in effect, "represent merely a rationalised nationalism, with wider limits for the individual units, but otherwise reproducing the working characteristics of the system of national states" (19) – an argument that held much sway at a time when the Soviet Union was the West's key partner in the fight against the Axis Powers.

The alternative was to let go of all thoughts of "traditional organisation on the basis of a set of constitutional division of jurisdiction of rights and powers," and instead to focus on "specific ends and needs, (...) according to the conditions of their time and place"[4] (Mitrany 20). This kind of "functional practice" (24) would allow cooperating governments to steer clear of "the Scylla of power and the Charybdis of sovereignty" (27).

Functionalism was introduced into the debate at Strasbourg in a speech by Labour MP Maurice Edelman, who used it exactly as Mitrany had defined it: as an alternative to federal union, not a complement to it. What he proposed was to grant the Council the authority to act as a kind of coordinator in specific economic sectors, a "planning by consent" that left the sovereignty of the member states fully intact (Walton 379).

These two concepts would take on a life of their own in the years after the great Council of Europe debate. Supranational, which had been used by the federalist delegates as a mere synonym, came to be seen as something qualitatively different, "standing midway between international and federal organs" (Mason vii). Functionalism, for its part, was seized

---

4   Mitrany seemed unaware of the existence of the European tradition in federal theory, going back to Kant and Saint-Simon, which had used schemes such as the ones he proposed as levers for further federalisation. In the view of theorists working within this tradition, the two approaches went together.

on by the federalist camp and turned into a means to a federal end, "the possible establishment of a series of supranational authorities each having a particular purpose or 'function'" (Zurcher 51).

The first meaningful move in that direction came at the end of a particularly acrimonious debate in the early spring of 1950. At one point the Swedish delegate professor Bertil Ohlin challenged the federalist camp: if they were so keen to form a federal union, why didn't they go and form one of their own "along the lines that so many speakers had advocated" (Walton 383). Paul Reynaud, the man who had briefly been Prime Minister at the start of the German invasion of France in May 1940, responded with a famous outburst: "Some say 'Frenchmen, take the risk and start first'. (...) Take the risk! Well, ladies and gentlemen, we shall take the risk" (Walton 383). He proceeded by tabling an amendment asking for the creation of supranational authorities in a number of key sectors of the European economy, including coal and steel production.

Like all other resolutions, this one too was defeated by the assembly. The endless series of no votes ended up killing one of the leading ideas for the unification of the continent. Not the French idea though, but the British one. All countries involved would eventually recognise that a union that was incapable of producing policy was a pointless organisation. As Reynaud observed, it was effectively home to two different approaches, working against each other: "The Council of Europe consists of two bodies, one of them *for* Europe, the other *against* it" (Zurcher 55). In his resignation speech, Paul-Henri Spaak apportioned the blame more evenly:

> Some Germans will not support a united Europe until the whole of Germany is united. Some Belgians will do so only if the United Kingdom joins in. Some Frenchmen are against a unification of Europe if it entails their being left to negotiate directly with the Germans. The British will not form part of a united Europe so long as they have not found a solution acceptable both to themselves and the Commonwealth. Our Scandinavian friends look on at all this in a somewhat disillusioned and disinterested manner, or so it appears.
> (Spaak, "Statement after his resignation as President of the Consultative Assembly")

As a result, "[t]oday, whether we like it or not, interest in the cause of a united Europe no longer lies, I am sorry to say, within this Assembly. (...) We can no longer do to-day what we could have done a year or two ago, for people are beginning to make fun of us and are speaking of our inability to achieve anything" (Spaak, "Statement after his resignation").

By the end of 1951 the Assembly itself concluded in a report by a special committee that it was "passing through a crisis, that it had not produced the results which its sponsors had expected, that little progress had been made in building a united Europe" (Walton 386).

—

The debates in the Council of Europe generally left the federalist camp disappointed. The European Union of Federalists summarised the feeling among its members when it wrote that the debates in the Assembly had "marked the end of the illusion that the aim of European unity can be achieved without political machinery on a supranational level. The time has now come to draw the necessary conclusions" (Zurcher 53).

There is another way to look at the Assembly debates though. If they failed to produce any significant decisions, they did at least lead to a reappraisal of its basic assumptions on the part of the federal camp. The war seemed to have persuaded people that a great leap forward was desirable, and more than a few had assumed that such a leap was also possible. The Ventotene Manifesto held up the American constitution as an example. What the authors forgot, however, was that the delegates at the Philadelphia Convention had a very different starting position. There already was an American union, established through the Articles of Confederation. The question for the Philadelphia delegates was if they could find a way to save it by perfecting it. On the European side, a union would first have to be created. The required leap forward was therefore qualitatively of a completely different order than the American one.

One man who realised this was Spaak. In his *Foreign Affairs* article, he acknowledged that "[t]here are points in common between America at the end of the eighteenth century and Europe today, and I believe that the farsightedness and courage of Hamilton, Madison, Jay and the others hold great lessons for Europeans" (Spaak, "The Integration of Europe" 95). But, he warned, "the two situations are not analogous" (95). Unlike the American union, the European one would not be built all at once. In the process to come, "the precondition of success" would therefore be "the awareness that this is a long-term undertaking" (100).

European theoreticians since Kant had always accepted this fact and had devised their plans accordingly. Through trial and error, the postwar federalist movement had now ended up in the same position. It accepted that the building of a European federal union might not be the work of a moment but of generations, that it might have to start with a small vanguard of committed countries and focus on a particular economic sector. It was a lesson it needed to learn. And having learned it, it was ready for what came next.

The Monnet Moment

The birth of an eventual successful European federal union owed much to the French businessman, diplomat, and civil servant Jean Monnet (1888–1979). At age sixteen, his parents forced him to leave school so he could go into the family cognac sales business. Family connections then helped him land a job in the French wartime administration, where he distinguished himself to such an extent that he was eventually invited to take up the position of deputy secretary-general of the secretariat of the new League of Nations.

In Monnet's view, the League Covenant was a document full of high ideals. But in its day-to-day operations, it had a number of obvious shortcomings. One was the lack of an effective institutional framework to help prepare and execute the Council's decisions: "[T]he tasks of reconstruction, which needed a genuine supranational power, were now to be tackled by an organisation whose only permanent element was its Secretariat" (Monnet, *Memoirs* 238). Another was the Council's efficiency in decision-making, which was significantly limited by the unanimity rule. In all, though, the feeling in the early days of the League seemed to be that "it was bound to prevail, by sheer moral strength, by the appeal of public opinion, and by the force of habit" (81).

Looking back fifty years later, Monnet was more critical. He described the League as a "switchboard" authority, a mere channel "through which nations communicate with each other" (Monnet, *Memoirs* 222). Bringing nations together was pointless if there was no means of getting them to take, and adhere to, common decisions: "Getting national officials to cooperate is well-intentioned enough; but the method breaks down as soon as national interests conflict, unless there is an independent body that can take a common view of the problem and arrive at a common decision" (75). The root cause of the League's problems, he concluded, was national sovereignty: "The veto was at once the cause and the symbol of this inability to go beyond national self-interest" (96).

Still, his criticism of the organisation was tempered by a sense of realism: "[I]n 1921 the time was not yet ripe for the delegation of sovereignty to a common High Authority" (Monnet, *Memoirs* 87). And on balance, he felt that within the limited setting created by the Covenant, "[t]he League Secretariat and its contacts worked well" (94).

—

Monnet was not the kind of man to look to literature for inspiration. His was a life of action, not of contemplation. His biographer described his attitude as "anti-historicism" and claimed he "suspect[ed] history of being a crutch for those who hoped relying on it would be easier than thinking for themselves" (Duchênes 29). That does not mean that he was completely unaffected by the three canons of federal union. There are traces of the peace plan tradition in his writings, for example in his reference to "a 'political grand design'," when describing his hopes at the end of the First World War for a League of Nations to institute lasting peace (Monnet, *Memoirs* 78), and to Briand's proposal for "'a federal link' between the peoples of Europe" (282). More obvious was his connection to the canon of actual experiments with transnational federal unions. He personally worked in, and helped give structure to, the League of Nations. He was also on good personal terms with Leon Bourgeois, who as he put it "took part in every stage of the fight for peace in the first quarter of the century" – an implicit reference to the two The Hague peace conferences at which Bourgeois was an active participant (83).

As for the canon of greater and lesser-known thinkers: though obviously not academically inclined, there are traces of it in his writings and recorded thoughts as well. Monnet's former assistant, and the co-author of his autobiography, François Fontaine, claimed that the only three political thinkers with whom Monnet was familiar were Hamilton, Madison, and Jay. He also revealed that during his time at the ECSC's High Commission, Monnet kept a pile of copies of the *Federalist Papers* in his office to hand out to visitors (Fransen 5, fn 1). There are, however, no references to the contents of the essays in his speeches or his memoirs, nor any personal notes or records of conversations in which the book or its authors came up as a topic of conversation.[5] The same goes for the European federal tradition.

On balance, Monnet's thinking on federal union seemed more American than European in its orientation. Though it's impossible to say with certainty what caused this, one plausible explanation is that his only personal link with a federal theoretician was with the author of *Union Now*, Clarence Streit. Though their paths may well have crossed before – either in Paris when both were there for the Versailles peace talks, or in Geneva at the League of

---

5   The only unambiguous reference to the *Federalist Papers* came in his *Memoirs*, when he remarked about the "mid-century period" that it was characterised by "extraordinary ferment in men's minds about the idea of European unity" (Monnet, *Memoirs* 281), and that "The London *Times* and *The Economist* published admirable editorials worthy of Jay's, Madison's and Hamilton's *Federalist Papers*" (281–282).

Nations, though Monnet was no longer working at the Secretariat General by the time Streit took up his post as *New York Times* correspondent – personal contact between them seems to have been established only in the late 1930s through their mutual friend, John Foster Dulles. Together, the three men spent the summer of 1940 working on a transatlantic federal constitution (Imlay 114, fn 82). After that, the relationship seems to have continued mainly through correspondence. Monnet did write a recommendation for Streit's book which appeared on the back cover of the 1948 edition. In it, he remarked that it had been "[t]en years (...) since I first read *Union Now* "and observed that there was "reason to hope" because "'Union' is now a rallying cry for millions".

There are certainly traces of Streit's – and by extension Hamilton's and Madison's – thinking in Monnet's own ideas and statements: the rejection of an absolute status for national sovereignty and of any non-federal type of international organisation, the importance of a direct relationship between the federal government and the citizen, and the embrace of a transatlantic scheme as an ultimate objective. The latter idea was included, for example, in a letter to Robert Schuman written in April 1948 during a visit to the United States: "All my reflections and my observations lead me to one conclusion which is now for me a profound conviction: the effort of the countries of western Europe, in order to match up to the circumstances – both the dangers which threaten us and the American effort – must become a true European effort which alone the existence of a Federation of the West will render possible" (Fransen 92).[6]

Monnet's thinking was no mere carbon copy of Streit's though. If the letter to Schuman contained a clear reference to the Streitian concept of a transatlantic federation, there was also the suggestion of an idea that Streit had explicitly rejected, and that seemed closer to the concept of a world order propagated by Churchill: a European organisation that would serve as a separate pillar of a transatlantic community ("a true European

---

6   His biographer, Jean Dûchenes, notes that, though Monnet "did not explain what he meant by a 'Federation of the West'," in 1950 Monnet would define it as consisting of "western Europe, Britain, the United States and British Dominions" (Dûchenes 289). The idea would remain part of his political thought. In 1961, for example, Monnet gave an address at Dartmouth College in which he made the case for a European Union embedded in a Transatlantic Union. In that speech the term "the West" was used to refer to the trans-Atlantic community: "[J]ust as Europe is now in the process of uniting, so the West must move towards some kind of union." Worth noting is that a copy of the speech was reprinted with Monnet's permission in *Freedom & Union*, the magazine run by Clarence Streit. See Jean Monnet, "Peace Needs Quick Steps to Atlantic Union," in *Freedom & Union*, July-August, 1961.

effort") (Fransen 90). The latter idea he had already articulated several years earlier, in a conversation with fellow national commissioner in the French Committee for National Liberation (FCNL), Hervé Alphand. He distinguished two different options for a European union: it was to be either a broad economic union or more specifically based on a sectoral cooperation in the fields of coal and steel production. Though the initial focus of his scheme was a regional union involving France, Belgium, The Netherlands and Luxembourg, the ultimate goal was "to include within the Union all the States of Europe except the U.S.S.R." (90).

Apart from the Soviet Union, he also noted "the special case of the British Isles" (Fransen 90). The fact that he treated these two as independent powers was consistent with what he had written earlier that year, in a note on the postwar situation, drafted in Algiers while he was there to work for the FCNL. The note made the case for Europe as a separate power in its relations with the existing three Great Powers.[7] It also contained a clear statement of principles about what he saw as necessary steps for the reconstruction of Europe: "[T]he re-establishment or establishment of a democratic regime in Europe, and the economic and political organisation of a 'European entity'" (Monnet, "Thoughts on the future"). In a next section of the note, he made it clear what he meant by the term "entity": "Prosperity for the States of Europe and the social developments that must go with it will only be possible if they form a *federation* or a 'European entity' that makes them into a common economic unit" (Monnet, "Thoughts on the future"; my emphasis). He fully understood that this required a break with the dogma of sovereignty: "There will be no peace in Europe if the States are reconstituted on the basis of national sovereignty, with all that that entails in terms of prestige politics and economic protectionism" (Monnet, "'Thoughts on the future").

The Algiers note also contains the first reference to a version of the gradualist approach that would be more fully developed in his conversation with Alphand: "It will obviously not be possible to achieve this 'European result' immediately. A fairly long period will be necessary to allow for the requisite discussions and the conclusion of the necessary agreements. But it is vital to make immediate provision for measures which at the very least will

---

7   In 1953, Robert Schuman would produce a similar geopolitical analysis, when looking back at the turn of the 1950s. The three main powers were "North America, the Soviet bloc, the British Commonwealth." Against this kind of Great Powers competition, 20 individual Western European nations would be powerless, unless they found a way of cooperating: "The challenge was for us [France] to organise Europe as a unifying project" (Robert Schuman, lecture to the College of Europe, Bruges, 22 October 1953).

ensure that it remains possible to achieve such a result" (Monnet, "Thoughts on the future"). This approach, which he had developed independently of the prewar European federal tradition, put him in a different camp from most of the other wartime supporters of federal union, who tended to think in terms of a giant leap forward. It would put him front of the queue when the more ambitious schemes had all burned themselves out, and British functionalist attempts had failed to receive sufficient backing in the Council of Europe.

There was one other remarkable thing about the Algiers note: even in 1943, when victory was still far from assured, he already talked about Germany's future status in fairly open terms. It would be a Germany, though, deprived of its industrial heartlands of the Ruhr, Saar and Rhineland. In Monnet's plans, those would be used to form a new "European industrial country" at the service of all of Western Europe – what Alphand described in his diary as "a kind of Lotharingia" (Fransen 91).

It wasn't until early 1950, when repeated attempts to win the British government for his scheme had failed, that he reached the conclusion that the kind of union he proposed would only work if France could somehow find a way of working *with* Germany for the unification of Western Europe. When, in March 1950, Schuman asked him what could be done to improve the frosty relations with the new German government, Monnet told him that "[p]eace can be founded only on equality. (...) We failed in 1919 because we introduced discrimination and a sense of superiority. Now we are beginning to make the same mistake again" (Monnet, *Memoirs* 283).

This idea of making a peace pact with Germany the cornerstone of French security had of course been propagated by Churchill as early as 1946, but in France itself the idea was nothing short of revolutionary. Not only did it have to ignore the obvious pain, still omnipresent in French society, caused by the German occupation, and the fact that it had fought three large scale wars with the Germans in the previous eighty years, it also had to go against a fifty year old French geostrategic doctrine which was based on two premises: alliance *with* Great Britain, and alliance *against* Germany (Fransen 90–91, 94).

Monnet's mission was to find a way to get first his own government, and then other European governments, to accept a joint Western European authority, with French–German cooperation as its cornerstone, and then get them to accept that it needed to be invested with its own claim to sovereignty. It seemed an impossible task, but just as in 1918, the stars in their courses would align for his idea. And when they did, he had the good fortune of finding at the heart of the French government exactly the right man to take the idea forward.

Europe united: the Schuman Plan

The breakthrough for Europe's federal unification required a number of puzzle pieces to fall into place. One was the restoration of Germany, or at least the free part of it, to full statehood. Without it, no union of any kind would have had a chance to succeed. Even though their European allies saw renewed German statehood mainly as a potential problem, by 1948 American policymakers had become convinced that the geostrategic situation left them no choice but to push forward with it. They feared a divided Germany would make an easy target for Soviet infiltration and communist-led revolution. That scenario constituted "the greatest threat to the security of all Western nations, including the US," according to Secretary of State George Marshall (Isaacson and Thomas 454). If containment of the Soviet threat was the aim, keeping the Western parts of Germany out of Russian hands was key.

It was George Kennan who had set out what would eventually become the standard Western approach to the German question. It was based on accepting the facts on the ground, specifically the partition of the country into an Eastern and a Western zone:

> We have no choice but to lead our section of Germany to a form of independence so prosperous, so secure, so superior, that the East cannot threaten it. (...) Better a dismembered Germany in which the West, at least, can act as a buffer to the forces of totalitarianism than a united Germany which again brings those forces to the North Sea.
> (Isaacson and Thomas 290)

Just as in the case of Europe as a whole, the debate about Germany was no longer whether it could remain united, but whether any part of it could remain free. The division of both country and continent was accepted as a political fact.

As early as October 1946, Bevin had articulated the British government's preference for a German constitutional solution that would leave it less centralised but not so weak that it would form an easy prey for Soviet aggression: "We countenance a German constitution which would avoid the two extremes of a loose confederation of autonomous states and a unitary centralised state" (Friedrich 467). To this federal blueprint, his American colleague Marshall then added a further characteristic when addressing the subject of German unity at the Moscow summit in the spring of 1947. He stressed the importance of any new German constitution containing a bill of rights, to protect German citizens from the kind of arbitrary abuses that were so commonplace under the Nazis. He specifically mentioned "protection from arbitrary arrest, search and seizure, and (...) equality under the law" (467).

By the time the British and American governments used the Six Power Conference in June 1948 to start the process leading to the formation of a new German state, it was therefore already clear what kind of constitution they had in mind for it. If it was one that closely fitted the German federal constitutional tradition, that was in a sense a coincidence. Still, in its details, the Basic Law (*Grundgesetz*) that was adopted in the spring of 1949 was very much a product of that tradition (Basic Law of the FRG).[8] As a federal republic, it arranged for a distribution of powers between the federal centre and the states (now called *Länder*), whose constitutions were supposed to be based on the same principles as the federal government: the rule of law (*Rechtsstaat*) and democracy (Art. 28) It also contained a supremacy clause that declared federal law superior to state law (Art. 31). The legislative power was divided between a *Bundestag* elected by the people, and a *Bundesrat* nominated by the governments of the various states. The executive was in charge of foreign policy, though not of defence. Not that the states had any competence here. It was rather that Germany was not allowed, at this stage, to have its own defence policy. If the situation demanded it, it was allowed to join an international "system of mutual collective security" (Art. 24).

If the final text was the product of an attempt to reconnect with the pre-1933 federal constitutional past, it was also a conscious attempt to repair some of the damage done by twelve years of Nazi rule. Article 1 declared that "the dignity of man shall be inviolable." It made it "the duty of all state authority" to "respect and protect it." These "inviolable and inalienable human rights" were declared to form "the basis of every human community, of peace and of justice in the world." It then set out a number of human rights which were considered to be "binding as directly valid law" (Art. 1). Among them were many of the same rights included in the Universal Declaration, which had been drafted explicitly with Nazi abuses in mind: the right to life and physical inviolability (Art. 2), equality before the law and freedom from discrimination (Art. 3), freedom of conscience and religion (Art. 4), freedom of speech (Art. 5), freedom of assembly (Art. 8) and freedom of association (Art. 9). Among the other rights, several seemed intended specifically to prevent a repeat of Nazi abuses: the protection of secrecy of the mail and telecommunications (Art. 10), the ban on compulsory labour

---

8   All subsequent quotes in this section come from this document unless indicated otherwise.

(Art. 12), the inviolable status of a person's home (Art. 13), and crucially: of their citizenship (Art. 16).

One thing the Basic Law was clearly not was a *national* law. The German lands under Russian control were blocked from joining the new state. The prime ministers of the Western states therefore decided that the word "constitution" (*Verfassung*) was to be avoided. It could only be used once the text covered all of Germany, not merely its western parts. From the start, the West German states were therefore focused on reunification. To underline this, the preamble talked about the duty of "the entire German people" to achieve its "unity and freedom." Similarly Article 23 stated that though the text would "for the time being" apply only to the West German states, it would become applicable to "other parts of Germany" upon their accession to the Union.

—

Two important questions remained to be answered. Both had been raised by Carl Schmitt during the Weimar years. One was the question of the revision of the constitution. It was through the old Article 76 of the Weimar Constitution that the Nazi's had tightened their grip on power. That clause had contained a loophole that had been ruthlessly exploited by Hitler. The vote would stand if two-thirds of the *Reichstag's* members present voted in favour, *and* at least two thirds of members were present during the vote. This gave him the idea of blocking just under one-third of members by locking them up or otherwise preventing their attendance, so that his own 45 percent of the seats was suddenly almost enough to get his amendment adopted. In the new Article 79, the demand was increased to two-thirds of *all* members, in *both* houses.

Even with this change, though, the clause might still be open to abuse. This raised Schmitt's other question, the one that he had debated with Hans Kelsen: who was going to be the guardian of this new constitution? For the state constitutions, the text offered a clear answer through the third provision of Article 28: "The Federation shall guarantee that the constitutional order of the *Länder* shall correspond to the basic rights and the provisions of paragraphs (1) and (2)." And for normal cases, the Federal Constitutional Court would act as a guarantor of fundamental rights and constitutional propriety. For extraordinary cases, however, where the legal order was used against itself effectively to abolish itself, the text provided no clear solution.

It would come from a different source. In their Occupation Statute of 12 May 1949, the Military Governors and Commanders in Chief of the Western Zones of Germany declared that, "in order to ensure the accomplishment of the basic purposes of the occupation," they reserved for themselves a

number of special powers. Among them, Article 2 (f) listed the enforcement of "respect for the Basic Law" (Occupation Statute of Germany). The
new German union's constitutional integrity was therefore guarded over
by *foreign* powers. In other words: it was independent, but not sovereign
(Friedrich 474). It would become the mission of the first West-German
Chancellor, Konrad Adenauer, to remedy this situation.

—

As the British and American governments pushed for bringing the free
parts of Germany back into the Western community of nations as a single
federal republic, the French government found itself caught on the horns
of a dilemma. It saw the continued occupation of the French administered
part of Germany as a safeguard against a possible German resurgence,
and worse, German rearmament. On a more practical note, the continued
occupation of the Saar territory also gave the French access to its coal
reserves, thus ensuring a steady supply of affordable coke for the French
steel industry. The biggest fear among French policymakers was that a newly
independent Germany would decide to sell its coke elsewhere – a move that
would jeopardise France's fragile economic recovery. In short, it could not
afford to give up control of the Saar, but realistically it could also no longer
hold on to it (Roth 521–522).

In August 1949, French Foreign Secretary Robert Schuman was still
defending his government's crude attempt at a solution of this dilemma
(Roth 474). Under the French policy introduced in 1947, the Saar region
had become nominally independent, and economically integrated into the
French economy through a monetary and customs union. It was clear to him
that this position was not really tenable, given the American government's
position and German outright hostility to the idea. He needed to find a more
credible way to square the circle.

In an attempt to break the stalemate within the Western Alliance about
the future status of Germany's occupied industrial heartland, in September 1949 US Secretary of State Dean Acheson asked Schuman to produce a
constructive proposal (Roth 486). The thought behind it seemed to be that
making the most awkward member of the group responsible for coming
up with a solution was the most likely route to a breakthrough.[9] A French
failure to deliver would free the US to impose a solution of its own. When, in

9   An alternative explanation is that as a result of the sterling crisis of September 1949, Acheson
had concluded that the UK was no longer in a position to lead a possible effort to integrate

early 1950, there was still no visible progress on the French side, he proposed a deadline in the form of the next meeting of the French, American and British foreign ministers, mid-May, in London (498–498).

When Schuman struggled to come up with a plan that reconciled French ambitions (continued control over, or at least access to, German coal supplies) with Allied demands for restored German control over the region, the man tasked with leading the French economic reconstruction effort, Jean Monnet, seized the opportunity to present a plan of his own, a version of the one that he had first conceived in the early 1940s.

The core of it was formed by a proposal to put the coal and steel industries of Germany and France under a joint administration, for the benefit of both economies. This would effectively guarantee continued French access to German coke supplies, and it would do so under the guise of restoring (West) Germany's standing in Europe, while offering some sense of German control, albeit shared, over its own industries. At the heart of the plan was a concept of shared sovereignty: a newly created central authority would take decisions affecting both industries, and member states no longer had the individual veto power to block these decisions.

—

Schuman would immediately embrace the proposal, and not just for reasons of state or lack of alternatives, though time was certainly a factor by now – Monnet had only forwarded the proposal to Schuman on 28 April 1950, two weeks before Acheson's deadline (Monnet, *Memoirs* 951). If he was immediately convinced by the proposal, it was in part also because it appealed to his political–philosophical instincts. Unlike Monnet, whose federalism was more of a visceral nature, Schuman's federalism was a product of a studious mind. In Strasbourg, he had studied under the German constitutional law scholar Paul Laband, while in Berlin he studied Greek history under Friedrich Nietzsche's old rival, Ulrich von Wilamowitz-Möllendor. As an expression of his Catholic faith, he joined the *Görresgesellschaft*, a German catholic intellectual society (Roth 39–43). His reading tastes in later life reflected that same faith, from mediaeval classical texts like St Thomas Aquinas' *Summa Theologiae* to the works of the Catholic Personalist writers of his own era, some of whom (Jacques Maritain, Henri Brugmans) he knew personally (427).

Germany into the Western European economy. Given the importance of the overall objective, he had no option but to encourage France to take the lead. See Milward 473–474.

Personalism was first and foremost a theory about the essentially re-lational nature of human existence. It rejected both the totalitarian idea of a person's life belonging to the state (the "political soldier") and liberal individualism's atomistic view of society (the "isolated individual"). Against these it posited the concept of the person as inherently connected to others, "responsible for their actions, free and engaged," part of various communities that together constituted society and the world community (Brugmans 115).

To the extent that Personalism had a political creed, it was federalism. Not so much as a constitutional construct, as the Swiss Personalist author Denis de Rougemont (1906–1985) explained in a speech to the first annual congress of the Union of European Federalists in 1947: "[N]othing is more contrary to the essence of federalism than generalisations and a theoretical spirit"[10] (Rougemont, "l'Attitude Fédéraliste" 59). This federalism, which he called "more organic than rational" (61) was defined by the philosopher Emmanuel Mounier (1905–1950) as a "twofold orientation (...) towards im-mediate interests and towards universality" which characterised both the person and "the entire system" (Mounier 250).

Given the emphasis in Personalist thought on "the reality of the organic international community" (Mounier 260) it was no surprise that these authors rejected the concept of nationalism, "which places the fatherland above truth and justice and above the inalienable rights of the person" (255), as well as the imposition of an artificial upper limit on the sense of community in the form of what Rougemont called "the tyrannical dogma of national sovereignty" (Rougement, "The Adventure of the 20th Century").

—

The Personalist thinker who engaged most deeply with the latter topic was Jacques Maritain (1882–1973). In a series of lectures delivered at the University of Chicago in December 1949, published under the title *Man and the State*, he rejected both the concept of the nation state ("[T]he systematic identification of (...) *Nation* and *State* has been a woe to modern society") and the idea of sovereignty (Maritain 2).

The "original error" of the concept of sovereignty as developed by Bodin was that it had ignored what Maritain called its "vicariousness" – the fact that power should not be conceived of as absolute ("ab-solute, that is non-bound,

---

10   This would not stop De Rougemont from proposing a Swiss-style federal constitution for Europe. See for example his speech at the European Movement conference in The Hague, *Congress of Europe*, 39.

separate") and unlimited but as relational and therefore essentially social context-bound (Maritain 34–35). Bodin's conception of sovereignty was, he explained, based on an error of interpretation. Instead of seeing power as *"participation* in a right naturally possessed by the people" (37), Bodin had treated it as *possession* of a "total power of the commonwealth" (35) which was exercised independently from the community. This error allowed sovereignty to be turned into a concept which was above the community, and eventually even above right and wrong. From there, it was but a short jump for it to become a tool for the justification of totalitarian conceptions of the state: "The Sovereignty of the totalitarian state is the master of good and evil as well as of life and death. That is just which serves the interest of the Sovereign" (48). To free political thought from this deadly burden, there was only one option: "In order to think in a consistent manner in political philosophy, we have to discard the concept of Sovereignty, which is but one with the concept of Absolutism" (49).

Maritain would distinguish himself in postwar debate, not just as a leading exponent of federal thought but also as one of the principal intellectual forces behind the new Christian Democrat movement (Segers 84). The latter was born out of two separate religious initiatives. One was a wartime manifesto drafted by a group of Italian Catholic activists which included the later Prime Minister Alcide de Gasperi. The text was effectively a mix of the Catholic church's social teachings and the European federalism of the resistance movement. Its restatement of Christian humanist ideals of human dignity, social justice, and a sense of community experienced through intermediary institutions rather than statist collectivism, combined with an optimistic vision of European reconciliation, provided exactly the kind of inspiration that Catholics – until then effectively deserted by Pope Pius XII – were looking for (92). The other were the various Protestant initiatives to foster an ecumenical spirit which would eventually allow Catholic and Protestant politicians to join forces in united *Christian* rather than separate Catholic and Protestant parties.[11]

The fact that Monnet provided him with a proposal that allowed for the development of exactly the kind of solidarity-based European federal initiative that seemed to embody the ideals of this new Christian Democratic movement at the very moment when he needed it most, would probably not have surprised the devout Catholic Schuman: "We are all just imperfect

---

11   Interestingly, Segers notes that Maritain himself attended a number of meetings of one of the ecumenical initiatives, the Commission to study the bases of a Just and Durable Peace (CJDP), which was chaired by John Foster Dulles (Segers 92).

instruments of a Providence which uses us in the realisation of grand designs which surpass us" (Roth 682). Whether the word play was intended or not, there is little doubt that Schuman thought that by helping to deliver this new Grand Design, he was doing God's work.

—

Once he decided to take up Monnet's proposal and make it French government policy, what was left was to devise a strategy for its adoption. In his famous Declaration of 9 May 1950, he would state that *"L'Europe ne se fera pas d'un coup"* (Europe will not be built all at once). What he left unsaid though was that Europe was very much being built *through a coup.*

Secrecy was one of the essential ingredients of every successful coup in the federal tradition. Usually it served to throw a veil over the true intentions behind an action, or to obfuscate the meaning of a compromise formula. In the case of the Schuman plan, the secrecy *was* the coup. The reasons for this were obvious: not only were they keen to avoid a storm of nationalist protests over the suggestion of close cooperation with Germany, but they also wanted to make sure neither the French Foreign Ministry nor some of France's allies – especially the British government – would kill it, or at least water it down, before it could be put to the test. Most of all, they were counting on the psychological effect of a dramatic announcement on both public opinion and the main actors involved (Gerbet 552).

In total, until the day of the announcement, only nine people were fully informed of the content of the plan (Monnet, *Memoirs* 300). It was kept secret from just about everybody, including Schuman's own civil servants at the Foreign Office and the *corps diplomatique*, most of his colleagues in the French cabinet, and most allies (only Acheson was briefed during a visit to Paris). The German Chancellor Konrad Adenauer received a copy of the plan and a personal letter from Schuman explaining its "highly political" purpose on the morning of the 9th, while the German cabinet was in session (302). It had been delivered through a secret visit that very morning by Schuman's personal envoy, Robert Mischlich, who had stressed the "exceptional urgency" of the matter. Schuman had deliberately chosen Mischlich as his courier so that they could avoid having to go through official diplomatic channels (301). Through Adenauer, the German cabinet was briefed and lined up behind the plan.

The French cabinet was not informed about the plan's existence until Schuman received confirmation by phone that the German government was on board.[12] This was around lunchtime on the 9th. A few hours later, he stood before a gathering of international newspaper correspondents in the *Salle de l'Horloge* in the French Ministry of Foreign Affairs (the same room where both the League's Covenant and the Briand-Kellogg pact had been announced) and read his famous declaration.

—

Schuman opened the press conference with a statement that sounded as both a wish and a prophecy: "France has acted, and the consequences of its action could be immense. We hope they will be" (The Schuman Declaration).[13] He then proceeded to read a text that had been drafted and redrafted numerous times over the previous weeks, every word carefully chosen for maximum effect on public opinion and allied governments.

It started with an act of homage to Aristide Briand and a claim that the Second World War was directly linked to the failure to implement his proposal for a United States of Europe: "In taking upon herself for more than 20 years the role of champion of a united Europe, France has always had as her essential aim the service of peace. A united Europe was not achieved and we had war." After first raising the stakes, Schuman then injected a sense of calm by explaining that what he asked for was not a revolution but a small initial commitment: "Europe will not be made all at once, or according to a single plan. It will be built through concrete achievements which first create a de facto solidarity." This action was focused on "one limited but decisive point": placing "Franco-German production of coal and steel as a whole under a common higher authority, within the framework of an organisation open to the participation of the other countries of Europe."

Schuman made no secret of the fact that he intended this plan to serve as "a first step in the federation of Europe." Though he did not use the words "national sovereignty," it was clear that what he proposed was a decisive move beyond it: "[B]y instituting a new higher authority, whose decisions will bind France, Germany, and other member countries, this proposal will lead to the realisation of the first concrete foundation of a European

---

12   To make sure that the plan met the deadline of 10 May, when Schuman was supposed to meet Acheson and Bevin in London to reveal whatever solution for the Saar he had come up with, the two ministers who were in on the plot – René Pleven and René Mayer – worked to have the weekly cabinet meeting moved from Wednesday the 10th to Tuesday the 9th. This is probably why, like the German cabinet, the French cabinet also only first heard of the existence of the plan on the day of its announcement. See Monnet, *Memoirs*, p. 300.

13   All subsequent quotes in this section come from this speech unless indicated otherwise.

federation indispensable to the preservation of peace." If successful, this plan could "change the destinies of those regions which have long been devoted to the manufacture of munitions of war, of which they have been the most constant victims."

—

There were several complicating factors that could have derailed the plan. One was a personality issue. Though Prime Minister Georges Bidault was a declared supporter of the idea of a European federal union, and on record that he accepted that this would have to involve a transfer of sovereignty to the federal level (Walton 379, fn 49), he was also an acknowledged supporter of the idea of a transatlantic union. In early May 1950, his own focus was fully on the latter. Just weeks prior to Schuman's presentation in cabinet, Bidault had given a speech in which he had argued for the creation of a High Atlantic Council with a military and economic focus – and eventually even a political one (Gerbet 543). Though there seemed to be little support for the idea outside the French Prime Minister's office – Acheson dismissed it as "stillborn" (Acheson 383) – its mere existence, and the Prime Minister's attachment to it, could have complicated the attempt to gain support for Schuman's alternative proposal.

Especially because there was also a potential problem on the personal level. Bidault and Schuman were competitors rather than colleagues. At Bidault's end, their rivalry for the high offices of state had at times spilled over into personal animosity. Schuman's biographer recorded one such incident in which the two traded barbs. After Bidault had described Schuman as a "lean gas engine" (suggesting that like the fuel, he was suffering from an excess of air), the latter replied that "not everyone can have an engine running on alcohol" (Roth 439). This double clash of proposals and characters could have proven to be a significant obstacle, if it had not been for one crucial detail. As Jean Monnet put it in his memoirs: "The fact is that there was no Bidault plan, but a Schuman plan" (Monnet, *Memoirs* 298). In the cabinet meeting in which Schuman presented his proposal, Bidault made no statement of support, but he did not veto it either (Roth 510).

Another potential stumbling block was formed by the American government. It had obviously repeatedly paid lip service to the idea of a united Europe, but that did not make it an immediate supporter of the plan. There were two concerns that both had to be addressed to secure American buy-in. One surfaced during the meeting between Schuman and Acheson in Paris. The American Foreign Secretary seemed mostly supportive of the French proposal, but did express one concern: "[W]as the plan cover for a gigantic European cartel?" (Acheson 383). To clarify that this was not the case, a section was added at the end of Schuman's statement: "The institution of the higher authority will in no way prejudge the methods of ownership of enterprises" (The Schuman Declaration).

More fundamental was a concern that emerged in American policy making circles in the days after Schuman's press conference. John Foster Dulles sent a note of warning to Jean Monnet that some in Washington, DC suspected that France intended to use the new organisation to "build up a 'third force', which will be 'neutral'" (Dulles). He urged Monnet to get the French government to provide clarification on the "'neutrality' view (...) which could have an unfavourable effect upon the relation of our two countries" (Dulles to Monnet, May 23, 1950). The French government would make frequent statements rejecting neutrality, enough to placate America's political class, which would eventually give the Schuman Plan its strongest support. The idea of a European union as a neutral third force, however, would take on a life of its own in French politics.

The most important potential obstacle was formed by the reception of the plan among France's European allies. The aim of the launch strategy was to bounce them into accepting the idea, and then use the negotiations to find enough common ground to allow them to sign on. The strategy of minimal information used to get the plan through the French and German cabinets was combined with a strategy of no information towards its allies. The full force of *fait accompli* was brought to bear on the Dutch, Belgian, Luxembourgeois and Italian cabinets, whose ambassadors were only briefed about the existence of the plan moments before the press conference. Their responses varied from outright enthusiasm (Spaak stated that he had wished he had written Schuman's declaration himself) to diplomatic hesitancy, especially on the part of the Dutch. None of the four governments, however, would turn down the invitation for the negotiations.

A more complicated calculation confronted the men behind the plan when it came to the British government. On the one hand British participation in the negotiations could increase credibility of the scheme in the eyes of other European governments (especially the Dutch, and potentially the Northern European governments). On the other hand, as the debate in the Strasbourg Assembly had shown, British participation might also negatively impact the chances of the scheme succeeding. In the end they solved it by making the British government an offer it couldn't possibly accept: to settle the details of the new authority's constitution only during negotiations between the participating states, but to commit *in advance* to the principle that it would involve a "partial fusion of sovereignty" – something that had only been the *outcome* of the negotiations during the Philadelphia Convention (Monnet, *Memoirs* 311).

Keen to avoid the impression of not wanting to join a European unification effort, the British government tried to put the blame on the French proposal. It did so by focusing on a single word in the French description of the negotiations: "commitment." By arguing that to give such a commitment in advance was impossible, it asked for a special position in the negotiations, effectively half in, half out: participating in the drafting of the new treaty but not in any way accepting its content until all of it was on the table.

Monnet urged Schuman to refuse the request. Accepting the British demand would inevitably mean "the replacement of the French proposal by something that would merely travesty it, (...) some kind of OEEC. In the end, a time would come when France would have to take the responsibility of breaking off the negotiations and taking the blame" (Monnet, *Memoirs* 312). The French delegation replied to the British request by replacing the word "commitment" with "immediate objective," but it left the proposal otherwise intact. The British government, forced to choose, then opted out of the negotiations, claiming that it could not agree to "terms which committed them in advance of such consideration to pool the production of coal and steel and to institute a new high authority whose decisions would bind the Governments concerned" (House of Commons resolution, 27 June 1950).

Europe United: the European Coal and Steel Community

Having outmanoeuvred the British government, and secured the German government's enthusiastic support, Monnet had every reason to look forward to the coming treaty negotiations with confidence. When the negotiators gathered in Paris on 20 June 1950, he had three priorities: he wanted the new organisation to be based on a transfer of sovereignty from the member states to the centre; he wanted the centre to be as strong as possible in order to guarantee its success in the near term, which would boost its chances of survival in the medium term; and he wanted the treaty to be concluded quickly in order to capitalise on the momentum created by the successful launch. In the end he would achieve most of the first objective, some of the second, and precious little of the third. It would take nearly a year before the negotiations were finally completed.

—

The French hosts opened proceedings with not one but two audacious moves. The first was an attempt to radically change the perspective of the various country delegations, who would have arrived there chiefly to defend their national interests. Schuman used his speech at the opening of the negotiations on 20 June to suggest that those present must be prepared to move beyond mere domestic priorities if they wanted to serve their countries well. In an echo of Saint-Pierre, he used the language of *raison d'état* to make the case for a European approach: "Without losing sight of the specific necessities of our own countries, we must be aware that the national interest today consists precisely in finding beyond our national boundaries the means of achieving a more rational structure for the economy. (...) Our negotiations will be better and more than selfish haggling that refuses both risk and trust" (Schuman, "Address given at the opening of the conference on the Schuman Plan"; my emphasis). By repeatedly appealing to the group character of the gathering through the use of personal pronouns like 'us', 'we', and 'our', he tried to instil in them a sense of shared destiny: "[I]t is an awe-inspiring task that *our* governments have allocated to *us* and entrusted *us* with. *We* will undertake it with respect, conscious of *our* responsibility. *We* feel that *we* are not allowed to fail this task, to abandon without concluding an agreement" (Schuman).

It was a variation on the theme used by Briand in his 1930 memorandum, creating the suggestion that a union of sorts had already been established even before the talks had started, at least at the moral level. It was more than just a rhetorical ploy though. The only way the talks could succeed was if the hosts could prevent discussions getting bogged down in technical details. The best way of doing that would be to focus on constitutional issues first, and leave the dealing with technical issues to the High Authority once it was fully established. But if the other negotiators were to accept this approach, they would first have to take a mental leaIt required them to act *as if* the High Authority already existed – only that way could they delegate issues to it. The most effective way of preparing them for that leap was to make them *want* it to exist.

For his part, to maximise the chances of a collective identity emerging among the negotiators, Monnet tried to create optimal conditions for it. Negotiations were moved from the beautiful but formal Foreign Office building at the Quay d'Orsay to Monnet's personal offices in the much smaller building of the Commissariat Général du Plan. He then proposed that the chief negotiators would meet separately, and that there would be no official stenographic report of their discussions. The idea was that being able to speak freely, without intervention from technical experts, would allow the diplomats to move beyond their countries' official instructions (effectively the same method that had been used by the American Founders at the Philadelphia Convention).

It is a testament to Monnet's character and powers of persuasion that even the most hard-nosed among the negotiators were eventually positively affected by his approach. In the course of the negotiations, there were several moments where the talks could have failed if participants did not share a desire to find compromise solutions for the common European good. This European spirit would repeatedly win out over the will to defend national priorities at all cost. The man who would be Monnet's main opponent during the first part of the conference, the Dutch chief negotiator Dirk Spierenburg (1909–2001), later admitted that because of Monnet's efforts to create the right setting, he remembered them taking place in "an atmosphere of consultations rather than one of negotiations" (Spierenburg and Poidevin 16).

—

The second French proposal was truly explosive. The High Authority that was to become the executive of the new organisation would receive virtually absolute powers. The only check on its actions came in the form of an assembly, made up of delegations selected by national parliaments. The assembly's powers were limited though. It would meet only once a year, and then only to review and approve or reject (by two-thirds majority) the High Authority's work in the previous year. It had no right of initiative or scrutiny, or even of consultation on planned decisions by the High Authority. It was, in short, not so much a legislature as a parliamentary version of a court of auditors.

Superficially, Monnet's opening move resembled that of Alexander Hamilton in Philadelphia. Like Monnet, Hamilton had also proposed the creation of a central government that was so strong that it left no role for the states. Both men seemed intent on creating the preconditions for the survival of their union, and clearly agreed that only a strong central government would be able to deliver the kind of successes that would secure its existence in the medium term. That is where the similarities ended though. For Hamilton, proposing an almost absolute central authority likely served the tactical purpose of enabling a compromise over sovereignty to appear. Monnet had no need for such tactics. The acceptance of the idea of a central authority with its own claim to sovereignty had been made a precondition for participation in the talks. Everyone present knew what they were there to do.

Or so he thought. Because it quickly transpired that at least one of the delegations was not in any way inclined to follow Monnet's lead on this issue.

On the first day of the actual negotiations, Spierenburg asked two questions that Monnet would later describe as "the most serious obstacles the conference faced" (Monnet, *Memoirs* 325). One was what relationship there would be between the new authority and the Council of Europe. Monnet described it as "a trap" (325) and it clearly was. If the ECSC ended up being integrated into the decision-making structures of the Council of Europe, the chance of it delivering the desired breakthrough on divided sovereignty would be negligible. The final compromise over this issue was not entirely to Monnet's liking – the member states would use their Strasbourg delegations to convene a separate ECSC Assembly within the same building, though with extra representatives for some of the small member states – but he would at least succeed in keeping the High Authority outside the Council of Europe's grasp.

Spierenburg's other question dealt with the role of member states: "The French plan as at present described will revolutionise many things. How will governments react? If we are to carry them with us, they must be given a role in the system and wider powers, even if they are to give up some of their sovereignty" (Monnet, *Memoirs* 325). In his autobiography, Monnet remarked that when he heard Spierenburg's question, he "was not quite clear as to what it might imply" (325). But the same question had arisen, in various forms, in discussions within the OEEC and in the debate during the conference of the European Movement in The Hague. On both occasions, it was the Dutch delegation that had raised it. The question could therefore hardly have come as a surprise. At stake was the position of the smaller states, an issue that had also been a major theme in Philadelphia: how could they defend their interests after the abolition of the veto?

In the following weeks, Spierenburg worked in tandem with his Belgian and Luxembourg colleagues to maximise the pressure on Monnet. The Belgian negotiator, Ambassador Max Suetens, was the one who put the concrete Benelux demand on the table. Given that his government was "not prepared to give the High Authority excessive powers," he suggested that it should be overseen by a "supervisory body" of "Ministers, who effectively exercise power" (Monnet, *Memoirs* 326). Spierenburg built on this by suggesting there should be a qualified majority of two-thirds to validate any High Authority decision. To add to the weight of the demand, he added that "this is a point on which I see no possibility of compromise." In other words, as Monnet concluded, "[t]he Benelux countries were clearly thinking in terms of blocking minorities" (326).

The member states versus High Authority issue was now fully dominating the discussion. It was up to Monnet to find a way to deal with it. He started by slowing down the pace of the talks: "I realised I had to play for time, and get my colleagues used to discussing problems of national sovereignty without flinching from the thought" (Monnet, *Memoirs* 327). He used a procedural trick to buy himself the time he needed by setting up a number of technical working groups. This clearly meant that his third objective of "conducting the negotiations with a decent amount of haste in order to achieve immediate concrete results" (327) as set out in a memorandum to the inter-ministerial committee on the Schuman plan in early June 1950 would have to be let go of.

A compromise between the two positions was eventually worked out. The negotiators came to it in two stages. The first one was Monnet suggesting there was a way of giving both sides what they wanted by introducing a division of competencies: "[T]hose which the Treaty, by a collective decision of our national Parliaments, will expressly entrust to the High Authority; and those which spill over into the responsibility of Governments, and in which Governments should be empowered to intervene, provided that they act collectively" (Monnet, *Memoirs* 331). When Spierenburg insisted that even in the first case "ministers ought to be able to give the High Authority political directives," Hallstein spoke up to defend its independence: "In the eyes of my Government (...) the High Authority is the keystone of the European Community" (331).

The standoff was about the relative status of the institutions. Would one be placed above the other in the institutional hierarchy, or would they be placed next to each other? In his only meaningful intervention in the negotiations, Robert Schuman stressed that the institutions that had been created ought to function on the basis of equality. This meant, first and foremost, an independent High Authority. If a Council of Ministers was also to be included in the constitutional framework, it would be next to it, not above it. One week later Spierenburg, who had clearly taken on board Schuman's message that it was Monnet's compromise proposal or no deal, came back with final confirmation that the Dutch government was willing to continue the negotiations on the basis suggested by the French Foreign Secretary.

—

The fact that the Dutch government eventually decided to accept a transfer of sovereignty to the High Authority as a price for participation in the ECSC was strongly influenced by another issue that dominated Western European political debate in the immediate postwar period: decolonisation. The first few years after the war saw Great Britain lose control over the entire Indian subcontinent and Burma. In French Indochina, the Vietminh started a war of independence that would eventually see the colonial power suffer a decisive defeat at the battle of Dien Bien Phu, in May 1954. The Dutch had fought and lost a similar bloody war against the Indonesian independence movement. Though the Indonesians themselves had declared their independence as early as August 1945, the Dutch government would not recognise this fact until it had finally accepted military defeat. The formal handover of power took place on 27 December 1949.

The loss of what was by far the largest part of its colonial empire meant the Dutch faced a significant economic challenge. In his *Memoires*, the Dutch Foreign Secretary (and later NATO Secretary–General) Dirk Stikker explained what losing Indonesia meant for the Dutch economy: "We needed to thoroughly – and quickly – restructure our economy in keeping with our new position in the world order" (Stikker147; my translation throughout) If for the British government colonial considerations were an important factor in its decision not to join the ECSC negotiations, for the Dutch government they were probably the single most important reason behind its decision to participate. As Stikker put it: "We needed to find a replacement for Indonesia and the only possibility I saw was that we would pour all our energy into creating free-er trade and larger markets in Europe, based on higher production. If this failed, we would no longer be able to maintain our standard of living" (147).

In the end it was the "two Dirks" (Stikker and Spierenburg) who persuaded the reluctant Dutch Prime Minister, Willem Drees, to accept the idea of joining the ECSC on the basis of divided sovereignty. It was an essential step in what would become the reinvention of the Dutch economic model, from being the centre of a colonial empire to becoming *"Europoort,"* the gateway to Europe for global (mainly American) imports.[14]

———

The final distribution of powers and responsibilities between the High Authority and Council was settled in a number of expert committee

14   Though European colonialism clearly was a political factor of the first order in the immediate postwar period, it affected the calculations of the various countries involved in different ways. If for The Netherlands the loss of Indonesia was a reason for entering into the talks to form the ECSC, for the British government the continued existence of the Commonwealth was a prime factor in staying out of these same talks. Meanwhile, unlike their stance during the negotiations leading to the NATO treaty, the French government tried to keep the administration of its colonies out of the scope of the ECSC treaty, against efforts by the Italians and the Dutch to have them included to get access to north and west African iron ore reserves. See Kundnani, *Euro Whiteness* 72.

meetings. There would be three different categories of issues. On coal and steel production, the High Authority would receive an exclusive competence. On pricing policy, the High Authority was required to consult the Council before acting. And on issues like production quotas and import restrictions, it was only allowed to act if the Council had expressly agreed (Salzmann 245). In other words: the two institutions were both equal *and* unequal to each other, with checks on each other's powers.

Within this complicated framework of distributed powers, there were some clear concessions by the states to the new central authority. It received, for example, under Article 86 of the Treaty (Treaty Establishing the ECSC) the power to perform inspections of coal and steel facilities in the member states – exactly the kind of power that Woodrow Wilson had refused to include in the Covenant. The High Authority was also given certain powers that Hamilton had argued for in the American context. Article 49 allowed it to contract loans by borrowing on the capital markets. The delegates agreed that they would get better terms there if they negotiated collectively, through the High Authority, than if they approached the markets individually (Zurcher 77). To finance the loans, and to cover administrative expenditures, the same article and the next one (Article 50) also gave the High Authority the power of "imposing levies on the production of coal and steel."

These powers – of inspection, borrowing for investment, and taxation – were part of a number of powers that collectively achieved the very thing Tocqueville had described as the decisive difference between the American Constitution and the old Articles of Confederation: "The old confederate governments presided over communities (...) that of the Union presides over individuals" (see page 297 above). There was one other power that added to this effect. It was not a power *of* the High Authority however, but a power *against* it: the ability of producers to bring a case against its decision to the Court of Justice.

As part of their proposals, the Benelux countries were the first to suggest the creation of an independent Court. They promoted it for the same reason that Monnet had omitted it from his original plan: it could serve as a check on executive power. His idea had been to allow for the option of *ad hoc* arbitration panels to settle conflicts between the member states, or between the states and the centre, in a political process of conciliation. It would effectively give the High Authority a free hand, leaving it unbound by any legal review of its decisions.

He might have gotten away with that approach, if it hadn't been for the German delegation. Fresh from founding their own federal constitution, Walter Hallstein (1901–1982) and his team of legal advisers had come to

Paris with a certain ideal conception of a European union in mind. Their mission was, as Hallstein put it, to "anticipate the institutions of the future all-in federation of Europe" (Boerger-De Smedt 342 fn 12). In late April 1951 Hallstein, later the president of the first European Commission, used a lecture at the Goethe University in Frankfurt am Main to reflect on the treaty that had just been signed. If his mission had been to create the framework for a future European federal union, he would be satisfied with what had been agreed. Reviewing what he called its "institutional, one could even say constitutional issues," he observed that "if one considers the various analogies available to help characterise this new entity, the aptest image remains the federal model" (Hallstein). The High Authority "could be likened to a federal ministry," the Council of Ministers "to the federal council of a federal state" (in German a *Bundesrat*). The Assembly in turn "could be seen as a first step towards a European Parliament" (Hallstein).

The final element in the constitutional framework was the one to which Hallstein had contributed the most: the Court. Its structure and remit was the outcome of a protracted battle that took place in the summer of 1950. It pitted the French against the German delegation, in what was as much a clash of legal traditions as a clash of political interests. The French delegation rejected the idea of constitutional review as a 'government by judges'. It was keen to limit the court to a kind of administrative review role in line with established French legal practice. The Court would be allowed to set aside High Authority decisions, but not to replace them – that kind of "political" decision should remain the prerogative of the executive. It also did not want to allow an appeal on broader economic grounds, let alone on the basis of (lack of) compliance with the treaty. Any appeal to the Court should limit itself to the question if regulations had been correctly applied in the case at hand, not whether the regulations themselves were in line with the Treaty. Crucially, it also wanted to limit access to the court to member states only (Boerger-De Smedt 345–346).

Against this, the Germans wanted a court that had a broad constitutional remit, while taking into account the economic consequences of High Authority actions (or inactions). To assure its federal constitutional character, it also had to grant direct access to individual companies or industry organisations (Boerger-De Smedt 346). This was in line with the new constitutional review principles included in Article 100 of the German Basic Law of 1949, which in 1951 would lead to the creation of the German Federal Constitutional Court (*Bundesverfassungsgericht*).

In a way this was a replay of the debate that Schmitt and Kelsen had conducted in the early 1930s, with Schmitt arguing for the primacy of the executive and Kelsen making the case for the Court as the guardian of the constitution.[15] The difference with that debate was that, in this case, the delegates were actively trying to find a formula that could bridge the divide between the two approaches. Inevitably, the final compromise was a halfway house between an administrative and a constitutional court. The French delegation had succeeded in limiting the grounds for appeal, and in restricting access to the court for companies to a certain extent. In conflicts between the High Authority and member states, the court would also work more as an arbitration panel. Still, Hallstein greeted the final compromise as a success. Not only was it, in his eyes, a constitutional court in the traditional sense "in so far as it offers those affected by an abuse of its powers by the European administrative authority – those affected being producers and states – the opportunity to bring an action to have the contested decision declared void"; it was also a constitutional court in the American sense of offering something close to judicial review by "ensur[ing] compliance with the constitutional limits placed on the actions of the various organs" (Hallstein).

—

Around the time that Monnet was struggling to reach a compromise with the Benelux delegations, halfway round the world war broke out on the Korean peninsula. He realised immediately what the consequences of this could be for his negotiations: "[S]elf-protective reactions to the return of violence encouraged purely nationalistic attitudes which set us back several years and threatened the constructive efforts" (Monnet, *Memoirs* 337). "[O]ur only hope of salvation," he concluded, "lay in continuing and accelerating the process of change we had begun" (339).

In Bonn, Konrad Adenauer had seized up the situation and drawn a rather different conclusion. He realised that the Americans, who considered the Korean conflict part of a wider conflict with communism, would inevitably increase their demand for European troops (Williams 365). It gave him the opening he had been looking for to put an entirely different issue on the table: that of German sovereignty, and linked to it, the topic of German NATO membership (Williams 373). He correctly assumed that the Americans would be willing to discuss anything under the changed circumstances.

---

15   It's worth noting that at this point in the discussion, the German delegates on several occasions deliberately replaced the word "treaty" with "constitution," as if to drive home their message (Boerger-De Smedt 346).

This introduced a new risk for Monnet: "[I]f the Germans get what the Schuman Plan offers them, but without the Plan itself, we shall run the risk of their turning their backs on us" (Monnet, *Memoirs* 340). When Acheson used a meeting of the Three Powers in New York in September 1950 to put the idea of German troops under NATO command on the agenda, Monnet had to make a strategic decision. He saw three options for France: "To do nothing – but is that possible? To treat Germany on a national basis – but that would stop the Schuman Plan and the building of Europe. Or to integrate Germany into Europe by means of a broader Schuman Plan." He opted for the third, accepting that "the federation of Europe would have to become an immediate objective" (342).

Projecting the method of the Schuman Plan on military affairs, he suggested "that the solution of the German problem in its military aspect be sought in the same spirit and by the same method as for coal and steel; the establishment of a European Army with a single High Command"[16] (Monnet *Memoirs* 345). Not as part of the same negotiations though. Monnet proposed creating a separate negotiating framework for the military talks. Crucially, he demanded that they only start "after the Schuman Treaty is signed" (345). Given that he knew Adenauer was keen to find a European solution for the issue of German rearmament, he assumed this would help persuade the Germans to cooperate with bringing the talks to a speedy conclusion.

This was another miscalculation on the part of Monnet. Adenauer was a personal supporter of the ideas contained in the Schuman Plan, but he was also a German politician answerable to his constituents. These constituents, especially the business community, were putting increasing pressure on him to protect Germany's Ruhr-based coal cartel DKV from the effects of the ECSC's antitrust regulations, something that Monnet categorically ruled out. Adenauer decided to respond to this pressure by placing a reserve on the antitrust clause of the treaty, and to wait for the Americans to make up their mind about what they wanted most: German participation in NATO, or German integration in Europe. With all other issues resolved, by January 1951 the talks ground to a halt.

The completed treaty lay on Monnet's desk for three months, without any further progress to report (Monnet *Memoirs* 351). He had no room for compromise on this issue – he could not reasonably ask the French parliament to vote for a deal that effectively left German coal outside the High Authority's grasp (US Department of State, Office of the Historian,

---

16   This idea would take the form of the European Defence Community. Its negotiations and eventual failed ratification fall outside the scope of this book.

"Cable by the American Ambassador in France to the Secretary of State,"
21 February 1951). The negotiations might well have failed, if Monnet did
not have one more ace to play: his personal connections with the American
government. He asked his friend, the American High Commissioner for
Occupied Germany, John McCloy, to persuade Adenauer to lift his reserve
and allow the Schuman Plan to be ratified. Under American pressure, the
German Chancellor gave way (Fransen 110–111).

—

Though the political drama was now over, the treaty was not strictly speaking
the finished article. The issue of representation had been settled only in
part. Through the Council, the smaller states had seemed to secure equal
representation, which Monnet called "the natural result of the unanimity
rule which governs international relations when there is no Community
structure" (Monnet, *Memoirs* 352). But there *was* a community structure,
and it was clear that there could be no use of national vetoes in the High
Authority, whose members were supposed to be acting independently from
member state pressures (Art. 10: "… whose independence is beyond doubt").
A final compromise would therefore be required.

The delegates would meet one more time, on 12 April 1951, to work out
the details. In this debate, France and Germany united against the other
four prospective member states. The argument they gave was one of relative
weight: "Four of the six countries – Italy and the three Benelux countries –
accounted for only a quarter of the Community's coal and steel production.
It would not have been reasonable for them to be able to hold back France
and Germany" (Monnet, *Memoirs* 352). They therefore suggested a system
of weighted voting in the Council, and proportional representation in the
High Authority and Assembly.

In the Council, the final compromise proposed a double weighting formula
for majority decisions: by number of member states and by coal production.
In practice, this meant that France and Germany together were given a
blocking minority. The principle of equal representation was preserved
through the rotating presidency, where each member state would be entitled
to a six-month period in the chair. France and Germany were given the
exact same voting weight, as well as the same number of members of the
High Authority and Strasbourg Assembly. This way, the Treaty enshrined
the German demand for "perfect equality" (with France, that is).

—

The finished treaty was signed a week later, on 18 April 1951, in the same Salle de l'Horloge at the French Ministry of Foreign Affairs where the talks had also begun. The final text clearly fell short of Monnet's initial expectations. Though he had succeeded in securing the transfer of sovereignty to a new collective (Western) European organisation, the High Authority was far from the all-powerful institution he wanted it to be. But if the Treaty failed to deliver on that point, it was because it was a much more federal construct than he had set out to create.

In its institutional details, the ECSC resembled the American constitution of 1787 in one crucial aspect: both had four powers instead of the usual three in the separated powers scheme: executive, legislative, judiciary *and* the states. More relevant were the differences, not just in scope but also in detail. The European version did not have a unitary executive but rather a board with a president who functioned merely as *primus inter pares*. The legislative power was much less developed than the American Congress. Whereas the ECSC's Council did have a right of consultation over some High Authority decisions, and a veto power over others, the Assembly merely had the power to reject the High Authority's collective body of decisions after the fact (though that kind of rejection would have resulted in the High Authority's dismissal and replacement, itself a considerable if largely theoretical power). The Court of Justice was probably most similar to the American Supreme Court, though it too faced some practical constraints. And though decisions taken by the High Authority were binding (Art. 14) there was no supremacy clause.[17] The rules governing the expansion of the two unions also differed markedly. In the American union, membership applications of potential new states required a simple majority of both houses of Congress. The ECSC Treaty's Article 98 stated that while any European country could apply for membership, the decision on admission was subject to a veto of every individual existing member state. This would make the process of enlargement of the European union much more complicated going forward (though as we have seen, the fact that it was easier in theory did not make the American process of enlargement any less problematic in practice).

The one thing the European treaty most obviously did not do was create a new nation. There was no European equivalent of "We The People "– the treaty only spoke of the plural "peoples." Article 20 did describe the Assembly as consisting of "the representatives of the peoples," but these delegates were not directly elected. They were instead selected in the same way senators

---

17   This gap in the constitutional design would eventually be filled by the European Court of Justice through its ruling in Costa v Enel, C-6/64.

had been appointed under the 1787 US Constitution: "[D]esignated by their respective parliaments"[18] (Art. 21).

For all its limitations, Monnet looked on his work with pride: "What we are doing (...) is proving that an authority freely created by six nations who were separated over long centuries by their national sovereignty can take decisions in the interest of the six and see them executed by companies and nations" (Monnet, *Les États-Unis D'Europe Ont Commencé* 57). As such, the ECSC formed "the first step towards a European federation."

Bibliography

Acheson, Dean. *Present at the Creation: My Years in the State Department.* W. W. Norton, 1969.

Basic Law of the Federal Republic of Germany. 23 May 1949, Bonn. https://www.cvce.eu/content/publication/1999/1/1/7fa618bb-604e-4980-b667-76bf0cd0dd9b/publishable_en.pdf. Accessed 6 March 2024.

Boerger-De Smedt, Anne. "Negotiating the Foundations of European Law, 1950–1957: The Legal History of the Treaties of Paris and Rome." *Contemporary European History*, vol. 21, no. 3, Aug. 2012, pp. 339–356.

Brugmans, Henri. *Panorama de la Pensée Fédéraliste.* La Colombe, 1956.

Council of Europe. *Congress of Europe, The Hague, 7–11 May, 1948*, The Council of Europe Publishing,.1999

Dammen, Melle van. *De Vooruitstrevende Partij voor Wereldregering 1947–1952: Idealisme in de marge van de naoorlogse politiek.* Radboud Universiteit, 2018.

Duchênes, François. *Jean Monnet: The First Statesman of Interdependence.* 1994. Plunkett Lake Press, 2022.

Dulles, John Foster. Letter to Jean Monnet, 23 May 1950. John Foster Dulles Papers, Seely G. Mudd Manuscript Library, Princeton University, Series 1, Selected Correspondence 1891–1960, box Jean Monnet, 1950 (reel), pp. 2–3.

Fransen, Frederic. *The Supranational Politics of Jean Monnet.* Bloomsbury Publishing, 2001.

Friedrich, Carl. "Rebuilding The German Constitution, I." *The American Political Science Review*, vol. 43, no. 3., June 1949, pp. 461–482.

Gerbet, Pierre. "La genèse du plan Schuman: Des origines à la déclaration du 9 mai 1950." *Revue Française de Science Politique*, vol. 6–3, 1956, pp. 525–553.

18 In the US Constitution, Article 1 section 3 talked about "two senators from each state, chosen by the legislature thereof." The indirect election method was replaced 125 years later by a direct election through the 17th Amendment, adopted in 1913.

Hallstein, Walter. "The Schuman Plan." 28 April 1951, Johann Wolfgang Goethe University, Frankfurt. Address. https://www.cvce.eu/en/obj/address_given_ by_walter_hallstein_on_the_schuman_plan_28_april_1951-en-81868a56-1b45- 446e-a572-f14085701773.html. Accessed 6 March 2024.

Hansard, House of Commons resolution, 27 June 1950, vol. 476, 2104

Imlay, Talbot C, *Clarence Streit and Twentieth Century American Internationalism.* Cambridge University Press, 2023.

Isaacson, Walter and Evan Thomas. *The Wise Men: Six Friends and the World They Made.* 1986. Simon & Schuster, 1997.

Kundnani, Hans. *Euro Whiteness: Culture, Empire and Race in the European Project.* Hurst, 2023.

Maritain, Jacques. *Man and the State.* University of Chicago Press, 1951.

Mason, Henry L, *The European Coal and Steel Community: Experiment in Supra-nationalism.* Springer, 1955.

Milward, Alan S, *The Reconstruction of Western Europe 1945–1951.* 1984. Routledge, 2006.

Mitrany, David. *A Working Peace System: An Argument for the Functional Development of International Organization.* Oxford University Press, 1943.

Monnet, Jean. *Les États-Unis D'Europe Ont Commencé: La Communauté Européenne Du Charbon et L'Acier. Discours et Allocutions.* Robert Laffont, 1962.

Monnet, Jean. *Memoirs.* Doubleday & Company, 1978.

Monnet, Jean. "Peace Needs Quick Steps to Atlantic Union." *Freedom & Union,* Jul.–Aug. 1961, pp. 12–14.

Monnet, Jean. "Jean Monnet's Thoughts on the future." 5 August 1943, Algiers. https://www.cvce.eu/content/publication/1997/10/13/b61a8924-57bf-4890-9e4b- 73bf4d882549/publishable_en.pdf. Accessed 6 March 2024.

Mounier, Emmanuel. *A Personalist Manifesto.* Longmans, Green & Co, 1938.

Occupation Statute of Germany. "Text of Occupation Statute promulgated on the 12th May 1949 by the Military Governors and Commanders in Chief of the Western Zone. 12 May 1949, Bonn. https://www.cvce.eu/ content/publication/2003/10/21/6750efd3-4b34-4fec-9a4a-dfoff125d302/ publishable_en.pdf

Price, Harry Bayard. *The Marshall Plan and Its Meaning.* Cornell University Press, 1955.

Richter, Hedwig. *Demokratie, Eine Deutsche Affäre: Vom 18. Jahrhundert bis zur Gegenwart.* C. H. Beck, 2020.

Roth, François. *Robert Schuman: Du Lorrain des frontières au père de l'Europe.* Fayard, 2008.

Rougemont, Denis de. "The Adventure of the 20th Century." 22 April 1948, Paris. Lecture. https://www.cvce.eu/content/publication/2008/1/18/ff3d3e3a-0f5b-41bf- 961a-067822bb65ee/publishable_en.pdf. Accessed 6 March 2024.

Rougemont, Denis de. "L'Attitude Fédéraliste." *Revue Economique et Sociale*, October 1947, pp. 49–60.

Salzmann, Walter H. *D. Spierenburg en de Buitenlandse Economische Betrekkingen van Nederland 1945–1952*. Sdu Uitgevers, 1999.

Schuman, Robert. "Address given at the opening of the conference on the Schuman Plan.", 20 June 1950, Paris. https://www.cvce.eu/en/obj/address_given_by_robert_schuman_at_the_opening_of_the_conference_on_the_schuman_plan_paris_20_june_1950-en-411d38eb-3475-4a98-b0b3-aecce8ca60a7.html. Accessed 6 March 2024.

Schuman, Robert. "The Coming Century of Supranational Communities. , 16 May 1949, Strasbourg Festival Hall. Speech. https://www.schuman.info/Strasbourg549.htm. Accessed 6 March 2024.

Schuman, Robert. "The Schuman Declaration." 9 May 1950, Paris. https://www.cvce.eu/en/obj/the_schuman_declaration_paris_9_may_1950-en-9cc6ac38-32f5-4c0a-a337-9a8ae4d5740f.html. Accessed 6 March 2024.

Schuman, Robert, Lecture to the College of Europe, Bruges, 22 October 1953 Address given by Robert Schuman on the origin and elaboration of the Schuman Plan (Bruges, 22–23 October 1953) – CVCE Website

Segers, Mathieu. *The Origins of European Integration: The Prehistory of Today's European Union, 1937–1951*. Cambridge University Press, 2023.

Spaak, Paul-Henri. "The Integration of Europe, Dreams and Realities." *Foreign Affairs*, 1 Oct. 1950, pp. 94–100.

Spaak, Paul-Henri. "Statement by Mr. Paul-Henri Spaak after his resignation as President of the Consultative Assembly." 11 December 1951. https://pace.coe.int/en/verbatim/1951-12-11/am/en#speech-9455. Accessed 6 March 2024.

Spaak, Paul-Henri. "Western Union: U.S.E." *Time Magazine*, 23 Mar. 1953. https://content.time.com/time/subscriber/article/0,33009,806614,00.html. Accessed 6 March 2024.

Spierenburg, Dirk and Raymond Poidevin. *Histoire de la Haute Autorité de la Communauté Européenne du Charbon et de l'Acier*. Bruylant, 1993

US Department of State, Office of the Historian, "Cable by the American Ambassador in France to the Secretary of State," 21 February 1951.

Statute of the Council of Europe. https://rm.coe.int/1680306052. Accessed 6 March 2024.

Stikker, Dirk. *Memoires: Herinneringen uit de lange jaren waarin ik betrokken was bij de voortdurende wereldcrisis*. Nijgh & van Ditmar, 1966.

Treaty Establishing the European Coal and Steel Community. 18 April 1951, Paris. https://www.cvce.eu/en/obj/treaty_establishing_the_european_coal_and_steel_community_paris_18_april_1951-en-11a21305-941e-49d7-a171-ed5be548cd58.html. Accessed 6 March 2024.

Walton, Clarence C, "The Fate of Neo-Federalism in Western Europe." *The Western Political Quarterly*, vol. 5, no. 3, pp. 366–390.

Williams, Charles. *Konrad Adenauer: The Father of the New Germany*. Abacus, 2003.

Zurcher, Arnold. *The Struggle to Unite Europe: 1940–1958*. Greenwood Press, 1958.

Conclusion

This book started with a hypothesis: the people who negotiated the earliest version of the European Union, the European Coal and Steel Community, would have worked with concepts that contained numerous historical layers of meaning. Irrespective of whether they were aware of their existence, these hidden layers would have impacted the outcome of the negotiations, by influencing what the negotiators would reasonably have expected to be able to achieve through them. And so I set out to uncover the various layers of meaning contained in what Koselleck called the "sediments of time."

This voyage of dis-covery started with the first early modern analysis of a regime type at least somewhat similar to the European Union: the league as described in Machiavelli's *Discourses*. In his analysis of the historical examples of the league (including his personal favourite, the pre-Roman Etruscan League), and of the ones existing while he wrote his treatise (chiefly the Swiss Confederation) he identified a number of core qualities that would later become associated with federal union: its being based on the equal status of the participating states, its link with a political culture of freedom, and its functioning as a collective defence arrangement.

It did not serve a defensive purpose only though. In spite of the fact that he claimed a league had an optimal size in terms of territory and number of members beyond which it was difficult to sustain organisationally, he also included it in his overview of methods for territorial expansion. Here the league, or "Tuscan method," competed with two others: "violent union," which he linked to the Athenians and the Spartans, and what he called "the method of Rome," of forming an alliance where the other members effectively served the dominant power. This then was what the oldest layer contributed to the concept of federal union: equality, freedom, security ànd expansion.

The second oldest layer of meaning was formed by reflections on the practical experiences of various regional leagues that existed around the time of writing of the *Discourses* or were founded in the century after Machiavelli's death: the Swiss Confederation, the Polish-Lithuanian Commonwealth (1569), the Dutch United Provinces (1579–1581), and the Holy Roman Empire in the format that was constituted through the Peace Treaty of Westphalia

Livestro, Joshua: *A More Perfect Union. Federal Union in Political Theory and Practice, 1500-1951.* Amsterdam: Amsterdam University Press, 2024.
DOI: 10.5117/9789048563777_CONC

(1648). Though these leagues all developed institutions to facilitate collective action, their weaknesses were obvious to commentators writing at the time: to Simler commenting on the Swiss Confederation, Grotius on the Dutch United Provinces, Pufendorf on the Holy Roman Empire, and Konarski on the Polish-Lithuanian Commonwealth. Their main addition to the concept of federal union was the factor that allowed these leagues to survive for several centuries in spite of their institutional shortcomings: their cultural foundation, a republican system of ethics or virtues that emphasised the need for togetherness (*concordia*). If these leagues had a relationship with the outside world, it was based on a striving for *equilibrium*. Towards their neighbours, their unions were defensive in nature, and as such, within Europe at least, they offered alternatives to the dominant mode of expansion called universal monarchy, as practised and celebrated first in Spain and later in France. Where the model of universal monarchy stressed the importance of order and hierarchy, the early modern federal unions valued liberty and equality above everything else.

In the end though, a cultural foundation alone was not enough for a league or union to survive and flourish. Improvised quasi-constitutional solutions like the organisation of confederated sejms in the Polish–Lithuanian case or the selective ignoring of the veto rule by Dutch decision-makers helped to prevent more acute crises. They did not, however, prevent the process of slow erosion of the constitutional framework (in fact, as Madison argued in his reflection on these European leagues in *Federalist* 20, they may well have contributed to it). The worst affected of the four, the Polish–Lithuanian Commonwealth, would see its institutions infiltrated by foreign powers that exploited the inherent weaknesses of its royal electoral system and the *liberum veto* in its parliamentary decision-making process. Its inability to either increase its internal cohesion or expand its territory to a scale that would have made it safe from potential attacks meant it ended up getting conquered by more assertive neighbouring powers. The others would disappear in the historical maelstrom that accompanied the French Revolution and the subsequent, seemingly unstoppable march to universal empire by Napoleon Bonaparte.

—

It was the century-long debate about the methods of expansion in the context of the English–Scottish Union of the Crowns that gave birth to the new term "federal union." Though there was initially some confusion about its meaning, commentators would eventually settle on the idea that it served as the replacement of the old Machiavellian term "league." It came to be seen as the term that best fitted the "something in between" as described by the German jurist and philosopher Samuel Pufendorf: a "federal union" was more politically integrated than a mere military alliance, but less than a fully incorporating union.

The conceptual space of "federal unions" was eventually filled by plans for European unification. In their earliest form, these were mainly schemes that envisaged unification by military force. Later there was a shift to plans that accepted only unification by peaceful means. The latter idea, of peaceful unification through the creation of a European Council or Parliament that could help settle conflicts between its member states and even take decisions on their behalf, presented itself as the main rival of the dominant doctrine of the Balance of Power. Though it would not persuade any of the major powers contesting the political spaces of eighteenth century Europe, the ideal of a continent-wide federal union as a peace scheme did succeed in establishing itself as the permanent alternative to – and critique of – a system that treated war as a legitimate method for settling conflicts between states. It would add a further layer of meaning in the form of the idea of federal union being intrinsically linked to peace – without, though, renouncing the idea of territorial expansion.

If it was the merit of European authors like Henri IV/Sully, William Penn, and the Abbé de Saint-Pierre to have developed the idea of a federal union on a continental scale, it was to the credit of the American Founders that they managed to find a way of actually creating not one, but two such unions. The essential difference between the first of 1777 and the second of 1787 was that, whereas the first move towards federation by the thirteen colonies, immediately after declaring independence in 1776, was entirely based on the old idea of a shared cultural and ethical foundation as a presumed sufficient guarantee of the union's flourishing, the second move, culminating in the Federalist debates on the constitution, was based on the realisation that the union's survival actually required additional constitutional safeguards. To achieve it, the American Founders had to strike a double compromise: on the distribution of sovereignty between the states and the central federal authority, and on the representation of larger and smaller states in the legislative power at federal level, a compromise that was framed along lines of equality and proportionality. Building on the work of the seventeenth century English radical Whigs, as interpreted by the great French constitutional thinker and political theorist Montesquieu, and the practical experiences with it in the constitutions of the states, the American Founders also managed to construct a mixed regime based entirely on the principle that people is a legal and political unity of equal persons. The American federal union had a mixed regime based on a division of powers, not on a division of estates or classes.

The final result was a constitutional framework that established a balance between the various powers in the centre, and between the centre and the states. Its cornerstone was an idea that had been around since classical antiquity: the rule of law. This was the unique contribution of the American layer: switching from a cultural to an institutional safeguarding of the federal union, and making the rule of law the ultimate check in a system of separated powers with checks and balances that prevented any of the institutions from overpowering the others. As a final check, adopted during the ratification process of the new constitution, the American Founders also took up, elaborated, and refined an idea from English constitutional practice: a bill of rights. The idea was to give the citizens an extra layer of protection against the powers of the new federal government they, as citizens, had helped to create.

On paper, the American constitution seemed to have solved the three problematics of federal union that Machiavelli first identified in his *Discourses*: of decision-making, of extent, and of duration. In practice though, the newly created federal union needed one other element to enable it to function properly. It was the same element that had served as the foundation of the earlier federal unions, though with a twist: the culture of compromise, married to *raison d'état* thinking, creating a kind of doctrine of "the necessity of compromise." It was through a number of calculated, and sometimes downright cynical, compromises that the union was held together in the first seventy years of its existence. Once the fatal Dred Scott ruling made compromise on the most troublesome issue, that of slavery, impossible, civil war inevitably followed.

—

The main compromise that had made the American constitution possible was on the counter-concept of sovereignty, giving up the idea, cherished especially by Europe's would-be absolute monarchs, that sovereign power had to be indivisible. On the European side of the Atlantic, it would take half a century before this started to be fully understood (the fact that it eventually did sink in was largely thanks to the work of Alexis de Tocqueville). Even then, its impact on European political theory and practice remained limited. When the Swiss adopted a new constitution in 1848 based on the American model, they copied the system of dual representation in parliament (equal and proportional), but not the compromise on sovereignty. In Europe, the other federal unions created in the nineteenth century were also still based on an undivided conception of sovereignty: the European Congress System established in Vienna, the German *Bund*, the North German *Bund*, and the German *Reich*. Perhaps it should not come as a surprise, then, that the wave of European federal peace plans produced from the 1830s onwards were based on the same idea of undivided sovereignty.

The most important novelty of what can be called the nineteenth century European layer in the development of federal union was a reflection on the question of how to establish a union in the first place. Having banned the idea of a final war to establish perpetual peace, Europe's federal thinkers and politicians looked for ways to at least create an opening towards federal union in the here and now. To that end, they introduced two innovations. One was the redefinition of federal union from an end state, or a state of being, to a process – a working towards, rather than an immediate achieving of, federal union. The intended effect here was to make the first step towards federal union seemingly less political, and therefore less daunting for those who were encouraged to take it. The other innovation was that Europe's nineteenth century federalists invented various practical schemes for this initial stage of moving towards federal union. Some looked to a vanguard of like-minded or politically similar states, others hoped rather for the unifying dynamic created by seemingly limited economic cooperative schemes.

There was also a geographical innovation. Whereas the old European peace plans involved only the European continent, American involvement in the European peace movement stimulated the development of a new strand of federal union thinking in the form of transatlantic union. The arrival of this new idea meant that from the 1840s onwards, the concept of federal union would always have a transatlantic component. European unification would no longer be contemplated in isolation.

The European hesitancy to accept the American solution of divided sovereignty was down largely to the fact that the continent was, at that time, still dominated by empires and monarchies. The rulers of these territories considered their sovereignty to be a personal possession, derived not from The People but from God. It made the idea of divided sovereignty difficult even to contemplate, let alone to accept. Perhaps it also had something to do with the fact that one active part of the federal union coalition was formed by the various budding nationalist movements. To them, national sovereignty and federal union were components of the same utopian vision of the continent's future, one in which federal union facilitated the birth of free and democratic *nation*-states. The arrival of the nationalist revolutionaries in the peace movement of the 1830s also brought with it a new counter-conceptual pairing. Democratic federal union, which stressed the rights of the individual citizen, came to be seen as the opponent, indeed the *enemy*, of a very different kind of federal union that had been created on the continent: the Holy Alliance of Monarchs, which emphasised above all the importance of international order and stability.

From the 1860s onwards, democratic federal union was then redefined again, this time as the counter-concept of a new regime type that also claimed to have democratic roots: caesarism. The core difference between the two regime types concerned the way they treated the three powers: legislature, executive, and judiciary. In caesarist theory and practice, the three were considered indivisible. They were unified in a single person, the new Caesar, who represented both the People and the State. Against this, federal union theorists stressed the vital importance for a free society of the separation of powers in any constitutional set-up, of checks and balances between them, of certain inalienable individual rights, and of the rule of law rather than the rule of one man.

In all, the nineteenth century added a complex layer of multiple meanings to the concept of federal union on the European side. Federalism came to be seen as working towards an end state, as well as the end state itself (a tension that would never be fully resolved). It also became associated with a method for this "working towards": the formation of a small group of founding states, and/or the use of a (usually economic) limited cooperative project that could serve as a kind of lever for the achievement of the ultimate objective of federal union. It took on a transatlantic aspect, and became firmly associated with democracy and individual rights. To distinguish it from the other democratic movement of the century, caesarism, it stressed the fundamental importance of the American idea of linking federal union to separation of powers and the rule of law, though it stayed clear of the American idea of divided sovereignty.

The first part of the twentieth century would not add a new layer of its own. It would instead build on two ideas that formed part of the nineteenth century notions of federal union: transatlantic, or indeed global, federation, and anti-caesarism. The former was implemented through the The Hague Peace Conferences of 1899 and 1907, and through the League of Nations. The League immediately ran into trouble because its founding idea was based on a logical contradiction. It was to be founded as a league of sovereign states, but these sovereign states were then asked to commit themselves to their mutual defence. This would have required them to sacrifice at least some of their sovereign power freely to decide on issues of war and peace, which had been seen as a hallmark of sovereignty since the late sixteenth century. The US Senate, which saw the power to declare war and peace as its prerogative and indeed its constitutional duty, refused to ratify the treaty. The British political class, which did vote to ratify, refused to accept the consequences of its vote. The League, therefore, could not deliver in practice what it promised to do on paper. In its decision-making, it also failed to overcome another hurdle sovereignty threw up: the veto rights of individual member states. Here the main contribution to the rethinking of federal union was a recognition and confirmation of an older lesson first formulated by the American Founders: if a federal union was based on nothing but the good intentions of its fully sovereign constituent states, it was doomed to fail.

In the Interbellum, what was federal anti-Caesarism became federal anti-totalitarianism, first in Italy, later in all of Europe. During the Second World War, federal unionist resistance writers and political thinkers like the German Jewish refugee Arendt added one more element to the anti-Caesarism layer. Whereas nineteenth century federalists started from the premise that nationalism was part of the solution to the problem created by the suppression of democracy and liberty in multinational empires, the Second World War federal unionists defined nationalism, more specifically *national sovereignty*, as part of the problem, and perhaps even the core of the problem. In their view, there was a direct link between the embrace of the idea of national sovereignty in the aftermath of the First World War and the rise of totalitarianism during the 1920s and 1930s. Federal union therefore came to be associated with the denial of the primacy of national sovereignty. For liberty to survive, the continent's states needed to be embedded in a federal union, invested with its own sovereign powers.

—-

Running vertically through these layers were three strands of political thinking and acting that eventually served as canons that would be studied to inspire, or invoked to justify, the creation of the various federal union schemes. First was the canon of greater and lesser thinkers who engaged with federal union as a regime form for civil government. This tradition ran all the way from Machiavelli to Arendt. Second was a canon of schemes for the unification or pacification of the European continent, which started with George of Bohemia and ended with the flurry of proposals for the formation of some form of European or trans-Atlantic union in the post Second World War period. The final one was the strand that united the various actual experiences with the formation of leagues or federal unions, from ancient Greece to the postwar era.

The collected wisdom of these three canonical strands would be a significant source of inspiration for the generation of politicians that conducted the various post-war experiments with different forms of federal union in Europe and the Atlantic area. The influence of the canon of political philosophers was visible at both the personal level and in public debate. Most prominent here were the American Founders in the form of the authors of the *Federalist Papers*: Alexander Hamilton, James Madison, and John Jay. Their views were disseminated through British liberal free-market thinkers like Robbins, the writers of the resistance movement, and the American author Clarence Streit, whose work influenced both Jean Monnet and the American architects of the NATO treaty. The core idea adopted from the American tradition was the importance of shared sovereignty as a necessary condition for the viability of a federal union. This attack on national sovereignty was also supported by the Catholic philosophical movement called personalism, with authors like Rougemont, Brugmans, and Maritain, which had its roots in a long tradition of Thomist and Neo-Scholastic thought. The influence of these authors was most significant among the Catholic politicians who helped shape the postwar order, first and foremost Robert Schuman.

The influence of the canon of federal blueprints was equally clear. The figures of Henry IV and Duc de Sully seemed omnipresent in the speeches of the leading politicians of the postwar era, who presented themselves as "servants of the Grand Design." Among other peace schemes, Aristide Briand's attempt to pave the way for the creation of a United States of Europe was the most important, although authors like Saint-Pierre and Kant were also mentioned.

Just as impactful were the practical experiences contained in the third canon – that of actually implemented federal projects. Experiences with the League of Nations were a factor in all deliberations on shaping the political order of postwar Europe. The general conclusion was that the League of Nations had failed, though there was no consensus on the causes of that failure. British politicians pointed to a lack of goodwill in the implementation on the part of member states, while their continental counterparts emphasised the structural deficiencies that had made success impossible. According to the latter group, the main shortcoming was that the League was based on the absolute sovereignty of member states, with the veto as a symbol of the flaws of that design. This conclusion received further confirmation through proceedings in the Council of Europe, whose inability to produce meaningful decisions effectively ended the national sovereignty-based federation as a viable option.

One conclusion that can be drawn on the basis of the available evidence is that the European Founding was as much a constitutional event as the US Founding. It dealt with the same issues, and came up with remarkably similar structures, though with one fundamental difference: it was based on the Kantian idea of the Founding as a long-term process that could take generations to complete, rather than a single event. Another important similarity is that the European Founders were also no less involved in an investigation of the nature and feasibility of a federal union on a continental scale than their American counterparts had been. The principled debates at the founding Congress of the European Movement in The Hague and in the Council of Europe were instrumental in helping the Founders reach a consensus on the most likely way forward in building a federal union on a European scale.

—

Just as it informed and inspired the postwar generation of European and trans-Atlantic Founders, so the collected wisdom of these three canons of federalist thought could help to inform debate on a number of issues vexing today's European politicians. Take the ongoing discussion in some European member states about the so-called *Kompetenz-Kompetenz* issue in relation to the European Court of Justice. As Hamilton and, later, Tocqueville stated in no uncertain terms, allowing an individual member state supreme court rather than the European Court of Justice to determine where to draw the line between federal and member state competences would, from the perspective of the union, be like "allowing foreign judges to preside over the nation" (Tocqueville 141). A union is an empire of laws. More than anything, it needs consistency in the interpretation of its rules, and in the demarcation of jurisdictions. That kind of clarity can only come from a supreme court at the federal level. To quote Tocqueville again: "To suppose that a state can exist when its fundamental laws are subjected to four-and-twenty different interpretations at the same time is to advance a proposition contrary alike to reason and to experience" (141).

Related to this discussion is another topic on which there still seems to be a lot of European confusion, even three quarters of a century after the ECSC's founding: sovereignty. The canons of federalist thought and practice offer plenty of useful material for study here. The philosophical canon runs, roughly speaking, from Ludolf Hugo and the American Founders via Tocqueville to Kelsen, Arendt, and Maritain. At the practical level, the debates at the 1787 US convention and during the 1950–51 ECSC negotiations are also worth studying. Such a study should leave no room for doubt, by the way, that the European project was based on a conception of *shared* sovereignty between the centre and the member states – all participants knew it and accepted it as an essential quality of the union they were creating. In fact, it was exactly for this reason that the British government decided not to join the negotiations.

On this topic, one of the leading historians of Europe's twentieth century, Timothy Snyder, has argued somewhat provocatively that it is an error to talk about *national* sovereignty in a European context. Along the lines of the American Founder James Wilson (and later American politicians like Daniel Webster and Abraham Lincoln) he argues that most European states were never properly sovereign in an individual capacity:

> *In history there was no era of the nation-state. Generally (...) empire ended where integration began. In the indispensable cases of Germany, France, Britain, Italy, The Netherlands, Spain, and Portugal there was no moment between empire and integration when the nation was sovereign and the state flourished in isolation. Citizens of these countries unreflectively believe that their country has a history as a nation-state; generally, after a moment of reflection, they realise that this is not the case*
> (Snyder 76–77).

What goes for these Western and Southern European countries, also goes for the Eastern European ones who moved straight from Soviet domination to European integration.

Snyder has a point that, in terms of governance, very few European states actually managed to fully realise sovereignty according to Jean Bodin's maximalist definition. The problem of the Interbellum period was that aspirations of absolute sovereignty were mixed with virulent nationalism.

As Hannah Arendt and the resistance writers explained, this toxic combination was an important cause, and perhaps even the main cause, of the Second World War.

As the example of the American Union's pre-Civil War history shows, though, even a perfectly workable federal compromise on sovereignty like the one negotiated in Philadelphia in 1787 won't necessarily prevent conflicts between the centre and the states. Both have a rightful claim to sovereignty, and they may well look for ways to increase their share of it. A federal constitution is a way of managing this tension, not of cancelling it altogether. Especially worth studying here are the debates about states' rights during the 1832 South Carolina nullification crisis. It was proof, if proof were needed, that, as Alexander Hamilton concluded in *Federalist* 15 after studying the European federal examples, the main threat to any union is not an excessive degree of centralisation of power, but the "perpetual effort in each [member state] to fly off from the common centre" (Hamilton et al. 150).

The three canons of federal thought and practice also show the significance of the idea of separation of powers to federal unions, both within the central federal government and between the centre and the states. The division that the participants at both the US Constitutional Convention and the ECSC negotiations eventually settled on was the product of hard-fought compromises over every one of their institutions. Studying the nature of those compromises gives us a better understanding of the relationship between the three powers, and of their significance. The philosophical tradition on this issue runs from the seventeenth century British radical Whigs (Harrington and Locke), via Montesquieu, the American Founders, Kant, and Saint-Simon, the thinkers involved in the nineteenth century peace movement (chiefly Lemonnier), via Kelsen, to the wartime resistance writers.

Another established principle developed through the three canons is that a federal union cannot exist as a mix of different types of regimes, part free and part unfree. Over the course of the nineteenth century, the Kantian idea of a federation of republics (a democratic or monarchical regime with separation of powers) became the consensus position. Through the efforts of the authors of the first two peace movements, it was eventually narrowed down to *democratic* republics only. A European federal union, they argued, should only accept as member states democratic countries founded on the principles of liberty, equality, and separation of powers.

The experience of the German monarchical federal union created by Bismarck in 1871 teaches another important lesson: separation of powers alone is not enough. Every power also needs the means to check and counter-balance the other powers. Seen from this perspective, it is definitely a concern that within the European Union there are insufficient checks at the European level on the power of the Council of Heads of State and Government. The system may currently work in practice (though the veto problem within it is becoming increasingly difficult to ignore and will certainly overwhelm the union in case of an expansion to thirty-five member states), but the federal tradition has shown that the fact that it doesn't work in theory will inevitably become a major problem in due course. As James Madison observed in *Federalist* 20: "A weak constitution must necessarily terminate in dissolution. (...) Tyranny has perhaps oftener grown out of the assumptions of power called for, on pressing exigencies, by a defective constitution, than out of the full service of the largest constitutional authorities" (Hamilton et al. 171).

On the issue of checks and balances, the canonical writings of Madison, specifically *Federalist Papers* 47 to 51, deserve closer study in Europe. Additional sources worth studying are Max Weber's reflections on the shortcomings of the Bismarckian constitution, and Hans Kelsen's observations in his debate with Carl Schmitt about the importance of certain legislative powers for the judiciary. It is important, though, that a move to limit or abolish the national veto should not initiate a slide into crude majoritarianism. A federal union must always show a healthy respect for the rights of the individual and the minority. In fact it is designed for just that purpose. Just like the American union, the EU is a *compound* democracy.[1] As explained by Madison in his fifty-first *Federalist Paper*, "it is of great importance in a republic not only to guard the society against the oppression of its rulers, but to guard one part of the society against the injustice of the other part"(Hamilton et al. 321). The extended republic can hold many different interests that will combine in different majorities on different issues. This means there is less likelihood of a permanent majority violating the rights of the minority.

If the union is to survive, it is also essential that the member states grasp the truth of Hamilton's contention – expanded upon by Tocqueville, and embraced by the authors of the Ventotene Manifesto, and indeed the authors of the ECSC Treaty – that the central authority must be allowed to develop its own direct relationship with the people, not just through access to the Court but also through executive policies, ranging from taxation to the execution of federal public works and the distribution of benefits to companies and citizens. The relationship should also be built the other way: from the citizens to the centre's executive, through the strengthening of democratic accountability at all levels of decision-making.

———

The story of the dramatic failure of some of the early modern experiments with federal union offers an important warning. The same combination of factors that slowly killed the Polish–Lithuanian Commonwealth is manifesting itself in today's EU: individual member state vetoes that slow down or block federal decision-making, in combination with foreign powers

---

1   On this, see also Sergio Fabbrini, *Compound Democracies: Why the United States and Europe are Becoming Similar,* specifically pp. 3–4. The nature of the European compound republic is shown most clearly in the European Parliament, which currently holds seven different party groups as well as a number of smaller clusters of independent MEPs. It reflects the presence in European societies of many different factions with their own platforms of political priorities.

encouraging member states to enter into agreements that undermine the collective interest. The strategy employed by today's Kremlin is no different from the one designed by Peter I and applied to deadly effect by Catherine II. The aim is to weaken a large neighbouring union by fomenting internal dissent and exploiting the veto rule to get client factions within the union to prevent any decisions aimed at making its policy more effective. Less dramatic, but no less decisive, was the failure of the Dutch United Provinces to give both a clear mandate and the means to implement it to their joint central authority. Burdening it with the war debts run up on behalf of the collective without ever granting it the means to repay those debts, they condemned their union to slow but inevitable decline.

Here the federal union canons offer two useful sources of insight. One is the writings of Alexander Hamilton, who more than any other thinker stressed the link between internal cohesion and external security.[2] As he pointed out, all attempts to secure a sense of unity in foreign policy culturally rather than constitutionally – that is: *without* abolishing the individual state veto – eventually failed. That said, he accepted that it was important not to dismiss the cultural idea of unity or concord. The tradition of reflection on the latter concept, and the core virtue of compromise, runs from Grotius via Leibniz and the American Founders' embrace of the necessity of compromise, to Lincoln, Weber, and ultimately to Schuman and the Catholic personalist thinkers that inspired him. As the notorious Dred Scott Supreme Court ruling showed, a union robbed of the possibility of compromise will not long survive.

The other lesson concerns what else would be required to safeguard a union against foreign intervention. Abolishing the veto would do much to limit the ability of foreign states to destabilise the union, but it would leave untouched the problem of individual states conducting their own foreign policy at the expense of the union. The canon of practical examples presents three different solutions here. One was contained in the Treaty of Westphalia of 1648. Its Article 65 stated that "it shall be free perpetually to each of the States of the Empire, to make Alliances with Strangers for their Preservation and Safety; *provided, nevertheless*, such Alliances be not against the emperor, and the Empire" (my emphasis). Instead of this "yes, provided...", the American Articles of Confederation of 1777 proposed a "no unless..." (Art. 6): "No State, *without the Consent of the united States,*

---

2   In the words of one of his intellectual biographers: "The interdependence of forms of government and the conduct of foreign policy is one of the great issues in the debate on the nature of republican government, and Hamilton has been very much in the middle of this debate" (Stourz 6).

in congress assembled, shall send any embassy to, or receive any embassy from, or enter into any conference, agreement, alliance, or treaty, with any King, prince or state" (my emphasis). The latter version seems more effective, because more easily enforceable. Even more direct was Article 10 of the 1787 Constitution, which simply stated: "No State shall enter into any Treaty, Alliance, or Confederation."

As important as guarding itself against external intervention is the internal safeguarding of the rule of law and separation of powers against attempts at dismantling by anti-constitutional forces. Here, the canon of political thinkers runs from Kant, via the writers of the Second Peace Movement, to Kelsen and Arendt. Also worth studying are the post-war Universal Declaration on Human Rights and the German Constitution of 1949, both of which offered considered attempts to protect the rule of law and the rights of the individual against any form of totalitarianism. A separate tradition worth studying here is that of classical republicanism – in a sense the other, non-constitutional part of the Machiavellian Moment as described by J. G. A. Pocock. With its strong emphasis on liberty, equality, civic virtue, and education, it could help to create a citizenry that would be willing and able to defend its constitutions and the rights contained within them against any attacks, foreign or domestic.

—

The work of Machiavelli offers some lessons of its own. The first is that it is essential for the health of a union periodically to recreate and strengthen the union through reform of its constitutional arrangements. When a union lapses into the error of treating the status quo as unchangeable, it risks terminal decline. *Riddure ai principi* is a core task for a union that wants to survive and thrive.

The second lesson is that democracy is not an optional extra. The people have a way of forcing themselves into any constitutional setup. Within the European Union this should not be seen as a problem that requires managing, but as a source of vitality that needs to be embraced. A directly elected president of the Commission, for example, would become at once the single most important popularly elected figure in the entire Union. This would not just create a check on the powers of the European Council (the one institution currently lacking any such check) but would also put the people at the heart of the European decision-making process, thereby increasing its power to influence the overall course of the Union. An alternative would be to have the Commissioners directly elected and then get them to choose the president from among themselves. In that case, the main challenge would be to design an electoral system that would allow individual Commissioners to function as European representatives rather than national ones.

Not allowing the people (Machiavelli's *popolo*) to play its own role can be counterproductive, as we saw in the last few decades. Since the early 1990s, it has used the one power at its disposal, the vote, as a kind of veto power in order to influence European political decision-making.

On the topic of the people, it is important to dispel any notions from German Romanticism that a constitution can only be the product of a pre-existing *Volk* giving itself a political structure, and that "therefore" the EU cannot be, or ever become, a federal union. This certainly wasn't true in the case of the United States, as the German historian Dieter Langewiesche recently pointed out, and even in the case of Germany itself it wasn't necessarily accurate: "In the beginning there was no German people from which was founded a German *Reich* and German states. Put succinctly, ethnogenesis followed constitution-building, not the other way round" (Langewiesche 23–24). Worth reading here are the wartime resistance writers, specifically the reflections of authors like Spinelli and Romein, on new European myths and traditions logically having to follow the act of creation of a new union. Perhaps the best description of the complex nature of the issue of national identity in a federal union comes once again from James Madison, in a letter written towards the end of his life, on 28 August 1830, to the later Secretary of State Edward Everett. Rather than the Constitution either being based on, or eventually leading to, the creation of a single We The People, Madison suggested the peoples of the several states constituted a single people "for certain purposes," while remaining citizens of their individual states for others (Madison). In other words: the correct terms to use are not "people" (singular) or "peoples" (plural), but both. Any person is a citizen of their member state *and* a citizen of the Union.

Finally, a point about the fraught relationship of the European Union with that most Machiavellian of concepts: power. The EU is, and of right ought to be, a geopolitical entity. Like any federal union, it is *pulled* outwards by border states that seek to join it, because there are clear benefits to union membership. At the same time it can be forced to *push* outwards because there is a legitimate need to stop other actors from claiming territories that could otherwise serve to constrict or threaten the union. Here, the EU has much to learn. It seems to operate from a kind of Sartrian belief: *"Geopolitique, c'est les autres."* Other great powers practice geopolitics, the EU merely sees it as its duty to shield itself from it. This is a poor excuse for a strategy. Better would be to have a clear-eyed view of European interests, and to decide from there what is required in terms of geopolitical action.

There is a rich federal tradition worth studying here. It starts with Machiavelli himself, then runs via the *raison d'état* authors, Henri IV and his counsellor Sully, Hamilton, Metternich, and Bismarck, to the early geopolitical writers and the federalist politicians of the post Second World War period (chiefly Churchill). This tradition offers a number of important lessons. One is that geopolitics is, first and foremost, about control of territory. It is as true today as it was when Sir Halford Mackinder first formulated it as a maxim: who controls Eastern Europe, controls the Heartland. In its confrontation with Russian expansionism, EU-membership of Ukraine, Moldova, Georgia, and ultimately also Belarus is therefore, to quote Rudolf Kjellén, a categorical geopolitical imperative. Accepting that necessity as a fact means the member states must also undertake serious efforts to give their union the tools to achieve it. both diplomatic and military. And even though Europeans today may not possess the level of paranoia required to believe in a geostrategic concept like encirclement, their opponents most definitely do. It would therefore be wise to assume that they are actively trying to do to the EU what they fear the EU would do to them, and develop a strategy to counter it.

Since conflicts between large powers tend to be decided by philosophical arguments as often as by force of arms (no weapon has ever stopped an idea), it would also be worth revisiting the debates of the nineteenth and twentieth century in which federal union was developed as the great theoretical challenge to the dominant system of the day, which was always a form of authoritarianism. The idea here would be to weaponise the arguments in favour of federal union used at the time against these precursors of today's authoritarian regimes.

We see this ideological conflict repeated in the twenty-first century, both within the EU itself and in its confrontation with the global forces of authoritarianism. To win it, the forces of unionism will have to develop a political agenda that turns the constitutional principles on which the EU was founded into a coherent political agenda for mass mobilisation. They need, in other words, to weaponize their founding documents and the constitutional principles enshrined in them: separation of powers, checks and balances, and human rights. And they need to do so not just because these things are inherently good and worth defending, but also because they are the most effective antidote to authoritarianism.

Here the experiences with the mobilisation of public opinion from consecutive generations of nineteenth and early twentieth century peace activists are worth studying – if not for their methods, which need an update to make them suitable for a twenty-first century setting, then at least for their ability to inspire a willingness to work towards a goal greater than themselves in an army of political activists, journalists, thinkers, and politicians.

Another part of a counter-strategy to the active attempts by the likes of China and Russia to destabilise the world order must be to build stronger relationships with other federal unions around the world. The logic here is that federal unions make natural allies, since they are based on the same fundamental principles of freedom, equality, and the rule of law. Such a strategy should focus in part on developing the closest possible relationship with the African Union. A plausible step here would be for Europe to help Africa develop its own internal market and its own *Zollverein* (customs union). This would allow the rule of law to grow deeper roots on the continent. In the short term, it would make it a more attractive partner to trade with. In the long term, developing an attachment to federal principles might make it more likely to choose fellow federations over authoritarian coalition partners. In the second half of the twenty-first century, the decisions made by Africa on the issue of its strategic partnerships may well end up determining the fate of the world.

The EU should also focus on ways of strengthening the ties with its sister Union, the United States of America, through the North Atlantic Treaty Organisation. Kissinger's remarks about the Washington treaty containing some openings for the creation of a kind of North Atlantic confederation may be worth studying here, as well as the original Canadian ambitions for Article 2 of the founding treaty. Alternatively, it could be worth exploring options for the founding of a kind of union of unions – the federations of the world united in a single body, whose members are all committed to the principle of rejecting war as a means of settling conflicts between states, and of respecting the rule of law. This meta-union could unite not just the EU, US and African Union, but also federal unions like Canada, Australia, Brazil, and India. By creating a zone that covers more than half the world's population built entirely on the rule of law, it would offer the beginning of a solution to the problem of the present continuing erosion of international norms and institutions.

———

The final lesson will probably be the most difficult to accept for today's European political class: this time is *not* different. The worst mistake member states could make is to assume that a mere "government of governments" rather than a government of, by, and for the people could be made to work after all. History offers no example of a federal union formed on that basis that actually lasted the course. It offers plenty of examples to the contrary – a number of them are included in this book.

There is no historical evidence to suggest that undivided national sovereignty can provide a workable basis for a collective order on the European continent. The last time this idea was tried was the Interbellum. By the end of it, totalitarian regimes had sprung up everywhere, and the whole world found itself at war. The *only* reason that peace has lasted since 1945 between Europe's larger states, and that the smaller states have endured with a semblance of independence, is because of their being embedded in a union that has, since its founding, been based on *shared* sovereignty between the member states and the centre.

It is in the existential interest of all member states to create the preconditions for the flourishing of their common union. There is nothing unique about the European Union that makes it likelier to survive its present imperfections than, say, the Polish–Lithuanian Commonwealth or the League of Nations. The choice is simple: either they form a more perfect union, or it will fail.

Bibliography

Articles of Confederation. 1777. https://www.archives.gov/milestone-documents/articles-of-confederation. Accessed 6 March 2024.

Constitution of the United States of America. 1787. https://uscode.house.gov/static/constitution.pdf. Accessed 6 March 2024.

Fabbrini, Sergio. *Compound Democracies: Why the United States and Europe are becoming similar.* Oxford University Press, 2010.

Hamilton, Alexander, James Madison and John Jay. *The Federalist Papers.* 1787. Penguin, 1987.

Langewiesche, Dieter. *Vom Vielstaatlichen Reich zum Föderativen Bundesstaat* Heidelberger Akademische Bibliothek, 2020.

Madison, James. Letter to Edward Evertt. 28 August 1830. https://founders.archives.gov/documents/Madison/99-02-02-2138#:~:text=A%20political%20system%20that%20does,for%20uncertainty%20confusion%20and%20violence. Accessed 6 March 2024.

Snyder, Timothy. *The Road to Unfreedom: Russia, Europe, America.* Vintage, 2019.

Stourz, Gerald. *Alexander Hamilton and the Idea of Republican Government.* Stanford University Press, 1970.

Tocqueville, Alexis de. *Democracy in America.* 1835. Everyman, 1994.

Treaty of Westphalia. 1648. https://avalon.law.yale.edu/17th_century/westphal.asp. Accessed 6 March 2024.

Epilogue: The United States of Europe

After fleeing to Brussels in the aftermath of his failed attempt to stop the coup that saw Louis Napoleon tighten his grip on power, Victor Hugo spent the next twenty years in exile – initially because he had to, eventually because he chose to (in the late 1850s he rejected an offer of amnesty by the French court with the message "When liberty returns, I will return.") He left Brussels and settled in the Channel Islands, which gave him a feeling of physical proximity to France while also allowing him to maintain a critical distance from proceedings there. For a while his home was on the larger island of Jersey, until he decided to leave before being pushed out when he sided with the editors of a local French refugee newspaper who had criticised Queen Victoria for fraternising with Napoleon III. He moved to the nearby island of Guernsey, which would remain his home for the next fifteen years (Stephens 256–257).

Hugo would turn his exile phase into a period of incredible productivity. He published a successful collection of poems in the shape of his 1856 *Contemplations*. The receipts from this book allowed him to buy a townhouse in Guernsey's little capital city St Peter Port (Stephens 275). He spent years redesigning the property's interior, making the house a reflection of his artistic and philosophical inclinations. In it, he would also complete arguably his most famous work, *Les Miserables* (1862).

If exile could not stop him from increasing his fame as an artist and a writer, it also did nothing to diminish his faith in his ideals of liberty, equality, and European unity. He peppered newspaper editors with letters of support for a range of causes, from the Polish uprising of 1863–1864 to the Irish Fenians, and sponsored Garibaldi's revolutionary brigade (Stephens 317–318). He became involved with the second peace movement, acting as honorary chair of the 1869 conference in Lausanne. It was this movement that, even more than the first, devoted itself to the cause of a united Europe.

With the rumours of war again growing – this time between Napoleon III's French Empire and the North German Bund led by Bismarck – Hugo felt that the movement needed an act of inspiration to rally its spirits. To that end, he used 14 July 1870 to organise a ceremony in the garden of his

Livestro, Joshua: *A More Perfect Union. Federal Union in Political Theory and Practice, 1500-1951.* Amsterdam: Amsterdam University Press, 2024.

DOI: 10.5117/9789048563777_EPI

house in Guernsey. In the presence of family and some close friends, he planted an acorn and read a poem he had written for the occasion. Naming the tree The United States of Europe, he used the poem to call for his great idea to grow roots and reach across the continent: "Grow, tree; reign, idea; may the idea become life, the tree eternity!" ("To the Outlaws," July 14th, 1870; my translation).

Five days later, war broke out. It was the first of many historic events the oak would experience in its lifetime. It would live through wars, the fall of empires, the rise of tyrants, and the triumph of liberty. Eventually, eighty years later, it would see the planting of another acorn – one made of coal and steel. That one too received its dedication – not by a poet, but by a man who had devoted his life to business and politics. His name was Jean Monnet. Praising the "democratic and pacific revolution" that Europe was going through, he predicted that the organisation he had helped to found would eventually lead to "the creation of the United States of Europe" (Monnet 58–59).

The poet and the businessman are long gone. But their dream survives.

Bibliography

Hugo, Victor. "Aux Proscrits." 14 July 1870. https://www.bonjourpoesie.fr/lesgrand-sclassiques/poemes/victor_hugo/aux_proscrits. Accessed 6 March 2024.

Monnet, Jean. *Les États-Unis D'Europe Ont Commencé: La Communauté Européenne Du Charbon et L'Acier. Discours et Allocutions*. Robert Laffont, 1962.

Stephens, Bradley. *Victor Hugo*. Reaktion Books, 2019.

Acknowledgements

First of all I'd like to thank professor Martin van Gelderen, for being sufficiently interested in the hypothesis that I had originally formulated to encourage me to continue my research, and then for taking time out of his busy schedule to read the individual chapters and provide me with valuable feedback on them. Many thanks also to professor Catherine de Vries, for encouraging me to undertake the kind of research that could lead to a book like this, and for the many stimulating conversations in the margin of the meetings of the Europe panel of the Dutch Council on Foreign Relations.

A number of experts were kind enough to answer questions about specific aspects of the trans-Atlantic federal tradition that I have tried to reconstruct in this book: professor Maartje Abbenhuis of the University of Auckland about the early twentieth century peace movement, professor Carole Dornier of the Université de Caen on the work of Saint-Pierre and Montesquieu, Dr. Tomasz Gromelski of the University of Oxford about the place of Machiavelli in Polish Renaissance debate, emeritus professor David Hendrickson of the Colorado College about the influence of the European federal tradition on the Amerikan Founding, professor Talbot Imlay of the Université Laval in Quebec about the ties between the American writer Clarence Streit and the European Founder Jean Monnet, Dr. Joanna Kenty (now at The Citizens Campaign in New Jersey, previously at the Radboud University in Nijmegen, The Netherlands, and at Temple University in Rome) about the influence of Tacitism on the American Founders, and Regina Wasowicz of the library of the Polish Parliament about the nineteenth century Polish tradition of European federalism.

Further words of thanks go to Hans Kribbe, who helped me think through the original hypothesis, and later read and discussed a number of chapters of the book – may his new think tank become a Big success (pun intended).

A special word of thanks also to my publisher, Amsterdam University Press, for giving me the platform to publish this book.

Last but not least, many thanks to my family in Holland: Anna and Merel, Lotte, Leon, Richard, Bart and Sofie, Daan, Liet, Juuk and Piet, Benjamin and Kelly. To my in-laws in England: Jerry and Jenny, Emily, Kevin, Aniela and Sofia, Bec, Paul, Izzie and Jake. And of course to my wife Sarah and my children Daniel, Hannah and Ruben, whose seemingly endless patience made it possible for me to spend several years working on this book – I hope it was worth the wait.

Index

For Product Safety Concerns and Information please contact our EU
representative GPSR@taylorandfrancis.com
Taylor & Francis Verlag GmbH, Kaufingerstraße 24, 80331 München, Germany

www.ingramcontent.com/pod-product-compliance
Lightning Source LLC
Chambersburg PA
CBHW070712280326
41926CB00087B/1783